THE PHILOSOPHY OF NIETZSCHE

THUS SPAKE ZARATHUSTRA

BEYOND GOOD AND EVIL

THE GENEALOGY OF MORALS

ECCE HOMO

THE BIRTH OF TRAGEDY

THE MODERN LIBRARY · NEW YORK

THE MODERN LIBRARY

IS PUBLISHED BY

RANDOM HOUSE, INC.

GENERAL CONTENTS

INTRODUCTION

No PHILOSOPHER since Kant has left so undeniable an imprint on modern thought as has Friedrich Nietzsche. Even Schopenhauer, whose influence colored the greater part of Europe, made no such widespread impression. Not only in ethics and literature do we find the molding hand of Nietzsche at work, invigorating and solidifying; but in pedagogics and in art, in politics and religion, the influence of his doctrines is to be encountered.

The facts relating to Nietzsche's life are few and simple. He was born at Röcken, a little village in the Prussian province of Saxony, on October 15, 1844; and it is an interesting paradox that this most terrible and devastating critic of Christianity and its ideals was the culmination of two long collateral lines of theologians. There were two other children in the Nietzsche household—a girl born in 1846, and a son born in 1850. The girl was named Therese Elizabeth Alexandra, and afterward she became the philosopher's closest companion and guardian and his most voluminous biographer. The boy, Joseph, did not survive his first year. When Nietzsche's father died the family moved to Naumburg; and Friedrich, then only six years old, was sent to a local Municipal Boys' School. Later he was withdrawn and entered in a private institution which prepared the younger students for the Cathedral Grammar School. After a few years here Nietzsche successfully passed his examinations for the well-known Landes-Schule at Pforta, where he remained until 1864, enrolling the following term at the University of Bonn.

It was at Bonn that a decided change came over his religious views; and it was here also that his great friendship for Friedrich Wilhelm Ritschl, the philologist, developed. When Ritschl was transferred to the University of Leipzig, Nietzsche followed him. Leipzig was the turning point of his life. Here he met Wagner; became acquainted with Erwin Rohde; and discovered Schopenhauer. An interest in politics also developed in him; and the war between Prussia and Austria fanned his youthful ardor to an almost extravagant degree. Twice he offered his services to the military, but both times was rejected on account of his shortsightedness. In the autumn of 1867, however, a new army regulation resulted in his being called to the colors, and he joined the artillery at Naumburg. But he was thrown from his horse in training and received a severe injury to his chest, which necessitated his permanent withdrawal from service.

In October, 1868, Nietzsche returned to his work at Leipzig, and shortly after, although but twenty-four, he was offered the post of Classical Philology at Bâle. Two years later came the Franco-Prussian War, and he secured service as an ambulance attendant in the Hospital Corps. But his health was poor, and the work proved too much for him. He contracted diphtheria and severe dysentery, and it was necessary for him to discontinue his duties entirely. His sister tells us that this illness greatly undermined his health, and was the first cause of his subsequent condition. He did not wait until he was well before resuming his duties at the University; and this new strain imposed on his already depleted condition had much to do with bringing on his final breakdown.

In 1872, Nietzsche's first important work appeared—"The Birth of Tragedy from the Spirit of Music"; and in 1873 he began a series of famous pamphlets which later were put into book form under the title of "Thoughts Out of Season." His

health was steadily declining, and during the holidays he
alternated between Switzerland and Italy in an endeavor to
recuperate. In the former place he was with Wagner, but in
1876 his friendship for the composer began to cool. He had
gone to Bayreuth, and there, after hearing *"Der Ring des
Nibelungen,"* he became bitter and disgusted at what he believed to be Wagner's compromise with Christianity. But so
strong was his affection for Wagner the man that it was not
until ten years had passed that he could bring himself to write
the now famous attack which he had long had in mind.

The year after the appearance of "Human All-Too-Human"
(*"Menschliches Allzu Menschliches"*), Nietzsche's illness
compelled him to resign his professorship at Bâle; and two
more years saw the appearance of "The Dawn of Day" (*"Mor-
genröten"*), his first book of constructive thinking. The remainder of his life was spent in a fruitless endeavor to regain
his health. For eight years, during all of which time he was
busily engaged in writing, he sought a climate that would
revive him—visiting in turn Sils-Maria in Switzerland, Genoa,
Monaco, Messina, Grunewald, Tautenburg, Rome, Naumburg,
Nice, Venice, Mentone, and the Riviera. But to no avail. He
was constantly ill and for the most part alone, and this per-
turbed and restless period of his life resolved itself into a continuous struggle against melancholy and physical suffering.
During these eight years Nietzsche had written "Thus Spake
Zarathustra" (*"Also Sprach Zarathustra"*), "The Joyful Wisdom" (*"La Gaya Scienza"*), "Beyond Good and Evil" (*"Jen-
seits Gute und Böse"*), "The Genealogy of Morals" (*"Zur
Genealogie der Moral"*), "The Case of Wagner," "The Twilight of the Idols" (*"Götzendämmerung"*), "The Antichrist"
(*"Der Antichrist"*), "Ecce Homo," "Nietzsche *contra* Wag-

ner," and an enormous number of notes which were to constitute his final and culminating work, "The Will to Power" (*"Die Wille zur Macht"*). The events during this period of Nietzsche's career were few. Perhaps the most important was his meeting with Lou Salomé. But even this episode had small bearing on his life, and has been greatly emphasised by biographers because of its isolation in an existence outwardly drab and uneventful.

In January, 1889, an apoplectic fit marked the beginning of the end. Nietzsche's manner suddenly became alarming. He exhibited numerous eccentricities, so grave as to mean but one thing: his mind was seriously affected. There has long been a theory that his insanity was of gradual growth, that, in fact, he was unbalanced from birth. But there is no evidence to substantiate this theory. The statement that his books were those of a madman is entirely without foundation. His works were thought out in the most clarified manner; in his intercourse with his friends he was restrained and normal; and his voluminous correspondence showed no change toward the end either in sentiment or tone. His insanity was sudden; it came without warning; and it is puerile to point to his state of mind during the last years of his life as a criticism of his philosophy. His books must stand or fall on internal evidence. Judged from that standpoint they are scrupulously sane.

The cause of Nietzsche's breakdown was due to a number of influences—his excessive use of chloral which he took for insomnia, the tremendous strain to which he put his intellect, his constant disappointments and privations, his mental solitude, his prolonged physical suffering. We know little of his last days before he went insane. Overbeck, in answer to a mad note, found him in Turin, broken. Nietzsche was put in a private sanitarium at Jena. Recovering somewhat he returned to Naumburg. Later his sister, Frau Förster-Nietzsche, removed him to a villa at Weimar; and three years after, on the twenty-fifth of August, 1900, he died. He was buried at Röcken, his native village.

WILLARD HUNTINGTON WRIGHT

THUS SPAKE ZARATHUSTRA

Translated by Thomas Common

CONTENTS

[*xv*]

CONTENTS

SECOND PART

THIRD PART

CONTENTS

INTRODUCTION

By Mrs. Förster-Nietzsche

HOW ZARATHUSTRA CAME INTO BEING

"Zarathustra is my brother's most personal work; it is the history of his most individual experiences, of his friendships, ideals, raptures, bitterest disappointments and sorrows. Above it all, however, there soars, transfiguring it, the image of his greatest hopes and remotest aims. My brother had the figure of Zarathustra in his mind from his very earliest youth: he once told me that even as a child he had dreamt of him. At different periods in his life, he would call this haunter of his dreams by different names; "but in the end," he declares in a note on the subject, "I had to do a *Persian* the honor of identifying him with this creature of my fancy. Persians were the first to take a broad and comprehensive view of history. Every series of evolutions, according to them, was presided over by a prophet; and every prophet had his 'Hazar'—his dynasty of a thousand years."

All Zarathustra's views, as also his personality, were early conceptions of my brother's mind. Whoever reads his posthumously published writings for the years 1869-82 with care, will constantly meet with passages suggestive of Zarathustra's thoughts and doctrines. For instance, the ideal of the Superman is put forth quite clearly in all his writings during the years 1873-75; and in "We Philologists," the following remarkable observations occur:—

"How can one praise and glorify a nation as a whole?—

Even among the Greeks, it was the *individuals* that counted.

"The Greeks are interesting and extremely important because they reared such a vast number of great individuals. How was this possible? The question is one which ought to be studied.

"I am interested only in the relations of a people to the rearing of the individual man, and among the Greeks the conditions were unusually favorable for the development of the individual; not by any means owing to the goodness of the people, but because of the struggles of their evil instincts.

"With the help of favorable measures great individuals might be reared who would be both different from and higher than those who heretofore have owed their existence to mere chance. Here we may still be hopeful: in the rearing of exceptional men."

The notion of rearing the Superman is only a new form of an ideal Nietzsche already had in his youth, that *"the object of mankind should lie in its highest individuals"* (or, as he writes in "Schopenhauer as Educator": "Mankind ought constantly to be striving to produce great men—this and nothing else is its duty."). But the ideals he most revered in those days are no longer held to be the highest types of men. No, around this future ideal of a coming humanity—the Superman—the poet spread the veil of becoming. Who can tell to what glorious heights man can still ascend? That is why, after having tested the worth of our noblest ideal—that of the Saviour, in the light of the new valuations, the poet cries with passionate emphasis in "Zarathustra":

"Never yet hath there been a Superman. Naked have I seen both of them, the greatest and the smallest man:—

"All-too-similar are they still to each other. Verily even the greatest found I—all-too-human!"—

[*xx*]

The phrase "the rearing of the Superman," has very often been misunderstood. By the word "rearing," in this case, is meant the act of modifying by means of new and higher values —values which, as laws and guides of conduct and opinion, are now to rule over mankind. In general the doctrine of the Superman can only be understood correctly in conjunction with other ideas of the author's, such as:—the Order of Rank, the Will to Power, and the Transvaluation of All Values. He assumes that Christianity, as a product of the resentment of the botched and the weak, has put in ban all that is beautiful, strong, proud, and powerful, in fact all the qualities resulting from strength, and that, in consequence, all forces which tend to promote or elevate life have been seriously undermined. Now, however, a new table of valuations must be placed over mankind—namely, that of the strong, mighty, and magnificent man, overflowing with life and elevated to his zenith—the Superman, who is now put before us with overpowering passion as the aim of our life, hope, and will. And just as the old system of valuing, which only extolled the qualities favorable to the weak, the suffering, and the oppressed, has succeeded in producing a weak, suffering, and "modern" race, so this new and reversed system of valuing ought to rear a healthy, strong, lively, and courageous type, which would be a glory to life itself. Stated briefly, the leading principle of this new system of valuing would be: "All that proceeds from power is good, all that springs from weakness is bad."

This type must not be regarded as a fanciful figure: it is not a nebulous hope which is to be realized at some indefinitely remote period, thousands of years hence; nor is it a new species (in the Darwinian sense) of which we can know nothing, and which it would therefore be somewhat absurd to strive after. But it is meant to be a possibility which men of the present could realize with all their spiritual and physical energies, provided they adopted the new values.

The author of "Zarathustra" never lost sight of that egregious example of a transvaluation of all values through Christianity, whereby the whole of the deified mode of life and thought of the Greeks, as well as strong Romedom, was almost annihilated or transvalued in a comparatively short time. Could not a rejuvenated Græco-Roman system of valuing (once it had been refined and made more profound by the schooling which two thousand years of Christianity had provided) effect another such revolution within a calculable period of time, until that glorious type of manhood shall finally appear which is to be our new faith and hope, and in the creation of which Zarathustra exhorts us to participate?

In his private notes on the subject the author uses the expression "Superman" (always in the singular, by-the-bye), as signifying "the most thoroughly well-constituted type," as opposed to "modern man"; above all, however, he designates Zarathustra himself as an example of the Superman. In "Ecce Homo" he is careful to enlighten us concerning the precursors and prerequisites to the advent of this highest type, in referring to a certain passage in "The Joyful Wisdom":—

"In order to understand this type, we must first be quite clear in regard to the leading physiological condition on which it depends: this condition is what I call *great healthiness*. I know not how to express my meaning more plainly or more personally than I have done already in one of the last chapters (Aphorism 382) of the fifth book of "The Joyful Wisdom":

"We, the new, the nameless, the hard-to-understand"—it says there— "we firstlings of a yet untried future—we require for a new end also a new means, namely, a new healthiness, stronger, sharper, tougher, bolder and merrier than all healthiness hitherto. He whose soul longeth to experience the whole range of hitherto recognized values and desirabilities, and to circumnavigate all the coasts of this ideal 'Mediterranean Sea,' who, from the adventures of his most personal experience, wants to know how it feels to be a conqueror, and discoverer of the ideal—as likewise how it is with the artist, the saint, the legislator, the sage, the scholar, the devotee, the prophet, and the godly non-conformist of the old style— requires one thing above all for that purpose, *great healthiness*—such healthiness as one not only possesses, but also constantly acquires and must acquire, because one unceasingly sacrifices it again, and must sacrifice it! —And now, after having been long on the way in this fashion, we Argonauts of the ideal, more courageous perhaps than prudent, and often enough shipwrecked and brought to grief, nevertheless dangerously healthy, always healthy again—it would seem as if, in recompense for it all, that we have a still undiscovered country before us, the boundaries of which no one has yet seen, a beyond to all countries and corners of the ideal known hitherto, a world so over-rich in the beautiful, the strange, the questionable, the frightful, and the divine, that our curiosity as well as our thirst for possession thereof, have got out of hand—alas! that nothing will now any longer satisfy us!—

"How could we still be content with *the man of the present day* after such outlooks, and with such a craving in our conscience and consciousness? Sad enough; but it is unavoidable that we should look on the worthiest aims and hopes of the man of the present day with ill-concealed amusement, and perhaps should no longer look at them. Another ideal runs on before us, a strange, tempting ideal full of danger, to which we should not like to persuade any one, because we do not so readily acknowledge any one's *right thereto:* the ideal of a spirit who plays naïvely (that is to say involuntarily and from overflowing abundance and power) with everything that has hitherto been called holy, good, intangible, or divine; to whom the loftiest conception which the people have reasonably made their measure of value, would already practically imply danger, ruin, abasement, or at least relaxation, blindness, or temporary self-forgetfulness; the ideal of a humanly superhuman welfare and benevolence, which will often enough appear *inhuman,* for example, when put alongside of all past seriousness on earth, and alongside of all past solemnities in bearing, word, tone, look, morality, and pursuit, as their truest involuntary parody—and *with* which, nevertheless, perhaps *the great seriousness* only commences, when the proper interrogative mark is set up, the fate of the soul changes, the hour-hand moves, and tragedy begins. . . ."

Although the figure of Zarathustra and a large number of the leading thoughts in this work had appeared much earlier in the dreams and writings of the author, "Thus Spake Zarathustra" did not actually come into being until the month of August, 1881, in Sils-Maria; and it was the idea of the Eternal Recurrence of all things which finally induced my brother to set forth his new views in poetic language. In regard to his first conception of this idea, his autobiographical sketch, "Ecce, Homo," written in the autumn of 1888, contains the following passage:—

"The fundamental idea of my work—namely, the Eternal Recurrence of all things—this highest of all possible formulæ of a Yea-saying philosophy, first occurred to me in August, 1881. I made a note of the thought on a sheet of paper, with the postscript: 6,000 feet beyond men and time! That day I happened to be wandering through the woods alongside of the lake of Silvaplana, and I halted beside a huge, pyramidal and towering rock not far from Surlei. It was then that the thought struck me. Looking back now, I find that exactly two months previous to this inspiration, I had had an omen of its coming in the form of a sudden and decisive alteration in my tastes—more particularly in music. It would even be possible to consider all 'Zarathustra' as a musical composition. At all events, a very necessary condition in its production was a renaissance in myself of the art of hearing. In a small mountain resort (Recoaro) near Vicenza, where I spent the spring of 1881, I and my friend and Maëstro, Peter Gast—also one who had been born again—discovered that the phœnix music that hovered over us, wore lighter and brighter plumes than it had done theretofore."

[*xxiv*]

During the month of August, 1881, my brother resolved to reveal the teaching of the Eternal Recurrence, in dithyrambic and psalmodic form, through the mouth of Zarathustra. Among the notes of this period, we found a page on which is written the first definite plan of "Thus Spake Zarathustra":—

"MIDDAY AND ETERNITY."

"GUIDE-POSTS TO A NEW WAY OF LIVING."

Beneath this is written:—

"Zarathustra born on lake Urmi; left his home in his thirtieth year; went into the province of Aria, and, during ten years of solitude in the mountains, composed the Zend-Avesta."

"The sun of knowledge stands once more at midday; and the serpent of eternity lies coiled in its light——: It is *your* time, ye midday brethren."

In that summer of 1881, my brother, after many years of steadily declining health, began at last to rally, and it is to this first gush of the recovery of his once splendid bodily condition that we owe not only "The Joyful Wisdom," which in its mood may be regarded as a prelude to "Zarathustra," but also "Zarathustra" itself. Just as he was beginning to recuperate his health, however, an unkind destiny brought him a number of most painful personal experiences. His friends caused him many disappointments, which were the more bitter to him, inasmuch as he regarded friendship as such a sacred institution; and for the first time in his life he realized the whole horror of that loneliness to which, perhaps, all greatness is condemned. But to be forsaken is something very different from deliberately choosing blessed loneliness. How he longed, in those days, for the ideal friend who would thoroughly understand him, to whom he would be able to say all, and whom he imagined he had found at various periods in his life from his earliest youth onwards. Now, however, that the way he had chosen grew ever more perilous and steep, he found nobody who could follow him: he therefore created a perfect friend for himself in the ideal form of a majestic philosopher, and made this creation the preacher of his gospel to the world.

Whether my brother would ever have written "Thus Spake Zarathustra" according to the first plan sketched in the summer of 1881, if he had not had the disappointments already referred to, is now an idle question; but perhaps where "Zarathustra" is concerned, we may also say with Master Eckhardt: "The fleetest beast to bear you to perfection is suffering."

My brother writes as follows about the origin of the first part of "Zarathustra":—"In the winter of 1882-83, I was living on the charming little Gulf of Rapallo, not far from Genoa, and between Chiavari and Cape Porto Fino. My health was not very good; the winter was cold and exceptionally rainy; and the small inn in which I lived was so close to the water that at night my sleep would be disturbed if the sea were high. These circumstances were surely the very reverse of favorable; and yet in spite of it all, and as if in demonstration of my belief that everything decisive comes to life in spite of every obstacle, it was precisely during this winter and in the midst of these unfavorable circumstances that my 'Zarathustra' originated. In the morning I used to start out in a southerly direction up the glorious road to Zoagli, which rises aloft through a forest of pines and gives one a view far out into the sea. In the afternoon, as often as my health permitted, I walked round the whole bay from Santa Margherita to beyond Porto Fino. This spot was all the more interesting to me, inasmuch as it was so dearly loved by the Emperor Frederick III. In the autumn of 1886 I chanced to be there again when he was revisiting this small, forgotten world of happiness for the last time. It was on these two roads that all 'Zarathustra' came to me, above all Zarathustra himself as a type;—I ought rather to say that it was on these walks that these ideas waylaid me."

The first part of "Zarathustra" was written in about ten days—that is to say, from the beginning to about the middle of February, 1883. "The last lines were written precisely in the hallowed hour when Richard Wagner gave up the ghost in Venice."

With the exception of the ten days occupied in composing the first part of this book, my brother often referred to this winter as the hardest and sickliest he had ever experienced. He did not, however, mean thereby that his former disorders were troubling him, but that he was suffering from a severe attack of influenza which he had caught in Santa Margherita, and which tormented him for several weeks after his arrival in Genoa. As a matter of fact, however, what he complained of most was his spiritual condition—that indescribable forsaken-ness—to which he gives such heartrending expression in "Zarathustra." Even the reception which the first part met with at the hands of friends and acquaintances was extremely disheartening: for almost all those to whom he presented copies of the work misunderstood it. "I found no one ripe for many of my thoughts; the case of 'Zarathustra' proves that one can speak with the utmost clearness, and yet not be heard by any one." My brother was very much discouraged by the feeble-ness of the response he was given, and as he was striving just then to give up the practice of taking hydrate of chloral—a drug he had begun to take while ill with influenza—the fol-lowing spring, spent in Rome, was a somewhat gloomy one for him. He writes about it as follows:—"I spent a melancholy spring in Rome, where I only just managed to live—and this was no easy matter. This city, which is absolutely unsuited to the poet-author of 'Zarathustra,' and for the choice of which I was not responsible, made me inordinately miserable. I tried to leave it. I wanted to go to Aquila—the opposite of Rome in every respect, and actually founded in a spirit of enmity towards that city (just as I also shall found a city some day), as a memento of an atheist and genuine enemy of the Church—a person very closely related to me—the great Hohenstaufen, the Emperor Frederick II. But Fate lay behind it all: I had to return again to Rome. In the end I was obliged to be satisfied with the Piazza Barberini, after I had exerted myself in vain to find an anti-Christian quarter. I fear that on one occasion, to avoid bad smells as much as possible, I actually inquired at the Palazzo del Quirinale whether they could not provide a quiet room for a philosopher. In a chamber high above the Piazza just mentioned, from which one obtained a general view of Rome and could hear the fountains plashing far below, the loneliest of all songs was composed—'The Night-Song.' About this time I was obsessed by an unspeakably sad melody, the refrain of which I recognised in the words, 'dead through immortality.' "

We remained somewhat too long in Rome that spring, and what with the effect of the increasing heat and the discouraging circumstances already described, my brother resolved not to write any more, or in any case, not to proceed with "Zarathustra," although I offered to relieve him of all trouble in connection with the proofs and the publisher. When, however, we returned to Switzerland towards the end of June, and he found himself once more in the familiar and exhilarating air of the mountains, all his joyous creative powers revived, and in a note to me announcing the dispatch of some manuscript, he wrote as follows: "I have engaged a place here for three months: forsooth, I am the greatest fool to allow my courage to be sapped from me by the climate of Italy. Now and again I am troubled by the thought: *what next?* My 'future' is the darkest thing in the world to me, but as there still remains a great deal for me to do, I suppose I ought rather to think of doing this than of my future, and leave the rest to *thee* and the gods."

The second part of "Zarathustra" was written between the 26th of June and the 6th July. "This summer, finding myself once more in the sacred place where the first thought of 'Zarathustra' flashed across my mind, I conceived the second part. Ten days sufficed. Neither for the second, the first, nor the third part, have I required a day longer."

He often used to speak of the ecstatic mood in which he wrote "Zarathustra"; how in his walks over hill and dale the ideas would crowd into his mind, and how he would note them down hastily in a notebook from which he would transcribe them on his return, sometimes working till midnight. He says in a letter to me: "You can have no idea of the vehemence of such composition," and in "Ecce Homo" (autumn 1888) he describes as follows with passionate enthusiasm the incomparable mood in which he created Zarathustra:—

"—Has any one at the end of the nineteenth century any distinct notion of what poets of a stronger age understood by the word inspiration? If not, I will describe it. If one had the smallest vestige of superstition in one, it would hardly be possible to set aside completely the idea that one is the mere incarnation, mouthpiece or medium of an almighty power. The idea of revelation in the sense that something becomes suddenly visible and audible with indescribable certainty and accuracy, which profoundly convulses and upsets one—describes simply the matter of fact. One hears—one does not seek; one takes—one does not ask who gives: a thought sud-

denly flashes up like lightning, it comes with necessity, unhesitatingly—I have never had any choice in the matter. There
is an ecstasy such that the immense strain of it is sometimes
relaxed by a flood of tears, along with which one's steps either
rush or involuntarily lag, alternately. There is the feeling that
one is completely out of hand, with the very distinct consciousness of an endless number of fine thrills and quiverings to the
very toes;—there is a depth of happiness in which the pain-
fullest and gloomiest do not operate as antitheses, but as conditioned, as demanded in the sense of necessary shades of
colour in such an overflow of light. There is an instinct for
rhythmic relations which embraces wide areas of forms
(length, the need of a wide-embracing rhythm, is almost the
measure of the force of an inspiration, a sort of counterpart
to its pressure and tension). Everything happens quite involuntarily, as if in a tempestuous outburst of freedom, of absoluteness, of power and divinity. The involuntariness of the figures
and similes is the most remarkable thing; one loses all perception of what constitutes the figure and what constitutes the
simile; everything seems to present itself as the readiest, the
correctest and the simplest means of expression. It actually
seems, to use one of Zarathustra's own phrases, as if all things
came unto one, and would fain be similes: 'Here do all things
come caressingly to thy talk and flatter thee, for they want to
ride upon thy back. On every simile dost thou here ride to
every truth. Here fly open unto thee all being's words and
word-cabinets; here all being wanteth to become words, here
all becoming wanteth to learn of thee how to talk.' This is *my*
experience of inspiration. I do not doubt but that one would
have to go back thousands of years in order to find some one
who could say to me: It is mine also!—''

In the autumn of 1883 my brother left the Engadine for

Germany and stayed there a few weeks. In the following winter, after wandering somewhat erratically through Stresa, Genoa, and Spezia, he landed in Nice, where the climate so happily promoted his creative powers that he wrote the third part of "Zarathustra." "In the winter, beneath the halcyon sky of Nice, which then looked down upon me for the first time in my life, I found the third 'Zarathustra'—and came to the end of my task; the whole having occupied me scarcely a year. Many hidden corners and heights in the landscapes round about Nice are hallowed to me by unforgettable moments. That decisive chapter entitled 'Old and New Tables' was composed in the very difficult ascent from the station to Eza—that wonderful Moorish village in the rocks. My most creative moments were always accompanied by unusual muscular activity. The body is inspired: let us waive the question of the 'soul.' I might often have been seen dancing in those days. Without a suggestion of fatigue I could then walk for seven or eight hours on end among the hills. I slept well and laughed well —I was perfectly robust and patient."

As we have seen, each of the three parts of "Zarathustra" was written, after a more or less short period of preparation in about ten days. The composition of the fourth part alone was broken by occasional interruptions. The first notes relating to this part were written while he and I were staying together in Zurich in September 1884. In the following November, while staying at Mentone, he began to elaborate these notes, and after a long pause, finished the manuscript at Nice between the end of January and the middle of February 1885. My brother then called this part the fourth and last; but even before, and shortly after it had been privately printed, he wrote to me saying that he still intended writing a fifth and sixth part, and notes relating to these parts are now in my possession. This

[*xxxi*]

fourth part (the original MS. of which contains this note: "Only for my friends, not for the public") is written in a particularly personal spirit, and those few to whom he presented a copy of it, he pledged to the strictest secrecy concerning its contents. He often thought of making this fourth part public also, but doubted whether he would ever be able to do so without considerably altering certain portions of it. At all events he resolved to distribute this manuscript production, of which only forty copies were printed, only among those who had proved themselves worthy of it, and it speaks eloquently of his utter loneliness and need of sympathy in those days, that he had occasion to present only seven copies of his book according to this resolution.

Already at the beginning of this history I hinted at the reasons which led my brother to select a Persian as the incarnation of his ideal of the majestic philosopher. His reasons, however, for choosing Zarathustra of all others to be his mouthpiece, he gives us in the following words:——"People have never asked me, as they should have done, what the name Zarathustra precisely means in my mouth, in the mouth of the first Immoralist; for what distinguishes that philosopher from all others in the past is the very fact that he was exactly the reverse of an immoralist. Zarathustra was the first to see in the struggle between good and evil the essential wheel in the working of things. The translation of morality into the metaphysical, as force, cause, end in itself, was *his* work. But the very question suggests its own answer. Zarathustra *created* the most portentous error, *morality*, consequently he should also be the first to *perceive* that error, not only because he has had longer and greater experience of the subject than any other thinker—all history is the experimental refutation of the theory of the so-called moral order of things:—the more important point is that Zarathustra was more truthful than any other thinker. In his teaching alone do we meet with truthfulness upheld as the highest virtue—*i.e.:* the reverse of the *cowardice* of the 'idealist' who flees from reality. Zarathustra had more courage in his body than any other thinker before or after him. To tell the truth and *to aim straight:* that is the first Persian virtue. Am I understood? . . . The overcoming of morality through itself —through truthfulness, the overcoming of the moralist through his opposite—*through me*—: that is what the name Zarathustra means in my mouth."

ELIZABETH FÖRSTER-NIETZSCHE

NIETZSCHE ARCHIVES,
  WEIMAR, *December* 1905.

Zarathustra's Prologue

1

WHEN Zarathustra was thirty years old, he left his home and the lake of his home, and went into the mountains. There he enjoyed his spirit and his solitude, and for ten years did not weary of it. But at last his heart changed,—and rising one morning with the rosy dawn, he went before the sun, and spake thus unto it:

Thou great star! What would be thy happiness if thou hadst not those for whom thou shinest!

For ten years hast thou climbed hither unto my cave: thou wouldst have wearied of thy light and of the journey, had it not been for me, mine eagle, and my serpent.

But we awaited thee every morning, took from thee thine overflow, and blessed thee for it.

Lo! I am weary of my wisdom, like the bee that hath gathered too much honey; I need hands outstretched to take it.

I would fain bestow and distribute, until the wise have once more become joyous in their folly, and the poor happy in their riches.

Therefore must I descend into the deep: as thou doest in the evening, when thou goest behind the sea, and givest light also to the nether-world, thou exuberant star!

Like thee must I *go down,* as men say, to whom I shall descend.

Bless me, then, thou tranquil eye, that canst behold even the greatest happiness without envy!

Bless the cup that is about to overflow, that the water may flow golden out of it, and carry everywhere the reflection of thy bliss!

Lo! This cup is again going to empty itself, and Zarathustra is again going to be a man.

Thus began Zarathustra's down-going.

2

Zarathustra went down the mountain alone, no one meeting him. When he entered the forest, however, there suddenly stood before him an old man, who had left his holy cot to seek roots. And thus spake the old man to Zarathustra:

"No stranger to me is this wanderer: many years ago passed he by. Zarathustra he was called; but he hath altered.

Then thou carriedst thine ashes into the mountains: wilt thou now carry thy fire into the valleys? Fearest thou not the incendiary's doom?

Yea, I recognize Zarathustra. Pure is his eye, and no loathing lurketh about his mouth. Goeth he not along like a dancer?

Altered is Zarathustra; a child hath Zarathustra become; an awakened one is Zarathustra: what wilt thou do in the land of the sleepers?

As in the sea hast thou lived in solitude, and it hath borne thee up. Alas, wilt thou now go ashore? Alas, wilt thou again drag thy body thyself?"

Zarathustra answered: "I love mankind."

"Why," said the saint, "did I go into the forest and the desert? Was it not because I loved men far too well?

Now I love God: men, I do not love. Man is a thing too imperfect for me. Love to man would be fatal to me."

Zarathustra answered: "What spake I of love! I am bringing gifts unto men."

"Give them nothing," said the saint. "Take rather part of their load, and carry it along with them—that will be most agreeable unto them: if only it be agreeable unto thee!

If, however, thou wilt give unto them, give them no more than an alms, and let them also beg for it!"

"No," replied Zarathustra, "I give no alms. I am not poor enough for that."

The saint laughed at Zarathustra, and spake thus: "Then see to it that they accept thy treasures! They are distrustful of anchorites, and do not believe that we come with gifts.

The fall of our footsteps ringeth too hollow through their streets. And just as at night, when they are in bed and hear a man abroad long before sunrise, so they ask themselves concerning us: Where goeth the thief?

Go not to men, but stay in the forest! Go rather to the animals! Why not be like me—a bear amongst bears, a bird amongst birds?"

"And what doeth the saint in the forest?" asked Zarathustra.

The saint answered: "I make hymns and sing them; and in making hymns I laugh and weep and mumble: thus do I praise God.

With singing, weeping, laughing, and mumbling do I praise the God who is my God. But what dost thou bring us as a gift?"

When Zarathustra had heard these words, he bowed to the saint and said: "What should I have to give thee! Let me rather hurry hence lest I take aught away from thee!"— And thus

[5]

they parted from one another, the old man and Zarathustra, laughing like schoolboys.

When Zarathustra was alone, however, he said to his heart: "Could it be possible! This old saint in the forest hath not yet heard of it, that *God is dead!*"

3

When Zarathustra arrived at the nearest town which adjoineth the forest, he found many people assembled in the market-place; for it had been announced that a rope-dancer would give a performance. And Zarathustra spake thus unto the people:

I teach you the Superman. Man is something that is to be surpassed. What have ye done to surpass man?

All beings hitherto have created something beyond themselves: and ye want to be the ebb of that great tide, and would rather go back to the beast than surpass man?

What is the ape to man? A laughing-stock, a thing of shame. And just the same shall man be to the Superman: a laughing-stock, a thing of shame.

Ye have made your way from the worm to man, and much within you is still worm. Once were ye apes, and even yet man is more of an ape than any of the apes.

Even the wisest among you is only a disharmony and hybrid of plant and phantom. But do I bid you become phantoms or plants?

Lo, I teach you the Superman!

The Superman is the meaning of the earth. Let your will say: The Superman *shall be* the meaning of the earth!

I conjure you, my brethren, *remain true to the earth,* and believe not those who speak unto you of superearthly hopes! Poisoners are they, whether they know it or not.

Despisers of life are they, decaying ones and poisoned ones themselves, of whom the earth is weary: so away with them!

Once blasphemy against God was the greatest blasphemy; but God died, and therewith also those blasphemers. To blaspheme the earth is now the dreadfulest sin, and to rate the heart of the unknowable higher than the meaning of the earth!

Once the soul looked contemptuously on the body, and then that contempt was the supreme thing:—the soul wished the body meagre, ghastly, and famished. Thus it thought to escape from the body and the earth.

Oh, that soul was itself meagre, ghastly, and famished; and cruelty was the delight of that soul!

But ye, also, my brethren, tell me: What doth your body say about your soul? Is your soul not poverty and pollution and wretched self-complacency?

Verily, a polluted stream is man. One must be a sea, to receive a polluted stream without becoming impure.

Lo, I teach you the Superman: he is that sea; in him can your great contempt be submerged.

What is the greatest thing ye can experience? It is the hour of great contempt. The hour in which even your happiness becometh loathsome unto you, and so also your reason and virtue.

The hour when ye say: "What good is my happiness! It is poverty and pollution and wretched self-complacency. But my happiness should justify existence itself!"

The hour when ye say: "What good is my reason! Doth it long for knowledge as the lion for his food? It is poverty and pollution and wretched self-complacency!"

The hour when ye say: "What good is my virtue! As yet it hath not made me passionate. How weary I am of my good

[7]

and my bad! It is all poverty and pollution and wretched self-complacency!"

The hour when ye say: "What good is my justice! I do not see that I am fervour and fuel. The just, however, are fervour and fuel!"

The hour when we say: "What good is my pity! Is not pity the cross on which he is nailed who loveth man? But my pity is not a crucifixion."

Have ye ever spoken thus? Have ye ever cried thus? Ah! would that I had heard you crying thus!

It is not your sin—it is your self-satisfaction that crieth unto heaven; your very sparingness in sin crieth unto heaven!

Where is the lightning to lick you with its tongue? Where is the frenzy with which ye should be inoculated?

Lo, I teach you the Superman: he is that lightning, he is that frenzy!—

When Zarathustra had thus spoken, one of the people called out: "We have now heard enough of the rope-dancer; it is time now for us to see him!" And all the people laughed at Zarathustra. But the rope-dancer, who thought the words applied to him, began his performance.

4

Zarathustra, however, looked at the people and wondered. Then he spake thus:

Man is a rope stretched between the animal and the Superman—a rope over an abyss.

A dangerous crossing, a dangerous wayfaring, a dangerous looking-back, a dangerous trembling and halting.

What is great in man is that he is a bridge and not a goal:

what is lovable in man is that he is an *over-going* and a *down-going*.

I love those that know not how to live except as down-goers, for they are the over-goers.

I love the great despisers, because they are the great adorers, and arrows of longing for the other shore.

I love those who do not first seek a reason beyond the stars for going down and being sacrifices, but sacrifice themselves to the earth, that the earth of the Superman may hereafter arrive.

I love him who liveth in order to know, and seeketh to know in order that the Superman may hereafter live. Thus seeketh he his own down-going.

I love him who laboureth and inventeth, that he may build the house for the Superman, and prepare for him earth, animal, and plant: for thus seeketh he his own down-going.

I love him who loveth his virtue: for virtue is the will to down-going, and an arrow of longing.

I love him who reserveth no share of spirit for himself, but wanteth to be wholly the spirit of his virtue: thus walketh he as spirit over the bridge.

I love him who maketh his virtue his inclination and destiny: thus, for the sake of his virtue, he is willing to live on, or live no more.

I love him who desireth not too many virtues. One virtue is more of a virtue than two, because it is more of a knot for one's destiny to cling to.

I love him whose soul is lavish, who wanteth no thanks and doth not give back: for he always bestoweth, and desireth not to keep for himself.

I love him who is ashamed when the dice fall in his favour, and who then asketh: "Am I a dishonest player?"—for he is willing to succumb.

[*9*]

I love him who scattereth golden words in advance of his deeds, and always doeth more than he promiseth: for he seeketh his own down-going.

I love him who justifieth the future ones, and redeemeth the past ones: for he is willing to succumb through the present ones.

I love him who chasteneth his God, because he loveth his God: for he must succumb through the wrath of his God.

I love him whose soul is deep even in the wounding, and may succumb through a small matter: thus goeth he willingly over the bridge.

I love him whose soul is so overfull that he forgetteth himself, and all things are in him: thus all things become his down-going.

I love him who is of a free spirit and a free heart: thus is his head only the bowels of his heart; his heart, however, causeth his down-going.

I love all who are like heavy drops falling one by one out of the dark cloud that lowereth over man: they herald the coming of the lightning, and succumb as heralds.

Lo, I am a herald of the lightning, and a heavy drop out of the cloud: the lightning, however, is the *Superman*.—

5

When Zarathustra had spoken these words, he again looked at the people, and was silent. "There they stand," said he to his heart; "there they laugh: they understand me not; I am not the mouth for these ears.

Must one first batter their ears, that they may learn to hear with their eyes? Must one clatter like kettledrums and penitential preachers? Or do they only believe the stammerer?

They have something whereof they are proud. What do they call it, that which maketh them proud? Culture, they call it; it distinguisheth them from the goatherds.

They dislike, therefore, to hear of 'contempt' of themselves. So I will appeal to their pride.

I will speak unto them of the most contemptible thing: that, however, is *the last man!*"

And thus spake Zarathustra unto the people:

It is time for man to fix his goal. It is time for man to plant the germ of his highest hope.

Still is his soil rich enough for it. But that soil will one day be poor and exhausted, and no lofty tree will any longer be able to grow thereon.

Alas! there cometh the time when man will no longer launch the arrow of his longing beyond man—and the string of his bow will have unlearned to whizz!

I tell you: one must still have chaos in one, to give birth to a dancing star. I tell you: ye have still chaos in you.

Alas! There cometh the time when man will no longer give birth to any star. Alas! There cometh the time of the most despicable man, who can no longer despise himself.

Lo! I show you *the last man.*

"What is love? What is creation? What is longing? What is a star?"—so asketh the last man and blinketh.

The earth hath then become small, and on it there hoppeth the last man who maketh everything small. His species is ineradicable like that of the ground-flea; the last man liveth longest.

"We have discovered happiness"—say the last men, and blink thereby.

They have left the regions where it is hard to live; for they

[*11*]

need warmth. One still loveth one's neighbour and rubbeth against him; for one needeth warmth.

Turning ill and being distrustful, they consider sinful: they walk warily. He is a fool who still stumbleth over stones or men!

A little poison now and then: that maketh pleasant dreams. And much poison at last for a pleasant death.

One still worketh, for work is a pastime. But one is careful lest the pastime should hurt one.

One no longer becometh poor or rich; both are too burdensome. Who still wanteth to rule? Who still wanteth to obey? Both are too burdensome.

No shepherd, and one herd! Everyone wanteth the same; everyone is equal: he who hath other sentiments goeth voluntarily into the madhouse.

"Formerly all the world was insane,"—say the subtlest of them, and blink thereby.

They are clever and know all that hath happened: so there is no end to their raillery. People still fall out, but are soon reconciled—otherwise it spoileth their stomachs.

They have their little pleasures for the day, and their little pleasures for the night, but they have a regard for health.

"We have discovered happiness,"—say the last men, and blink thereby.—

And here ended the first discourse of Zarathustra, which is also called "The Prologue", for at this point the shouting and mirth of the multitude interrupted him. "Give us this last man, O Zarathustra,"—they called out—"make us into these last men! Then will we make thee a present of the Superman!" And all the people exulted and smacked their lips. Zarathustra, however, turned sad, and said to his heart:

"They understand me not: I am not the mouth for these ears.

Too long, perhaps, have I lived in the mountains; too much have I hearkened unto the brooks and trees: now do I speak unto them as unto the goatherds.

Calm is my soul, and clear, like the mountains in the morn·ing. But they think me cold, and a mocker with terrible jests.

And now do they look at me and laugh: and while they laugh they hate me too. There is ice in their laughter."

6

Then, however, something happened which made every mouth mute and every eye fixed. In the meantime, of course, the rope-dancer had commenced his performance: he had come out at a little door, and was going along the rope which was stretched between two towers, so that it hung above the market-place and the people. When he was just midway across, the little door opened once more, and a gaudily-dressed fellow like a buffoon sprang out, and went rapidly after the first one. "Go on, halt-foot," cried his frightful voice, "go on, lazy-bones, interloper, sallow-face!—lest I tickle thee with my heel! What dost thou here between the towers? In the tower is the place for thee, thou shouldst be locked up; to one better than thyself thou blockest the way!"—And with every word he came nearer and nearer the first one. When, however, he was but a step behind, there happened the frightful thing which made every mouth mute and every eye fixed—he uttered a yell like a devil, and jumped over the other who was in his way. The latter, however, when he thus saw his rival triumph, lost at the same time his head and his footing on the rope; he threw his pole away, and shot downward faster than it, like an eddy of arms and legs, into the depth. The market-place and the people were like the sea when the storm cometh on: they all flew apart and in disorder, especially where the body was about to fall.

Zarathustra, however, remained standing, and just beside him fell the body, badly injured and disfigured, but not yet dead. After a while consciousness returned to the shattered man, and he saw Zarathustra kneeling beside him. "What art thou doing there?" said he at last, "I knew long ago that the devil would trip me up. Now he draggeth me to hell: wilt thou prevent him?"

"On mine honour, my friend," answered Zarathustra, "there is nothing of all that whereof thou speakest: there is no devil and no hell. Thy soul will be dead even sooner than thy body; fear, therefore, nothing any more!"

The man looked up distrustfully. "If thou speakest the truth," said he, "I lose nothing when I lose my life. I am not much more than an animal which hath been taught to dance by blows and scanty fare."

"Not at all," said Zarathustra, "thou hast made danger thy calling; therein there is nothing contemptible. Now thou perishest by thy calling: therefore will I bury thee with mine own hands."

When Zarathustra had said this the dying one did not reply further; but he moved his hand as if he sought the hand of Zarathustra in gratitude.

7

Meanwhile the evening came on, and the market-place veiled itself in gloom. Then the people dispersed, for even curiosity and terror become fatigued. Zarathustra, however, still sat beside the dead man on the ground, absorbed in thought: so he forgot the time. But at last it became night, and a cold wind blew upon the lonely one. Then arose Zarathustra and said to his heart:

Verily, a fine catch of fish hath Zarathustra made to-day! It is not a man he hath caught, but a corpse.

Sombre is human life, and as yet without meaning: a buffoon may be fateful to it.

I want to teach men the sense of their existence, which is the Superman, the lightning out of the dark cloud—man.

But still am I far from them, and my sense speaketh not unto their sense. To men I am still something between a fool and a corpse.

Gloomy is the night, gloomy are the ways of Zarathustra. Come, thou cold and stiff companion! I carry thee to the place where I shall bury thee with mine own hands.

<hr>

8

When Zarathustra had said this to his heart, he put the corpse upon his shoulders and set out on his way. Yet had he not gone a hundred steps, when there stole a man up to him and whispered in his ear—and lo! he that spake was the buffoon from the tower. "Leave this town, O Zarathustra," said he, "there are too many here who hate thee. The good and just hate thee, and call thee their enemy and despiser; the believers in the orthodox belief hate thee, and call thee a danger to the multitude. It was thy good fortune to be laughed at: and verily thou spakest like a buffoon. It was thy good fortune to associate with the dead dog; by so humiliating thyself thou hast saved thy life today. Depart, however, from this town,—or tomorrow I shall jump over thee, a living man over a dead one." And when he had said this, the buffoon vanished; Zarathustra, how-ever, went on through the dark streets.

At the gate of the town the grave-diggers met him: they shone their torch on his face, and, recognising Zarathustra, they sorely derided him. "Zarathustra is carrying away the dead dog: a fine thing that Zarathustra hath turned a grave-digger! For our hands are too cleanly for that roast. Will Zarathustra steal the bite from the devil? Well then, good luck to the re-past! If only the devil is not a better thief than Zarathustra!—he will steal them both, he will eat them both!" And they laughed among themselves, and put their heads together.

Zarathustra made no answer thereto, but went on his way. When he had gone on for two hours, past forests and swamps, he had heard too much of the hungry howling of the wolves, and he himself became hungry. So he halted at a lonely house in which a light was burning.

"Hunger attacketh me," said Zarathustra, "like a robber. Among forests and swamps my hunger attacketh me, and late in the night.

"Strange humours hath my hunger. Often it cometh to me only after a repast, and all day it hath failed to come: where hath it been?"

And thereupon Zarathustra knocked at the door of the house. An old man appeared, who carried a light, and asked: "Who cometh unto me and my bad sleep?"

"A living man and a dead one," said Zarathustra. "Give me something to eat and drink, I forgot it during the day. He that feedeth the hungry refresheth his own soul, saith wisdom."

The old man withdrew, but came back immediately and offered Zarathustra bread and wine. "A bad country for the hungry," said he; "that is why I live here. Animal and man come unto me, the anchorite. But bid thy companion eat and drink also, he is wearier than thou." Zarathustra answered: "My companion is dead; I shall hardly be able to persuade him to eat." "That doth not concern me," said the old man sullenly; "he that knocketh at my door must take what I offer him. Eat, and fare ye well!"——

Thereafter Zarathustra again went on for two hours, trust-ing to the path and the light of the stars: for he was an experi-enced night-walker, and liked to look into the face of all that slept. When the morning dawned, however, Zarathustra found himself in a thick forest, and no path was any longer visible. He then put the dead man in a hollow tree at his head—for he wanted to protect him from the wolves—and laid himself down on the ground and moss. And immediately he fell asleep, tired in body, but with a tranquil soul.

9

Long slept Zarathustra; and not only the rosy dawn passed over his head, but also the morning. At last, however, his eyes opened, and amazedly he gazed into the forest and the stillness, amazedly he gazed into himself. Then he arose quickly, like a seafarer who all at once seeth the land; and he shouted for joy: for he saw a new truth. And he spake thus to his heart:

A light hath dawned upon me: I need companions—living ones; not dead companions and corpses, which I carry with me where I will.

But I need living companions, who will follow me because they want to follow themselves—and to the place where I will. A light hath dawned upon me. Not to the people is Zarathustra to speak, but to companions! Zarathustra shall not be the herd's herdsman and hound!

[17]

To allure many from the herd—for that purpose have I come. The people and the herd must be angry with me: a robber shall Zarathustra be called by the herdsmen.

Herdsmen, I say, but they call themselves the good and just. Herdsmen, I say, but they call themselves the believers in the orthodox belief.

Behold the good and just! Whom do they hate most? Him who breaketh up their tables of values, the breaker, the law-breaker:—he, however, is the creator.

Behold the believers of all beliefs! Whom do they hate most? Him who breaketh up their tables of values, the breaker, the law-breaker—he, however, is the creator.

Companions, the creator seeketh, not corpses—and not herds or believers either. Fellow-creators the creator seeketh—those who grave new values on new tables.

Companions, the creator seeketh, and fellow-reapers: for everything is ripe for the harvest with him. But he lacketh the hundred sickles: so he plucketh the ears of corn and is vexed.

Companions, the creator seeketh, and such as know how to whet their sickles. Destroyers, will they be called, and despisers of good and evil. But they are the reapers and rejoicers.

Fellow-creators, Zarathustra seeketh; fellow-reapers and fellow-rejoicers, Zarathustra seeketh: what hath he to do with herds and herdsmen and corpses!

And thou, my first companion, rest in peace! Well have I buried thee in thy hollow tree; well have I hid thee from the wolves.

But I part from thee; the time hath arrived. 'Twixt rosy dawn and rosy dawn there came unto me a new truth.

I am not to be a herdsman, I am not to be a grave-digger. Not any more will I discourse unto the people; for the last time have I spoken unto the dead.

[*18*]

With the creators, the reapers, and the rejoicers will I associate: the rainbow will I show them, and all the stairs to the Superman.

To the lone-dwellers will I sing my song, and to the twain-dwellers; and unto him who hath still ears for the unheard, will I make the heart heavy with my happiness.

I make for my goal, I follow my course; over the loitering and tardy will I leap. Thus let my on-going be their down-going!

10

This had Zarathustra said to his heart when the sun stood at noon-tide. Then he looked inquiringly aloft,—for he heard above him the sharp call of a bird. And behold! An eagle swept through the air in wide circles, and on it hung a serpent, not like a prey, but like a friend: for it kept itself coiled round the eagle's neck.

"They are mine animals," said Zarathustra, and rejoiced in his heart.

"The proudest animal under the sun, and the wisest animal under the sun,—they have come out to reconnoitre.

They want to know whether Zarathustra still liveth. Verily, do I still live?

More dangerous have I found it among men than among animals; in dangerous paths goeth Zarathustra. Let mine animals lead me!"

When Zarathustra had said this, he remembered the words of the saint in the forest. Then he sighed and spake thus to his heart:

"Would that I were wiser! Would that I were wise from the very heart, like my serpent!

But I am asking the impossible. Therefore do I ask my pride to go always with my wisdom!

And if my wisdom should some day forsake me:—alas! it loveth to fly away!—may my pride then fly with my folly!"

Thus began Zarathustra's down-going.

THUS SPAKE ZARATHUSTRA

FIRST PART

1. The Three Metamorphoses

THREE metamorphoses of the spirit do I designate to you: how the spirit becometh a camel, the camel a lion, and the lion at last a child.

Many heavy things are there for the spirit, the strong load-bearing spirit in which reverence dwelleth: for the heavy and the heaviest longeth its strength.

What is heavy? so asketh the load-bearing spirit; then kneeleth it down like the camel, and wanteth to be well laden.

What is the heaviest thing, ye heroes? asketh the load-bearing spirit, that I may take it upon me and rejoice in my strength.

Is it not this: To humiliate oneself in order to mortify one's pride? To exhibit one's folly in order to mock at one's wisdom?

Or is it this: To desert our cause when it celebrateth its triumph? To ascend high mountains to tempt the tempter?

Or is it this: To feed on the acorns and grass of knowledge, and for the sake of truth to suffer hunger of soul?

Or is it this: To be sick and dismiss comforters, and make friends of the deaf, who never hear thy requests?

Or is it this: To go into foul water when it is the water of truth, and not disclaim cold frogs and hot toads?

Or is it this: To love those who despise us, and give one's hand to the phantom when it is going to frighten us?

All these heaviest things the load-bearing spirit taketh upon itself: and like the camel, which, when laden, hasteneth into the wilderness, so hasteneth the spirit into its wilderness.

But in the loneliest wilderness happeneth the second meta-morphosis: here the spirit becometh a lion; freedom will it capture, and lordship in its own wilderness.

Its last Lord it here seeketh: hostile will it be to him, and to its last God; for victory will it struggle with the great dragon.

What is the great dragon which the spirit is no longer inclined to call Lord and God? "Thou-shalt," is the great dragon called. But the spirit of the lion saith, "I will."

"Thou-shalt," lieth in its path, sparkling with gold—a scale-covered beast; and on every scale glittereth golden, "Thou shalt!"

The values of a thousand years glitter on those scales, and thus speaketh the mightiest of all dragons: "All the values of things—glitter on me.

All values have already been created, and all created values—do I represent. Verily, there shall be no 'I will' any more." Thus speaketh the dragon.

My brethren, wherefore is there need of the lion in the spirit? Why sufficeth not the beast of burden, which renounceth and is reverent?

To create new values—that, even the lion cannot yet accomplish: but to create itself freedom for new creating—that can the might of the lion do.

To create itself freedom, and give a holy Nay even unto duty: for that, my brethren, there is need of the lion.

To assume the ride to new values—that is the most formidable assumption for a load-bearing and reverent spirit. Verily, unto such a spirit it is preying, and the work of a beast of prey.

As its holiest, it once loved "Thou-shalt": now is it forced to find illusion and arbitrariness even in the holiest things, that it may capture freedom from its love: the lion is needed for this capture.

[24]

But tell me, my brethren, what the child can do, which even the lion could not do? Why hath the preying lion still to become a child?

Innocence is the child, and forgetfulness, a new beginning, a game, a self-rolling wheel, a first movement, a holy Yea.

Aye, for the game of creating, my brethren, there is needed a holy Yea unto life: *its own* will, willeth now the spirit; *his own* world winneth the world's outcast.

Three metamorphoses of the spirit have I designated to you: how the spirit became a camel, the camel a lion, and the lion at last a child.——

Thus spake Zarathustra. And at that time he abode in the town which is called The Pied Cow.

2. *The Academic Chairs of Virtue*

PEOPLE commended unto Zarathustra a wise man, as one who could discourse well about sleep and virtue: greatly was he honoured and rewarded for it, and all the youths sat before his chair. To him went Zarathustra, and sat among the youths before his chair. And thus spake the wise man:

Respect and modesty in presence of sleep! That is the first thing! And to go out of the way of all who sleep badly and keep awake at night!

Modest is even the thief in presence of sleep: he always stealeth softly through the night. Immodest, however, is the night-watchman; immodestly he carrieth his horn.

No small art is it to sleep: it is necessary for that purpose to keep awake all day.

Ten times a day must thou overcome thyself: that causeth wholesome weariness, and is poppy to the soul.

Ten times must thou reconcile again with thyself; for overcoming is bitterness, and badly sleep the unreconciled.

Ten truths must thou find during the day; otherwise wilt thou seek truth during the night, and thy soul will have been hungry.

Ten times must thou laugh during the day, and be cheerful; otherwise thy stomach, the father of affliction, will disturb thee in the night.

Few people know it, but one must have all the virtues in order to sleep well. Shall I bear false witness? Shall I commit adultery?

Shall I covet my neighbour's maidservant? All that would ill accord with good sleep.

And even if one have all the virtues, there is still one thing needful: to send the virtues themselves to sleep at the right time.

That they may not quarrel with one another, the good females! And about thee, thou unhappy one!

Peace with God and thy neighbour: so desireth good sleep. And peace also with thy neighbour's devil! Otherwise it will haunt thee in the night.

Honour to the government. and obedience, and also to the crooked government! So desireth good sleep. How can I help it, if power liketh to walk on crooked legs?

He who leadeth his sheep to the greenest pasture, shall always be for me the best shepherd: so doth it accord with good sleep.

Many honours I want not, nor great treasures: they excite the spleen. But it is bad sleeping without a good name and a little treasure.

A small company is more welcome to me than a bad one: but they must come and go at the right time. So doth it accord with good sleep.

Well, also, do the poor in spirit please me: they promote sleep. Blessed are they, especially if one always give in to them.

Thus passeth the day unto the virtuous. When night cometh, then take I good care not to summon sleep. It disliketh to be summoned—sleep, the lord of the virtues!

But I think of what I have done and thought during the day. Thus ruminating, patient as a cow, I ask myself: What were thy ten overcomings?

And what were the ten reconciliations, and the ten truths, and the ten laughters with which my heart enjoyed itself?

Thus pondering, and cradled by forty thoughts, it overtaketh me all at once—sleep, the unsummoned, the lord of the virtues.

Sleep tappeth on mine eye, and it turneth heavy. Sleep toucheth my mouth, and it remaineth open.

Verily, on soft soles doth it come to me, the dearest of thieves, and stealeth from me my thoughts: stupid do I then stand, like this academic chair.

But not much longer do I then stand: I already lie.—

When Zarathustra heard the wise man thus speak, he laughed in his heart: for thereby had a light dawned upon him. And thus spake he to his heart:

A fool seemeth this wise man with his forty thoughts: but I believe he knoweth well how to sleep.

Happy even is he who liveth near this wise man! Such sleep is contagious—even through a thick wall it is contagious.

A magic resideth even in his academic chair. And not in vain did the youths sit before the preacher of virtue.

His wisdom is to keep awake in order to sleep well. And verily, if life had no sense, and had I to choose nonsense, this would be the desirablest nonsense for me also.

Now know I well what people sought formerly above all else when they sought teachers of virtue. Good sleep they sought for themselves, and poppy-head virtues to promote it!

To all those belauded sages of the academic chairs, wisdom was sleep without dreams: they knew no higher significance of life.

Even at present, to be sure, there are some like this preacher of virtue, and not always so honourable: but their time is past. And not much longer do they stand: there they already lie.

Blessed are those drowsy ones: for they shall soon nod to sleep.—

Thus spake Zarathustra.

3. Backworldsmen

ONCE on a time, Zarathustra also cast his fancy beyond man, like all backworldsmen. The work of a suffering and tortured God, did the world then seem to me.

The dream—and diction—of a God, did the world then seem to me; coloured vapours before the eyes of a divinely dissatisfied one.

Good and evil, and joy and woe, and I and thou—coloured

vapours did they seem to me before creative eyes. The creator wished to look away from himself,—thereupon he created the world.

Intoxicating joy is it for the sufferer to look away from his suffering and forget himself. Intoxicating joy and self-forgetting, did the world once seem to me.

This world, the eternally imperfect, an eternal contradiction's image and imperfect image—an intoxicating joy to its imperfect creator:—thus did the world once seem to me.

Thus, once on a time, did I also cast my fancy beyond man, like all backworldsmen. Beyond man, forsooth?

Ah, ye brethren, that God whom I created was human work and human madness, like all the gods!

A man was he, and only a poor fragment of a man and ego. Out of mine own ashes and glow it came unto me, that phantom. And verily, it came not unto me from the beyond!

What happened, my brethren? I surpassed myself, the suffering one; I carried mine own ashes to the mountain; a brighter flame I contrived for myself. And lo! Thereupon the phantom *withdrew* from me!

To me the convalescent would it now be suffering and torment to believe in such phantoms: suffering would it now be to me, and humiliation. Thus speak I to backworldsmen.

Suffering was it, and impotence—that created all backworlds; and the short madness of happiness, which only the greatest sufferer experienceth.

Weariness, which seeketh to get to the ultimate with one leap, with a death-leap; a poor ignorant weariness, unwilling even to will any longer: that created all gods and backworlds.

Believe me, my brethren! It was the body which despaired of the body—it groped with the fingers of the infatuated spirit at the ultimate walls.

Believe me, my brethren! It was the body which despaired of the earth—it heard the bowels of existence speaking unto it.

And then it sought to get through the ultimate walls with its head—and not with its head only—into "the other world."

But that "other world" is well concealed from man, that dehumanised, inhuman world, which is a celestial naught; and the bowels of existence do not speak unto man, except as man.

Verily, it is difficult to prove all being, and hard to make it speak. Tell me, ye brethren, is not the strangest of all things best proved?

Yea, this ego, with its contradiction and perplexity, speaketh most uprightly of its being—this creating, willing, evaluing ego, which is the measure and value of things.

And this most upright existence, the ego—it speaketh of the body, and still implieth the body, even when it museth and raveth and fluttereth with broken wings.

Always more uprightly learneth it to speak, the ego; and the more it learneth, the more doth it find titles, and honours for the body and the earth.

A new pride taught me mine ego, and that teach I unto men: no longer to thrust one's head into the sand of celestial things, but to carry it freely, a terrestrial head, which giveth meaning to the earth!

A new will teach I unto men: to choose that path which man hath followed blindly, and to approve of it—and no longer to slink aside from it, like the sick and perishing!

The sick and perishing—it was they who despised the body and the earth, and invented the heavenly world, and the redeeming blood-drops; but even those sweet and sad poisons they borrowed from the body and the earth!

From their misery they sought escape, and the stars were

too remote for them. Then they sighed: "O that there were heavenly paths by which to steal into another existence and into happiness!" Then they contrived for themselves their by-paths and bloody draughts!

Beyond the sphere of their body and this earth they now fancied themselves transported, these ungrateful ones. But to what did they owe the convulsion and rapture of their transport? To their body and this earth.

Gentle is Zarathustra to the sickly. Verily, he is not indignant at their modes of consolation and ingratitude. May they become convalescents and overcomers, and create higher bodies for themselves!

Neither is Zarathustra indignant at a convalescent who looketh tenderly on his delusions, and at midnight stealeth round the grave of his God; but sickness and a sick frame remain even in his tears.

Many sickly ones have there always been among those who muse, and languish for God; violently they hate the discerning ones, and the latest of virtues, which is uprightness.

Backward they always gaze toward dark ages: then, indeed, were delusion and faith something different. Raving of the reason was likeness to God, and doubt was sin.

Too well do I know those godlike ones: they insist on being believed in, and that doubt is sin. Too well, also, do I know what they themselves most believe in.

Verily, not in backworlds and redeeming blood-drops: but in the body do they also believe most; and their own body is for them the thing-in-itself.

But it is a sickly thing to them, and gladly would they get out of their skin. Therefore hearken they to the preachers of death, and themselves preach backworlds.

Hearken rather, my brethren, to the voice of the healthy body; it is a more upright and pure voice.

More uprightly and purely speaketh the healthy body, perfect and square-built; and it speaketh of the meaning of the earth.—

Thus spake Zarathustra.

4. The Despisers of the Body

To the despisers of the body will I speak my word. I wish them neither to learn afresh, nor teach anew, but only to bid farewell to their own bodies,—and thus be dumb.

"Body am I, and soul"—so saith the child. And why should one not speak like children?

But the awakened one, the knowing one, saith: "Body am I entirely, and nothing more; and soul is only the name of something in the body."

The body is a big sagacity, a plurality with one sense, a war and a peace, a flock and a shepherd.

An instrument of thy body is also thy little sagacity, my brother, which thou callest "spirit"—a little instrument and plaything of thy big sagacity.

"Ego," sayest thou, and art proud of that word. But the greater thing—in which thou art unwilling to believe—is thy body with its big sagacity; it saith not "ego," but doeth it.

What the sense feeleth, what the spirit discerneth, hath never its end in itself. But sense and spirit would fain persuade thee that they are the end of all things: so vain are they.

[*32*]

Instruments and playthings are sense and spirit: behind them there is still the Self. The Self seeketh with the eyes of the senses, it hearkeneth also with the ears of the spirit.

Ever hearkeneth the Self, and seeketh; it compareth, mastereth, conquereth, and destroyeth. It ruleth, and is also the ego's ruler.

Behind thy thoughts and feelings, my brother, there is a mighty lord, an unknown sage—it is called Self; it dwelleth in thy body, it is thy body.

There is more sagacity in thy body than in thy best wisdom. And who then knoweth why thy body requireth just thy best wisdom?

Thy Self laugheth at thine ego, and its proud prancings. "What are these prancings and flights of thought unto me?" it saith to itself. "A by-way to my purpose. I am the leading-string of the ego, and the prompter of its notions."

The Self saith unto the ego: "Feel pain!" And thereupon it suffereth, and thinketh how it may put an end thereto—and for that very purpose it *is meant* to think.

The Self saith unto the ego: "Feel pleasure!" Thereupon it rejoiceth, and thinketh how it may ofttimes rejoice—and for that very purpose it *is meant* to think.

To the despisers of the body will I speak a word. That they despise is caused by their esteem. What is it that created esteeming and despising and worth and will?

The creating Self created for itself esteeming and despising, it created for itself joy and woe. The creating body created for itself spirit, as a hand to its will.

Even in your folly and despising ye each serve your Self, ye despisers of the body. I tell you, your very Self wanteth to die, and turneth away from life.

No longer can your Self do that which it desireth most:—

[*33*]

create beyond itself. That is what it desireth most; that is all its fervour.

But it is now too late to do so:—so your Self wisheth to succumb, ye despisers of the body.

To succumb—so wisheth your Self; and therefore have ye become despisers of the body. For ye can no longer create beyond yourselves.

And therefore are ye now angry with life and with the earth. And unconscious envy is in the sidelong look of your contempt.

I go not your way, ye despisers of the body! Ye are no bridges for me to the Superman!—

Thus spake Zarathustra.

5. *Joys and Passions*

MY BROTHER, when thou hast a virtue, and it is thine own virtue, thou hast it in common with no one.

To be sure, thou wouldst call it by name and caress it; thou wouldst pull its ears and amuse thyself with it.

And lo! Then hast thou its name in common with the people, and hast become one of the people and the herd with thy virtue!

Better for thee to say: "Ineffable is it, and nameless, that which is pain and sweetness to my soul, and also the hunger of my bowels."

Let thy virtue be too high for the familiarity of names, and if thou must speak of it, be not ashamed to stammer about it.

Thus speak and stammer: "That is *my* good, that do I love, thus doth it please me entirely, thus only do *I* desire the good.

Not as the law of a God do I desire it, not as a human law or a human need do I desire it; it is not to be a guide-post for me to superearths and paradises.

An earthly virtue is it which I love: little prudence is therein, and the least everyday wisdom.

But that bird built its nest beside me: therefore, I love and cherish it—now sitteth it beside me on its golden eggs."

Thus shouldst thou stammer, and praise thy virtue.

Once hadst thou passions and calledst them evil. But now hast thou only thy virtues: they grew out of thy passions.

Thou implantedst thy highest aim into the heart of those passions: then became they thy virtues and joys.

And though thou wert of the race of the hot-tempered, or of the voluptuous, or of the fanatical, or the vindictive;

All thy passions in the end became virtues, and all thy devils angels.

Once hadst thou wild dogs in thy cellar: but they changed at last into birds and charming songstresses.

Out of thy poisons brewedst thou balsam for thyself; thy cow, affliction, milkedst thou—now drinketh thou the sweet milk of her udder.

And nothing evil groweth in thee any longer, unless it be the evil that groweth out of the conflict of thy virtues.

My brother, if thou be fortunate, then wilt thou have one virtue and no more: thus goest thou easier over the bridge.

Illustrious is it to have many virtues, but a hard lot; and many a one hath gone into the wilderness and killed himself, because he was weary of being the battle and battlefield of virtues.

My brother, are war and battle evil? Necessary, however, is the evil; necessary are the envy and the distrust and the back-biting among the virtues.

Lo! how each of thy virtues is covetous of the highest place; it wanteth thy whole spirit to be *its* herald, it wanteth thy whole power, in wrath, hatred, and love.

Jealous is every virtue of the others, and a dreadful thing is jealousy. Even virtues may succumb by jealousy.

He whom the flame of jealousy encompasseth, turneth at last, like the scorpion, the poisoned sting against himself.

Ah! my brother, hast thou never seen a virtue backbite and stab itself?

Man is something that hath to be surpassed: and therefore shalt thou love thy virtues,—for thou wilt succumb by them.—

Thus spake Zarathustra.

6. *The Pale Criminal*

YE DO not mean to slay, ye judges and sacrificers, until the animal hath bowed its head? Lo! the pale criminal hath bowed his head: out of his eye speaketh the great contempt.

"Mine ego is something which is to be surpassed: mine ego is to me the great contempt of man": so speaketh it out of that eye.

When he judged himself—that was his supreme moment; let not the exalted one relapse again into his low estate!

There is no salvation for him who thus suffereth from himself, unless it be speedy death.

Your slaying, ye judges, shall be pity, and not revenge; and in that ye slay, see to it that ye yourselves justify life!

It is not enough that ye should reconcile with him whom ye slay. Let your sorrow be love to the Superman: thus will ye justify your own survival!

"Enemy" shall ye say but not "villain," "invalid" shall ye say but not "wretch," "fool" shall ye say but not "sinner."

And thou, red judge, if thou would say audibly all thou hast done in thought, then would every one cry: "Away with the nastiness and the virulent reptile!"

But one thing is the thought, another thing is the deed, and another thing is the idea of the deed. The wheel of causality doth not roll between them.

An idea made this pale man pale. Adequate was he for his deed when he did it, but the idea of it, he could not endure when it was done.

Evermore did he now see himself as the doer of one deed. Madness, I call this: the exception reversed itself to the rule in him.

The streak of chalk bewitcheth the hen; the stroke he struck bewitched his weak reason. Madness *after* the deed, I call this.

Hearken, ye judges! There is another madness besides, and it is *before* the deed. Ah! ye have not gone deep enough into this soul!

Thus speaketh the red judge: "Why did this criminal commit murder? He meant to rob." I tell you, however, that his soul wanted blood, not booty: he thirsted for the happiness of the knife!

But his weak reason understood not this madness, and it persuaded him. "What matter about blood!" it said; "wishest thou not, at least, to make booty thereby? Or take revenge?"

And he hearkened unto his weak reason: like lead lay its words upon him—thereupon he robbed when he murdered. He did not mean to be ashamed of his madness.

And now once more lieth the lead of his guilt upon him, and once more is his weak reason so benumbed, so paralysed, and so dull.

Could he only shake his head, then would his burden roll off; but who shaketh that head?

What is this man? A mass of diseases that reach out into the world through the spirit; there they want to get their prey.

What is this man? A coil of wild serpents that are seldom at peace among themselves—so they go forth apart and seek prey in the world.

Look at that poor body! What it suffered and craved, the poor soul interpreted to itself—it interpreted it as murderous desire, and eagerness for the happiness of the knife.

Him who now turneth sick, the evil overtaketh which is now the evil: he seeketh to cause pain with that which causeth him pain. But there have been other ages, and another evil and good.

Once was doubt evil, and the will to Self. Then the invalid became a heretic or sorcerer; as heretic or sorcerer he suffered, and sought to cause suffering.

But this will not enter your ears; it hurteth your good people, ye tell me. But what doth it matter to me about your good people!

Many things in your good people cause me disgust, and verily, not their evil. I would that they had a madness by which they succumbed, like this pale criminal!

Verily, I would that their madness were called truth, or

fidelity, or justice: but they have their virtue in order to live long, and in wretched self-complacency.

I am a railing alongside the torrent; whoever is able to grasp me may grasp me! Your crutch, however, I am not.—

Thus spake Zarathustra.

7. *Reading and Writing*

OF ALL that is written, I love only what a person hath written with his blood. Write with blood, and thou wilt find that blood is spirit.

It is no easy task to understand unfamiliar blood; I hate the reading idlers.

He who knoweth the reader, doeth nothing more for the reader. Another century of readers—and spirit itself will stink.

Every one being allowed to learn to read, ruineth in the long run not only writing but also thinking.

Once spirit was God, then it became man, and now it even becometh populace.

He that writeth in blood and proverbs doth not want to be read, but learnt by heart.

In the mountains the shortest way is from peak to peak, but for that route thou must have long legs. Proverbs should be peaks, and those spoken to should be big and tall.

The atmosphere rare and pure, danger near and the spirit full of a joyful wickedness: thus are things well matched.

I want to have goblins about me, for I am courageous. The

courage which scareth away ghosts, createth for itself goblins
—it wanteth to laugh.

I no longer feel in common with you; the very cloud which I
see beneath me, the blackness and heaviness at which I laugh
—that is your thunder-cloud.

Ye look aloft when ye long for exaltation; and I look downward because I am exalted.

Who among you can at the same time laugh and be exalted?

He who climbeth on the highest mountains, laugheth at all
tragic plays and tragic realities.

Courageous, unconcerned, scornful, coercive—so wisdom
wisheth us; she is a woman, and ever loveth only a warrior.

Ye tell me, "Life is hard to bear." But for what purpose
should ye have your pride in the morning and your resignation in the evening?

Life is hard to bear: but do not affect to be so delicate! We
are all of us fine sumpter asses and she-asses.

What have we in common with the rose-bud, which
trembleth because a drop of dew hath formed upon it?

It is true we love life; not because we are wont to live, but
because we are wont to love.

There is always some madness in love. But there is always,
also, some method in madness.

And to me also, who appreciate life, the butterflies, and
soap-bubbles, and whatever is like them amongst us, seem most
to enjoy happiness.

To see these light, foolish, pretty, lively little sprites flit
about—that moveth Zarathustra to tears and songs.

I should only believe in a God that would know how to
dance.

And when I saw my devil, I found him serious, thorough,

profound, solemn: he was the spirit of gravity—through him all things fall.

Not by wrath, but by laughter, do we slay. Come, let us slay the spirit of gravity!

I learned to walk; since then have I let myself run. I learned to fly; since then I do not need pushing in order to move from a spot.

Now am I light, now do I fly; now do I see myself under myself. Now there danceth a God in me.—

Thus spake Zarathustra.

8. The Tree on the Hill

ZARATHUSTRA's eye had perceived that a certain youth avoided him. And as he walked alone one evening over the hills surrounding the town called "The Pied Cow," behold, there found he the youth sitting leaning against a tree, and gazing with wearied look into the valley. Zarathustra thereupon laid hold of the tree beside which the youth sat, and spake thus:

"If I wished to shake this tree with my hands, I should not be able to do so.

But the wind, which we see not, troubleth and bendeth it as it listeth. We are sorest bent and troubled by invisible hands."

Thereupon the youth arose disconcerted, and said: "I hear Zarathustra, and just now was I thinking of him!" Zarathustra answered:

"Why art thou frightened on that account?—But it is the same with man as with the tree.

The more he seeketh to rise into the height and light, the more vigorously do his roots struggle earthward, downward, into the dark and deep—into the evil."

"Yea, into the evil!" cried the youth. "How is it possible that thou hast discovered my soul?"

Zarathustra smiled, and said: "Many a soul one will never discover, unless one first invent it."

"Yea, into the evil!" cried the youth once more.

"Thou saidst the truth, Zarathustra. I trust myself no longer since I sought to rise into the height, and nobody trusteth me any longer; how doth that happen?

I change too quickly: my to-day refuteth my yesterday. I often overleap the steps when I clamber; for so doing, none of the steps pardons me.

When aloft, I find myself always alone. No one speaketh unto me; the frost of solitude maketh me tremble. What do I seek on the height?

My contempt and my longing increase together; the higher I clamber, the more do I despise him who clambereth. What doth he seek on the height?

How ashamed I am of my clambering and stumbling! How I mock at my violent panting! How I hate him who flieth! How tired I am on the height!"

Here the youth was silent. And Zarathustra contemplated the tree beside which they stood, and spake thus:

"This tree standeth lonely here on the hills; it hath grown up high above man and beast.

And if it wanted to speak, it would have none who could understand it: so high hath it grown.

Now it waiteth and waiteth,—for what doth it wait? It dwelleth too close to the seat of the clouds; it waiteth perhaps for the first lightning?"

When Zarathustra had said this, the youth called out with violent gestures: "Yea, Zarathustra, thou speakest the truth My destruction I longed for, when I desired to be on the height, and thou art the lightning for which I waited! Lo. what have I been since thou hast appeared amongst us? It is mine envy of thee that hath destroyed me!"—Thus spake the youth, and wept bitterly. Zarathustra, however, put his arm about him, and led the youth away with him.

And when they had walked a while together, Zarathustra began to speak thus:

It rendeth my heart. Better than thy words express it, thine eyes tell me all thy danger.

As yet thou art not free; thou still *seekest* freedom. Too unslept hath thy seeking made thee, and too wakeful.

On the open height wouldst thou be; for the stars thirsteth thy soul. But thy bad impulses also thirst for freedom.

Thy wild dogs want liberty; they bark for joy in their cellar when thy spirit endeavoureth to open all prison doors.

Still art thou a prisoner—it seemeth to me—who deviseth liberty for himself: ah! sharp becometh the soul of such prisoners, but also deceitful and wicked.

To purify himself, is still necessary for the freedman of the spirit. Much of the prison and the mould still remaineth in him: pure hath his eye still to become.

Yea, I know thy danger. But by my love and hope I conjure thee: cast not thy love and hope away!

Noble thou feelest thyself still, and noble others also feel thee still, though they bear thee a grudge and cast evil looks Know this, that to everybody a noble one standeth in the way.

Also to the good, a noble one standeth in the way: and even when they call him a good man, they want thereby to put him aside.

The new, would the noble man create, and a new virtue. The old, wanteth the good man, and that the old should be conserved.

But it is not the danger of the noble man to turn a good man, but lest he should become a blusterer, a scoffer, or a destroyer.

Ah! I have known noble ones who lost their highest hope. And then they disparaged all high hopes.

Then lived they shamelessly in temporary pleasures, and beyond the day had hardly an aim.

"Spirit is also voluptuousness,"—said they. Then broke the wings of their spirit; and now it creepeth about, and defileth where it gnaweth.

Once they thought of becoming heroes; but sensualists are they now. A trouble and a terror is the hero to them.

But by my love and hope I conjure thee: cast not away the hero in thy soul! Maintain holy thy highest hope!—

Thus spake Zarathustra.

9. *The Preachers of Death*

THERE are preachers of death: and the earth is full of those to whom desistance from life must be preached.

Full is the earth of the superfluous; marred is life by the many-too-many. May they be decoyed out of this life by the "life eternal"!

"The yellow ones": so are called the preachers of death, or

"the black ones." But I will show them unto you in other colours besides.

There are the terrible ones who carry about in themselves the beast of prey, and have no choice except lusts or self-laceration. And even their lusts are self-laceration.

They have not yet become men, those terrible ones: may they preach desistance from life, and pass away themselves!

There are the spiritually consumptive ones: hardly are they born when they begin to die, and long for doctrines of lassitude and renunciation.

They would fain be dead, and we should approve of their wish! Let us beware of awakening those dead ones, and of damaging those living coffins!

They meet an invalid, or an old man, or a corpse—and immediately they say: "Life is refuted!"

But they only are refuted, and their eye, which seeth only one aspect of existence.

Shrouded in thick melancholy, and eager for the little casualties that bring death: thus do they wait, and clench their teeth.

Or else, they grasp at sweetmeats, and mock at their childishness thereby: they cling to their straw of life, and mock at their still clinging to it.

Their wisdom speaketh thus: "A fool, he who remaineth alive; but so far are we fools! And that is the foolishest thing in life!"

"Life is only suffering": so say others, and lie not. Then see to it that ye cease! See to it that the life ceaseth which is only suffering!

And let this be the teaching of your virtue: "Thou shalt slay thyself! Thou shalt steal away from thyself!"—

[45]

"Lust is sin,"—so say some who preach death—"let us go apart and beget no children!"

"Giving birth is troublesome,"—say others—"why still give birth? One beareth only the unfortunate!" And they also are preachers of death.

"Pity is necessary,"—so saith a third party. "Take what I have! Take what I am! So much less doth life bind me!"

Were they consistently pitiful, then would they make their neighbours sick of life. To be wicked—that would be their true goodness.

But they want to be rid of life; what care they if they bind others still faster with their chains and gifts!—

And ye also, to whom life is rough labour and disquiet, are ye not very tired of life? Are ye not very ripe for the sermon of death?

All ye to whom rough labour is dear, and the rapid, new, and strange—ye put up with yourselves badly; your diligence is flight, and the will to self-forgetfulness.

If ye believed more in life, then would ye devote yourselves less to the momentary. But for waiting, ye have not enough of capacity in you—nor even for idling!

Everywhere resoundeth the voices of those who preach death; and the earth is full of those to whom death hath to be preached.

Or "life eternal"; it is all the same to me—if only they pass away quickly!—

Thus spake Zarathustra.

10. War and Warriors

BY OUR best enemies we do not want to be spared, nor by those either whom we love from the very heart. So let me tell you the truth!

My brethren in war! I love you from the very heart. I am, and was ever, your counterpart. And I am also your best enemy. So let me tell you the truth!

I know the hatred and envy of your hearts. Ye are not great enough not to know of hatred and envy. Then be great enough not to be ashamed of them!

And if ye cannot be saints of knowledge, then, I pray you, be at least its warriors. They are the companions and forerunners of such saintship.

I see many soldiers; could I but see many warriors! "Uniform" one calleth what they wear; may it not be uniform what they therewith hide!

Ye shall be those whose eyes ever seek for an enemy—for *your* enemy. And with some of you there is hatred at first sight.

Your enemy shall ye seek; your war shall ye wage, and for the sake of your thoughts! And if your thoughts succumb, your uprightness shall still shout triumph thereby!

Ye shall love peace as a means to new wars—and the short peace more than the long.

You I advise not to work, but to fight. You I advise not to peace, but to victory. Let your work be a fight, let your peace be a victory!

One can only be silent and sit peacefully when one hath arrow and bow; otherwise one prateth and quarrelleth. Let your peace be a victory!

Ye say it is the good cause which halloweth even war? I say unto you: it is the good war which halloweth every cause.

War and courage have done more great things than charity. Not your sympathy, but your bravery hath hitherto saved the victims.

"What is good?" ye ask. To be brave is good. Let the little girls say: "To be good is what is pretty, and at the same time touching."

They call you heartless: but your heart is true, and I love the bashfulness of your goodwill. Ye are ashamed of your flow, and others are ashamed of their ebb.

Ye are ugly? Well then, my brethren, take the sublime about you, the mantle of the ugly!

And when your soul becometh great, then doth it become haughty, and in your sublimity there is wickedness. I know you.

In wickedness the haughty man and the weakling meet. But they misunderstand one another. I know you.

Ye shall only have enemies to be hated, but not enemies to be despised. Ye must be proud of your enemies; then, the successes of your enemies are also your successes.

Resistance—that is the distinction of the slave. Let your distinction be obedience. Let your commanding itself be obeying!

To the good warrior soundeth "thou shalt" pleasanter than "I will." And all that is dear unto you, ye shall first have it commanded unto you.

Let your love to life be love to your highest hope; and let your highest hope be the highest thought of life!

Your highest thought, however, ye shall have it commanded unto you by me—and it is this: man is something that is to be surpassed.

[48]

So live your life of obedience and of war! What matter about long life! What warrior wisheth to be spared!

I spare you not, I love you from my very heart, my brethren in war!—

Thus spake Zarathustra.

11. *The New Idol*

SOMEWHERE there are still peoples and herds, but not with us, my brethren: here there are states.

A state? What is that? Well! open now your ears unto me, for now will I say unto you my word concerning the death of peoples.

A state, is called the coldest of all cold monsters. Coldly lieth it also; and this lie creepeth from its mouth: "I, the state, am the people."

It is a lie! Creators were they who created peoples, and hung a faith and a love over them: thus they served life.

Destroyers, are they who lay snares for many, and call it the state: they hang a sword and a hundred cravings over them.

Where there is still a people, there the state is not understood, but hated as the evil eye, and as sin against laws and customs.

This sign I give unto you: every people speaketh its language of good and evil: this its neighbour understandeth not. Its language hath it devised for itself in laws and customs.

But the state lieth in all languages of good and evil; and whatever it saith it lieth; and whatever it hath it hath stolen.

False is everything in it; with stolen teeth it biteth, the biting one. False are even its bowels.

Confusion of language of good and evil; this sign I give unto you as the sign of the state. Verily, the will to death, indicateth this sign! Verily, it beckoneth unto the preachers of death!

Many too many are born: for the superfluous ones was the state devised!

See just how it enticeth them to it, the many-too-many! How it swalloweth and cheweth and recheweth them!

"On earth there is nothing greater than I: it is I who am the regulating finger of God"—thus roareth the monster. And not only the long-eared and short-sighted fall upon their knees!

Ah! even in your ears, ye great souls, it whispereth its gloomy lies! Ah! it findeth out the rich hearts which willingly lavish themselves!

Yea, it findeth you out too, ye conquerors of the old God! Weary ye became of the conflict, and now your weariness serveth the new idol!

Heroes and honourable ones, it would fain set up around it, the new idol! Gladly it basketh in the sunshine of good consciences,—the cold monster!

Everything will it give *you,* if *ye* worship it, the new idol: thus it purchaseth the lustre of your virtue, and the glance of your proud eyes.

It seeketh to allure by means of you, the many-too-many! Yea, a hellish artifice hath here been devised, a death-horse jingling with the trappings of divine honours!

Yea, a dying for many hath here been devised, which glorifieth itself as life: verily, a hearty service unto all preachers of death!

The state, I call it, where all are poison-drinkers, the good and the bad: the state, where all lose themselves, the good and the bad: the state, where the slow suicide of all—is called "life."

Just see these superfluous ones! They steal the works of the inventors and the treasures of the wise. Culture, they call their theft—and everything becometh sickness and trouble unto them!

Just see these superfluous ones! Sick are they always; they vomit their bile and call it a newspaper. They devour one another, and cannot even digest themselves.

Just see these superfluous ones! Wealth they acquire and become poorer thereby. Power they seek for, and above all, the lever of power, much money—these impotent ones!

See them clamber, these nimble apes! They clamber over one another, and thus scuffle into the mud and the abyss.

Towards the throne they all strive: it is their madness—as if happiness sat on the throne! Ofttimes sitteth filth on the throne. —and ofttimes also the throne on filth.

Madmen they all seem to me, and clambering apes, and too eager. Badly smelleth their idol to me, the cold monster: badly they all smell to me, these idolaters.

My brethren, will ye suffocate in the fumes of their maws and appetites! Better break the windows and jump into the open air!

Do go out of the way of the bad odour! Withdraw from the idolatry of the superfluous!

Do go out of the way of the bad odour! Withdraw from the steam of these human sacrifices!

Open still remaineth the earth for great souls. Empty are still many sites for lone ones and twain ones, around which floateth the odour of tranquil seas.

Open still remaineth a free life for great souls. Verily, he who possesseth little is so much the less possessed: blessed be moderate poverty!

There, where the state ceaseth—there only commenceth the man who is not superfluous: there commenceth the song of the necessary ones, the single and irreplaceable melody.

There, where the state *ceaseth*—pray look thither, my brethren! Do ye not see it, the rainbow and the bridges of the Superman?—

Thus spake Zarathustra.

12. The Flies in the Market-Place

FLEE, my friend, into thy solitude! I see thee deafened with the noise of the great men, and stung all over with the stings of the little ones.

Admirably do forest and rock know how to be silent with thee. Resemble again the tree which thou lovest, the broad-branched one—silently and attentively it o'erhangeth the sea.

Where solitude endeth, there beginneth the market-place; and where the market-place beginneth, there beginneth also the noise of the great actors, and the buzzing of the poison-flies.

In the world even the best things are worthless without those who represent them: those representers, the people call great men.

Little do the people understand what is great—that is to say, the creating agency. But they have a taste for all repre-senters and actors of great things.

Around the devisers of new values revolveth the world:—. invisibly it revolveth. But around the actors revolve the people and the glory: such is the course of things.

Spirit, hath the actor, but little conscience of the spirit. He believeth always in that wherewith he maketh believe most strongly—in *himself!*

Tomorrow he hath a new belief, and the day after, one still newer. Sharp perceptions hath he, like the people, and change-able humours.

To upset—that meaneth with him to prove. To drive mad—that meaneth with him to convince. And blood is counted by him as the best of all arguments.

A truth which only glideth into fine ears, he calleth false-hood and trumpery. Verily, he believeth only in gods that make a great noise in the world!

Full of clattering buffoons is the market-place,—and the people glory in their great men! These are for them the masters of the hour.

But the hour presseth them; so they press thee. And also from thee they want Yea or Nay. Alas! thou wouldst set thy chair betwixt For and Against?

On account of those absolute and impatient ones, be not jealous, thou lover of truth! Never yet did truth cling to the arm of an absolute one.

On account of those abrupt ones, return into thy security: only in the market-place is one assailed by Yea? or Nay?

Slow is the experience of all deep fountains: long have they to wait until they know *what* hath fallen into their depths.

Away from the market-place and from fame taketh place all that is great: away from the market-place and from fame have ever dwelt the devisers of new values.

Flee, my friend, into thy solitude: I see thee stung all over by the poisonous flies. Flee thither, where a rough, strong breeze bloweth!

Flee into thy solitude! Thou hast lived too closely to the small and the pitiable. Flee from their invisible vengeance! Towards thee they have nothing but vengeance.

Raise no longer an arm against them! Innumerable are they, and it is not thy lot to be a fly-flap.

Innumerable are the small and pitiable ones; and of many a proud structure, rain-drops and weeds have been the ruin.

Thou art not stone; but already hast thou become hollow by the numerous drops. Thou wilt yet break and burst by the numerous drops.

Exhausted I see thee, by poisonous flies; bleeding I see thee, and torn at a hundred spots; and thy pride will not even upbraid.

Blood they would have from thee in all innocence; blood their bloodless souls crave for—and they sting, therefore, in all innocence.

But thou, profound one, thou sufferest too profoundly even from small wounds; and ere thou hadst recovered, the same poison-worm crawled over thy hand.

Too proud art thou to kill these sweet-tooths. But take care lest it be thy fate to suffer all their poisonous injustice!

They buzz around thee also with their praise: obtrusiveness is their praise. They want to be close to thy skin and thy blood.

They flatter thee, as one flattereth a God or devil; they whimper before thee, as before a God or devil. What doth it come to! Flatterers are they, and whimperers, and nothing more.

Often, also, do they show themselves to thee as amiable ones.

But that hath ever been the prudence of the cowardly. Yea! the cowardly are wise!

They think much about thee with their circumscribed souls —thou art always suspected by them! Whatever is much thought about is at last thought suspicious.

They punish thee for all thy virtues. They pardon thee in their inmost hearts only—for thine errors.

Because thou art gentle and of upright character, thou sayest: "Blameless are they for their small existence." But their circumscribed souls think: "Blamable is all great existence."

Even when thou art gentle towards them, they still feel themselves despised by thee; and they repay thy beneficence with secret maleficence.

Thy silent pride is always counter to their taste; they rejoice if once thou be humble enough to be frivolous.

What we recognise in a man, we also irritate in him. Therefore be on your guard against the small ones!

In thy presence they feel themselves small, and their baseness gleameth and gloweth against thee in invisible vengeance.

Sawest thou not how often they became dumb when thou approachedst them, and how their energy left them like the smoke of an extinguishing fire?

Yea, my friend, the bad conscience art thou of thy neighbours; for they are unworthy of thee. Therefore they hate thee, and would fain suck thy blood.

Thy neighbours will always be poisonous flies; what is great in thee—that itself must make them more poisonous, and always more fly-like.

Flee, my friend, into thy solitude—and thither, where a rough strong breeze bloweth. It is not thy lot to be a fly-flap.—

Thus spake Zarathustra.

13. Chastity

1 LOVE the forest. It is bad to live in cities: there, there are too many of the lustful.

Is it not better to fall into the hands of a murderer than into the dreams of a lustful woman?

And just look at these men: their eye saith it—they know nothing better on earth than to lie with a woman.

Filth is at the bottom of their souls; and alas! if their filth hath still spirit in it!

Would that ye were perfect—at least as animals! But to animals belongeth innocence.

Do I counsel you to slay your instincts? I counsel you to innocence in your instincts.

Do I counsel you to chastity? Chastity is a virtue with some, but with many almost a vice.

These are continent, to be sure: but doggish lust looketh enviously out of all that they do.

Even into the heights of their virtue and into their cold spirit doth this creature follow them, with its discord.

And how nicely can doggish lust beg for a piece of spirit, when a piece of flesh is denied it!

Ye love tragedies and all that breaketh the heart? But I am distrustful of your doggish lust.

Ye have too cruel eyes, and ye look wantonly towards the sufferers. Hath not your lust just disguised itself and taken the name of fellow-suffering?

And also this parable give I unto you: Not a few who meant to cast out their devil, went thereby into the swine themselves.

To whom chastity is difficult, it is to be dissuaded: lest it become the road to hell—to filth and lust of soul.

Do I speak of filthy things? That is not the worst thing for me to do.

Not when the truth is filthy, but when it is shallow, doth the discerning one go unwillingly into its waters.

Verily, there are chaste ones from their very nature; they are gentler of heart, and laugh better and oftener than you.

They laugh also at chastity, and ask: "What is chastity?

Is chastity not folly? But the folly came unto us, and not we unto it.

We offered that guest harbour and heart: now it dwelleth with us—let it stay as long as it will!"—

Thus spake Zarathustra.

14. The Friend

"ONE is always too many about me"—thinketh the anchorite. "Always once one—that maketh two in the long run!"

I and me are always too earnestly in conversation: how could it be endured, if there were not a friend?

The friend of the anchorite is always the third one: the third one is the cork which preventeth the conversation of the two sinking into the depth.

Ah! there are too many depths for all anchorites. Therefore, do they long so much for a friend and for his elevation.

Our faith in others betrayeth wherein we would fain have faith in ourselves. Our longing for a friend is our betrayer.

And often with our love we want merely to overleap envy. And often we attack and make ourselves enemies, to conceal that we are vulnerable.

"Be at least mine enemy!"—thus speaketh the true reverence, which doth not venture to solicit friendship.

If one would have a friend, then must one also be willing to wage war for him: and in order to wage war, one must be *capable* of being an enemy.

One ought still to honour the enemy in one's friend. Canst thou go nigh unto thy friend, and not go over to him?

In one's friend one shall have one's best enemy. Thou shalt be closest unto him with thy heart when thou withstandest him.

Thou wouldst wear no raiment before thy friend? It is in honour of thy friend that thou showest thyself to him as thou art? But he wisheth thee to the devil on that account!

He who maketh no secret of himself shocketh: so much reason have ye to fear nakedness! Aye, if ye were gods, ye could then be ashamed of clothing!

Thou canst not adorn thyself fine enough for thy friend; for thou shalt be unto him an arrow and a longing for the Superman.

Sawest thou ever thy friend asleep—to know how he looketh? What is usually the countenance of thy friend? It is thine own countenance, in a coarse and imperfect mirror.

Sawest thou ever thy friend asleep? Wert thou not dismayed at thy friend looking so? O my friend, man is something that hath to be surpassed.

In divining and keeping silence shall the friend be a master: not everything must thou wish to see. Thy dream shall disclose unto thee what thy friend doeth when awake.

Let thy pity be a divining: to know first if thy friend

wanteth pity. Perhaps he loveth in thee the unmoved eye, and the look of eternity.

Let thy pity for thy friend be hid under a hard shell; thou shalt bite out a tooth upon it. Thus will it have delicacy and sweetness.

Art thou pure air and solitude and bread and medicine to thy friend? Many a one cannot loosen his own fetters, but i. nevertheless his friend's emancipator.

Art thou a slave? Then thou canst not be a friend. Art thou a tyrant? Then thou canst not have friends.

Far too long hath there been a slave and a tyrant concealed in woman. On that account woman is not yet capable of friendship: she knoweth only love.

In woman's love there is injustice and blindness to all she doth not love. And even in woman's conscious love, there is still always surprise and lightning and night, along with the light.

As yet woman is not capable of friendship: women are still cats and birds. Or at the best, cows.

As yet woman is not capable of friendship. But tell me, ye men, who of you is capable of friendship?

Oh! your poverty, ye men, and your sordidness of soul! As much as ye give to your friend, will I give even to my foe, and will not have become poorer thereby.

There is comradeship: may there be friendship!

Thus spake Zarathustra.

15. *The Thousand and One Goals*

MANY lands saw Zarathustra, and many peoples: thus he discovered the good and bad of many peoples. No greater power did Zarathustra find on earth than good and bad.

No people could live without first valuing; if a people will maintain itself, however, it must not value as its neighbour valueth.

Much that passed for good with one people was regarded with scorn and contempt by another: thus I found it. Much found I here called bad, which was there decked with purple honours.

Never did the one neighbour understand the other: ever did his soul marvel at his neighbour's delusion and wickedness.

A table of excellencies hangeth over every people. Lo! it is the table of their triumphs; lo! it is the voice of their Will to Power.

It is laudable, what they think hard; what is indispensable and hard they call good; and what relieveth in the direst distress, the unique and hardest of all,—they extol as holy.

Whatever maketh them rule and conquer and shine, to the dismay and envy of their neighbours, they regard as the high and foremost thing, the test and the meaning of all else.

Verily, my brother, if thou knewest but a people's need, its land, its sky, and its neighbour, then wouldst thou divine the law of its surmountings, and why it climbeth up that ladder to its hope.

"Always shalt thou be the foremost and prominent above others: no one shall thy jealous soul love, except a friend"—

that made the soul of a Greek thrill: thereby went he his way to greatness.

"To speak truth, and be skilful with bow and arrow"—so seemed it alike pleasing and hard to the people from whom cometh my name—the name which is alike pleasing and hard to me.

"To honour father and mother, and from the root of the soul to do their will"—this table of surmounting hung another people over them, and became powerful and permanent thereby.

"To have fidelity, and for the sake of fidelity to risk honour and blood, even in evil and dangerous courses"—teaching itself so, another people mastered itself, and thus mastering itself, became pregnant and heavy with great hopes.

Verily, men have given unto themselves all their good and bad. Verily, they took it not, they found it not, it came not unto them as a voice from heaven.

Values did man only assign to things in order to maintain himself—he created only the significance of things, a human significance! Therefore, calleth he himself "man," that is, the valuator.

Valuing is creating: hear it, ye creating ones! Valuation itself is the treasure and jewel of the valued things.

Through valuation only is there value; and without valuation the nut of existence would be hollow. Hear it, ye creating ones!

Change of values—that is, change of the creating ones. Always doth he destroy who hath to be a creator.

Creating ones were first of all peoples, and only in late times individuals; verily, the individual himself is still the latest creation.

Peoples once hung over them tables of the good. Love which

would rule and love which would obey, created for themselves such tables.

Older is the pleasure in the herd than the pleasure in the ego: and as long as the good conscience is for the herd, the bad conscience only saith: ego.

Verily, the crafty ego, the loveless one, that seeketh its advantage in the advantage of many—it is not the origin of the herd, but its ruin.

Loving ones, was it always, and creating ones, that created good and bad. Fire of love gloweth in the names of all the virtues, and fire of wrath.

Many lands saw Zarathustra, and many peoples: no greater power did Zarathustra find on earth than the creations of the loving ones—"good" and "bad" are they called.

Verily, a prodigy is this power of praising and blaming. Tell me, ye brethren, who will master it for me? Who will put a fetter upon the thousand necks of this animal?

A thousand goals have there been hitherto, for a thousand peoples have there been. Only the fetter for the thousand necks is still lacking; there is lacking the one goal. As yet humanity hath not a goal.

But pray tell me, my brethren, if the goal of humanity be still lacking, is there not also still lacking—humanity itself?—

Thus spake Zarathustra.

16. Neighbour-Love

YE CROWD around your neighbour, and have fine words for it. But I say unto you: your neighbour-love is your bad love of yourselves.

Ye flee unto your neighbour from yourselves, and would fain make a virtue thereof: but I fathom your "unselfishness."

The *Thou* is older than the *I;* the *Thou* hath been consecrated, but not yet the *I:* so man presseth nigh unto his neighbour.

Do I advise you to neighbour-love? Rather do I advise you to neighbour-flight and to furthest love!

Higher than love to your neighbour is love to the furthest and future ones; higher still than love to men, is love to things and phantoms.

The phantom that runneth on before thee, my brother, is fairer than thou; why dost thou not give unto it thy flesh and thy bones? But thou fearest, and runnest unto thy neighbour.

Ye cannot endure it with yourselves, and do not love yourselves sufficiently: so ye seek to mislead your neighbour into love, and would fain gild yourselves with his error.

Would that ye could not endure it with any kind of near ones, or their neighbours; then would ye have to create your friend and his overflowing heart out of yourselves.

Ye call in a witness when ye want to speak well of yourselves; and when ye have misled him to think well of you, ye also think well of yourselves.

Not only doth he lie, who speaketh contrary to his knowledge, but more so, he who speaketh contrary to his ignorance.

And thus speak ye of yourselves in your intercourse, and belie your neighbour with yourselves.

Thus saith the fool: "Association with men spoileth the character, especially when one hath none."

The one goeth to his neighbour because he seeketh himself, and the other because he would fain lose himself. Your bad love to yourselves maketh solitude a prison to you.

The furthest ones are they who pay for your love to the near ones; and when there are but five of you together, a sixth must always die.

I love not your festivals either: too many actors found I there, and even the spectators often behaved like actors.

Not the neighbour do I teach you, but the friend. Let the friend be the festival of the earth to you, and a foretaste of the Superman.

I teach you the friend and his overflowing heart. But one must know how to be a sponge, if one would be loved by overflowing hearts.

I teach you the friend in whom the world standeth complete, a capsule of the good,—the creating friend, who hath always a complete world to bestow.

And as the world unrolled itself for him, so rolleth it together again for him in rings, as the growth of good through evil, as the growth of purpose out of chance.

Let the future and the furthest be the motive of thy today; in thy friend shalt thou love the Superman as thy motive.

My brethren, I advise you not to neighbour-love—I advise you to furthest love!—

Thus spake Zarathustra.

17. The Way of the Creating One

WOULDST thou go into isolation, my brother? Wouldst thou seek the way unto thyself? Tarry yet a little and hearken unto me.

"He who seeketh may easily get lost himself. All isolation is wrong": so say the herd. And long didst thou belong to the herd.

The voice of the herd will still echo in thee. And when thou sayest, "I have no longer a conscience in common with you," then will it be a plaint and a pain.

Lo, that pain itself did the same conscience produce; and the last gleam of that conscience still gloweth on thine affliction.

But thou wouldst go the way of thine affliction, which is the way unto thyself? Then show me thine authority and thy strength to do so!

Art thou a new strength and a new authority? A first motion? A self-rolling wheel? Canst thou also compel stars to revolve around thee?

Alas! there is so much lusting for loftiness! There are so many convulsions of the ambitions! Show me that thou art not a lusting and ambitious one!

Alas! there are so many great thoughts that do nothing more than the bellows: they inflate, and make emptier than ever.

Free, dost thou call thyself? Thy ruling thought would I hear of, and not that thou hast escaped from a yoke.

Art thou one *entitled* to escape from a yoke? Many a one hath cast away his final worth when he hath cast away his servitude.

Free from what? What doth that matter to Zarathustra! Clearly, however, shall thine eye show unto me: free *for what?*

Canst thou give unto thyself thy bad and thy good, and set up thy will as a law over thee? Canst thou be judge for thyself, and avenger of thy law?

Terrible is aloneness with the judge and avenger of one's own law. Thus is a star projected into desert space, and into the icy breath of aloneness.

To-day sufferest thou still from the multitude, thou individual; to-day hast thou still thy courage unabated, and thy hopes.

But one day will the solitude weary thee; one day will thy pride yield, and thy courage quail. Thou wilt one day cry: "I am alone!"

One day wilt thou see no longer thy loftiness, and see too closely thy lowliness; thy sublimity itself will frighten thee as a phantom. Thou wilt one day cry: "All is false!"

There are feelings which seek to slay the lonesome one; if they do not succeed, then must they themselves die! But art thou capable of it—to be a murderer?

Hast thou ever known, my brother, the word "disdain"? And the anguish of thy justice in being just to those that disdain thee?

Thou forcest many to think differently about thee; that, charge they heavily to thine account. Thou camest nigh unto them, and yet wentest past: for that they never forgive thee.

Thou goest beyond them: but the higher thou risest, the smaller doth the eye of envy see thee. Most of all, however, is the flying one hated.

"How could ye be just unto me!"—must thou say—"I choose your injustice as my allotted portion."

Injustice and filth cast they at the lonesome one: but, my

brother, if thou wouldst be a star, thou must shine for then, none the less on that account!

And be on thy guard against the good and just! They would fain crucify those who devise their own virtue—they hate the lonesome ones.

Be on thy guard, also, against holy simplicity! All is unholy to it that is not simple; fain, likewise, would it play with the fire—of the fagot and stake.

And be on thy guard, also, against the assaults of thy love! Too readily doth the recluse reach his hand to any one who meeteth him.

To many a one mayest thou not give thy hand, but only thy paw; and I wish thy paw also to have claws.

But the worst enemy thou canst meet, wilt thou thyself always be; thou waylayest thyself in caverns and forests.

Thou lonesome one, thou goest the way to thyself! And past thyself and thy seven devils leadeth thy way!

A heretic wilt thou be to thyself, and a wizard and a sooth-sayer, and a fool, and a doubter, and a reprobate, and a villain.

Ready must thou be to burn thyself in thine own flame; how couldst thou become new if thou have not first become ashes!

Thou lonesome one, thou goest the way of the creating one: a God wilt thou create for thyself out of thy seven devils!

Thou lonesome one, thou goest the way of the loving one: thou lovest thyself, and on that account despisest thou thyself, as only the loving ones despise.

To create, desireth the loving one, because he despiseth! What knoweth he of love who hath not been obliged to despise just what he loved!

With thy love, go into thine isolation, my brother, and with thy creating; and late only will justice limp after thee.

With my tears, go into thine isolation, my brother. I love him who seeketh to create beyond himself, and thus succumbeth.——

Thus spake Zarathustra.

18. Old and Young Women

WHY stealest thou along so furtively in the twilight, Zarathustra? And what hidest thou so carefully under thy mantle?

Is it a treasure that hath been given thee? Or a child that hath been born thee? Or goest thou thyself on a thief's errand, thou friend of the evil?——

Verily, my brother, said Zarathustra, it is a treasure that hath been given me: it is a little truth which I carry.

But it is naughty, like a young child; and if I hold not its mouth, it screameth too loudly.

As I went on my way alone today, at the hour when the sun declineth, there met me an old woman, and she spake thus unto my soul:

"Much hath Zarathustra spoken also to us women, but never spake he unto us concerning woman."

And I answered her: "Concerning woman, one should only talk unto men."

"Talk also unto me of woman," said she; "I am old enough to forget it presently."

And I obliged the old woman and spake thus unto her:

Everything in woman is a riddle, and everything in woman hath one solution—it is called pregnancy.

Man is for woman a means: the purpose is always the child.
But what is woman for man?

Two different things wanteth the true man: danger and
diversion. Therefore wanteth he woman, as the most dangerous plaything.

Man shall be trained for war, and woman for the recreation
of the warrior: all else is folly.

Too sweet fruits—these the warrior liketh not. Therefore
liketh he woman;—bitter is even the sweetest woman.

Better than man doth woman understand children, but man
is more childish than woman.

In the true man there is a child hidden: it wanteth to play.
Up then, ye women, and discover the child in man!

A plaything let woman be, pure and fine like the precious
stone, illumined with the virtues of a world not yet come.

Let the beam of a star shine in your love! Let your hope say:
"May I bear the Superman!"

In your love let there be valour! With your love shall ye
assail him who inspireth you with fear!

In your love be your honour! Little doth woman understand
otherwise about honour. But let this be your honour: always
to love more than ye are loved, and never be the second.

Let man fear woman when she loveth: then maketh she
every sacrifice, and everything else she regardeth as worthless.

Let man fear woman when she hateth: for man in his innermost soul is merely evil; woman, however, is mean.

Whom hateth woman most?—Thus spake the iron to the
loadstone: "I hate thee most, because thou attractest, but art
too weak to draw unto thee."

The happiness of man is, "I will." The happiness of woman
is, "He will."

"Lo! now hath the world become perfect!"—thus thinketh every woman when she obeyeth with all her love.

Obey, must the woman, and find a depth for her surface. Surface is woman's soul, a mobile, stormy film on shallow water.

Man's soul, however, is deep, its current gusheth in subterranean caverns: woman surmiseth its force, but comprehendeth it not.—

Then answered me the old woman: "Many fine things hath Zarathustra said, especially for those who are young enough for them.

Strange! Zarathustra knoweth little about woman, and yet he is right about them! Doth this happen, because with women nothing is impossible?

And now accept a little truth by way of thanks! I am old enough for it!

Swaddle it up and hold its mouth: otherwise it will scream too loudly, the little truth."

"Give me, woman, thy little truth!" said I. And thus spake the old woman:

"Thou goest to women? Do not forget thy whip!"—

Thus spake Zarathustra.

19. The Bite of the Adder

ONE day had Zarathustra fallen asleep under a fig-tree, owing to the heat, with his arm over his face. And there came an adder and bit him in the neck, so that Zarathustra screamed with pain. When he had taken his arm from his face he looked at the serpent; and then did it recognise the eyes of Zarathustra, wriggled awkwardly, and tried to get away. "Not at all," said Zarathustra, "as yet hast thou not received my thanks! Thou hast awakened me in time; my journey is yet long." "Thy journey is short," said the adder sadly; "my poison is fatal." Zarathustra smiled. "When did ever a dragon die of a serpent's poison?"—said he. "But take thy poison back! Thou art not rich enough to present it to me." Then fell the adder again on his neck, and licked his wound.

When Zarathustra once told this to his disciples they asked him: "And what, O Zarathustra, is the moral of thy story?" And Zarathustra answered them thus:

The destroyer of morality, the good and just call me: my story is immoral.

When, however, ye have an enemy, then return him not good for evil: for that would abash him. But prove that he hath done something good to you.

And rather be angry than abash any one! And when ye are cursed, it pleaseth me not that ye should then desire to bless. Rather curse a little also!

And should a great injustice befall you, then do quickly five small ones besides. Hideous to behold is he on whom injustice presseth alone.

Did ye ever know this? Shared injustice is half justice. And he who can bear it, shall take the injustice upon himself!

A small revenge is humaner than no revenge at all. And if the punishment be not also a right and an honour to the transgressor, I do not like your punishing.

Nobler is it to own oneself in the wrong than to establish one's right, especially if one be in the right. Only, one must be rich enough to do so.

I do not like your cold justice; out of the eye of your judges there always glanceth the executioner and his cold steel.

Tell me: where find we justice, which is love with seeing eyes?

Devise me, then, the love which not only beareth all punishment, but also all guilt!

Devise me, then, the justice which acquitteth every one except the judge!

And would ye hear this likewise? To him who seeketh to be just from the heart, even the lie becometh philanthropy.

But how could I be just from the heart! How can I give every one his own! Let this be enough for me: I give unto every one mine own.

Finally, my brethren, guard against doing wrong to any anchorite. How could an anchorite forget! How could he requite!

Like a deep well is an anchorite. Easy is it to throw in a stone: if it should sink to the bottom, however, tell me, who will bring it out again?

Guard against injuring the anchorite! If ye have done so, however, well then, kill him also!—

Thus spake Zarathustra.

20. Child and Marriage

I HAVE a question for thee alone, my brother: like a sounding-lead, cast I this question into thy soul, that I may know its depth.

Thou art young, and desirest child and marriage. But I ask thee: Art thou a man *entitled* to desire a child?

Art thou the victorious one, the self-conqueror, the ruler of thy passions, the master of thy virtues? Thus do I ask thee.

Or doth the animal speak in thy wish, and necessity? Or isolation? Or discord in thee?

I would have thy victory and freedom long for a child. Living monuments shalt thou build to thy victory and emancipation.

Beyond thyself shalt thou build. But first of all must thou be built thyself, rectangular in body and soul.

Not only onward shalt thou propagate thyself, but upward! For that purpose may the garden of marriage help thee!

A higher body shalt thou create, a first movement, a spontaneously rolling wheel—a creating one shalt thou create.

Marriage: so call I the will of the twain to create the one that is more than those who created it. The reverence for one another, as those exercising such a will, call I marriage.

Let this be the significance and the truth of thy marriage. But that which the many-too-many call marriage, those superfluous ones—ah, what shall I call it?

Ah, the poverty of soul in the twain! Ah, the filth of soul in the twain! Ah, the pitiable self-complacency in the twain!

Marriage they call it all; and they say their marriages are made in heaven.

Well, I do not like it, that heaven of the superfluous! No, I do not like them, those animals tangled in the heavenly toils!

Far from me also be the God who limpeth thither to bless what he hath not matched!

Laugh not at such marriages! What child hath not had reason to weep over its parents?

Worthy did this man seem, and ripe for the meaning of the earth: but when I saw his wife, the earth seemed to me a home for madcaps.

Yea, I would that the earth shook with convulsions when a saint and a goose mate with one another.

This one went forth in quest of truth as a hero, and at last got for himself a small decked-up lie: his marriage he calleth it.

That one was reserved in intercourse and chose choicely. But one time he spoilt his company for all time: his marriage he calleth it.

Another sought a handmaid with the virtues of an angel. But all at once he became the handmaid of a woman, and now would he need also to become an angel.

Careful, have I found all buyers, and all of them have astute eyes. But even the astutest of them buyeth his wife in a sack.

Many short follies—that is called love by you. And your marriage putteth an end to many short follies, with one long stupidity.

Your love to woman, and woman's love to man—ah, would that it were sympathy for suffering and veiled deities! But generally two animals alight on one another.

But even your best love is only an enraptured simile and a painful ardour. It is a torch to light you to loftier paths.

Beyond yourselves shall ye love some day! Then *learn* first of all to love. And on that account ye had to drink the bitter cup of your love.

Bitterness is in the cup even of the best love; thus doth it cause longing for the Superman; thus doth it cause thirst in thee, the creating one!

Thirst in the creating one, arrow and longing for the Superman: tell me, my brother, is this thy will to marriage?

Holy call I such a will, and such a marriage.—

Thus spake Zarathustra.

21. *Voluntary Death*

MANY die too late, and some die too early. Yet strange
soundeth the precept: "Die at the right time!"

Die at the right time: so teacheth Zarathustra.

To be sure, he who never liveth at the right time, how could
he ever die at the right time? Would that he might never be
born!—Thus do I advise the superfluous ones.

But even the superfluous ones make much ado about their
death, and even the hollowest nut wanteth to be cracked.

Every one regardeth dying as a great matter: but as yet death
is not a festival. Not yet have people learned to inaugurate the
finest festivals.

The consummating death I show unto you, which becometh
a stimulus and promise to the living.

His death, dieth the consummating one triumphantly, surrounded by hoping and promising ones.

Thus should one learn to die; and there should be no festival
at which such a dying one doth not consecrate the oaths of the
living!

Thus to die is best; the next best, however, is to die in battle,
and sacrifice a great soul.

But to the fighter equally hateful as to the victor, is your
grinning death which stealeth nigh like a thief,—and yet
cometh as master.

My death, praise I unto you, the voluntary death, which
cometh unto me because *I* want it.

And when shall I want it?—He that hath a goal and an heir,
wanteth death at the right time for the goal and the heir.

[75]

And out of reverence for the goal and the heir, he will hang up no more withered wreaths in the sanctuary of life.

Verily, not the rope-makers will I resemble: they lengthen out their cord, and thereby go ever backward.

Many a one, also, waxeth too old for his truths and triumphs; a toothless mouth hath no longer the right to every truth.

And whoever wanteth to have fame, must take leave of honour betimes, and practise the difficult art of—going at the right time.

One must discontinue being feasted upon when one tasteth best: that is known by those who want to be long loved.

Sour apples are there, no doubt, whose lot is to wait until the last day of autumn: and at the same time they become ripe, yellow, and shrivelled.

In some ageth the heart first, and in others the spirit. And some are hoary in youth, but the late young keep long young.

To many men life is a failure; a poison-worm gnaweth at their heart. Then let them see to it that their dying is all the more a success.

Many never become sweet; they rot even in the summer. It is cowardice that holdeth them fast to their branches.

Far too many live, and far too long hang they on their branches. Would that a storm came and shook all this rottenness and worm-eatenness from the tree!

Would that there came preachers of *speedy* death! Those would be the appropriate storms and agitators of the trees of life! But I hear only slow death preached, and patience with all that is "earthly."

Ah! ye preach patience with what is earthly? This earthly is it that hath too much patience with you, ye blasphemers!

Verily, too early died that Hebrew whom the preachers of slow death honour: and to many hath it proved a calamity that he died too early.

As yet had he known only tears, and the melancholy of the Hebrews, together with the hatred of the good and just —the Hebrew Jesus: then was he seized with the longing for death.

Had he but remained in the wilderness, and far from the good and just! Then, perhaps, would he have learned to live, and love the earth—and laughter also!

Believe it, my brethren! He died too early; he himself would have disavowed his doctrine had he attained to my age! Noble enough was he to disavow!

But he was still immature. Immaturely loveth the youth, and immaturely also hateth he man and earth. Confined and awk· ward are still his soul and the wings of his spirit.

But in man there is more of the child than in the youth, and less of melancholy: better understandeth he about life and death.

Free for death, and free in death; a holy Naysayer, when there is no longer time for Yea: thus understandeth he about death and life.

That your dying may not be a reproach to man and the earth, my friends: that do I solicit from the honey of your soul.

In your dying shall your spirit and your virtue still shine like an evening after-glow around the earth: otherwise your dying hath been unsatisfactory.

Thus will I die myself, that ye friends may love the earth more for my sake; and earth will I again become, to have rest in her that bore me.

[77]

Verily, a goal had Zarathustra; he threw his ball. Now be ye friends the heirs of my goal; to you throw I the golden ball.

Best of all, do I see you, my friends, throw the golden ball! And so tarry I still a little while on the earth—pardon me for it!

Thus spake Zarathustra.

22. *The Bestowing Virtue*

1

WHEN Zarathustra had taken leave of the town to which his heart was attached, the name of which is "The Pied Cow," there followed him many people who called themselves his disciples, and kept him company. Thus came they to a cross-roads. Then Zarathustra told them that he now wanted to go alone; for he was fond of going alone. His disciples, however, presented him at his departure with a staff, on the golden handle of which a serpent twined round the sun. Zarathustra rejoiced on account of the staff, and supported himself thereon; then spake he thus to his disciples:

Tell me, pray: how came gold to the highest value? Because it is uncommon, and unprofiting, and beaming, and soft in lustre; it always bestoweth itself.

Only as image of the highest virtue came gold to the highest value. Goldlike, beameth the glance of the bestower. Gold-lustre maketh peace between moon and sun.

Uncommon is the highest virtue, and unprofiting, beaming is it, and soft of lustre: a bestowing virtue is the highest virtue.

Verily, I divine you well, my disciples: ye strive like me for the bestowing virtue. What should ye have in common with cats and wolves?

It is your thirst to become sacrifices and gifts yourselves: and therefore have ye the thirst to accumulate all riches in your soul.

Insatiably striveth your soul for treasures and jewels, because your virtue is insatiable in desiring to bestow.

Ye constrain all things to flow towards you and into you, so that they shall flow back again out of your fountain as the gifts of your love.

Verily, an appropriator of all values must such bestowing love become; but healthy and holy, call I this selfishness.—

Another selfishness is there, an all-too-poor and hungry kind, which would always steal—the selfishness of the sick, the sickly selfishness.

With the eye of the thief it looketh upon all that is lustrous; with the craving of hunger it measureth him who hath abundance; and ever doth it prowl round the tables of bestowers.

Sickness speaketh in such craving, and invisible degeneration; of a sickly body, speaketh the larcenous craving of this selfishness.

Tell me, my brother, what do we think bad, and worst of all? Is it not *degeneration?*—And we always suspect degeneration when the bestowing soul is lacking.

Upward goeth our course from genera on to super-genera. But a horror to us is the degenerating sense, which saith: "All for myself."

Upward soareth our sense: thus is it a simile of our body, a simile of an elevation. Such similes of elevations are the names of the virtues.

Thus goeth the body through history, a becomer and fighter.

And the spirit—what is it to the body? Its fights' and victories' herald, its companion and echo.

Similes, are all names of good and evil; they do not speak out, they only hint. A fool who seeketh knowledge from them!

Give heed, my brethren, to every hour when your spirit would speak in similes: there is the origin of your virtue.

Elevated is then your body, and raised up; with its delight, enraptureth it the spirit; so that it becometh creator, and valuer, and lover, and everything's benefactor.

When your heart overfloweth broad and full like the river, a blessing and a danger to the lowlanders: there is the origin of your virtue.

When ye are exalted above praise and blame, and your will would command all things, as a loving one's will: there is the origin of your virtue.

When ye despise pleasant things, and the effeminate couch, and cannot couch far enough from the effeminate: there is the origin of your virtue.

When ye are willers of one will, and when that change of every need is needful to you: there is the origin of your virtue.

Verily, a new good and evil is it! Verily, a new deep murmuring, and the voice of a new fountain!

Power is it, this new virtue; a ruling thought is it, and around it a subtle soul: a golden sun, with the serpent of knowledge around it.

2
———

Here paused Zarathustra awhile, and looked lovingly on his disciples. Then he continued to speak thus—and his voice had changed:

Remain true to the earth, my brethren, with the power of your virtue! Let your bestowing love and your knowledge be devoted to be the meaning of the earth! Thus do I pray and conjure you.

Let it not fly away from the earthly and beat against eternal walls with its wings! Ah, there hath always been so much flown-away virtue!

Lead, like me, the flown-away virtue back to the earth—yea, back to body and life: that it may give to the earth its meaning, a human meaning!

A hundred times hitherto hath spirit as well as virtue flown away and blundered. Alas! in our body dwelleth still all this delusion and blundering: body and will hath it there become.

A hundred times hitherto hath spirit as well as virtue attempted and erred. Yea, an attempt hath man been. Alas, much ignorance and error hath become embodied in us!

Not only the rationality of millennia—also their madness, breaketh out in us. Dangerous is it to be an heir.

Still fight we step by step with the giant Chance, and over all mankind hath hitherto ruled nonsense, the lack-of-sense.

Let your spirit and your virtue be devoted to the sense of the earth, my brethren: let the value of everything be determined anew by you! Therefore shall ye be fighters! Therefore shall ye be creators!

Intelligently doth the body purify itself; attempting with intelligence it exalteth itself; to the discerners all impulses sanctify themselves; to the exalted the soul becometh joyful.

Physician, heal thyself: then wilt thou also heal thy patient. Let it be his best cure to see with his eyes him who maketh himself whole.

A thousand paths are there which have never yet been trodden; a thousand salubrities and hidden islands of life.

Unexhausted and undiscovered is still man and man's world.

Awake and hearken, ye lonesome ones! From the future come winds with stealthy pinions, and to fine ears good tidings are proclaimed.

Ye lonesome ones of today, ye seceding ones, ye shall one day be a people: out of you who have chosen yourselves, shall a chosen people arise:—and out of it the Superman.

Verily, a place of healing shall the earth become! And already is a new odour diffused around it, a salvation-bringing odour—and a new hope!

3

When Zarathustra had spoken these words, he paused, like one who had not said his last word; and long did he balance the staff doubtfully in his hand. At last he spake thus—and his voice had changed:

I now go alone, my disciples! Ye also now go away, and alone! So will I have it.

Verily, I advise you: depart from me, and guard yourselves against Zarathustra! And better still: be ashamed of him! Perhaps he hath deceived you.

The man of knowledge must be able not only to love his enemies, but also to hate his friends.

One requiteth a teacher badly if one remain merely a scholar. And why will ye not pluck at my wreath?

Ye venerate me; but what if your veneration should some day collapse? Take heed lest a statue crush you!

Ye say, ye believe in Zarathustra? But of what account is Zarathustra! Ye are my believers: but of what account are all believers!

Ye had not yet sought yourselves: then did ye find me. So do all believers; therefore all belief is of so little account.

Now do I bid you lose me and find yourselves; and only when ye have all denied me, will I return unto you.

Verily, with other eyes, my brethren, shall I then seek my lost ones; with another love shall I then love you.

And once again shall ye have become friends unto me, and children of one hope: then will I be with you for the third time, to celebrate the great noontide with you.

And it is the great noontide, when man is in the middle of his course between animal and Superman, and celebrateth his advance to the evening as his highest hope: for it is the advance to a new morning.

At such time will the down-goer bless himself, that he should be an over-goer; and the sun of his knowledge will be at noontide.

"Dead are all the Gods: now do we desire the Superman to live."—Let this be our final will at the great noontide!—

Thus spake Zarathustra.

THUS SPAKE ZARATHUSTRA

SECOND PART

"—and only when ye have all denied
me, will I return unto you.

Verily, with other eyes, my brethren,
shall I then seek my lost ones; with
another love shall I then love you."—
ZARATHUSTRA, I., "The Bestowing
Virtue" (p. 92).

23. *The Child with the Mirror*

AFTER this Zarathustra returned again into the mountains to the solitude of his cave, and withdrew himself from men, waiting like a sower who hath scattered his seed. His soul, however, became impatient and full of longing for those whom he loved: because he had still much to give them. For this is hardest of all: to close the open hand out of love, and keep modest as a giver.

Thus passed with the lonesome one months and years; his wisdom meanwhile increased, and caused him pain by its abundance.

One morning, however, he awoke ere the rosy dawn, and having meditated long on his couch, at last spake thus to his heart:

Why did I startle in my dream, so that I awoke? Did not a child come to me, carrying a mirror?

"O Zarathustra"—said the child unto me—"look at thyself in the mirror!"

But when I looked into the mirror, I shrieked, and my heart throbbed: for not myself did I see therein, but a devil's grimace and derision.

Verily, all too well do I understand the dream's portent and monition: my *doctrine* is in danger; tares want to be called wheat!

Mine enemies have grown powerful and have disfigured the

likeness of ıy doctrine, so that my dearest ones have to blush for the gifts that I gave them.

Lost are my friends; the hour hath come for me to seek my lost ones!—

With these words Zarathustra started up, not however like a person in anguish seeking relief, but rather like a seer and a singer whom the spirit inspireth. With amazement did his eagle and serpent gaze upon him: for a coming bliss overspread his countenance like the rosy dawn.

What hath happened unto me, mine animals?—said Zarathustra. Am I not transformed? Hath not bliss come unto me like a whirlwind?

Foolish is my happiness, and foolish things will it speak: it is still too young—so have patience with it!

Wounded am I by my happiness: all sufferers shall be physicians unto me!

To my friends can I again go down, and also to mine enemies! Zarathustra can again speak and bestow, and show his best love to his loved ones!

My impatient love overfloweth in streams,—down towards sunrise and sunset. Out of silent mountains and storms of affliction, rusheth my soul into the valleys.

Too long have I longed and looked into the distance. Too long hath solitude possessed me: thus have I unlearned to keep silence.

Utterance have I become altogether, and the brawling of a brook from high rocks: downward into the valleys will I hurl my speech.

And let the stream of my love sweep into unfrequented channels! How should a stream not finally find its way to the sea!

Forsooth, there is a lake in me, sequestered and self-sufficing; but the stream of my love beareth this along with it, down—to the sea!

New paths do I tread, a new speech cometh unto me; tired have I become—like all creators—of the old tongues. No longer will my spirit walk on worn-out soles.

Too slowly runneth all speaking for me:—into thy chariot, O storm, do I leap! And even thee will I whip with my spite!

Like a cry and an huzza will I traverse wide seas, till I find the Happy Isles where my friends sojourn;—

And mine enemies amongst them! How I now love every one unto whom I may but speak! Even mine enemies pertain to my bliss.

And when I want to mount my wildest horse, then doth my spear always help me up best: it is my foot's ever ready servant:—

The spear which I hurl at mine enemies! How grateful am I to mine enemies that I may at last hurl it!

Too great hath been the tension of my cloud: 'twixt laughters of lightnings will I cast hail-showers into the depths.

Violently will my breast then heave; violently will it blow its storm over the mountains: thus cometh its assuagement.

Verily, like a storm cometh my happiness, and my freedom! But mine enemies shall think that *the evil one* roareth over their heads.

Yea, ye also, my friends, will be alarmed by my wild wisdom; and perhaps ye will flee therefrom, along with mine enemies.

Ah, that I knew how to lure you back with shepherds' flutes! Ah, that my lioness wisdom would learn to roar softly! And much have we already learned with one another!

My wild wisdom became pregnant on the lonesome mountains; on the rough stones did she bear the youngest of her young.

Now runneth she foolishly in the arid wilderness, and seeketh and seeketh the soft sward—mine old, wild wisdom!

On the soft sward of your hearts, my friends!—on your love, would she fain couch her dearest one!—

Thus spake Zarathustra.

24. In the Happy Isles

THE figs fall from the trees, they are good and sweet; and in falling the red skins of them break. A north wind am I to ripe figs.

Thus, like figs, do these doctrines fall for you, my friends: imbibe now their juice and their sweet substance! It is autumn all around, and clear sky, and afternoon.

Lo, what fullness is around us! And out of the midst of superabundance, it is delightful to look out upon distant seas.

Once did people say God, when they looked out upon distant seas; now, however, have I taught you to say, Superman.

God is a conjecture: but I do not wish your conjecturing to reach beyond your creating will.

Could ye *create* a God?—Then, I pray you, be silent about all gods! But ye could well create the Superman.

Not perhaps ye yourselves, my brethren! But into fathers and forefathers of the Superman could ye transform yourselves: and let that be your best creating!—

God is a conjecture: but I should like your conjecturing restricted to the conceivable.

Could ye *conceive* a God?—But let this mean Will to Truth unto you, that everything be transformed into the humanly conceivable, the humanly visible, the humanly sensible! Your own discernment shall ye follow out to the end!

And what ye have called the world shall but be created by you: your reason, your likeness, your will, your love, shall it itself become! And verily, for your bliss, ye discerning ones!

And how would ye endure life without that hope, ye discerning ones? Neither in the inconceivable could ye have been born, nor in the irrational.

But that I may reveal my heart entirely unto you, my friends: *if* there were gods, how could I endure it to be no God! *Therefore* there are no gods.

Yea, I have drawn the conclusion; now, however, doth it draw me.—

God is a conjecture: but who could drink all the bitterness of this conjecture without dying? Shall his faith be taken from the creating one, and from the eagle his flights into eagle-heights?

God is a thought—it maketh all the straight crooked, and all that standeth reel. What? Time would be gone, and all the perishable would be but a lie?

To think this is giddiness and vertigo to human limbs, and even vomiting to the stomach: verily, the reeling sickness do I call it, to conjecture such a thing.

Evil do I call it and misanthropic: all that teaching about the one, and the plenum, and the unmoved, and the sufficient, and the imperishable!

All the imperishable—that's but a simile, and the poets lie too much.—

But of time and of becoming shall the best similes speak: a praise shall they be, and a justification of all perishableness!

Creating—that is the great salvation from suffering, and life's alleviation. But for the creator to appear, suffering itself is needed, and much transformation.

Yea, much bitter dying must there be in your life, ye creators! Thus are ye advocates and justifiers of all perishableness.

For the creator himself to be the new-born child, he must also be willing to be the child-bearer, and endure the pangs of the child-bearer.

Verily, through a hundred souls went I my way, and through a hundred cradles and birth-throes. Many a farewell have I taken; I know the heart-breaking last hours.

But so willeth it my creating Will, my fate. Or, to tell you it more candidly: just such a fate—willeth my Will.

All *feeling* suffereth in me, and is in prison: but my *willing* ever cometh to me as mine emancipator and comforter.

Willing emancipateth: that is the true doctrine of will and emancipation—so teacheth you Zarathustra.

No longer willing, and no longer valuing, and no longer creating! Ah, that that great debility may ever be far from me!

And also in discerning do I feel only my will's procreating and evolving delight; and if there be innocence in my knowledge, it is because there is will to procreation in it.

Away from God and gods did this will allure me; what would there be to create if there were—gods!

But to man doth it ever impel me anew, my fervent creative will; thus impelleth it the hammer to the stone.

Ah, ye men, within the stone slumbereth an image for me, the image of my visions! Ah, that it should slumber in the hardest, ugliest stone!

[*92*]

Now rageth my hammer ruthlessly against its prison. From the stone fly the fragments: what's that to me?

I will complete it: for a shadow came unto me—the stillest and lightest of all things once came unto me!

The beauty of the superman came unto me as a shadow. Ah, my brethren! Of what account now are—the gods to me!—

Thus spake Zarathustra.

25. *The Pitiful*

MY FRIENDS, there hath arisen a satire on your friend: "Behold Zarathustra! Walketh he not amongst us as if amongst animals?"

But it is better said in this wise: "The discerning one walketh amongst men *as* amongst animals."

Man himself is to the discerning one: the animal with red cheeks.

How hath that happened unto him? Is it not because he hath had to be ashamed too oft?

O my friends! Thus speaketh the discerning one: shame, shame, shame—that is the history of man!

And on that account doth the noble one enjoin on himself not to abash: bashfulness doth he enjoin himself in presence of all sufferers.

Verily, I like them not, the merciful ones, whose bliss is in their pity: too destitute are they of bashfulness.

If I must be pitiful, I dislike to be called so; and if I be so, it is preferably at a distance.

Preferably also do I shroud my head, and flee, before being recognised: and thus do I bid you do, my friends!

May my destiny ever lead unafflicted ones like you across my path, and those with whom I *may* have hope and repast and honey in common!

Verily, I have done this and that for the afflicted: but something better did I always seem to do when I had learned to enjoy myself better.

Since humanity came into being, man hath enjoyed himself too little: that alone, my brethren, is our original sin!

And when we learn better to enjoy ourselves, then do we unlearn best to give pain unto others, and to contrive pain.

Therefore do I wash the hand that hath helped the sufferer; therefore do I wipe also my soul.

For in seeing the sufferer suffering—thereof was I ashamed on account of his shame; and in helping him, sorely did I wound his pride.

Great obligations do not make grateful, but revengeful; and when a small kindness is not forgotten, it becometh a gnawing worm.

"Be shy in accepting! Distinguish by accepting!"—thus do I advise those who have naught to bestow.

I, however, am a bestower: willingly do I bestow as friend to friends. Strangers, however, and the poor, may pluck for themselves the fruit from my tree: thus doth it cause less shame.

Beggars, however, one should entirely do away with! Verily, it annoyeth one to give unto them, and it annoyeth one not to give unto them.

And likewise sinners and bad consciences! Believe me, my friends: the sting of conscience teacheth one to sting.

The worst things, however, are the petty thoughts. Verily, better to have done evilly than to have thought pettily!

To be sure, ye say: "The delight in petty evils spareth one many a great evil deed." But here one should not wish to be sparing.

Like a boil is the evil deed: it itcheth and irritateth and breaketh forth—it speaketh honourably.

"Behold, I am disease," saith the evil deed: that is its honourableness.

But like infection is the petty thought: it creepeth and hideth, and wanteth to be nowhere—until the whole body is decayed and withered by the petty infection.

To him however, who is possessed of a devil, I would whisper this word in the ear: "Better for thee to rear up thy devil! Even for thee there is still a path to greatness!"—

Ah, my brethren! One knoweth a little too much about every one! And many a one becometh transparent to us, but still we can by no means penetrate him.

It is difficult to live among men because silence is so difficult.

And not to him who is offensive to us are we most unfair, but to him who doth not concern us at all.

If, however, thou hast a suffering friend, then be a resting-place for his suffering; like a hard bed, however, a camp-bed: thus wilt thou serve him best.

And if a friend doeth thee wrong, then say: "I forgive thee what thou hast done unto me; that thou hast done it unto *thyself,* however—how could I forgive that!"

Thus speaketh all great love: it surpasseth even forgiveness and pity.

One should hold fast one's heart; for when one letteth it go, how quickly doth one's head run away!

Ah, where in the world have there been greater follies than

with the pitiful? And what in the world hath caused more suffering than the follies of the pitiful?

Woe unto all loving ones who have not an elevation which is above their pity!

Thus spake the devil unto me, once on a time: "Even God hath his hell: it is his love for man."

And lately, did I hear him say these words: "God is dead: of his pity for man hath God died."—

So be ye warned against pity: *from thence* there yet cometh unto men a heavy cloud! Verily, I understand weather-signs!

But attend also to this word: All great love is above all its pity: for it seeketh—to create what is loved!

"Myself do I offer unto my love, *and my neighbour as myself*"—such is the language of all creators.

All creators, however, are hard.—

Thus spake Zarathustra.

26. The Priests

AND one day Zarathustra made a sign to his disciples and spake these words unto them:

"Here are priests: but although they are mine enemies, pass them quietly and with sleeping swords!

Even among them there are heroes; many of them have suffered too much:— so they want to make others suffer.

Bad enemies are they: nothing is more revengeful than their meekness. And readily doth he soil himself who toucheth them.

But my blood is related to theirs; and I want withal to see my blood honoured in theirs."—

And when they had passed, a pain attacked Zarathustra; but not long had he struggled with the pain, when he began to speak thus:

It moveth my heart for those priests. They also go against my taste; but that is the smallest matter unto me, since I am among men.

But I suffer and have suffered with them: prisoners are they unto me, and stigmatised ones. He whom they call Saviour put them in fetters:—

In fetters of false values and fatuous words! Oh, that some one would save them from their Saviour!

On an isle they once thought they had landed, when the sea tossed them about; but behold, it was a slumbering monster!

False values and fatuous words: these are the worst monsters for mortals—long slumbereth and waiteth the fate that is in them.

But at last it cometh and awaketh and devoureth and engulfeth whatever hath built tabernacles upon it.

Oh, just look at those tabernacles which those priests have built themselves! Churches, they call their sweet-smelling caves!

Oh, that falsified light, that mustified air! Where the soul—may not fly aloft to its height!

But so enjoineth their belief: "On your knees, up the stair, ye sinners!"

Verily, rather would I see a shameless one than the distorted eyes of their shame and devotion!

Who created for themselves such caves and penitence-stairs? Was it not those who sought to conceal themselves, and were ashamed under the clear sky?

And only when the clear sky looketh again through ruined roofs, and down upon grass and red poppies on ruined walls—will I again turn my heart to the seats of this God.

They called God that which opposed and afflicted them: and verily, there was much hero-spirit in their worship!

And they knew not how to love their God otherwise than by nailing men to the cross!

As corpses they thought to live; in black draped they their corpses; even in their talk do I still feel the evil flavour of charnel-houses.

And he who liveth nigh unto them liveth nigh unto black pools, wherein the toad singeth his song with sweet gravity.

Better songs would they have to sing, for me to believe in their Saviour: more like saved ones would his disciples have to appear unto me!

Naked, would I like to see them: for beauty alone should preach penitence. But whom would that disguised affliction convince!

Verily, their saviours themselves came not from freedom and freedom's seventh heaven! Verily, they themselves never trod the carpets of knowledge!

Of defects did the spirit of those saviours consist; but into every defect had they put their illusion, their stop-gap, which they called God.

In their pity was their spirit drowned; and when they swelled and o'erswelled with pity, there always floated to the surface a great folly.

Eagerly and with shouts drove they their flock over their foot-bridge; as if there were but one foot-bridge to the future! Verily, those shepherds also were still of the flock!

Small spirits and spacious souls had those shepherds: but,

my brethren, what small domains have even the most spacious souls hitherto been!

Characters of blood did they write on the way they went, and their folly taught that truth is proved by blood.

But blood is the very worst witness to truth; blood tainteth the purest teaching, and turneth it into delusion and hatred of heart.

And when a person goeth through fire for his teaching— what doth that prove! It is more, verily, when out of one's own burning cometh one's own teaching!

Sultry heart and cold head; where these meet, there ariseth the blusterer, the "Saviour."

Greater ones, verily, have there been, and higher-born ones, than those whom the people call saviours, those rapturous blusterers!

And by still greater ones than any of the saviours must ye be saved, my brethren, if ye would find the way to freedom!

Never yet hath there been a Superman. Naked have I seen both of them, the greatest man and the smallest man:—

All-too-similar are they still to each other. Verily, even the greatest found I—all-too-human!—

Thus spake Zarathustra.

27. The Virtuous

WITH thunder and heavenly fireworks must one speak to indolent and somnolent senses.

But beauty's voice speaketh gently: it appealeth only to the most awakened souls.

[99]

Gently vibrated and laughed unto me to-day my buckler; it was beauty's holy laughing and thrilling.

At you, ye virtuous ones, laughed my beauty to-day. And thus came its voice unto me: "They want—to be paid besides!"

Ye want to be paid besides, ye virtuous ones! Ye want reward for virtue, and heaven for earth, and eternity for your to-day?

And now ye upbraid me for teaching that there is no reward-giver, nor paymaster? And verily, I do not even teach that virtue is its own reward.

Ah! this is my sorrow: into the basis of things have reward and punishment been insinuated—and now even into the basis of your souls, ye virtuous ones!

But like the snout of the boar shall my word grub up the basis of your souls; a ploughshare will I be called by you.

All the secrets of your heart shall be brought to light; and when ye lie in the sun, grubbed up and broken, then will also your falsehood be separated from your truth.

For this is your truth: ye are *too pure* for the filth of the words: vengeance, punishment, recompense, retribution.

Ye love your virtue as a mother loveth her child; but when did one hear of a mother wanting to be paid for her love?

It is your dearest Self, your virtue. The ring's thirst is in you: to reach itself again struggleth every ring, and turneth itself.

And like the star that goeth out, so is every work of your virtue: ever is its light on its way and travelling—and when will it cease to be on its way?

Thus is the light of your virtue still on its way, even when its work is done. Be it forgotten and dead, still its ray of light liveth and travelleth.

That your virtue is your Self, and not an outward thing, a

skin, or a cloak: that is the truth from the basis of your souls, ye virtuous ones!——

But sure enough there are those to whom virtue meaneth writhing under the lash: and ye have hearkened too much unto their crying!

And others are there who call virtue the slothfulness of their vices; and when once their hatred and jealousy relax the limbs, their "justice" becometh lively and rubbeth its sleepy eyes.

And others are there who are drawn downwards: their devils draw them. But the more they sink, the more ardently gloweth their eye, and the longing for their God.

Ah! their crying also hath reached your ears, ye virtuous ones: "What I am *not*, that, that is God to me, and virtue!"

And others are there who go along heavily and creakingly, like carts taking stones downhill: they talk much of dignity and virtue—their drag they call virtue!

And others are there who are like eight-day clocks when wound up; they tick, and want people to call ticking—virtue.

Verily, in those have I mine amusement: wherever I find such clocks I shall wind them up with my mockery, and they shall even whirr thereby!

And others are proud of their modicum of righteousness, and for the sake of it do violence to all things: so that the world is drowned in their unrighteousness.

Ah! how ineptly cometh the word "virtue" out of their mouth! And when they say: "I am just," it always soundeth like: "I am just—revenged!"

With their virtues they want to scratch out the eyes of their enemies; and they elevate themselves only that they may lower others.

And again there are those who sit in their swamp, and speak

thus from among the bulrushes: "Virtue—that is to sit quietly in the swamp.

We bite no one, and go out of the way of him who would bite; and in all matters we have the opinion that is given us."

And again there are those who love attitudes, and think that virtue is a sort of attitude.

Their knees continually adore, and their hands are eulogies of virtue, but their heart knoweth naught thereof.

And again there are those who regard it as virtue to say: "Virtue is necessary"; but after all they believe only that policemen are necessary.

And many a one who cannot see men's loftiness, calleth it virtue to see their baseness far too well: thus calleth he his evil eye virtue.—

And some want to be edified and raised up, and call it virtue: and others want to be cast down,—and likewise call it virtue.

And thus do almost all think that they participate in virtue; and at least every one claimeth to be an authority on "good" and "evil."

But Zarathustra came not to say unto all those liars and fools: "What do *ye* know of virtue! What *could* ye know of virtue!"—

But that ye, my friends, might become weary of the old words which ye have learned from the fools and liars:

That ye might become weary of the words "reward," "retribution," "punishment," "righteous vengeance."—

That ye might become weary of saying: "That an action is good is because it is unselfish."

Ah! my friends! That *your* very Self be in your action, as the mother is in the child: let that be *your* formula of virtue!

Verily, I have taken from you a hundred formulæ and your virtue's favourite playthings; and now ye upbraid me, as children upbraid.

They played by the sea—then came there a wave and swept their playthings into the deep: and now do they cry.

But the same wave shall bring them new playthings, and spread before them new speckled shells!

Thus will they be comforted; and like them shall ye also, my friends, have your comforting—and new speckled shells!—

Thus spake Zarathustra.

28. The Rabble

LIFE is a well of delight; but where the rabble also drink, there all fountains are poisoned.

To everything cleanly am I well disposed; but I hate to see the grinning mouths and the thirst of the unclean.

They cast their eye down into the fountain: and now glanceth up to me their odious smile out of the fountain.

The holy water have they poisoned with their lustfulness; and when they called their filthy dreams delight, then poisoned they also the words.

Indignant becometh the flame when they put their damp hearts to the fire; the spirit itself bubbleth and smoketh when the rabble approach the fire.

Mawkish and over-mellow becometh the fruit in their hands: unsteady, and withered at the top, doth their look make the fruit-tree.

And many a one who hath turned away from life, hath only turned away from the rabble: he hated to share with them fountain, flame, and fruit.

And many a one who hath gone into the wilderness and suffered thirst with beasts of prey, disliked only to sit at the cistern with filthy camel-drivers.

And many a one who hath come along as a destroyer, and as a hailstorm to all cornfields, wanted merely to put his foot into the jaws of the rabble, and thus stop their throat.

And it is not the mouthful which hath most choked me, to know that life itself requireth enmity and death and torture-crosses:—

But I asked once, and suffocated almost with my question: What? Is the rabble also *necessary* for life?

Are poisoned fountains necessary, and stinking fires, and filthy dreams, and maggots in the bread of life?

Not my hatred, but my loathing, gnawed hungrily at my life! Ah, ofttimes became I weary of spirit, when I found even the rabble spiritual!

And on the rulers turned I my back, when I saw what they now call ruling: to traffic and bargain for power—with the rabble!

Amongst peoples of a strange language did I dwell, with stopped ears: so that the language of their trafficking might remain strange unto me, and their bargaining for power.

And holding my nose, I went morosely through all yesterdays and todays: verily, badly smell all yesterdays and todays of the scribbling rabble!

Like a cripple become deaf, and blind, and dumb—thus have I lived long; that I might not live with the power-rabble, the scribe-rabble, and the pleasure-rabble.

Toilsomely did my spirit mount stairs, and cautiously; alms

of delight were its refreshment; on the staff did life creep along with the blind one.

What hath happened unto me? How have I freed myself from loathing? Who hath rejuvenated mine eye? How have I flown to the height where no rabble any longer sit at the wells?

Did my loathing itself create for me wings and fountain-divining powers? Verily, to the loftiest height had I to fly, to find again the well of delight!

Oh, I have found it, my brethren! Here on the loftiest height bubbleth up for me the well of delight! And there is a life at whose waters none of the rabble drink with me!

Almost too violently dost thou flow for me, thou fountain of delight! And often emptiest thou the goblet again, in wanting to fill it!

And yet must I learn to approach thee more modestly: far too violently doth my heart still flow towards thee:—

My heart on which my summer burneth, my short, hot, melancholy, over-happy summer: how my summer heart longeth for thy coolness!

Past, the lingering distress of my spring! Past, the wickedness of my snowflakes in June! Summer have I become entirely, and summer-noontide!

A summer on the loftiest height, with cold fountains and blissful stillness: oh, come, my friends, that the stillness may become more blissful!

For this is *our* height and our home: too high and steep do we here dwell for all uncleanly ones and their thirst.

Cast but your pure eyes into the well of my delight, my friends! How could it become turbid thereby! It shall laugh back to you with *its* purity.

On the tree of the future build we our nest; eagles shall bring us lone ones food in their beaks!

Verily, no food of which the impure could be fellow-partakers! Fire, would they think they devoured, and burn their mouths!

Verily, no abodes do we here keep ready for the impure! An ice-cave to their bodies would our happiness be, and to their spirits!

And as strong winds will we live above them, neighbours to the eagles, neighbours to the snow, neighbours to the sun: thus live the strong winds.

And like a wind will I one day blow amongst them, and with my spirit, take the breath from their spirit: thus willeth my future.

Verily, a strong wind is Zarathustra to all low places; and this counsel counselleth he to his enemies, and to whatever spitteth and speweth: "Take care not to spit *against* the wind!"—

Thus spake Zarathustra.

29. The Tarantulas

LO, THIS is the tarantula's den! Would'st thou see the tarantula itself? Here hangeth its web: touch this, so that it may tremble.

There cometh the tarantula willingly: Welcome, tarantula! Black on thy back is thy triangle and symbol; and I know also what is in thy soul.

Revenge is in thy soul: wherever thou bitest, there ariseth black scab; with revenge, thy poison maketh the soul giddy!

Thus do I speak unto you in parable, ye who make the soul giddy, ye preachers of *equality!* Tarantulas are ye unto me, and secretly revengeful ones!

But I will soon bring your hiding-places to the light: therefore do I laugh in your face my laughter of the height.

Therefore do I tear at your web, that your rage may lure you out of your den of lies, and that your revenge may leap forth from behind your word "justice."

Because, *for man to be redeemed from revenge*—that is for me the bridge to the highest hope, and a rainbow after long storms.

Otherwise, however, would the tarantulas have it. "Let it be very justice for the world to become full of the storms of our vengeance"—thus do they talk to one another.

"Vengeance will we use, and insult, against all who are not like us"—thus do the tarantula-hearts pledge themselves.

"And 'Will to Equality'—that itself shall henceforth be the name of virtue; and against all that hath power will we raise an outcry!"

Ye preachers of equality, the tyrant-frenzy of impotence crieth thus in you for "equality": your most secret tyrant-longings disguise themselves thus in virtue-words!

Fretted conceit and suppressed envy—perhaps your fathers' conceit and envy: in you break they forth as flame and frenzy of vengeance.

What the father hath hid cometh out in the son; and oft have I found in the son the father's revealed secret.

Inspired ones they resemble: but it is not the heart that inspireth them—but vengeance. And when they become subtle and cold, it is not spirit, but envy, that maketh them so.

Their jealousy leadeth them also into thinkers' paths; and this is the sign of their jealousy—they always go too far: so that their fatigue hath at last to go to sleep on the snow.

In all their lamentations soundeth vengeance, in all their eulogies is maleficence; and being judge seemeth to them bliss.

But thus do I counsel you, my friends: distrust all in whom the impulse to punish is powerful!

They are people of bad race and lineage; out of their countenances peer the hangman and the sleuth-hound.

Distrust all those who talk much of their justice! Verily, in their souls not only honey is lacking.

And when they call themselves "the good and just," forget not, that for them to be Pharisees, nothing is lacking but—power!

My friends, I will not be mixed up and confounded with others.

There are those who preach my doctrine of life, and are at the same time preachers of equality, and tarantulas.

That they speak in favour of life, though they sit in their den, these poison-spiders, and withdrawn from life—is because they would thereby do injury.

To those would they thereby do injury who have power at present: for with those the preaching of death is still most at home.

Were it otherwise, then would the tarantulas teach otherwise: and they themselves were formerly the best world-maligners and heretic-burners.

With these preachers of equality will I not be mixed up and confounded. For thus speaketh justice *unto me:* "Men are not equal."

And neither shall they become so! What would be my love to the Superman, if I spake otherwise?

On a thousand bridges and piers shall they throng to the future, and always shall there be more war and inequality among them: thus doth my great love make me speak!

Inventors of figures and phantoms shall they be in their hostilities; and with those figures and phantoms shall they yet fight with each other the supreme fight!

Good and evil, and rich and poor, and high and low, and all names of values: weapons shall they be, and sounding signs, that life must again and again surpass itself!

Aloft will it build itself with columns and stairs—life itself: into remote distances would it gaze, and out towards blissful beauties—*therefore* doth it require elevation!

And because it requireth elevation, therefore doth it require steps, and variance of steps and climbers! To rise striveth life, and in rising to surpass itself.

And just behold, my friends! Here where the tarantula's den is, riseth aloft an ancient temple's ruins—just behold it with enlightened eyes!

Verily, he who here towered aloft his thoughts in stone, knew as well as the wisest ones about the secret of life!

That there is struggle and inequality even in beauty, and war for power and supremacy: that doth he here teach us in the plainest parable.

How divinely do vault and arch here contrast in the struggle: how with light and shade they strive against each other, the divinely striving ones.—

Thus, steadfast and beautiful, let us also be enemies, my friends! Divinely will we strive *against* one another!—

Alas! There hath the tarantula bit me myself, mine old enemy! Divinely steadfast and beautiful, it hath bit me on the finger!

"Punishment must there be, and justice"—so thinketh it·

"not gratuitously shall he here sing songs in honour of enmity!"

Yea, it hath revenged itself! And alas! now will it make my soul also dizzy with revenge!

That I may *not* turn dizzy, however, bind me fast, my friends, to this pillar! Rather will I be a pillar-saint than a whirl of vengeance!

Verily, no cyclone or whirlwind is Zarathustra: and if he be a dancer, he is not at all a tarantula-dancer!—

Thus spake Zarathustra.

30. The Famous Wise Ones

THE people have ye served and the people's superstition—*not* the truth!—all ye famous wise ones! And just on that account did they pay you reverence.

And on that account also did they tolerate your unbelief, because it was a pleasantry and a by-path for the people. Thus doth the master give free scope to his slaves, and even enjoyeth their presumptuousness.

But he who is hated by the people, as the wolf by the dogs —is the free spirit, the enemy of fetters, the non-adorer, the dweller in the woods.

To hunt him out of his lair—that was always called "sense of right" by the people: on him do they still hound their sharpest-toothed dogs.

"For there the truth is, where the people are! Woe, woe to the seeking ones!"—thus hath it echoed through all time.

Your people would ye justify in their reverence: that called ye "Will to Truth," ye famous wise ones!

And your heart hath always said to itself: "From the people have I come: from thence came to me also the voice of God."

Stiff-necked and artful, like the ass, have ye always been, as the advocates of the people.

And many a powerful one who wanted to run well with the people, hath harnessed in front of his horses—a donkey, a famous wise man.

And now, ye famous wise ones, I would have you finally throw off entirely the skin of the lion!

The skin of the beast of prey, the speckled skin, and the dishevelled locks of the investigator, the searcher, and the conqueror!

Ah! for me to learn to believe in your "conscientiousness," ye would first have to break your venerating will.

Conscientious—so call I him who goeth into God-forsaken wildernesses, and hath broken his venerating heart.

In the yellow sands and burnt by the sun, he doubtless peereth thirstily at the isles rich in fountains, where life reposeth under shady trees.

But his thirst doth not persuade him to become like those comfortable ones: for where there are oases, there are also idols.

Hungry, fierce, lonesome, God-forsaken: so doth the lion-will wish itself.

Free from the happiness of slaves, redeemed from deities and adorations, fearless and fear-inspiring, grand and lonesome: so is the will of the conscientious.

In the wilderness have ever dwelt the conscientious, the free spirits, as lords of the wilderness; but in the cities dwell the well-foddered, famous wise ones—the draught-beasts.

For, always do they draw, as asses—the *people's* carts!

Not that I on that account upbraid them: but serving ones do they remain, and harnessed ones, even though they glitter in golden harness.

And often have they been good servants and worthy of their hire. For thus saith virtue: "If thou must be a servant, seek him unto whom thy service is most useful!

The spirit and virtue of thy master shall advance by thou being his servant: thus wilt thou thyself advance with his spirit and virtue!"

And verily, ye famous wise ones, ye servants of the people! Ye yourselves have advanced with the people's spirit and virtue—and the people by you! To your honour do I say it!

But the people ye remain for me, even with your virtues, the people with purblind eyes—the people who know not what *spirit* is!

Spirit is life which itself cutteth into life: by its own torture doth it increase its own knowledge,—did ye know that before?

And the spirit's happiness is this: to be anointed and consecrated with tears as a sacrificial victim,—did ye know that before?

And the blindness of the blind one, and his seeking and groping, shall yet testify to the power of the sun into which he hath gazed,—did ye know that before?

And with mountains shall the discerning one learn to *build!* It is a small thing for the spirit to remove mountains,—did ye know that before?

Ye know only the sparks of the spirit: but ye do not see the anvil which it is, and the cruelty of its hammer!

Verily, ye know not the spirit's pride! But still less could ye endure the spirit's humility, should it ever want to speak!

And never yet could ye cast your spirit into a pit of snow:

ye are not hot enough for that! Thus are ye unaware, also, of the delight of its coldness.

In all respects, however, ye make too familiar with the spirit; and out of wisdom have ye often made an alms-house and a hospital for bad poets.

Ye are not eagles: thus have ye never experienced the happiness of the alarm of the spirit. And he who is not a bird should not camp above abysses.

Ye seem to me lukewarm ones: but coldly floweth all deep knowledge. Ice-cold are the innermost wells of the spirit: a refreshment to hot hands and handlers.

Respectable do ye there stand, and stiff, and with straight backs, ye famous wise ones!—no strong wind or will impelleth you.

Have ye ne'er seen a sail crossing the sea, rounded and inflated, and trembling with the violence of the wind?

Like the sail trembling with the violence of the spirit, doth my wisdom cross the sea—my wild wisdom!

But ye servants of the people, ye famous wise ones—how *could* ye go with me!—

Thus spake Zarathustra.

31. *The Night-Song*

'TIS night: now do all gushing fountains speak louder. And my soul also is a gushing fountain.

'Tis night: now only do all songs of the loving ones awake. And my soul also is the song of a loving one.

Something unappeased, unappeasable, is within me; it

longeth to find expression. A craving for love is within me, which speaketh itself the language of love.

Light am I: ah, that I were night! But it is my lonesomeness to be begirt with light!

Ah, that I were dark and nightly! How would I suck at the breasts of light!

And you yourselves would I bless, ye twinkling starlets and glow-worms aloft!—and would rejoice in the gifts of your light.

But I live in mine own light, I drink again into myself the flames that break forth from me.

I know not the happiness of the receiver; and oft have I dreamt that stealing must be more blessed than receiving.

It is my poverty that my hand never ceaseth bestowing; it is mine envy that I see waiting eyes and the brightened nights of longing.

Oh, the misery of all bestowers! Oh, the darkening of my sun! Oh, the craving to crave! Oh, the violent hunger in satiety!

They take from me: but do I yet touch their soul? There is a gap 'twixt giving and receiving; and the smallest gap hath finally to be bridged over.

A hunger ariseth out of my beauty: I should like to injure those I illumine; I should like to rob those I have gifted:—thus do I hunger for wickedness.

Withdrawing my hand when another hand already stretcheth out to it; hesitating like the cascade, which hesitateth even in its leap:—thus do I hunger for wickedness!

Such revenge doth mine abundance think of: such mischief welleth out of my lonesomeness.

My happiness in bestowing died in bestowing; my virtue became weary of itself by its abundance!

He who ever bestoweth is in danger of losing his shame; to

him who ever dispenseth, the hand and heart become callous by very dispensing.

Mine eye no longer overfloweth for the shame of suppliants; my hand hath become too hard for the trembling of filled hands.

Whence have gone the tears of mine eye, and the down of my heart? Oh, the lonesomeness of all bestowers! Oh, the silence of all shining ones!

Many suns circle in desert space: to all that is dark do they speak with their light—but to me they are silent.

Oh, this is the hostility of light to the shining one: un-pityingly doth it pursue its course.

Unfair to the shining one in its innermost heart, cold to the suns:—thus travelleth every sun.

Like a storm do the suns pursue their courses: that is their travelling. Their inexorable will do they follow: that is their coldness.

Oh, ye only is it, ye dark, nightly ones, that extract warmth from the shining ones! Oh, ye only drink milk and refreshment from the light's udders!

Ah, there is ice around me; my hand burneth with the iciness! Ah, there is thirst in me; it panteth after your thirst!

'Tis night: alas, that I have to be light! And thirst for the nightly! And lonesomeness!

'Tis night: now doth my longing break forth in me as a fountain,—for speech do I long.

'Tis night: now do all gushing fountains speak louder. And my soul also is a gushing fountain.

'Tis night: now do all songs of loving ones awake. And my soul also is the song of a loving one.—

Thus sang Zarathustra.

32. The Dance-Song

ONE evening went Zarathustra and his disciples through the forest; and when he sought for a well, lo, he lighted upon a green meadow peacefully surrounded by trees and bushes, where maidens were dancing together. As soon as the maidens recognised Zarathustra, they ceased dancing; Zarathustra, however, approached them with friendly mien and spake these words:

Cease not your dancing, ye lovely maidens! No game-spoiler hath come to you with evil eye, no enemy of maidens.

God's advocate am I with the devil: he, however, is the spirit of gravity. How could I, ye light-footed ones, be hostile to divine dances? Or to maidens' feet with fine ankles?

To be sure, I am a forest, and a night of dark trees: but he who is not afraid of my darkness, will find banks full of roses under my cypresses.

And even the little God may he find, who is dearest to maidens: beside the well lieth he quietly, with closed eyes.

Verily, in broad daylight did he fall asleep, the sluggard! Had he perhaps chased butterflies too much?

Upbraid me not, ye beautiful dancers, when I chasten the little God somewhat! He will cry, certainly, and weep—but he is laughable even when weeping!

And with tears in his eyes shall he ask you for a dance; and I myself will sing a song to his dance:

A dance-song and satire on the spirit of gravity my supremest, powerfulest devil, who is said to be "lord of the world."—

And this is the song that Zarathustra sang when Cupid and the maidens danced together:

Of late did I gaze into thine eye, O Life! And into the unfathomable did I there seem to sink.

But thou pulledst me out with a golden angle; derisively didst thou laugh when I called thee unfathomable.

"Such is the language of all fish," saidst thou; "what *they* do not fathom is unfathomable.

But changeable am I only, and wild, and altogether a woman, and no virtuous one:

Though I be called by you men the 'profound one,' or the 'faithful one,' 'the eternal one,' 'the mysterious one.'

But ye men endow us always with your own virtues—alas, ye virtuous ones!"

Thus did she laugh, the unbelievable one; but never do I believe her and her laughter, when she speaketh evil of herself.

And when I talked face to face with my wild Wisdom, she said to me angrily: "Thou willest, thou cravest, thou lovest; on that account alone dost thou *praise* Life!"

Then had I almost answered indignantly and told the truth to the angry one; and one cannot answer more indignantly than when one "telleth the truth" to one's Wisdom.

For thus do things stand with us three. In my heart do I love only Life—and verily, most when I hate her!

But that I am fond of Wisdom, and often too fond, is because she remindeth me very strongly of Life!

She hath her eye, her laugh, and even her golden angle-rod: am I responsible for it that both are so alike?

And when once Life asked me: "Who is she then, this Wisdom?"—then said I eagerly: "Ah, yes! Wisdom!

One thirsteth for her and is not satisfied, one looketh through veils, one graspeth through nets.

Is she beautiful? What do I know! But the oldest carps are still lured by her.

Changeable is she, and wayward; often have I seen her bite her lip, and pass the comb against the grain of her hair.

Perhaps she is wicked and false, and altogether a woman; but when she speaketh ill of herself, just then doth she seduce most."

When I had said this unto Life, then laughed she maliciously, and shut her eyes. "Of whom dost thou speak?" said she. "Perhaps of me?

And if thou wert right—is it proper to say *that* in such wise to my face! But now, pray, speak also of thy Wisdom!"

Ah, and now hast thou again opened thine eyes, O beloved Life! And into the unfathomable have I again seemed to sink.—

Thus sang Zarathustra. But when the dance was over and the maidens had departed, he became sad.

"The sun hath been long set," said he at last, "the meadow is damp, and from the forest cometh coolness.

An unknown presence is about me, and gazeth thoughtfully. What! Thou livest still, Zarathustra?

Why? Wherefore? Whereby? Whither? Where? How? Is it not folly still to live?—

Ah, my friends; the evening is it which thus interrogateth in me. Forgive me my sadness!

Evening hath come on: forgive me that evening hath come on!"

Thus sang Zarathustra.

33. The Grave-Song

"YONDER is the grave-island, the silent isle; yonder also are the graves of my youth. Thither will I carry an evergreen wreath of life."

Resolving thus in my heart, did I sail o'er the sea.—

Oh, ye sights and scenes of my youth! Oh, all ye gleams of love, ye divine fleeting gleams! How could ye perish so soon for me! I think of you to-day as my dead ones.

From you, my dearest dead ones, cometh unto me a sweet savour, heart-opening and melting. Verily, it convulseth and openeth the heart of the lone seafarer.

Still am I the richest and most to be envied—I, the lonesomest one! For I *have possessed* you, and ye possess me still. Tell me: to whom hath there ever fallen such rosy apples from the tree as have fallen unto me?

Still am I your love's heir and heritage, blooming to your memory with many-hued, wild-growing virtues, O ye dearest ones!

Ah, we were made to remain nigh unto each other, ye kindly strange marvels; and not like timid birds did ye come to me and my longing—nay, but as trusting ones to a trusting one!

Yea, made for faithfulness, like me, and for fond eternities, must I now name you by your faithlessness, ye divine glances and fleeting gleams: no other name have I yet learnt.

Verily, too early did ye die for me, ye fugitives. Yet did ye not flee from me, nor did I flee from you: innocent are we to each other in our faithlessness.

To kill *me,* did they strangle you, ye singing birds of my

hopes! Yea, at you, ye dearest ones, did malice ever shoot its arrows—to hit my heart!

And they hit it! Because ye were always my dearest, my possession and my possessedness: *on that account* had ye to die young, and far too early!

At my most vulnerable point did they shoot the arrow—namely, at you, whose skin is like down—or more like the smile that dieth at a glance!

But this word will I say unto mine enemies: What is all manslaughter in comparison with what ye have done unto me!

Worse evil did ye do unto me than all manslaughter; the irretrievable did ye take from me:—thus do I speak unto you, mine enemies!

Slew ye not my youth's visions and dearest marvels! My playmates took ye from me, the blessed spirits! To their memory do I deposit this wreath and this curse.

This curse upon you, mine enemies! Have ye not made mine eternal short, as a tone dieth away in a cold night! Scarcely, as the twinkle of divine eyes, did it come to me—as a fleeting gleam!

Thus spake once in a happy hour my purity: "Divine shall everything be unto me."

Then did ye haunt me with foul phantoms; ah, whither hath that happy hour now fled!

"All days shall be holy unto me"—so spake once the wisdom of my youth: verily, the language of a joyous wisdom!

But then did ye enemies steal my nights, and sold them to sleepless torture: ah, whither hath that joyous wisdom now fled?

Once did I long for happy auspices: then did ye lead an owl-monster across my path, an adverse sign. Ah, whither did my tender longing then flee?

All loathing did I once vow to renounce: then did ye change my nigh ones and nearest ones into ulcerations. Ah, whither did my noblest vow then flee?

As a blind one did I once walk in blessed ways: then did ye cast filth on the blind one's course: and now is he disgusted with the old footpath.

And when I performed my hardest task, and celebrated the triumph of my victories, then did ye make those who loved me call out that I then grieved them most.

Verily, it was always your doing: ye embittered to me my best honey, and the diligence of my best bees.

To my charity have ye ever sent the most impudent beggars; around my sympathy have ye ever crowded the incurably shameless. Thus have ye wounded the faith of my virtue.

And when I offered my holiest as a sacrifice, immediately did your "piety" put its fatter gifts beside it: so that my holiest suffocated in the fumes of your fat.

And once did I want to dance as I had never yet danced: beyond all heavens did I want to dance. Then did ye seduce my favourite minstrel.

And now hath he struck up an awful, melancholy air: alas, he tooted as a mournful horn to mine ear!

Murderous minstrel, instrument of evil, most innocent instrument! Already did I stand prepared for the best dance: then didst thou slay my rapture with thy tones!

Only in the dance do I know how to speak the parable of the highest things:—and now hath my grandest parable remained unspoken in my limbs!

Unspoken and unrealised hath my highest hope remained! And there have perished for me all the visions and consolations of my youth!

How did I ever bear it? How did I survive and surmount such wounds? How did my soul rise again out of those sepulchres?

Yea, something invulnerable, unburiable is with me, something that would rend rocks asunder: it is called *my Will*. Silently doth it proceed, and unchanged throughout the years.

Its course will it go upon my feet, mine old Will; hard of heart is its nature and invulnerable.

Invulnerable am I only in my heel. Ever livest thou there, and art like thyself, thou most patient one! Ever hast thou burst all shackles of the tomb!

In thee still liveth also the unrealisedness of my youth; and as life and youth sittest thou here hopeful on the yellow ruins of graves.

Yea, thou art still for me the demolisher of all graves: Hail to thee, my Will! And only where there are graves are there resurrections.—

Thus sang Zarathustra.

34. Self-Surpassing

"WILL to Truth" do ye call it, ye wisest ones, that which impelleth you and maketh you ardent?

Will for the thinkableness of all being: thus do *I* call your will!

All being would ye *make* thinkable: for ye doubt with good reason whether it be already thinkable.

But it shall accommodate and bend itself to you! So willeth

your will. Smooth shall it become and subject to the spirit, as its mirror and reflection.

That is your entire will, ye wisest ones, as a Will to Power; and even when ye speak of good and evil, and of estimates of value.

Ye would still create a world before which ye can bow the knee: such is your ultimate hope and ecstasy.

The ignorant, to be sure, the people—they are like a river on which a boat floateth along: and in the boat sit the estimates of value, solemn and disguised.

Your will and your valuations have ye put on the river of becoming; it betrayeth unto me an old Will to Power, what is believed by the people as good and evil.

It was ye, ye wisest ones, who put such guests in this boat, and gave them pomp and proud names—ye and your ruling Will!

Onward the river now carrieth your boat: it *must* carry it. A small matter if the rough wave foameth and angrily resisteth its keel!

It is not the river that is your danger and the end of your good and evil, ye wisest ones: but that Will itself, the Will to Power—the unexhausted, procreating life-will.

But that ye may understand my gospel of good and evil, for that purpose will I tell you my gospel of life, and of the nature of all living things.

The living thing did I follow; I walked in the broadest and narrowest paths to learn its nature.

With a hundred-faced mirror did I catch its glance when its mouth was shut, so that its eye might speak unto me. And its eye spake unto me.

But wherever I found living things, there heard I also the language of obedience. All living things are obeying things.

[*123*]

And this heard I secondly: Whatever cannot obey itself, is commanded. Such is the nature of living things.

This, however, is the third thing which I heard—namely, that commanding is more difficult than obeying. And not only because the commander beareth the burden of all obeyers, and because this burden readily crusheth him:—

An attempt and a risk seemed all commanding unto me; and whenever it commandeth, the living thing risketh itself thereby.

Yea, even when it commandeth itself, then also must it atone for its commanding. Of its own law must it become the judge and avenger and victim.

How doth this happen! So did I ask myself. What persuadeth the living thing to obey, and command, and even be obedient in commanding?

Hearken now unto my word, ye wisest ones! Test it seriously, whether I have crept into the heart of life itself, and into the roots of its heart!

Wherever I found a living thing, there found I Will to Power; and even in the will of the servant found I the will to be master.

That to the stronger the weaker shall serve—thereto persuadeth he his will who would be master over a still weaker one. That delight alone he is unwilling to forego.

And as the lesser surrendereth himself to the greater that he may have delight and power over the least of all, so doth even the greatest surrender himself, and staketh—life, for the sake of power.

It is the surrender of the greatest to run risk and danger, and play dice for death.

And where there is sacrifice and service and love-glances, there also is the will to be master. By by-ways doth the weaker then slink into the fortress, and into the heart of the mightier one—and there stealeth power.

And this secret spake Life herself unto me. "Behold," said she, "I am that *which must ever surpass itself.*

To be sure, ye call it will to procreation, or impulse towards a goal, towards the higher, remoter, more manifold: but all that is one and the same secret.

Rather would I succumb than disown this one thing; and verily, where there is succumbing and leaf-falling, lo, there doth Life sacrifice itself—for power!

That I have to be struggle, and becoming, and purpose, and cross-purpose—ah, he who divineth my will, divineth well also on what *crooked* paths it hath to tread!

Whatever I create, and however much I love it,—soon must I be adverse to it, and to my love: so willeth my will.

And even thou, discerning one, art only a path and footstep of my will: verily, my Will to Power walketh even on the feet of thy Will to Truth!

He certainly did not hit the truth who shot at it the formula: "Will to existence": that will—doth not exist!

For what is not, cannot will; that, however, which is in existence—how could it still strive for existence!

Only where there is life, is there also will: not, however, Will to Life, but—so teach I thee—Will to Power!

Much is reckoned higher than life itself by the living one; but out of the very reckoning speaketh—the Will to Power!"—

Thus did Life once teach me: and thereby, ye wisest ones, do I solve you the riddle of your hearts.

Verily, I say unto you: good and evil which would be everlasting—it doth not exist! Of its own accord must it ever surpass itself anew.

With your values and formulæ of good and evil, ye exercise power, ye valuing ones: and that is your secret love, and the sparkling, trembling, and overflowing of your souls.

But a stronger power groweth out of your values, and a new surpassing: by it breaketh egg and egg-shell.

And he who hath to be a creator in good and evil—verily, he hath first to be a destroyer, and break values in pieces.

Thus doth the greatest evil pertain to the greatest good: that, however, is the creating good.—

Let us *speak* thereof, ye wisest ones, even though it be bad. To be silent is worse; all suppressed truths become poisonous.

And let everything break up which—can break up by our truths! Many a house is still to be built!—

Thus spake Zarathustra.

35. *The Sublime Ones*

CALM is the bottom of my sea: who would guess that it hideth droll monsters!

Unmoved is my depth: but it sparkleth with swimming enigmas and laughters.

A sublime one saw I today, a solemn one, a penitent of the spirit: Oh, how my soul laughed at his ugliness!

With upraised breast, and like those who draw in their breath: thus did he stand, the sublime one, and in silence:

O'erhung with ugly truths, the spoil of his hunting, and rich in torn raiment; many thorns also hung on him—but I saw no rose.

Not yet had he learned laughing and beauty. Gloomy did this hunter return from the forest of knowledge.

From the fight with wild beasts returned he home: but even yet a wild beast gazeth out of his seriousness—an unconquered wild beast!

As a tiger doth he ever stand, on the point of springing; but I do not like those strained souls; ungracious is my taste towards all those self-engrossed ones.

And ye tell me, friends, that there is to be no dispute about taste and tasting? But all life is a dispute about taste and tasting!

Taste: that is weight at the same time, and scales and weigher; and alas for every living thing that would live without dispute about weight and scales and weigher!

Should he become weary of his sublimeness, this sublime one, then only will his beauty begin—and then only will I taste him and find him savoury.

And only when he turneth away from himself will he o'erleap his own shadow—and verily! into *his* sun.

Far too long did he sit in the shade; the cheeks of the penitent of the spirit became pale; he almost starved on his expectations.

Contempt is still in his eye, and loathing hideth in his mouth. To be sure, he now resteth, but he hath not yet taken rest in the sunshine.

As the ox ought he to do; and his happiness should smell of the earth, and not of contempt for the earth.

As a white ox would I like to see him, which, snorting and lowing, walketh before the plough-share: and his lowing should also laud all that is earthly!

Dark is still his countenance; the shadow of his hand danceth upon it. O'ershadowed is still the sense of his eye.

His deed itself is still the shadow upon him: his doing obscureth the doer. Not yet hath he overcome his deed.

To be sure, I love in him the shoulders of the ox: but now do I want to see also the eye of the angel.

Also his hero-will hath he still to unlearn: an exalted one shall he be, and not only a sublime one:—the ether itself should raise him, the will-less one!

He hath subdued monsters, he hath solved enigmas. But he should also redeem his monsters and enigmas; into heavenly children should he transform them.

As yet hath his knowledge not learned to smile, and to be without jealousy; as yet hath his gushing passion not become calm in beauty.

Verily, not in satiety shall his longing cease and disappear, but in beauty! Gracefulness belongeth to the munificence of the magnanimous.

His arm across his head: thus should the hero repose; thus should he also surmount his repose.

But precisely to the hero is *beauty* the hardest thing of all. Unattainable is beauty by all ardent wills.

A little more, a little less: precisely this is much here, it is the most here.

To stand with relaxed muscles and with unharnessed will: that is the hardest for all of you, ye sublime ones!

When power becometh gracious and descendeth into the visible—I call such condescension, beauty.

And from no one do I want beauty so much as from thee, thou powerful one: let thy goodness be thy last self-conquest.

All evil do I accredit to thee: therefore do I desire of thee the good.

Verily, I have often laughed at the weaklings, who think themselves good because they have crippled paws!

[*128*]

The virtue of the pillar shalt thou strive after: more beautiful doth it ever become, and more graceful—but internally harder and more sustaining—the higher it riseth.

Yea, thou sublime one, one day shalt thou also be beautiful, and hold up the mirror to thine own beauty.

Then will thy soul thrill with divine desires; and there will be adoration even in thy vanity!

For this is the secret of the soul: when the hero hath abandoned it, then only approacheth it in dreams—the super-hero.—

Thus spake Zarathustra.

36. The Land of Culture

Too far did I fly into the future: a horror seized upon me.

And when I looked around me, lo! there time was my sole contemporary.

Then did I fly backwards, homewards—and always faster. Thus did I come unto you: ye present-day men, and into the land of culture.

For the first time brought I an eye to see you, and good desire: verily, with longing in my heart did I come.

But how did it turn out with me? Although so alarmed—I had yet to laugh! Never did mine eye see anything so motley-coloured!

I laughed and laughed, while my foot still trembled, and my heart as well. "Here forsooth, is the home of all the paint-pots,"—said I.

With fifty patches painted on faces and limbs—so sat ye there to mine astonishment, ye present-day men!

And with fifty mirrors around you, which flattered your play of colours, and repeated it!

Verily, ye could wear no better masks, ye present-day men, than your own faces! Who could—*recognise* you!

Written all over with the characters of the past, and these characters also pencilled over with new characters—thus have ye concealed yourselves well from all decipherers!

And though one be a trier of the reins, who still believeth that ye have reins! Out of colours ye seem to be baked, and out of glued scraps.

All times and peoples gaze divers-coloured out of your veils; all customs and beliefs speak divers-coloured out of your gestures.

He who would strip you of veils and wrappers, and paints and gestures, would just have enough left to scare the crows.

Verily, I myself am the scared crow that once saw you naked, and without paint; and I flew away when the skeleton ogled at me.

Rather would I be a day-labourer in the nether-world, and among the shades of the by-gone!—Fatter and fuller than ye, are forsooth the nether-worldlings!

This, yea this, is bitterness to my bowels, that I can neither endure you naked nor clothed, ye present-day men!

All that is unhomelike in the future, and whatever maketh strayed birds shiver, is verily more homelike and familiar than your "reality."

For thus speak ye: "Real are we wholly, and without faith and superstition": thus do ye plume yourselves—alas! even without plumes!

Indeed, how would ye be *able* to believe, ye divers-coloured ones!—ye who are pictures of all that hath ever been believed!

Perambulating refutations are ye, of belief itself, and a dislocation of all thought. *Untrustworthy ones:* thus do *I* call you, ye real ones!

All periods prate against one another in your spirits; and the dreams and pratings of all periods were even realer than your awakeness!

Unfruitful are ye: *therefore* do ye lack belief. But he who had to create, had always his presaging dreams and astral premonitions—and believed in believing!—

Half-open doors are ye, at which grave-diggers wait. And this is *your* reality: "Everything deserveth to perish."

Alas, how ye stand there before me, ye unfruitful ones; how lean your ribs! And many of you surely have had knowledge thereof.

Many a one hath said: "There hath surely a God filched something from me secretly whilst I slept? Verily, enough to make a girl for himself therefrom!

"Amazing is the poverty of my ribs!" thus hath spoken many a present-day man.

Yea, ye are laughable unto me, ye present-day men! And especially when ye marvel at yourselves!

And woe unto me if I could not laugh at your marvelling, and had to swallow all that is repugnant in your platters!

As it is, however, I will make lighter of you, since I have to carry *what is heavy;* and what matter if beetles and May-bugs also alight on my load!

Verily, it shall not on that account become heavier to me! And not from you, ye present-day men, shall my great weariness arise.—

Ah, whither shall I now ascend with my longing! From all mountains do I look out for fatherlands and motherlands.

[*131*]

But a home have I found nowhere: unsettled am I in all cities, and decamping at all gates.

Alien to me, and a mockery, are the present-day men, to whom of late my heart impelled me; and exiled am I from fatherlands and motherlands.

Thus do I love only my *children's land,* the undiscovered in the remotest sea: for it do I bid my sails search and search.

Unto my children will I make amends for being the child of my fathers: and unto all the future—for *this* present-day!—

Thus spake Zarathustra.

37. *Immaculate Perception*

WHEN yester-eve the moon arose, then did I fancy it about to bear a sun: so broad and teeming did it lie on the horizon.

But it was a liar with its pregnancy; and sooner will I believe in the man in the moon than in the woman.

To be sure, little of a man is he also, that timid night-reveller. Verily, with a bad conscience doth he stalk over the roofs.

For he is covetous and jealous, the monk in the moon; covetous of the earth, and all the joys of lovers.

Nay, I like him not, that tom-cat on the roofs! Hateful unto me are all that slink around half-closed windows!

Piously and silently doth he stalk along on the star-carpets: —but I like no light-treading human feet, on which not even a spur jingleth.

Every honest one's step speaketh; the cat however, stealeth

along over the ground. Lo! cat-like doth the moon come along, and dishonestly.——

This parable speak I unto you sentimental dissemblers, unto you, the "pure discerners!" You do I call——covetous ones!

Also ye love the earth, and the earthly: I have divined you well!——but shame is in your love, and a bad conscience——ye are like the moon!

To despise the earthly hath your spirit been persuaded, but not your bowels: these, however, are the strongest in you!

And now is your spirit ashamed to be at the service of your bowels, and goeth in by-ways and lying ways to escape its own shame.

"That would be the highest thing for me"——so saith your lying spirit unto itself——"to gaze upon life without desire, and not like the dog, with hanging-out tongue:

To be happy in gazing: with dead will, free from the grip and greed of selfishness——cold and ashy-grey all over, but with intoxicated moon-eyes!

That would be the dearest thing to me"——thus doth the seduced one seduce himself,——"to love the earth as the moon loveth it, and with the eye only to feel its beauty.

And this do I call *immaculate* perception of all things: to want nothing else from them, but to be allowed to lie before them as a mirror with a hundred facets."——

Oh, ye sentimental dissemblers, ye covetous ones! Ye lack innocence in your desire: and now do ye defame desiring on that account!

Verily, not as creators, as procreators, or as jubilators do ye love the earth!

Where is innocence? Where there is will to procreation. And he who seeketh to create beyond himself, hath for me the purest will.

[*133*]

Where is beauty? Where I *must will* with my whole Will; where I will love and perish, that an image may not remain merely an image.

Loving and perishing: these have rhymed from eternity. Will to love: that is to be ready also for death. Thus do I speak unto you cowards!

But now doth your emasculated ogling profess to be "contemplation!" And that which can be examined with cowardly eyes is to be christened "beautiful!" Oh, ye violators of noble names!

But it shall be your curse, ye immaculate ones, ye pure discerners, that ye shall never bring forth, even though ye lie broad and teeming on the horizon!

Verily, ye fill your mouth with noble words: and we are to believe that your heart overfloweth, ye cozeners?

But *my* words are poor, contemptible, stammering words: gladly do I pick up what falleth from the table at your repasts.

Yet still can I say therewith the truth—to dissemblers! Yea, my fish-bones, shells, and prickly leaves shall—tickle the noses of dissemblers!

Bad air is always about you and your repasts: your lascivious thoughts, your lies, and secrets are indeed in the air!

Dare only to believe in yourselves—in yourselves and in your inward parts! He who doth not believe in himself always lieth.

A God's mask have ye hung in front of you, ye "pure ones". into a God's mask hath your execrable coiling snake crawled.

Verily ye deceive, ye "contemplative ones!" Even Zarathustra was once the dupe of your godlike exterior; he did not divine the serpent's coil with which it was stuffed.

A God's soul, I once thought I saw playing in your games,

ye pure discerners! No better arts did I once dream of than your arts!

Serpents' filth and evil odour, the distance concealed from me: and that a lizard's craft prowled thereabouts lasciviously.

But I came *nigh* unto you: then came to me the day,—and now cometh it to you,—at an end is the moon's love affair!

See there! Surprised and pale doth it stand—before the rosy dawn!

For already she cometh, the glowing one,—*her* love to the earth cometh! Innocence, and creative desire, is all solar love!

See there, how she cometh impatiently over the sea! Do ye not feel the thirst and the hot breath of her love?

At the sea would she suck, and drink its depths to her height: now riseth the desire of the sea with its thousand breasts.

Kissed and sucked *would* it be by the thirst of the sun; vapour *would* it become, and height, and path of light, and light itself!

Verily, like the sun do I love life, and all deep seas.

And this meaneth *to me* knowledge: all that is deep shall ascend—to my height!—

Thus spake Zarathustra.

38. Scholars

WHEN I lay asleep, then did a sheep eat at the ivy-wreath on my head,—it ate, and said thereby: "Zarathustra is no longer a scholar."

It said this, and went away clumsily and proudly. A child told it to me.

I like to lie here where the children play, beside the ruined wall, among thistles and red poppies.

A scholar am I still to the children, and also to the thistles and red poppies. Innocent are they, even in their wickedness.

But to the sheep I am no longer a scholar: so willeth my lot —blessings upon it!

For this is the truth: I have departed from the house of the scholars, and the door have I also slammed behind me.

Too long did my soul sit hungry at their table: not like them have I got the knack of investigating, as the knack of nut-cracking.

Freedom do I love, and the air over fresh soil; rather would I sleep on ox-skins than on their honours and dignities.

I am too hot and scorched with mine own thought: often is it ready to take away my breath. Then have I to go into the open air, and away from all dusty rooms.

But they sit cool in the cool shade: they want in everything to be merely spectators, and they avoid sitting where the sun burneth on the steps.

Like those who stand in the street and gape at the passers-by: thus do they also wait, and gape at the thoughts which others have thought.

Should one lay hold of them, then do they raise a dust like flour-sacks, and involuntarily: but who would divine that their dust came from corn, and from the yellow delight of the summer fields?

When they give themselves out as wise, then do their petty sayings and truths chill me: in their wisdom there is often an odour as if it came from the swamp; and verily, I have even heard the frog croak in it!

Clever are they—they have dexterous fingers: what doth *my*

simplicity pretend to beside their multiplicity! All threading and knitting and weaving do their fingers understand: thus do they make the hose of the spirit!

Good clockworks are they: only be careful to wind them up properly! Then do they indicate the hour without mistake, and make a modest noise thereby.

Like millstones do they work, and like pestles: throw only seed-corn unto them!—they know well how to grind corn small, and make white dust out of it.

They keep a sharp eye on one another, and do not trust each other the best. Ingenious in little artifices, they wait for those whose knowledge walketh on lame feet,—like spiders do they wait.

I saw them always prepare their poison with precaution; and always did they put glass gloves on their fingers in doing so.

They also know how to play with false dice; and so eagerly did I find them playing, that they perspired thereby.

We are alien to each other, and their virtues are even more repugnant to my taste than their falsehoods and false dice.

And when I lived with them, then did I live above them. Therefore did they take a dislike to me.

They want to hear nothing of any one walking above their heads; and so they put wood and earth and rubbish betwixt me and their heads.

Thus did they deafen the sound of my tread: and least have I hitherto been heard by the most learned.

All mankind's faults and weaknesses did they put betwixt themselves and me:—they call it "false ceiling" in their houses.

But nevertheless I walk with my thoughts *above* their heads;

and even should I walk on mine own errors, still would I be above them and their heads.

For men are *not* equal: so speaketh justice. And what I will, *they* may not will!—

Thus spake Zarathustra.

39. *Poets*

"SINCE I have known the body better"—said Zarathustra to one of his disciples—"the spirit hath only been to me symbolically spirit; and all the 'imperishable'—that is also but a simile."

"So have I heard thee say once before," answered the disciple, "and then thou addedst: 'But the poets lie too much.' Why didst thou say that the poets lie too much?"

"Why?" said Zarathustra. "Thou askest why? I do not belong to those who may be asked after their Why.

Is my experience but of yesterday? It is long ago that I experienced the reasons for mine opinions.

Should I not have to be a cask of memory, if I also wanted to have my reasons with me?

It is already too much for me even to retain mine opinions; and many a bird flieth away.

And sometimes, also, do I find a fugitive creature in my dovecote, which is alien to me, and trembleth when I lay my hand upon it.

But what did Zarathustra once say unto thee? That the poets lie too much?—But Zarathustra also is a poet.

Believest thou that he there spake the truth? Why dost thou believe it?"

The disciple answered: "I believe in Zarathustra." But Zarathustra shook his head and smiled.—

Belief doth not sanctify me, said he, least of all the belief in myself.

But granting that some one did say in all seriousness that the poets lie too much: he was right—*we* do lie too much.

We also know too little, and are bad learners: so we are obliged to lie.

And which of us poets hath not adulterated his wine? Many a poisonous hotchpotch hath evolved in our cellars: many an indescribable thing hath there been done.

And because we know little, therefore are we pleased from the heart with the poor in spirit, especially when they are young women!

And even of those things are we desirous, which old women tell one another in the evening. This do we call the eternally feminine in us.

And as if there were a special secret access to knowledge, which *choketh up* for those who learn anything, so do we believe in the people and in their "wisdom."

This, however, do all poets believe: that whoever pricketh up his ears when lying in the grass or on lonely slopes, learneth something of the things that are betwixt heaven and earth.

And if there come unto them tender emotions, then do the poets always think that nature herself is in love with them:

And that she stealeth to their ear to whisper secrets into it, and amorous flatteries: of this do they plume and pride themselves, before all mortals!

Ah, there are so many things betwixt heaven and earth of which only the poets have dreamed!

And especially *above* the heavens: for all gods are poet-symbolisations, poet-sophistications!

Verily, ever are we drawn aloft—that is, to the realm of the clouds: on these do we set our gaudy puppets, and then call them gods and Supermen:—

Are not they light enough for those chairs!—all these gods and Supermen?—

Ah, how I am weary of all the inadequate that is insisted on as actual! Ah, how I am weary of the poets!

When Zarathustra so spake, his disciple resented it, but was silent. And Zarathustra also was silent; and his eye directed itself inwardly, as if it gazed into the far distance. At last he sighed and drew breath.—

I am of today and heretofore, said he thereupon; but something is in me that is of the morrow, and the day following, and the hereafter.

I became weary of the poets, of the old and of the new: superficial are they all unto me, and shallow seas.

They did not think sufficiently into the depth; therefore their feeling did not reach to the bottom.

Some sensation of voluptuousness and some sensation of tedium: these have as yet been their best contemplation.

Ghost-breathing and ghost-whisking, seemeth to me all the jingle-jangling of their harps; what have they known hitherto of the fervour of tones!—

They are also not pure enough for me: they all muddle their water that it may seem deep.

And fain would they thereby prove themselves reconcilers: but mediaries and mixers are they unto me, and half-and-half, and impure!—

Ah, I cast indeed my net into their sea, and meant to catch

good fish; but always did I draw up the head of some ancient God.

Thus did the sea give a stone to the hungry one. And they themselves may well originate from the sea.

Certainly, one findeth pearls in them: thereby they are the more like hard molluscs. And instead of a soul, I have often found in them salt slime.

They have learned from the sea also its vanity: is not the sea the peacock of peacocks?

Even before the ugliest of all buffaloes doth it spread out its tail; never doth it tire of its lace-fan of silver and silk.

Disdainfully doth the buffalo glance thereat, nigh to the sand with its soul, nigher still to the thicket, nighest, however, to the swamp.

What is beauty and sea and peacock-splendour to it! This parable I speak unto the poets.

Verily, their spirit itself is the peacock of peacocks, and a sea of vanity!

Spectators seeketh the spirit of the poet—should they even be buffaloes!—

But of this spirit became I weary; and I see the time coming when it will become weary of itself.

Yea, changed have I seen the poets, and their glance turned towards themselves.

Penitents of the spirit have I seen appearing; they grew out of the poets.—

Thus spake Zarathustra.

40. Great Events

THERE is an isle in the sea—not far from the Happy Isles of Zarathustra—on which a volcano ever smoketh; of which isle the people, and especially the old women amongst them, say that it is placed as a rock before the gate of the nether-world; but that through the volcano itself the narrow way leadeth downwards which conducteth to this gate.

Now about the time that Zarathustra sojourned on the Happy Isles, it happened that a ship anchored at the isle on which standeth the smoking mountain, and the crew went ashore to shoot rabbits. About the noontide hour, however, when the captain and his men were together again, they saw suddenly a man coming towards them through the air, and a voice said distinctly: "It is time! It is the highest time!" But when the figure was nearest to them (it flew past quickly, however, like a shadow, in the direction of the volcano), then did they recognise with the greatest surprise that it was Zarathustra; for they had all seen him before except the captain himself, and they loved him as the people love: in such wise that love and awe were combined in equal degree.

"Behold!" said the old helmsman, "there goeth Zarathustra to hell!"

About the same time that these sailors landed on the fire-isle, there was a rumour that Zarathustra had disappeared; and when his friends were asked about it, they said that he had gone on board a ship by night, without saying whither he was going.

Thus there arose some uneasiness. After three days, how-ever, there came the story of the ship's crew in addition to this uneasiness—and then did all the people say that the devil had taken Zarathustra. His disciples laughed, sure enough, at this talk; and one of them said even: "Sooner would I believe that Zarathustra hath taken the devil." But at the bottom of their hearts they were all full of anxiety and longing: so their joy was great when on the fifth day Zarathustra appeared amongst them.

And this is the account of Zarathustra's interview with the fire-dog:

The earth, said he, hath a skin; and this skin hath diseases. One of these diseases, for example, is called "man."

And another of these diseases is called "the fire-dog": concerning *him* men have greatly deceived themselves, and let themselves be deceived.

To fathom this mystery did I go o'er the sea; and I have seen the truth naked, verily! barefooted up to the neck.

Now do I know how it is concerning the fire-dog; and likewise concerning all the spouting and subversive devils, of which not only old women are afraid.

"Up with thee, fire-dog, out of thy depth!" cried I, "and confess how deep that depth is! Whence cometh that which thou snortest up?

Thou drinkest copiously at the sea: that doth thine embittered eloquence betray! In sooth, for a dog of the depth, thou takest thy nourishment too much from the surface!

At the most, I regard thee as the ventriloquist of the earth: and ever, when I have heard subversive and spouting devils speak, I have found them like thee: embittered, mendacious, and shallow.

Ye understand how to roar and obscure with ashes! Ye are the best braggarts, and have sufficiently learned the art of making dregs boil.

Where ye are, there must always be dregs at hand, and much that is spongy, hollow, and compressed: it wanteth to have freedom.

'Freedom' ye all roar most eagerly: but I have unlearned the belief in 'great events,' when there is much roaring and smoke about them.

And believe me, friend Hullabaloo! The greatest events— are not our noisiest, but our stillest hours.

Not around the inventors of new noise, but around the inventors of new values, doth the world revolve; *inaudibly* it revolveth.

And just own to it! Little had ever taken place when thy noise and smoke passed away. What, if a city did become a mummy, and a statue lay in the mud!

And this do I say also to the o'erthrowers of statues: It is certainly the greatest folly to throw salt into the sea, and statues into the mud.

In the mud of your contempt lay the statue: but it is just its law, that out of contempt, its life and living beauty grow again!

With diviner features doth it now arise, seducing by its suffering; and verily! it will yet thank you for o'erthrowing it, ye subverters!

This counsel, however, do I counsel to kings and churches, and to all that is weak with age or virtue—let yourselves be o'erthrown! That ye may again come to life, and that virtue— may come to you!—"

Thus spake I before the fire-dog: then did he interrupt me sullenly, and asked: "Church? What is that?"

"Church?" answered I, "that is a kind of state, and indeed the most mendacious. But remain quiet, thou dissembling dog! Thou surely knowest thine own species best!

Like thyself the state is a dissembling dog; like thee doth

it like to speak with smoke and roaring—to make believe, like thee, that it speaketh out of the heart of things.

For it seeketh by all means to be the most important creature on earth, the state; and people think it so."

When I had said this, the fire-dog acted as if mad with envy. "What!" cried he, "the most important creature on earth? And people think it so?" And so much vapour and terrible voices came out of his throat, that I thought he would choke with vexation and envy.

At last he became calmer and his panting subsided; as soon, however, as he was quiet, I said laughingly:

"Thou art angry, fire-dog: so I am in the right about thee!

And that I may also maintain the right, hear the story of another fire-dog; he speaketh actually out of the heart of the earth.

Gold doth his breath exhale, and golden rain: so doth his heart desire. What are ashes and smoke and hot dregs to him!

Laughter flitteth from him like a variegated cloud; adverse is he to thy gargling and spewing and grips in the bowels!

The gold, however, and the laughter—these doth he take out of the heart of the earth: for, that thou mayst know it,— *the heart of the earth is of gold.*"

When the fire-dog heard this, he could no longer endure to listen to me. Abashed did he draw in his tail, said "bow-wow!" in a cowed voice, and crept down into his cave.—

Thus told Zarathustra. His disciples, however, hardly listened to him: so great was their eagerness to tell him about the sailors, the rabbits, and the flying man.

"What am I to think of it!" said Zarathustra. "Am I indeed a ghost?

But it may have been my shadow. Ye have surely heard something of the Wanderer and his Shadow?

One thing, however, is certain: I must keep a tighter hold of it; otherwise it will spoil my reputation."

And once more Zarathustra shook his head and wondered. "What am I to think of it!" said he once more.

"Why did the ghost cry: 'It is time! It is the highest time!' *For what* is it then—the highest time?"—

Thus spake Zarathustra.

41. *The Soothsayer*

"—AND I saw a great sadness come over mankind. The best turned weary of their works.

A doctrine appeared, a faith ran beside it: 'All is empty, all is alike, all hath been!'

And from all hills there re-echoed: 'All is empty, all is alike, all hath been!'

To be sure we have harvested: but why have all our fruits become rotten and brown? What was it fell last night from the evil moon?

In vain was all our labour, poison hath our wine become, the evil eye hath singed yellow our fields and hearts.

Arid have we all become; and fire falling upon us, then do we turn dust like ashes:—yea, the fire itself have we made aweary.

All our fountains have dried up, even the sea hath receded. All the ground trieth to gape, but the depth will not swallow!

'Alas! where is there still a sea in which one could be drowned?' so soundeth our plaint—across shallow swamps.

Verily, even for dying have we become too weary; now do we keep awake and live on—in sepulchres."

Thus did Zarathustra hear a soothsayer speak; and the foreboding touched his heart and transformed him. Sorrowfully did he go about and wearily; and he became like unto those of whom the soothsayer had spoken.—

Verily, said he unto his disciples, a little while, and there cometh the long twilight. Alas, how shall I preserve my light through it!

That it may not smother in this sorrowfulness! To remoter worlds shall it be a light, and also to remotest nights!

Thus did Zarathustra go about grieved in his heart, and for three days he did not take any meat or drink: he had no rest, and lost his speech. At last it came to pass that he fell into a deep sleep. His disciples, however, sat around him in long night-watches, and waited anxiously to see if he would awake, and speak again, and recover from his affliction.

And this is the discourse that Zarathustra spake when he awoke; his voice, however, came unto his disciples as from afar:

Hear, I pray you, the dream that I dreamed, my friends, and help me to divine its meaning!

A riddle is it still unto me, this dream; the meaning is hidden in it and encaged, and doth not yet fly above it on free pinions.

All life had I renounced, so I dreamed. Night-watchman and grave-guardian had I become, aloft, in the lone mountain-fortress of Death.

There did I guard his coffins: full stood the musty vaults of those trophies of victory. Out of glass coffins did vanquished life gaze upon me.

The odour of dust-covered eternities did I breathe: sultry

and dust-covered lay my soul. And who could have aired his soul there!

Brightness of midnight was ever around me; lonesomeness cowered beside her; and as a third, death-rattle stillness, the worst of my female friends.

Keys did I carry, the rustiest of all keys; and I knew how to open with them the most creaking of all gates.

Like a bitterly angry croaking ran the sound through the long corridors when the leaves of the gate opened: ungraciously did this bird cry, unwillingly was it awakened.

But more frightful even, and more heart-strangling was it, when it again became silent and still all around, and I alone sat in that malignant silence.

Thus did time pass with me, and slip by, if time there still was: what do I know thereof! But at last there happened that which awoke me.

Thrice did there peal peals at the gate like thunders, thrice did the vaults resound and howl again: then did I go to the gate.

Alpa! cried I, who carrieth his ashes unto the mountain? Alpa! Alpa! who carrieth his ashes unto the mountain?

And I pressed the key, and pulled at the gate, and exerted myself. But not a finger's-breadth was it yet open:

Then did a roaring wind tear the folds apart: whistling, whizzing, and piercing, it threw unto me a black coffin.

And in the roaring and whistling and whizzing, the coffin burst open, and spouted out a thousand peals of laughter.

And a thousand caricatures of children, angels, owls, fools, and child-sized butterflies laughed and mocked, and roared at me.

Fearfully was I terrified thereby: it prostrated me. And I cried with horror as I ne'er cried before.

But mine own crying awoke me:—and I came to myself.—

Thus did Zarathustra relate his dream, and then was silent: for as yet he knew not the interpretation thereof. But the disciple whom he loved most arose quickly, seized Zarathustra's hand, and said:

"Thy life itself interpreteth unto us this dream, O Zarathustra!

Art thou not thyself the wind with shrill whistling, which bursteth open the gates of the fortress of Death?

Art thou not thyself the coffin full of many-hued malices and angel-caricatures of life?

Verily, like a thousand peals of children's laughter cometh Zarathustra into all sepulchres, laughing at those night-watchmen and grave-guardians, and whoever else rattleth with sinister keys.

With thy laughter wilt thou frighten and prostrate them: fainting and recovering wilt thou demonstrate thy power over them.

And when the long twilight cometh and the mortal weariness, even then wilt thou not disappear from our firmament, thou advocate of life!

New stars hast thou made us see, and new nocturnal glories: verily, laughter itself hast thou spread out over us like a many-hued canopy.

Now will children's laughter ever from coffins flow; now will a strong wind ever come victoriously unto all mortal weariness: of this thou art thyself the pledge and the prophet!

Verily, *they themselves didst thou dream,* thine enemies: that was thy sorest dream.

But as thou awokest from them and camest to thyself, so shall they awaken from themselves—and come unto thee!"

Thus spake the disciple; and all the others then thronged

[*149*]

around Zarathustra, grasped him by the hands, and tried to persuade him to leave his bed and his sadness, and return unto them. Zarathustra, however, sat upright on his couch, with an absent look. Like one returning from long foreign sojourn did he look on his disciples, and examined their features; but still he knew them not. When, however, they raised him, and set him upon his feet, behold, all on a sudden his eye changed; he understood everything that had happened, stroked his beard, and said with a strong voice:

"Well! this hath just its time; but see to it, my disciples, that we have a good repast, and without delay! Thus do I mean to make amends for bad dreams!

The soothsayer, however, shall eat and drink at my side: and verily, I will yet show him a sea in which he can drown himself!"—

Thus spake Zarathustra. Then did he gaze long into the face of the disciple who had been the dream-interpreter, and shook his head.—

42. Redemption

WHEN Zarathustra went one day over the great bridge, then did the cripples and beggars surround him, and a hunchback spake thus unto him:

"Behold, Zarathustra! Even the people learn from thee, and acquire faith in thy teaching: but for them to believe fully in thee, one thing is still needful—thou must first of all convince us cripples! Here hast thou now a fine selection, and verily, an opportunity with more than one forelock! The blind canst thou heal, and make the lame run; and from him who hath too much behind, couldst thou well, also, take away a little;—that, I think, would be the right method to make the cripples believe in Zarathustra!"

Zarathustra, however, answered thus unto him who so spake: When one taketh his hump from the hunchback, then doth one take from him his spirit—so do the people teach. And when one giveth the blind man eyes, then doth he see too many bad things on the earth: so that he curseth him who healed him. He, however, who maketh the lame man run, inflicteth upon him the greatest injury; for hardly can he run, when his vices run away with him—so do the people teach concerning cripples. And why should not Zarathustra also learn from the people, when the people learn from Zarathustra?

It is, however, the smallest thing unto me since I have been amongst men, to see one person lacking an eye, another an ear, and a third a leg, and that others have lost the tongue, or the nose, or the head.

I see and have seen worse things, and divers things so hideous, that I should neither like to speak of all matters, nor even keep silent about some of them: namely, men who lack everything, except that they have too much of one thing—men who are nothing more than a big eye, or a big mouth, or a big belly, or something else big,—reversed cripples, I call such men.

And when I came out of my solitude, and for the first time passed over this bridge, then I could not trust mine eyes, but looked again and again, and said at last: "That is an ear! An ear as big as a man!" I looked still more attentively—and actually there did move under the ear something that was pitiably small and poor and slim. And in truth this immense ear was perched on a small thin stalk—the stalk, however, was a man! A person putting a glass to his eyes, could even recognise further a small envious countenance, and also that a bloated soullet dangled at the stalk. The people told me, however, that the big ear was not only a man, but a great man, a genius. But I never believed in the people when they spake of great men —and I hold to my belief that it was a reversed cripple, who had too little of everything, and too much of one thing.

When Zarathustra had spoken thus unto the hunchback, and unto those of whom the hunchback was the mouthpiece and advocate, then did he turn to his disciples in profound dejection, and said:

Verily, my friends, I walk amongst men as amongst the fragments and limbs of human beings!

This is the terrible thing to mine eye, that I find man broken up, and scattered about, as on a battle- and butcher-ground.

And when mine eye fleeth from the present to the bygone, it findeth ever the same: fragments and limbs and fearful chances—but no men!

The present and the bygone upon earth—ah! my friends—that is *my* most unbearable trouble; and I should not know how to live, if I were not a seer of what is to come.

A seer, a purposer, a creator, a future itself, and a bridge to the future—and alas! also as it were a cripple on this bridge: all that is Zarathustra.

And ye also asked yourselves often: "Who is Zarathustra to us? What shall he be called by us?" And like me, did ye give yourselves questions for answers.

Is he a promiser? Or a fulfiller? A conqueror? Or an inheritor? A harvest? Or a ploughshare? A physician? Or a healed one?

Is he a poet? Or a genuine one? An emancipator? Or a subjugator? A good one? Or an evil one?

I walk amongst men as the fragments of the future: that future which I contemplate.

And it is all my poetisation and aspiration to compose and collect into unity what is fragment and riddle and fearful chance.

And how could I endure to be a man, if man were not also the composer, and riddle-reader, and redeemer of chance!

To redeem what is past, and to transform every "It was" into "Thus would I have it!"—that only do I call redemption!

Will—so is the emancipator and joy-bringer called: thus have I taught you, my friends! But now learn this likewise: the Will itself is still a prisoner.

Willing emancipateth: but what is that called which still putteth the emancipator in chains?

"It was": thus is the Will's teeth-gnashing and lonesomest tribulation called. Impotent towards what hath been done—it is a malicious spectator of all that is past.

Not backward can the Will will; that it cannot break time and time's desire—that is the Will's lonesomest tribulation.

Willing emancipateth: what doth Willing itself devise in order to get free from its tribulation and mock at its prison?

Ah, a fool becometh every prisoner! Foolishly delivereth itself also the imprisoned Will.

That time doth not run backward—that is its animosity: "That which was": so is the stone which it cannot roll called.

And thus doth it roll stones out of animosity and ill-humour, and taketh revenge on whatever doth not, like it, feel rage and ill-humour.

Thus did the Will, the emancipator, become a torturer; and on all that is capable of suffering it taketh revenge, because it cannot go backward.

This, yea, this alone is *revenge* itself: the Will's antipathy to time, and its "It was."

Verily, a great folly dwelleth in our Will; and it became a curse unto all humanity, that this folly acquired spirit!

The spirit of revenge: my friends, that hath hitherto been man's best contemplation; and where there was suffering, it was claimed there was always penalty.

"Penalty," so calleth itself revenge. With a lying word it feigneth a good conscience.

And because in the willer himself there is suffering, because he cannot will backwards—thus was Willing itself, and all life, claimed—to be penalty!

And then did cloud after cloud roll over the spirit, until at last madness preached: "Everything perisheth, therefore everything deserveth to perish!"

"And this itself is justice, the law of time—that he must devour his children:" thus did madness preach.

"Morally are things ordered according to justice and penalty. Oh, where is there deliverance from the flux of things and from the 'existence' of penalty?" Thus did madness preach.

"Can there ·be deliverance when there is eternal justice? Alas, unrollable is the stone, 'It was': eternal must also be all penalties!" Thus did madness preach.

"No deed can be annihilated: how could it be undone by the penalty! This, this is what is eternal in the 'existence' of penalty, that existence also must be eternally recurring deed and guilt!

Unless the Will should at last deliver itself, and Willing

become non-Willing——:" but ye know, my brethren, this fabulous song of madness!

Away from those fabulous songs did I lead you when I taught you: "The Will is a creator."

All "It was" is a fragment, a riddle, a fearful chance—until the creating Will saith thereto: "But thus would I have it."——

Until the creating Will saith thereto: "But thus do I will it! Thus shall I will it!"

But did it ever speak thus? And when doth this take place? Hath the Will been unharnessed from its own folly?

Hath the Will become its own deliverer and joy-bringer? Hath it unlearned the spirit of revenge and all teeth-gnashing?

And who hath taught it reconciliation with time, and something higher than all reconciliation?

Something higher than all reconciliation must the Will will which is the Will to Power——: but how doth that take place? Who hath taught it also to will backwards?

——But at this point in his discourse it chanced that Zarathustra suddenly paused, and looked like a person in the greatest alarm. With terror in his eyes did he gaze on his disciples; his glances pierced as with arrows their thoughts and arrearthoughts. But after a brief space he again laughed, and said soothedly:

"It is difficult to live amongst men, because silence is so difficult—especially for a babbler."——

Thus spake Zarathustra. The hunchback, however, had listened to the conversation and had covered his face during the time; but when he heard Zarathustra laugh, he looked up with curiosity, and said slowly:

"But why doth Zarathustra speak otherwise unto us than unto his disciples?"

Zarathustra answered: "What is there to be wondered at! With hunchbacks one may well speak in a hunchbacked way!"

"Very good," said the hunchback; "and with pupils one may well tell tales out of school.

But why doth Zarathustra speak otherwise unto his pupils— than unto himself?"—

43. Manly Prudence

NOT the height, it is the declivity that is terrible!

The declivity, where the gaze shooteth *downwards,* and the hand graspeth *upwards.* There doth the heart become giddy through its double will.

Ah, friends, do ye divine also my heart's double will?

This, this is *my* declivity and my danger, that my gaze shooteth towards the summit, and my hand would fain clutch and lean—on the depth!

To man clingeth my will; with chains do I bind myself to man, because I am pulled upwards to the Superman: for thither doth mine other will tend.

And *therefore* do I live blindly among men, as if I knew them not: that my hand may not entirely lose belief in firmness.

I know not you men: this gloom and consolation is often spread around me.

I sit at the gateway for every rogue, and ask: Who wisheth to deceive me?

This is my first manly prudence, that I allow myself to be deceived, so as not to be on my guard against deceivers.

Ah, if I were on my guard against man, how could man be an anchor to my ball! Too easily would I be pulled upwards and away!

This providence is over my fate, that I have to be without foresight.

And he who would not languish amongst men, must learn to drink out of all glasses; and he who would keep clean amongst men, must know how to wash himself even with dirty water.

And thus spake I often to myself for consolation: "Courage! Cheer up! old heart! An unhappiness hath failed to befall thee: enjoy that as thy—happiness!"

This, however, is mine other manly prudence: I am more forbearing to the *vain* than to the proud.

Is not wounded vanity the mother of all tragedies? Where, however, pride is wounded, there there groweth up something better than pride.

That life may be fair to behold, its game must be well played; for that purpose, however, it needeth good actors.

Good actors have I found all the vain ones: they play, and wish people to be fond of beholding them—all their spirit is in this wish.

They represent themselves, they invent themselves; in their neighbourhood I like to look upon life—it cureth of melancholy.

Therefore am I forbearing to the vain, because they are the physicians of my melancholy, and keep me attached to man as to a drama.

And further, who conceiveth the full depth of the modesty of the vain man! I am favourable to him, and sympathetic on account of his modesty.

From you would he learn his belief in himself; he feedeth upon your glances, he eateth praise out of your hands.

Your lies doth he even believe when you lie favourably about him: for in its depths sigheth his heart: "What am *I*?"

And if that be the true virtue which is unconscious of itself —well, the vain man is unconscious of his modesty!—

This is, however, my third manly prudence: I am not put out of conceit with the *wicked* by your timorousness.

I am happy to see the marvels the warm sun hatcheth: tigers and palms and rattlesnakes.

Also amongst men there is a beautiful brood of the warm sun, and much that is marvellous in the wicked.

In truth, as your wisest did not seem to me so very wise, so found I also human wickedness below the fame of it.

And oft did I ask with a shake of the head: Why still rattle, ye rattlesnakes?

Verily, there is still a future even for evil! And the warmest south is still undiscovered by man.

How many things are now called the worst wickedness, which are only twelve feet broad and three months long! Some day, however, will greater dragons come into the world.

For that the Superman may not lack his dragon, the super-dragon that is worthy of him, there must still much warm sun glow on moist virgin forests!

Out of your wild cats must tigers have evolved, and out of your poison-toads, crocodiles: for the good hunter shall have a good hunt!

And verily, ye good and just! In you there is much to be laughed at, and especially your fear of what hath hitherto been called "the devil!"

So alien are ye in your souls to what is great, that to you the Superman would be *frightful* in his goodness!

And ye wise and knowing ones, ye would flee from the solar-glow of the wisdom in which the Superman joyfully batheth his nakedness!

Ye highest men who have come within my ken! this is my doubt of you, and my secret laughter: I suspect ye would call my Superman—a devil!

Ah, I became tired of those highest and best ones: from their "height" did I long to be up, out, and away to the Super-man!

A horror came over me when I saw those best ones naked: then there grew for me the pinions to soar away into distant futures.

Into more distant futures, into more southern souths than ever artist dreamed of: thither, where gods are ashamed of all clothes!

But disguised do I want to see *you,* ye neighbours and fellowmen, and well-attired and vain and estimable, as "the good and just;"—

And disguised will I myself sit amongst you—that I may *mistake* you and myself: for that is my last manly prudence.—

Thus spake Zarathustra.

44. *The Stillest Hour*

WHAT hath happened unto me, my friends? Ye see me troubled, driven forth, unwillingly obedient, ready to go— alas, to go away from *you!*

Yea, once more must Zarathustra retire to his solitude: but unjoyously this time doth the bear go back to his cave!

What hath happened unto me? Who ordereth this?—**Ah, mine** angry mistress wisheth it so; she spake unto me. Have I ever named her name to you?

Yesterday towards evening there spake unto me *my stillest hour:* that is the name of my terrible mistress.

And thus did it happen—for everything must I tell you, that your heart may not harden against the suddenly departing one!

Do ye know the terror of him who falleth asleep?—

To the very toes he is terrified, because the ground giveth way under him, and the dream beginneth.

This do I speak unto you in parable. Yesterday at the stillest hour did the ground give way under me: the dream began.

The hour-hand moved on, the timepiece of my life drew breath—never did I hear such stillness around me, so that my heart was terrified.

Then was there spoken unto me without voice: *"Thou knowest it, Zarathustra?"*—

And I cried in terror at this whispering, and the blood left my face: but I was silent.

Then was there once more spoken unto me without voice: "Thou knowest it, Zarathustra, but thou dost not speak it!"—

And at last I answered, like one defiant: "Yea, I know it, but I will not speak it!"

Then was there again spoken unto me without voice: "Thou *wilt* not, Zarathustra? Is this true? Conceal thyself not behind thy defiance!"—

And I wept and trembled like a child, and said: "Ah, I would indeed, but how can I do it! Exempt me only from this! It is beyond my power!"

Then was there again spoken unto me without voice: "What

matter about thyself, Zarathustra! Speak thy word, and succumb!"

And I answered: "Ah, is it *my* word? Who am *I?* I await the worthier one; I am not worthy even to succumb by it."

Then was there again spoken unto me without voice: "What matter about thyself? Thou art not yet humble enough for me. Humility hath the hardest skin."—

And I answered: "What hath not the skin of my humility endured! At the foot of my height do I dwell: how high are my summits, no one hath yet told me. But well do I know my valleys."

Then was there again spoken unto me without voice: "O Zarathustra, he who hath to remove mountains removeth also valleys and plains."—

And I answered: "As yet hath my word not removed mountains, and what I have spoken hath not reached man. I went, indeed, unto men, but not yet have I attained unto them."

Then was there again spoken unto me without voice: "What knowest thou *thereof!* The dew falleth on the grass when the night is most silent."—

And I answered: "They mocked me when I found and walked in mine own path; and certainly did my feet then tremble.

And thus did they speak unto me: Thou forgottest the path before, now dost thou also forget how to walk!"

Then was there again spoken unto me without voice: "What matter about their mockery! Thou art one who hast unlearned to obey: now shalt thou command!

Knowest thou not who is most needed by all? He who commandeth great things.

To execute great things is difficult: but the more difficult task is to command great things.

This is thy most unpardonable obstinacy: thou hast the power, and thou wilt not rule."—

And I answered: "I lack the lion's voice for all commanding."

Then was there again spoken unto me as a whispering: "It is the stillest words which bring the storm. Thoughts that come with doves' footsteps guide the world.

O Zarathustra, thou shalt go as a shadow of that which is to come: thus wilt thou command, and in commanding go foremost."—

And I answered: "I am ashamed."

Then was there again spoken unto me without voice: "Thou must yet become a child, and be without shame.

The pride of youth is still upon thee; late hast thou become young: but he who would become a child must surmount even his youth."—

And I considered a long while, and trembled. At last, however, did I say what I had said at first. "I will not."

Then did a laughing take place all around me. Alas, how that laughing lacerated my bowels and cut into my heart!

And there was spoken unto me for the last time: "O Zarathustra, thy fruits are ripe, but thou art not ripe for thy fruits!

So must thou go again into solitude: for thou shalt yet become mellow."—

And again was there a laughing, and it fled: then did it become still around me, as with a double stillness. I lay, however, on the ground, and the sweat flowed from my limbs.

—Now have ye heard all, and why I have to return into my solitude. Nothing have I kept hidden from you, my friends.

But even this have ye heard from me, *who* is still the most reserved of men—and will be so!

Ah, my friends! I should have something more to say unto

you! I should have something more to give unto you! Why do
I not give it? Am I then a niggard?—

When, however, Zarathustra had spoken these words, the
violence of his pain, and a sense of the nearness of his departure from his friends came over him, so that he wept aloud;
and no one knew how to console him. In the night, however,
he went away alone and left his friends.

THUS SPAKE ZARATHUSTRA

THIRD PART

"Ye look aloft when ye long for exaltation, and I look downward because I am exalted.

"Who among you can at the same time laugh and be exalted?

"He who climbeth on the highest mountains, laugheth at all tragic plays and tragic realities."—ZARATHUSTRA, I., "Reading and Writing" (p. 56).

45. *The Wanderer*

THEN, when it was about midnight, Zarathustra went his way over the ridge of the isle, that he might arrive early in the morning at the other coast; because there he meant to embark. For there was a good roadstead there, in which foreign ships also liked to anchor: those ships took many people with them, who wished to cross over from the Happy Isles. So when Zarathustra thus ascended the mountain, he thought on the way of his many solitary wanderings from youth onwards, and how many mountains and ridges and summits he had already climbed.

I am a wanderer and mountain-climber, said he to his heart. I love not the plains, and it seemeth I cannot long sit still.

And whatever may still overtake me as fate and experience —a wandering will be therein, and a mountain-climbing: in the end one experienceth only oneself.

The time is now past when accidents could befall me; and what *could* now fall to my lot which would not already be mine own!

It returneth only, it cometh home to me at last—mine own Self, and such of it as hath been long abroad, and scattered among things and accidents.

And one thing more do I know: I stand now before my last summit, and before that which hath been longest reserved for me. Ah, my hardest path must I ascend! Ah, I have begun my lonesomest wandering!

He, however, who is of my nature doth not avoid such an hour: the hour that saith unto him: Now only dost thou go the way to thy greatness! Summit and abyss—these are now comprised together!

Thou goest the way to thy greatness: now hath it become thy last refuge, what was hitherto thy last danger!

Thou goest the way to thy greatness: it must now be thy best courage that there is no longer any path behind thee!

Thou goest the way to thy greatness: here shall no one steal after thee! Thy foot itself hath effaced the path behind thee, and over it standeth written: Impossibility.

And if all ladders henceforth fail thee, then must thou learn to mount upon thine own head: how couldst thou mount upward otherwise?

Upon thine own head, and beyond thine own heart! Now must the gentlest in thee become the hardest.

He who hath always much-indulged himself, sickeneth at last by his much-indulgence. Praises on what maketh hardy! I do not praise the land where butter and honey—flow!

To learn *to look away from* oneself, is necessary in order to see *many things*:—this hardiness is needed by every mountain-climber.

He, however, who is obtrusive with his eyes as a discerner, how can he ever see more of anything than its foreground!

But thou, O Zarathustra, wouldst view the ground of everything, and its background: thus must thou mount even above thyself—up, upwards, until thou hast even thy stars *under* thee!

Yea! To look down upon myself, and even upon my stars: that only would I call my *summit*, that hath remained for me as my *last* summit!—

Thus spake Zarathustra to himself while ascending, comforting his heart with harsh maxims: for he was sore at heart as he had never been before. And when he had reached the top of the mountain-ridge, behold, there lay the other sea spread out before him; and he stood still and was long silent. The night, however, was cold at this height, and clear and starry.

I recognise my destiny, said he at last, sadly. Well! I am ready. Now hath my last lonesomeness begun.

Ah, this sombre, sad sea, below me! Ah, this sombre nocturnal vexation! Ah, fate and sea! To you must I now *go down!*

Before my highest mountain do I stand, and before my longest wandering: therefore must I first go deeper down than I ever ascended:

—Deeper down into pain than I ever ascended, even into its darkest flood! So willeth my fate. Well! I am ready.

Whence come the highest mountains? so did I once ask. Then did I learn that they come out of the sea.

That testimony is inscribed on their stones, and on the walls of their summits. Out of the deepest must the highest come to its height.—

Thus spake Zarathustra on the ridge of the mountain where it was cold: when, however, he came into the vicinity of the sea, and at last stood alone amongst the cliffs, then had he become weary on his way, and eagerer than ever before.

Everything as yet sleepeth, said he; even the sea sleepeth. Drowsily and strangely doth its eye gaze upon me.

But it breatheth warmly—I feel it. And I feel also that it dreameth. It tosseth about dreamily on hard pillows.

Hark! Hark! How it groaneth with evil recollections! Or evil expectations?

[*169*]

Ah, I am sad along with thee, thou dusky monster, and angry with myself even for thy sake.

Ah, that my hand hath not strength enough! Gladly, indeed, would I free thee from evil dreams!—

And while Zarathustra thus spake, he laughed at himself with melancholy and bitterness. What! Zarathustra, said he, wilt thou even sing consolation to the sea?

Ah, thou amiable fool, Zarathustra, thou too-blindly confiding one! But thus hast thou ever been: ever hast thou approached confidently all that is terrible.

Every monster wouldst thou caress. A whiff of warm breath, a little soft tuft on its paw:—and immediately wert thou ready to love and lure it.

Love is the danger of the lonesomest one, love to anything, *if it only live!* Laughable, verily, is my folly and my modesty in love!—

Thus spake Zarathustra, and laughed thereby a second time. Then, however, he thought of his abandoned friends—and as if he had done them a wrong with his thoughts, he upbraided himself because of his thoughts. And forthwith it came to pass that the laugher wept—with anger and longing wept Zarathustra bitterly.

46. The Vision and the Enigma

1

WHEN it got abroad among the sailors that Zarathustra was on board the ship—for a man who came from the Happy Isles had gone on board along with him,—there was great curiosity and expectation. But Zarathustra kept silent for two days, and was cold and deaf with sadness; so that he neither answered looks nor questions. On the evening of the second day, however, he again opened his ears, though he still kept silent: for there were many curious and dangerous things to be heard on board the ship, which came from afar, and was to go still further. Zarathustra, however, was fond of all those who make distant voyages, and dislike to live without danger. And behold! when listening, his own tongue was at last loosened, and the ice of his heart broke. Then did he begin to speak thus:

To you, the daring venturers and adventurers, and whoever hath embarked with cunning sails upon frightful seas,—

To you the enigma-intoxicated, the twilight-enjoyers, whose souls are allured by flutes to every treacherous gulf:

—For ye dislike to grope at a thread with cowardly hand; and where ye can *divine,* there do ye hate to *calculate*—

To you only do I tell the enigma that I *saw*—the vision of the lonesomest one.—

Gloomily walked I lately in corpse-coloured twilight—gloomily and sternly, with compressed lips. Not only one sun had set for me.

A path which ascended daringly among boulders, an evil, lonesome path, which neither herb nor shrub any longer

[*171*]

cheered, a mountain-path, crunched under the daring of my foot.

Mutely marching over the scornful clinking of pebbles, trampling the stone that let it slip: thus did my foot force its way upwards.

Upwards:——in spite of the spirit that drew it downwards, towards the abyss, the spirit of gravity, my devil and arch-enemy.

Upwards:——although it sat upon me, half-dwarf, half-mole; paralysed, paralysing; dripping lead in mine ear, and thoughts like drops of lead into my brain.

"O Zarathustra," it whispered scornfully, syllable by syllable, "thou stone of wisdom! Thou threwest thyself high, but every thrown stone must——fall!

O Zarathustra, thou stone of wisdom, thou sling-stone, thou star-destroyer! Thyself threwest thou so high,——but every thrown stone——must fall!

Condemned of thyself, and to thine own stoning: O Zarathustra, far indeed threwest thou thy stone——but upon *thyself* will it recoil!"

Then was the dwarf silent; and it lasted long. The silence, however, oppressed me; and to be thus in pairs, one is verily lonesomer than when alone!

I ascended, I ascended, I dreamt, I thought,——but everything oppressed me. A sick one did I resemble, whom bad torture wearieth, and a worse dream reawakeneth out of his first sleep.——

But there is something in me which I call courage: it hath hitherto slain for me every dejection. This courage at last bade me stand still and say: "Dwarf! Thou! Or I!"——

For courage is the best slayer,——courage which *attacketh:* for in every attack there is sound of triumph.

[*172*]

Man, however, is the most courageous animal: thereby hath he overcome every animal. With sound of triumph hath he overcome every pain; human pain, however, is the sorest pain.

Courage slayeth also giddiness at abysses: and where doth man not stand at abysses! Is not seeing itself—seeing abysses?

Courage is the best slayer: courage slayeth also fellow-suffering. Fellow-suffering, however, is the deepest abyss: as deeply as man looketh into life, so deeply also doth he look into suffering.

Courage, however, is the best slayer, courage which attacketh: it slayeth even death itself; for it saith: *"Was that life? Well! Once more!"*

In such speech, however, there is much sound of triumph. He who hath ears to hear, let him hear.—

2

"Halt, dwarf!" said I. "Either I—or thou! I, however, am the stronger of the two:—thou knowest not mine abysmal thought! *It*—couldst thou not endure!"

Then happened that which made me lighter: for the dwarf sprang from my shoulder, the prying sprite! And it squatted on a stone in front of me. There was however a gateway just where we halted.

"Look at this gateway! Dwarf!" I continued, "it hath two faces. Two roads come together here: these hath no one yet gone to the end of.

This long lane backwards: it continueth for an eternity. And that long lane forward—that is another eternity.

They are antithetical to one another, these roads; they directly abut on one another:—and it is here, at this gateway, that they come together. The name of the gateway is inscribed above: 'This Moment.'

But should one follow them further—and ever further and further on, thinkest thou, dwarf, that these roads would be eternally antithetical?"—

"Everything straight lieth," murmured the dwarf, contemptuously. "All truth is crooked; time itself is a circle."

"Thou spirit of gravity!" said I wrathfully, "do not take it too lightly! Or I shall let thee squat where thou squattest, Haltfoot,—and I carried thee *high*!"

"Observe," continued I, "This Moment! From the gateway, This Moment, there runneth a long eternal lane *backwards:* behind us lieth an eternity.

Must not whatever *can* run its course of all things, have already run along that lane? Must not whatever *can* happen of all things have already happened, resulted, and gone by?

And if everything has already existed, what thinkest thou, dwarf, of This Moment? Must not this gateway also—have already existed?

And are not all things closely bound together in such wise that This Moment draweth all coming things after it? *Consequently*—itself also?

For whatever *can* run its course of all things, also in this long lane *outward—must* it once more run!—

And this slow spider which creepeth in the moonlight, and this moonlight itself, and thou and I in this gateway whispering together, whispering of eternal things—must we not all have already existed?

—And must we not return and run in that other lane out before us, that long weird lane—must we not eternally return?"—

Thus did I speak, and always more softly: for I was afraid

[*174*]

of mine own thoughts, and arrear-thoughts. Then, suddenly did I hear a dog *howl* near me.

Had I ever heard a dog howl thus? My thoughts ran back. Yes! When I was a child, in my most distant childhood:

—Then did I hear a dog howl thus. And saw it also, with hair bristling, its head upwards, trembling in the stillest midnight, when even dogs believe in ghosts:

—So that it excited my commiseration. For just then went the full moon, silent as death, over the house; just then did it stand still, a glowing globe—at rest on the flat roof, as if on some one's property:—

Thereby had the dog been terrified: for dogs believe in thieves and ghosts. And when I again heard such howling, then did it excite my commiseration once more.

Where was now the dwarf? And the gateway? And the spider? And all the whispering? Had I dreamt? Had I awakened? 'Twixt rugged rocks did I suddenly stand alone, dreary in the dreariest moonlight.

But there lay a man! And there! The dog leaping, bristling, whining—now did it see me coming—then did it howl again, then did it *cry:*—had I ever heard a dog cry so for help?

And verily, what I saw, the like had I never seen. A young shepherd did I see, writhing, choking, quivering, with distorted countenance, and with a heavy black serpent hanging out of his mouth.

Had I ever seen so much loathing and pale horror on one countenance? He had perhaps gone to sleep? Then had the serpent crawled into his throat—there had it bitten itself fast.

My hand pulled at the serpent, and pulled:—in vain! I failed to pull the serpent out of his throat. Then there cried out of me: "Bite! Bite!

Its head off! Bite!"—so cried it out of me; my horror, my

hatred, my loathing, my pity, all my good and my bad cried with one voice out of me.——

Ye daring ones around me! Ye venturers and adventurers, and whoever of you have embarked with cunning sails on unexplored seas! Ye enigma-enjoyers!

Solve unto me the enigma that I then beheld, interpret unto me the vision of the lonesomest one!

For it was a vision and a foresight:——*what* did I then behold in parable? And *who* is it that must come some day?

Who is the shepherd into whose throat the serpent thus crawled? *Who* is the man into whose throat all the heaviest and blackest will thus crawl?

——The shepherd however bit as my cry had admonished him; he bit with a strong bite! Far away did he spit the head of the serpent:——and sprang up.——

No longer shepherd, no longer man—a transfigured being, a light-surrounded being, that *laughed!* Never on earth laughed a man as *he* laughed!

O my brethren, I heard a laughter which was no human laughter,——and now gnaweth a thirst at me, a longing that is never allayed.

My longing for that laughter gnaweth at me: oh, how can I still endure to live! And how could I endure to die at present!——

Thus spake Zarathustra.

47. *Involuntary Bliss*

WITH such enigmas and bitterness in his heart did Zarathustra sail o'er the sea. When, however, he was four day-journeys from the Happy Isles and from his friends, then had he surmounted all his pain:—triumphantly and with firm foot did he again accept his fate. And then talked Zarathustra in this wise to his exulting conscience:

Alone am I again, and like to be so, alone with the pure heaven, and the open sea; and again is the afternoon around me.

On an afternoon did I find my friends for the first time; on an afternoon, also, did I find them a second time:—at the hour when all light becometh stiller.

For whatever happiness is still on its way 'twixt heaven and earth, now seeketh for lodging a luminous soul: *with happiness* hath all light now become stiller.

O afternoon of my life! Once did my happiness also descend to the valley that it might seek a lodging: then did it find those open hospitable souls.

O afternoon of my life! What did I not surrender that I might have one thing: this living plantation of my thoughts, and this dawn of my highest hope!

Companions did the creating one once seek, and children of *his* hope: and lo, it turned out that he could not find them, except he himself should first create them.

Thus am I in the midst of my work, to my children going, and from them returning: for the sake of his children must Zarathustra perfect himself.

For in one's heart one loveth only one's child and one's work; and where there is great love to oneself, then is it the sign of pregnancy: so have I found it.

Still are my children verdant in their first spring, standing nigh one another, and shaken in common by the winds, the trees of my garden and of my best soil.

And verily, where such trees stand beside one another, there *are* Happy Isles!

But one day will I take them up, and put each by itself alone: that it may learn lonesomeness and defiance and prudence.

Gnarled and crooked and with flexible hardness shall it then stand by the sea, a living lighthouse of unconquerable life.

Yonder where the storms rush down into the sea, and the snout of the mountain drinketh water, shall each on a time have his day and night watches, for *his* testing and recognition.

Recognised and tested shall each be, to see if he be of my type and lineage:—if he be master of a long will, silent even when he speaketh, and giving in such wise that he *taketh* in giving:—

—So that he may one day become my companion, a fellow-creator and fellow-enjoyer with Zarathustra:—such a one as writeth my will on my tables, for the fuller perfection of all things.

And for his sake and for those like him, must I perfect *myself:* therefore do I now avoid my happiness, and present myself to every misfortune—for *my* final testing and recognition.

And verily, it were time that I went away; and the wanderer's shadow and the longest tedium and the stillest hour—have all said unto me: "It is the highest time!"

The word blew to me through the keyhole and said "Come!" The door sprang subtly open unto me, and said "Go!"

But I lay enchained to my love for my children: desire spread this snare for me—the desire for love—that I should become the prey of my children, and lose myself in them.

Desiring—that is now for me to have lost myself. *I possess you, my children!* In this possessing shall everything be assurance and nothing desire.

But brooding lay the sun of my love upon me, in his own juice stewed Zarathustra,—then did shadows and doubts fly past me.

For frost and winter I now longed: "Oh, that frost and winter would again make me crack and crunch!" sighed I: —then arose icy mist out of me.

My past burst its tomb, many pains buried alike woke up:— fully slept had they merely, concealed in corpse-clothes.

So called everything unto me in signs: "It is time!" But I— heard not, until at last mine abyss moved, and my thought bit me.

Ah, abysmal thought, which art *my* thought! When shall I find strength to hear thee burrowing, and no longer tremble?

To my very throat throbbeth my heart when I hear them burrowing! Thy muteness even is like to strangle me, thou abysmal mute one!

As yet have I never ventured to call thee *up;* it hath been enough that I—have carried thee about with me! As yet have I not been strong enough for my final lion-wantonness and playfulness.

Sufficiently formidable unto me hath thy weight ever been: but one day shall I yet find the strength and the lion's voice which will call thee up!

When I shall have surmounted myself therein, then will I surmount myself also in that which is greater; and a *victory* shall be the seal of my perfection!——

Meanwhile do I sail along on uncertain seas; chance flattereth me, smooth-tongued chance; forward and backward do I gaze—, still see I no end.

As yet hath the hour of my final struggle not come to me— or doth it come to me perhaps just now? Verily, with insidious beauty do sea and life gaze upon me round about:

O afternoon of my life! O happiness before eventide! O haven upon high seas! O peace in uncertainty! How I distrust all of you!

Verily, distrustful am I of your insidious beauty! Like the lover am I, who distrusteth too sleek smiling.

As he pusheth the best-beloved before him—tender even in severity, the jealous one—, so do I push this blissful hour before me.

Away with thee, thou blissful hour! With thee hath there come to me an involuntary bliss! Ready for my severest pain do I here stand:—at the wrong time hast thou come!

Away with thee, thou blissful hour! Rather harbour there— with my children! Hasten! and bless them before eventide with *my* happiness!

There, already approacheth eventide: the sun sinketh. Away—my happiness!—

Thus spake Zarathustra. And he waited for his misfortune the whole night; but he waited in vain. The night remained clear and calm, and happiness itself came nigher and nigher unto him. Towards morning, however, Zarathustra laughed to his heart, and said mockingly: "Happiness runneth after me. That is because I do not run after women. Happiness, however, is a woman."

48. Before Sunrise

O HEAVEN above me, thou pure, thou deep heaven! Thou abyss of light! Gazing on thee, I tremble with divine desires.

Up to thy height to toss myself—that is *my* depth! In thy purity to hide myself—that is *mine* innocence!

The God veileth his beauty: thus hidest thou thy stars. Thou speakest not: *thus* proclaimest thou thy wisdom unto me.

Mute o'er the raging sea hast thou risen for me to-day; thy love and thy modesty make a revelation unto my raging soul.

In that thou camest unto me beautiful, veiled in thy beauty, in that thou spakest unto me mutely, obvious in thy wisdom:

Oh, how could I fail to divine all the modesty of thy soul! *Before* the sun didst thou come unto me—the lonesomest one.

We have been friends from the beginning: to us are grief, gruesomeness, and ground common; even the sun is common to us.

We do not speak to each other, because we know too much—: we keep silent to each other, we smile our knowledge to each other.

Art thou not the light of my fire? Hast thou not the sister-soul of mine insight?

Together did we learn everything; together did we learn to ascend beyond ourselves to ourselves, and to smile uncloudedly:—

—Uncloudedly to smile down out of luminous eyes and out of miles of distance, when under us constraint and purpose and guilt stream like rain.

And wandered I alone, for *what* did my soul hunger by night and in labyrinthine paths? And climbed I mountains, *whom* did I ever seek, if not thee, upon mountains?

And all my wandering and mountain-climbing: a necessity was it merely, and a makeshift of the unhandy one:—to *fly* only, wanteth mine entire will, to fly into *thee!*

And what have I hated more than passing clouds, and whatever tainteth thee? And mine own hatred have I even hated, because it tainted thee!

The passing clouds I detest—those stealthy cats of prey: they take from thee and me what is common to us—the vast unbounded Yea- and Amen-saying.

These mediators and mixers we detest—the passing clouds. those half-and-half ones, that have neither learned to bless nor to curse from the heart.

Rather will I sit in a tub under a closed heaven, rather will I sit in the abyss without heaven, than see thee, thou luminous heaven, tainted with passing clouds!

And oft have I longed to pin them fast with the jagged gold-wires of lightning, that I might, like the thunder, beat the drum upon their kettle-bellies:—

—An angry drummer, because they rob me of thy Yea and Amen!—thou heaven above me, thou pure, thou luminous heaven! Thou abyss of light!—because they rob thee of *my* Yea and Amen.

For rather will I have noise and thunders and tempest-blasts, than this discreet, doubting cat-repose; and also amongst men do I hate most of all the soft-treaders, and half-and-half ones, and the doubting, hesitating, passing clouds.

And "he who cannot bless shall *learn* to curse!"—this clear teaching dropt unto me from the clear heaven; this star standeth in my heaven even in dark nights.

I, however, am a blesser and a Yea-sayer, if thou be but around me, thou pure, thou luminous heaven! Thou abyss of light!—into all abysses do I then carry my beneficent Yea-saying

A blesser have I become and a Yea-sayer: and therefore strove I long and was a striver, that I might one day get my hands free for blessing.

This, however, is my blessing: to stand above everything as its own heaven, its round roof, its azure bell and eternal security: and blessed is he who thus blesseth!

For all things are baptized at the font of eternity, and beyond good and evil; good and evil themselves, however, are but fugitive shadows and damp afflictions and passing clouds.

Verily, it is a blessing and not a blasphemy when I teach that "above all things there standeth the heaven of chance, the heaven of innocence, the heaven of hazard, the heaven of wantonness."

"Of Hazard"—that is the oldest nobility in the world; that gave I back to all things; I emancipated them from bondage under purpose.

This freedom and celestial serenity did I put like an azure bell above all things, when I taught that over them and through them, no "eternal Will"—willeth.

This wantonness and folly did I put in place of that Will, when I taught that "In everything there is one thing impossible —rationality!"

A *little* reason, to be sure, a germ of wisdom scattered from star to star—this leaven is mixed in all things: for the sake of folly, wisdom is mixed in all things!

A little wisdom is indeed possible; but this blessed security have I found in all things, that they prefer—*to dance* on the feet of chance.

O heaven above me! thou pure, thou lofty heaven! This is now thy purity unto me, that there is no eternal reason-spider and reason-cobweb:—

[*183*]

—That thou art to me a dancing-floor for divine chances, that thou art to me a table of the Gods, for divine dice and dice-players!—

But thou blushest? Have I spoken unspeakable things? Have I abused, when I meant to bless thee?

Or is it the shame of being two of us that maketh thee blush! —Dost thou bid me go and be silent, because now—*day* cometh?

The world is deep:—and deeper than e'er the day could read. Not everything may be uttered in presence of day. But day cometh: so let us part!

O heaven above me, thou modest one! thou glowing one! O thou, my happiness before sunrise! The day cometh: so let us part!—

Thus spake Zarathustra.

49. *The Bedwarfing Virtue*

1

WHEN Zarathustra was again on the continent, he did not go straightway to his mountains and his cave, but made many wanderings and questionings, and ascertained this and that; so that he said of himself jestingly: "Lo, a river that floweth back unto its source in many windings!" For he wanted to learn what had taken place *among men* during the interval: whether they had become greater or smaller. And once, when he saw a row of new houses, he marvelled, and said:

[*184*]

"What do these houses mean? Verily, no great soul put them up as its simile!

Did perhaps a silly child take them out of its toy-box? Would that another child put them again into the box!

And these rooms and chambers—can *men* go out and in there? They seem to be made for silk dolls; or for dainty-eaters, who perhaps let others eat with them."

And Zarathustra stood still and meditated. At last he said sorrowfully: "There hath *everything* become smaller!

Everywhere do I see lower doorways: he who is of *my* type can still go therethrough, but—he must stoop!

Oh, when shall I arrive again at my home, where I shall no longer have to stoop—shall no longer have to stoop *before the small ones!*"—And Zarathustra sighed, and gazed into the distance.—

The same day, however, he gave his discourse on the bedwarfing virtue.

2

I pass through this people and keep mine eyes open: they do not forgive me for not envying their virtues.

They bite at me, because I say unto them that for small people, small virtues are necessary—and because it is hard for me to understand that small people are *necessary!*

Here am I still like a cock in a strange farm-yard, at which even the hens peck: but on that account I am not unfriendly to the hens.

I am courteous towards them, as towards all small annoyances; to be prickly towards what is small, seemeth to me wisdom for hedgehogs.

They all speak of me when they sit around their fire in the evening—they speak of me, but no one thinketh—of me!

This is the new stillness which I have experienced: their noise around me spreadeth a mantle over my thoughts.

They shout to one another: "What is this gloomy cloud about to do to us? Let us see that it doth not bring a plague upon us!"

And recently did a woman seize upon her child that was coming unto me: "Take the children away," cried she, "such eyes scorch children's souls."

They cough when I speak: they think coughing an objection to strong winds—they divine nothing of the boisterousness of my happiness!

"We have not yet time for Zarathustra"—so they object; but what matter about a time that "hath no time" for Zarathustra?

And if they should altogether praise me, how could I go to sleep on *their* praise? A girdle of spines is their praise unto me: it scratcheth me even when I take it off.

And this also did I learn among them: the praiser doeth as if he gave back; in truth, however, he wanteth more to be given him!

Ask my foot if their lauding and luring strains please it! Verily, to such measure and ticktack, it liketh neither to dance nor to stand still.

To small virtues would they fain lure and laud me; to the ticktack of small happiness would they fain persuade my foot.

I pass through this people and keep mine eyes open; they have become *smaller,* and ever become smaller:—*the reason thereof is their doctrine of happiness and virtue.*

For they are moderate also in virtue,—because they want comfort. With comfort, however, moderate virtue only is compatible.

To be sure, they also learn in their way to stride on and stride forward: that, I call their *hobbling*.—Thereby they become a hindrance to all who are in haste.

And many of them go forward, and look backwards thereby, with stiffened necks: those do I like to run up against.

Foot and eye shall not lie, nor give the lie to each other. But there is much lying among small people.

Some of them *will*, but most of them are *willed*. Some of them are genuine, but most of them are bad actors.

There are actors without knowing it amongst them, and actors without intending it—, the genuine ones are always rare, especially the genuine actors.

Of man there is little here: therefore do their women masculinise themselves. For only he who is man enough, will—*save the woman* in woman.

And this hypocrisy found I worst amongst them, that even those who command feign the virtues of those who serve.

"I serve, thou servest, we serve"—so chanteth here even the hypocrisy of the rulers—and alas! if the first lord be *only* the first servant!

Ah, even upon their hypocrisy did mine eyes' curiosity alight; and well did I divine all their fly-happiness, and their buzzing around sunny window-panes.

So much kindness, so much weakness do I see. So much justice and pity, so much weakness.

Round, fair, and considerate are they to one another, as grains of sand are round, fair, and considerate to grains of sand.

Modestly to embrace a small happiness—that do they call "submission"! and at the same time they peer modestly after a new small happiness.

In their hearts they want simply one thing most of all: that no one hurt them. Thus do they anticipate every one's wishes and do well unto every one.

That, however, is *cowardice,* though it be called "virtue."—

And when they chance to speak harshly, those small people, then do *I* hear therein only their hoarseness—every draught of air maketh them hoarse.

Shrewd indeed are they, their virtues have shrewd fingers. But they lack fists: their fingers do not know how to creep behind fists.

Virtue for them is what maketh modest and tame: therewith have they made the wolf a dog, and man himself man's best domestic animal.

"We set our chair in the *midst*"—so saith their smirking unto me—"and as far from dying gladiators as from satisfied swine."

That, however, is—*mediocrity,* though it be called moderation.—

3

I pass through this people and let fall many words: but they know neither how to take nor how to retain them.

They wonder why I came not to revile venery and vice; and verily, I came not to warn against pickpockets either!

They wonder why I am not ready to abet and whet their wisdom: as if they had not yet enough of wiseacres, whose voices grate on mine ear like slate-pencils!

And when I call out: "Curse all the cowardly devils in you, that would fain whimper and fold the hands and adore"— then do they shout: "Zarathustra is godless."

And especially do their teachers of submission shout this;—but precisely in their ears do I love to cry: "Yea! I *am* Zarathustra, the godless!"

Those teachers of submission! Wherever there is aught puny, or sickly, or scabby, there do they creep like lice; and only my disgust preventeth me from cracking them.

Well! This is my sermon for *their* ears: I am Zarathustra the godless, who saith: "Who is more godless than I, that I may enjoy his teaching?"

I am Zarathustra the godless: where do I find mine equal? And all those are mine equals who give unto themselves their Will, and divest themselves of all submission.

I am Zarathustra the godless! I cook every chance in *my* pot. And only when it hath been quite cooked do I welcome it as *my* food.

And verily, many a chance came imperiously unto me: but still more imperiously did my *Will* speak unto it,—then did it lie imploringly upon its knees—

—Imploring that it might find home and heart with me, and saying flatteringly: "See, O Zarathustra, how friend only cometh unto friend!"—

But why talk I, when no one hath *mine* ears! And so will I shout it out unto all the winds:

Ye ever become smaller, ye small people! Ye crumble away, ye comfortable ones! Ye will yet perish—

—By your many small virtues, by your many small omissions, and by your many small submissions!

Too tender, too yielding: so is your soil! But for a tree to become *great,* it seeketh to twine hard roots around hard rocks!

Also what ye omit weaveth at the web of all the human future; even your naught is a cobweb, and a spider that liveth on the blood of the future.

And when ye take, then is it like stealing, ye small virtuous ones; but even among knaves *honour* saith that "one shall only steal when one cannot rob."

"It giveth itself"—that is also a doctrine of submission. But I say unto you, ye comfortable ones, that *it taketh to itself*, and will ever take more and more from you!

Ah, that ye would renounce all *half*-willing, and would decide for idleness as ye decide for action!

Ah, that ye understood my word: "Do ever what ye will— but first be such as *can will*.

Love ever your neighbour as yourselves—but first be such as *love themselves*—

—Such as love with great love, such as love with great contempt!" Thus speaketh Zarathustra the godless.—

But why talk I, when no one hath *mine* ears! It is still an hour too early for me here.

Mine own forerunner am I among this people, mine own cockcrow in dark lanes.

But *their* hour cometh! And there cometh also mine! Hourly do they become smaller, poorer, unfruitfuller,—poor herbs! poor earth!

And *soon* shall they stand before me like dry grass and prairie, and verily, weary of themselves—and panting for *fire*, more than for water!

O blessed hour of the lightning! O mystery before noontide! —Running fires will I one day make of them, and heralds with flaming tongues:—

—Herald shall they one day with flaming tongues: It cometh, it is nigh, *the great noontide!*

Thus spake Zarathustra.

50. On the Olive-Mount

WINTER, a bad guest, sitteth with me at home; blue are my hands with his friendly hand-shaking.

I honour him, that bad guest, but gladly leave him alone. Gladly do I run away from him; and when one runneth *well*, then one escapeth him!

With warm feet and warm thoughts do I run where the wind is calm—to the sunny corner of mine olive-mount.

There do I laugh at my stern guest, and am still fond of him; because he cleareth my house of flies, and quieteth many little noises.

For he suffereth it not if a gnat wanteth to buzz, or even two of them; also the lanes maketh he lonesome, so that the moonlight is afraid there at night.

A hard guest is he,—but I honour him, and do not worship, like the tenderlings, the pot-bellied fire-idol.

Better even a little teeth-chattering than idol-adoration!—so willeth my nature. And especially have I a grudge against all ardent, steaming, steamy fire-idols.

Him whom I love, I love better in winter than in summer; better do I now mock at mine enemies, and more heartily, when winter sitteth in my house.

Heartily, verily, even when I *creep* into bed—: there, still laugheth and wantoneth my hidden happiness; even my deceptive dream laugheth.

I, a—creeper? Never in my life did I creep before the powerful; and if ever I lied, then did I lie out of love. Therefore am I glad even in my winter-bed.

A poor bed warmeth me more than a rich one, for I am jealous of my poverty. And in winter she is most faithful unto me.

With a wickedness do I begin every day: I mock at the winter with a cold bath: on that account grumbleth my stern house-mate.

Also do I like to tickle him with a wax-taper, that he may finally let the heavens emerge from ashy-grey twilight.

For especially wicked am I in the morning: at the early hour when the pail rattleth at the well, and horses neigh warmly in grey lanes:—

Impatiently do I then wait, that the clear sky may finally dawn for me, the snow-bearded winter-sky, the hoary one, the white-head,—

—The winter-sky, the silent winter-sky, which often stifleth even its sun!

Did I perhaps learn from it the long clear silence? Or did it learn it from me? Or hath each of us devised it himself?

Of all good things the origin is a thousandfold,—all good roguish things spring into existence for joy: how could they always do so—for once only!

A good roguish thing is also the long silence, and to look, like the winter-sky, out of a clear, round-eyed countenance:—

—Like it to stifle one's sun, and one's inflexible solar will: verily, this art and this winter-roguishness have I learned *well*!

My best-loved wickedness and art is it, that my silence hath learned not to betray itself by silence.

Clattering with diction and dice, I outwit the solemn assistants: all those stern watchers, shall my will and purpose elude.

That no one might see down into my depth and into mine ultimate will—for that purpose did I devise the long clear silence.

Many a shrewd one did I find: he veiled his countenance and made his water muddy, that no one might see therethrough and thereunder.

But precisely unto him came the shrewder distrusters and nut-crackers: precisely from him did they fish his best-concealed fish!

But the clear, the honest, the transparent—these are for me the wisest silent ones: in them, so *profound* is the depth that even the clearest water doth not—betray it.—

Thou snow-bearded, silent, winter-sky, thou round-eyed whitehead above me! Oh, thou heavenly simile of my soul and its wantonness!

And *must* I not conceal myself like one who hath swallowed gold—lest my soul should be ripped up?

Must I not wear stilts, that they may *overlook* my long legs —all those enviers and injurers around me?

Those dingy, fire-warmed, used-up, green-tinted, ill-natured souls—how *could* their envy endure my happiness!

Thus do I show them only the ice and winter of my peaks— and *not* that my mountain windeth all the solar girdles around it!

They hear only the whistling of my winter-storms: and know *not* that I also travel over warm seas, like longing, heavy, hot south-winds.

They commiserate also my accidents and chances:—but *my* word saith: "Suffer the chance to come unto me: innocent is it as a little child!"

How *could* they endure my happiness, if I did not put around it accidents, and winter-privations, and bear-skin caps, and enmantling snowflakes!

—If I did not myself commiserate their *pity*, the pity of those enviers and injurers!

-If I did not myself sigh before them, and chatter with cold, and patiently *let* myself be swathed in their pity!

This is the wise waggish-will and good-will of my soul, that it *concealeth not* its winters and glacial storms; it concealeth not its chilblains either.

To one man, lonesomeness is the flight of the sick one; to another, it is the flight *from* the sick ones.

Let them *hear* me chattering and sighing with winter-cold, all those poor squinting knaves around me! With such sighing and chattering do I flee from their heated rooms.

Let them sympathise with me and sigh with me on account of my chilblains: "At the ice of knowledge will he yet *freeze to death!*"—so they mourn.

Meanwhile do I run with warm feet hither and thither on mine olive-mount: in the sunny corner of mine olive-mount do I sing, and mock at all pity.—

Thus sang Zarathustra.

51. On Passing-By

THUS slowly wandering through many peoples and divers cities, did Zarathustra return by round-about roads to his mountains and his cave. And behold, thereby came he unawares also to the gate of the *great city*. Here, however, a foaming fool, with extended hands, sprang forward to him and stood in his way. It was the same fool whom the people called "the ape of Zarathustra:" for he had learned from him something of the expression and modulation of language, and perhaps liked also to borrow from the store of his wisdom. And the fool talked thus to Zarathustra:

O Zarathustra, here is the great city: here hast thou nothing to seek and everything to lose.

Why wouldst thou wade through this mire? Have pity upon thy foot! Spit rather on the gate of the city, and—turn back!

Here is the hell for anchorites' thoughts: here are great thoughts seethed alive and boiled small.

Here do all great sentiments decay: here may only rattle-boned sensations rattle!

Smellest thou not already the shambles and cookshops of the spirit? Steameth not this city with the fumes of slaughtered spirit?

Seest thou not the souls hanging like limp dirty rags?—And they make newspapers also out of these rags!

Hearest thou not how spirit hath here become a verbal game? Loathsome verbal swill doth it vomit forth!—And they make newspapers also out of this verbal swill.

They hound one another, and know not whither! They inflame one another, and know not why! They tinkle with their pinchbeck, they jingle with their gold.

They are cold, and seek warmth from distilled waters: they are inflamed, and seek coolness from frozen spirits; they are all sick and sore through public opinion.

All lusts and vices are here at home; but here there are also the virtuous; there is much appointable appointed virtue:—

Much appointable virtue with scribe-fingers, and hardy sitting-flesh and waiting-flesh, blessed with small breast-stars, and padded, haunchless daughters.

There is here also much piety, and much faithful spittle-licking and spittle-backing, before the God of Hosts.

"From on high," drippeth the star, and the gracious spittle; for the high, longeth every starless bosom.

The moon hath its court, and the court hath its moon-calves: unto all, however, that cometh from the court do the mendicant people pray, and all appointable mendicant virtues.

"I serve, thou servest, we serve"—so prayeth all appointable virtue to the prince: that the merited star may at last stick on the slender breast!

But the moon still revolveth around all that is earthly: so revolveth also the prince around what is earthliest of all—that, however, is the gold of the shopman.

The God of the Hosts of war is not the God of the golden bar; the prince proposeth, but the shopman—disposeth!

By all that is luminous and strong and good in thee, O Zarathustra! Spit on this city of shopmen and return back!

Here floweth all blood putridly and tepidly and frothily through all veins: spit on the great city, which is the great slum where all the scum frotheth together!

Spit on the city of compressed souls and slender breasts, or pointed eyes and sticky fingers—

—On the city of the obtrusive, the brazen-faced, the pen-demagogues and tongue-demagogues, the overheated ambitious:—

Where everything maimed, ill-famed, lustful, untrustful, over-mellow, sickly-yellow and seditious, festereth perniciously:—

—Spit on the great city and turn back!—

Here, however, did Zarathustra interrupt the foaming fool, and shut his mouth.—

Stop this at once! called out Zarathustra, long have thy speech and thy species disgusted me!

Why didst thou live so long by the swamp, that thou thyself hadst to become a frog and a toad?

Floweth there not a tainted, frothy, swamp-blood in thine own veins, when thou hast thus learned to croak and revile?

Why wentest thou not into the forest? Or why didst thou not till the ground? Is the sea not full of green islands?

I despise thy contempt; and when thou warnedst me—why didst thou not warn thyself?

Out of love alone shall my contempt and my warning bird take wing; but not out of the swamp!—

They call thee mine ape, thou foaming fool: but I call thee my grunting-pig,—by thy grunting, thou spoilest even my praise of folly.

What was it that first made thee grunt? Because no one sufficiently *flattered* thee:—therefore didst thou seat thyself beside this filth, that thou mightest have cause for much grunting,—

—That thou mightest have cause for much *vengeance!* For vengeance, thou vain fool, is all thy foaming; I have divined thee well!

But thy fools'-word injureth *me,* even when thou art right! And even if Zarathustra's word *were* a hundred times justified, thou wouldst ever—*do* wrong with my word!

Thus spake Zarathustra. Then did he look on the great city and sighed, and was long silent. At last he spake thus:

I loathe also this great city, and not only this fool. Here and there—there is nothing to better, nothing to worsen.

Woe to this great city!—And I would that I already saw the pillar of fire in which it will be consumed!

For such pillars of fire must precede the great noontide. But this hath its time and its own fate.—

This precept, however, give I unto thee, in parting, thou fool: Where one can no longer love, there should one—*pass by!*—

Thus spake Zarathustra, and passed by the fool and the great city.

52. *The Apostates*

1

AH, LIETH everything already withered and grey which but lately stood green and many-hued on this meadow! And how much honey of hope did I carry hence into my beehives!

Those young hearts have already all become old—and not old even! only weary, ordinary, comfortable:—they declare it: "We have again become pious."

Of late did I see them run forth at early morn with valorous steps: but the feet of their knowledge became weary, and now do they malign even their morning valour!

Verily, many of them once lifted their legs like the dancer to them winked the laughter of my wisdom:—then did they bethink themselves. Just now have I seen them bent down—to creep to the cross.

Around light and liberty did they once flutter like gnats and young poets. A little older, a little colder: and already are they mystifiers, and mumblers and mollycoddles.

Did perhaps their hearts despond, because lonesomeness had swallowed me like a whale? Did their ear perhaps hearken yearningly-long for me *in vain,* and for my trumpet-notes and herald-calls?

—Ah! Ever are there but few of those whose hearts have persistent courage and exuberance; and in such remaineth also the spirit patient. The rest, however, are *cowardly.*

The rest: these are always the great majority, the common-place, the superfluous, the far-too many—those all are cowardly!—

Him who is of my type, will also the experiences of my type meet on the way: so that his first companions must be corpses and buffoons.

His second companions, however—they will call themselves his *believers,*—will be a living host, with much love, much folly, much unbearded veneration.

To those believers shall he who is of my type among men not bind his heart; in those spring-times and many-hued meadows shall he not believe, who knoweth the fickly faint-hearted human species!

Could they do otherwise, then would they also *will* otherwise. The half-and-half spoil every whole. That leaves become withered,—what is there to lament about that!

Let them go and fall away, O Zarathustra, and do not lament! Better even to blow amongst them with rustling winds,—

—Blow amongst those leaves, O Zarathustra, that everything *withered* may run away from thee the faster!—

2

"We have again become pious"—so do those apostates confess; and some of them are still too pusillanimous thus to confess.

Unto them I look into the eye,—before them I say it unto their face and unto the blush on their cheeks: Ye are those who again *pray!*

It is however a shame to pray! Not for all, but for thee, and me, and whoever hath his conscience in his head. For *thee* it is a shame to pray!

Thou knowest it well: the faint-hearted devil in thee, which would fain fold its arms, and place its hands in its bosom, and take it easier:—this faint-hearted devil persuadeth thee that "there *is* a God!"

Thereby, however, dost thou belong to the light-dreading type, to whom light never permitteth repose: now must thou daily thrust thy head deeper into obscurity and vapour!

And verily, thou choosest the hour well: for just now do the nocturnal birds again fly abroad. The hour hath come for all light-dreading people, the vesper hour and leisure hour, when they do not—"take leisure."

I hear it and smell it: it hath come—their hour for hunt and procession, not indeed for a wild hunt, but for a tame, lame, snuffling, soft-treaders', soft-prayers' hunt,—

—For a hunt after susceptible simpletons: all mouse-traps for the heart have again been set! And whenever I lift a curtain, a night-moth rusheth out of it.

Did it perhaps squat there along with another night-moth? For everywhere do I smell small concealed communities; and wherever there are closets there are new devotees therein, and the atmosphere of devotees.

They sit for long evenings beside one another, and say: "Let us again become like little children and say, 'good God!'"— ruined in mouths and stomachs by the pious confectioners.

Or they look for long evenings at a crafty, lurking cross-spider, that preacheth prudence to the spiders themselves, and teacheth that "under crosses it is good for cobweb-spinning!"

Or they sit all day at swamps with angle-rods, and on that account think themselves *profound;* but whoever fisheth where there are no fish, I do not even call him superficial!

Or they learn in godly-gay style to play the harp with a hymn-poet, who would fain harp himself into the heart of young girls:—for he hath tired of old girls and their praises.

Or they learn to shudder with a learned semi-madcap, who waiteth in darkened rooms for spirits to come to him—and the spirit runneth away entirely!

Or they listen to an old roving howl- and growl-piper, who hath learned from the sad winds the sadness of sounds; now pipeth he as the wind, and preacheth sadness in sad strains.

And some of them have even become night-watchmen: they know now how to blow horns, and go about at night and awaken old things which have long fallen asleep.

Five words about old things did I hear yesternight at the garden-wall: they came from such old, sorrowful, arid night-watchmen.

"For a father he careth not sufficiently for his children: human fathers do this better!"—

"He is too old! He now careth no more for his children,"—answered the other night-watchman.

"*Hath* he then children? No one can prove it unless he himself prove it! I have long wished that he would for once prove it thoroughly."

"Prove? As if *he* had ever proved anything! Proving is difficult to him; he layeth great stress on one's *believing* him."

"Ay! Ay! Belief saveth him; belief in him. That is the way with old people! So it is with us also!"—

—Thus spake to each other the two old night-watchmen and light-scarers, and tooted thereupon sorrowfully on their horns: so did it happen yesternight at the garden-wall.

To me, however, did the heart writhe with laughter, and was like to break; it knew not where to go, and sunk into the midriff.

Verily, it will be my death yet—to choke with laughter when I see asses drunken, and hear night-watchmen thus doubt about God.

Hath the time not *long* since passed for all such doubts? Who may nowadays awaken such old slumbering, light shunning things!

With the old Deities hath it long since come to an end:— and verily, a good joyful Deity-end had they!

They did not "begloom" themselves to death—that do people fabricate! On the contrary, they—*laughed* themselves to death once on a time!

That took place when the ungodliest utterance came from a God himself—the utterance: "There is but one God! Thou shalt have no other gods before me!"—

—An old grim-beard of a God, a jealous one, forgot himself in such wise:—

And all the gods then laughed, and shook upon their thrones, and exclaimed: "Is it not just divinity that there are gods, but no God?"

He that hath an ear let him hear.—

Thus talked Zarathustra in the city he loved, which is surnamed "The Pied Cow." For from here he had but two days to travel to reach once more his cave and his animals; his soul, however, rejoiced unceasingly on account of the nighness of his return home.

53. *The Return Home*

O LONESOMENESS! my *home*, lonesomeness! Too long have I lived wildly in wild remoteness, to return to thee without tears!

Now threaten me with the finger as mothers threaten; now smile upon me as mothers smile; now say just: "Who was it that like a whirlwind once rushed away from me?—

—Who when departing called out: 'Too long have I sat with lonesomeness; there have I unlearned silence!' *That* hast thou learned now—surely?

O Zarathustra, everything do I know; and that thou wert *more forsaken* amongst the many, thou unique one, than thou ever wert with me!

One thing is forsakenness, another matter is lonesomeness: *that* hast thou now learned! And that amongst men thou wilt ever be wild and strange:

—Wild and strange even when they love thee: for above all they want to be *treated indulgently!*

Here, however, art thou at home and house with thyself; here canst thou utter everything, and unbosom all motives; nothing is here ashamed of concealed, congealed feelings.

Here do all things come caressingly to thy talk and flatter thee: for they want to ride upon thy back. On every simile dost thou here ride to every truth.

Uprightly and openly mayest thou here talk to all things: and verily, it soundeth as praise in their ears, for one to talk to all things—directly!

Another matter, however, is forsakenness. For, dost thou remember, O Zarathustra? When thy bird screamed overhead, when thou stoodest in the forest, irresolute, ignorant where to go, beside a corpse:—

—When thou spakest: 'Let mine animals lead me! More dangerous have I found it among men than among animals:' —*That* was forsakenness!

And dost thou remember, O Zarathustra? When thou sattest in thine isle, a well of wine giving and granting amongst empty buckets, bestowing and distributing amongst the thirsty:

—Until at last thou alone sattest thirsty amongst the drunken ones, and wailedst nightly: 'Is taking not more blessed than giving? And stealing yet more blessed than taking?'—*That* was forsakenness!

And dost thou remember, O Zarathustra? When thy stillest hour came and drove thee forth from thyself, when with wicked whispering it said: 'Speak and succumb!'—

—When it disgusted thee with all thy waiting and silence, and discouraged thy humble courage: *That* was forsakenness!"—

O lonesomeness! My home, lonesomeness! How blessedly and tenderly speaketh thy voice unto me!

We do not question each other, we do not complain to each other; we go together openly through open doors.

For all is open with thee and clear; and even the hours run here on lighter feet. For in the dark, time weigheth heavier upon one than in the light.

Here fly open unto me all beings' words and word-cabinets: here all being wanteth to become words, here all becoming wanteth to learn of me how to talk.

Down there, however—all talking is in vain! There, forgetting and passing-by are the best wisdom: *that* have I learned now!

He who would understand everything in man must handle everything. But for that I have too clean hands.

I do not like even to inhale their breath; alas! that I have lived so long among their noise and bad breaths!

O blessed stillness around me! O pure odours around me! How from a deep breast this stillness fetcheth pure breath! How it hearkeneth, this blessed stillness!

But down there—there speaketh everything, there is everything misheard. If one announce one's wisdom with bells, the shopmen in the market-place will out-jingle it with pennies!

Everything among them talketh; no one knoweth any longer how to understand. Everything falleth into the water; nothing falleth any longer into deep wells.

Everything among them talketh, nothing succeedeth any longer and accomplisheth itself. Everything cackleth, but who will still sit quietly on the nest and hatch eggs?

Everything among them talketh, everything is out-talked. And that which yesterday was still too hard for time itself and its tooth, hangeth today, outchamped and outchewed, from the mouths of the men of today.

Everything among them talketh, everything is betrayed. And what was once called the secret and secrecy of profound souls, belongeth to-day to the street-trumpeters and other butterflies.

O human hubbub, thou wonderful thing! Thou noise in dark streets! Now art thou again behind me:—my greatest danger lieth behind me!

In indulging and pitying lay ever my greatest danger; and all human hubbub wisheth to be indulged and tolerated.

With suppressed truths, with fool's hand and befooled heart, and rich in petty lies of pity:—thus have I ever lived among men.

[205]

Disguised did I sit amongst them, ready to misjudge *myself* that I might endure *them,* and willingly saying to myself: "Thou fool, thou dost not know men!"

One unlearneth men when one liveth amongst them: there is too much foreground in all men—what can far-seeing, far-longing eyes do *there!*

And, fool that I was, when they misjudged me, I indulged them on that account more than myself, being habitually hard on myself, and often even taking revenge on myself for the indulgence.

Stung all over by poisonous flies, and hollowed like the stone by many drops of wickedness: thus did I sit among them, and still said to myself: "Innocent is everything petty of its pettiness!"

Especially did I find those who call themselves "the good," the most poisonous flies; they sting in all innocence, they lie in all innocence; how *could* they—be just towards me!

He who liveth amongst the good—pity teacheth him to lie. Pity maketh stifling air for all free souls. For the stupidity of the good is unfathomable.

To conceal myself and my riches—*that* did I learn down there: for every one did I still find poor in spirit. It was the lie of my pity, that I knew in every one.

—That I saw and scented in every one, what was *enough* of spirit for him, and what was *too much!*

Their stiff wise men: I call them wise, not stiff—thus did I learn to slur over words.

The grave-diggers dig for themselves diseases. Under old rubbish rest bad vapours. One should not stir up the marsh. One should live on mountains.

With blessed nostrils do I again breathe mountain-freedom.

Freed at last is my nose from the smell of all human hubbub!

With sharp breezes tickled, as with sparkling wine, *sneezeth* my soul—sneezeth, and shouteth self-congratulatingly: "Health to thee!"

Thus spake Zarathustra.

54. *The Three Evil Things*

1

IN MY dream, in my last morning-dream, I stood today on a promontory—beyond the world; I held a pair of scales, and *weighed* the world.

Alas, that the rosy dawn came too early to me: she glowed me awake, the jealous one! Jealous is she always of the glows of my morning-dream.

Measurable by him who hath time, weighable by a good weigher, attainable by strong pinions, divinable by divine nut-crackers: thus did my dream find the world:—

My dream, a bold sailor, half-ship, half-hurricane, silent as the butterfly, impatient as the falcon: how had it the patience and leisure to-day for world-weighing!

Did my wisdom perhaps speak secretly to it, my laughing, wide-awake day-wisdom, which mocketh at all "infinite worlds"? For it saith: "Where force is, there becometh *number* the master: it hath more force."

How confidently did my dream contemplate this finite

world, not new-fangledly, not old-fangledly, not timidly, not entreatingly:—

—As if a big round apple presented itself to my hand, a ripe golden apple, with a coolly-soft, velvety skin:—thus did the world present itself unto me:—

—As if a tree nodded unto me, a broad-branched, strong-willed tree, curved as a recline and a foot-stool for weary travellers: thus did the world stand on my promontory:—

—As if delicate hands carried a casket towards me—a casket open for the delectation of modest adoring eyes: thus did the world present itself before me today:—

—Not riddle enough to scare human love from it, not solution enough to put to sleep human wisdom:—a humanly good thing was the world to me to-day, of which such bad things are said!

How I thank my morning-dream that I thus at today's dawn, weighed the world! As a humanly good thing did it come unto me, this dream and heart-comforter!

And that I may do the like by day, and imitate and copy its best, now will I put the three worst things on the scales, and weigh them humanly well.—

He who taught to bless taught also to curse: what are the three best cursed things in the world? These will I put on the scales.

Voluptuousness, passion for power, and *selfishness:* these three things have hitherto been best cursed, and have been in worst and falsest repute—these three things will I weigh humanly well.

Well! here is my promontory, and there is the sea—*it* rolleth hither unto me, shaggily and fawningly, the old, faithful, hundred-headed dog-monster that I love!—

Well! Here will I hold the scales over the weltering sea: and also a witness do I choose to look on——thee, the anchorite-tree, thee, the strong-odoured, broad-arched tree that I love!——

On what bridge goeth the now to the hereafter? By what constraint doth the high stoop to the low? And what enjoineth even the highest still——to grow upwards?——

Now stand the scales poised and at rest: three heavy questions have I thrown in; three heavy answers carrieth the other scale.

2

Voluptuousness: unto all hair-shirted despisers of the body, a sting and stake; and, cursed as "the world," by all back-worldsmen: for it mocketh and befooleth all erring, misin-ferring teachers.

Voluptuousness: to the rabble, the slow fire at which it is burnt; to all wormy wood, to all stinking rags, the prepared heat and stew furnace.

Voluptuousness: to free hearts, a thing innocent and free, the garden-happiness of the earth, all the future's thanks-over-flow to the present.

Voluptuousness: only to the withered a sweet poison; to the lion-willed, however, the great cordial, and the reverently saved wine of wines.

Voluptuousness: the great symbolic happiness of a higher happiness and highest hope. For to many is marriage promised, and more than marriage,——

——To many that are more unknown to each other than man and woman:——and who hath fully understood *how unknown* to each other are man and woman!

Voluptuousness:——but I will have hedges around my

[*209*]

thoughts, and even around my words, lest swine and libertine should break into my gardens!—

Passion for power: the glowing scourge of the hardest of the heart-hard; the cruel torture reserved for the cruellest themselves; the gloomy flame of living pyres.

Passion for power: the wicked gadfly which is mounted on the vainest peoples; the scorner of all uncertain virtue; which rideth on every horse and on every pride.

Passion for power: the earthquake which breaketh and up-breaketh all that is rotten and hollow; the rolling, rumbling, punitive demolisher of whited sepulchres; the flashing interrogative-sign beside premature answers.

Passion for power: before whose glance man creepeth and croucheth and drudgeth, and becometh lower than the serpent and the swine:—until at last great contempt crieth out of him—,

Passion for power: the terrible teacher of great contempt, which preacheth to their face to cities and empires: "Away with thee!"—until a voice crieth out of themselves: "Away with *me!*"

Passion for power: which, however, mounteth alluringly even to the pure and lonesome, and up to self-satisfied elevations, glowing like a love that painteth purple felicities alluringly on earthly heavens.

Passion for power: but who would call it *passion,* when the height longeth to stoop for power! Verily, nothing sick or diseased is there in such longing and descending!

That the lonesome height may not forever remain lonesome and self-sufficing; that the mountains may come to the valleys and the winds of the heights to the plains:—

Oh, who could find the right prenomen and honouring name

for such longing! "Bestowing virtue"—thus did Zarathustra once name the unnamable.

And then it happened also,—and verily, it happened for the first time!—that his word blessed *selfishness,* the wholesome, healthy selfishness, that springeth from the powerful soul:—

—From the powerful soul, to which the high body appertaineth, the handsome, triumphing, refreshing body, around which everything becometh a mirror:

—The pliant, persuasive body, the dancer, whose symbol and epitome is the self-enjoying soul. Of such bodies and souls the self-enjoyment calleth itself "virtue."

With its words of good and bad doth such self-enjoyment shelter itself as with sacred groves; with the names of its happiness doth it banish from itself everything contemptible.

Away from itself doth it banish everything cowardly; it saith: "Bad—*that is* cowardly!" Contemptible seem to it the ever-solicitous, the sighing, the complaining, and whoever pick up the most trifling advantage.

It despiseth also all bitter-sweet wisdom: for verily, there is also wisdom that bloometh in the dark, a night-shade wisdom, which ever sigheth: "All is vain!"

Shy distrust is regarded by it as base, and every one who wanteth oaths instead of looks and hands: also all over-distrustful wisdom,—for such is the mode of cowardly souls.

Baser still it regardeth the obsequious, doggish one, who immediately lieth on his back, the submissive one; and there is also wisdom that is submissive, and doggish, and pious, and obsequious.

Hateful to it altogether, and a loathing, is he who will never defend himself, he who swalloweth down poisonous spittle and bad looks, the all-too-patient one, the all-endurer, the all-satisfied one: for that is the mode of slaves.

[*211*]

Whether they be servile before gods and divine spurnings, or before men and stupid human opinions: at *all* kinds of slaves doth it spit, this blessed selfishness!

Bad: thus doth it call all that is spirit-broken, and sordidly-servile—constrained, blinking eyes, depressed hearts, and the false submissive style, which kisseth with broad cowardly lips.

And spurious wisdom: so doth it call all the wit that slaves, and hoary-headed and weary ones affect; and especially all the cunning, spurious-witted, curious-witted foolishness of priests!

The spurious wise, however, all the priests, the world-weary, and those whose souls are of feminine and servile nature—oh, how hath their game all along abused selfishness!

And precisely *that* was to be virtue and was to be called virtue—to abuse selfishness! And "selfless"—so did they wish themselves with good reason, all those world-weary cowards and cross-spiders!

But to all those cometh now the day, the change, the sword of judgment, *the great noontide:* then shall many things be revealed!

And he who proclaimeth the *ego* wholesome and holy, and selfishness blessed, verily, he, the prognosticator, speaketh also what he knoweth: *"Behold, it cometh, it is night, the great noontide!"*

Thus spake Zarathustra.

55. *The Spirit of Gravity*

1

MY MOUTHPIECE—is of the people: too coarsely and cordially do I talk for Angora rabbits. And still stranger soundeth my word unto all ink-fish and pen-foxes.

My hand—is a fool's hand: woe unto all tables and walls, and whatever hath room for fool's sketching, fool's scrawling!

My foot—is a horse-foot; therewith do I trample and trot over stick and stone, in the fields up and down, and am bedevilled with delight in all fast racing.

My stomach—is surely an eagle's stomach? For it preferreth lamb's flesh. Certainly it is a bird's stomach.

Nourished with innocent things, and with few, ready and impatient to fly, to fly away—that is now my nature: why should there not be something of bird-nature therein!

And especially that I am hostile to the spirit of gravity, that is bird-nature:—verily, deadly hostile, supremely hostile, originally hostile! Oh, whither hath my hostility not flown and misflown!

Thereof could I sing a song— —and *will* sing it: though I be alone in an empty house, and must sing it to mine own ears.

Other singers are there, to be sure, to whom only the full house maketh the voice soft, the hand eloquent, the eye expressive, the heart wakeful:—those do I not resemble.—

2

He who one day teacheth men to fly will have shifted all landmarks; to him will all landmarks themselves fly into the air; the earth will he christen anew—as "the light body."

The ostrich runneth faster than the fastest horse, but it also thrusteth its head heavily into the heavy earth: thus is it with the man who cannot yet fly.

Heavy unto him are earth and life, and so *willeth* the spirit of gravity! But he who would become light, and be a bird, must love himself:—thus do *I* teach.

Not, to be sure, with the love of the sick and infected, for with them stinketh even self-love!

One must learn to love oneself—thus do I teach—with a wholesome and healthy love: that one may endure to be with oneself, and not go roving about.

Such roving about christeneth itself "brotherly love"; with these words hath there hitherto been the best lying and dissembling, and especially by those who have been burdensome to every one.

And verily, it is no commandment for today and tomorrow to *learn* to love oneself. Rather is it of all arts the finest, subtlest, last and patientest.

For to its possessor is all possession well concealed, and of all treasure-pits one's own is last excavated—so causeth the spirit of gravity.

Almost in the cradle are we apportioned with heavy words and worths: "good" and "evil"—so calleth itself this dowry. For the sake of it we are forgiven for living.

And therefore suffereth one little children to come unto one, to forbid them betimes to love themselves—so causeth the spirit of gravity.

And we—we bear loyally what is apportioned unto us, on hard shoulders, over rugged mountains! And when we sweat, then do people say to us: "Yea, life is hard to bear!"

But man himself only is hard to bear! The reason thereof is that he carrieth too many extraneous things on his shoulders. Like the camel kneeleth he down, and letteth himself be well laden.

Especially the strong load-bearing man in whom reverence resideth. Too many *extraneous* heavy words and worths loadeth he upon himself—then seemeth life to him a desert!

And verily! Many a thing also that is *our own* is hard to bear! And many internal things in man are like the oyster—repulsive and slippery and hard to grasp;—

So that an elegant shell, with elegant adornment, must plead for them. But this art also must one learn: to *have* a shell, and a fine appearance, and sagacious blindness!

Again, it deceiveth about many things in man, that many a shell is poor and pitiable, and too much of a shell. Much concealed goodness and power is never dreamt of; the choicest dainties find no tasters!

Women know that, the choicest of them: a little fatter a little leaner—oh, how much fate is in so little!

Man is difficult to discover, and unto himself most difficult of all; often lieth the spirit concerning the soul. So causeth the spirit of gravity.

He, however, hath discovered himself who saith: This is *my* good and evil: therewith hath he silenced the mole and the dwarf, who say: "Good for all, evil for all."

Verily, neither do I like those who call everything good, and this world the best of all. Those do I call the all-satisfied.

All-satisfiedness, which knoweth how to taste everything,—that is not the best taste! I honour the refractory, fastidious tongues and stomachs, which have learned to say "I" and "Yea" and "Nay."

To chew and digest everything, however—that is the genuine swine-nature! Ever to say YE-A—that hath only the ass learned, and those like it!—

Deep yellow and hot red—so wanteth *my* taste—it mixeth blood with all colours. He, however, who whitewasheth his house, betrayeth unto me a whitewashed soul.

With mummies, some fall in love; others with phantoms: both alike hostile to all flesh and blood—oh, how repugnant are both to my taste! For I love blood.

And there will I not reside and abide where every one spitteth and speweth: that is now *my* taste,—rather would I live amongst thieves and perjurers. Nobody carrieth gold in his mouth.

Still more repugnant unto me, however, are all lick-spittles; and the most repugnant animal of man that I found, did I christen "parasite": it would not love, and would yet live by love.

Unhappy do I call all those who have only one choice: either to become evil beasts, or evil beast-tamers. Amongst such would I not build my tabernacle.

Unhappy do I also call those who have ever to *wait*,—they are repugnant to my taste—all the toll-gatherers and traders, and kings, and other landkeepers and shopkeepers.

Verily, I learned waiting also, and thoroughly so,—but only waiting for *myself*. And above all did I learn standing and walking and running and leaping and climbing and dancing.

This however is my teaching: he who wisheth one day to fly,

must first learn standing and walking and running and climbing and dancing:—one doth not fly into flying!

With rope-ladders learned I to reach many a window, with nimble legs did I climb high masts: to sit on high masts of perception seemed to me no small bliss;—

—To flicker like small flames on high masts: a small light, certainly, but a great comfort to cast-away sailors and ship-wrecked ones!

By divers ways and wendings did I arrive at my truth; not by one ladder did I mount to the height where mine eye roveth into my remoteness.

And unwillingly only did I ask my way—that was always counter to my taste! Rather did I question and test the ways themselves.

A testing and a questioning hath been all my travelling:— and verily, one must also *learn* to answer such questioning! That, however,—is my taste:

—Neither a good nor a bad taste, but *my* taste, of which I have no longer either shame or secrecy.

"This—is now *my* way,—where is yours?" Thus did I answer those who asked me "the way." For *the* way—it doth not exist!

Thus spake Zarathustra.

56. Old and New Tables

1

HERE do I sit and wait, old broken tables around me and also new half-written tables. When cometh mine hour?

—The hour of my descent, of my down-going: for once more will I go unto men.

For that hour do I now wait: for first must the signs come unto me that it is *mine* hour—namely, the laughing lion with the flock of doves.

Meanwhile do I talk to myself as one who hath time. No one telleth me anything new, so I tell myself mine own story.

2

When I came unto men, then found I them resting on an old infatuation: all of them thought they had long known what was good and bad for men.

An old wearisome business seemed to them all discourse about virtue; and he who wished to sleep well spake of "good" and "bad" ere retiring to rest.

This somnolence did I disturb when I taught that *no one yet knoweth* what is good and bad:—unless it be the creating one!

—It is he, however, who createth man's goal, and giveth to the earth its meaning and its future: he only *effecteth* it *that* aught is good or bad.

And I bade them upset their old academic chairs, and

wherever that old infatuation had sat; I bade them laugh at their great moralists, their saints, their poets, and their saviours.

At their gloomy sages did I bid them laugh, and whoever had sat admonishing as a black scarecrow on the tree of life.

On their great grave-highway did I seat myself, and even beside the carrion and vultures—and I laughed at all their bygone and its mellow decaying glory.

Verily, like penitential preachers and fools did I cry wrath and shame on all their greatness and smallness. Oh, that their best is so very small! Oh, that their worst is so very small! Thus did I laugh.

Thus did my wise longing, born in the mountains, cry and laugh in me; a wild wisdom, verily!—my great pinion-rustling longing.

And oft did it carry me off and up and away and in the midst of laughter; then flew I quivering like an arrow with sun-intoxicated rapture:

—Out into distant futures, which no dream hath yet seen, into warmer souths than ever sculptor conceived,—where gods in their dancing are ashamed of all clothes:

(That I may speak in parables and halt and stammer like the poets: and verily I am ashamed that I have still to be a poet!)

Where all becoming seemed to me dancing of gods, and wantoning of gods, and the world unloosed and unbridled and fleeing back to itself:—

—As an eternal self-fleeing and re-seeking of one another of many gods, as the blessed self-contradicting, recommuning, and refraternising with one another of many gods:—

Where all time seemed to me a blessed mockery of moments, where necessity was freedom itself, which played happily with the goad of freedom:—

[219]

Where I also found again mine old devil and arch-enemy, the spirit of gravity, and all that it created: constraint, law, necessity and consequence and purpose and will and good and evil:—

For must there not be that which is danced *over*, danced beyond? Must there not, for the sake of the nimble, the nimblest, —be moles and clumsy dwarfs?——

3

There was it also where I picked up from the path the word "Superman," and that man is something that must be surpassed.

—That man is a bridge and not a goal—rejoicing over his noontides and evenings, as advances to new rosy dawns:

—The Zarathustra word of the great noontide, and whatever else I have hung up over men like purple evening-afterglows.

Verily, also new stars did I make them see, along with new nights; and over cloud and day and night, did I spread out laughter like a gay-coloured canopy.

I taught them all *my* poetisation and aspiration: to compose and collect into unity what is fragment in man, and riddle and fearful chance;——

—As composer, riddle-reader, and redeemer of chance, did I teach them to create the future, and all that *hath been*—to redeem by creating.

The past of man to redeem, and every "It was" to transform, until the Will saith: "But so did I will it! So shall I will it—"

—This did I call redemption; this alone taught I them to call redemption.— —

Now do I await *my* redemption—that I may go unto them for the last time.

For once more will I go unto men: *amongst* them will my sun set; in dying will I give them my choicest gift!

From the sun did I learn this, when it goeth down, the exuberant one: gold doth it then pour into the sea, out of inexhaustible riches,—

—So that the poorest fisherman roweth even with *golden* oars! For this did I once see, and did not tire of weeping in beholding it.— —

Like the sun will also Zarathustra go down: now sitteth he here and waiteth, old broken tables around him, and also new tables—half-written.

4

Behold, here is a new table; but where are my brethren who will carry it with me to the valley and into hearts of flesh?—

Thus demandeth my great love to the remotest ones: *be not considerate of thy neighbour!* Man is something that must be surpassed.

There are many divers ways and modes of surpassing: see *thou* thereto! But only a buffoon thinketh: "man can also be *overleapt*."

Surpass thyself even in thy neighbour: and a right which thou canst seize upon, shalt thou not allow to be given thee!

What thou doest can no one do to thee again. Lo, there is no requital.

He who cannot command himself shall obey. And many a one *can* command himself, but still sorely lacketh self-obedience!

5

Thus wisheth the type of noble souls: they desire to have nothing *gratuitously,* least of all, life.

He who is of the populace wisheth to live gratuitously; we others, however, to whom life hath given itself—we are ever considering *what* we can best give *in return!*

And verily, it is a noble dictum which saith: "What life promiseth *us,* that promise will *we* keep—to life!"

One should not wish to enjoy where one doth not contribute to the enjoyment. And one should not *wish* to enjoy!

For enjoyment and innocence are the most bashful things. Neither like to be sought for. One should *have* them,—but one should rather *seek* for guilt and pain!—

6

O my brethren, he who is a firstling is ever sacrificed. Now, however, are we firstlings!

We all bleed on secret sacrificial altars, we all burn and broil in honour of ancient idols.

Our best is still young: this exciteth old palates. Our flesh is tender, our skin is only lambs' skin:—how could we not excite old idol-priests!

In ourselves dwelleth he still, the old idol-priest, who broileth our best for his banquet. Ah, my brethren, how could firstlings fail to be sacrifices!

But so wisheth our type; and I love those who do not wish to preserve themselves, the down-going ones do I love with mine entire love: for they go beyond.—

7

To be true—that *can* few be! And he who can, will not! Least of all, however, can the good be true.

Oh, those good ones! *Good men never speak the truth.* For the spirit, thus to be good, is a malady.

They yield, those good ones, they submit themselves; their heart repeateth, their soul obeyeth: *he,* however, who obeyeth, *doth not listen to himself!*

All that is called evil by the good, must come together in order that one truth may be born. O my brethren, are ye also evil enough for *this* truth?

The daring venture, the prolonged distrust, the cruel Nay, the tedium, the cutting-into-the-quick—how seldom do *these* come together! Out of such seed, however—is truth produced!

Beside the bad conscience hath hitherto grown all *knowledge!* Break up, break up, ye discerning ones, the old tables!

8

When the water hath planks, when gangways and railings o'erspan the stream, verily, he is not believed who then saith: "All is in flux."

But even the simpletons contradict him. "What?" say the simpletons, "all in flux? Planks and railings are still *over* the stream!

"*Over* the stream all is stable, all the values of things, the bridges and bearings, all 'good' and 'evil': these are all stable!"—

[223]

Cometh, however, the hard winter, the stream-tamer, then learn even the wittiest distrust, and verily, not only the simpletons then say: "Should not everything—*stand still?*"

"Fundamentally standeth everything still"—that is an appropriate winter doctrine, good cheer for an unproductive period, a great comfort for winter-sleepers and fireside-loungers.

"Fundamentally standeth everything still"—: but *contrary* thereto, preacheth the thawing wind!

The thawing wind, a bullock, which is no ploughing bullock —a furious bullock, a destroyer, which with angry horns breaketh the ice! The ice however— —*breaketh gangways!*

O my brethren, is not everything *at present in flux?* Have not all railings and gangways fallen into the water? Who would still *hold on* to "good" and "evil"?

"Woe to us! Hail to us! The thawing wind bloweth!"— Thus preach, my brethren, through all the streets!

9

There is an old illusion—it is called good and evil. Around soothsayers and astrologers hath hitherto revolved the orbit of this illusion.

Once did one *believe* in soothsayers and astrologers; and *therefore* did one believe, "Everything is fate: thou shalt, for thou must!"

Then again did one distrust all soothsayers and astrologers; and *therefore* did one believe, "Everything is freedom: thou canst, for thou willest!"

O my brethren, concerning the stars and the future there

hath hitherto been only illusion, and not knowledge; and *therefore* concerning good and evil there hath hitherto been only illusion and not knowledge!

10

"Thou shalt not rob! Thou shalt not slay!"—such precepts were once called holy; before them did one bow the knee and the head, and take off one's shoes.

But I ask you: Where have there ever been better robbers and slayers in the world than such holy precepts?

Is there not even in all life—robbing and slaying? And for such precepts to be called holy, was not *truth* itself thereby—slain?

—Or was it a sermon of death that called holy what contradicted and dissuaded from life?—O my brethren, break up, break up for me the old tables!

11

It is my sympathy with all the past that I see it is abandoned,—

—Abandoned to the favour, the spirit and the madness of every generation that cometh, and reinterpreteth all that hath been as its bridge!

A great potentate might arise, an artful prodigy, who with approval and disapproval could strain and constrain all the past, until it became for him a bridge, a harbinger, a herald, and a cock-crowing.

This however is the other danger, and mine other sympathy:
—he who is of the populace, his thoughts go back to his grand-father,—with his grandfather, however, doth time cease.

Thus is all the past abandoned: for it might some day happen for the populace to become master, and drown all time in shallow waters.

Therefore, O my brethren, a *new nobility* is needed, which shall be the adversary of all populace and potentate rule, and shall inscribe anew the word "noble" on new tables.

For many noble ones are needed, and many kinds of noble ones, *for a new nobility!* Or, as I once said in parable: "That is just divinity, that there are gods, but no God!"

12

O my brethren, I consecrate you and point you to a new nobility: ye shall become procreators and cultivators and sowers of the future;—

—Verily, not to a nobility which ye could purchase like traders with traders' gold; for little worth is all that hath its price.

Let it not be your honour henceforth whence ye come, but whither ye go! Your Will and your feet which seek to surpass you—let these be your new honour!

Verily, not that ye have served a prince—of what account are princes now!—nor that ye have become a bulwark to that which standeth, that it may stand more firmly.

Not that your family have become courtly at courts, and that ye have learned—gay-coloured, like the flamingo—to stand long hours in shallow pools:

(For *ability*-to-stand is a merit in courtiers; and all courtiers believe that unto blessedness after death pertaineth—*permission*-to-sit!*)

Nor even that a Spirit called Holy, led your forefathers into promised lands, which I do not praise: for where the worst of all trees grew—the cross,—in that land there is nothing to praise!—

—And verily, wherever this "Holy Spirit" led its knights, always in such campaigns did—goats and geese, and wry-heads and guy-heads run *foremost!*—

O my brethren, not backward shall your nobility gaze, but *outward!* Exiles shall ye be from all fatherlands and forefatherlands!

Your *children's land* shall ye love: let this love be your new nobility,—the undiscovered in the remotest seas! For it do I bid your sails search and search!

Unto your children shall ye *make amends* for being the children of your fathers: all the past shall ye *thus* redeem! This new table do I place over you!

13

"Why should one live? All is vain! To live—that is to thresh straw; to live—that is to burn oneself and yet not get warm."—

Such ancient babbling still passeth for "wisdom"; because it is old, however, and smelleth mustily, *therefore* is it the more honoured. Even mould ennobleth.—

Children might thus speak: they *shun* the fire because it hath burnt them! There is much childishness in the old books of wisdom.

And he who ever "thresheth straw," why should he be allowed to rail at threshing! Such a fool one would have to muzzle!

Such persons sit down to the table and bring nothing with them, not even good hunger:—and then do they rail: "All is vain!"

But to eat and drink well, my brethren, is verily no vain art! Break up, break up for me the tables of the never-joyous ones!

14

"To the clean are all things clean"—thus say the people. I, however, say unto you: To the swine all things become swinish!

Therefore preach the visionaries and bowed-heads (whose hearts are also bowed down): "The world itself is a filthy monster."

For these are all unclean spirits; especially those, however, who have no peace or rest, unless they see the world *from the backside*—the backworldsmen!

To those do I say it to the face, although it sound unpleasantly: the world resembleth man, in that it hath a backside,— *so much* is true!

There is in the world much filth: *so much* is true! But the world itself is not therefore a filthy monster!

There is wisdom in the fact that much in the world smelleth badly: loathing itself createth wings, and fountain-divining powers!

In the best there is still something to loathe; and the best is still something that must be surpassed!—

O my brethren, there is much wisdom in the fact that much filth is in the world!—

15

Such sayings did I hear pious backworldsmen speak to their consciences, and verily without wickedness or guile,—although there is nothing more guileful in the world, or more wicked.

"Let the world be as it is! Raise not a finger against it!"

"Let whoever will choke and stab and skin and scrape the people: raise not a finger against it! Thereby will they learn to renounce the world."

"And thine own reason—this shalt thou thyself stifle and choke; for it is a reason of this world,—thereby wilt thou learn thyself to renounce the world."—

—Shatter, shatter, O my brethren, those old tables of the pious! Tatter the maxims of the world-maligners!—

16

"He who learneth much unlearneth all violent cravings"—that do people now whisper to one another in all the dark lanes.

"Wisdom wearieth, nothing is worth while; thou shalt not crave!"—this new table found I hanging even in the public markets.

Break up for me, O my brethren, break up also that *new* table! The weary-o'-the-world put it up, and the preachers of death and the jailer: for lo, it is also a sermon for slavery:—

Because they learned badly and not the best, and everything too early and everything too fast; because they *ate* badly: from thence hath resulted their ruined stomach;—

—For a ruined stomach, is their spirit: *it* persuadeth to death! For verily, my brethren, the spirit *is* a stomach!

Life is a well of delight, but to him in whom the ruined stomach speaketh, the father of affliction, all fountains are poisoned.

To discern: that is *delight* to the lion-willed! But he who hath become weary, is himself merely "willed"; with him play all the waves.

And such is always the nature of weak men: they lose themselves on their way. And at last asketh their weariness: "Why did we ever go on the way? All is indifferent!"

To them soundeth it pleasant to have preached in their ears: "Nothing is worth while! Ye shall not will!" That, however, is a sermon for slavery.

O my brethren, a fresh blustering wind cometh Zarathustra unto all way-weary ones; many noses will he yet make sneeze!

Even through walls bloweth my free breath, and into prisons and imprisoned spirits!

Willing emancipateth: for willing is creating: so do I teach. And *only* for creating shall ye learn!

And also the learning shall ye *learn* only from me, the learning well!—He who hath ears let him hear!

17

There standeth the boat—thither goeth it over, perhaps into vast nothingness—but who willeth to enter into this "Perhaps"?

None of you want to enter into the death-boat! How should ye then be *world-weary* ones!

World-weary ones! And have not even withdrawn from the

earth! Eager did I ever find you for the earth, amorous still of your own earth-weariness!

Not in vain doth your lip hang down:—a small worldly wish still sitteth thereon! And in your eye—floateth there not a cloudlet of unforgotten earthly bliss?

There are on the earth many good inventions, some useful, some pleasant: for their sake is the earth to be loved.

And many such good inventions are there, that they are like woman's breasts: useful at the same time, and pleasant.

Ye world-weary ones, however! Ye earth-idlers! You, shall one beat with stripes! With stripes shall one again make you sprightly limbs.

For if ye be not invalids, or decrepit creatures, of whom the earth is weary, then are ye sly sloths, or dainty, sneaking pleasure-cats. And if ye will not again *run* gaily, then shall ye —pass away!

To the incurable shall one not seek to be a physician: thus teacheth Zarathustra:—so shall ye pass away!

But more *courage* is needed to make an end than to make a new verse: that do all physicians and poets know well.—

18

O my brethren, there are tables which weariness framed, and tables which slothfulness framed, corrupt slothfulness: although they speak similarly, they want to be heard differently.—

See this languishing one! Only a span-breadth is he from his goal; but from weariness hath he lain down obstinately in the dust, this brave one!

From weariness yawneth he at the path, at the earth, at the

goal, and at himself: not a step further will he go,—this brave one!

Now gloweth the sun upon him, and the dogs lick at his sweat: but he lieth there in his obstinacy and preferreth to languish:—

—A span-breadth from his goal, to languish! Verily, ye will have to drag him into his heaven by the hair of his head— this hero!

Better still that ye let him lie where he hath lain down, that sleep may come unto him, the comforter, with cooling patter-rain.

Let him lie, until of his own accord he awakeneth,—until of his own accord he repudiateth all weariness, and what weariness hath taught through him!

Only, my brethren, see that ye scare the dogs away from him, the idle skulkers, and all the swarming vermin:—

—All the swarming vermin of the "cultured," that—feast on the sweat of every hero!—

19

I form circles around me and holy boundaries; ever fewer ascend with me ever higher mountains: I build a mountain-range out of ever holier mountains.—

But wherever ye would ascend with me, O my brethren, take care lest a *parasite* ascend with you!

A parasite: that is a reptile, a creeping, cringing reptile, that trieth to fatten on your infirm and sore places.

And *this* is its art: it divineth where ascending souls are weary, in your trouble and dejection, in your sensitive modesty, doth it build its loathsome nest.

Where the strong are weak, where the noble are all-too-gentle—there buildeth it its loathsome nest; the parasite liveth where the great have small sore-places.

What is the highest of all species of being, and what is the lowest? The parasite is the lowest species; he, however, who is of the highest species feedeth most parasites.

For the soul which hath the longest ladder, and can go deepest down: how could there fail to be most parasites upon it?—

—The most comprehensive soul, which can run and stray and rove furthest in itself; the most necessary soul, which out of joy flingeth itself into chance:—

—The soul in Being, which plungeth into Becoming; the possessing soul, which *seeketh* to attain desire and longing:—

—The soul fleeing from itself, which overtaketh itself in the widest circuit; the wisest soul, unto which folly speaketh most sweetly:—

—The soul most self-loving, in which all things have their current and counter-current, their ebb and their flow:—oh, how could *the loftiest soul* fail to have the worst parasites?

20

O my brethren, am I then cruel? But I say: What falleth, that shall one also push!

Everything of today—it falleth, it decayeth; who would preserve it! But I—I wish also to push it!

Know ye the delight which rolleth stones into precipitous depths?—Those men of today, see just how they roll into my depths!

A prelude am I to better players, O my brethren! An example! *Do* according to mine example!

And him whom ye do not teach to fly, teach I pray you—*to fall faster!*—

21

I love the brave: but it is not enough to be a swordsman,—one must also know *whereon* to use swordsmanship!

And often is it greater bravery to keep quiet and pass by, that *thereby* one may reserve oneself for a worthier foe!

Ye shall only have foes to be hated; but not foes to be despised: ye must be proud of your foes. Thus have I already taught.

For the worthier foe, O my brethren, shall ye reserve yourselves: therefore must ye pass by many a one,—

—Especially many of the rabble, who din your ears with noise about people and peoples.

Keep your eye clear of their For and Against! There is there much right, much wrong: he who looketh on becometh wroth.

Therein viewing, therein hewing—they are the same thing: therefore depart into the forests and lay your sword to sleep!

Go *your* ways! and let the people and peoples go theirs!—gloomy ways, verily, on which not a single hope glinteth any more!

Let there the trader rule, where all that still glittereth is—traders' gold. It is the time of kings no longer: that which now calleth itself the people is unworthy of kings.

See how these peoples themselves now do just like the traders: they pick up the smallest advantage out of all kinds of rubbish!

They lay lures for one another, they lure things out of one another,—that they call "good neighbourliness." O blessed remote period when a people said to itself: "I will be—*master* over peoples!"

For, my brethren, the best shall rule, the best also *willeth* to rule! And where the teaching is different, there—the best *is lacking*.

22

If *they* had—bread for nothing, alas! for what would *they* cry! Their maintainment—that is their true entertainment; and they shall have it hard!

Beasts of prey, are they: in their "working"—there is even plundering, in their "earning"—there is even over-reaching! Therefore shall they have it hard!

Better beasts of prey shall they thus become, subtler, cleverer, *more man-like:* for man is the best beast of prey.

All the animals hath man already robbed of their virtues: that is why of all animals it hath been hardest for man.

Only the birds are still beyond him. And if man should yet learn to fly, alas! *to what height*—would his rapacity fly!

23

Thus would I have man and woman: fit for war, the one; fit for maternity, the other; both, however, fit for dancing with head and legs.

And lost be the day to us in which a measure hath not been danced. And false be every truth which hath not had laughter along with it!

24

Your marriage-arranging: see that it be not a bad *arranging!* Ye have arranged too hastily: so there *followeth* therefrom—marriage-breaking!

And better marriage-breaking than marriage-bending, marriage-lying!—Thus spake a woman unto me: "Indeed, I broke the marriage, but first did the marriage break—me!"

The badly paired found I ever the most revengeful: they make every one suffer for it that they no longer run singly.

On that account want I the honest ones to say to one another: "We love each other: let us *see to it* that we maintain our love! Or shall our pledging be blundering?"

—"Give us a set term and a small marriage, that we may see if we are fit for the great marriage! It is a great matter always to be twain."

Thus do I counsel all honest ones; and what would be my love to the Superman, and to all that is to come, if I should counsel and speak otherwise!

Not only to propagate yourselves onwards but *upwards*—thereto, O my brethren, may the garden of marriage help you!

25

He who hath grown wise concerning old origins, lo, he will at last seek after the fountains of the future and new origins.—

O my brethren, not long will it be until *new peoples* shall arise and new fountains shall rush down into new depths.

For the earthquake—it choketh up many wells, it causeth much languishing: but it bringeth also to light inner powers and secrets.

The earthquake discloseth new fountains. In the earthquake of old peoples new fountains burst forth.

And whoever calleth out: "Lo, here is a well for many thirsty ones, one heart for many longing ones, one will for many instruments":—around him collecteth a *people,* that is to say, many attempting ones.

Who can command, who must obey—*that is there attempted!* Ah, with what long seeking and solving and failing and learning and re-attempting!

Human society: it is an attempt—so I teach—a long seeking: it seeketh however the ruler!—

—An attempt, my brethren! And *no* "contract"! Destroy, I pray you, destroy that word of the soft-hearted and half-and-half!

26

O my brethren! With whom lieth the greatest danger to the whole human future? Is it not with the good and just?—

—As those who say and feel in their hearts: "We already know what is good and just, we possess it also; woe to those who still seek thereafter!"

And whatever harm the wicked may do, the harm of the good is the harmfulest harm!

And whatever harm the world-maligners may do, the harm of the good is the harmfulest harm!

O my brethren, into the hearts of the good and just looked some one once on a time, who said: "They are the Pharisees." But people did not understand him.

The good and just themselves were not free to understand him; their spirit was imprisoned in their good conscience. The stupidity of the good is unfathomably wise.

[237]

It is the truth, however, that the good *must* be Pharisees—
they have no choice!

The good *must* crucify him who deviseth his own virtue!
That *is* the truth!

The second one, however, who discovered their country—
the country, heart and soil of the good and just,—it was he
who asked: "Whom do they hate most?"

The *creator,* hate they most, him who breaketh the tables
and old values, the breaker,—him they call the law-breaker.

For the good—they *cannot* create; they are always the beginning of the end:—

—They crucify him who writeth new values on new tables,
they sacrifice *unto themselves* the future—they crucify the
whole human future!

The good—they have always been the beginning of the
end.—

27

O my brethren, have ye also understood this word? And
what I once said of the "last man"?— —

With whom lieth the greatest danger to the whole human
future? Is it not with the good and just?

Break up, break up, I pray you, the good and just!—O my
brethren, have ye understood also this word?

28

Ye flee from me? Ye are frightened? Ye tremble at this
word?

O my brethren, when I enjoined you to break up the good, and the tables of the good, then only did I embark man on his high seas.

And now only cometh unto him the great terror, the great outlook, the great sickness, the great nausea, the great sea-sickness.

False shores and false securities did the good teach you; in the lies of the good were ye born and bred. Everything hath been radically contorted and distorted by the good.

But he who discovered the country of "man," discovered also the country of "man's future." Now shall ye be sailors for me, brave, patient!

Keep yourselves up betimes, my brethren, learn to keep yourselves up! The sea stormeth: many seek to raise themselves again by you.

The sea stormeth: all is in the sea. Well! Cheer up! Ye old seaman-hearts!

What of fatherland! *Thither* striveth our helm where our *children's land* is! Thitherwards, stormier than the sea, stormeth our great longing!—

29

"Why so hard!"—said to the diamond one day the charcoal; "are we then not near relatives?"—

Why so soft? O my brethren; thus do *I* ask you: are ye then not—my brethren?

Why so soft, so submissive and yielding? Why is there so much negation and abnegation in your hearts? Why is there so little fate in your looks?

[239]

And if ye will not be fates and inexorable ones, how can ye one day—conquer with me?

And if your hardness will not glance and cut and chip to pieces, how can ye one day—create with me?

For the creators are hard. And blessedness must it seem to you to press your hand upon millenniums as upon wax,—

—Blessedness to write upon the will of millenniums as upon brass,—harder than brass, nobler than brass. Entirely hard is only the noblest.

This new table, O my brethren, put I up over you: *Become hard!*—

30

O thou, my Will! Thou change of every need, *my* needfulness! Preserve me from all small victories!

Thou fatedness of my soul, which I call fate! Thou In-me! Over-me! Preserve and spare me for one great fate!

And thy last greatness, my Will, spare it for thy last—that thou mayest be inexorable *in* thy victory! Ah, who hath not succumbed to his victory!

Ah, whose eye hath not bedimmed in this intoxicated twilight! Ah, whose foot hath not faltered and forgotten in victory—how to stand!—

—That I may one day be ready and ripe in the great noontide: ready and ripe like the glowing ore, the lightning-bearing cloud, and the swelling milk-udder:—

—Ready for myself and for my most hidden Will: a bow eager for its arrow, an arrow eager for its star:—

—A star, ready and ripe in its noontide, glowing, pierced, blessed, by annihilating sun-arrows:—

[*240*]

—A sun itself, and an inexorable sun-will, ready for annihilation in victory!

O Will, thou change of every need, *my* needfulness! Spare
me for one great victory!———

Thus spake Zarathustra.

57. *The Convalescent*

1

ONE morning, not long after his return to his cave, Zarathustra sprang up from his couch like a madman, crying with a
frightful voice, and acting as if some one still lay on the couch
who did not wish to rise. Zarathustra's voice also resounded
in such a manner that his animals came to him frightened, and
out of all the neighbouring caves and lurking-places all the
creatures slipped away—flying, fluttering, creeping or leaping,
according to their variety of foot or wing. Zarathustra, however, spake these words:

Up, abysmal thought out of my depth! I am thy cock and
morning dawn, thou overslept reptile: Up! Up! My voice shall
soon crow thee awake!

Unbind the fetters of thine ears: listen! For I wish to hear
thee! Up! Up! There is thunder enough to make the very graves
listen!

And rub the sleep and all the dimness and blindness out of

thine eyes! Hear me also with thine eyes: my voice is a medicine even for those born blind.

And once thou art awake, then shalt thou ever remain awake. It is not *my* custom to awake great-grandmothers out of their sleep that I may bid them—sleep on!

Thou stirrest, stretchest thyself, wheezest? Up! Up! Not wheeze, shalt thou,—but speak unto me! Zarathustra calleth thee, Zarathustra the godless!

I, Zarathustra, the advocate of living, the advocate of suffering, the advocate of the circuit—thee do I call, my most abysmal thought!

Joy to me! Thou comest,—I hear thee! Mine abyss *speaketh*, my lowest depth have I turned over into the light!

Joy to me! Come hither! Give me thy hand— —ha! let be! aha!— —Disgust, disgust, disgust— — —alas to me!

2

Hardly, however, had Zarathustra spoken these words, when he fell down as one dead, and remained long as one dead. When however he again came to himself, then was he pale and trembling, and remained lying; and for long he would neither eat nor drink. This condition continued for seven days; his animals, however, did not leave him day nor night, except that the eagle flew forth to fetch food. And what it fetched and foraged, it laid on Zarathustra's couch: so that Zarathustra at last lay among yellow and red berries, grapes, rosy apples, sweet-smelling herbage, and pine-cones. At his feet, however, two lambs were stretched, which the eagle had with difficulty carried off from their shepherds.

At last, after seven days, Zarathustra raised himself upon his couch, took a rosy apple in his hand, smelt it and found its smell pleasant. Then did his animals think the time had come to speak unto him.

"O Zarathustra," said they, "now hast thou lain thus for seven days with heavy eyes: wilt thou not set thyself again upon thy feet?

Step out of thy cave: the world waiteth for thee as a garden. The wind playeth with heavy fragrance which seeketh for thee; and all brooks would like to run after thee.

All things long for thee, since thou hast remained alone for seven days—step forth out of thy cave! All things want to be thy physicians!

Did perhaps a new knowledge come to thee, a bitter, grievous knowledge? Like leavened dough layest thou, thy soul arose and swelled beyond all its bounds.—"

—O mine animals, answered Zarathustra, talk on thus and let me listen! It refresheth me so to hear your talk: where there is talk, there is the world as a garden unto me.

How charming it is that there are words and tones; are not words and tones rainbows and seeming bridges 'twixt the eternally separated?

To each soul belongeth another world; to each soul is every other soul a back-world.

Among the most alike doth semblance deceive most delightfully: for the smallest gap is most difficult to bridge over.

For me—how could there be an outside-of-me? There is no outside! But this we forget on hearing tones; how delightful it is that we forget!

Have not names and tones been given unto things that man may refresh himself with them? It is a beautiful folly, speaking; therewith danceth man over everything.

How lovely is all speech and all falsehoods of tones! With tones danceth our love on variegated rainbows.——

——"O Zarathustra," said then his animals, "to those who think like us, things all dance themselves: they come and hold out the hand and laugh and flee—and return.

Everything goeth, everything returneth; eternally rolleth the wheel of existence. Everything dieth, everything blossometh forth again; eternally runneth on the year of existence.

Everything breaketh, everything is integrated anew; eternally buildeth itself the same house of existence. All things separate, all things again greet one another; eternally true to itself remaineth the ring of existence.

Every moment beginneth existence, around every 'Here' rolleth the ball 'There.' The middle is everywhere. Crooked is the path of eternity."——

——O ye wags and barrel-organs! answered Zarathustra, and smiled once more, how well do ye know what had to be fulfilled in seven days:——

——And how that monster crept into my throat and choked me! But I bit off its head and spat it away from me.

And ye—ye have made a lyre-lay out of it? Now, however, do I lie here, still exhausted with that biting and spitting-away, still sick with mine own salvation.

And ye looked on at it all? O mine animals, are ye also cruel? Did ye like to look at my great pain as men do? For man is the cruellest animal.

At tragedies, bull-fights, and crucifixions hath he hitherto been happiest on earth; and when he invented his hell, behold, that was his heaven on earth.

When the great man crieth—: immediately runneth the little man thither, and his tongue hangeth out of his mouth for very lusting. He, however, calleth it his "pity."

The little man, especially the poet—how passionately doth he accuse life in words! Hearken to him, but do not fail to hear the delight which is in all accusation!

Such accusers of life—them life overcometh with a glance of the eye. "Thou lovest me?" saith the insolent one; "wait a little, as yet have I no time for thee."

Towards himself man is the cruellest animal; and in all who call themselves "sinners" and "bearers of the cross" and "penitents," do not overlook the voluptuousness in their plaints and accusations!

And I myself—do, I thereby want to be man's accuser? Ah, mine animals, this only have I learned hitherto, that for man his baddest is necessary for his best,—

—That all that is baddest is the best *power,* and the hardest stone for the highest creator; and that man must become better *and* badder:—

Not to *this* torture-stake was I tied, that I know man is bad, —but I cried, as no one hath yet cried:

"Ah, that his baddest is so very small! Ah, that his best is so very small!"

The great disgust at man—*it* strangled me and had crept into my throat: and what the soothsayer had presaged: "All is alike, nothing is worth while, knowledge strangleth."

A long twilight limped on before me, a fatally weary, fatally intoxicated sadness, which spake with yawning mouth.

"Eternally he returneth, the man of whom thou art weary, the small man"—so yawned my sadness, and dragged its foot and could not go to sleep.

A cavern, became the human earth to me; its breast caved in; everything living became to me human dust and bones and mouldering past.

My sighing sat on all human graves, and could no longer

arise: my sighing and questioning croaked and choked, and gnawed and nagged day and night:

—"Ah, man returneth eternally! The small man returneth eternally!"

Naked had I once seen both of them, the greatest man and the smallest man: all too like one another—all too human, even the greatest man!

All too small, even the greatest man!—that was my disgust at man! And the eternal return also of the smallest man!—that was my disgust at all existence!

Ah, Disgust! Disgust! Disgust!— —Thus spake Zarathustra, and sighed and shuddered; for he remembered his sickness. Then did his animals prevent him from speaking further.

"Do not speak further, thou convalescent!"—so answered his animals, "but go out where the world waiteth for thee like a garden.

Go out unto the roses, the bees, and the flocks of doves! Especially, however, unto the singing-birds, to learn *singing* from them!

For singing is for the convalescent; the sound ones may talk. And when the sound also want songs, then want they other songs than the convalescent."

—"O ye wags and barrel-organs, do be silent!" answered Zarathustra, and smiled at his animals. "How well ye know what consolation I devised for myself in seven days!

That I have to sing once more—*that* consolation did I devise for myself, and *this* convalescence: would ye also make another lyre-lay thereof?"

—"Do not talk further," answered his animals once more; "rather, thou convalescent, prepare for thyself first a lyre, a new lyre!

For behold, O Zarathustra! For thy new lays there are needed new lyres.

Sing and bubble over, O Zarathustra, heal thy soul with new lays: that thou mayest bear thy great fate, which hath not yet been any one's fate!

For thine animals know it well, O Zarathustra, who thou art and must become: behold, *thou art the teacher of the eternal return,*—that is now *thy* fate!

That thou must be the first to teach this teaching—how could this great fate not be thy greatest danger and infirmity!

Behold, we know what thou teachest: that all things eternally return, and ourselves with them, and that we have already existed times without number, and all things with us.

Thou teachest that there is a great year of Becoming, a prodigy of a great year; it must, like a sand-glass, ever turn up anew, that it may anew run down and run out:—

—So that all those years are like one another in the greatest and also in the smallest, so that we ourselves, in every great year, are like ourselves in the greatest and also in the smallest.

And if thou wouldst now die, O Zarathustra, behold, we know also how thou wouldst then speak to thyself:—but thine animals beseech thee not to die yet!

Thou wouldst speak, and without trembling, buoyant rather with bliss, for a great weight and worry would be taken from thee, thou patientest one!—

'Now do I die and disappear,' wouldst thou say, 'and in a moment I am nothing. Souls are as mortal as bodies.

But the plexus of causes returneth in which I am intertwined,—it will again create me! I myself pertain to the causes of the eternal return.

I come again with this sun, with this earth, with this eagle, with this serpent—*not* to a new life, or a better life, or a similar life:

—I come again eternally to this identical and selfsame life, in its greatest and its smallest, to teach again the eternal return of all things,—

—To speak again the word of the great noontide of earth and man, to announce again to man the Superman.

I have spoken my word. I break down by my word: so willeth mine eternal fate—as announcer do I succumb!

The hour hath now come for the down-goer to bless himself. Thus—*endeth* Zarathustra's down-going.' "——

When the animals had spoken these words they were silent and waited, so that Zarathustra might say something to them; but Zarathustra did not hear that they were silent. On the contrary, he lay quietly with closed eyes like a person sleeping, although he did not sleep; for he communed just then with his soul. The serpent, however, and the eagle, when they found him silent in such wise, respected the great stillness around him, and prudently retired.

58. The Great Longing

O MY soul, I have taught thee to say "today" as "once on a time" and "formerly," and to dance thy measure over every Here and There and Yonder.

O my soul, I delivered thee from all by-places, I brushed down from thee dust and spiders and twilight.

O my soul, I washed the petty shame and the by-place virtue

[*248*]

from thee, and persuaded thee to stand naked before the eyes of the sun.

With the storm that is called "spirit" did I blow over thy surging sea; all clouds did I blow away from it; I strangled even the strangler called "sin."

O my soul, I gave thee the right to say Nay like the storm, and to say Yea as the open heaven saith Yea: calm as the light remainest thou, and now walkest through denying storms.

O my soul, I restored to thee liberty over the created and the uncreated; and who knoweth, as thou knowest, the voluptuousness of the future?

O my soul, I taught thee the contempt which doth not come like worm-eating, the great, the loving contempt, which loveth most where it contemneth most.

O my soul, I taught thee so to persuade that thou persuadest even the grounds themselves to thee: like the sun, which persuadeth even the sea to its height.

O my soul, I have taken from thee all obeying and knee-bending and homage-paying; I have myself given thee the names, "Change of need" and "Fate."

O my soul, I have given thee new names and gay-coloured playthings, I have called thee "Fate" and "the Circuit of circuits" and "the Navel-string of time" and "the Azure bell."

O my soul, to thy domain gave I all wisdom to drink all new wines, and also all immemorially old strong wines of wisdom.

O my soul, every sun shed I upon thee, and every night and every silence and every longing:—then grewest thou up for me as a vine.

O my soul, exuberant and heavy dost thou now stand forth, a vine with swelling udders and full clusters of brown golden grapes:—

—Filled and weighted by thy happiness, waiting from superabundance, and yet ashamed of thy waiting.

O my soul, there is nowhere a soul which could be more loving and more comprehensive and more extensive! Where could future and past be closer together than with thee?

O my soul, I have given thee everything, and all my hands have become empty by thee:—and now! Now sayest thou to me, smiling and full of melancholy: "Which of us oweth thanks?—

—Doth the giver not owe thanks because the receiver received? Is bestowing not a necessity? Is receiving not—pitying?"

O my soul, I understand the smiling of thy melancholy: thine over-abundance itself now stretcheth out longing hands!

Thy fulness looketh forth over raging seas, and seeketh and waiteth: the longing of over-fulness looketh forth from the smiling heaven of thine eyes!

And verily, O my soul! Who could see thy smiling and not melt into tears? The angels themselves melt into tears through the over-graciousness of thy smiling.

Thy graciousness and over-graciousness, is it which will not complain and weep: and yet, O my soul, longeth thy smiling for tears, and thy trembling mouth for sobs.

"Is not all weeping complaining? And all complaining, accusing?" Thus speakest thou to thyself; and therefore, O my soul, wilt thou rather smile than pour forth thy grief—

—Than in gushing tears pour forth all thy grief concerning thy fulness, and concerning the craving of the vine for the vintager and vintage-knife!

But wilt thou not weep, wilt thou not weep forth thy purple melancholy, then wilt thou have to *sing,* O my soul!—Behold, I smile myself, who foretell thee this:

[*250*]

—Thou wilt have to sing with passionate song, until all seas turn calm to hearken unto thy longing,—

—Until over calm longing seas the bark glideth, the golden marvel, around the gold of which all good, bad, and marvellous things frisk:—

—Also many large and small animals, and everything that hath light marvellous feet, so that it can run on violet-blue paths,—

—Towards the golden marvel, the spontaneous bark, and its master: he, however, is the vintager who waiteth with the diamond vintage-knife,—

—Thy great deliverer, O my soul, the nameless one—for whom future songs only will find names! And verily, already hath thy breath the fragrance of future songs,—

—Already glowest thou and dreamest, already drinkest thou thirstily at all deep echoing wells of consolation, already reposeth thy melancholy in the bliss of future songs!— —

O my soul, now have I given thee all, and even my last possession, and all my hands have become empty by thee: —*that I bade thee sing,* behold, that was my last thing to give!

That I bade thee sing,—say now, say: *which* of us now—oweth thanks?—Better still, however: sing unto me, sing, O my soul! And let me thank thee!—

Thus spake Zarathustra.

59. *The Second Dance Song*

1

"INTO thine eyes gazed I lately, O Life: gold saw I gleam in thy night-eyes,—my heart stood still with delight:

—A golden bark saw I gleam on darkened waters, a sinking, drinking, reblinking, golden swing-bark!

At my dance-frantic foot, dost thou cast a glance, a laughing, questioning, melting, thrown glance:

Twice only movedst thou thy rattle with thy little hands— then did my feet swing with dance-fury.—

My heels reared aloft, my toes they hearkened,—thee they would know: hath not the dancer his ear—in his toe!

Unto thee did I spring: then fledst thou back from my bound; and towards me waved thy fleeing, flying tresses round!

Away from thee did I spring, and from thy snaky tresses: then stoodst thou there half-turned, and in thine eye caresses.

With crooked glances—dost thou teach me crooked courses; on crooked courses learn my feet—crafty fancies!

I fear thee near, I love thee far; thy flight allureth me, thy seeking secureth me:—I suffer, but for thee, what would I not gladly bear!

For thee, whose coldness inflameth, whose hatred misleadeth, whose flight enchaineth, whose mockery—pleadeth:

—Who would not hate thee, thou great bindress, in-windress, temptress, seekress, findress! Who would not love thee, thou innocent, impatient, wind-swift, child-eyed sinner!

Whither pullest thou me now, thou paragon and tomboy? And now foolest thou me fleeing; thou sweet romp dost annoy!

I dance after thee, I follow even faint traces lonely. Where
art thou? Give me thy hand! Or thy finger only!

Here are caves and thickets: we shall go astray!—Halt!
Stand still! Seest thou not owls and bats in fluttering fray?

Thou bat! Thou owl! Thou wouldst play me foul? Where
are we? From the dogs hast thou learned thus to bark and howl.

Thou gnashest on me sweetly with little white teeth; thine
evil eyes shoot out upon me, thy curly little mane from under
neath!

This is a dance over stock and stone: I am the hunter,—wilt
thou be my hound, or my chamois anon?

Now beside me! And quickly, wickedly springing! Now up!
And over!—Alas! I have fallen myself overswinging!

Oh, see me lying, thou arrogant one, and imploring grace!
Gladly would I walk with thee—in some lovelier place!

—In the paths of love, through bushes variegated, quiet,
trim! Or there along the lake, where gold-fishes dance and
swim!

Thou art now a-weary? There above are sheep and sun-set
stripes: is it not sweet to sleep—the shepherd pipes?

Thou art so very weary? I carry thee thither; let just thine
arm sink! And art thou thirsty—I should have something; but
thy mouth would not like it to drink!—

—Oh, that cursed, nimble, supple serpent and lurking-
witch! Where art thou gone? But in my face do I feel through
thy hand, two spots and red blotches itch!

I am verily weary of it, ever thy sheepish shepherd to be.
Thou witch, if I have hitherto sung unto thee, now shalt *thou*
—cry unto me!

To the rhythm of my whip shalt thou dance and cry! I forget not my whip?—Not I!"—

[*253*]

Then did Life answer me thus, and kept thereby her fine ears closed:

"O Zarathustra! Crack not so terribly with thy whip! Thou knowest surely that noise killeth thought,—and just now there came to me such delicate thoughts.

We are both of us genuine ne'er-do-wells and ne'er-do-ills. Beyond good and evil found we our island and our green meadow—we two alone! Therefore must we be friendly to each other!

And even should we not love each other from the bottom of our hearts,—must we then have a grudge against each other if we do not love each other perfectly?

And that I am friendly to thee, and often too friendly, that knowest thou: and the reason is that I am envious of thy Wisdom. Ah, this mad old fool, Wisdom!

If thy Wisdom should one day run away from thee, ah! then would also my love run away from thee quickly."—

Thereupon did Life look thoughtfully behind and around, and said softly: "O Zarathustra, thou art not faithful enough to me!

Thou lovest me not nearly so much as thou sayest; I know thou thinkest of soon leaving me.

There is an old heavy, heavy, booming-clock: it boometh by night up to thy cave:—

—When thou hearest this clock strike the hours at midnight, then thinkest thou between one and twelve thereon—

—Thou thinkest thereon, O Zarathustra, I know it—of soon leaving me!"—

"Yea," answered I, hesitatingly, "but thou knowest it also"
—And I said something into her ear, in amongst her confused,
yellow, foolish tresses.

"Thou *knowest* that, O Zarathustra? That knoweth no
one— —"

And we gazed at each other, and looked at the green
meadow o'er which the cool evening was just passing, and we
wept together.—Then, however, was Life dearer unto me than
all my Wisdom had ever been.—

Thus spake Zarathustra.

3

One!

O man! Take heed!

Two!

What saith deep midnight's voice indeed?

Three!

"I slept my sleep—

Four!

"From deepest dream I've woke and plead:—

Five!

"The world is deep,

Six!

"And deeper than the day could read.

[255]

Seven!

"Deep is its woe—

Eight!

"Joy—deeper still than grief can be:

Nine!

"Woe saith: Hence! Go!

Ten!

"But joys all want eternity—

Eleven!

"Want deep profound eternity!"

Twelve!

60. *The Seven Seals*

(OR THE YEA AND AMEN LAY.)

1

IF I be a diviner and full of the divining spirit which wan
dereth on high mountain-ridges, 'twixt two seas,—

Wandereth 'twixt the past and the future as a heavy cloud—
hostile to sultry plains, and to all that is weary and can neither
die nor live:

Ready for lightning in its dark bosom, and for the redeeming flash of light, charged with lightnings which say Yea! which laugh Yea! ready for divining flashes of lightning:—

—Blessed, however, is he who is thus charged! And verily, long must he hang like a heavy tempest on the mountain, who shall one day kindle the light of the future!—

Oh, how could I not be ardent for Eternity and for the marriage-ring of rings—the ring of the return?

Never yet have I found the woman by whom I should like to have children, unless it be this woman whom I love: for I love thee, O Eternity!

For I love thee, O Eternity!

2
———

If ever my wrath hath burst graves, shifted landmarks, or rolled old shattered tables into precipitous depths:

If ever my scorn hath scattered mouldered words to the winds, and if I have come like a besom to cross-spiders, and as a cleansing wind to old charnel-houses:

If ever I have sat rejoicing where old gods lie buried, world-blessing, world-loving, beside the monuments of old world-maligners:—

—For even churches and gods'-graves do I love, if only heaven looketh through their ruined roofs with pure eyes; gladly do I sit like grass and red poppies on ruined churches—

Oh, how could I not be ardent for Eternity, and for the marriage-ring of rings—the ring of the return?

Never yet have I found the woman by whom I should like to have children, unless it be this woman whom I love: for I love thee, O Eternity!

For I love thee, O Eternity!

3

If ever a breath hath come to me of the creative breath, and of the heavenly necessity which compelleth even chances to dance star-dances:

If ever I have laughed with the laughter of the creative lightning, to which the long thunder of the deed followeth, grumblingly, but obediently:

If ever I have played dice with the gods at the divine table of the earth, so that the earth quaked and ruptured, and snorted forth fire-streams:—

—For a divine table is the earth, and trembling with new creative dictums and dice-casts of the gods:

Oh, how could I not be ardent for Eternity, and for the marriage-ring of rings—the ring of the return?

Never yet have I found the woman by whom I should like to have children, unless it be this woman whom I love: for I love thee, O Eternity!

For I love thee, O Eternity!

4

If ever I have drunk a full draught of the foaming spice- and confection-bowl in which all things are well mixed:

If ever my hand hath mingled the furthest with the nearest, fire with spirit, joy with sorrow, and the harshest with the kindest:

If I myself am a grain of the saving salt which maketh everything in the confection-bowl mix well:—

—For there is a salt which uniteth good with evil; and even the evilest is worthy, as spicing and as final over-foaming:—

Oh, how could I not be ardent for Eternity, and for the marriage-ring of rings—the ring of the return?

Never yet have I found the woman by whom I should like to have children, unless it be this woman whom I love: for I love thee, O Eternity!

For I love thee, O Eternity!

5

If I be fond of the sea, and all that is sealike, and fondest of it when it angrily contradicteth me:

If the exploring delight be in me, which impelleth sails to the undiscovered, if the seafarer's delight be in my delight:

If ever my rejoicing hath called out: "The shore hath vanished,—now hath fallen from me the last chain—

The boundless roareth around me, far away sparkle for me space and time,—well! cheer up! old heart!"—

Oh, how could I not be ardent for Eternity, and for the marriage-ring of rings—the ring of the return?

Never yet have I found the woman by whom I should like to have children, unless it be this woman whom I love: for I love thee, O Eternity!

For I love thee, O Eternity!

6

If my virtue be a dancer's virtue, and if I have often sprung with both feet into golden-emerald rapture:

If my wickedness be a laughing wickedness, at home among rose-banks and hedges of lilies:

—or in laughter is all evil present, but it is sanctified and absolved by its own bliss:—

And if it be my Alpha and Omega that everything heavy shall become light, everybody a dancer, and every spirit a bird: and verily, that is my Alpha and Omega!—

Oh, how could I not be ardent for Eternity, and for the marriage-ring of rings—the ring of the return?

Never yet have I found the woman by whom I should like to have children, unless it be this woman whom I love: for I love thee, O Eternity!

For I love thee, O Eternity!

7

If ever I have spread out a tranquil heaven above me, and have flown into mine own heaven with mine own pinions:

If I have swum playfully in profound luminous distances, and if my freedom's avian wisdom hath come to me:—

—Thus however speaketh avian wisdom:—"Lo, there is no above and no below! Throw thyself about,—outward, backward, thou light one! Sing! speak no more!

—Are not all words made for the heavy? Do not all words lie to the light ones? Sing! speak no more!"—

Oh, how could I not be ardent for Eternity, and for the marriage-ring of rings—the ring of the return?

Never yet have I found the woman by whom I should like to have children, unless it be this woman whom I love: for I love thee, O Eternity!

For I love thee, O Eternity!

THUS SPAKE ZARATHUSTRA

FOURTH AND LAST PART

Ah, where in the world have there been greater follies than with the pitiful? And what in the world hath caused more suffering than the follies of the pitiful?

Woe unto all loving ones who have not an elevation which is above their pity!

Thus spake the devil unto me, once on a time: "Ever God hath his hell: it is his love for man."

And lately did I hear him say these words: "God is dead: of his pity for man hath God died."—ZARATHUSTRA, II., "The Pitiful" (p. 102).

61. *The Honey Sacrifice*

—AND again passed moons and years over Zarathustra's soul,
and he heeded it not; his hair, however, became white. One
day when he sat on a stone in front of his cave, and gazed
calmly into the distance—one there gazeth out on the sea, and
away beyond sinuous abysses,—then went his animals thoughtfully round about him, and at last set themselves in front of
him.

"O Zarathustra," said they, "gazest thou out perhaps for thy
happiness?"—"Of what account is my happiness!" answered
he, "I have long ceased to strive any more for happiness, I
strive for my work."—"O Zarathustra," said the animals once
more, "that sayest thou as one who hath overmuch of good
things. Liest thou not in a sky-blue lake of happiness?"—"Ye
wags," answered Zarathustra, and smiled, "how well did ye
choose the simile! But ye know also that my happiness is heavy,
and not like a fluid wave of water: it presseth me and will not
leave me, and is like molten pitch."—

Then went his animals again thoughtfully around him, and
placed themselves once more in front of him. "O Zarathustra,"
said they, "it is consequently *for that reason* that thou thyself always becometh yellower and darker, although thy hair
looketh white and flaxen? Lo, thou sittest in thy pitch!"—
"What do ye say, mine animals?" said Zarathustra, laughing;
"verily I reviled when I spake of pitch. As it happeneth with

me, so is it with all fruits that turn ripe. It is the *honey* in my veins that maketh my blood thicker, and also my soul stiller."
—"So will it be, O Zarathustra," answered his animals, and pressed up to him; "but wilt thou not today ascend a high mountain? The air is pure, and today one seeth more of the world than ever."—"Yea, mine animals," answered he, "ye counsel admirably and according to my heart: I will today ascend a high mountain! But see that honey is there ready to hand, yellow, white, good, ice-cool, golden-comb-honey. For know that when aloft I will make the honey-sacrifice."—

When Zarathustra, however, was aloft on the summit, he sent his animals home that had accompanied him, and found that he was now alone:—then he laughed from the bottom of his heart, looked around him, and spake thus:

That I spake of sacrifices and honey-sacrifices, it was merely a ruse in talking and verily, a useful folly! Here aloft can I now speak freer than in front of mountain-caves and anchorites' domestic animals.

What to sacrifice! I squander what is given me, a squanderer with a thousand hands: how could I call that—sacrificing?

And when I desired honey I only desired bait, and sweet mucus and mucilage, for which even the mouths of growling bears, and strange, sulky, evil birds, water:

—The best bait, as huntsmen and fishermen require it. For if the world be as a gloomy forest of animals, and a pleasure-ground for all wild huntsmen, it seemeth to me rather—and preferably—a fathomless, rich sea;

—A sea full of many-hued fishes and crabs, for which even the gods might long, and might be tempted to become fishers in it, and casters of nets,—so rich is the world in wonderful things, great and small!

Especially the human world, the human sea:—towards *it* do I now throw out my golden angle-rod and say: Open up, thou human abyss!

Open up, and throw unto me thy fish and shining crabs! With my best bait shall I allure to myself today the strangest human fish!

—My happiness itself do I throw out into all places far and wide 'twixt orient, noontide, and occident, to see if many human fish will not learn to hug and tug at my happiness;—

Until, biting at my sharp hidden hooks, they have to come up unto *my* height, the motleyest abyss-groundlings, to the wickedest of all fishers of men.

For *this* am I from the heart and from the beginning—drawing, hither-drawing, upward-drawing, upbringing; a drawer, a trainer, a training-master, who not in vain counselled himself once on a time: "Become what thou art!"

Thus may men now come *up* to me; for as yet do I await the signs that it is time for my down-going; as yet do I not myself go down, as I must do, amongst men.

Therefore do I here wait, crafty and scornful upon high mountains, no impatient one, no patient one; rather one who hath even unlearnt patience,—because he no longer "suffereth."

For my fate giveth me time: it hath forgotten me perhaps? Or doth it sit behind a big stone and catch flies?

And verily, I am well-disposed to mine eternal fate, because it doth not hound and hurry me, but leaveth me time for merriment and mischief; so that I have to-day ascended this high mountain to catch fish.

Did ever any one catch fish upon high mountains? And though it be a folly what I here seek and do, it is better so than that down below I should become solemn with waiting, and green and yellow—

—A posturing wrath-snorter with waiting, a holy howl-storm from the mountains, an impatient one that shouteth down into the valleys: "Hearken, else I will scourge you with the scourge of God!"

Not that I would have a grudge against such wrathful ones on that account: they are well enough for laughter to me! Impatient must they now be, those big alarm-drums, which find a voice now or never!

Myself, however, and my fate—we do not talk to the Present, neither do we talk to the Never: for talking we have patience and time and more than time. For one day must it yet come, and may not pass by.

What must one day come and may not pass by? Our great Hazar, that is to say, our great, remote human-kingdom, the Zarathustra-kingdom of a thousand years— —

How remote may such "remoteness" be? What doth it concern me? But on that account it is none the less sure unto me—, with both feet stand I secure on this ground;

—On an eternal ground, on hard primary rock, on this highest, hardest, primary mountain-ridge, unto which all winds come, as unto the storm-parting, asking Where? and Whence? and Whither?

Here laugh, laugh, my hearty, healthy wickedness! From high mountains cast down thy glittering scorn-laughter! Allure for me with thy glittering the finest human fish!

And whatever belongeth unto *me* in all seas, my in-and-for-me in all things—fish *that* out for me, bring *that* up to me: for that do I wait, the wickedest of all fish-catchers.

Out! out! my fishing-hook! In and down, thou bait of my happiness! Drip thy sweetest dew, thou honey of my heart! Bite, my fishing-hook, into the belly of all black affliction!

Look out, look out, mine eye! Oh, how many seas round about me, what dawning human futures! And above me—what rosy red stillness! What unclouded silence!

62. The Cry of Distress

THE next day sat Zarathustra again on the stone in front of his cave, whilst his animals roved about in the world outside to bring home new food,—also new honey: for Zarathustra had spent and wasted the old honey to the very last particle. When he thus sat, however, with a stick in his hand, tracing the shadow of his figure on the earth, and reflecting—verily! not upon himself and his shadow,—all at once he startled and shrank back: for he saw another shadow beside his own. And when he hastily looked around and stood up, behold, there stood the soothsayer beside him, the same whom he had once given to eat and drink at his table, the proclaimer of the great weariness, who taught: "All is alike, nothing is worth while, the world is without meaning, knowledge strangleth." But his face had changed since then; and when Zarathustra looked into his eyes, his heart was startled once more: so much evil announcement and ashy-grey lightnings passed over that countenance.

The soothsayer, who had perceived what went on in Zarathustra's soul, wiped his face with his hand, as if he would wipe out the impression; the same did also Zarathustra. And when both of them had thus silently composed and strengthened themselves, they gave each other the hand, as a token that they wanted once more to recognise each other.

"Welcome hither," said Zarathustra, "thou soothsayer of the great weariness, not in vain shalt thou once have been my messmate and guest. Eat and drink also with me to-day, and forgive it that a cheerful old man sitteth with thee at table!"—"A cheerful old man?" answered the soothsayer, shaking his head, "but whoever thou art, or wouldst be, O Zarathustra, thou hast been here aloft the longest time,—in a little while thy bark shall no longer rest on dry land!"—"Do I then rest on dry land?"—asked Zarathustra, laughing.—"The waves around thy mountain," answered the soothsayer, "rise and rise, the waves of great distress and affliction: they will soon raise thy bark also and carry thee away."—Thereupon was Zarathustra silent and wondered.—"Dost thou still hear nothing?" continued the soothsayer: "doth it not rush and roar out of the depth?"—Zarathustra was silent once more and listened: then heard he a long, long cry, which the abysses threw to one another and passed on; for none of them wished to retain it: so evil did it sound.

"Thou ill announcer," said Zarathustra at last, "that is a cry of distress, and the cry of a man; it may come perhaps out of a black sea. But what doth human distress matter to me! My last sin which hath been reserved for me,—knowest thou what it is called?"

—"*Pity!*" answered the soothsayer from an overflowing heart, and raised both his hands aloft—"O Zarathustra, I have come that I may seduce thee to thy last sin!"—

And hardly had those words been uttered when there sounded the cry once more, and longer and more alarming than before—also much nearer. "Hearest thou? Hearest thou, O Zarathustra?" called out the soothsayer, "the cry concerneth thee, it calleth thee: Come, come, come; it is time, it is the highest time!"—

Zarathustra was silent thereupon, confused and staggered; at last he asked, like one who hesitateth in himself: "And who is it that there calleth me?"

"But thou knowest it, certainly," answered the soothsayer warmly, "why dost thou conceal thyself? It is *the higher man* that crieth for thee!"

"The higher man?" cried Zarathustra, horror-stricken: "what wanteth *he*? What wanteth *he*? The higher man! What wanteth he here?"—and his skin covered with perspiration.

The soothsayer, however, did not heed Zarathustra's alarm, but listened and listened in the downward direction. When, however, it had been still there for a long while, he looked behind, and saw Zarathustra standing trembling.

"O Zarathustra," he began, with sorrowful voice, "thou dost not stand there like one whose happiness maketh him giddy: thou wilt have to dance lest thou tumble down!

But although thou shouldst dance before me, and leap all thy side-leaps, no one may say unto me: 'Behold, here danceth the last joyous man!'

In vain would any one come to this height who sought *him* here: caves would he find, indeed, and back-caves, hiding-places for hidden ones; but not lucky mines, nor treasure-chambers, nor new gold-veins of happiness.

Happiness—how indeed could one find happiness among such buried-alive and solitary ones! Must I yet seek the last happiness on the Happy Isles, and far away among forgotten seas?

But all is alike, nothing is worth while, no seeking is of service, there are no longer any Happy Isles!"——

Thus sighed the soothsayer; with his last sigh, however, Zarathustra again became serene and assured, like one who hath come out of a deep chasm into the light. "Nay! Nay! Three times Nay!" exclaimed he with a strong voice, and stroked his beard—"*that* do I know better! There are still Happy Isles! Silence *thereon,* thou sighing sorrow-sack!

Cease to splash *thereon,* thou rain-cloud of the forenoon! Do I not already stand here wet with thy misery, and drenched like a dog?

Now do I shake myself and run away from thee, that I may again become dry: thereat mayest thou not wonder! Do I seem to thee discourteous? Here however is *my* court.

But as regards the higher man: well! I shall seek him at once in those forests: *from thence* came his cry. Perhaps he is there hard beset by an evil beast.

He is in *my* domain: therein shall he receive no scath! And verily, there are many evil beasts about me."—

With those words Zarathustra turned around to depart. Then said the soothsayer: "O Zarathustra, thou art a rogue!

I know it well: thou wouldst fain be rid of me! Rather wouldst thou run into the forest and lay snares for evil beasts!

But what good will it do thee? In the evening wilt thou have me again: in thine own cave will I sit, patient and heavy like a block—and wait for thee!"

"So be it!" shouted back Zarathustra, as he went away: "and what is mine in my cave belongeth also unto thee, my guest!

Shouldst thou however find honey therein, well! just lick it up, thou growling bear, and sweeten thy soul! For in the evening we want both to be in good spirits;

—In good spirits and joyful, because this day hath come to an end! And thou thyself shalt dance to my lays, as my dancing-bear.

Thou dost not believe this? Thou shakest thy head? Well! Cheer up, old bear! But I also—am a soothsayer."

Thus spake Zarathustra.

63. Talk with the Kings

1

ERE Zarathustra had been an hour on his way in the mountains and forests, he saw all at once a strange procession. Right on the path which he was about to descend came two kings walking, bedecked with crowns and purple girdles, and variegated like flamingoes: they drove before them a laden ass. "What do these kings want in my domain?" said Zarathustra in astonishment to his heart, and hid himself hastily behind a thicket. When however the kings approached to him, he said half-aloud, like one speaking only to himself: "Strange! Strange! How doth this harmonise? Two kings do I see—and only one ass!"

Thereupon the two kings made a halt; they smiled and looked towards the spot whence the voice proceeded, and afterwards looked into each other's faces. "Such things do we also think among ourselves," said the king on the right, "but we do not utter them."

The king on the left, however, shrugged his shoulders and

answered: "That may perhaps be a goat-herd. Or an anchorite who hath lived too long among rocks and trees. For no society at all spoileth also good manners."

"Good manners?" replied angrily and bitterly the other king: "what then do we run out of the way of? Is it not 'good manners'? Our 'good society'?

Better, verily, to live among anchorites and goat-herds, than with our gilded, false, over-rouged populace—though it call itself 'good society.'

—Though it call itself 'nobility.' But there all is false and foul, above all the blood—thanks to old evil diseases and worse curers.

The best and dearest to me at present is still a sound peasant, coarse, artful, obstinate and enduring: that is at present the noblest type.

The peasant is at present the best; and the peasant type should be master! But it is the kingdom of the populace—I no longer allow anything to be imposed upon me. The populace, however—that meaneth, hodgepodge.

Populace-hodgepodge: therein is everything mixed with everything, saint and swindler, gentleman and Jew, and every beast out of Noah's ark.

Good manners! Everything is false and foul with us. No one knoweth any longer how to reverence: it is *that* precisely that we run away from. They are fulsome obtrusive dogs; they gild palm-leaves.

This loathing choketh me, that we kings ourselves have become false, draped and disguised with the old faded pomp of our ancestors, show-pieces for the stupidest, the craftiest, and whosoever at present trafficketh for power.

We *are not* the first men—and have nevertheless to *stand for* them: of this imposture have we at last become weary and disgusted.

From the rabble have we gone out of the way, from all those bawlers and scribe-blowflies, from the trader-stench, the ambition-fidgeting, the bad breath—: fie, to live among the rabble;

—Fie, to stand for the first men among the rabble! Ah, loathing! Loathing! Loathing! What doth it now matter about us kings!"—

"Thine old sickness seizeth thee," said here the king on the left, "thy loathing seizeth thee, my poor brother. Thou knowest, however, that some one heareth us."

Immediately thereupon, Zarathustra, who had opened ears and eyes to this talk, rose from his hiding-place, advanced towards the kings, and thus began:

"He who hearkeneth unto you, he who gladly hearkeneth unto you, is called Zarathustra.

I am Zarathustra who once said: 'What doth it now matter about kings!' Forgive me; I rejoiced when ye said to each other: 'What doth it matter about us kings!'

Here, however, is *my* domain and jurisdiction: what may ye be seeking in my domain? Perhaps, however, ye have *found* on your way what I seek: namely, the higher man."

When the kings heard this, they beat upon their breasts and said with one voice: "We are recognised!

With the sword of thine utterance severest thou the thickest darkness of our hearts. Thou hast discovered our distress; for lo! we are on our way to find the higher man—

—The man that is higher than we, although we are kings. To him do we convey this ass. For the highest man shall also be the highest lord on earth.

There is no sorer misfortune in all human destiny, than when the mighty of the earth are not also the first men. Then everything becometh false and distorted and monstrous.

And when they are even the last men, and more beast than man, then riseth and riseth the populace in honour, and at last saith even the populace-virtue: 'Lo, I alone am virtue!' "—

What have I just heard? answered Zarathustra. What wisdom in kings! I am enchanted, and verily, I have already promptings to make a rhyme thereon:—

—Even if it should happen to be a rhyme not suited for every one's ears. I unlearned long ago to have consideration for long ears. Well then! Well now!

(Here, however, it happened that the ass also found utterance: it said distinctly and with malevolence, Y-E-A.)

'Twas once—methinks year one of our blessed Lord,—
Drunk without wine, the Sybil thus deplored:—
"How ill things go!
Decline! Decline! Ne'er sank the world so low!
Rome now hath turned harlot and harlot-stew,
Rome's Cæsar a beast, and God—hath turned Jew!"

2

With those rhymes of Zarathustra the kings were delighted; the king on the right, however, said: "O Zarathustra, how well it was that we set out to see thee!

For thine enemies showed us thy likeness in their mirror: there lookedst thou with the grimace of a devil, and sneeringly: so that we were afraid of thee.

But what good did it do! Always didst thou prick us anew in heart and ear with thy sayings. Then did we say at last: What doth it matter how he look!

We must *hear* him; him who teacheth: 'Ye shall love peace as a means to new wars, and the short peace more than the long!'

No one ever spake such warlike words: 'What is good? To be brave is good. It is the good war that halloweth every cause.'

O Zarathustra, our fathers' blood stirred in our veins at such words: it was like the voice of spring to old wine-casks.

When the swords ran among one another like red-spotted serpents, then did our fathers become fond of life; the sun of every peace seemed to them languid and lukewarm, the long peace, however, made them ashamed.

How they sighed, our fathers, when they saw on the wall brightly furbished, dried-up swords! Like those they thirsted for war. For a sword thirsteth to drink blood, and sparkleth with desire."—— —

—When the kings thus discoursed and talked eagerly of the happiness of their fathers, there came upon Zarathustra no little desire to mock at their eagerness: for evidently they were very peaceable kings whom he saw before him, kings with old and refined features. But he restrained himself. "Well!" said he, "thither leadeth the way, there lieth the cave of Zarathustra; and this day is to have a long evening! At present, however, a cry of distress calleth me hastily away from you.

It will honour my cave if kings want to sit and wait in it: but, to be sure, ye will have to wait long!

Well! What of that! Where doth one at present learn better to wait than at courts? And the whole virtue of kings that hath remained unto them—is it not called to-day: *Ability* to wait?"

Thus spake Zarathustra.

64. The Leech

AND Zarathustra went thoughtfully on, further and lower down, through forests and past moory bottoms; as it happeneth, however, to every one who meditateth upon hard matters, he trod thereby unawares upon a man. And lo, there spurted into his face all at once a cry of pain, and two curses and twenty bad invectives, so that in his fright he raised his stick and also struck the trodden one. Immediately afterwards, however, he regained his composure, and his heart laughed at the folly he had just committed.

"Pardon me," said he to the trodden one, who had got up enraged, and had seated himself, "pardon me, and hear first of all a parable.

As a wanderer who dreameth of remote things on a lonesome highway, runneth unawares against a sleeping dog, a dog which lieth in the sun:

—As both of them then start up and snap at each other, like deadly enemies, those two beings mortally frightened—so did it happen unto us.

And yet! And yet—how little was lacking for them to caress each other, that dog and that lonesome one! Are they not both—lonesome ones!"

—"Whoever thou art," said the trodden one, still enraged, "thou treadest also too nigh me with thy parable, and not only with thy foot!

Lo! am I then a dog?"—And thereupon the sitting one got up, and pulled his naked arm out of the swamp. For at first he had lain outstretched on the ground, hidden and indiscernible, like those who lie in wait for swamp-game.

"But whatever art thou about!" called out Zarathustra in alarm, for he saw a deal of blood streaming over the naked arm,—"what hath hurt thee? Hath an evil beast bit thee, thou unfortunate one?"

The bleeding one laughed, still angry, "What matter is it to thee!" said he, and was about to go on. "Here am I at home and in my province. Let him question me whoever will: to a dolt, however, I shall hardly answer."

"Thou art mistaken," said Zarathustra sympathetically, and held him fast; "thou art mistaken. Here thou art not at home, but in my domain, and therein shall no one receive any hurt.

Call me however what thou wilt—I am who I must be. I call myself Zarathustra.

Well! Up thither is the way to Zarathustra's cave: it is not far,—wilt thou not attend to thy wounds at my home?

It hath gone badly with thee, thou unfortunate one, in this life: first a beast bit thee, and then—a man trod upon thee!"— —

When however the trodden one had heard the name of Zarathustra he was transformed. "What happeneth unto me!" he exclaimed, "*who* preoccupieth me so much in this life as this one man, namely Zarathustra, and that one animal that liveth on blood, the leech?

For the sake of the leech did I lie here by this swamp, like a fisher, and already had mine outstretched arm been bitten ten times, when there biteth a still finer leech at my blood, Zarathustra himself!

O happiness! O miracle! Praised be this day which enticed me into the swamp! Praised be the best, the livest cupping-glass, that at present liveth; praised be the great conscience-leech Zarathustra!"—

Thus spake the trodden one, and Zarathustra rejoiced at his words and their refined reverential style. "Who art thou?" asked he, and gave him his hand, "there is much to clear up and elucidate between us, but already methinketh pure clear day is dawning."

"I am *the spiritually conscientious one*," answered he who was asked, "and in matters of the spirit it is difficult for any one to take it more rigorously, more restrictedly, and more severely than I, except him from whom I learnt it, Zarathustra himself.

Better know nothing than half-know many things! Better be a fool on one's own account, than a sage on other people's approbation! I—go to the basis:

—What matter if it be great or small? If it be called swamp or sky? A handbreadth of basis is enough for me, if it be actually basis and ground!

—A handbreadth of basis: thereon can one stand. In the true knowing-knowledge there is nothing great and nothing small."

"Then thou art perhaps an expert on the leech?" asked Zarathustra; "and thou investigatest the leech to its ultimate basis, thou conscientious one?"

"O Zarathustra," answered the trodden one, "that would be something immense; how could I presume to do so!

That, however, of which I am master and knower, is the *brain* of the leech:—that is *my* world!

And it is also a world! Forgive it, however, that my pride here findeth expression, for here I have not mine equal. Therefore said I: 'here am I at home.'

How long have I investigated this one thing, the brain of the leech, so that here the slippery truth might no longer slip from me! Here is *my* domain!

—For the sake of this did I cast everything else aside, for

the sake of this did everything else become indifferent to me; and close beside my knowledge lieth my black ignorance.

My spiritual conscience requireth from me that it should be so—that I should know one thing, and not know all else: they are a loathing unto me, all the semi-spiritual, all the hazy, hovering, and visionary.

Where mine honesty ceaseth, there am I blind, and want also to be blind. Where I want to know, however, there want I also to be honest—namely, severe, rigorous, restricted, cruel and inexorable.

Because *thou* once saidest, O Zarathustra: 'Spirit is life which itself cutteth into life';—that led and allured me to thy doctrine. And verily, with mine own blood have I increased mine own knowledge!''

—"As the evidence indicateth," broke in Zarathustra; for still was the blood flowing down on the naked arm of the conscientious one. For there had ten leeches bitten into it.

"O thou strange fellow, how much doth this very evidence teach me—namely, thou thyself! And not all, perhaps, might I pour into thy rigorous ear!

Well then! We part here! But I would fain find thee again. Up thither is the way to my cave: to-night shalt thou there by my welcome guest!

Fain would I also make amends to thy body for Zarathustra treading upon thee with his feet: I think about that. Just now, however, a cry of distress calleth me hastily away from thee."

Thus spake Zarathustra.

65. The Magician

1

WHEN however Zarathustra had gone round a rock, then saw he on the same path, not far below him, a man who threw his limbs about like a maniac, and at last tumbled to the ground on his belly. "Halt!" said then Zarathustra to his heart, "he there must surely be the higher man, from him came that dreadful cry of distress,—I will see if I can help him." When, however, he ran to the spot where the man lay on the ground, he found a trembling old man with fixed eyes; and in spite of all Zarathustra's efforts to lift him and set him again on his feet, it was all in vain. The unfortunate one, also, did not seem to notice that some one was beside him; on the contrary, he continually looked around with moving gestures, like one forsaken and isolated from all the world. At last, however, after much trembling, and convulsion, and curling-himself-up, he began to lament thus:

Who warm'th me, who lov'th me still?
　Give ardent fingers!
　Give heartening charcoal-warmers!
Prone, outstretched, trembling,
Like him, half dead and cold, whose feet one warm'th—
And shaken, ah! by unfamiliar fevers,
Shivering with sharpened, icy-cold frost-arrows,
　By thee pursued, my fancy!
Ineffable! Recondite! Sore-frightening!
　Thou huntsman 'hind the cloud-banks!

Now lightning-struck by thee,
Thou mocking eye that me in darkness watcheth:
-—Thus do I lie,
Bend myself, twist myself, convulsed
With all eternal torture,
   And smitten
By thee, cruellest huntsman,
Thou unfamiliar—*God* . . .

Smite deeper!
Smite yet once more!
Pierce through and rend my heart!
What mean'th this torture
With dull, indented arrows?
Why look'st thou hither,
Of human pain not weary,
With mischief-loving, godly flash-glances?
Not murder wilt thou,
But torture, torture?
For why—*me* torture,
Thou mischief-loving, unfamiliar God?—

Ha! Ha!
Thou stealest nigh
In midnight's gloomy hour? . . .
What wilt thou?
Speak!
Thou crowdst me, pressest—
Ha! now far too closely!
Thou hearst me breathing,
Thou o'erhearst my heart,
Thou ever jealous one!

—Of what, pray, ever jealous?
Off! Off!
For why the ladder?
Wouldst thou *get in?*
To heart in-clamber?
To mine own secretest
Conceptions in-clamber?
Shameless one! Thou unknown one!—Thief!
What seekst thou by thy stealing?
What seekst thou by thy hearkening?
What seekst thou by thy torturing?
Thou torturer!
Thou—hangman-God!
Or shall I, as the mastiffs do,
Roll me before thee?
And cringing, enraptured, frantical,
My tail friendly—waggle!

In vain!
Goad further!
Cruellest goader!
No dog—thy game just am I,
Cruellest huntsman!
Thy proudest of captives,
Thou robber 'hind the cloud-banks . . .
Speak finally!
Thou lightning-veiled one! Thou unknown one! Speak!
What wilt thou, highway-ambusher, from—*me?*
What *wilt* thou, unfamiliar—God?
What?
Ransom-gold?
How much of ransom-gold?

[*282*]

Solicit much—that bid'th my pride!
And be concise—that bid'th mine other pride!

Ha! Ha!
Me—wantst thou? me?
—Entire? . . .

Ha! Ha!
And torturest me, fool that thou art,
Dead-torturest quite my pride?
Give *love* to me—who warm'th me still?
    Who lov'th me still?—
Give ardent fingers
Give heartening charcoal-warmers,
Give me, the lonesomest,
The ice (ah! seven-fold frozen ice
For very enemies,
For foes, doth make one thirst).
Give, yield to me,
Cruellest foe,
—*Thyself!*——

Away!
There fled he surely,
My final, only comrade,
My greatest foe,
Mine unfamiliar—
My hangman-God! . . .

—Nay!
Come thou back!
With all of thy great tortures!

To me the last of lonesome ones,
Oh, come thou back!
All my hot tears in streamlets trickle
Their course to thee!
And all my final hearty fervour—
Up-glow'th to *thee!*
Oh, come thou back,
 Mine unfamiliar God! my *pain!*
 My final bliss!

2

—Here, however, Zarathustra could no longer restrain himself; he took his staff and struck the wailer with all his might.
"Stop this," cried he to him with wrathful laughter, "stop this,
thou stage-player! Thou false coiner! Thou liar from the very
heart! I know thee well!

I will soon make warm legs to thee, thou evil magician: I
know well how—to make it hot for such as thou!"

—"Leave off," said the old man, and sprang up from the
ground, "strike me no more, O Zarathustra! I did it only for
amusement!

That kind of thing belongeth to mine art. Thee thyself, I
wanted to put to the proof when I gave this performance. And
verily, thou hast well detected me!

But thou thyself—hast given me no small proof of thyself:
thou art *hard,* thou wise Zarathustra! Hard strikest thou with
thy 'truths,' thy cudgel forceth from me—*this* truth!"

—"Flatter not," answered Zarathustra, still excited and
frowning, "thou stage-player from the heart! Thou art false:
why speakest thou—of truth!

[*284*]

Thou peacock of peacocks, thou sea of vanity; *what* didst thou represent before me, thou evil magician; *whom* was I meant to believe in when thou wailedst in such wise?"

"*The penitent in spirit*," said the old man, "it was him—I represented; thou thyself once devisedst this expression—

—The poet and magician who at last turneth his spirit against himself, the transformed one who freezeth to death by his bad science and conscience.

And just acknowledge it: it was long, O Zarathustra, before thou discoveredst my trick and lie! Thou *believedst* in my distress when thou heldest my head with both thy hands,—

—I heard thee lament 'we have loved him too little, loved him too little!' Because I so far deceived thee, my wickedness rejoiced in me."

"Thou mayest have deceived subtler ones than I," said Zarathustra sternly. "I am not on my guard against deceivers; I *have to be* without precaution: so willeth my lot.

Thou, however,—*must* deceive: so far do I know thee! Thou must ever be equivocal, trivocal, quadrivocal, and quinquivocal! Even what thou hast now confessed, is not nearly true enough nor false enough for me!

Thou bad false coiner, how couldst thou do otherwise! Thy very malady wouldst thou whitewash if thou showed thyself naked to thy physician.

Thus didst thou whitewash thy lie before me when thou saidst: 'I did so *only* for amusement!' There was also *seriousness* therein, thou *art* something of a penitent-in-spirit!

I divine thee well: thou hast become the enchanter of all the world; but for thyself thou hast no lie or artifice left,— thou art disenchanted to thyself!

Thou hast reaped disgust as thy one truth. No word in thee

is any longer genuine, but thy mouth is so: that is to say, the disgust that cleaveth unto thy mouth."———

——"Who art thou at all!" cried here the old magician with defiant voice, "who dareth to speak thus unto *me,* the greatest man now living?"—and a green flash shot from his eye at Zarathustra. But immediately after he changed, and said sadly:

"O Zarathustra, I am weary of it, I am disgusted with mine arts, I am not *great,* why do I dissemble! But thou knowest it well—I sought for greatness!

A great man I wanted to appear, and persuaded many; but the lie hath been beyond my power. On it do I collapse.

O Zarathustra, everything is a lie in me; but that I collapse—this my collapsing is *genuine!*"——

"It honoureth thee," said Zarathustra gloomily, looking down with sidelong glance, "it honoureth thee that thou soughtest for greatness, but it betrayeth thee also. Thou art not great.

Thou bad old magician, *that* is the best and the honestest thing I honour in thee, that thou hast become weary of thyself, and hast expressed it: 'I am not great.'

Therein do I honour thee as a penitent-in-spirit, and although only for the twinkling of an eye, in that one moment wast thou—genuine.

But tell me, what seekest thou here in *my* forests and rocks? And if thou hast put thyself in *my* way, what proof of me wouldst thou have?—

——Wherein didst thou put *me* to the test?"

Thus spake Zarathustra, and his eyes sparkled. But the old magician kept silence for a while; then said he: "Did I put thee to the test? I—seek only.

O Zarathustra, I seek a genuine one, a right one, a simple

one, an unequivocal one, a man of perfect honesty, a vessel of wisdom, a saint of knowledge, a great man!

Knowest thou it not, O Zarathustra? *I seek Zarathustra."*

—And here there arose a long silence between them: Zarathustra, however, became profoundly absorbed in thought, so that he shut his eyes. But afterwards coming back to the situation, he grasped the hand of the magician, and said, full of politeness and policy:

"Well! Up thither leadeth the way, there is the cave of Zarathustra. In it mayest thou seek him whom thou wouldst fain find.

And ask counsel of mine animals, mine eagle and my serpent: they shall help thee to seek. My cave however is large.

I myself, to be sure—I have as yet seen no great man. That which is great, the acutest eye is at present insensible to it. It is the kingdom of the populace.

Many a one have I found who stretched and inflated himself, and the people cried: 'Behold; a great man!' But what good do all bellows do! The wind cometh out at last.

At last bursteth the frog which hath inflated itself too long: then cometh out the wind. To prick a swollen one in the belly, I call good pastime. Hear that, ye boys!

Our today is of the popular: who still *knoweth* what is great and what is small! Who could there seek successfully for greatness! A fool only: it succeedeth with fools.

Thou seekest for great men, thou strange fool? Who *taught* that to thee? Is today the time for it? Oh, thou bad seeker, why dost thou—tempt me?"———

Thus spake Zarathustra, comforted in his heart, and went laughing on his way.

66. Out of Service

NOT long, however, after Zarathustra had freed himself from
the magician, he again saw a person sitting beside the path
which he followed, namely a tall, black man, with a haggard,
pale countenance: *this man* grieved him exceedingly. "Alas,"
said he to his heart, "there sitteth disguised affliction; methinketh he is of the type of the priests: what do *they* want in
my domain?

What! Hardly have I escaped from that magician, and must
another necromancer again run across my path,—

—Some sorcerer with laying-on-of-hands, some sombre
wonder-worker by the grace of God, some anointed world-
maligner, whom, may the devil take!

But the devil is never at the place which would be his right
place: he always cometh too late, that cursed dwarf and club-
foot!"—

Thus cursed Zarathustra impatiently in his heart, and considered how with averted look he might slip past the black
man. But behold, it came about otherwise. For at the same
moment had the sitting one already perceived him; and not
unlike one whom an unexpected happiness overtaketh, he
sprang to his feet, and went straight towards Zarathustra.

"Whoever thou art, thou traveller," said he, "help a strayed
one, a seeker, an old man, who may here easily come to grief!

The world here is strange to me, and remote; wild beasts
also did I hear howling; and he who could have given me protection—he is himself no more.

I was seeking the last pious man, a saint and an anchorite,

who, alone in his forest, had not yet heard of what all the world knoweth at present."

"*What* doth all the world know at present?" asked Zarathustra. "Perhaps that the old God no longer liveth, in whom all the world once believed?"

"Thou sayest it," answered the old man sorrowfully. "And I served that old God until his last hour.

Now, however, am I out of service, without master, and yet not free; likewise am I no longer merry even for an hour, except it be in recollections.

Therefore did I ascend into these mountains, that I might finally have a festival for myself once more, as becometh an old pope and church-father: for know it, that I am the last pope!—a festival of pious recollections and divine services.

Now, however, is he himself dead, the most pious of men, the saint in the forest, who praised his God constantly with singing and mumbling.

He himself found I no longer when I found his cot—but two wolves found I therein, which howled on account of his death,—for all animals loved him. Then did I haste away.

Had I thus come in vain into these forests and mountains? Then did my heart determine that I should seek another, the most pious of all those who believe not in God—, my heart determined that I should seek Zarathustra!"

Thus spake the hoary man, and gazed with keen eyes at him who stood before him. Zarathustra however seized the hand of the old pope and regarded it a long while with admiration.

"Lo! thou venerable one," said he then, "what a fine and long hand! That is the hand of one who hath ever dispensed blessings. Now, however, doth it hold fast him whom thou seekest, me, Zarathustra.

[*289*]

It is I, the ungodly Zarathustra, who saith: 'Who is un-godlier than I, that I may enjoy his teaching?' "—

Thus spake Zarathustra, and penetrated with his glances the thoughts and arrear-thoughts of the old pope. At last the latter began:

"He who most loved and possessed him hath now also lost him most—:

—Lo, I myself am surely the most godless of us at present? But who could rejoice at that!"—

—"Thou servedst him to the last?" asked Zarathustra thoughtfully, after a deep silence, "thou knowest *how* he died? Is it true what they say, that sympathy choked him;

—That he saw how *man* hung on the cross, and could not endure it;—that his love to man became his hell, and at last his death?"— —

The old pope however did not answer, but looked aside timidly, with a painful and gloomy expression.

"Let him go," said Zarathustra, after prolonged meditation, still looking the old man straight in the eye.

"Let him go, he is gone. And though it honoureth thee that thou speakest only in praise of this dead one, yet thou knowest as well as I *who* he was, and that he went curious ways."

"To speak before three eyes," said the old pope cheerfully (he was blind of one eye), "in divine matters I am more en-lightened than Zarathustra himself—and may well be so.

My love served him long years, my will followed all his will. A good servant, however, knoweth everything, and many a thing even which a master hideth from himself.

He was a hidden God, full of secrecy. Verily, he did not come by his son otherwise than by secret ways. At the door of his faith standeth adultery.

Whoever extolleth him as a God of love, doth not think

[*290*]

highly enough of love itself. Did not that God want also to be judge? But the loving one loveth irrespective of reward and requital.

When he was young, that God out of the Orient, then was he harsh and revengeful, and built himself a hell for the delight of his favourites.

At last, however, he became old and soft and mellow and pitiful, more like a grandfather than a father, but most like a tottering old grandmother.

There did he sit shrivelled in his chimney-corner, fretting on account of his weak legs, world-weary, will-weary, and one day he suffocated of his all-too-great pity."— —

"Thou old pope," said here Zarathustra interposing, "hast thou seen *that* with thine eyes? It could well have happened in that way: in that way, *and* also otherwise. When gods die they always die many kinds of death.

Well! At all events, one way or other—he is gone! He was counter to the taste of mine ears and eyes; worse than that I should not like to say against him.

I love everything that looketh bright and speaketh honestly. But he—thou knowest it, forsooth, thou old priest, there was something of thy type in him, the priest-type—he was equivocal.

He was also indistinct. How he raged at us, this wrath-snorter, because we understood him badly! But why did he not speak more clearly?

And if the fault lay in our ears, why did he give us ears that heard him badly? If there was dirt in our ears, well! who put it in them?

Too much miscarried with him, this potter who had not learned thoroughly! That he took revenge on his pots and creations, however, because they turned out badly—that was a sin against *good taste*.

There is also good taste in piety: *this* at last said: 'Away with *such* a God! Better to have no God, better to set up destiny on one's own account, better to be a fool, better to be God oneself!' "

—"What do I hear!" said then the old pope, with intent ears; "O Zarathustra, thou art more pious than thou believest, with such an unbelief! Some god in thee hath converted thee to thine ungodliness.

Is it not thy piety itself which no longer letteth thee believe in a God? And thine over-great honesty will yet lead thee even beyond good and evil!

Behold, what hath been reserved for thee? Thou hast eyes and hands and mouth, which have been predestined for blessing from eternity. One doth not bless with the hand alone.

Nigh unto thee, though thou professest to be the ungodliest one, I feel a hale and holy odour of long benedictions: I feel glad and grieved thereby.

Let me be thy guest, O Zarathustra, for a single night! Nowhere on earth shall I now feel better than with thee!"—

"Amen! So shall it be!" said Zarathustra, with great astonishment; "up thither leadeth the way, there lieth the cave of Zarathustra.

Gladly, forsooth, would I conduct thee thither myself, thou venerable one; for I love all pious men. But now a cry of distress calleth me hastily away from thee.

In my domain shall no one come to grief; my cave is a good haven. And best of all would I like to put every sorrowful one again on firm land and firm legs.

Who, however, could take *thy* melancholy off thy shoulders? For that I am too weak. Long, verily, should we have to wait until some one re-awoke thy God for thee.

For that old God liveth no more: he is indeed dead."—

Thus spake Zarathustra.

67. *The Ugliest Man*

—AND again did Zarathustra's feet run through mountains and forests, and his eyes sought and sought, but nowhere was he to be seen whom they wanted to see—the sorely distressed sufferer and crier. On the whole way, however, he rejoiced in his heart and was full of gratitude. "What good things," said he, "hath this day given me, as amends for its bad beginning! What strange interlocutors have I found!

At their words will I now chew a long while as at good corn; small shall my teeth grind and crush them, until they flow like milk into my soul!"—

When, however, the path again curved round a rock, all at once the landscape changed, and Zarathustra entered into a realm of death. Here bristled aloft black and red cliffs, without any grass, tree, or bird's voice. For it was a valley which all animals avoided, even the beasts of prey, except that a species of ugly, thick, green serpent came here to die when they became old. Therefore the shepherds called this valley: "Serpent-death."

Zarathustra, however, became absorbed in dark recollections, for it seemed to him as if he had once before stood in this valley. And much heaviness settled on his mind, so that he walked slowly and always more slowly, and at last stood still. Then, however, when he opened his eyes, he saw something sitting by the wayside shaped like a man, and hardly like a man, something nondescript. And all at once there came over Zarathustra a great shame, because he had gazed on such a thing. Blushing up to the very roots of his white hair, he turned aside his glance, and raised his foot that he might leave this ill-starred place. Then, however, became the dead wilderness vocal: for from the ground a noise welled up, gurgling and rattling, as water gurgleth and rattleth at night through stopped-up water-pipes; and at last it turned into human voice and human speech:—it sounded thus:

"Zarathustra! Zarathustra! Read my riddle! Say, say! *What is the revenge on the witness?*

I entice thee back; here is smooth ice! See to it, see to it, that thy pride does not here break its legs!

Thou thinkest thyself wise, thou proud Zarathustra! Read then the riddle, thou hard nut-cracker,—the riddle that I am! Say then: who am *I!*"

—When however Zarathustra had heard these words,—what think ye then took place in his soul? *Pity overcame him;* and he sank down all at once, like an oak that hath long withstood many tree-fellers,—heavily, suddenly, to the terror even of those who meant to fell it. But immediately he got up again from the ground, and his countenance became stern.

"I know thee well," said he, with a brazen voice, *"thou art the murderer of God!* Let me go.

Thou couldst not *endure* him who beheld *thee,*—who ever beheld thee through and through, thou ugliest man. Thou tookest revenge on this witness!"

Thus spake Zarathustra and was about to go; but the non-

descript grasped at a corner of his garment and began anew
to gurgle and seek for words. "Stay," said he at last—

—"Stay! Do not pass by! I have divined what axe it was
that struck thee to the ground: hail to thee, O Zarathustra, that
thou art again upon thy feet!

Thou hast divined, I know it well, how the man feeleth who
killed him,—the murderer of God. Stay! Sit down here beside me; it is not to no purpose.

To whom would I go but unto thee? Stay, sit down! Do not
however look at me! Honour thus—mine ugliness!

They persecute me: now art *thou* my last refuge. *Not* with
their hatred, *not* with their bailiffs;—Oh, such persecution
would I mock at, and be proud and cheerful!

Hath not all success hitherto been with the well-persecuted
ones? And he who persecuteth well learneth readily to be
obsequent—when once he is—put behind! But it is their *pity*—

—Their pity is it from which I flee away and flee to thee. O
Zarathustra, protect me, thou, my last refuge, thou sole one
who divinedst me:

—Thou hast divined how the man feeleth who killed *him*.
Stay! And if thou wilt go, thou impatient one, go not the way
that I came. *That* way is bad.

Art thou angry with me because I have already racked language too long? Because I have already counselled thee? But
know that it is I, the ugliest man,

—Who have also the largest, heaviest feet. Where *I* have
gone, the way is bad. I tread all paths to death and destruction.

But that thou passedst me by in silence, that thou blushedst
—I saw it well: thereby did I know thee as Zarathustra.

Every one else would have thrown to me his alms, his pity,
in look and speech. But for that—I am not beggar enough: that
didst thou divine.

[*295*]

For that I am too *rich,* rich in what is great, frightful, ugliest, most unutterable! Thy shame, O Zarathustra, *honoured* me!

With difficulty did I get out of the crowd of the pitiful,— that I might find the only one who at present teacheth that 'pity is obtrusive'—thyself, O Zarathustra!

—Whether it be the pity of a God, or whether it be human pity, it is offensive to modesty. And unwillingness to help may be nobler than the virtue that rusheth to do so.

That however—namely, pity—is called virtue itself at present by all petty people:—they have no reverence for great misfortune, great ugliness, great failure.

Beyond all these do I look, as a dog looketh over the backs of thronging flocks of sheep. They are petty, good-wooled, good-willed, grey people.

As the heron looketh contemptuously at shallow pools, with backward-bent head, so do I look at the throng of grey little waves and wills and souls.

Too long have we acknowledged them to be right, those petty people: *so* we have at last given them power as well;— and now do they teach that 'good is only what petty people call good.'

And 'truth' is at present what the preacher spake who himself sprang from them, that singular saint and advocate of the petty people, who testified of himself: 'I—am the truth.'

That immodest one hath long made the petty people greatly puffed up,—he who taught no small error when he taught: 'I —am the truth.'

Hath an immodest one ever been answered more courteously?—Thou, however, O Zarathustra, passedst him by, and saidst: 'Nay! Nay! Three times Nay!'

Thou warnedst against his error; thou warnedst—the first

to do so—against pity:—not every one, not none, but thyself and thy type.

Thou art ashamed of the shame of the great sufferer; and verily when thou sayest: 'From pity there cometh a heavy cloud; take heed, ye men!'

—When thou teachest: 'All creators are hard, all great love is beyond their pity:' O Zarathustra, how well versed dost thou seem to me in weather-signs!

Thou thyself, however,—warn thyself also against *thy* pity! For many are on their way to thee, many suffering, doubting, despairing, drowning, freezing ones—

I warn thee also against myself. Thou hast read my best, my worst riddle, myself, and what I have done. I know the axe that felleth thee.

But he—*had to* die: he looked with eyes which beheld *everything,*—he beheld men's depths and dregs, all his hidden ignominy and ugliness.

His pity knew no modesty: he crept into my dirtiest corners. This most prying, over-intrusive, over-pitiful one had to die.

He ever beheld *me:* on such a witness I would have revenge —or not live myself.

The God who beheld everything, *and also man:* that God had to die! Man cannot *endure* it that such a witness should live."

Thus spake the ugliest man. Zarathustra however got up, and prepared to go on: for he felt frozen to the very bowels.

"Thou nondescript," said he, "thou warnedst me against thy path. As thanks for it I praise mine to thee. Behold, up thither is the cave of Zarathustra.

My cave is large and deep and hath many corners; there findeth he that is most hidden his hiding-place. And close beside it, there are a hundred lurking-places and by-places for creeping, fluttering, and hopping creatures.

Thou outcast, who hast cast thyself out, thou wilt not live amongst men and men's pity? Well then, do like me! Thus wilt thou learn also from me; only the doer learneth.

And talk first and foremost to mine animals! The proudest animal and the wisest animal—they might well be the right counsellors for us both!"——

Thus spake Zarathustra and went his way, more thoughtfully and slowly even than before: for he asked himself many things, and hardly knew what to answer.

"How poor indeed is man," thought he in his heart, "how ugly, how wheezy, how full of hidden shame!

They tell me that man loveth himself. Ah, how great must that self-love be! How much contempt is opposed to it!

Even this man hath loved himself, as he hath despised himself,—a great lover methinketh he is, and a great despiser.

No one have I yet found who more thoroughly despised himself: even *that* is elevation. Alas, was *this* perhaps the higher man whose cry I heard?

I love the great despisers. Man is something that hath to be surpassed."——

68. The Voluntary Beggar

WHEN Zarathustra had left the ugliest man, he was chilled and felt lonesome: for much coldness and lonesomeness came over his spirit, so that even his limbs became colder thereby. When, however, he wandered on and on, uphill and down, at times past green meadows, though also sometimes over wild stony couches where formerly perhaps an impatient brook had made its bed, then he turned all at once warmer and heartier again.

"What hath happened unto me?" he asked himself, "something warm and living quickeneth me; it must be in the neighbourhood.

Already am I less alone; unconscious companions and brethren rove around me; their warm breath toucheth my soul."

When, however, he spied about and sought for the comforters of his lonesomeness, behold, there were kine there standing together on an eminence, whose proximity and smell had warmed his heart. The kine, however, seemed to listen eagerly to a speaker, and took no heed of him who approached. When, however, Zarathustra was quite nigh unto them, then did he hear plainly that a human voice spake in the midst of the kine, and apparently all of them had turned their heads towards the speaker.

Then ran Zarathustra up speedily and drove the animals aside; for he feared that some one had here met with harm, which the pity of the kine would hardly be able to relieve. But in this he was deceived; for behold, there sat a man on the ground who seemed to be persuading the animals to have no fear of him, a peaceable man and Preacher-on-the-Mount, out of whose eyes kindness itself preached. "What dost thou seek here?" called out Zarathustra in astonishment.

"What do I here seek?" answered he: "the same that thou seekest, thou mischief-maker; that is to say, happiness upon earth.

To that end, however, I would fain learn of these kine. For I tell thee that I have already talked half a morning unto them, and just now were they about to give me their answer. Why dost thou disturb them?

Except we be converted and become as kine, we shall in no wise enter into the kingdom of heaven. For we ought to learn from them one thing: ruminating.

And verily, although a man should gain the whole world, and yet not learn one thing, ruminating, what would it profit him! He would not be rid of his affliction,

—His great affliction: that, however, is at present called *disgust*. Who hath not at present his heart, his mouth and his eyes full of disgust? Thou also! Thou also! But behold these kine!"—

Thus spake the Preacher-on-the-Mount, and turned then his own look towards Zarathustra—for hitherto it had rested lovingly on the kine—: then, however, he put on a different expression. "Who is this with whom I talk?" he exclaimed, frightened, and sprang up from the ground.

"This is the man without disgust, this is Zarathustra himself, the surmounter of the great disgust, this is the eye, this is the mouth, this is the heart of Zarathustra himself."

And whilst he thus spake he kissed with o'erflowing eyes the hands of him with whom he spake, and behaved altogether like one to whom a precious gift and jewel hath fallen unawares from heaven. The kine, however, gazed at it all and wondered.

"Speak not of me, thou strange one; thou amiable one!" said Zarathustra, and restrained his affection, "speak to me firstly of thyself! Art thou not the voluntary beggar who once cast away great riches,—

—Who was ashamed of his riches and of the rich, and fled to the poorest to bestow upon them his abundance and his heart? But they received him not."

"But they received me not," said the voluntary beggar, "thou knowest it, forsooth. So I went at last to the animals and to those kine."

"Then learnedst thou," interrupted Zarathustra, "how much harder it is to give properly than to take properly, and that bestowing well is an *art*—the last, subtlest master-art of kindness."

"Especially nowadays," answered the voluntary beggar: "at present, that is to say, when everything low hath become rebellious and exclusive and haughty in its manner—in the manner of the populace.

For the hour hath come, thou knowest it forsooth, for the great, evil, long, slow mob-and-slave-insurrection: it extendeth and extendeth!

Now doth it provoke the lower classes, all benevolence and petty giving; and the overrich may be on their guard!

Whoever at present drip, like bulgy bottles out of all-too-small necks:—of such bottles at present one willingly breaketh the necks.

Wanton avidity, bilious envy, careworn revenge, populace-pride: all these struck mine eye. It is no longer true that the poor are blessed. The kingdom of heaven, however, is with the kine."

"And why is it not with the rich?" asked Zarathustra temptingly, while he kept back the kine which sniffed familiarly at the peaceful one.

"Why dost thou tempt me?" answered the other. "Thou knowest it thyself better even than I. What was it drove me to the poorest, O Zarathustra? Was it not my disgust at the richest?

—At the culprits of riches, with cold eyes and rank thoughts, who pick up profit out of all kinds of rubbish—at this rabble that stinketh to heaven,

—At this gilded, falsified populace, whose fathers were pickpockets, or carrion-crows, or rag-pickers, with wives compliant, lewd and forgetful:—for they are all of them not far different from harlots—

Populace above, populace below! What are 'poor' and 'rich' at present! That distinction did I unlearn,—then did I flee away further and ever further, until I came to those kine."

Thus spake the peaceful one, and puffed himself and perspired with his words: so that the kine wondered anew. Zarathustra, however, kept looking into his face with a smile, all the time the man talked so severely—and shook silently his head.

"Thou doest violence to thyself, thou Preacher-on-the-Mount, when thou usest such severe words. For such severity neither thy mouth nor thine eye have been given thee.

Nor, methinketh, hath thy stomach either: unto *it* all such rage and hatred and foaming-over is repugnant. Thy stomach wanteth softer things: thou art not a butcher.

Rather seemest thou to me a plant-eater and a root-man. Perhaps thou grindest corn. Certainly, however, thou art averse to fleshly joys, and thou lovest honey."

"Thou hast divined me well," answered the voluntary beggar, with lightened heart. "I love honey, I also grind corn; for I have sought out what tasteth sweetly and maketh pure breath:

—Also what requireth a long time, a day's-work and a mouth's-work for gentle idlers and sluggards.

Furthest, to be sure, have those kine carried it: they have devised ruminating and lying in the sun. They also abstain from all heavy thoughts which inflate the heart."

—"Well!" said Zarathustra, "thou shouldst also see *mine*

animals, mine eagle and my serpent,—their like do not at present exist on earth.

Behold, thither leadeth the way to my cave: be tonight its guest. And talk to mine animals of the happiness of animals,—

—Until I myself come home. For now a cry of distress calleth me hastily away from thee. Also, shouldst thou find new honey with me, ice-cold, golden-comb-honey, eat it!

Now, however, take leave at once of thy kine, thou strange one! thou amiable one! though it be hard for thee. For they are thy warmest friends and preceptors!"—

—"One excepted, whom I hold still dearer," answered the voluntary beggar. "Thou thyself art good, O Zarathustra, and better even than a cow!"

"Away, away with thee! thou evil flatterer!" cried Zarathustra mischievously, "why dost thou spoil me with such praise and flattery-honey?

"Away, away from me!" cried he once more, and heaved his stick at the fond beggar, who, however, ran nimbly away.

69. The Shadow

SCARCELY however was the voluntary beggar gone in haste, and Zarathustra again alone, when he heard behind him a new voice which called out: "Stay! Zarathustra! Do wait! It is myself, forsooth, O Zarathustra, myself, thy shadow!" But Zarathustra did not wait; for a sudden irritation came over him on account of the crowd and the crowding in his mountains. "Whither hath my lonesomeness gone?" spake he.

"It is verily becoming too much for me; these mountains swarm; my kingdom is no longer of *this* world; I require new mountains.

My shadow calleth me? What matter about my shadow! Let it run after me! I—run away from it."

Thus spake Zarathustra to his heart and ran away. But the one behind followed after him, so that immediately there were three runners, one after the other—namely, foremost the voluntary beggar, then Zarathustra, and thirdly, and hindmost, his shadow. But not long had they run thus when Zarathustra became conscious of his folly, and shook off with one jerk all his irritation and detestation.

"What!" said he, "have not the most ludicrous things always happened to us old anchorites and saints?

Verily, my folly hath grown big in the mountains! Now do I hear six old fools' legs rattling behind one another!

But doth Zarathustra need to be frightened by his shadow? Also, methinketh that after all it hath longer legs than mine."

Thus spake Zarathustra, and, laughing with eyes and entrails, he stood still and turned round quickly—and behold, he almost thereby threw his shadow and follower to the ground, so closely had the latter followed at his heels, and so weak was he. For when Zarathustra scrutinised him with his glance he was frightened as by a sudden apparition, so slender, swarthy, hollow and worn-out did this follower appear.

"Who art thou?" asked Zarathustra vehemently, "what doest thou here? And why callest thou thyself my shadow? Thou art not pleasing unto me."

"Forgive me," answered the shadow, "that it is I; and if I please thee not—well, O Zarathustra! therein do I admire thee and thy good taste.

A wanderer am I, who have walked long at thy heels; always on the way, but without a goal, also without a home: so that verily, I lack little of being the eternally Wandering Jew, except that I am not eternal and not a Jew.

What? Must I ever be on the way? Whirled by every wind, unsettled, driven about? O earth, thou hast become too round for me!

On every surface have I already sat, like tired dust have I fallen asleep on mirrors and window-panes: everything taketh from me, nothing giveth; I become thin——I am almost equal to a shadow.

After thee, however, O Zarathustra, did I fly and hie longest; and though I hid myself from thee, I was nevertheless thy best shadow: wherever thou hast sat, there sat I also.

With thee have I wandered about in the remotest, coldest worlds, like a phantom that voluntarily haunteth winter roofs and snows.

With thee have I pushed into all the forbidden, all the worst and the furthest: and if there be anything of virtue in me, it is that I have had no fear of any prohibition.

With thee have I broken up whatever my heart revered; all boundary-stones and statues have I o'erthrown; the most dangerous wishes did I pursue,——verily, beyond every crime did I once go.

With thee did I unlearn the belief in words and worths and in great names. When the devil casteth his skin, doth not his name also fall away? It is also skin. The devil himself is perhaps——skin.

'Nothing is true, all is permitted': so said I to myself. Into the coldest water did I plunge with head and heart. Ah, how oft did I stand there naked on that account, like a red crab!

Ah, where have gone all my goodness and all my shame and all my belief in the good! Ah, where is the lying innocence which I once possessed, the innocence of the good and of their noble lies!

Too oft, verily, did I follow close to the heels of truth: then did it kick me on the face. Sometimes I meant to lie, and behold! then only did I hit—the truth.

Too much hath become clear unto me: now it doth not concern me any more. Nothing liveth any longer that I love,—how should I still love myself?

'To live as I incline, or not to live at all': so do I wish; so wisheth also the holiest. But alas! how have *I* still—inclination?

Have *I*—still a goal? A haven towards which *my* sail is set?

A good wind? Ah, he only who knoweth *whither* he saileth, knoweth what wind is good, and a fair wind for him.

What still remaineth to me? A heart weary and flippant; an unstable will; fluttering wings; a broken backbone.

This seeking for *my* home: O Zarathustra, dost thou know that this seeking hath been *my* home-sickening; it eateth me up.

'*Where* is—*my* home?' For it do I ask and seek, and have sought, but have not found it. O eternal everywhere, O eternal nowhere, O eternal—in-vain!"

Thus spake the shadow, and Zarathustra's countenance lengthened at his words. "Thou art my shadow!" said he at last sadly.

"Thy danger is not small, thou free spirit and wanderer! Thou hast had a bad day: see that a still worse evening doth not overtake thee!

To such unsettled ones as thou, seemeth at last even a

prisoner blessed. Didst thou ever see how captured criminals sleep? They sleep quietly, they enjoy their new security.

Beware lest in the end a narrow faith capture thee, a hard, rigorous delusion! For now everything that is narrow and fixed seduceth and tempteth thee.

Thou hast lost thy goal. Alas, how wilt thou forego and forget that loss? Thereby—hast thou also lost thy way!

Thou poor rover and rambler, thou tired butterfly! wilt thou have a rest and a home this evening? Then go up to my cave!

Thither leadeth the way to my cave. And now will I run quickly away from thee again. Already lieth as it were a shadow upon me.

I will run alone, so that it may again become bright around me. Therefore must I still be a long time merrily upon my legs. In the evening, however, there will be—dancing with me!"— —

Thus spake Zarathustra.

70. *Noontide*

—AND Zarathustra ran and ran, but he found no one else, and was alone and ever found himself again; he enjoyed and quaffed his solitude, and thought of good things—for hours. About the hour of noontide, however, when the sun stood exactly over Zarathustra's head, he passed an old, bent and gnarled tree, which was encircled round by the ardent love of a vine, and hidden from itself; from this there hung yellow grapes in abundance, confronting the wanderer. Then he felt inclined to quench a little thirst, and to break off for himself a cluster of grapes. When, however, he had already his arm outstretched for that purpose, he felt still more inclined for something else—namely, to lie down beside the tree at the hour of perfect noontide and sleep.

This Zarathustra did; and no sooner had he laid himself on the ground in the stillness and secrecy of the variegated grass, than he had forgotten his little thirst, and fell asleep. For as the proverb of Zarathustra saith: "One thing is more necessary than the other." Only that his eyes remained open:—for they never grew weary of viewing and admiring the tree and the love of the vine. In falling asleep, however, Zarathustra spake thus to his heart:

"Hush! Hush! Hath not the world now become perfect? What hath happened unto me?

As a delicate wind danceth invisibly upon parqueted seas, light, feather-light, so—danceth sleep upon me.

No eye doth it close to me, it leaveth my soul awake. Light is it, verily, feather-light.

It persuadeth me, I know not how, it toucheth me inwardly with a caressing hand, it constraineth me. Yea, it constraineth me, so that my soul stretcheth itself out:—

—How long and weary it becometh, my strange soul! Hath a seventh-day evening come to it precisely at noontide? Hath it already wandered too long, blissfully, among good and ripe things?

It stretcheth itself out, long—longer! it lieth still, my strange soul. Too many good things hath it already tasted; this golden sadness oppresseth it, it distorteth its mouth.

—As a ship that putteth into the calmest cove:—it now

draweth up to the land, weary of long voyages and uncertain seas. Is not the land more faithful?

As such a ship huggeth the shore, tuggeth the shore:—then it sufficeth for a spider to spin its thread from the ship to the land. No stronger ropes are required there.

As such a weary ship in the calmest cove, so do I also now repose, nigh to the earth, faithful, trusting, waiting, bound to it with the lightest threads.

O happiness! O happiness! Wilt thou perhaps sing, O my soul? Thou liest in the grass. But this is the secret, solemn hour, when no shepherd playeth his pipe.

Take care! Hot noontide sleepeth on the fields. Do not sing! Hush! The world is perfect.

Do not sing, thou prairie-bird, my soul! Do not even whisper! Lo—hush! The old noontide sleepeth, it moveth its mouth: doth it not just now drink a drop of happiness—

—An old brown drop of golden happiness, golden wine? Something whisketh over it, its happiness laugheth. Thus— laugheth a God. Hush!—

—'For happiness, how little sufficeth for happiness!' Thus spake I once and thought myself wise. But it was a blasphemy: *that* have I now learned. Wise fools speak better.

The least thing precisely, the gentlest thing, the lightest thing, a lizard's rustling, a breath, a whisk, an eye-glance— *little* maketh up the *best* happiness. Hush!

—What hath befallen me: Hark! Hath time flown away? Do I not fall? Have I not fallen—hark! into the well of eternity?

—What happeneth to me? Hush! It stingeth me—alas—to the heart? To the heart! Oh, break up, break up, my heart, after such happiness, after such a sting!

—What? Hath not the world just now become perfect? Round and ripe? Oh, for the golden round ring—whither doth it fly? Let me run after it! Quick!

Hush— —" (and here Zarathustra stretched himself, and felt that he was asleep.)

"Up!" said he to himself, "thou sleeper! Thou noontide sleeper! Well then, up, ye old legs! It is time and more than time; many a good stretch of road is still awaiting you—

Now have ye slept your fill; for how long a time? A half-eternity! Well then, up now, mine old heart! For how long after such a sleep mayest thou—remain awake?"

(But then did he fall asleep anew, and his soul spake against him and defended itself, and lay down again)—"Leave me alone! Hush! Hath not the world just now become perfect? Oh, for the golden round ball!"—

"Get up," said Zarathustra, "thou little thief, thou slug-gard! What! Still stretching thyself, yawning, sighing, falling into deep wells?

Who art thou then, O my soul!" (and here he became frightened, for a sunbeam shot down from heaven upon his face.)

"O heaven above me," said he sighing, and sat upright, "thou gazest at me? Thou hearkenest unto my strange soul?

When wilt thou drink this drop of dew that fell down upon all earthly things,—when wilt thou drink this strange soul—

—When, thou well of eternity! thou joyous, awful, noon-tide abyss! when wilt thou drink my soul back into thee?"

Thus spake Zarathustra, and rose from his couch beside the tree, as if awakening from a strange drunkenness: and behold! there stood the sun still exactly above his head. One might, however, rightly infer therefrom that Zarathustra had not then slept long.

71. *The Greeting*

IT WAS late in the afternoon only when Zarathustra, after long useless searching and strolling about, again came home to his cave. When, however, he stood over against it, not more than twenty paces therefrom, the thing happened which he now least of all expected: he heard anew the great *cry of distress.* And extraordinary! this time the cry came out of his own cave. It was a long, manifold, peculiar cry, and Zarathustra plainly distinguished that it was composed of many voices: although heard at a distance it might sound like the cry out of a single mouth.

Thereupon Zarathustra rushed forward to his cave, and behold! what a spectacle awaited him after that concert! For there did they all sit together whom he had passed during the day: the king on the right and the king on the left, the old magician, the pope, the voluntary beggar, the shadow, the intellectually conscientious one, the sorrowful soothsayer, and the ass; the ugliest man, however, had set a crown on his head, and had put round him two purple girdles,—for he liked, like all ugly ones, to disguise himself and play the handsome person. In the midst, however, of that sorrowful company stood Zarathustra's eagle, ruffled and disquieted, for it had been called upon to answer too much for which its pride had not any answer; the wise serpent however hung round its neck.

All this did Zarathustra behold with great astonishment; then however he scrutinised each individual guest with courteous curiosity, read their souls and wondered anew. In the meantime the assembled ones had risen from their seats, and waited with reverence for Zarathustra to speak. Zarathustra however spake thus:

"Ye despairing ones! Ye strange ones! So it was *your* cry of distress that I heard? And now do I know also where he is to be sought, whom I have sought for in vain today: *the higher man*—:

—In mine own cave sitteth he, the higher man! But why do I wonder! Have not I myself allured him to me by honey-offerings and artful lure-calls of my happiness?

But it seemeth to me that ye are badly adapted for company: ye make one another's hearts fretful, ye that cry for help, when ye sit here together? There is one that must first come,

—One who will make you laugh once more, a good jovial buffoon, a dancer, a wind, a wild romp, some old fool:— what think ye?

Forgive me, however, ye despairing ones, for speaking such trivial words before you, unworthy, verily, of such guests! But ye do not divine *what* maketh my heart wanton:—

—Ye yourselves do it, and your aspect, forgive it me! For every one becometh courageous who beholdeth a despairing one. To encourage a despairing one—every one thinketh himself strong enough to do so.

To myself have ye given this power,—a good gift, mine honourable guests! An excellent guest's-present! Well, do not then upbraid when I also offer you something of mine.

This is mine empire and my dominion: that which is mine, however, shall this evening and tonight be yours. Mine animals shall serve you: let my cave be your resting-place!

At house and home with me shall no one despair: in my purlieus do I protect every one from his wild beasts. And that is the first thing which I offer you: security!

The second thing, however, is my little finger. And when ye

have *that,* then take the whole hand also, yea and the heart with it! Welcome here, welcome to you, my guests!"

Thus spake Zarathustra, and laughed with love and mischief. After this greeting his guests bowed once more and were reverentially silent; the king on the right, however, answered him in their name.

"O Zarathustra, by the way in which thou hast given us thy hand and thy greeting, we recognise thee as Zarathustra. Thou hast humbled thyself before us; almost hast thou hurt our reverence—:

—Who however could have humbled himself as thou hast done, with such pride? *That* uplifteth us ourselves; a refreshment is it, to our eyes and hearts.

To behold this, merely, gladly would we ascend higher mountains than this. For as eager beholders have we come; we wanted to see what brighteneth dim eyes.

And lo! now is it all over with our cries of distress. Now are our minds and hearts open and enraptured. Little is lacking for our spirits to become wanton.

There is nothing, O Zarathustra, that groweth more pleasingly on earth than a lofty, strong will: it is the finest growth. An entire landscape refresheth itself at one such tree.

To the pine do I compare him, O Zarathustra, which groweth up like thee—tall, silent, hardy, solitary, of the best, supplest wood, stately,—

—In the end, however, grasping out for *its* dominion with strong, green branches, asking weighty questions of the wind, the storm, and whatever is at home on high places;

—Answering more weightily, a commander, a victor! Oh! who should not ascend high mountains to behold such growths?

At thy tree, O Zarathustra, the gloomy and ill-constituted

also refresh themselves; at thy look even the wavering become steady and heal their hearts.

And verily, towards thy mountain and thy tree do many eyes turn to-day; a great longing hath arisen, and many have learned to ask: 'Who is Zarathustra?'

And those into whose ears thou hast at any time dripped thy song and thy honey: all the hidden ones, the lone-dwellers and the twain-dwellers, have simultaneously said to their hearts:

'Doth Zarathustra still live? It is no longer worth while to live, everything is indifferent, everything is useless: or else— we must live with Zarathustra!'

'Why doth he not come who hath so long announced himself?' thus do many people ask; 'hath solitude swallowed him up? Or should we perhaps go to him?'

Now doth it come to pass that solitude itself becometh fragile and breaketh open, like a grave that breaketh open and can no longer hold its dead. Everywhere one seeth resurrected ones.

Now do the waves rise and rise around thy mountain, O Zarathustra. And however high be thy height, many of them must rise up to thee: thy boat shall not rest much longer on dry ground.

And that we despairing ones have now come into thy cave, and already no longer despair:—it is but a prognostic and a presage that better ones are on the way to thee,—

—For they themselves are on the way to thee, the last remnant of God among men—that is to say, all the men of great longing, of great loathing, of great satiety,

—All who do not want to live unless they learn again to *hope*—unless they learn from thee, O Zarathustra, the *great* hope!"

Thus spake the king on the right, and seized the hand of Zarathustra in order to kiss it; but Zarathustra checked his veneration, and stepped back frightened, fleeing as it were, silently and suddenly into the far distance. After a little while, however, he was again at home with his guests, looked at them with clear scrutinising eyes, and said:

"My guests, ye higher men, I will speak plain language and plainly with you. It is not for *you* that I have waited here in these mountains."

(" 'Plain language and plainly?' Good God!" said here the king on the left to himself; "one seeth he doth not know the good Occidentals, this sage out of the Orient!

But he meaneth 'blunt language and bluntly'—well! That is not the worst taste in these days!")

"Ye may, verily, all of you be higher men," continued Zara· thustra; "but for me—ye are neither high enough, nor strong enough.

For me, that is to say, for the inexorable which is now silent in me, but will not always be silent. And if ye appertain to me, still it is not as my right arm.

For he who himself standeth, like you, on sickly and tender legs, wisheth above all to be *treated indulgently,* whether he be conscious of it or hide it from himself.

My arms and my legs, however, I do not treat indulgently, *I do not treat my warriors indulgently:* how then could ye be fit for *my* warfare?

With you I should spoil all my victories. And many of you would tumble over if ye but heard the loud beating of my drums.

Moreover, ye are not sufficiently beautiful and well-born for me. I require pure, smooth mirrors for my doctrines; on your surface even mine own likeness is distorted.

On your shoulders presseth many a burden, many a recol
lection; many a mischievous dwarf squatteth in your corners
There is concealed populace also in you.

And though ye be high and of a higher type, much in you
is crooked and misshapen. There is no smith in the world that
could hammer you right and straight for me.

Ye are only bridges: may higher ones pass over upon you
Ye signify steps: so do not upbraid him who ascendeth beyond
you into *his* height!

Out of your seed there may one day arise for me a genuine
son and perfect heir: but that time is distant. Ye yourselves
are not those unto whom my heritage and name belong.

Not for you do I wait here in these mountains; not with you
may I descend for the last time. Ye have come unto me only
as a presage that higher ones are on the way to me,—

—*Not* the men of great longing, of great loathing, of great
satiety, and that which ye call the remnant of God;

—Nay! Nay! Three times Nay! For *others* do I wait here
in these mountains, and will not lift my foot from thence
without them;

—For higher ones, stronger ones, triumphanter ones,
merrier ones, for such as are built squarely in body and soul:
laughing lions must come!

O my guests, ye strange ones—have ye yet heard nothing of
my children? And that they are on the way to me?

Do speak unto me of my gardens, of my Happy Isles, of my
new beautiful race—why do ye not speak unto me thereof?

This guests'-present do I solicit of your love, that ye speak
unto me of my children. For them am I rich, for them I became
poor: what have I not surrendered.

What would I not surrender that I might have one thing:

hese children, *this* living plantation, *these* life-trees of my
vill and of my highest hope!"

Thus spake Zarathustra, and stopped suddenly in his dis-
ourse: for his longing came over him, and he closed his eyes
nd his mouth, because of the agitation of his heart. And all
iis guests also were silent, and stood still and confounded:
xcept only that the old soothsayer made signs with his hands
nd his gestures.

72. The Supper

'OR at this point the soothsayer interrupted the greeting of
Zarathustra and his guests: he pressed forward as one who had
io time to lose, seized Zarathustra's hand and exclaimed: "But
Zarathustra!

One thing is more necessary than the other, so sayest thou
hyself: well, one thing is now more necessary *unto me* than
ll others.

A word at the right time: didst thou not invite me to *table?*
And here are many who have made long journeys. Thou dost
iot mean to feed us merely with discourses?

Besides, all of you have thought too much about freezing,
lrowning, suffocating, and other bodily dangers: none of you,
iowever, have thought of *my* danger, namely, perishing of
iunger—"

(Thus spake the soothsayer. When Zarathustra's animals,
iowever, heard these words, they ran away in terror. For they
aw that all they had brought home during the day would not
ie enough to fill the one soothsayer.)

"Likewise perishing of thirst," continued the soothsayer.
'And although I hear water splashing here like words of wis-

[*317*]

dom—-that is to say, plenteously and unweariedly, I—want
wine!

Not every one is a born water-drinker like Zarathustra.
Neither doth water suit weary and withered ones: *we* deserve
wine—*it* alone giveth immediate vigour and improvised
health!''

On this occasion, when the soothsayer was longing for wine,
it happened that the king on the left, the silent one, also found
expression for once. *''We* took care,'' said he, ''about wine, I,
along with my brother the king on the right: we have enough
of wine,—a whole ass-load of it. So there is nothing lacking
but bread.''

''Bread,'' replied Zarathustra, laughing when he spake, ''it
is precisely bread that anchorites have not. But man doth not
live by bread alone, but also by the flesh of good lambs, of
which I have two:

—*These* shall we slaughter quickly, and cook spicily with
sage: it is so that I like them. And there is also no lack of
roots and fruits, good enough even for the fastidious and
dainty,—nor of nuts and other riddles for cracking.

Thus will we have a good repast in a little while. But whoever wisheth to eat with us must also give a hand to the work,
even the kings. For with Zarathustra even a king may be a
cook.''

This proposal appealed to the hearts of all of them, save
that the voluntary beggar objected to the flesh and wine and
spices.

''Just hear this glutton Zarathustra!'' said he jokingly: ''doth
one go into caves and high mountains to make such repasts?

Now indeed do I understand what he once taught us:
'Blessed be moderate poverty!' And why he wisheth to do
away with beggars.''

"Be of good cheer," replied Zarathustra, "as I am. Abide by thy customs, thou excellent one: grind thy corn, drink thy water, praise thy cooking,—if only it make thee glad!

I am a law only for mine own; I am not a law for all. He, however, who belongeth unto me must be strong of bone and light of foot,—

—Joyous in fight and feast, no sulker, no John o' Dreams, ready for the hardest task as for the feast, healthy and hale.

The best belongeth unto mine and me; and if it be not given us, then do we take it:—the best food, the purest sky, the strongest thoughts, the fairest women!"—

Thus spake Zarathustra; the king on the right however answered and said: "Strange! Did one ever hear such sensible things out of the mouth of a wise man?

And verily, it is the strangest thing in a wise man, if over and above, he be still sensible, and not an ass."

Thus spake the king on the right and wondered; the ass however, with ill-will, said YE-A to his remark. This however was the beginning of that long repast which is called "The Supper" in the history-books. At this there was nothing else spoken of but *the higher man*.

73. The Higher Man

1

WHEN I came unto men for the first time, then did I commit the anchorite folly, the great folly: I appeared on the market-place.

And when I spake unto all, I spake unto none. In the evening, however, rope-dancers were my companions, and corpses; and I myself almost a corpse.

With the new morning, however, there came unto me a new truth: then did I learn to say: "Of what account to me are market-place and populace and populace-noise and long populace-ears!"

Ye higher men, learn *this* from me: On the market-place no one believeth in higher men. But if ye will speak there, very well! The populace, however, blinketh: "We are all equal."

"Ye higher men,"—so blinketh the populace—"there are no higher men, we are all equal; man is man, before God— we are all equal!"

Before God!—Now, however, this God hath died. Before the populace, however, we will not be equal. Ye higher men, away from the market-place!

2

Before God!—Now however this God hath died! Ye higher men, this God was your greatest danger.

Only since he lay in the grave have ye again arisen. Now only cometh the great noontide, now only doth the higher man become—master!

Have ye understood this word, O my brethren? Ye are frightened: do your hearts turn giddy? Doth the abyss here yawn for you? Doth the hell-hound here yelp at you?

Well! Take heart! ye higher men! Now only travaileth the mountain of the human future. God hath died: now do *we* desire—the Superman to live.

3

The most careful ask to-day: "How is man to be maintained?" Zarathustra however asketh, as the first and only one: "How is man to be *surpassed?*"

The Superman, I have at heart; *that* is the first and only thing to me—and *not* man: not the neighbour, not the poorest, not the sorriest, not the best.—

O my brethren, what I can love in man is that he is an overgoing and a down-going. And also in you there is much that maketh me love and hope.

In that ye have despised, ye higher men, that maketh me hope. For the great despisers are the great reverers.

In that ye have despaired, there is much to honour. For ye have not learned to submit yourselves, ye have not learned petty policy.

For to-day have the petty people become master: they all preach submission and humility and policy and diligence and consideration and the long *et cetera* of petty virtues.

Whatever is of the effeminate type, whatever originateth from the servile type, and especially the populace-mishmash: —*that* wisheth now to be master of all human destiny—O disgust! Disgust! Disgust!

That asketh and asketh and never tireth: "How is man to maintain himself best, longest, most pleasantly?" Thereby— are they the masters of today.

These masters of today—surpass them, O my brethren— these petty people: *they* are the Superman's greatest danger!

Surpass, ye higher men, the petty virtues, the petty policy, the sand-grain considerateness, the ant-hill trumpery, the pitiable comfortableness, the "happiness of the greatest number"—!

And rather despair than submit yourselves. And verily, I love you, because ye know not today how to live, ye higher men! For thus do *ye* live—best!

4

Have ye courage, O my brethren? Are ye stout-hearted? *Not* the courage before witnesses, but anchorite and eagle courage, which not even a God any longer beholdeth?

Cold souls, mules, the blind and the drunken, I do not call stout-hearted. He hath heart who knoweth fear, but *vanquisheth* it; who seeth the abyss, but with *pride*.

He who seeth the abyss, but with eagle's eyes,—he who with eagle's talons *graspeth* the abyss: he hath courage.— —

5

"Man is evil"—so said to me for consolation, all the wisest ones. Ah, if only it be still true today! For the evil is man's best force.

"Man must become better and eviler"—so do *I* teach. The evilest is necessary for the Superman's best.

It may have been well for the preacher of the petty people to suffer and be burdened by men's sin. I, however, rejoice in great sin as my great *consolation*.—

Such things, however, are not said for long ears. Every word, also, is not suited for every mouth. These are fine far-away things: at them sheep's claws shall not grasp!

6

Ye higher men, think ye that I am here to put right what ye have put wrong?

Or that I wished henceforth to make snugger couches for you sufferers? Or show you restless, miswandering, misclimbing ones, new and easier footpaths?

Nay! Nay! Three times Nay! Always more, always better ones of your type shall succumb,—for ye shall always have it worse and harder. Thus only—

—Thus only groweth man aloft to the height where the lightning striketh and shattereth him: high enough for the lightning!

Towards the few, the long, the remote go forth my soul and my seeking: of what account to me are your many little, short miseries!

Ye do not yet suffer enough for me! For ye suffer from yourselves, ye have not yet suffered *from man.* Ye would lie if ye spake otherwise! None of you suffereth from what *I* have suffered.——

7

It is not enough for me that the lightning no longer doeth harm. I do not wish to conduct it away: it shall learn—to work for *me.*—

My wisdom hath accumulated long like a cloud, it becometh stiller and darker. So doeth all wisdom which shall one day bear *lightnings.*—

[*323*]

Unto these men of today will I not be *light,* nor be called light. *Them*—will I blind: lightning of my wisdom! put out their eyes!

8

Do not will anything beyond your power: there is a bad falseness in those who will beyond their power.

Especially when they will great things! For they awaken distrust in great things, these subtle false-coiners and stage-players:—

—Until at last they are false towards themselves, squint-eyed, whited cankers, glossed over with strong words, parade virtues and brilliant false deeds.

Take good care there, ye higher men! For nothing is more precious to me, and rarer, than honesty.

Is this today not that of the populace? The populace however knoweth not what is great and what is small, what is straight and what is honest: it is innocently crooked, it ever lieth.

9

Have a good distrust today, ye higher men, ye enheartened ones! Ye open-hearted ones! And keep your reasons secret! For this today is that of the populace.

What the populace once learned to believe without reasons, who could—refute it to them by means of reasons?

And on the market-place one convinceth with gestures. But reasons make the populace distrustful.

And when truth hath once triumphed there, then ask your-

selves with good distrust: "What strong error hath fought
for it?"

Be on your guard also against the learned! They hate you,
because they are unproductive! They have cold, withered eyes
before which every bird is unplumed.

Such persons vaunt about not lying: but inability to lie is
still far from being love to truth. Be on your guard!

Freedom from fever is still far from being knowledge!
Refrigerated spirits I do not believe in. He who cannot lie,
doth not know what truth is.

10

If ye would go up high, then use your own legs! Do not get
yourselves *carried* aloft; do not seat yourselves on other people's backs and heads!

Thou hast mounted, however, on horseback? Thou now
ridest briskly up to thy goal? Well, my friend! But thy lame
foot is also with thee on horseback!

When thou reachest thy goal, when thou alightest from thy
horse: precisely on thy *height,* thou higher man,—then wilt
thou stumble!

11

Ye creating ones, ye higher men! One is only pregnant with
one's own child.

Do not let yourselves be imposed upon or put upon! Who
then is *your* neighbour? Even if ye act "for your neighbour"—
ye still do not create for him!

Unlearn, I pray you, this "for," ye creating ones: your very virtue wisheth you to have naught to do with "for" and "on account of" and "because." Against these false little words shall ye stop your ears.

"For one's neighbour," is the virtue only of the petty people: there it is said "like and like," and "hand washeth hand":— they have neither the right nor the power for *your* self-seeking!

In your self-seeking, ye creating ones, there is the foresight and foreseeing of the pregnant! What no one's eye hath yet seen, namely, the fruit—this, sheltereth and saveth and nourisheth your entire love.

Where your entire love is, namely, with your child, there is also your entire virtue! Your work, your will is *your* "neighbour": let no false values impose upon you!

12

Ye creating ones, ye higher men! Whoever hath to give birth is sick; whoever hath given birth, however, is unclean.

Ask women: one giveth birth, not because it giveth pleasure. The pain maketh hens and poets cackle.

Ye creating ones, in you there is much uncleanness. That is because ye have had to be mothers.

A new child: oh, how much new filth hath also come into the world! Go apart! He who hath given birth shall wash his soul!

13

Be not virtuous beyond your powers! And seek nothing from yourselves opposed to probability!

Walk in the footsteps in which your fathers' virtue hath already walked! How would ye rise high, if your fathers' will should not rise with you?

He, however, who would be a firstling, let him take care lest he also become a lastling! And where the vices of your fathers are, there should ye not set up as saints!

He whose fathers were inclined for women, and for strong wine and flesh of wildboar swine; what would it be if he demanded chastity of himself?

A folly would it be! Much, verily, doth it seem to me for such a one, if he should be the husband of one or of two or of three women.

And if he founded monasteries, and inscribed over their portals: "The way to holiness,"—I should still say: What good is it! it is a new folly!

He hath founded for himself a penance-house and refuge-house: much good may it do! But I do not believe in it.

In solitude there groweth what any one bringeth into it—also the brute in one's nature. Thus is solitude inadvisable unto many.

Hath there ever been anything filthier on earth than the saints of the wilderness? *Around them* was not only the devil loose—but also the swine.

14

Shy, ashamed, awkward, like the tiger whose spring hath failed—thus, ye higher men, have I often seen you slink aside. A *cast* which ye made had failed.

But what doth it matter, ye dice-players! Ye had not learned to play and mock, as one must play and mock! Do we not ever sit at a great table of mocking and playing?

And if great things have been a failure with you, have ye yourselves therefore—been a failure? And if ye yourselves have been a failure, hath man therefore—been a failure? If man, however, hath been a failure: well then! never mind!

15

The higher its type, always the seldomer doth a thing succeed. Ye higher men here, have ye not all—been failures?

Be of good cheer; what doth it matter? How much is still possible! Learn to laugh at yourselves, as ye ought to laugh!

What wonder even that ye have failed and only half-succeeded, ye half-shattered ones! Doth not—man's *future* strive and struggle in you?

Man's furthest, profoundest, star-highest issues, his prodigious powers—do not all these foam through one another in your vessel?

What wonder that many a vessel shattereth! Learn to laugh at yourselves, as ye ought to laugh! Ye higher men, Oh, how much is still possible!

And verily, how much hath already succeeded! How rich is this earth in small, good, perfect things, in well-constituted things!

Set around you small, good, perfect things, ye higher men. Their golden maturity healeth the heart. The perfect teacheth one to hope.

16

What hath hitherto been the greatest sin here on earth? Was it not the word of him who said: "Woe unto them that laugh now!"

Did he himself find no cause for laughter on the earth? Then he sought badly. A child even findeth cause for it.

He—did not love sufficiently: otherwise would he also have loved us, the laughing ones! But he hated and hooted us; wailing and teeth-gnashing did he promise us.

Must one then curse immediately, when one doth not love? That—seemeth to me bad taste. Thus did he, however, this absolute one. He sprang from the populace.

And he himself just did not love sufficiently; otherwise would he have raged less because people did not love him. All great love doth not *seek* love:—it seeketh more.

Go out of the way of all such absolute ones! They are a poor sickly type, a populace-type: they look at this life with ill-will, they have an evil eye for this earth.

Go out of the way of all such absolute ones! They have heavy feet and sultry hearts:—they do not know how to dance. How could the earth be light to such ones!

17

Tortuously do all good things come nigh to their goal. Like cats they curve their backs, they purr inwardly with their approaching happiness,—all good things laugh.

His step betrayeth whether a person already walketh on *his own* path: just see me walk! He, however, who cometh nigh to his goal, danceth.

And verily, a statue have I not become, not yet do I stand there stiff, stupid and stony, like a pillar; I love fast racing.

And though there be on earth fens and dense afflictions, he who hath light feet runneth even across the mud, and danceth, as upon well-swept ice.

Lift up your hearts, my brethren, high, higher! And do not forget your legs! Lift up also your legs, ye good dancers, and better still, if ye stand upon your heads!

18

This crown of the laughter, this rose-garland crown: I my-self have put on this crown, I myself have consecrated my laughter. No one else have I found to-day potent enough for this.

Zarathustra the dancer, Zarathustra the light one, who beck-oneth with his pinions, one ready for flight, beckoning unto all birds, ready and prepared, a blissfully light-spirited one:—

Zarathustra the soothsayer, Zarathustra the sooth-laugher, no impatient one, no absolute one, one who loveth leaps and side-leaps; I myself have put on this crown!

19

Lift up your hearts, my brethren, high, higher! And do not forget your legs! Lift up also your legs, ye good dancers, and better still if ye stand upon your heads!

There are also heavy animals in a state of happiness, there are club-footed ones from the beginning. Curiously do they exert themselves, like an elephant which endeavoureth to stand upon its head.

Better, however, to be foolish with happiness than foolish with misfortune, better to dance awkwardly than walk lamely. So learn, I pray you, my wisdom, ye higher men: even the worst thing hath two good reverse sides,—

—Even the worst thing hath good dancing-legs: so learn, I pray you, ye higher men, to put yourselves on your proper legs!

So unlearn, I pray you, the sorrow-sighing, and all the populace-sadness! Oh, how sad the buffoons of the populace seem to me today! This today, however, is that of the populace.

20

Do like unto the wind when it rusheth forth from its mountain-caves: unto its own piping will it dance; the seas tremble and leap under its footsteps.

That which giveth wings to asses, that which milketh the lionesses:—praised be that good, unruly spirit, which cometh like a hurricane unto all the present and unto all the populace,—

—Which is hostile to thistle-heads and puzzle-heads, and to all withered leaves and weeds:—praised be this wild, good, free spirit of the storm, which danceth upon fens and afflictions, as upon meadows!

Which hateth the consumptive populace-dogs, and all the ill-constituted, sullen brood:—praised be this spirit of all free spirits, the laughing storm, which bloweth dust into the eyes of all the melanopic and melancholic!

Ye higher men, the worst thing in you is that ye have none of you learned to dance as ye ought to dance—to dance beyond yourselves! What doth it matter that ye have failed!

How many things are still possible! So *learn* to laugh beyond yourselves! Lift up your hearts, ye good dancers, high! higher! And do not forget the good laughter!

This crown of the laughter, this rose-garland crown: to you, my brethren, do I cast this crown! Laughing have I consecrated; ye higher men, *learn,* I pray you—to laugh!

74. *The Song of Melancholy*

1

WHEN Zarathustra spake these sayings, he stood nigh to the entrance of his cave; with the last words, however, he slipped away from his guests, and fled for a little while into the open air.

"O pure odours around me," cried he, "O blessed stillness around me! But where are mine animals? Hither, hither, mine eagle and my serpent!

Tell me, mine animals: these higher men, all of them—do they perhaps not *smell* well? O pure odours around me! Now only do I know and feel how I love you, mine animals."

—And Zarathustra said once more: "I love you, mine animals!" The eagle, however, and the serpent pressed close to him when he spake these words, and looked up to him. In this attitude were they all three silent together, and sniffed and sipped the good air with one another. For the air here outside was better than with the higher men.

2

Hardly, however, had Zarathustra left the cave when the old magician got up, looked cunningly about him, and said: "He is gone!

And already, ye higher men—let me tickle you with this complimentary and flattering name, as he himself doeth—already doth mine evil spirit of deceit and magic attack me, my melancholy devil,

—Which is an adversary to this Zarathustra from the very heart: forgive it for this! Now doth it wish to conjure before you, it hath just *its* hour; in vain do I struggle with this evil spirit.

Unto all of you, whatever honours ye like to assume in your names, whether ye call yourselves 'the free spirits' or 'the conscientious,' or 'the penitents of the spirit,' or 'the unfettered,' or 'the great longers,'—

—Unto all of you, who like me suffer *from the great loathing,* to whom the old God hath died, and as yet no new God lieth in cradles and swaddling clothes—unto all of you is mine evil spirit and magic-devil favourable.

I know you, ye higher men, I know him,—I know also this fiend whom I love in spite of me, this Zarathustra: he himself often seemeth to me like the beautiful mask of a saint,

—Like a new strange mummery in which mine evil spirit, the melancholy devil, delighteth:—I love Zarathustra, so doth it often seem to me, for the sake of mine evil spirit.—

[*333*]

But already doth *it* attack me and constrain me, this spirit of melancholy, this evening-twilight devil: and verily, ye higher men, it hath a longing—

—Open your eyes!—it hath a longing to come *naked,* whether male or female, I do not yet know: but it cometh, it constraineth me, alas! open your wits!

The day dieth out, unto all things cometh now the evening, also unto the best things; hear now, and see, ye higher men, what devil—man or woman—this spirit of evening-melancholy is!''

Thus spake the old magician, looked cunningly about him, and then seized his harp.

3

In evening's limpid air,
What time the dew's soothings
Unto the earth downpour,
Invisibly and unheard—
For tender shoe-gear wear
The soothing dews, like all that's kind-gentle—:
Bethinkst thou then, bethinkst thou, burning heart,
How once thou thirstedest,
For heaven's kindly teardrops and dew's down-drop-
          pings,
All singed and weary thirstedest,
What time on yellow grass-pathways
Wicked, occidental sunny glances
Through sombre trees about thee sported,
Blindingly sunny glow-glances, gladly-hurting?

"Of *truth* the wooer? Thou?"—so taunted they—
"Nay! Merely poet!
A brute insidious, plundering, grovelling,
That aye must lie,
That wittingly, wilfully, aye must lie:
For booty lusting,
Motley masked,
Self-hidden, shrouded,
Himself his booty—
He—of truth the wooer?
Nay! Mere fool! Mere poet!
Just motley speaking,
From mask of fool confusedly shouting,
Circumambling on fabricated word-bridges,
On motley rainbow-arches,
'Twixt the spurious heavenly,
And spurious earthly,
Round us roving, round us soaring,—
Mere fool! Mere poet!

He—of truth the wooer?
Not still, stiff, smooth and cold,
Become an image,
A godlike statue,
Set up in front of temples,
As a God's own door-guard:
Nay! hostile to all such truthfulness-statues,
In every desert homelier than at temples,
With cattish wantonness,
Through every window leaping
Quickly into chances,

Every wild forest a-sniffing,
Greedily-longingly, sniffing,
That thou, in wild forests,
'Mong the motley-speckled fierce creatures,
Shouldest rove, sinful-sound and fine-coloured,
With longing lips smacking,
Blessedly mocking, blessedly hellish, blessedly blood-
　　thirsty,
Robbing, skulking, lying—roving:——

Or unto eagles like which fixedly,
Long adown the precipice look,
Adown *their* precipice:—— —
Oh, how they whirl down now,
Thereunder, therein,
To ever deeper profoundness whirling!——
Then,
Sudden,
With aim aright,
With quivering flight,
On *lambkins* pouncing,
Headlong down, sore-hungry,
For lambkins longing,
Fierce 'gainst all lamb-spirits,
Furious-fierce 'gainst all that look
Sheeplike, or lambeyed, or crisp-woolly,
—Grey, with lambsheep kindliness!

Even thus,
Eaglelike, pantherlike,
Are the poet's desires,
Are *thine own* desires 'neath a thousand guises.

Thou fool! Thou poet!
Thou who all mankind viewedst—
So God, as sheep—:
The God *to rend* within mankind,
As the sheep in mankind,
And in rending *laughing*—

That, that is thine own blessedness!
Of a panther and eagle—blessedness!
Of a poet and fool—the blessedness!"— —

In evening's limpid air,
What time the moon's sickle,
Green, 'twixt the purple-glowings,
And jealous, steal'th forth:
—Of day the foe,
With every step in secret,
The rosy garland-hammocks
Downsickling, till they've sunken
Down nightwards, faded, downsunken:—

Thus had I sunken one day
From mine own truth-insanity,
From mine own fervid day-longings,
Of day aweary, sick of sunshine,
—Sunk downwards, evenwards, shadowwards:
By one sole trueness
All scorched and thirsty:
—Bethinkst thou still, bethinkst thou, burning heart,
How then thou thirstedest?—
That I should banned be
From all the trueness!
Mere fool! Mere poet!

75. Science

THUS sang the magician; and all who were present went like birds unawares into the net of his artful and melancholy voluptuousness. Only the spiritually conscientious one had not been caught: he at once snatched the harp from the magician and called out: "Air! Let in good air! Let in Zarathustra! Thou makest this cave sultry and poisonous, thou bad old magician!

Thou seducest, thou false one, thou subtle one, to unknown desires and deserts. And alas, that such as thou should talk and make ado about the *truth!*

Alas, to all free spirits who are not on their guard against *such* magicians! It is all over with their freedom: thou teachest and temptest back into prisons,—

—Thou old melancholy devil, out of thy lament soundeth a lurement: thou resemblest those who with their praise of chastity secretly invite to voluptuousness!"

Thus spake the conscientious one; the old magician, however, looked about him, enjoying his triumph, and on that account put up with the annoyance which the conscientious one caused him. "Be still!" said he with modest voice, "good songs want to re-echo well; after good songs one should be long silent.

Thus do all those present, the higher men. Thou, however, hast perhaps understood but little of my song? In thee there is little of the magic spirit."

"Thou praisest me," replied the conscientious one, "in that thou separatest me from thyself; very well! But, ye others, what do I see? Ye still sit there, all of you, with lusting eyes—:

Ye free spirits, whither hath your freedom gone! Ye almost seem to me to resemble those who have long looked at bad girls dancing naked: your souls themselves dance!

In you, ye higher men, there must be more of that which the magician calleth his evil spirit of magic and deceit:—we must indeed be different.

And verily, we spake and thought long enough together ere Zarathustra came home to his cave, for me not to be unaware that we *are* different.

We *seek* different things even here aloft, ye and I. For I seek more *security;* on that account have I come to Zarathustra. For he is still the most steadfast tower and will—

—Today, when everything tottereth, when all the earth quaketh. Ye, however, when I see what eyes ye make, it almost seemeth to me that ye seek *more insecurity,*

—More horror, more danger, more earthquake. Ye long (it almost seemeth so to me—forgive my presumption, ye higher men)—

—Ye long for the worst and dangerousest life, which frighteneth *me* most,—for the life of wild beasts, for forests, caves, steep mountains and labyrinthine gorges.

And it is not those who lead *out of* danger that please you best, but those who lead you away from all paths, the misleaders. But if such longing in you be *actual,* it seemeth to me nevertheless to be *impossible.*

For fear—that is man's original and fundamental feeling; through fear everything is explained, original sin and original virtue. Through fear there grew also *my* virtue, that is to say: Science.

For fear of wild animals—that hath been longest fostered in man, inclusive of the animal which he concealeth and feareth in himself:—Zarathustra calleth it 'the beast inside.'

[*339*]

Such prolonged ancient fear, at last become subtle, spiritual and intellectual—at present, me thinketh, it is called *Science.*"—

Thus spake the conscientious one; but Zarathustra, who had just come back into his cave and had heard and divined the last discourse, threw a handful of roses to the conscientious one, and laughed on account of his "truths." "Why!" he exclaimed, "what did I hear just now? Verily, it seemeth to me, thou art a fool, or else I myself am one: and quietly and quickly will I put thy 'truth' upside down.

For *fear*—is an exception with us. Courage, however, and adventure, and delight in the uncertain, in the unattempted— *courage* seemeth to me the entire primitive history of man.

The wildest and most courageous animals hath he envied and robbed of all their virtues: thus only did he become—man.

This courage, at last become subtle, spiritual and intellectual, this human courage, with eagle's pinions and serpent's wisdom: *this,* it seemeth to me, is called at present—"

"*Zarathustra!*" cried all of them there assembled, as if with one voice, and burst out at the same time into a great laughter; there arose, however, from them as it were a heavy cloud. Even the magician laughed, and said wisely: "Well! It is gone, mine evil spirit!

And did I not myself warn you against it when I said that it was a deceiver, a lying and deceiving spirit?

Especially when it showeth itself naked. But what can *I* do with regard to its tricks! Have *I* created it and the world?

Well! Let us be good again, and of good cheer! And although Zarathustra looketh with evil eye—just see him! he disliketh me—:

—Ere night cometh will he again learn to love and laud me; he cannot live long without committing such follies.

He—loveth his enemies: this art knoweth he better than any one I have seen. But he taketh revenge for it—on his friends!"

Thus spake the old magician, and the higher men applauded him; so that Zarathustra went round, and mischievously and lovingly shook hands with his friends,—like one who hath to make amends and apologise to every one for something. When however he had thereby come to the door of his cave, lo, then had he again a longing for the good air outside, and for his animals,—and wished to steal out.

67. *Among Daughters of the Desert*

1

"Go NOT away!" said then the wanderer who called himself Zarathustra's shadow, "abide with us—otherwise the old gloomy affliction might again fall upon us.

Now hath that old magician given us of his worst for our good, and lo! the good, pious pope there hath tears in his eyes, and hath quite embarked again upon the sea of melancholy.

Those kings may well put on a good air before us still: for that have *they* learned best of us all at present! Had they however no one to see them, I wager that with them also the bad game would again commence,—

—The bad game of drifting clouds, of damp melancholy, of curtained heavens, of stolen suns, of howling autumn-winds,

—The bad game of our howling and crying for help! Abide with us, O Zarathustra! Here there is much concealed misery that wisheth to speak, much evening, much cloud, much damp air!

Thou hast nourished us with strong food for men, and powerful proverbs: do not let the weakly, womanly spirits attack us anew at dessert!

Thou alone makest the air around thee strong and clear. Did I ever find anywhere on earth such good air as with thee in thy cave?

Many lands have I seen, my nose hath learned to test and estimate many kinds of air: but with thee do my nostrils taste their greatest delight!

Unless it be,—unless it be—, do forgive an old recollection! Forgive me an old after-dinner song, which I once composed amongst daughters of the desert:—

For with them was there equally good, clear, Oriental air; there was I furthest from cloudy, damp, melancholy Old-Europe!

Then did I love such Oriental maidens and other blue kingdoms of heaven, over which hang no clouds and no thoughts.

Ye would not believe how charmingly they sat there, when they did not dance, profound, but without thoughts, like little secrets, like beribboned riddles, like dessert-nuts—

Many-hued and foreign, forsooth! but without clouds: riddles which can be guessed: to please such maidens I then composed an after-dinner psalm."

Thus spake the wanderer who called himself Zarathustra's shadow; and before any one answered him, he had seized the harp of the old magician, crossed his legs, and looked calmly and sagely around him:—with his nostrils, however, he inhaled the air slowly and questioningly, like one who in new countries tasteth new foreign air. Afterward he began to sing with a kind of roaring.

2

The deserts grow: woe him who doth them hide!
   —Ha!
Solemnly!
In effect solemnly!
A worthy beginning!
Afric manner, solemnly!
Of a lion worthy,
Or perhaps of a virtuous howl-monkey—
—But it's naught to you,
Ye friendly damsels dearly loved,
At whose own feet to me,
The first occasion,
To a European under palm-trees,
At seat is now granted. Selah.

Wonderful, truly!
Here do I sit now,
The desert nigh, and yet I am
So far still from the desert,
Even in naught yet deserted:
That is, I'm swallowed down
By this the smallest oasis—:
—It opened up just yawning,
Its loveliest mouth agape,
Most sweet-odoured of all mouthlets:
Then fell I right in,
Right down, right through—in 'mong you,
Ye friendly damsels dearly loved! Selah.

[*343*]

Hail! hail! to that whale, fishlike,
If it thus for its guest's convenience
Made things nice!—(ye well know,
Surely, my learned allusion?)
Hail to its belly,
If it had e'er
A such loveliest oasis-belly
As this is: though however I doubt about it,
—With this come I out of Old-Europe,
That doubt'th more eagerly than doth any
Elderly married woman.
May the Lord improve it!
Amen!

Here do I sit now,
In this the smallest oasis,
Like a date indeed,
Brown, quite sweet, gold-suppurating,
For rounded mouth of maiden longing,
But yet still more for youthful, maidlike,
Ice-cold and snow-white and incisory
Front teeth: and for such assuredly,
Pine the hearts all of ardent date-fruits. **Selah.**

To the there-named south-fruits now,
Similar, all-too-similar,
Do I lie here; by little
Flying insects
Round-sniffled and round-played,
And also by yet littler,
Foolisher, and peccabler
Wishes and phantasies,—

Environed by you,
Ye silent, presentientest
Maiden-kittens,
Dudu and Suleika,
—*Roundsphinxed*, that into one word
I may crowd much feeling:
(Forgive me, O God,
All such speech-sinning!)
—Sit I here the best of air sniffling,
Paradisal air, truly,
Bright and buoyant air, golden-mottled,
As goodly air as ever
From lunar orb downfell—
Be it by hazard,
Or supervened it by arrogancy?
As the ancient poets relate it.
But doubter, I'm now calling it
In question: with this do I come indeed
Out of Europe,
That doubt'th more eagerly than doth any
Elderly married woman.
May the Lord improve it!
Amen.

This the finest air drinking,
With nostrils out-swelled like goblets,
Lacking future, lacking remembrances,
Thus do I sit here, ye
Friendly damsels dearly loved,
And look at the palm-tree there,
How it, to a dance-girl, like,

Doth bow and bend and on its haunches bob,
—One doth it too, when one view'th it long!—
To a dance-girl like, who as it seem'th to me,
Too long, and dangerously persistent,
Always, always, just on *single* leg hath stood?
—Then forgot she thereby, as it seem'th to me,
The *other* leg?
For vainly I, at least,
Did search for the amissing
Fellow-jewel
—Namely, the other leg—
In the sanctified precincts,
Nigh her very dearest, very tenderest,
Flapping and fluttering and flickering skirting.
Yea, if ye should, ye beauteous friendly ones,
Quite take my word:
She hath, alas! *lost* it!
Hu! Hu! Hu! Hu! Hu!
It is away!
For ever away!
The other leg!
Oh, pity for that loveliest other leg!
Where may it now tarry, all-forsaken weeping?
The lonesomest leg?
In fear perhaps before a
Furious, yellow, blond and curled
Leonine monster? Or perhaps even
Gnawed away, nibbled badly—
Most wretched, woeful! woeful! nibbled badly! Selah.

Oh, weep ye not,
Gentle spirits!

Weep ye not, ye
Date-fruit spirits! Milk-bosoms!
Ye sweetwood-heart
Purselets!
Weep ye no more,
Pallid Dudu!
Be a man, Suleika! Bold! Bold!
—Or else should there perhaps
Something strengthening, heart-strengthening,
Here most proper be?
Some inspiring text?
Some solemn exhortation?—
Ha! Up now! honour!
Moral honour! European honour!
Blow again, continue,
Bellows-box of virtue!
Ha!
Once more thy roaring,
Thy moral roaring!
As a virtuous lion
Nigh the daughters of deserts roaring!
—For virtue's out-howl,
Ye very dearest maidens,
Is more than every
European fervour, European hot-hunger!
And now do I stand here,
As European,
I can't be different, God's help to me!
Amen!

The deserts grow: woe him who doth them hide!

[*347*]

77. *The Awakening*

1

AFTER the song of the wanderer and shadow, the cave became all at once full of noise and laughter: and since the assembled guests all spake simultaneously, and even the ass, encouraged thereby, no longer remained silent, a little aversion and scorn for his visitors came over Zarathustra, although he rejoiced at their gladness. For it seemed to him a sign of convalescence. So he slipped out into the open air and spake to his animals.

"Whither hath their distress now gone?" said he, and already did he himself feel relieved of his petty disgust— "with me, it seemeth that they have unlearned their cries of distress!

—Though, alas! not yet their crying." And Zarathustra stopped his ears, for just then did the YE-A of the ass mix strangely with the noisy jubilation of those higher men.

"They are merry," he began again, "and who knoweth? perhaps at their host's expense; and if they have learned of me to laugh, still it is not *my* laughter they have learned.

But what matter about that! They are old people: they recover in their own way, they laugh in their own way; mine ears have already endured worse and have not become peevish.

This day is a victory: he already yieldeth, he fleeth, *the spirit of gravity,* mine old arch-enemy! How well this day is about to end, which began so badly and gloomily!

And it is *about to* end. Already cometh the evening: over the sea rideth it hither, the good rider! How it bobbeth, the blessed one, the home-returning one, in its purple saddles!

The sky gazeth brightly thereon, the world lieth deep. Oh, all ye strange ones who have come to me, it is already worth while to have lived with me!"

Thus spake Zarathustra. And again came the cries and laughter of the higher men out of the cave: then began he anew:

"They bite at it, my bait taketh, there departeth also from them their enemy, the spirit of gravity. Now do they learn to laugh at themselves: do I hear rightly?

My virile food taketh effect, my strong and savoury sayings: and verily, I did not nourish them with flatulent vegetables! But with warrior-food, with conqueror-food: new desires did I awaken.

New hopes are in their arms and legs, their hearts expand. They find new words, soon will their spirits breathe wantonness.

Such food may sure enough not be proper for children, nor even for longing girls old and young. One persuadeth their bowels otherwise; I am not their physician and teacher.

The *disgust* departeth from these higher men; well! that is my victory. In my domain they become assured; all stupid shame fleeth away; they empty themselves.

They empty their hearts, good times return unto them, they keep holiday and ruminate,—they become *thankful*.

That do I take as the best sign: they become thankful. Not long will it be ere they devise festivals, and put up memorials to their old joys.

They are *convalescents!*" Thus spake Zarathustra joyfully to his heart and gazed outward; his animals, however, pressed up to him, and honoured his happiness and his silence.

[*349*]

2

All on a sudden however, Zarathustra's ear was frightened: for the cave which had hitherto been full of noise and laughter, became all at once still as death;—his nose, however, smelt a sweet-scented vapour and incense-odour, as if from burning pine-cones.

"What happeneth? What are they about?" he asked himself, and stole up to the entrance, that he might be able unobserved to see his guests. But wonder upon wonder! what was he then obliged to behold with his own eyes!

"They have all of them become *pious* again, they *pray,* they are mad!"—said he, and was astonished beyond measure. And forsooth! all these higher men, the two kings, the pope out of service, the evil magician, the voluntary beggar, the wanderer and shadow, the old soothsayer, the spiritually conscientious one, and the ugliest man—they all lay on their knees like children and credulous old women, and worshipped the ass. And just then began the ugliest man to gurgle and snort, as if something unutterable in him tried to find expression; when, however, he had actually found words, behold! it was a pious, strange litany in praise of the adored and censed ass. And the litany sounded thus:

Amen! And glory and honour and wisdom and thanks and praise and strength be to our God, from everlasting to everlasting!

—The ass, however, here brayed YE-A.

He carried our burdens, he hath taken upon him the form of a servant, he is patient of heart and never saith Nay; and he who loveth his God chastiseth him.

—The ass, however, here brayed YE-A.

He speaketh not: except that he ever saith Yea to the world which he created: thus doth he extol his world. It is his artfulness that speaketh not: thus is he rarely found wrong.

—The ass, however, here brayed YE-A.

Uncomely goeth he through the world. Grey is the favourite colour in which he wrappeth his virtue. Hath he spirit, then doth he conceal it; every one, however, believeth in his long ears.

—The ass, however, here brayed YE-A.

What hidden wisdom it is to wear long ears, and only to say Yea and never Nay! Hath he not created the world in his own image, namely, as stupid as possible?

—The ass, however, here brayed YE-A.

Thou goest straight and crooked ways; it concerneth thee little what seemeth straight or crooked unto us men. Beyond good and evil is thy domain. It is thine innocence not to know what innocence is.

—The ass, however, here brayed YE-A.

Lo! how thou spurnest none from thee, neither beggars noi kings. Thou sufferest little children to come unto thee, and when the bad boys decoy thee, then sayest thou simply, YE-A.

—The ass, however, here brayed YE-A.

Thou lovest she-asses and fresh figs, thou art no food-despiser. A thistle tickleth thy heart when thou chancest to be hungry. There is the wisdom of a God therein.

—The ass, however, here brayed YE-A.

78. The Ass-Festival

1

AT THIS place in the litany, however, Zarathustra could no longer control himself; he himself cried out YE-A, louder even than the ass, and sprang into the midst of his maddened guests. "Whatever are you about, ye grown-up children?" he exclaimed, pulling up the praying ones from the ground. "Alas, if any one else, except Zarathustra, had seen you:

Every one would think you the worst blasphemers, or the very foolishest old women, with your new belief!

And thou thyself, thou old pope, how is it in accordance with thee, to adore an ass in such a manner as God?"—

"O Zarathustra," answered the pope, "forgive me, but in divine matters I am more enlightened even than thou. And it is right that it should be so.

Better to adore God so, in this form, than in no form at all! Think over this saying, mine exalted friend: thou wilt readily divine that in such a saying there is wisdom.

He who said 'God is a Spirit'—made the greatest stride and slide hitherto made on earth towards unbelief: such a dictum is not easily amended again on earth!

Mine old heart leapeth and boundeth because there is still something to adore on earth. Forgive it, O Zarathustra, to an old, pious pontiff-heart!—"

—"And thou," said Zarathustra to the wanderer and shadow, "thou callest and thinkest thyself a free spirit? And thou here practisest such idolatry and hierolatry?

Worse verily, doest thou here than with thy bad brown girls, thou bad, new believer!"

"It is sad enough," answered the wanderer and shadow, "thou art right: but how can I help it! The old God liveth again, O Zarathustra, thou mayst say what thou wilt.

The ugliest man is to blame for it all: he hath reawakened him. And if he say that he once killed him, with Gods *death* is always just a prejudice."

—"And thou," said Zarathustra, "thou bad old magician, what didst thou do! Who ought to believe any longer in thee in this free age, when *thou* believest in such divine donkeyism?

It was a stupid thing that thou didst; how couldst thou, a shrewd man, do such a stupid thing!"

"O Zarathustra," answered the shrewd magician, "thou art right, it was a stupid thing,—it was also repugnant to me."

—"And thou even," said Zarathustra to the spiritually con- scientious one, "consider, and put thy finger to thy nose! Doth nothing go against thy conscience here? Is thy spirit not too cleanly for this praying and the fumes of those devotees?"

"There is something therein," said the spiritually conscien- tious one, and put his finger to his nose, "there is something in this spectacle which even doeth good to my conscience.

Perhaps I dare not believe in God: certain it is however, that God seemeth to me most worthy of belief in this form.

God is said to be eternal, according to the testimony of the most pious: he who hath so much time taketh his time. As slow and as stupid as possible: *thereby* can such a one nevertheless go very far.

And he who hath too much spirit might well become infatu- ated with stupidity and folly. Think of thyself, O Zarathustra!

Thou thyself—verily! even thou couldst well become an ass through superabundance of wisdom.

Doth not the true sage willingly walk on the crookedest paths? The evidence teacheth it, O Zarathustra,—*thine own evidence!*"

—"And thou thyself, finally," said Zarathustra, and turned towards the ugliest man, who still lay on the ground stretching up his arm to the ass (for he gave it wine to drink). "Say, thou nondescript, what hast thou been about!

Thou seemest to me transformed, thine eyes glow, the mantle of the sublime covereth thine ugliness: *what* didst thou do?

Is it then true what they say, that thou hast again awakened him? And why? Was he not for good reasons killed and made away with?

Thou thyself seemest to me awakened: what didst thou do? why didst *thou* turn round? Why didst *thou* get converted? Speak, thou nondescript!"

"O Zarathustra," answered the ugliest man, "thou art a rogue!

Whether *he* yet liveth, or again liveth, or is thoroughly dead —which of us both knoweth that best? I ask thee.

One thing however do I know,—from thyself did I learn it once, O Zarathustra: he who wanteth to kill most thoroughly, *laugheth*.

'Not by wrath but by laughter doth one kill'—thus spakest thou once, O Zarathustra, thou hidden one, thou destroyer without wrath, thou dangerous saint,—thou art a rogue!"

2

Then, however, did it come to pass that Zarathustra, astonished at such merely roguish answers, jumped back to the door of his cave, and turning towards all his guests, cried out with a strong voice:

"O ye wags, all of you, ye buffoons! Why do ye dissemble and disguise yourselves before me!

How the hearts of all of you convulsed with delight and wickedness, because ye had at last become again like little children—namely, pious,—

—Because ye at last did again as children do—namely, prayed, folded your hands and said 'good God'!

But now leave, I pray you, *this* nursery, mine own cave, where today all childishness is carried on. Cool down, here outside, your hot child-wantonness and heart-tumult!

To be sure: except ye become as little children ye shall not enter into *that* kingdom of heaven." (And Zarathustra pointed aloft with his hands.)

"But we do not at all want to enter into the kingdom of heaven: we have become men,—*so we want the kingdom of earth.*"

3

And once more began Zarathustra to speak. "O my new friends," said he,—"ye strange ones, ye higher men, how well do ye now please me,—

—Since ye have again become joyful! Ye have, verily, all blossomed forth: it seemeth to me that for such flowers as you, *new festivals* are required.

—A little valiant nonsense, some divine service and ass-festival, some old joyful Zarathustra fool, some blusterer to blow your souls bright.

Forget not this night and this ass-festival, ye higher men! *That* did ye devise when with me, that do I take as a good omen,—such things only the convalescents devise!

And should ye celebrate it again, this ass-festival, do it from love to yourselves, do it also from love to me! And in remembrance of *me!"*

Thus spake Zarathustra.

79. *The Drunken Song*

1

MEANWHILE one after another had gone out into the open air, and into the cool, thoughtful night; Zarathustra himself, however, led the ugliest man by the hand, that he might show him his night-world, and the great round moon, and the silvery water-falls near his cave. There they at last stood still beside one another; all of them old people, but with comforted, brave hearts, and astonished in themselves that it was so well with them on earth; the mystery of the night, however, came nigher and nigher to their hearts. And anew Zarathustra thought to himself: "Oh, how well do they now please me, these higher men!"—but he did not say it aloud, for he respected their happiness and their silence.—

Then, however, there happened that which in this astonishing long day was most astonishing: the ugliest man began once more and for the last time to gurgle and snort, and when he had at length found expression, behold! there sprang a question plump and plain out of his mouth, a good, deep, clear question, which moved the hearts of all who listened to him.

"My friends, all of you," said the ugliest man, "what think ye? For the sake of this day—I am for the first time content to have lived mine entire life.

And that I testify so much is still not enough for me. It is worth while living on the earth: one day, one festival with Zarathustra, hath taught me to love the earth.

'Was *that*—life?' will I say unto death. 'Well! Once more!'

My friends, what think ye? Will ye not, like me, say unto death: 'Was *that*—life? For the sake of Zarathustra, well! Once more!' "— —

Thus spake the ugliest man; it was not, however, far from midnight. And what took place then, think ye? As soon as the higher men heard his question, they became all at once conscious of their transformation and convalescence, and of him who was the cause thereof: then did they rush up to Zarathustra, thanking, honouring, caressing him, and kissing his hands, each in his own peculiar way; so that some laughed and some wept. The old soothsayer, however, danced with delight; and though he was then, as some narrators suppose, full of sweet wine, he was certainly still fuller of sweet life, and had renounced all weariness. There are even those who narrate that the ass then danced: for not in vain had the ugliest man previously given it wine to drink. That may be the case, or it may be otherwise; and if in truth the ass did not dance that evening, there nevertheless happened then greater and rarer wonders than the dancing of an ass would have been. In short, as the proverb of Zarathustra saith: "What doth it matter!"

2

When, however, this took place with the ugliest man, Zarathustra stood there like one drunken: his glance dulled, his tongue faltered and his feet staggered. And who could divine what thoughts then passed through Zarathustra's soul? Apparently, however, his spirit retreated and fled in advance and was in remote distances, and as it were "wandering on high mountain-ridges," as it standeth written, " 'twixt two seas,

—Wandering 'twixt the past and the future as a heavy cloud." Gradually, however, while the higher men held him in their arms, he came back to himself a little, and resisted with his hands the crowd of the honouring and caring ones; but he did not speak. All at once, however, he turned his head quickly, for he seemed to hear something: then laid he his finger on his mouth and said: *"Come!"*

And immediately it became still and mysterious round about; from the depth however there came up slowly the sound of a clock-bell. Zarathustra listened thereto, like the higher men; then, however, laid he his finger on his mouth the second time, and said again: *"Come! Come! It is getting on to midnight!"*—and his voice had changed. But still he had not moved from the spot. Then it became yet stiller and more mysterious, and everything hearkened, even the ass, and Zarathustra's noble animals, the eagle and the serpent,—likewise the cave of Zarathustra and the big cool moon, and the night itself. Zarathustra, however, laid his hand upon his mouth for the third time, and said:

Come! Come! Come! Let us now wander! It is the hour: let us wander into the night!

3

Ye higher men, it is getting on to midnight: then will I say something into your ears, as that old clock-bell saith it into mine ear,—

—As mysteriously, as frightfully, and as cordially as that midnight clock-bell speaketh it to me, which hath experienced more than one man:

—Which hath already counted the smarting throbbings of your fathers' hearts—ah! ah! how it sigheth! how it laugheth in its dream! the old, deep, deep midnight!

Hush! Hush! Then is there many a thing heard which may not be heard by day; now however, in the cool air, when even all the tumult of your hearts hath become still,—

—Now doth it speak, now is it heard, now doth it steal into overwakeful, nocturnal souls: ah! ah! how the midnight sigheth! how it laugheth in its dream!

—Hearest thou not how it mysteriously, frightfully, and cordially speaketh unto *thee,* the old deep, deep midnight?

O man, take heed!

4

Woe to me! Whither hath time gone? Have I not sunk into deep wells? The world sleepeth—

Ah! Ah! The dog howleth, the moon shineth. Rather will I die, rather will I die, than say unto you what my midnight-heart now thinketh.

Already have I died. It is all over. Spider, why spinnest thou around me? Wilt thou have blood? Ah! Ah! The dew falleth, the hour cometh—

—The hour in which I frost and freeze, which asketh and asketh and asketh: "Who hath sufficient courage for it?

—Who is to be master of the world? Who is going to say: *Thus* shall ye flow, ye great and small streams!"

—The hour approacheth: O man, thou higher man, take heed! this talk is for fine ears, for thine ears—*what saith deep midnight's voice indeed?*

5

It carrieth me away, my soul danceth. Day's-work! Day's-work! Who is to be master of the world?

The moon is cool, the wind is still. Ah! Ah! Have ye already flown high enough? Ye have danced: a leg, nevertheless, is not a wing.

Ye good dancers, now is all delight over: wine hath become lees, every cup hath become brittle, the sepulchres mutter.

Ye have not flown high enough: now do the sepulchres mutter: "Free the dead! Why is it so long night? Doth not the moon make us drunken?"

Ye higher men, free the sepulchres, awaken the corpses! Ah, why doth the worm still burrow? There approacheth, there approacheth, the hour,—

—There boometh the clock-bell, there thrilleth still the heart, there burroweth still the wood-worm, the heart-worm. Ah! Ah! *The world is deep!*

6

Sweet lyre! Sweet lyre! I love thy tone, thy drunken, ranun-culine tone!—how long, how far hath come unto me thy tone, from the distance, from the ponds of love!

Thou old clock-bell, thou sweet lyre! Every pain hath torn thy heart, father-pain, fathers'-pain, forefathers'-pain; thy speech hath become ripe,—

—Ripe like the golden autumn and the afternoon, like mine anchorite heart—now sayest thou: The world itself hath become ripe, the grape turneth brown,

—Now doth it wish to die, to die of happiness. Ye higher men, do ye not feel it? There welleth up mysteriously an odour,

—A perfume and odour of eternity, a rosy-blessed, brown, gold-wine-odour of old happiness.

—Of drunken midnight-death happiness, which singeth: the world is deep, *and deeper than the day could read!*

7

Leave me alone! Leave me alone! I am too pure for thee. Touch me not! Hath not my world just now become perfect?

My skin is too pure for thy hands. Leave me alone, thou dull, doltish, stupid day! Is not the midnight brighter?

The purest are to be masters of the world, the least known, the strongest, the midnight-souls, who are brighter and deeper than any day.

O day, thou gropest for me? Thou feelest for my happiness? For thee am I rich, lonesome, a treasure-pit, a gold chamber?

O world, thou wantest *me*? Am I worldly for thee? Am I spiritual for thee? Am I divine for thee? But day and world, ye are too coarse,—

—Have cleverer hands, grasp after deeper happiness, after deeper unhappiness, grasp after some God; grasp not after me:

—Mine unhappiness, my happiness is deep, thou strange day, but yet am I no God, no God's-hell: *deep is its woe.*

8

God's woe is deeper, thou strange world! Grasp at God's woe, not at me! What am I! A drunken sweet lyre,—

—A midnight-lyre, a bell-frog, which no one understandeth, but which *must* speak before deaf ones, ye higher men! For ye do not understand me!

Gone! Gone! O youth! O noontide! O afternoon! Now have come evening and night and midnight,—the dog howleth, the wind:

—Is the wind not a dog? It whineth, it barketh, it howleth. Ah! Ah! how she sigheth! how she laugheth, how she wheezeth and panteth, the midnight!

How she just now speaketh soberly, this drunken poetess! hath she perhaps overdrunk her drunkenness? hath she become overawake? doth she ruminate?

—Her woe doth she ruminate over, in a dream, the old, deep midnight—and still more her joy. For joy, although woe be deep, *joy is deeper still than grief can be.*

9

Thou grape-vine! Why dost thou praise me? Have I not cut thee! I am cruel, thou bleedest—: what meaneth thy praise of my drunken cruelty?

"Whatever hath become perfect, everything mature—wanteth to die!" so sayest thou. Blessed, blessed be the vintner's knife! But everything immature wanteth to live: alas!

Woe saith: "Hence! Go! Away, thou woe!" But everything that suffereth wanteth to live, that it may become mature and lively and longing,

—Longing for the further, the higher, the brighter. "I want heirs," so saith everything that suffereth, "I want children, I do not want *myself*,"—

Joy, however, doth not want heirs, it doth not want children. —joy wanteth itself, it wanteth eternity, it wanteth recurrence, it wanteth everything eternally-like-itself.

Woe saith: "Break, bleed, thou heart! Wander, thou leg! Thou wing, fly! Onward! upward! thou pain!" Well! Cheer up! O mine old heart: *Woe saith: "Hence! Go!"*

10

Ye higher men, what think ye? Am I a soothsayer? Or a dreamer? Or a drunkard? Or a dream-reader? Or a midnight-bell?

Or a drop of dew? Or a fume and fragrance of eternity? Hear ye it not? Smell ye it not? Just now hath my world become perfect, midnight is also mid-day,—

Pain is also a joy, curse is also a blessing, night is also a sun,—go away! or ye will learn that a sage is also a fool.

Said ye ever Yea to one joy? O my friends, then said ye Yea also unto *all* woe. All things are enlinked, enlaced and enamoured,—

—Wanted ye ever once to come twice; said ye ever: "Thou pleasest me, happiness! Instant! Moment!" then wanted ye *all* to come back again!

—All anew, all eternal, all enlinked, enlaced and enamoured, Oh, then did ye *love* the world,—

—Ye eternal ones, ye love it eternally and for all time: and also unto woe do ye say: Hence! Go! but come back! *For joys all want—eternity!*

11

All joy wanteth the eternity of all things, it wanteth honey, it wanteth lees, it wanteth drunken midnight, it wanteth graves, it wanteth grave-tears' consolation, it wanteth gilded evening-red—

—*What* doth not joy want! it is thirstier, heartier, hungrier, more frightful, more mysterious, than all woe: it wanteth *itself,* it biteth into *itself,* the ring's will writheth in it,—

—It wanteth love, it wanteth hate, it is over-rich, it bestoweth, it throweth away, it beggeth for some one to take from it, it thanketh the taker, it would fain be hated,—

—So rich is joy that it thirsteth for woe, for hell, for hate, for shame, for the lame, for the *world,*—for this world, Oh, ye know it indeed!

Ye higher men, for you doth it long, this joy, this irrepressible, blessed joy—for your woe, ye failures! For failures, longeth all eternal joy.

For joys all want themselves, therefore do they also want grief! O happiness, O pain! Oh break, thou heart! Ye higher men, do learn it, that joys want eternity.

—Joys want the eternity of *all* things, they *want deep, profound eternity!*

12

Have ye now learned my song? Have ye divined what it would say? Well! Cheer up! Ye higher men, sing now my roundelay!

Sing now yourselves the song, the name of which is "Once more," the signification of which is "Unto all eternity!"—sing, ye higher men, Zarathustra's roundelay!

O man! Take heed!
What saith deep midnight's voice indeed?
"I slept my sleep—,
"From deepest dream I've woke, and plead:—
"The world is deep,
"And deeper than the day could read.
"Deep is its woe—,
"Joy—deeper still than grief can be:
"Woe saith: Hence! Go!
"But joys all want eternity—,
"—Want deep, profound eternity!"

80. The Sign

IN THE morning, however, after this night, Zarathustra jumped up from his couch, and, having girded his loins, he came out of his cave glowing and strong, like a morning sun coming out of gloomy mountains.

"Thou great star," spake he, as he had spoken once before, "thou deep eye of happiness, what would be all thy happiness if thou hadst not *those* for whom thou shinest!

And if they remained in their chambers whilst thou art already awake, and comest and bestowest and distributest, how would thy proud modesty upbraid for it!

Well! they still sleep, these higher men, whilst *I* am awake: *they* are not my proper companions! Not for them do I wait here in my mountains.

At my work I want to be, at my day: but they understand

not what are the signs of my morning, my step—is not for them the awakening-call.

They still sleep in my cave; their dream still drinketh at my drunken songs. The audient ear for *me*—the *obedient* ear, is yet lacking in their limbs."

—This had Zarathustra spoken to his heart when the sun arose: then looked he inquiringly aloft, for he heard above him the sharp call of his eagle. "Well!" called he upwards, "thus is it pleasing and proper to me. Mine animals are awake, for I am awake.

Mine eagle is awake, and like me honoureth the sun. With eagle-talons doth it grasp at the new light. Ye are my proper animals; I love you.

But still do I lack my proper men!"—

Thus spake Zarathustra; then, however, it happened that all on a sudden he became aware that he was flocked around and fluttered around, as if by innumerable birds,—the whizzing of so many wings, however, and the crowding around his head was so great that he shut his eyes. And verily, there came down upon him as it were a cloud, like a cloud of arrows which poureth upon a new enemy. But behold, here it was a cloud of love, and showered upon a new friend.

"What happeneth unto me?" thought Zarathustra in his astonished heart, and slowly seated himself on the big stone which lay close to the exit from his cave. But while he grasped about with his hands, around him, above him and below him, and repelled the tender birds, behold, there then happened to him something still stranger: for he grasped thereby unawares into a mass of thick, warm, shaggy hair; at the same time, however, there sounded before him a roar,—a long, soft lion-roar.

"The sign cometh," said Zarathustra, and a change came

over his heart. And in truth, when it turned clear before him, there lay a yellow, powerful animal at his feet, resting its head on his knee,—unwilling to leave him out of love, and doing like a dog which again findeth its old master. The doves, however, were no less eager with their love than the lion; and whenever a dove whisked over its nose, the lion shook its head and wondered and laughed.

When all this went on Zarathustra spake only a word: *"My children are nigh, my children"*—, then he became quite mute. His heart, however, was loosed, and from his eyes there dropped down tears and fell upon his hands. And he took no further notice of anything, but sat there motionless, without repelling the animals further. Then flew the doves to and fro, and perched on his shoulder, and caressed his white hair, and did not tire of their tenderness and joyousness. The strong lion, however, licked always the tears that fell on Zarathustra's hands, and roared and growled shyly. Thus did these animals do.—

All this went on for a long time, or a short time: for properly speaking, there is *no* time on earth for such things—. Meanwhile, however, the higher men had awakened in Zarathustra's cave, and marshalled themselves for a procession to go to meet Zarathustra, and give him their morning greeting: for they had found when they awakened that he no longer tarried with them. When, however, they reached the door of the cave and the noise of their steps had preceded them, the lion started violently; it turned away all at once from Zarathustra, and roaring wildly, sprang towards the cave. The higher men, however, when they heard the lion roaring, cried all aloud as with one voice, fled back and vanished in an instant.

Zarathustra himself, however, stunned and strange, rose from his seat, looked around him, stood there astonished, in-

quired of his heart, bethought himself, and remained alone.
"What did I hear?" said he at last, slowly, "what happened
unto me just now?"

But soon there came to him his recollection, and he took in
at a glance all that had taken place between yesterday and today. "Here is indeed the stone," said he, and stroked his beard,
"on *it* sat I yester-morn; and here came the soothsayer unto me,
and here heard I first the cry which I heard just now, the great
cry of distress.

O ye higher men, *your* distress was it that the old soothsayer
foretold to me yester-morn,—

—Unto your distress did he want to seduce and tempt me:
'O Zarathustra,' said he to me, 'I come to seduce thee to thy
last sin.'

To my last sin?" cried Zarathustra, and laughed angrily at
his own words: "*what* hath been reserved for me as my last
sin?"

—And once more Zarathustra became absorbed in himself,
and sat down again on the big stone and meditated. Suddenly
he sprang up,—

"*Fellow-suffering! Fellow-suffering with the higher men!*"
he cried out, and his countenance changed into brass. "Well!
That—hath had its time!

My suffering and my fellow-suffering—what matter about
them! Do I then strive after *happiness?* I strive after my *work!*

Well! The lion hath come, my children are nigh, Zarathustra
hath grown ripe, mine hour hath come:—

This is *my* morning, *my* day beginneth: *arise now, arise,
thou great noontide!*"— —

Thus spake Zarathustra and left his cave, glowing and
strong, like a morning sun coming out of gloomy mountains.

BEYOND GOOD AND EVIL

Translated by HELEN ZIMMERN

CONTENTS

INTRODUCTION

A DOUBLE purpose animated Friedrich Nietzsche in his writing of "Beyond Good and Evil" which was begun in the summer of 1885 and finished the following winter. It is at once an explanation and an elucidation of "Thus Spake Zarathustra," and a preparatory book for his greatest and most important work, "The Will to Power." In it Nietzsche attempts to define the relative terms of "good" and "evil," and to draw a line of distinction between immorality and unmorality. He saw the inconsistencies involved in the attempt to harmonize an ancient moral code with the needs of modern life, and recognized the compromises which were constantly being made between moral theory and social practice. His object was to establish a relationship between morality and necessity and to formulate a workable basis for human conduct. Consequently "Beyond Good and Evil" is one of his most important contributions to a new system of ethics, and touches on many of the deepest principles of his philosophy.

Nietzsche opens "Beyond Good and Evil" with a long chapter headed "Prejudices of Philosophers," in which he outlines the course to be taken by his dialectic. The exposition is accomplished by two methods; first, by an analysis and a refutation of the systems of thinking made use of by antecedent doctrinaires, and secondly, by defining the hypotheses on which his own philosophy is built. This chapter is a most important

[371]

one, setting forth, as it does, the *rationale* of his doctrine of the will to power. It establishes Nietzsche's philosophic position and presents a closely knit explanation of the course pursued in the following chapters. The relativity of all truth —the hypothesis so often assumed in his previous work— Nietzsche here defends by analogy and argument. Using other leading forms of philosophy as a ground for exploration, he questions the absolutism of truth and shows wherein lies the difficulty of a final definition. Nietzsche, in his analyses and criticisms, is not solely destructive: he is subterraneously constructing his own philosophical system founded on the "will to power." This phrase is used many times in the careful research of the first chapter. As the book proceeds, this doctrine develops.

Nietzsche's best definition of what he calls the "free spirit," namely: the thinking man, the intellectual aristocrat, the philosopher and ruler, is contained in the twenty-six pages of the second chapter of "Beyond Good and Evil." In a series of paragraphs—longer than is Nietzsche's wont—the leading characteristics of this superior man are described. The "free spirit," however, must not be confused with the superman. The former is the "bridge" which the present-day man must cross in the process of surpassing himself. In the delineation and analysis of him, as presented to us here, we can glimpse his most salient mental features. Heretofore, as in "Thus Spake Zarathustra," he has been but partially and provisionally defined. Now his instincts and desires, his habits and activities are outlined. Furthermore, we are given an explanation of his relation to the inferior man and to the organisms of his environment. The chapter is a most important one, for at many points it is a subtle elucidation of many of Nietzsche's dominant philosophic principles. By inference, the differences of class distinction are strictly drawn. The slave-morality (*sklav-moral*) and the master-morality (*herrenmoral*), though as yet undefined, are balanced against each other; and the deportmental standards of the masters and slaves are defined by way of distinguishing between these two opposing human factions.

A keen and far-reaching analysis of the various aspects assumed by religious faith constitutes a third section of "Beyond Good and Evil." Though touching upon various influences of Christianity, this section is more general in its religious scope than even "The Antichrist," many indications of which are to be found here. This chapter has to do with the numerous inner experiences of man, which are directly or indirectly attributable to religious doctrines. The origin of the instinct for faith itself is sought, and the results of this faith are balanced against the needs of the individuals and of the race. The relation between religious ecstasy and sensuality; the attempt on the part of religious practitioners to arrive at a negation of the will; the transition from religious gratitude to fear; the psychology at the bottom of saint worship;—to problems such as these Nietzsche devotes his energies in his inquiry of the religious mood. There is an illuminating exposition of the important stages in religious cruelty and of the motives underlying the various forms of religious sacrifices.

A very important phase of Nietzsche's teaching is contained in this criticism of the religious life. The detractors of the Nietzschean doctrine base their judgments on the assumption that the universal acceptance of his theories would result in social chaos. Nietzsche desired no such general adoption of his beliefs. In his bitterest diatribes against Christianity his object was not to shake the faith of the great majority of mankind in their idols. He sought merely to free the strong men from the restrictions of a religion which fitted the needs of only the weaker members of society. He neither hoped nor desired to wean the mass of humanity from Christianity or any similar dogmatic comfort. On the contrary, he denounced those superficial atheists who endeavored to weaken the foundations of religion. He saw the positive necessity of such religions as a basis for his slave-morality, and in the present chapter he exhorts the rulers to preserve the religious faith of the serving classes, and to use it as a means of government—as an instrument in the work of disciplining and educating. His entire system of ethics is built on the complete disseverance of the dominating class and the serving class; and his doctrine of "beyond good and evil" should be considered only as it pertains to the superior man. To apply it to all classes would be to reduce Nietzsche's whole system of ethics to impracticability, and therefore to an absurdity.

Passing from a consideration of the religious mood Nietzsche enters a broader sphere of ethical research, and endeavors to trace the history and development of morals. He accuses the philosophers of having avoided the real problem of morality, namely: the testing of the faith and motives which lie beneath moral beliefs. This is the task he sets for himself, and in his chapter, "The Natural History of Morals," he makes an examination of moral origins—an examination which is extended into an exhaustive treatise in his next book, "The Genealogy of Morals." However, his dissection here is carried out on a broader and far more general scale than in his previous books, such as "Human All-Too-Human" and "The Dawn of Day." Heretofore he had confined himself to codes and systems, to *acts* of morality and immorality, to judgments of conducts. In "Beyond Good and Evil" he treats of moral prejudices as forces working hand in hand with human progress. In addition, there is a definite attitude of constructive thinking here which is absent from his earlier work.

In the chapter, "We Scholars," Nietzsche continues his definition of the philosopher, whom he holds to be the highest type of man. Besides being a mere description of the intellectual traits of this "free spirit," the chapter is also an exposition of the shortcomings of those modern men who pose as philosophers. Also the man of science and the man of genius are analyzed and weighed as to their relative importance in the community. In fact, we have here Nietzsche's most concise and complete definition of the individuals upon whom rests the burden of progress. These valuations of the intellectual leaders are important to the student, for by one's understanding them, along with the reasons for such valuations, a comprehension of the ensuing volumes is facilitated.

Important material touching on many of the fundamental points of Nietzsche's philosophy is embodied in the chapter entitled "Our Virtues." The more general inquiries into conduct, and the research along the broader lines of ethics are supplanted by inquiries into specific moral attributes. The current virtues are questioned, and their historical significance is determined. The value of such virtues is tested in their relation to different types of men. Sacrifice, sympathy, brotherly love, service, loyalty, altruism, and similar ideals of conduct are examined, and the results of such virtues are shown to be incompatible with the demands of modern social intercourse. Nietzsche poses against these virtues the sterner and more rigid forms of conduct, pointing out wherein they meet with the present requirements of human progress. The chapter is a preparation for his establishment of a new morality and also an explanation of the dual ethical code which is one of the main pillars in his philosophical structure. Before presenting his precept of a dual morality, Nietzsche endeavors to determine woman's place in the political and social scheme, and points out the necessity, not only of individual feminine functioning, but of the preservation of a distinct polarity in sexual relationship.

In the final chapter many of Nietzsche's philosophical ideas take definite shape. The doctrine of slave-morality and master-morality, prepared for and partially defined in preceding chapters, is here directly set forth, and those virtues and attitudes which constitute the "nobility" of the master class are specifically defined. Nietzsche designates the duty of his aristocracy, and segregates the human attributes according to the rank of individuals. The Dionysian ideal, which underlies all the books that follow "Beyond Good and Evil," receives its first direct exposition and application. The hardier human traits, such as egotism, cruelty, arrogance, retaliation, and appropriation, are given ascendancy over the softer virtues, such as sympathy, charity, forgiveness, loyalty and humility, and are pronounced necessary constituents in the moral code of a natural aristocracy. At this point is begun the transvaluation of values which was to have been completed in "The Will to Power."

WILLARD HUNTINGTON WRIGHT

PREFACE

SUPPOSING that Truth is a woman—what then? Is there not ground for suspecting that all philosophers, in so far as they have been dogmatists, have failed to understand women—that the terrible seriousness and clumsy importunity with which they have usually paid their addresses to Truth, have been unskilled and unseemly methods for winning a woman? Certainly she has never allowed herself to be won; and at present every kind of dogma stands with sad and discouraged mien—*if*, indeed, it stands at all! For there are scoffers who maintain that it has fallen, that all dogma lies on the ground—nay more, that it is at its last gasp. But to speak seriously, there are good grounds for hoping that all dogmatising in philosophy, whatever solemn, whatever conclusive and decided airs it has assumed, may have been only a noble puerilism and tyronism; and probably the time is at hand when it will be once and again understood *what* has actually sufficed for the basis of such imposing and absolute philosophical edifices as the dogmatists have hitherto reared: perhaps some popular superstition of immemorial time (such as the soul-superstition, which, in the form of subject- and ego-superstition, has not yet ceased doing mischief) : perhaps some play upon words, a deception on the part of grammar, or an audacious generalisation of very restricted, very personal, very human—all-too-human facts. The philosophy of the dogmatists, it is to be hoped, was only a promise for thousands of years afterwards, as was astrology in still earlier times, in the service of which probably more labour, gold, acuteness, and patience have been spent than on any actual science hitherto: we owe to it, and to its "super-terrestrial" pretensions in Asia and Egypt, the grand style of architecture. It seems that in order to inscribe themselves upon the heart of humanity with everlasting claims, all great things have first to wander about the earth as enormous and awe-inspiring caricatures: dogmatic philosophy has been a caricature of this kind—for instance, the Vedanta doctrine in Asia, and Platonism in Europe. Let us not be ungrateful to it, although it must certainly be confessed that the worst, the most tiresome, and the most dangerous of errors hitherto has been a dogmatist error —namely, Plato's invention of Pure Spirit and the Good in Itself. But now when it has been surmounted, when Europe, rid of this nightmare, can again draw breath freely and at least enjoy a healthier—sleep, we, *whose duty is wakefulness itself,* are the heirs of all the strength which the struggle against this error has fostered. It amounted to the very inversion of truth, and the denial of the *perspective*—the fundamental condition—of life, to speak of Spirit and the Good as Plato spoke of them; indeed one might ask, as a physician: "How did such a malady attack that finest product of antiquity, Plato? Had the wicked Socrates really corrupted him? Was Socrates after all a corrupter of youths, and deserved his hemlock?" But the struggle against Plato, or—to speak plainer, and for the "people"—the struggle against the ecclesiastical oppression of millenniums of Christianity (for Christianity is Platonism for the "people"), produced in Europe a magnificent tension of soul, such as had not existed anywhere previously; with such a tensely-strained bow one can now aim at the furthest goals. As a matter of fact, the European feels this tension as a state of distress, and twice attempts have been made in grand style to unbend the bow: once by means of Jesuitism, and the second time by means of democratic enlightenment— which, with the aid of liberty of the press and newspaper-reading, might, in fact, bring it about that the spirit would not so easily find itself in "distress"! (The Germans invented gunpowder—all credit to them! but they again made things square —they invented printing.) But we, who are neither Jesuits, nor democrats, nor even sufficiently Germans, we *good Europeans,* and free, *very* free spirits—we have it still, all the distress of spirit and all the tension of its bow! And perhaps also the arrow, the duty, and, who knows? *the goal to aim at. . . .*

Sils Maria Upper Engadine, *June,* 1885.

1. Prejudices of Philosophers

1

THE Will to Truth, which is to tempt us to many a hazardous enterprise, the famous Truthfulness of which all philosophers have hitherto spoken with respect, what questions has this Will to Truth not laid before us! What strange, perplexing, questionable questions! It is already a long story; yet it seems as if it were hardly commenced. Is it any wonder if we at last grow distrustful, lose patience, and turn impatiently away? That this Sphinx teaches us at last to ask questions ourselves? *Who* is it really that puts questions to us here? *What* really is this "Will to Truth" in us? In fact we made a long halt at the question as to the origin of this Will—until at last we came to an absolute standstill before a yet more fundamental question. We inquired about the *value* of this Will. Granted that we want the truth: *why not rather* untruth? And uncertainty? Even ignorance? The problem of the value of truth presented itself before us—or was it we who presented ourselves before the problem? Which of us is the Œdipus here? Which the Sphinx? It would seem to be a rendezvous of questions and notes of interrogation. And could it be believed that it at last seems to us as if the problem had never been propounded before, as if we were the first to discern it, get a sight of it, and *risk raising* it. For there is risk in raising it; perhaps there is no greater risk.

2

"*How could* anything originate out of its opposite? For example, truth out of error? or the Will to Truth out of the will to deception? or the generous deed out of selfishness? or the pure sun-bright vision of the wise man out of covetousness? Such genesis is impossible; whoever dreams of it is a fool, nay, worse than a fool; things of the highest value must have a different origin, an origin of *their own*—in this transitory, seductive, illusory, paltry world, in this turmoil of delusion and cupidity, they cannot have their source. But rather in the lap of Being, in the intransitory, in the concealed God, in the 'Thing-in-itself'—*there* must be their source, and nowhere else!"—This mode of reasoning discloses the typical prejudice by which metaphysicians of all times can be recognised, this mode of valuation is at the back of all their logical procedure; through this "belief" of theirs, they exert themselves for their "knowledge," for something that is in the end solemnly christened "the Truth." The fundamental belief of metaphysicians is *the belief in antitheses of values*. It never occurred even to the wariest of them to doubt here on the very threshold (where doubt, however, was most necessary); though they had made a solemn vow, "*de omnibus dubitandum.*" For it may be doubted, firstly, whether antitheses exist at all; and secondly, whether the popular valuations and antitheses of value upon which metaphysicians have set their seal, are not perhaps merely superficial estimates, merely provisional perspectives, besides being probably made from some corner, perhaps from below—"frog perspectives," as it were, to borrow an expression current among painters. In spite of all the value which may belong to the true, the positive, and the unselfish, it might be possible that a higher and more fundamental value for life generally should be assigned to pretence, to the will to delusion, to selfishness, and cupidity. It might even be possible that *what* constitutes the value of those good and respected things, consists precisely in their being insidiously related, knotted, and crocheted to these evil and apparently opposed things— perhaps even in being essentially identical with them. Perhaps! But who wishes to concern himself with such dangerous "Perhapses"! For that investigation one must await the advent of a new order of philosophers, such as will have other tastes and inclinations, the reverse of those hitherto prevalent—philosophers of the dangerous "Perhaps" in every sense of the term. And to speak in all seriousness, I see sucn new philosophers beginning to appear.

3

Having kept a sharp eye on philosophers, and having read between their lines long enough, I now say to myself that the greater part of conscious thinking must be counted amongst the instinctive functions, and it is so even in the case of philosophical thinking; one has here to learn anew, as one learned anew about heredity and "innateness." As little as the act of birth comes into consideration in the whole process and procedure of heredity, just as little is "being-conscious" *opposed* to the instinctive in any decisive sense; the greater part of the conscious thinking of a philosopher is secretly influenced by his instincts, and forced into definite channels. And behind all logic and its seeming sovereignty of movement, there are valuations, or to speak more plainly, physiological demands, for the maintenance of a definite mode of life. For example, that the certain is worth more than the uncertain, that illusion is less valuable than "truth": such valuations, in spite of their regulative importance for *us,* might notwithstanding be only superficial valuations, special kinds of *niaiserie,* such as may be necessary for the maintenance of beings such as ourselves. Supposing, in effect, that man is not just the "measure of things." . . .

4

The falseness of an opinion is not for us any objection to it: it is here, perhaps, that our new language sounds most strangely. The question is, how far an opinion is life-furthering, life-preserving, species-preserving, perhaps species-rearing; and we are fundamentally inclined to maintain that the falsest opinions (to which the synthetic judgments *a priori* belong), are the most indispensable to us; that without a recognition of logical fictions, without a comparison of reality with the purely *imagined* world of the absolute and immutable, without a constant counterfeiting of the world by means of numbers, man could not live—that the renunciation of false opinions would be a renunciation of life, a negation of life. *To recognise untruth as a condition of life:* that is certainly to impugn the traditional ideas of value in a dangerous manner, and a philosophy which ventures to do so, has thereby alone placed itself beyond good and evil.

5

That which causes philosophers to be regarded half-distrustfully and half-mockingly, is not the oft-repeated discovery how innocent they are—how often and easily they make mistakes and lose their way, in short, how childish and childlike they are,—but that there is not enough honest dealing with them, whereas they all raise a loud and virtuous outcry when the problem of truthfulness is even hinted at in the remotest manner. They all pose as though their real opinions had been discovered and attained through the self-evolving of a cold, pure, divinely indifferent dialectic (in contrast to all sorts of mystics, who, fairer and foolisher, talk of "inspiration"); whereas, in fact, a prejudiced proposition, idea, or "suggestion," which is generally their heart's desire abstracted and refined, is defended by them with arguments sought out after the event. They are all advocates who do not wish to be regarded as such, generally astute defenders, also, of their prejudices, which they dub "truths,"—and *very* far from having the conscience which bravely admits this to itself; very far from having the good taste of the courage which goes so far as to let this be understood, perhaps to warn friend or foe, or in cheerful confidence and self-ridicule. The spectacle of the Tartuffery of old Kant, equally stiff and decent, with which he entices us into the dialectic by-ways that lead (more correctly mislead) to his "categorical imperative"—makes us fastidious ones smile, we who find no small amusement in spying out the subtle tricks of old moralists and ethical preachers. Or, still more so, the hocus-pocus in mathematical form, by means of which Spinoza has, as it were, clad his philosophy in mail and mask—in fact, the "love of *his* wisdom," to translate the term fairly and squarely—in order thereby to strike terror at once into the heart of the assailant who should dare to cast a glance on that invincible maiden, that Pallas Athene:—how much of personal timidity and vulnerability does this masquerade of a sickly recluse betray!

6

It has gradually become clear to me what every great philosophy up till now has consisted of—namely, the confession of its originator, and a species of involuntary and unconscious autobiography; and moreover that the moral (or immoral) purpose in every philosophy has constituted the true vital germ out of which the entire plant has always grown. Indeed, to understand how the abstrusest metaphysical assertions of a philosopher have been arrived at, it is always well (and wise) to first ask oneself: "What morality do they (or does he) aim at?" Accordingly, I do not believe that an "impulse to knowledge" is the father of philosophy; but that another impulse, here as elsewhere, has only made use of knowledge (and mistaken knowledge!) as an instrument. But whoever considers the fundamental impulses of man with a view to determining how far they may have here acted as *inspiring* genii (or as demons and cobolds), will find that they have all practised philosophy at one time or another, and that each one of them would have been only too glad to look upon itself as the ultimate end of existence and the legitimate *lord* over all the other impulses. For every impulse is imperious, and as *such,* attempts to philosophise. To be sure, in the case of scholars, in the case of really scientific men, it may be otherwise —"better," if you will; there there may really be such a thing as an "impulse to knowledge," some kind of small, independent clock-work, which, when well wound up, works away industriously to that end, *without* the rest of the scholarly impulses taking any material part therein. The actual "interests" of the scholar, therefore, are generally in quite another direction—in the family, perhaps, or in money-making, or in politics; it is, in fact, almost indifferent at what point of research his little machine is placed, and whether the hopeful young worker becomes a good philologist, a mushroom specialist, or a chemist; he is not *characterised* by becoming this or that. In the philosopher, on the contrary, there is absolutely nothing impersonal; and above all, his morality furnishes a decided and decisive testimony as to *who he is,*—that is to say, in what order the deepest impulses of his nature stand to each other.

7

How malicious philosophers can be! I know of nothing more stinging than the joke Epicurus took the liberty of making on Plato and the Platonists; he called them *Dionysiokolakes*. In its original sense, and on the face of it, the word signifies "Flatterers of Dionysius"—consequently, tyrants' accessories and lick-spittles; besides this, however, it is as much as to say, "They are all *actors,* there is nothing genuine about them" (for *Dionysiokolax* was a popular name for an actor). And the latter is really the malignant reproach that Epicurus cast upon Plato: he was annoyed by the grandiose manner, the *mise en scène* style of which Plato and his scholars were masters—of which Epicurus was not a master! He, the old school-teacher of Samos, who sat concealed in his little garden at Athens, and wrote three hundred books, perhaps out of rage and ambitious envy of Plato, who knows! Greece took a hundred years to find out who the garden-god Epicurus really was. Did she ever find out?

8

There is a point in every philosophy at which the "conviction" of the philosopher appears on the scene; or, to put it in the words of an ancient mystery:

> *Adventavit asinus,*
> *Pulcher et fortissimus.*

9

You desire to *live* "according to Nature"? Oh, you noble Stoics, what fraud of words! Imagine to yourselves a being like Nature, boundlessly extravagant, boundlessly indifferent, without purpose or consideration, without pity or justice, at once fruitful and barren and uncertain: imagine to yourselves *indifference* as a power—how *could* you live in accordance with such indifference? To live—is not that just endeavouring to be otherwise than this Nature? Is not living valuing, preferring, being unjust, being limited, endeavouring to be different? And granted that your imperative, "living according to Nature," means actually the same as "living according to life" —how could you do *differently?* Why should you make a principle out of what you yourselves are, and must be? In reality, however, it is quite otherwise with you: while you pretend to read with rapture the canon of your law in Nature, you want something quite the contrary, you extraordinary stage-players and self-deluders! In your pride you wish to dictate your morals and ideals to Nature, to Nature herself, and to incorporate them therein; you insist that it shall be Nature "according to the Stoa," and would like everything to be made after your own image, as a vast, eternal glorification and generalism of Stoicism! With all your love for truth, you have forced yourselves so long, so persistently, and with such hypnotic rigidity to see Nature *falsely,* that is to say, Stoically, that you are no longer able to see it otherwise—and to crown all, some unfathomable superciliousness gives you the Bedlamite hope that *because* you are able to tyrannise over yourselves—Stoicism is self-tyranny—Nature will also allow herself to be tyrannised over: is not the Stoic a *part* of Nature? . . . But this is an old and everlasting story: what happened in old times with the Stoics still happens today, as soon as ever a philosophy begins to believe in itself. It always creates the world in its own image; it cannot do otherwise; philosophy is this tyrannical impulse itself, the most spiritual Will to Power, the will to "creation of the world," the will to the *causa prima.*

10

The eagerness and subtlety, I should even say craftiness, with which the problem of "the real and the apparent world" is dealt with at present throughout Europe, furnishes food for thought and attention; and he who hears only a "Will to Truth" in the background, and nothing else, cannot certainly boast of the sharpest ears. In rare and isolated cases, it may really have happened that such a Will to Truth—a certain extravagant and adventurous pluck, a metaphysician's ambition of the forlorn hope—has participated therein: that which in the end always prefers a handful of "certainty" to a whole cartload of beautiful possibilities; there may even be puritanical fanatics of conscience, who prefer to put their last trust in a sure nothing, rather than in an uncertain something. But that is Nihilism, and the sign of a despairing, mortally wearied soul, notwithstanding the courageous bearing such a virtue may display. It seems, however, to be otherwise with stronger and livelier thinkers who are still eager for life. In that they side *against* appearance, and speak superciliously of "perspective," in that they rank the credibility of their own bodies about as low as the credibility of the ocular evidence that "the earth stands still," and thus, apparently, allowing with complacency their securest possession to escape (for what does one at present believe in more firmly than in one's body?),—who knows if they are not really trying to win back something which was formerly an even *securer* possession, something of the old domain of the faith of former times, perhaps the "immortal soul," perhaps "the old God," in short, ideas by which they could live better, that is to say, more vigorously and more joyously, than by "modern ideas"? There is *distrust* of these modern ideas in this mode of looking at things, a disbelief in all that has been constructed yesterday and today; there is perhaps some slight admixture of satiety and scorn, which can no longer endure the *bric-a-brac* of ideas of the most varied origin, such as so-called Positivism at present throws on the market; a disgust of the more refined taste at the village-fair motleyness and patchiness of all these reality-philosophasters, in whom there is nothing either new or true, except this motleyness. Therein it seems to me that we should agree with those sceptical anti-realists and knowledge-microscopists of the present day; their instinct, which repels them from *modern* reality, is unrefuted . . . what do their retrograde by-paths concern us! The main thing about them is *not* that they wish to go "back," but that they wish to get *away* therefrom. A little *more* strength, swing, courage, and artistic power, and they would be *off*—and not back!

11

It seems to me that there is everywhere an attempt at present to divert attention from the actual influence which Kant exercised on German philosophy, and especially to ignore prudently the value which he set upon himself. Kant was first and foremost proud of his Table of Categories; with it in his hand he said: "This is the most difficult thing that could ever be undertaken on behalf of metaphysics." Let us only understand this "could be"! He was proud of having *discovered* a new faculty in man, the faculty of synthetic judgment *a priori*. Granting that he deceived himself in this matter; the development and rapid flourishing of German philosophy depended nevertheless on his pride, and on the eager rivalry of the younger generation to discover if possible something—at all events "new faculties"—of which to be still prouder!—But let us reflect for a moment—it is high time to do so. "How are synthetic judgments *a priori possible?*" Kant asks himself—and what is really his answer? *"By means of a means* (faculty)"—but unfortunately not in five words, but so circumstantially, imposingly, and with such display of German profundity and verbal flourishes, that one altogether loses sight of the comical *niaiserie allemande* involved in such an answer. People were beside themselves with delight over this new faculty, and the jubilation reached its climax when Kant further discovered a moral faculty in man—for at that

[*391*]

time Germans were still moral, not yet dabbling in the "Politics of hard fact." Then came the honeymoon of German philosophy. All the young theologians of the Tübingen institution went immediately into the groves—all seeking for "faculties." And what did they not find—in that innocent, rich, and still youthful period of the German spirit, to which Romanticism, the malicious fairy, piped and sang, when one could not yet distinguish between "finding" and "inventing"! Above all a faculty for the "transcendental"; Schelling christened it, intellectual intuition, and thereby gratified the most earnest longings of the naturally pious-inclined Germans. One can do no greater wrong to the whole of this exuberant and eccentric movement (which was really youthfulness, notwithstanding that it disguised itself so boldly in hoary and senile conceptions), than to take it seriously, or even treat it with moral indignation. Enough, however—the world grew older, and the dream vanished. A time came when people rubbed their foreheads, and they still rub them to-day. People had been dreaming, and first and foremost—old Kant. "By means of a means (faculty)"—he had said, or at least meant to say. But, is that —an answer? An explanation? Or is it not rather merely a repetition of the question? How does opium induce sleep? "By means of a means (faculty)," namely the *virtus dormitiva,* replies the doctor in Molière,

> *Quia est in eo virtus dormitiva,*
> *Cujus est natura sensus assoupire.*

But such replies belong to the realm of comedy, and it is high time to replace the Kantian question, "How are synthetic judgments *a priori* possible?" by another question, "Why is belief in such judgments *necessary?*"—in effect, it is high time that we should understand that such judgments must be *believed* to be true, for the sake of the preservation of creatures like ourselves; though they still might naturally be *false* judgments! Or, more plainly spoken, and roughly and readily—synthetic judgments *a priori* should not "be possible" at all; we have no right to them; in our mouths they are nothing but false judgments. Only, of course, the belief in their truth is necessary, as plausible belief and ocular evidence belonging to the perspective view of life. And finally, to call to mind the enormous influence which "German philosophy"—I hope you understand its right to inverted commas (goosefeet)?—has exercised throughout the whole of Europe, there is no doubt that a certain *virtus dormitiva* had a share in it; thanks to German philosophy, it was a delight to the noble idlers, the virtuous, the mystics, the artists, the three-fourths Christians, and the political obscurantists of all nations, to find an antidote to the still overwhelming sensualism which overflowed from the last century into this, in short—"*sensus assoupire.*" . . .

12

As regards materialistic atomism, it is one of the best refuted theories that have been advanced, and in Europe there is now perhaps no one in the learned world so unscholarly as to attach serious signification to it, except for convenient everyday use (as an abbreviation of the means of expression)—thanks chiefly to the Pole Boscovich: he and the Pole Copernicus have hitherto been the greatest and most successful opponents of ocular evidence. For whilst Copernicus has persuaded us to believe, contrary to all the senses, that the earth does *not* stand fast, Boscovich has taught us to abjure the belief in the last thing that "stood fast" of the earth—the belief in "substance," in "matter," in the earth-residuum, and particle-atom: it is the greatest triumph over the senses that has hitherto been gained on earth. One must, however, go still further, and also declare war, relentless war to the knife, against the "atomistic requirements" which still lead a danger-ous after-life in places where no one suspects them, like the more celebrated "metaphysical requirements": one must also above all give the finishing stroke to that other and more por-tentous atomism which Christianity has taught best and longest, the *soul-atomism.* Let it be permitted to designate by this expression the belief which regards the soul as something inde-structible, eternal, indivisible, as a monad, as an *atomon: this* belief ought to be expelled from science! Between ourselves, it is not at all necessary to get rid of "the soul" thereby, and thus renounce one of the oldest and most venerated hypotheses —as happens frequently to the clumsiness of naturalists, who can hardly touch on the soul without immediately losing it. But the way is open for new acceptations and refinements of the soul-hypothesis; and such conceptions as "mortal soul," and "soul of subjective multiplicity," and "soul as social struc-ture of the instincts and passions," want henceforth to have legitimate rights in science. In that the *new* psychologist is about to put an end to the superstitions which have hitherto flourished with almost tropical luxuriance around the idea of the soul, he is really, as it were, thrusting himself into a new desert and a new distrust—it is possible that the older psychol-ogists had a merrier and more comfortable time of it; even-tually, however, he finds that precisely thereby he is also condemned to *invent*—and, who knows? perhaps to *discover* the new.

[*394*]

13

Psychologists should bethink themselves before putting down the instinct of self-preservation as the cardinal instinct of an organic being. A living thing seeks above all to *discharge* its strength—life itself is *Will to Power;* self-preservation is only one of the indirect and most frequent *results* thereof. In short, here, as everywhere else, let us beware of *superfluous* teleological principles!—one of which is the instinct of self-preservation (we owe it to Spinoza's inconsistency). It is thus, in effect, that method ordains, which must be essentially economy of principles.

14

It is perhaps just dawning on five or six minds that natural philosophy is only a world-exposition and world-arrangement (according to us, if I may say so!) and *not* a world-explanation; but in so far as it is based on belief in the senses, it is regarded as more, and for a long time to come must be regarded as more —namely, as an explanation. It has eyes and fingers of its own, it has ocular evidence and palpableness of its own: this operates fascinatingly, persuasively, and *convincingly* upon an age with fundamentally plebeian tastes—in fact, it follows instinctively the canon of truth of eternal popular sensualism. What is clear, what is "explained"? Only that which can be seen and felt— one must pursue every problem thus far. Obversely, however, the charm of the Platonic mode of thought, which was an *aristocratic* mode, consisted precisely in *resistance to* obvious sense-evidence—perhaps among men who enjoyed even stronger and more fastidious senses than our contemporaries, but who knew how to find a higher triumph in remaining masters of them: and this by means of pale, cold, grey conceptional networks which they threw over the motley whirl of the senses—the mob of the senses, as Plato said. In this overcoming of the world, and interpreting of the world in the manner of Plato, there was an *enjoyment* different from that which the physicists of today offer us—and likewise the Darwinists and antiteleologists among the physiological workers, with their principle of the "smallest possible effort," and the greatest possible blunder. "Where there is nothing more to see or to grasp, there is also nothing more for men to do"—that is certainly an imperative different from the Platonic one, but it may notwithstanding be the right imperative for a hardy, laborious race of machinists and bridge-builders of the future, who have nothing but *rough* work to perform.

15

To study physiology with a clear conscience, one must insist on the fact that the sense-organs are *not* phenomena in the sense of the idealistic philosophy; as such they certainly could not be causes! Sensualism, therefore, at least as regulative hypothesis, if not as heuristic principle. What? And others say even that the external world is the work of our organs? But then our body, as a part of this external world, would be the work of our organs! But then our organs themselves would be the work of our organs! It seems to me that this is a complete *reductio ad absurdum,* if the conception *causa sui* is something fundamentally absurd. Consequently, the external world is *not* the work of our organs—?

There are still harmless self-observers who believe that there are "immediate certainties"; for instance, "I think," or as the superstition of Schopenhauer puts it, "I will"; as though cognition here got hold of its object purely and simply as "the thing in itself," without any falsification taking place either on the part of the subject or the object. I would repeat it, however, a hundred times, that "immediate certainty," as well as "absolute knowledge" and the "thing in itself," involve a *contradictio in adjecto;* we really ought to free ourselves from the misleading significance of words! The people on their part may think that cognition is knowing all about things, but the philosopher must say to himself: "When I analyse the process that is expressed in the sentence, 'I think,' I find a whole series of daring assertions, the argumentative proof of which would be difficult, perhaps impossible: for instance, that it *is I* who think, that there must necessarily be something that thinks, that thinking is an activity and operation on the part of a being who is thought of as a cause, that there is an 'ego,' and finally, that it is already determined what is to be designated by thinking—that I *know* what thinking is. For if I had not already decided within myself what it is, by what standard could I determine whether that which is just happening is not perhaps 'willing' or 'feeling'? In short, the assertion 'I think,' assumes that I *compare* my state at the present moment with other states of myself which I know, in order to determine what it is; on account of this retrospective connection with further 'knowledge,' it has, at any rate, no immediate certainty for me."—In place of the "immediate certainty" in which the people may believe in the special case, the philosopher thus finds a series of metaphysical questions presented to him, veritable conscience questions of the intellect, to wit: "From whence did I get the notion of 'thinking'? Why do I believe in cause and effect? What gives me the right to speak of an 'ego,' and even of an 'ego' as cause, and finally of an 'ego' as cause of thought?" He who ventures to answer these metaphysical questions at once by an appeal to a sort of *intuitive* perception, like the person who says, "I think, and know that this, at least, is true, actual, and certain"—will encounter a smile and two notes of interrogation in a philosopher nowadays. "Sir," the philosopher will perhaps give him to understand, "it is improbable that you are not mistaken, but why should it be the truth?"

17

With regard to the superstitions of logicians, I shall never tire of emphasising a small, terse fact, which is unwillingly recognised by these credulous minds—namely, that a thought comes when "it" wishes, and not when "I" wish; so that it is a *perversion* of the facts of the case to say that the subject "I" is the condition of the predicate "think." *One* thinks; but that this "one" is precisely the famous old "ego," is, to put it mildly, only a supposition, an assertion, and assuredly not an "immediate certainty." After all, one has even gone too far with this "one thinks"—even the "one" contains an *interpretation* of the process, and does not belong to the process itself. One infers here according to the usual grammatical formula— "To think is an activity; every activity requires an agency that is active; consequently" . . . It was pretty much on the same lines that the older atomism sought, besides the operating "power," the material particle wherein it resides and out of which it operates—the atom. More rigorous minds, however, learned at last to get along without this "earth-residuum," and perhaps some day we shall accustom ourselves, even from the logician's point of view, to get along without the little "one" (to which the worthy old "ego" has refined itself).

18

It is certainly not the least charm of a theory that it is refutable; it is precisely thereby that it attracts the more subtle minds. It seems that the hundred-times-refuted theory of the "free will" owes its persistence to this charm alone; some one is always appearing who feels himself strong enough to refute it.

19

Philosophers are accustomed to speak of the will as though it were the best-known thing in the world; indeed, Schopenhauer has given us to understand that the will alone is really known to us, absolutely and completely known, without deduction or addition. But it again and again seems to me that in this case Schopenhauer also only did what philosophers are in the habit of doing—he seems to have adopted a *popular prejudice* and exaggerated it. Willing—seems to me to be above all something *complicated*, something that is a unity only in name—and it is precisely in a name that popular prejudice lurks, which has got the mastery over the inadequate precautions of philosophers in all ages. So let us for once be more cautious, let us be "unphilosophical": let us say that in all willing there is firstly a plurality of sensations, namely, the sensation of the condition *"away from which* we go," the sensation of the condition *"towards which* we go," the sensation of this *"from"* and *"towards"* itself, and then besides, an accompanying muscular sensation, which, even without our putting in motion "arms and legs," commences its action by force of habit, directly we "will" anything. Therefore, just as sensations (and indeed many kinds of sensations) are to be recognised as ingredients of the will, so, in the second place, thinking is also to be recognised; in every act of the will there is a ruling thought;—and let us not imagine it possible to sever this thought from the "willing," as if the will would then remain over! In the third place, the will is not only a complex of sensation and thinking, but it is above all an *emotion,* and in fact the emotion of the command. That which is termed "freedom of the will" is essentially the emotion of supremacy in respect to him who must obey: "I am free, 'he' must obey"— this consciousness is inherent in every will; and equally so the straining of the attention, the straight look which fixes itself exclusively on one thing, the unconditional judgment that "this and nothing else is necessary now," the inward certainty that obedience will be rendered—and whatever else pertains to the position of the commander. A man who *wills* commands something within himself which renders obedience, or which he believes renders obedience. But now let us notice what is the strangest thing about the will,—this affair so extremely complex, for which the people have only one name. Inasmuch as in the given circumstances we are at the same time the commanding *and* the obeying parties, and as the obeying party we know the sensations of constraint, impulsion, pressure, resistance, and motion, which usually commence immediately after the act of will; inasmuch as, on the other hand, we are accustomed to disregard this duality, and to deceive ourselves about

it by means of the synthetic term "I": a whole series of erroneous conclusions, and consequently of false judgments about the
will itself, has become attached to the act of willing—to such a
degree that he who wills believes firmly that willing *suffices*
for action. Since in the majority of cases there has only been
exercise of will when the effect of the command—consequently
obedience, and therefore action—was to be *expected,* the
appearance has translated itself into the sentiment, as if there
were a *necessity of effect;* in a word, he who wills believes with
a fair amount of certainty that will and action are somehow
one; he ascribes the success, the carrying out of the willing,
to the will itself, and thereby enjoys an increase of the sensation of power which accompanies all success. "Freedom of
Will"—that is the expression for the complex state of delight
of the person exercising volition, who commands and at the
same time identifies himself with the executor of the order—
who, as such, enjoys also the triumph over obstacles, but thinks
within himself that it was really his own will that overcame
them. In this way the person exercising volition adds the feelings of delight of his successful executive instruments, the
useful "underwills" or under-souls—indeed, our body is but a
social structure composed of many souls—to his feelings of
delight as commander. *L'effet c'est moi:* what happens here is
what happens in every well-constructed and happy commonwealth, namely, that the governing class identifies itself with
the successes of the commonwealth. In all willing it is absolutely a question of commanding and obeying, on the basis, as
already said, of a social structure composed of many "souls";
on which account a philosopher should claim the right to include willing-as-such within the sphere of morals—regarded
as the doctrine of the relations of supremacy under which the
phenomenon of "life" manifests itself.

20

That the separate philosophical ideas are not anything optional or autonomously evolving, but grow up in connection and relationship with each other; that, however suddenly and arbitrarily they seem to appear in the history of thought, they nevertheless belong just as much to a system as the collective members of the fauna of a Continent—is betrayed in the end by the circumstance: how unfailingly the most diverse philosophers always fill in again a definite fundamental scheme of *possible* philosophies. Under an invisible spell, they always revolve once more in the same orbit; however independent of each other they may feel themselves with their critical or systematic wills, something within them leads them, something impels them in definite order the one after the other—to wit, the innate methodology and relationship of their ideas. Their thinking is, in fact, far less a discovery than a re-recognising, a remembering, a return and a home-coming to a far-off, ancient common-household of the soul, out of which those ideas formerly grew: philosophising is so far a kind of atavism of the highest order. The wonderful family resemblance of all Indian, Greek, and German philosophising is easily enough explained. In fact, where there is affinity of language, owing to the common philosophy of grammar—I mean owing to the unconscious domination and guidance of similar grammatical functions—it cannot but be that everything is prepared at the outset for a similar development and succession of philosophical systems; just as the way seems barred against certain other possibilities of world-interpretation. It is highly probable that philosophers within the domain of the Ural-Altaic languages (where the conception of the subject is least developed) look otherwise "into the world," and will be found on paths of thought different from those of the Indo-Germans and Mussul-mans, the spell of certain grammatical functions is ultimately also the spell of *physiological* valuations and racial conditions. —So much by way of rejecting Locke's superficiality with regard to the origin of ideas.

21

The *causa sui* is the best self-contradiction that has yet been conceived, it is a sort of logical violation and unnaturalness; but the extravagant pride of man has managed to entangle itself profoundly and frightfully with this very folly. The desire for "freedom of will" in the superlative, metaphysical sense, such as still holds sway, unfortunately, in the minds of the half-educated, the desire to bear the entire and ultimate responsibility for one's actions oneself, and to absolve God, the world, ancestors, chance, and society therefrom, involves nothing less than to be precisely this *causa sui*, and, with more than Munchausen daring, to pull oneself up into existence by the hair, out of the slough of nothingness. If any one should find out in this manner the crass stupidity of the celebrated conception of "free will" and put it out of his head altogether, I beg of him to carry his "enlightenment" a step further, and also put out of his head the contrary of this monstrous conception of "free will": I mean "non-free will," which is tantamount to a misuse of cause and effect. One should not wrongly *materialise* "cause" and "effect," as the natural philosophers do (and whoever like them naturalises in thinking at present), according to the prevailing mechanical doltishness which makes the cause

[*403*]

press and push until it "effects" its end; one should use "cause" and "effect" only as pure *conceptions,* that is to say, as conventional fictions for the purpose of designation and mutual understanding,—*not* for explanation. In "being-in-itself" there is nothing of "casual-connection," of "necessity," or of "psychological non-freedom"; there the effect does *not* follow the cause, there "law" does not obtain. It is *we* alone who have devised cause, sequence, reciprocity, relativity, constraint, number, law, freedom, motive, and purpose; and when we interpret and intermix this symbol-world, as "being in itself," with things, we act once more as we have always acted—*mythologically.* The "non-free will" is mythology; in real life it is only a question of *strong* and *weak* wills.—It is almost always a symptom of what is lacking in himself, when a thinker, in every "casual-connection" and "psychological necessity," manifests something of compulsion, indigence, obsequiousness, oppression, and non-freedom; it is suspicious to have such feelings—the person betrays himself. And in general, if I have observed correctly, the "non-freedom of the will" is regarded as a problem from two entirely opposite standpoints, but always in a profoundly *personal* manner: some will not give up their "responsibility," their belief in *themselves,* the personal right to *their* merits, at any price (the vain races belong to this class); others on the contrary, do not wish to be answerable for anything, or blamed for anything, and owing to an inward self-contempt, seek *to get out of the business,* no matter how. The latter, when they write books, are in the habit at present of taking the side of criminals; a sort of socialistic sympathy is their favourite disguise. And as a matter of fact, the fatalism of the weak-willed embellishes itself surprisingly when it can pose as *"la religion de la souffrance humaine";* that is *its* "good taste."

on: interpretation—and you will be eager enough to make
this objection—well, so much the better.

22

Let me be pardoned, as an old philologist who cannot desist
from the mischief of putting his finger on bad modes of interpretation, but "Nature's conformity to law," of which you
physicists talk so proudly, as though—why, it exists only owing
to your interpretation and bad "philology." It is no matter of
fact, no "text," but rather just a naïvely humanitarian adjustment and perversion of meaning, with which you make abundant concessions to the democratic instincts of the modern
soul! "Everywhere equality before the law—Nature is not different in that respect, nor better than we:" a fine instance of
secret motive, in which the vulgar antagonism to everything
privileged and autocratic—likewise a second and more refined
atheism—is once more disguised. *"Ni Dieu, ni maître"*—that,
also, is what you want; and therefore "Cheers for natural
law!"—is it not so? But, as has been said, that is interpretation,
not text; and somebody might come along, who, with opposite
intentions and modes of interpretation, could read out of the
same "Nature," and with regard to the same phenomena, just
the tyrannically inconsiderate and relentless enforcement of
the claims of power—an interpreter who should so place the
unexceptionalness and unconditionalness of all "Will to
Power" before your eyes, that almost every word, and the word
"tyranny" itself, would eventually seem unsuitable, or like a
weakening and softening metaphor—as being too human; and
who should, nevertheless, end by asserting the same about this
world as you do, namely, that it has a "necessary" and "calculable" course, *not,* however, because laws obtain in it, but
because they are absolutely *lacking,* and every power effects its
ultimate consequences every moment. Granted that this also is

[*405*]

only interpretation—and you will be eager enough to make this objection?—well, so much the better.

23

All psychology hitherto has run aground on moral prejudices and timidities, it has not dared to launch out into the depths. In so far as it is allowable to recognise in that which has hitherto been written, evidence of that which has hitherto been kept silent, it seems as if nobody had yet harboured the notion of psychology as the Morphology and *Development-doctrine of the Will to Power,* as I conceive of it. The power of moral prejudices has penetrated deeply into the most intellectual world, the world apparently most indifferent and unprejudiced, and has obviously operated in an injurious, obstructive, blinding, and distorting manner. A proper physio-psychology has to contend with unconscious antagonism in the heart of the investigator, it has "the heart" against it: even a doctrine of the reciprocal conditionalness of the "good" and the "bad" impulses, causes (as refined immorality) distress and aversion in a still strong and manly conscience—still more so, a doctrine of the derivation of all good impulses from bad ones. If, however, a person should regard even the emotions of hatred, envy, covetousness, and imperiousness as life-conditioning emotions, as factors which must be present, fundamentally and essentially, in the general economy of life (which must, therefore, be further developed if life is to be further developed), he will suffer from such a view of things as from sea-sickness. And yet this hypothesis is far from being the strangest and most painful in this immense and almost new domain of dangerous knowledge; and there are in fact a hundred good reasons why every one should keep away from it who *can* do so! On the other hand, if one has once drifted hither with one's bark, well! very good! now let us set our teeth firmly! let us open our eyes and keep our hand fast on the helm! We sail away right *over* morality, we crush out, we destroy perhaps the remains of our own morality by daring to make our voyage thither—but what do *we* matter! Never yet did a *profounder* world of insight reveal itself to daring travellers and adventurers, and the psychologist who thus "makes a sacrifice"—it is *not* the *sacrifizio dell' intelletto*, on the contrary!—will at least be entitled to demand in return that psychology shall once more be recognised as the queen of the sciences, for whose service and equipment the other sciences exist. For psychology is once more the path to the fundamental problems.

2. *The Free Spirit*

24

O *sancta simplicitas!* In what strange simplification and falsification man lives! One can never cease wondering when once one has got eyes for beholding this marvel! How we have made everything around us clear and free and easy and simple! how we have been able to give our senses a passport to everything superficial, our thoughts a god-like desire for wanton pranks and wrong inferences!—how from the beginning, we have contrived to retain our ignorance in order to enjoy an almost inconceivable freedom, thoughtlessness, imprudence, heartiness, and gaiety—in order to enjoy life! And only on this solidified, granite-like foundation of ignorance could knowledge rear itself hitherto, the will to knowledge on the foundation of a far more powerful will, the will to ignorance, to the uncertain, to the untrue! Not as its opposite, but—as its refinement! It is to be hoped, indeed, that *language,* here as elsewhere, will not get over its awkwardness, and that it will continue to talk of opposites where there are only degrees and many refinements of gradation; it is equally to be hoped that the incarnated Tartuffery of morals, which now belongs to our unconquerable "flesh and blood," will turn the words round in the mouths of us discerning ones. Here and there we understand it, and laugh at the way in which precisely the best knowledge seeks most to retain us in this *simplified,* thoroughly artificial, suitably imagined and suitably falsified world: at the way in which, whether it will or not, it loves error, because, as living itself, it loves life!

25

After such a cheerful commencement, a serious word would fain be heard; it appeals to the most serious minds. Take care, ye philosophers and friends of knowledge, and beware of martyrdom! Of suffering "for the truth's sake"! even in your own defence! It spoils all the innocence and fine neutrality of your conscience; it makes you headstrong against objections and red rags; it stupefies, animalises, and brutalises, when in the struggle with danger, slander, suspicion, expulsion, and even worse consequences of enmity, ye have at last to play your last card as protectors of truth upon earth—as though "the Truth" were such an innocent and incompetent creature as to require protectors! and you of all people, ye knights of the sorrowful countenance, Messrs. Loafers and Cobweb-spinners of the spirit! Finally, ye know sufficiently well that it cannot be of any consequence if *ye* just carry your point; ye know that hitherto no philosopher has carried his point, and that there might be a more laudable truthfulness in every little interrogative mark which you place after your special words and favourite doctrines (and occasionally after yourselves) than in all the solemn pantomime and trumping games before accusers and law-courts! Rather go out of the way! Flee into concealment! And have your masks and your ruses, that ye may be mistaken for what you are, or somewhat feared! And pray, don't forget the garden, the garden with golden trellis-work! And have people around you who are as a garden—or as music on the waters at eventide, when already the day becomes a memory. Choose the *good* solitude, the free, wanton, lightsome solitude, which also gives you the right still to remain good in any sense whatsoever! How poisonous, how crafty, how bad, does every long war make one, which cannot be waged openly by means of force! How *personal* does a long fear make one, a long watching of enemies, of possible enemies! These pariahs of society, these long-pursued, badly-persecuted ones—also the compulsory recluses, the Spinozas or Giordano Brunos—always become in the end, even under the most intellectual masquerade, and perhaps without being themselves aware of it, refined vengeance-seekers and poison-brewers (just lay bare the foundation of Spinoza's ethics and theology!), not to speak of the stupidity of moral indignation, which is the unfailing sign in a philosopher that the sense of philosophical humour has left him. The martyrdom of the philosopher, his "sacrifice for the sake of truth," forces into the light whatever of the agitator and actor lurks in him; and if one has hitherto contemplated him only with artistic curiosity, with regard to many a philosopher it is easy to understand the dangerous desire to see him also in his deterioration (deteriorated into a "martyr," into a stage- and tribune-bawler). Only, that it is necessary with such a desire to be clear *what* spectacle one will see in any case—merely a satyric play, merely an epilogue farce, merely the continued proof that the long, real tragedy *is at an end,* supposing that every philosophy has been a long tragedy in its origin.

26

Every select man strives instinctively for a citadel and a privacy, where he is *free* from the crowd, the many, the majority—where he may forget "men who are the rule," as their exception;—exclusive only of the case in which he is pushed straight to such men by a still stronger instinct, as a discerner in the great and exceptional sense. Whoever, in intercourse with men, does not occasionally glisten in all the green and grey colours of distress, owing to disgust, satiety, sympathy, gloominess and solitariness, is assuredly not a man of elevated tastes; supposing, however, that he does not voluntarily take all this burden and disgust upon himself, that he persistently avoids it, and remains, as I said, quietly and proudly hidden in his citadel, one thing is then certain: he was not made, he was not predestined for knowledge. For as such, he would one day have to say to himself: "The devil take my good taste! but 'the rule' is more interesting than the exception—than myself, the exception!" And he would go *down,* and above all, he would go "inside." The long and serious study of the *average* man—and consequently much disguise, self-overcoming, familiarity,

and bad intercourse (all intercourse is bad intercourse except
with one's equals):—that constitutes a necessary part of the
life-history of every philosopher; perhaps the most disagreeable, odious, and disappointing part. If he is fortunate, however, as a favourite child of knowledge should be, he will meet
with suitable auxiliaries who will shorten and lighten his task;
I mean so-called cynics, those who simply recognise the animal,
the commonplace and "the rule" in themselves, and at the
same time have so much spirituality and ticklishness as to make
them talk of themselves and their like *before witnesses*—
sometimes they wallow, even in books, as on their own dung-
hill. Cynicism is the only form in which base souls approach
what is called honesty; and the higher man must open his ears
to all the coarser or finer cynicism, and congratulate himself
when the clown becomes shameless right before him, or the
scientific satyr speaks out. There are even cases where enchantment mixes with the disgust—namely, where by a freak of
nature, genius is bound to some such indiscreet billy-goat and
ape, as in the case of the Abbe Galiani, the profoundest,
acutest, and perhaps also filthiest man of his century—he was
far profounder than Voltaire, and consequently also, a good
deal more silent. It happens more frequently, as has been
hinted, that a scientific head is placed on an ape's body, a fine
exceptional understanding in a base soul, an occurrence by no
means rare, especially amongst doctors and moral physiologists. And whenever anyone speaks without bitterness, or
rather quite innocently of man, as a belly with two requirements, and a head with one; whenever any one sees, seeks and
wants to see only hunger, sexual instinct, and vanity as the real
and only motives of human actions; in short, when any one
speaks "badly"—and not even "ill"—of man, then ought the
lover of knowledge to hearken attentively and diligently; he

[*411*]

ought, in general, to have an open ear wherever there is talk without indignation. For the indignant man, and he who perpetually tears and lacerates himself with his own teeth (or, in place of himself, the world, God, or society), may indeed, morally speaking, stand higher than the laughing and self-satisfied satyr, but in every other sense he is the more ordinary, more indifferent, and less instructive case. And no one is such a *liar* as the indignant man.

27

It is difficult to be understood, especially when one thinks and lives *gangasrotogati* * among those only who think and live otherwise—namely, *kurmagati*,† or at best "froglike," *mandeikagati* ‡ (I do everything to be "difficultly understood" myself!)—and one should be heartily grateful for the good will to some refinement of interpretation. As regards "the good friends," however, who are always too easy-going, and think that as friends they have a right to ease, one does well at the very first to grant them a playground and romping-place for misunderstanding—one can thus laugh still; or get rid of them altogether, these good friends—and laugh then also!

28

What is most difficult to render from one language into another is the *tempo* of its style, which has its basis in the char-

---

* Like the river Ganges: *presto.*
† Like the tortoise: *lento.*
‡ Like the frog: *staccato.*

acter of the race, or to speak more physiologically, in the average *tempo* of the assimilation of its nutriment. There are honestly meant translations, which, as involuntary vulgarisations, are almost falsifications of the original, merely because its lively and merry *tempo* (which overleaps and obviates all dangers in word and expression) could not also be rendered. A German is almost incapacitated for *presto* in his language; consequently also, as may be reasonably inferred, for many of the most delightful and daring *nuances* of free, free-spirited thought. And just as the buffoon and satyr are foreign to him in body and conscience, so Aristophanes and Petronius are untranslatable for him. Everything ponderous, viscous, and pompously clumsy, all long-winded and wearying species of style, are developed in profuse variety among Germans— pardon me for stating the fact that even Goethe's prose, in its mixture of stiffness and elegance, is no exception, as a reflection of the "good old time" to which it belongs, and as an expression of German taste at a time when there was still a "German taste," which was a rococo-taste *in moribus et artibus.* Lessing is an exception, owing to his histrionic nature, which understood much, and was versed in many things; he who was not the translator of Bayle to no purpose, who took refuge willingly in the shadow of Diderot and Voltaire, and still more willingly among the Roman comedy-writers—Lessing loved also free-spiritism in the *tempo,* and flight out of Germany. But how could the German language, even in the prose of Lessing, imitate the *tempo* of Machiavelli, who in his "Principe" makes us breathe the dry, fine air of Florence, and cannot help presenting the most serious events in a boisterous *allegrissimo,* perhaps not without a malicious artistic sense of the contrast he ventures to present—long, heavy, difficult, dangerous thoughts, and a *tempo* of the gallop, and of the best,

[*413*]

wantonest humour? Finally, who would venture on a German translation of Petronius, who, more than any great musician hitherto, was a master of *presto* in invention, ideas, and words? What matter in the end about the swamps of the sick, evil world, or of the "ancient world," when like him, one has the feet of a wind, the rush, the breath, the emancipating scorn of a wind, which makes everything healthy, by making everything *run!* And with regard to Aristophanes—that transfiguring, complementary genius, for whose sake one *pardons* all Hellenism for having existed, provided one has understood in its full profundity *all* that there requires pardon and transfiguration; there is nothing that has caused me to meditate more on *Plato's* secrecy and sphinx-like nature, than the happily preserved *petit fait* that under the pillow of his death-bed there was found no "Bible," nor anything Egyptian, Pythagorean, or Platonic—but a book of Aristophanes. How could even Plato have endured life—a Greek life which he repudiated—without an Aristophanes?

29

It is the business of the very few to be independent; it is a privilege of the strong. And whoever attempts it, even with the best right, but without being *obliged* to do so, proves that he is probably not only strong, but also daring beyond measure. He enters into a labyrinth, he multiplies a thousandfold the dangers which life in itself already brings with it; not the least of which is that no one can see how and where he loses his way, becomes isolated, and is torn piecemeal by some minotaur of conscience. Supposing such a one comes to grief, it is so far from the comprehension of men that they neither feel it, nor sympathise with it. And he cannot any longer go back! He cannot even go back again to the sympathy of men!

30

Our deepest insights must—and should—appear as follies, and under certain circumstances as crimes, when they come unauthorisedly to the ears of those who are not disposed and predestined for them. The exoteric and the esoteric, as they were formerly distinguished by philosophers—among the Indians, as among the Greeks, Persians, and Mussulmans, in short, wherever people believed in gradations of rank and *not* in equality and equal rights—are not so much in contradistinction to one another in respect to the exoteric class, standing without, and viewing, estimating, measuring, and judging from the outside, and not from the inside; the more essential distinction is that the class in question views things from below upwards—while the esoteric class views things *from above downwards*. There are heights of the soul from which tragedy itself no longer appears to operate tragically; and if all the woe in the world were taken together, who would dare to decide whether the sight of it would *necessarily* seduce and constrain to sympathy, and thus to a doubling of the woe? . . . That which serves the higher class of men for nourishment or refreshment, must be almost poison to an entirely different and lower order of human beings. The virtues of the common man would perhaps mean vice and weakness in a philosopher; it might be possible for a highly developed man, supposing him to degenerate and go to ruin, to acquire qualities thereby alone, for the sake of which he would have to be honoured as a saint in the lower world into which he had sunk. There are books

which have an inverse value for the soul and the health according-
ing as the inferior soul and the lower vitality, or the higher and
more powerful, make use of them. In the former case they are
dangerous, disturbing, unsettling books, in the latter case they
are herald-calls which summon the bravest to *their* bravery.
Books for the general reader are always ill-smelling books, the
odour of paltry people clings to them. Where the populace eat
and drink, and even where they reverence, it is accustomed
to stink. One should not go into churches if one wishes to
breathe *pure* air.

31

In our youthful years we still venerate and despise without
the art of *nuance,* which is the best gain of life, and we have
rightly to do hard penance for having fallen upon men and
things with Yea and Nay. Everything is so arranged that the
worst of all tastes, *the taste for the unconditional,* is cruelly
befooled and abused, until a man learns to introduce a little
art into his sentiments, and prefers to try conclusions with the
artificial, as do the real artists of life. The angry and reverent
spirit peculiar to youth appears to allow itself no peace, until
it has suitably falsified men and things, to be able to vent its
passion upon them: youth in itself even, is something falsifying and deceptive. Later on, when the young soul, tortured
by continual disillusions, finally turns suspiciously against
itself—still ardent and savage even in its suspicion and remorse
of conscience: how it upbraids itself, how impatiently it tears
itself, how it revenges itself for its long self-blinding, as
though it had been a voluntary blindness! In this transition one

punishes oneself by distrust of one's sentiments; one tortures one's enthusiasm with doubt, one feels even the good conscience to be a danger, as if it were the self-concealment and lassitude of a more refined uprightness; and above all, one espouses upon principle the cause *against* "youth."—A decade later, and one comprehends that all this was also still—youth!

32

Throughout the longest period of human history—one calls it the prehistoric period—the value or non-value of an action was inferred from its *consequences;* the action in itself was not taken into consideration, any more than its origin; but pretty much as in China at present, where the distinction or disgrace of a child redounds to its parents, the retro-operating power of success or failure was what induced men to think well or ill of an action. Let us call this period the *pre-moral* period of mankind; the imperative, "know thyself!" was then still unknown. —In the last ten thousand years, on the other hand, on certain large portions of the earth, one has gradually got so far, that one no longer lets the consequences of an action, but its origin, decide with regard to its worth: a great achievement as a whole, an important refinement of vision and of criterion, the unconscious effect of the supremacy of aristocratic values and of the belief in "origin," the mark of a period which may be designated in the narrower sense as the *moral* one: the first attempt at self-knowledge is thereby made. Instead of the consequences, the origin—what an inversion of perspective! And assuredly an inversion effected only after long struggle and wavering! To be sure, an ominous new superstition, a peculiar narrowness of interpretation, attained supremacy precisely thereby: the origin of an action was interpreted in the most definite sense possible, as origin out of an *intention;* people were agreed in the belief that the value of an action lay in the value of its intention. The intention as the sole origin and antecedent history of an action: under the influence of this prejudice moral praise and blame have been bestowed, and men have judged and even philosophised almost up to the present day.—Is it not possible, however, that the necessity may now have arisen of again making up our minds with regard to the reversing and fundamental shifting of values, owing to a new self-consciousness and acuteness in man—is it not possible that we may be standing on the threshold of a period which to begin with, would be distinguished negatively as *ultra-moral:* nowadays when, at least amongst us immoralists, the suspicion arises that the decisive value of an action lies precisely in that which is *not intentional,* and that all its intentionalness, all that is seen, sensible, or "sensed" in it, belongs to its surface or skin—which, like every skin, betrays something, but *conceals* still more? In short, we believe that the intention is only a sign or symptom, which first requires an explanation—a sign, moreover, which has too many interpretations, and consequently hardly any meaning in itself alone: that morality, in the sense in which it has been understood hitherto, as intention-morality, has been a prejudice, perhaps a prematureness or preliminariness, probably something of the same rank as astrology and alchemy, but in any case something which must be surmounted. The surmounting of morality, in a certain sense even the self-mounting of morality—let that be the name for the long secret labour which has been reserved for the most refined, the most upright, and also the most wicked consciences of today, as the living touchstones of the soul.

[*418*]

33

It cannot be helped: the sentiment of surrender, of sacrifice for one's neighbour, and all self-renunciation-morality, must be mercilessly called to account, and brought to judgment; just as the æsthetics of "disinterested contemplation," under which the emasculation of art nowadays seeks insidiously enough to create itself a good conscience. There is far too much witchery and sugar in the sentiments "for others" and *"not* for myself," for one not needing to be doubly distrustful here, and for one asking promptly: "Are they not perhaps—*deceptions?"*—That they *please*—him who has them, and him who enjoys their fruit, and also the mere spectator—that is still no argument in their *favour,* but just calls for caution. Let us therefore be cautious!

34

At whatever standpoint of philosophy one may place oneself nowadays, seen from every position, the *erroneousness* of the world in which we think we live is the surest and most certain thing our eyes can light upon: we find proof after proof thereof, which would fain allure us into surmises concerning a deceptive principle in the "nature of things." He, however, who makes thinking itself, and consequently "the spirit," responsible for the falseness of the world—an honourable exit, which every conscious or unconscious *advocatus dei* avails himself of—he who regards this world, including space, time, form, and movement, as falsely *deduced,* would have at least good reason in the end to become distrustful also of all thinking; has it not hitherto been playing upon us the worst of

[*419*]

scurvy tricks? and what guarantee would it give that it would
not continue to do what it has always been doing? In all seriousness, the innocence of thinkers has something touching and
respect-inspiring in it, which even nowadays permits them to
wait upon consciousness with the request that it will give them
honest answers: for example whether it be "real" or not, and
why it keeps the outer world so resolutely at a distance, and
other questions of the same description. The belief in "immediate certainties" is a *moral naïveté* which does honour to us
philosophers; but—we have now to cease being *"merely
moral"* men! Apart from morality, such belief is a folly which
does little honour to us! If in middle-class life an ever-ready
distrust is regarded as the sign of a "bad character," and consequently as an imprudence, here amongst us, beyond the middle-
class world and its Yeas and Nays, what should prevent our
being imprudent and saying: the philosopher has at length a
right to "bad character," as the being who has hitherto been
most befooled on earth—he is now under *obligation* to dis-
trustfulness, to the wickedest squinting out of every abyss of
suspicion.—Forgive me the joke of this gloomy grimace and
turn of expression; for I myself have long ago learned to think
and estimate differently with regard to deceiving and being
deceived, and I keep at least a couple of pokes in the ribs
ready for the blind rage with which philosophers struggle
against being deceived. Why *not?* It is nothing more than a
moral prejudice that truth is worth more than semblance; it is,
in fact, the worst proved supposition in the world. *So* much
must be conceded: there could have been no life at all except
upon the basis of perspective estimates and semblances; and
if, with the virtuous enthusiasm and stupidity of many philosophers, one wished to do away altogether with the "seeming
world"—well, granted that *you* could do that,—at least noth-

ing of your "truth" would thereby remain! Indeed, what is it that forces us in general to the supposition that there is an essential opposition of "true" and "false"? Is it not enough to suppose degrees of seemingness, and as it were lighter and darker shades and tones of semblance—different *valeurs,* as the painters say? Why might not the world *which concerns us* —be a fiction? And to any one who suggested: "But to a fiction belongs an originator?"—might it not be bluntly replied: *Why?* May not this "belong" also belong to the fiction? Is it not at length permitted to be a little ironical towards the subject, just as towards the predicate and object? Might not the philosopher elevate himself above faith in grammar? All respect to governesses, but is it not time that philosophy should renounce governess-faith?

35

O Voltaire! O humanity! O idiocy! There is something ticklish in "the truth," and in the *search* for the truth; and if man goes about it too humanely—*"il ne cherche le vrai que pour faire le bien"*—I wager he finds nothing!

36

Supposing that nothing else is "given" as real but our world of desires and passions, that we cannot sink or rise to any other "reality" but just that of our impulses—for thinking is only a relation of these impulses to one another:—are we not permitted to make the attempt and to ask the question whether this which is "given" does not *suffice,* by means of our counter-arts, for the understanding even of the so-called mechanical (or "material") world? I do not mean as an illusion, a "semblance," a "representation" (in the Berkeleyan and Schopenhauerian sense), but as possessing the same degree of reality as our emotions themselves—as a more primitive form of the world of emotions, in which everything still lies locked in a mighty unity, which afterwards branches off and develops itself in organic processes (naturally also, refines and debilitates)—as a kind of instinctive life in which all organic functions, including self-regulation, assimilation, nutrition, secretion, and change of matter, are still synthetically united with one another—as a *primary form* of life?—In the end, it is not only permitted to make this attempt, it is commanded by the conscience of *logical method*. Not to assume several kinds of causality, so long as the attempt to get along with a single one has not been pushed to its furtherest extent (to absurdity, if I may be allowed to say so): that is a morality of method which one may not repudiate nowadays—it follows "from its definition," as mathematicians say. The question is ultimately whether we really recognise the will as *operating*, whether we believe in the causality of the will; if we do so—and fundamentally our belief *in this* is just our belief in causality itself—we *must* make the attempt to posit hypothetically the causality of the will as the only causality. "Will" can naturally only operate on "will"—and not on "matter" (not on "nerves," for instance): in short, the hypothesis must be hazarded, whether will does not operate on will wherever "effects" are recognised—and whether all mechanical action, inasmuch as a power operates therein, is not just the power of will, the effect of will. Granted, finally, that we succeeded in explaining our entire instinctive life as the development and ramification of

[*422*]

one fundamental form of will—namely, the Will to Power, as *my* thesis puts it; granted that all organic functions could be traced back to this Will to Power, and that the solution of the problem of generation and nutrition—it is one problem—could also be found therein: one would thus have acquired the right to define *all* active force unequivocally as *Will to Power*. The world seen from within, the world defined and designated according to its "intelligible character"—it would simply be "Will to Power," and nothing else.

37

"What? Does not that mean in popular language: God is disproved, but not the devil"?—On the contrary! On the contrary, my friends! And who the devil also compels you to speak popularly!

38

As happened finally in all the enlightenment of modern times with the French Revolution (that terrible farce, quite superfluous when judged close at hand, into which, however, the noble and visionary spectators of all Europe have interpreted from a distance their own indignation and enthusiasm so long and passionately, *until the text has disappeared under the interpretation*), so a noble posterity might once more misunderstand the whole of the past, and perhaps only thereby makes *its* aspect endurable.—Or rather, has not this already happened? Have not we ourselves been—that "noble posterity"? And, in so far as we now comprehend this, is it not—thereby already past?

Nobody will very readily regard a doctrine as true merely because it makes people happy or virtuous—excepting, perhaps,
the amiable "Idealists," who are enthusiastic about the good,
true, and beautiful, and let all kinds of motley, coarse, and
good-natured desirabilities swim about promiscuously in their
pond. Happiness and virtue are no arguments. It is willingly
forgotten, however, even on the part of thoughtful minds, that
to make unhappy and to make bad are just as little counter-
arguments. A thing could be *true,* although it were in the
highest degree injurious and dangerous; indeed, the fundamental constitution of existence might be such that one succumbed by a full knowledge of it—so that the strength of a
mind might be measured by the amount of "truth" it could
endure—or to speak more plainly, by the extent to which it
*require*d truth attenuated, veiled, sweetened, damped, and
falsified. But there is no doubt that for the discovery of certain
portions of truth the wicked and unfortunate are more favourably situated and have a greater likelihood of success; not to
speak of the wicked who are happy—a species about whom
moralists are silent. Perhaps severity and craft are more favourable conditions for the development of strong, independent
spirits and philosophers than the gentle, refined, yielding
good-nature, and habit of taking things easily, which are
prized, and rightly prized in a learned man. Presupposing
always, to begin with, that the term "philosopher" be not confined to the philosopher who writes books, or even introduces
his philosophy into books!—Stendhal furnishes a last feature
of the portrait of the free-spirited philosopher, which for the
sake of German taste I will not omit to underline—for it is

opposed to German taste. *"Pour être bon philosophe,"* says this last great psychologist, *"il faut être sec, clair, sans illusion. Un banquier, qui a fait fortune, a une partie du caractère requis pour faire des découvertes en philosophie, c'est-à-dire pour voir clair dans ce qui est."*

40

Everything that is profound loves the mask: the profoundest things have a hatred even of figure and likeness. Should not the *contrary* only be the right disguise for the shame of a God to go about in? A question worth asking!—it would be strange if some mystic has not already ventured on the same kind of thing. There are proceedings of such a delicate nature that it is well to overwhelm them with coarseness and make them unrecognisable; there are actions of love and of an extravagant magnanimity after which nothing can be wiser than to take a stick and thrash the witness soundly: one thereby obscures his recollection. Many a one is able to obscure and abuse his own memory, in order at least to have vengeance on this sole party in the secret: shame is inventive. They are not the worst things of which one is most ashamed: there is not only deceit behind a mask—there is so much goodness in craft. I could imagine that a man with something costly and fragile to conceal, would roll through life clumsily and rotundly like an old, green, heavily-hooped wine-cask: the refinement of his shame requiring it to be so. A man who has depths in his shame meets his destiny and his delicate decisions upon paths which few ever reach, and with regard to the existence of which his nearest and most intimate friends may be ignorant; his mortal danger conceals itself from their eyes, and equally so his regained security.

Such a hidden nature, which instinctively employs speech for silence and concealment, and is inexhaustible in evasion of communication, *desires* and insists that a mask of himself shall occupy his place in the hearts and heads of his friends; and supposing he does not desire it, his eyes will some day be opened to the fact that there is nevertheless a mask of him there—and that it is well to be so. Every profound spirit needs a mask; nay, more, around every profound spirit there continually grows a mask, owing to the constantly false, that is to say, *superficial* interpretation of every word he utters, every step he takes, every sign of life he manifests.

41

One must subject oneself to one's own tests that one is destined for independence and command, and do so at the right time. One must not avoid one's tests, although they constitute perhaps the most dangerous game one can play, and are in the end tests made only before ourselves and before no other judge. Not to cleave to any person, be it even the dearest—every person is a prison and also a recess. Not to cleave to a fatherland, be it even the most suffering and necessitous—it is even less difficult to detach one's heart from a victorious fatherland. Not to cleave to a sympathy, be it even for higher men, into whose peculiar torture and helplessness chance has given us an insight. Not to cleave to a science, though it tempt one with the most valuable discoveries, apparently specially reserved for *us*. Not to cleave to one's own liberation, to the voluptuous distance and remoteness of the bird, which always flies further aloft in order always to see more under it—the danger of the flier. Not to cleave to our own virtues, nor become as a whole a victim to any of our specialties, to our "hospitality" for instance, which is the danger of dangers for highly developed and wealthy souls, who deal prodigally, almost indifferently with themselves, and push the virtue of liberality so far that it becomes a vice. One must know how *to conserve oneself*—the best test of independence.

42

A new order of philosophers is appearing; I shall venture to baptize them by a name not without danger. As far as I understand them, as far as they allow themselves to be understood—for it is their nature to *wish* to remain something of a puzzle—these philosophers of the future might rightly, perhaps also wrongly, claim to be designated as *"tempters."* This name itself is after all only an attempt, or, if it be preferred, a temptation.

43

Will they be new friends of "truth," these coming philosophers? Very probably, for all philosophers hitherto have loved their truths. But assuredly they will not be dogmatists. It must be contrary to their pride, and also contrary to their taste, that their truth should still be truth for every one—that which has hitherto been the secret wish and ultimate purpose of all dogmatic efforts. "My opinion is *my* opinion: another person has not easily a right to it"—such a philosopher of the future will say, perhaps. One must renounce the bad taste of wishing to agree with many people. "Good" is no longer good when one's neighbour takes it into his mouth. And how could there be a "common good"! The expression contradicts itself; that which can be common is always of small value. In the end things must be as they are and have always been—the great things remain for the great, the abysses for the profound, the delicacies and thrills for the refined, and, to sum up shortly, everything rare for the rare.

44

Need I say expressly after all this that they will be free, *very* free spirits, these philosophers of the future—as certainly also they will not be merely free spirits, but something more, higher, greater, and fundamentally different, which does not wish to be misunderstood and mistaken? But while I say this, I feel under *obligation* almost as much to them as to ourselves (we free spirits who are their heralds and forerunners), to sweep away from ourselves altogether a stupid old prejudice and misunderstanding, which, like a fog, has too long made the conception of "free spirit" obscure. In every country of Europe, and the same in America, there is at present something which makes an abuse of this name: a very narrow, prepossessed, enchained class of spirits, who desire almost the opposite of what our intentions and instincts prompt—not to mention that in respect to the *new* philosophers who are appearing, they must still more be closed windows and bolted doors. Briefly and regrettably, they belong to the *levellers,* these wrongly named "free spirits"—as glib-tongued and scribe-fingered slaves of the democratic taste and its "modern ideas": all of them men without solitude, without personal solitude, blunt, honest fellows to whom neither courage nor honourable conduct ought to be denied; only, they are not free,

and are ludicrously superficial, especially in their innate par-
tiality for seeing the cause of almost *all* human misery and
failure in the old forms in which society has hitherto existed
—a notion which happily inverts the truth entirely! What they
would fain attain with all their strength, is the universal,
green-meadow happiness of the herd, together with security,
safety, comfort, and alleviation of life for every one; their two
most frequently chanted songs and doctrines are called "Equality of Rights" and "Sympathy with all Sufferers"—and suffering itself is looked upon by them as something which must be
done away with. We opposite ones, however, who have opened
our eye and conscience to the question how and where the
plant "man" has hitherto grown most vigorously, believe that
this has always taken place under the opposite conditions, that
for this end the dangerousness of his situation had to be increased enormously, his inventive faculty and dissembling
power (his "spirit") had to develop into subtlety and daring
under long oppression and compulsion, and his Will to Life
had to be increased to the unconditioned Will to Power:—we
believe that severity, violence, slavery, danger in the street
and in the heart, secrecy, stoicism, tempter's art and devilry of
every kind,—that everything wicked, terrible, tyrannical,
predatory, and serpentine in man, serves as well for the elevation of the human species as its opposite:—we do not even say
enough when we only say *this much*; and in any case we find
ourselves here, both with our speech and our science, at the
other extreme of all modern ideology and gregarious desira-
bility, as their antipodes perhaps? What wonder that we "free
spirits" are not exactly the most communicative spirits? that
we do not wish to betray in every respect *what* a spirit can free
itself from, and *where* perhaps it will then be driven? And as
to the import of the dangerous formula, "Beyond Good and

[*429*]

Evil," with which we at least avoid confusion, we *are* something else than *"libres-penseurs," "liberi pensatori,"* "freethinkers," and whatever these honest advocates of "modern ideas" like to call themselves. Having been at home, or at least guests, in many realms of the spirit; having escaped again and again from the gloomy, agreeable nooks in which preferences and prejudices, youth, origin, the accident of men and books, or even the weariness of travel seemed to confine us; full of malice against the seductions of dependency which lie concealed in honours, money, positions, or exaltation of the senses; grateful even for distress and the vicissitudes of illness, because they always free us from some rule, and its "prejudice," grateful to the God, devil, sheep, and worm in us; inquisitive to a fault, investigators to the point of cruelty, with unhesitating fingers for the intangible, with teeth and stomachs for the most indigestible, ready for any business that requires sagacity and acute senses, ready for every adventure, owing to an excess of "free will"; with anterior and posterior souls, into the ultimate intentions of which it is difficult to pry, with foregrounds and backgrounds to the end of which no foot may run; hidden ones under the mantles of light, appropriators, although we resemble heirs and spendthrifts, arrangers and collectors from morning till night, misers of our wealth and our full-crammed drawers, economical in learning and forgetting, inventive in scheming; sometimes proud of tables of categories, sometimes pedants, sometimes night-owls of work even in full day; yea, if necessary, even scarecrows—and it is necessary nowadays, that is to say, inasmuch as we are the born, sworn, jealous friends of *solitude,* of our own profoundest midnight and mid-day solitude:—such kind of men are we, we free spirits! And perhaps *ye* are also something of the same kind, ye coming ones, ye *new* philosophers?

3. *The Religious Mood*

45

THE human soul and its limits, the range of man's inner experiences hitherto attained, the heights, depths and distances of these experiences, the entire history of the soul *up to the present time,* and its still unexhausted possibilities: this is the preordained hunting-domain for a born psychologist and lover of a "big hunt." But how often must he say despairingly to himself: "A single individual! alas, only a single individual! and this great forest, this virgin forest!" So he would like to have some hundreds of hunting assistants, and fine trained hounds, that he could send into the history of the human soul, to drive *his* game together. In vain: again and again he experiences, profoundly and bitterly, how difficult it is to find assistants and dogs for all the things that directly excite his curiosity. The evil of sending scholars into new and dangerous hunting-domains, where courage, sagacity, and subtlety in every sense are required, is that they are no longer serviceable just when the *"big* hunt," and also the great danger commences,—it is precisely then that they lose their keen eye and nose. In order, for instance, to divine and determine what sort of history the problem of *knowledge and conscience* has hitherto had in the souls of *homines religiosi,* a person would perhaps himself have to possess as profound, as bruised, as immense an experience as the intellectual conscience of Pascal; and then he would still require that wide-spread heaven of clear, wicked spirituality, which, from above, would be able to oversee, arrange, and effectively formulise this mass of dangerous and painful experiences.—But who could do me this service! And who would have time to wait for such servants! —they evidently appear too rarely, they are so improbable at all times! Eventually one must do everything *oneself* in order to know something; which means that one has *much* to do!— But a curiosity like mine is once for all the most agreeable of vices—pardon me! I mean to say that the love of truth has its reward in heaven, and already upon earth.

46

Faith, such as early Christianity desired, and not infrequently achieved in the midst of a sceptical and southernly free-spirited world, which had centuries of struggle between philosophical schools behind it and in it, counting besides the education in tolerance which the *imperium Romanum* gave— this faith is *not* that sincere, austere slave-faith by which perhaps a Luther or a Cromwell, or some other northern barbarian of the spirit remained attached to his God and Christianity; it is much rather the faith of Pascal, which resembles in a terrible manner a continuous suicide of reason—a tough, long-lived, wormlike reason, which is not to be slain at once and with a single blow. The Christian faith from the beginning, is sacrifice: the sacrifice of all freedom, all pride, all self-confidence of spirit; it is at the same time subjection, self-derision, and self-mutilation. There is cruelty and religious Phœnicianism in this faith, which is adapted to a tender, many-sided, and very fastidious conscience; it takes for granted that the subjection of the spirit is indescribably *painful,* that all the past and all the habits of such a spirit resist the *absurdissimum,* in the form of which "faith" comes to it. Modern men, with their obtuseness as regards all Christian nomenclature, have no longer the sense for the terribly superlative conception which was implied to an antique taste by the paradox of the formula, "God on the Cross." Hitherto there had never and nowhere been such boldness in inversion, nor anything at once so dreadful, questioning, and questionable as this formula: it promised a transvaluation of all ancient values.——It was the Orient, the *profound* Orient, it was the Oriental slave who thus took revenge on Rome and its noble, light-minded toleration, on the Roman "Catholicism" of non-faith; and it was always, not the faith, but the freedom from the faith, the half-stoical and smiling indifference to the seriousness of the faith, which made the slaves indignant at their masters and revolt against them. "Enlightenment" causes revolt: for the slave desires the unconditioned, he understands nothing but the tyrannous, even in morals; he loves as he hates, without *nuance,* to the very depths, to the point of pain, to the point of sickness——his many *hidden* sufferings make him revolt against the noble taste which seems to *deny* suffering. The scepticism with regard to suffering, fundamentally only an attitude of aristocratic morality, was not the least of the causes, also, of the last great slave-insurrection which began with the French Revolution.

47

Wherever the religious neurosis has appeared on the earth so far, we find it connected with three dangerous prescriptions as to regimen: solitude, fasting, and sexual abstinence——but without its being possible to determine with certainty which is cause and which is effect, or *if* any relation at all of cause and effect exists there. This latter doubt is justified by the fact that one of the most regular symptoms among savage as well as among civilised peoples is the most sudden and excessive sensuality; which then with equal suddenness transforms into penitential paroxysms, world-renunciation, and will-renunciation: both symptoms perhaps explainable as disguised epilepsy? But nowhere is it *more* obligatory to put aside explanations: around no other type has there grown such a mass of absurdity and superstition, no other type seems to have been more interesting to men and even to philosophers—perhaps it is time to become just a little indifferent here, to learn caution, or, better still, to look away, *to go away.*—Yet in the background of the most recent philosophy, that of Schopenhauer, we find almost as the problem in itself, this terrible note of interrogation of the religious crisis and awakening. How is the negation of will *possible?* how is the saint possible?—that seems to have been the very question with which Schopenhauer made a start and became a philosopher. And thus it was a genuine Schopenhauerian consequence, that his most convinced adherent (perhaps also his last, as far as Germany is concerned), namely, Richard Wagner, should bring his own life-work to an end just here, and should finally put that terrible and eternal type upon the stage as Kundry, *type vécu,* and as it loved and lived, at the very time that the mad-doctors in almost all European countries had an opportunity to study the type close at hand, wherever the religious neurosis—or as I call it, "the religious mood"—made its latest epidemical outbreak and display as the "Salvation Army."—If it be a question, however, as to what has been so extremely interesting to men of all sorts in all ages, and even to philosophers, in the whole phenomenon of the saint, it is undoubtedly the appearance of the miraculous therein—namely, the immediate *succession of opposites,* of states of the soul regarded as morally antithetical: it was believed here to be self-evident that a "bad man" was all at once turned into a "saint," a good man. The hitherto existing psychology was wrecked at this point; is it not possible it may have happened principally because psychology had placed itself under the dominion of morals, because it *believed* in oppositions of moral values, and saw, read, and *interpreted* these oppositions into the text and facts of the case? What? "Miracle" only an error of interpretation? A lack of philology?

48

It seems that the Latin races are far more deeply attached to their Catholicism than we Northerners are to Christianity generally, and that consequently unbelief in Catholic countries means something quite different from what it does among Protestants—namely, a sort of revolt against the spirit of the race, while with us it is rather a return to the spirit (or non-spirit) of the race. We Northerners undoubtedly derive our origin from barbarous races, even as regards our talents for religion—we have *poor* talents for it. One may make an exception in the case of the Celts, who have theretofore furnished also the best soil for Christian infection in the north: the Christian ideal blossomed forth in France as much as ever the pale sun of the north would allow it. How strangely pious for our taste are still these later French sceptics, whenever there is any Celtic blood in their origin! How Catholic, how un-German does Auguste Comte's Sociology seem to us, with the Roman logic of its instincts! How Jesuitical, that amiable and shrewd cicerone of Port-Royal, Sainte-Beuve, in spite of all his hostility to Jesuits! And even Ernest Renan: how inaccessible to us Northerners does the language of such a Renan appear, in whom every instant the merest touch of religious thrill throws his refined voluptuous and comfortably couching soul off its balance! Let us repeat after him these fine sentences —and what wickedness and haughtiness is immediately aroused by way of answer in our probably less beautiful but harder souls, that is to say, in our more German souls!— *"Disons donc hardiment que la religion est un produit de l'homme normal, que l'homme est le plus dans le vrai quand il est le plus religieux et le plus assuré d'une destinée infinie. . . . C'est quand il est bon qu'il veut que la virtu corresponde à un order éternal, c'est quand il contemple les choses d'une manière désintéressée qu'il trouve la mort révoltante et absurde. Comment ne pas supposer que c'est dans ces moments-là, que l'homme voit le mieux?"* . . . These sentences are so extremely *antipodal* to my ears and habits of thought, that in my first impulse of rage on finding them, I wrote on the margin, *"la niaiserie religieuse par excellence!"*—until in my later rage I even took a fancy to them, these sentences with their truth absolutely inverted! It is so nice and such a distinction to have one's own antipodes!

49

That which is so astonishing in the religious life of the ancient Greeks is the irrestrainable stream of *gratitude* which it pours forth—it is a very superior kind of man who takes *such* an attitude towards nature and life.—Later on, when the populace got the upper hand in Greece, *fear* became rampant also in religion; and Christianity was preparing itself.

50

The passion for God: there are churlish, honest-hearted, and importunate kinds of it, like that of Luther—the whole of Protestantism lacks the southern *delicatezza*. There is an Oriental exaltation of the mind in it, like that of an undeservedly favoured or elevated slave, as in the case of St. Augustine, for instance, who lacks in an offensive manner, all nobility in bearing and desires. There is a feminine tenderness and sensuality in it, which modestly and unconsciously longs for a *unio mystica et physica*, as in the case of Madame de Guyon. In many cases it appears, curiously enough, as the disguise of a girl's or youth's puberty; here and there even as the hysteria of an old maid, also as her last ambition. The Church has frequently canonised the woman in such a case.

51

The mightiest men have hitherto always bowed reverently before the saint, as the enigma of self-subjugation and utter voluntary privation—why did they thus bow? They divined in him—and as it were behind the questionableness of his frail and wretched appearance—the superior force which wished to test itself by such a subjugation; the strength of will, in which they recognised their own strength and love of power, and knew how to honour it: they honoured something in themselves when they honoured the saint. In addition to this, the contemplation of the saint suggested to them a suspicion: such an enormity of self-negation and anti-naturalness will not have been coveted for nothing—they have said, inquiringly. There

[*437*]

is perhaps a reason for it, some very great danger, about which the ascetic might wish to be more accurately informed through his secret interlocutors and visitors? In a word, the mighty ones of the world learned to have a new fear before him, they divined a new power, a strange, still unconquered enemy:— it was the "Will to Power" which obliged them to halt before the saint. They had to question him.

52

In the Jewish "Old Testament," the book of divine justice, there are men, things, and sayings on such an immense scale, that Greek and Indian literature has nothing to compare with it. One stands with fear and reverence before those stupendous remains of what man was formerly, and one has sad thoughts about old Asia and its little out-pushed peninsula Europe, which would like, by all means, to figure before Asia as the "Progress of Mankind." To be sure, he who is himself only a slender, tame house-animal, and knows only the wants of a house-animal (like our cultured people of today, including the Christians of "cultured" Christianity), need neither be amazed nor even sad amid those ruins—the taste for the Old Testament is a touchstone with respect to "great" and "small": perhaps he will find that the New Testament, the book of grace, still appeals more to his heart (there is much of the odour of the genuine, tender, stupid beadsman and petty soul in it). To have bound up this New Testament (a kind of *rococo* of taste in every respect) along with the Old Testament into one book, as the "Bible," as "The Book in Itself," is perhaps the greatest audacity and "sin against the Spirit" which literary Europe has upon its conscience.

[*438*]

53

Why Atheism nowadays? "The father" in God is thoroughly refuted; equally so "the judge," "the rewarder." Also his "free will": he does not hear—and even if he did, he would not know how to help. The worst is that he seems incapable of communicating himself clearly: is he uncertain?—This is what I have made out (by questioning and listening at a variety of conversations) to be the cause of the decline of European theism; it appears to me that though the religious instinct is in vigorous growth,—it rejects the theistic satisfaction with pro found distrust.

54

What does all modern philosophy mainly do? Since Descartes—and indeed more in defiance of him than on the basis of his procedure—an *attentat* has been made on the part of all philosophers on the old conception of the soul, under the guise of a criticism of the subject and predicate conception —that is to say, an *attentat* on the fundamental presupposition of Christian doctrine. Modern philosophy, as epistemological scepticism, is secretly or openly *anti-Christian,* although (for keener ears, be it said) by no means anti-religious. Formerly, in effect, one believed in "the soul" as one believed in grammar and the grammatical subject: one said, "I" is the condition, "think" is the predicate and is conditioned—to think is an activity for which one *must* suppose a subject as cause. The attempt was then made, with marvellous tenacity and subtlety, to see if one could not get out of this net,—to see if the opposite was not perhaps true: "think" the condition, and "I" the conditioned; "I," therefore, only a synthesis which has been *made* by thinking itself. *Kant* really wished to prove that, starting from the subject, the subject could not be proved—nor the object either: the possibility of an *apparent existence* of the subject, and therefore of "the soul," may not always have been strange to him,—the thought which once had an immense power on earth as the Vedanta philosophy.

55

There is a great ladder of religious cruelty, with many rounds; but three of these are the most important. Once on a time men sacrificed human beings to their God, and perhaps just those they loved the best—to this category belong the firstling sacrifices of all primitive religions, and also the sacrifice of the Emperor Tiberius in the Mithra-Grotto on the Island of Capri, that most terrible of all Roman anachronisms. Then, during the moral epoch of mankind, they sacrificed to their God the strongest instincts they possessed, their "nature"; *this* festal joy shines in the cruel glances of ascetics and "anti-natural" fanatics. Finally, what still remained to be sacrificed? Was it not necessary in the end for men to sacrifice everything comforting, holy, healing, all hope, all faith in hidden harmonies, in future blessedness and justice? Was it not necessary to sacrifice God himself, and out of cruelty to themselves to worship stone, stupidity, gravity, fate, nothingness? To sacrifice God for nothingness—this paradoxical mystery of the ultimate cruelty has been reserved for the rising generation; we all know something thereof already.

[*440*]

56

Whoever, like myself, prompted by some enigmatical desire, has long endeavoured to go to the bottom of the question of pessimism and free it from the half-Christian, half-German narrowness and stupidity in which it has finally presented itself to this century, namely, in the form of Schopenhauer's philosophy; whoever, with an Asiatic and super-Asiatic eye, has actually looked inside, and into the most world-renouncing of all possible modes of thought—beyond good and evil, and no longer like Buddha and Schopenhauer, under the dominion and delusion of morality,—whoever has done this, has perhaps just thereby, without really desiring it, opened his eyes to behold the opposite ideal: the ideal of the most world-approving, exuberant and vivacious man, who has not only learned to compromise and arrange with that which was and is, but wishes to have it again *as it was and is,* for all eternity, insatiably calling out *de capo,* not only to himself, but to the whole piece and play; and not only the play, but actually to him who requires the play—and makes it necessary; because he always requires himself anew—and makes himself necessary.—What? And this would not be—*circulus vitiosus deus?*

57

The distance, and as it were the space around man, grows with the strength of his intellectual vision and insight: his world becomes profounder; new stars, new enigmas, and notions are ever coming into view. Perhaps everything on which the intellectual eye has exercised its acuteness and profundity has just been an occasion for its exercise, something of a game, something for children and childish minds. Perhaps the most solemn conceptions that have caused the most fighting and suffering, the conceptions "God" and "sin," will one day seem to us of no more importance than a child's plaything or a child's pain seems to an old man;—and perhaps another plaything and another pain will then be necessary once more for "the old man"—always childish enough, an eternal child!

58

Has it been observed to what extent outward idleness, or semi-idleness, is necessary to a real religious life (alike for its favourite microscopic labour of self-examination, and for its soft placidity called "prayer," the state of perpetual readiness for the "coming of God"), I mean the idleness with a good conscience, the idleness of olden times and of blood, to which the aristocratic sentiment that work is *dishonouring*—that it vulgarises body and soul—is not quite unfamiliar? And that consequently the modern, noisy, time-engrossing, conceited, foolishly proud laboriousness educates and prepares for "unbelief" more than anything else? Amongst these, for instance, who are at present living apart from religion in Germany, I find "free-thinkers" of diversified species and origin, but above all a majority of those in whom laboriousness from generation to generation has dissolved the religious instincts; so that they no longer know what purpose religions serve, and only note their existence in the world with a kind of dull astonishment. They feel themselves already fully occupied, these good people, be it by their business or by their pleasures, not to mention the "Fatherland," and the newspapers, and

their "family duties"; it seems that they have no time whatever
left for religion; and above all, it is not obvious to them
whether it is a question of a new business or a new pleasure—
for it is impossible, they say to themselves, that people should
go to church merely to spoil their tempers. They are by no
means enemies of religious customs; should certain circumstances, State affairs perhaps, require their participation in
such customs, they do what is required, as so many things are
done—with a patient and unassuming seriousness, and without
much curiosity or discomfort;—they live too much apart and
outside to feel even the necessity for a *for* or *against* in such
matters. Among those indifferent persons may be reckoned
nowadays the majority of German Protestants of the middle
classes, especially in the great laborious centres of trade and
commerce; also the majority of laborious scholars, and the
entire University personnel (with the exception of the theologians, whose existence and possibility there always give
psychologists new and more subtle puzzles to solve). On the
part of pious, or merely church-going people, there is seldom
any idea of *how much* good will, one might say arbitrary will,
is now necessary for a German scholar to take the problem of
religion seriously; his whole profession (and as I have said, his
whole workmanlike laboriousness, to which he is compelled
by his modern conscience) inclines him to a lofty and almost
charitable serenity as regards religion, with which is occasionally mingled a slight disdain for the "uncleanliness" of
spirit which he takes for granted wherever any one still pro-
fesses to belong to the Church. It is only with the help of
history (*not* through his own personal experience, therefore)
that the scholar succeeds in bringing himself to a respectful
seriousness, and to a certain timid deference in presence of

[*443*]

religions; but even when his sentiments have reached the stage of gratitude towards them, he has not personally advanced one step nearer to that which still maintains itself as Church or as piety; perhaps even the contrary. The practical indifference to religious matters in the midst of which he has been born and brought up, usually sublimates itself in his case into circumspection and cleanliness, which shuns contact with religious men and things; and it may be just the depth of his tolerance and humanity which prompts him to avoid the delicate trouble which tolerance itself brings with it.——Every age has its own divine type of naïveté, for the discovery of which other ages may envy it: and how much naïveté—adorable, childlike, and boundlessly foolish naïveté is involved in this belief of the scholar in his superiority, in the good conscience of his tolerance, in the unsuspecting, simple certainty with which his instinct treats the religious man as a lower and less valuable type, beyond, before, and *above* which he himself has developed— he, the little arrogant dwarf and mob-man, the sedulously alert, head-and-hand drudge of "ideas," of "modern ideas"!

59

Whoever has seen deeply into the world has doubtless divined what wisdom there is in the fact that men are superficial. It is their preservative instinct which teaches them to be flighty, lightsome, and false. Here and there one finds a passionate and exaggerated adoration of "pure forms" in philosophers as well as in artists: it is not to be doubted that whoever has *need* of the cult of the superficial to that extent, has at one time or another made an unlucky dive *beneath* it. Perhaps there is even an order of rank with respect to those burnt children, the born artists who find the enjoyment of life only in trying to *falsify* its image (as if taking wearisome revenge on it); one might guess to what degree life has disgusted them, by the extent to which they wish to see its image falsified, attenuated, ultrafied, and deified;—one might reckon the *homines religiosi* amongst the artists, as their *highest* rank. It is the profound, suspicious fear of an incurable pessimism which compels whole centuries to fasten their teeth into a religious interpretation of existence: the fear of the instinct which divines that truth might be attained *too soon,* before man has become strong enough, hard enough, artist enough. . . . Piety, the "Life in God," regarded in this light, would appear as the most elaborate and ultimate product of the *fear* of truth, as artist-adoration and artist-intoxication in presence of the most logical of all falsifications, as the will to the inversion of truth, to untruth at any price. Perhaps there has hitherto been no more effective means of beautifying man than piety; by means of it man can become so artful, so superficial, so iridescent, and so good, that his appearance no longer offends.

60

To love mankind *for God's sake*—this has so far been the noblest and remotest sentiment to which mankind has attained. That love to mankind, without any redeeming intention in the background, is only an *additional* folly and brutishness, that the inclination to this love has first to get its proportion, its delicacy, its grain of salt and sprinkling of ambergris from a higher inclination:—whoever first perceived and "experienced" this, however his tongue may have stammered as it at-

tempted to express such a delicate matter, let him for all time
be holy and respected, as the man who has so far flown highest
and gone astray in the finest fashion!

61

The philosopher, as *we* free spirits understand him—as the
man of the greatest responsibility, who has the conscience for
the general development of mankind,—will use religion for
his disciplining and educating work, just as he will use the
contemporary political and economic conditions. The selecting
and disciplining influence—destructive, as well as creative and
fashioning—which can be exercised by means of religion is
manifold and varied, according to the sort of people placed
under its spell and protection. For those who are strong and
independent, destined and trained to command, in whom the
judgment and skill of a ruling race is incorporated, religion
is an additional means for overcoming resistance in the exercise
of authority—as a bond which binds rulers and subjects in
common, betraying and surrendering to the former the conscience of the latter, their inmost heart, which would fain
escape obedience. And in the case of the unique natures of
noble origin, if by virtue of superior spirituality they should
incline to a more retired and contemplative life, reserving to
themselves only the more refined forms of government (over
chosen disciples or members of an order), religion itself may
be used as a means for obtaining peace from the noise and
trouble of managing *grosser* affairs, and for securing immunity
from the *unavoidable* filth of all political agitation. The
Brahmins, for instance, understood this fact. With the help of

a religious organisation, they secured to themselves the power of nominating kings for the people, while their sentiments prompted them to keep apart and outside, as men with a higher and super-regal mission. At the same time religion gives inducement and opportunity to some of the subjects to qualify themselves for future ruling and commanding: the slowly ascending ranks and classes, in which, through fortunate marriage customs, volitional power and delight in self-control are on the increase. To them religion offers sufficient incentives and temptations to aspire to higher intellectuality, and to experience the sentiments of authoritative self-control, of silence, and of solitude. Asceticism and Puritanism are almost indispensable means of educating and ennobling a race which seeks to rise above its hereditary baseness and work itself upward to future supremacy. And finally, to ordinary men, to the majority of the people, who exist for service and general utility, and are only so far entitled to exist, religion gives invaluable contentedness with their lot and condition, peace of heart, ennoblement of obedience, additional social happiness and sympathy, with something of transfiguration and embellishment, something of justification of all the commonplaceness, all the meanness, all the semi-animal poverty of their souls. Religion, together with the religious significance of life, sheds sunshine over such perpetually harassed men, and makes even their own aspect endurable to them; it operates upon them as the Epicurean philosophy usually operates upon sufferers of a higher order, in a refreshing and refining manner, almost *turning* suffering *to account,* and in the end even hallowing and vindicating it. There is perhaps nothing so admirable in Christianity and Buddhism as their art of teaching even the lowest to elevate themselves by piety to a seemingly higher order of things, and thereby to retain their satisfaction with the actual world in which they find it difficult enough to live—this very difficulty being necessary.

62

To be sure—to make also the bad counter-reckoning against such religions, and to bring to light their secret dangers—the cost is always excessive and terrible when religions do *not* operate as an educational and disciplinary medium in the hands of the philosopher, but rule voluntarily and *paramountly*, when they wish to be the final end, and not a means along with other means. Among men, as among all other animals, there is a surplus of defective, diseased, degenerating, infirm, and necessarily suffering individuals; the successful cases, among men also, are always the exception; and in view of the fact that man is *the animal not yet properly adapted to his environment*, the rare exception. But worse still. The higher the type a man represents, the greater is the improbability that he will *succeed*; the accidental, the law of irrationality in the general constitution of mankind, manifests itself most terribly in its destructive effect on the higher orders of men, the conditions of whose lives are delicate, diverse, and difficult to determine. What, then, is the attitude of the two greatest religions above-mentioned to the *surplus* of failures in life? They endeavour to preserve and keep alive whatever can be preserved; in fact, as the religions *for sufferers,* they take the part of these upon principle; they are always in favour of those who suffer from life as from a disease, and they would fain treat every other experience of life as false and impossible. However highly we may esteem this indulgent and preservative care (inasmuch as

in applying to others, it has applied, and applies also to the
highest and usually the most suffering type of man), the
hitherto *paramount* religions—to give a general appreciation
of them—are among the principal causes which have kept the
type of "man" upon a lower level—they have preserved too
much *that which should have perished*. One has to thank them
for invaluable services; and who is sufficiently rich in gratitude
not to feel poor at the contemplation of all that the "spiritual
men" of Christianity have done for Europe hitherto! But when
they had given comfort to the sufferers, courage to the oppressed and despairing, a staff and support to the helpless, and
when they had allured from society into convents and spiritual
penitentiaries the broken-hearted and distracted: what else had
they to do in order to work systematically in that fashion, and
with a good conscience, for the preservation of all the sick and
suffering, which means, in deed and in truth, to work for *the
deterioration of the European race?* To *reverse* all estimates of
value—*that* is what they had to do! And to shatter the strong,
to spoil great hopes, to cast suspicion on the delight in beauty,
to break down everything autonomous, manly, conquering,
and imperious—all instincts which are natural to the highest
and most successful type of "man"—into uncertainty, distress
of conscience, and self-destruction; forsooth, to invert all love
of the earthly and of supremacy over the earth, into hatred of
the earth and earthly things—*that* is the task the Church imposed on itself, and was obliged to impose, until, according
to its standard of value, "unworldliness," "unsensuousness,"
and "higher man" fused into one sentiment. If one could observe the strangely painful, equally coarse and refined comedy
of European Christianity with the derisive and impartial eye
of an Epicurean god, I should think one would never cease
marvelling and laughing; does it not actually seem that some

single will has ruled over Europe for eighteen centuries in order to make a *sublime abortion* of man? He, however, who, with opposite requirements (no longer Epicurean) and with some divine hammer in his hand, could approach this almost voluntary degeneration and stunting of mankind, as exemplified in the European Christian (Pascal, for instance), would he not have to cry aloud with rage, pity, and horror: "Oh, you bunglers, presumptuous pitiful bunglers, what have you done! Was that a work for your hands? How you have hacked and botched my finest stone! What have *you* presumed to do!" —I should say that Christianity has hitherto been the most portentous of presumptions. Men, not great enough, nor hard enough, to be entitled as artists to take part in fashioning *man;* men, not sufficiently strong and far-sighted to *allow,* with sublime self-constraint, the obvious law of the thousandfold failures and perishings to prevail; men, not sufficiently noble to see the radically different grades of rank and intervals of rank that separate man from man:—*such* men, with their "equality before God," have hitherto swayed the destiny of Europe; until at last a dwarfed, almost ludicrous species has been produced, a gregarious animal, something obliging, sickly, mediocre, the European of the present day.

4. *Apophthegms and Interludes*

63

He who is a thorough teacher takes things seriously—and even himself—only in relation to his pupils.

[*450*]

64

"Knowledge for its own sake"—that is the last snare laid by morality: we are thereby completely entangled in morals once more.

65

The charm of knowledge would be small, were it not that so much shame has to be overcome on the way to it.

65A

We are most dishonourable towards our God: he is not *permitted* to sin.

66

The tendency of a person to allow himself to be degraded, robbed, deceived, and exploited might be the diffidence of a God amongst men.

67

Love to one only is a barbarity, for it is exercised at the expense of all others. Love to God also!

68

"I did that," says my memory. "I could not have done that," says my pride, and remains inexorable. Eventually—the memory yields.

69

One has regarded life carelessly, if one has failed to see the hand that—kills with leniency.

70

If a man has character, he has also his typical experience, which always recurs.

71

The Sage as Astronomer.—So long as thou feelest the stars as an "above thee," thou lackest the eye of the discerning one.

72

It is not the strength, but the duration of great sentiments that makes great men.

73

He who attains his ideal, precisely thereby surpasses it.

73A

Many a peacock hides his tail from every eye—and calls it his pride.

[*452*]

74

A man of genius is unbearable, unless he possess at least two things besides: gratitude and purity.

75

The degree and nature of a man's sensuality extends to the highest altitudes of his spirit.

76

Under peaceful conditions the militant man attacks himself.

77

With his principles a man seeks either to dominate, or justify, or honour, or reproach, or conceal his habits: two men with the same principles probably seek fundamentally different ends therewith.

78

He who despises himself, nevertheless esteems himself thereby, as a despiser.

79

A soul which knows that it is loved, but does not itself love, betrays its sediment: its dregs come up.

80

A thing that is explained ceases to concern us.—What did the God mean who gave the advice, "Know thyself!" Did it perhaps imply: "Cease to be concerned about thyself! become objective!"—And Socrates?—And the "scientific man"?

81

It is terrible to die of thirst at sea. Is it necessary that you should so salt your truth that it will no longer—quench thirst?

82

"Sympathy for all"—would be harshness and tyranny for *thee*, my good neighbour!

83

Instinct.—When the house is on fire one forgets even the dinner.—Yes, but one recovers it from amongst the ashes.

84

Woman learns how to hate in proportion as she—forgets how to charm.

85

The same emotions are in man and woman, but in different *tempo;* on that account man and woman never cease to misunderstand each other.

[*454*]

86

In the background of all their personal vanity, women them-selves have still their impersonal scorn—for "woman."

87

Fettered Heart, Free Spirit.—When one firmly fetters one's heart and keeps it prisoner, one can allow one's spirit many liberties: I said this once before. But people do not believe it when I say so, unless they know it already.

88

One begins to distrust very clever persons when they become embarrassed.

89

Dreadful experiences raise the question whether he who experiences them is not something dreadful also.

90

Heavy, melancholy men turn lighter, and come temporarily to their surface, precisely by that which makes others heavy—by hatred and love.

91

So cold, so icy, that one burns one's finger at the touch of him! Every hand that lays hold of him shrinks back!—And for that very reason many think him red-hot.

92

Who has not, at one time or another—sacrificed himself for the sake of his good name?

93

In affability there is no hatred of men, but precisely on that account a great deal too much contempt of men.

94

The maturity of man—that means, to have reacquired the seriousness that one had as a child at play.

95

To be ashamed of one's immorality is a step on the ladder at the end of which one is ashamed also of one's morality.

96

One should part from life as Ulysses parted from Nausicaa--
blessing it rather than in love with it.

97

What? A great man? I always see merely the play-actor of his
own ideal.

98

When one trains one's conscience, it kisses one while it bites.

99

The Disappointed One Speaks.—"I listened for the echo and
I heard only praise."

100

We all feign to ourselves that we are simpler than we are; we
thus relax ourselves away from our fellows.

101

A discerning one might easily regard himself at present as the
animalisation of God.

102

Discovering reciprocal love should really disenchant the lover with regard to the beloved. "What! *She* is modest enough to love even you? Or stupid enough? Or—or———"

103

The Danger in Happiness.—"Everything now turns out best for me. I now love every fate:—who would like to be my fate?"

104

Not their love of humanity, but the impotence of their love, prevents the Christians of today—burning us.

105

The *pia fraus* is still more repugnant to the taste (*the "piety"*) of the free spirit (the "pious man of knowledge") than the *impia fraus*. Hence the profound lack of judgment, in comparison with the church, characteristic of the type "free spirit" —as *its* non-freedom.

106

By means of music the very passions enjoy themselves.

107

A sign of strong character, when once the resolution has been taken, to shut the ear even to the best counter-arguments. Occasionally, therefore, a will to stupidity.

108

There is no such thing as moral phenomena, but only a moral interpretation of phenomena.

109

The criminal is often enough not equal to his deed: he extenuates and maligns it.

110

The advocates of a criminal are seldom artists enough to turn the beautiful terribleness of the deed to the advantage of the doer.

111

Our vanity is most difficult to wound just when our pride has been wounded.

112

To him who feels himself preordained to contemplation and not to belief, all believers are too noisy and obtrusive; he guards against them.

113

"You want to prepossess him in your favour? Then you must be embarrassed before him."

114

The immense expectation with regard to sexual love, and the coyness in this expectation, spoils all the perspectives of women at the outset.

115

Where there is neither love nor hatred in the game, woman's play is mediocre.

116

The great epochs of our life are at the points when we gain courage to rebaptize our badness as the best in us.

117

The will to overcome an emotion, is ultimately only the will of another, or of several other, emotions.

118

There is an innocence of admiration: it is possessed by him to whom it has not yet occurred that he himself may be admired some day.

119

Our loathing of dirt may be so great as to prevent our cleaning ourselves—"justifying" ourselves.

120

Sensuality often forces the growth of love too much, so that its root remains weak, and is easily torn up.

121

It is a curious thing that God learned Greek when he wished to turn author—and that he did not learn it better.

122

To rejoice on account of praise is in many cases merely politeness of heart—and the very opposite of vanity of spirit.

123

Even concubinage has been corrupted—by marriage.

124

He who exults at the stake, does not triumph over pain, but because of the fact that he does not feel pain where he expected it. A parable.

125

When we have to change an opinion about any one, we charge heavily to his account the inconvenience he thereby causes us.

126

A nation is a detour of nature to arrive at six or seven great men.—Yes, and then to get round them.

127

In the eyes of all true women science is hostile to the sense of shame. They feel as if one wished to peep under their skin with it—or worse still! under their dress and finery.

128

The more abstract the truth you wish to teach, the more must you allure the senses to it.

129

The devil has the most extensive perspectives for God; on that account he keeps so far away from him:—the devil, in effect, as the oldest friend of knowledge.

130

What a person *is* begins to betray itself when his talent decreases,—when he ceases to show what he *can do*. Talent is also an adornment; an adornment is also a concealment.

131

The sexes deceive themselves about each other: the reason is that in reality they honour and love only themselves (or their own ideal, to express it more agreeably). Thus man wishes woman to be peaceable: but in fact woman is *essentially* unpeaceable, like the cat, however well she may have assumed the peaceable demeanour.

132

One is punished best for one's virtues.

133

He who cannot find the way to *his* ideal, lives more frivolously and shamelessly than the man without an ideal.

134

From the senses originate all trustworthiness, all good conscience, all evidence of truth.

135

Pharisaism is not a deterioration of the good man; a considerable part of it is rather an essential condition of being good.

136

The one seeks an accoucheur for his thoughts, the other seeks some one whom he can assist: a good conversation thus originates.

137

In intercourse with scholars and artists one readily makes mistakes of opposite kinds: in a remarkable scholar one not infrequently finds a mediocre man; and often even in a mediocre artist, one finds a very remarkable man.

138

We do the same when awake as when dreaming: we only invent and imagine him with whom we have intercourse—and forget it immediately.

[*464*]

139

In revenge and in love woman is more barbarous than man.

140

Advice as a Riddle.—"If the band is not to break, bite it first—secure to make!"

141

The belly is the reason why man does not so readily take himself for a God.

142

The chastest utterance I ever heard: *"Dans le véritable amour c'est l'âme qui enveloppe le corps."*

143

Our vanity would like what we do best to pass precisely for what is most difficult to us.—Concerning the origin of many systems of morals.

144

When a woman has scholarly inclinations there is generally something wrong with her sexual nature. Barrenness itself conduces to a certain virility of taste; man, indeed, if I may say so, is "the barren animal."

145

Comparing man and woman generally, one may say that woman would not have the genius for adornment, if she had not the instinct for the *secondary* role.

146

He who fights with monsters should be careful lest he thereby become a monster. And if thou gaze long into an abyss, the abyss will also gaze into thee.

147

From old Florentine novels—moreover, from life: *Buona femmina e mala femmina vuol bastone.*—Sacchetti, Nov. 86.

148

To seduce their neighbour to a favourable opinion, and afterwards to believe implicitly in this opinion of their neighbour—who can do this conjuring trick so well as women?

149

That which an age considers evil is usually an unseasonable echo of what was formerly considered good—the atavism of an old ideal.

150

Around the hero everything becomes a tragedy; around the demigod everything becomes a satyr-play; and around God everything becomes—what? perhaps a "world"?

151

It is not enough to possess a talent: one must also have your permission to possess it;—eh, my friends?

152

"Where there is the tree of knowledge, there is always Paradise:" so say the most ancient and the most modern serpents.

153

What is done out of love always takes place beyond good and evil.

154

Objection, evasion, joyous distrust, and love of irony are signs of health; everything absolute belongs to pathology.

155

The sense of the tragic increases and declines with sensuousness.

156

Insanity in individuals is something rare—but in groups, parties, nations, and epochs it is the rule.

157

The thought of suicide is a great consolation: by means of it one gets successfully through many a bad night.

158

Not only our reason, but also our conscience, truckles to our strongest impulse—the tyrant in us.

159

One *must* repay good and ill; but why just to the person who did us good or ill?

160

One no longer loves one's knowledge sufficiently after one has communicated it.

161

Poets act shamelessly towards their experiences: they exploit them.

162

"Our fellow-creature is not our neighbour, but our neighbour's neighbour:"—so thinks every nation.

163

Love brings to light the noble and hidden qualities of a lover— his rare and exceptional traits: it is thus liable to be deceptive as to his normal character.

164

Jesus said to his Jews: "The law was for servants;—love God as I love him, as his Son! What have we Sons of God to do with morals!"

165

In Sight of Every Party.—A shepherd has always need of a bellwether—or he has himself to be a wether occasionally.

166

One may indeed lie with the mouth; but with the accompanying grimace one nevertheless tells the truth.

[469]

167

To vigourous men intimacy is a matter of shame—and something precious.

168

Christianity gave Eros poison to drink; he did not die of it, certainly, but degenerated to Vice.

169

To talk much about oneself may also be a means of concealing oneself.

170

In praise there is more obtrusiveness than in blame.

171

Pity has an almost ludicrous effect on a man of knowledge, like tender hands on a Cyclops.

172

One occasionally embraces some one or other, out of love to mankind (because one cannot embrace all); but this is what one must never confess to the individual.

173

One does not hate as long as one disesteems, but only when one esteems equal or superior.

174

Ye Utilitarians—ye, too, love the *utile* only as a *vehicle* for your inclinations,—ye, too, really find the noise of its wheels insupportable!

175

One loves ultimately one's desires, not the thing desired.

176

The vanity of others is only counter to our taste when it is counter to our vanity.

177

With regard to what "truthfulness" is, perhaps nobody has ever been sufficiently truthful.

178

One does not believe in the follies of clever men: what a forfeiture of the rights of man!

[471]

179

The consequences of our actions seize us by the forelock, very indifferent to the fact that we have meanwhile "reformed."

180

There is an innocence in lying which is the sign of good faith in a cause.

181

It is inhuman to bless when one is being cursed.

182

The familiarity of superiors embitters one, because it may not be returned.

183

"I am affected, not because you have deceived me, but because I can no longer believe in you."

184

There is a haughtiness of kindness which has the appearance of wickedness.

[472]

185

"I dislike him."—Why?—"I am not a match for him."—Did any one ever answer so?

5. *The Natural History of Morals*

186

THE moral sentiment in Europe at present is perhaps as subtle, belated, diverse, sensitive, and refined, as the "Science of Morals" belonging thereto is recent, initial, awkward, and coarse-fingered:—an interesting contrast, which sometimes becomes incarnate and obvious in the very person of a moralist. Indeed, the expression, "Science of Morals" is, in respect to what is designated thereby, far too presumptuous and counter to *good* taste,—which is always a foretaste of more modest expressions. One ought to avow with the utmost fairness *what* is still necessary here for a long time, *what* is alone proper for the present: namely, the collection of material, the comprehensive survey and classification of an immense domain of delicate sentiments of worth, and distinctions of worth, which live, grow, propagate, and perish—and perhaps attempts to give a clear idea of the recurring and more common forms of these living crystallisations—as preparation for a *theory of types* of morality. To be sure, people have not hitherto been so modest. All the philosophers, with a pedantic and ridiculous seriousness, demanded of themselves something very much higher, more pretentious, and ceremonious, when they concerned themselves with morality as a science: they wanted to *give a basis* to morality—and every philosopher hitherto has believed that he has given it a basis; morality itself, however, has been regarded as something "given." How far from their awkward pride was the seemingly insignificant problem—left in dust and decay—of a description of forms of morality, notwithstanding that the finest hands and senses could hardly be fine enough for it! It was precisely owing to moral philosophers knowing the moral facts imperfectly, in an arbitrary epitome, or an accidental abridgement—perhaps as the morality of their environment, their position, their church, their *Zeitgeist,* their climate and zone—it was precisely because they were badly instructed with regard to nations, eras, and past ages, and were by no means eager to know about these matters, that they did not even come in sight of the real problems of morals—problems which only disclose themselves by a comparison of *many* kinds of morality. In every "Science of Morals" hitherto, strange as it may sound, the problem of morality itself has been *omitted;* there has been no suspicion that there was anything problematic there! That which philosophers called "giving a basis to morality," and endeavoured to realise, has, when seen in a right light, proved merely a learned form of good *faith* in prevailing morality, a new means of its *expression,* consequently just a matter-of-fact within the sphere of a definite morality, yea, in its ultimate motive, a sort of denial that it is *lawful* for this morality to be called in question—and in any case the reverse of the testing, analysing, doubting, and vivisecting of this very faith. Hear, for instance, with what innocence—almost worthy of honour—Schopenhauer represents his own task, and draw your conclusions concerning the scientificalness of a "Science" whose latest master

still talks in the strain of children and old wives: "The prin
ciple," he says (page 136 of the *Grundprobleme der Ethik**),
"the axiom about the purport of which all moralists are *practically* agreed: *neminem laede, immo omnes quantum potes
juva*—is *really* the proposition which all moral teachers strive
to establish, . . . the *real* basis of ethics which has been
sought, like the philosopher's stone, for centuries."—The difficulty of establishing the proposition referred to may indeed
be great—it is well known that Schopenhauer also was unsuc-
cessful in his efforts; and whoever has thoroughly realised how
absurdly false and sentimental this proposition is, in a world
whose essence is Will to Power, may be reminded that Schopenhauer, although a pessimist, *actually*—played the flute . . .
daily after dinner: one may read about the matter in his biography. A question by the way: a pessimist, a repudiator of God
and of the world, who *makes a halt* at morality—who assents
to morality, and plays the flute to *laede-neminem* morals, what?
Is that really—a pessimist?

187

Apart from the value of such assertions as "there is a categorical imperative in us," one can always ask: What does such
an assertion indicate about him who makes it? There are systems of morals which are meant to justify their author in the
eyes of other people; other systems of morals are meant to
tranquillise him, and make him self-satisfied; with other systems he wants to crucify and humble himself; with others he
wishes to take revenge; with others to conceal himself; with

* Pages 54-55 of Schopenhauer's *Basis of Morality*, translated by Arthur B.
Bullock, M.A. (1903).

others to glorify himself and gain superiority and distinction;
—this system of morals helps its author to forget, that system
makes him, or something of him, forgotten; many a moralist
would like to exercise power and creative arbitrariness over
mankind; many another, perhaps, Kant especially, gives us to
understand by his morals that "what is estimable in me, is that
I know how to obey—and with you it *shall* not be otherwise
than with me!" In short, systems of morals are only a *sign-
language of the emotions.*

188

In contrast to *laisser-aller,* every system of morals is a sort
of tyranny against "nature" and also against "reason"; that is,
however, no objection, unless one should again decree by some
system of morals, that all kinds of tyranny and unreasonableness are unlawful. What is essential and invaluable in every
system of morals, is that it is a long constraint. In order to
understand Stoicism, or Port-Royal, or Puritanism, one should
remember the constraint under which every language has attained to strength and freedom—the metrical constraint, the
tyranny of rhyme and rhythm. How much trouble have the
poets and orators of every nation given themselves!—not excepting some of the prose writers of today, in whose ear dwells
an inexorable conscientiousness—"for the sake of a folly," as
utilitarian bunglers say, and thereby deem themselves wise—
"from submission to arbitrary laws," as the anarchists say, and
thereby fancy themselves "free," even free-spirited. The singular fact remains, however, that everything of the nature of
freedom, elegance, boldness, dance, and masterly certainty,
which exists or has existed, whether it be in thought itself, or

in administration, or in speaking and persuading, in art just as in conduct, has only developed by means of the tyranny of such arbitrary law; and in all seriousness, it is not at all improbable that precisely this is "nature" and "natural"—and *not laisser-aller!* Every artist knows how different from the state of letting himself go, is his "most natural" condition, the free arranging, locating, disposing, and constructing in the moments of "inspiration"—and how strictly and delicately he then obeys a thousand laws, which, by their very rigidness and precision, defy all formulation by means of ideas (even the most stable idea has, in comparison therewith, something floating, manifold, and ambiguous in it). The essential thing "in heaven and in earth" is, apparently (to repeat it once more), that there should be long *obedience* in the same direction; there thereby results, and has always resulted in the long run, something which has made life worth living; for instance, virtue, art, music, dancing, reason, spirituality—anything whatever that is transfiguring, refined, foolish, or divine. The long bondage of the spirit, the distrustful constraint in the communicability of ideas, the discipline which the thinker imposed on himself to think in accordance with the rules of a church or a court, or conformable to Aristotelian premises, the persistent spiritual will to interpret everything that happened according to a Christian scheme, and in every occurrence to rediscover and justify the Christian God:—all this violence, arbitrariness, severity, dreadfulness, and unreasonableness, has proved itself the disciplinary means whereby the European spirit has attained its strength, its remorseless curiosity and subtle mobility; granted also that much irrecoverable strength and spirit had to be stifled, suffocated, and spoiled in the process (for here, as everywhere, "nature" shows herself as she is, in all her extravagant and *indifferent* magnificence, which is shocking, but nevertheless noble). That for centuries European thinkers only thought in order to prove something—nowadays, on the contrary, we are suspicious of every thinker who "wishes to prove something"—that it was always settled beforehand what *was to be* the result of their strictest thinking, as it was perhaps in the Asiatic astrology of former times, or as it is still at the present day in the innocent, Christian-moral explanation of immediate personal events "for the glory of God," or "for the good of the soul":—this tyranny, this arbitrariness, this severe and magnificent stupidity, has *educated* the spirit; slavery, both in the coarser and the finer sense, is apparently an indispensable means even of spiritual education and discipline. One may look at every system of morals in this light: it is "nature" therein which teaches to hate the *laisser-aller,* the too great freedom, and implants the need for limited horizons, for immediate duties—it teaches the *narrowing of perspectives,* and thus, in a certain sense, that stupidity is a condition of life and development. "Thou must obey some one, and for a long time; *otherwise* thou wilt come to grief, and lose all respect for thyself" —this seems to me to be the moral imperative of nature, which is certainly neither "categorical," as old Kant wished (consequently the "otherwise"), nor does it address itself to the individual (what does nature care for the individual!), but to nations, races, ages, and ranks, above all, however, to the animal "man" generally, to *mankind.*

189

Industrious races find it a great hardship to be idle: it was a master stroke of *English* instinct to hallow and begloom Sunday to such an extent that the Englishman unconsciously hankers for his week- and work-day again:—as a kind of cleverly devised, cleverly intercalated *fast,* such as is also frequently found in the ancient world (although, as is appropriate in southern nations, not precisely with respect to work). Many kinds of fasts are necessary; and wherever powerful influences and habits prevail, legislators have to see that intercalary days are appointed, on which such impulses are fettered, and learn to hunger anew. Viewed from a higher standpoint, whole generations and epochs, when they show themselves infected with any moral fanaticism, seem like those intercalated periods of restraint and fasting, during which an impulse learns to humble and submit itself—at the same time also to *purify* and *sharpen* itself; certain philosophical sects likewise admit of a similar interpretation (for instance, the Stoa, in the midst of Hellenic culture, with the atmosphere rank and overcharged with Aphrodisiacal odours).—Here also is a hint for the explanation of the paradox, why it was precisely in the most Christian period of European history, and in general only under the pressure of Christian sentiments, that the sexual impulse sublimated into love (*amour-passion*).

190

There is something in the morality of Plato which does not really belong to Plato, but which only appears in his philosophy, one might say, in spite of him: namely, Socratism, for which he himself was too noble. "No one desires to injure himself, hence all evil is done unwittingly. The evil man inflicts injury on himself; he would not do so, however, if he knew that evil is evil. The evil man, therefore, is only evil through error; if one free him from error one will necessarily make him—good."—This mode of reasoning savours of the *populace,* who perceive only the unpleasant consequences of evil-doing, and practically judge that "it is *stupid* to do wrong"; while they accept "good" as identical with "useful and pleasant," without further thought. As regards every system of utilitarianism, one may at once assume that it has the same origin, and follow the scent: one will seldom err.—Plato did all he could to interpret something refined and noble into the tenets of his teacher, and above all to interpret himself into them—he, the most daring of all interpreters, who lifted the entire Socrates out of the street, as a popular theme and song, to exhibit him in endless and impossible modifications— namely, in all his own disguises and multiplicities. In jest, and in Homeric language as well, what is the Platonic Socrates, if not—

πρόσθε Πλάτων ὄπισθέν τε Πλάτων μέσση τε Χίμαιρα.

191

The old theological problem of "Faith" and "Knowledge," or more plainly, of instinct and reason—the question whether, in respect to the valuation of things, instinct deserves more authority than rationality, which wants to appreciate and act according to motives, according to a "Why," that is to say, in conformity to purpose and utility—it is always the old moral problem that first appeared in the person of Socrates, and had divided men's minds long before Christianity. Socrates himself, following, of course, the taste of his talent—that of a surpassing dialectician—took first the side of reason; and, in fact, what did he do all his life but laugh at the awkward incapacity of the noble Athenians, who were men of instinct, like all noble men, and could never give satisfactory answers concerning the motives of their actions? In the end, however, though silently and secretly, he laughed also at himself: with his finer conscience and introspection, he found in himself the same difficulty and incapacity. "But why"—he said to himself —"should one on that account separate oneself from the instincts! One must set them right, and the reason *also*—one must follow the instincts, but at the same time persuade the reason to support them with good arguments." This was the real *falseness* of that great and mysterious ironist; he brought his conscience up to the point that he was satisfied with a kind of self-outwitting: in fact, he perceived the irrationality in the moral judgment.——Plato, more innocent in such matters, and without the craftiness of the plebeian, wished to prove to himself, at the expenditure of all his strength—the greatest strength a philosopher had ever expended—that reason and instinct lead spontaneously to one goal, to the good, to "God"; and since Plato, all theologians and philosophers have followed the same path—which means that in matters of morality, instinct (or as Christians call it, "Faith," or as I call it, "the herd") has hitherto triumphed. Unless one should make an exception in the case of Descartes, the father of rationalism (and consequently the grandfather of the Revolution), who recognised only the authority of reason: but reason is only a tool, and Descartes was superficial.

192

Whoever has followed the history of a single science, finds in its development a clue to the understanding of the oldest and commonest processes of all "knowledge and cognisance": there, as here, the premature hypotheses, the fictions, the good stupid will to "belief," and the lack of distrust and patience are first developed—our senses learn late, and never learn completely, to be subtle, reliable, and cautious organs of knowledge. Our eyes find it easier on a given occasion to produce a picture already often produced, than to seize upon the divergence and novelty of an impression: the latter requires more force, more "morality." It is difficult and painful for the ear to listen to anything new; we hear strange music badly. When we hear another language spoken, we involuntarily attempt to form the sounds into words with which we are more familiar and conversant—it was thus, for example, that the Germans modified the spoken word *arcubalista* into *armbrust* (crossbow). Our senses are also hostile and averse to the new; and generally, even in the "simplest" processes of sensation, the emotions *dominate*—such as fear, love, hatred, and the passive emotion of indolence.—As little as a reader nowadays reads all the single words (not to speak of syllables) of a page —he rather takes about five out of every twenty words at random, and "guesses" the probably appropriate sense to them— just as little do we see a tree correctly and completely in respect to its leaves, branches, colour, and shape; we find it so much easier to fancy the chance of a tree. Even in the midst of the most remarkable experiences, we still do just the same; we fabricate the greater part of the experience, and can hardly be made to contemplate any event, *except* as "inventors" thereof. All this goes to prove that from our fundamental nature and from remote ages we have been—*accustomed to lying*. Or, to express it more politely and hypocritically, in short, more pleasantly—one is much more of an artist than one is aware of.— In an animated conversation, I often see the face of the person with whom I am speaking so clearly and sharply defined before me, according to the thought he expresses, or which I believe to be evoked in his mind, that the degree of distinctness far exceeds the *strength* of my visual faculty—the delicacy of the play of the muscles and of the expression of the eyes *must* therefore be imagined by me. Probably the person put on quite a different expression, or none at all.

193

Quidquid luce fuit, tenebris agit: but also contrariwise. What we experience in dreams, provided we experience it often, pertains at last just as much to the general belongings of our soul as anything "actually" experienced; by virtue thereof we are richer or poorer, we have a requirement more or less, and finally, in broad daylight, and even in the brightest moments of our waking life, we are ruled to some extent by the nature of our dreams. Supposing that some one has often flown in his dreams, and that at last, as soon as he dreams, he is conscious of the power and art of flying as his privilege and his peculiarly enviable happiness; such a person, who believes that on the slightest impulse, he can actualise all sorts of curves and angles, who knows the sensation of a certain divine levity, an "upwards" without effort or constraint, a "downwards" without descending or lowering—without *trouble!*—how could the man with such dream-experiences and dream-habits fail to find "happiness" differently coloured and defined, even in his waking hours! How could he fail—to long *differently* for happiness? "Flight," such as is described by poets, must, when compared with his own "flying," be far too earthly, muscular, violent, far too "troublesome" for him.

194

The difference among men does not manifest itself only in the difference of their lists of desirable things——in their regarding different good things as worth striving for, and being disagreed as to the greater or less value, the order of rank, of the commonly recognised desirable things:——it manifests itself much more in what they regard as actually *having* and *possessing* a desirable thing. As regards a woman, for instance, the control over her body and her sexual gratification serves as an amply sufficient sign of ownership and possession to the more modest man; another with a more suspicious and ambitious thirst for possession, sees the "questionableness," the mere apparentness of such ownership, and wishes to have finer tests in order to know especially whether the woman not only gives herself to him, but also gives up for his sake what she has or would like to have——only *then* does he look upon her as "possessed." A third, however, has not even here got to the limit of his distrust and his desire for possession: he asks himself whether the woman, when she gives up everything for him, does not perhaps do so for a phantom of him; he wishes first to be thoroughly, indeed, profoundly well known; in order to be loved at all he ventures to let himself be found out. Only then does he feel the beloved one fully in his possession, when she no longer deceives herself about him, when she loves him just as much for the sake of his devilry and concealed insatiability, as for his goodness, patience, and spirituality. One man would like to possess a nation, and he finds all the higher arts of Cagliostro and Catalina suitable for his purpose. Another, with a more refined thirst for possession, says to himself: "One may not deceive where one desires to possess"——he is irritated and impatient at the idea that a mask of him should rule in the hearts of the people: "I must, therefore, *make* myself known, and first of all learn to know myself!" Amongst helpful and charitable people, one almost always finds the awkward craftiness which first gets up suitably him who has to be helped, as though, for instance, he should "merit" help, seek just *their* help, and would show himself deeply grateful, attached, and subservient to them for all help. With these conceits, they take control of the needy as a property, just as in general they are charitable and helpful out of a desire for property. One finds them jealous when they are crossed or forestalled in their charity. Parents involuntarily make something like themselves out of their children—they call that "education"; no mother doubts at the bottom of her heart that the child she has born is thereby her property, no father hesitates about his right to *his own* ideas and notions of worth. Indeed, in former times fathers deemed it right to use their discretion concerning the life or death of the newly born (as amongst the ancient Germans). And like the father, so also do the teacher, the class, the priest, and the prince still see in every new individual an unobjectionable opportunity for a new possession. The consequence is . . .

195

The Jews—a people "born for slavery," as Tacitus and the whole ancient world say of them; "the chosen people among the nations," as they themselves say and believe—the Jews performed the miracle of the inversion of valuations, by means of which life on earth obtained a new and dangerous charm for a couple of millenniums. Their prophets fused into one the expressions "rich," "godless," "wicked," "violent," "sensual," and for the first time coined the word "world" as a term of reproach. In this inversion of valuations (in which is also included the use of the word "poor" as synonymous with "saint" and "friend") the significance of the Jewish people is to be found; it is with *them* that the *slave-insurrection in morals* commences.

196

It is to be *inferred* that there are countless dark bodies near the sun—such as we shall never see. Amongst ourselves, this is an allegory; and the psychologist of morals reads the whole star-writing merely as an allegorical and symbolic language in which much may be unexpressed.

197

The beast of prey and the man of prey (for instance, Cæsar Borgia) are fundamentally misunderstood, "nature" is misunderstood, so long as one seeks a "morbidness" in the constitution of these healthiest of all tropical monsters and growths, or even an innate "hell" in them—as almost all moralists have done hitherto. Does it not seem that there is a hatred of the virgin forest and of the tropics among moralists? And that the "tropical man" must be discredited at all costs, whether as disease and deterioration of mankind, or as his own hell and self-torture? And why? In favour of the "temperate zones"? In favour of the temperate men? The "moral"? The mediocre? —This for the chapter: "Morals as Timidity."

198

All the systems of morals which address themselves with a view to their "happiness," as it is called—what else are they but suggestions for behaviour adapted to the degree of *danger* from themselves in which the individuals live; recipes for their passions, their good and bad propensities, in so far as such have the Will to Power and would like to play the master; small and great expediencies and elaborations, permeated with the musty odour of old family medicines and old-wife wisdom; all of them grotesque and absurd in their form—because they address themselves to "all," because they generalise where generalisation is not authorised; all of them speaking unconditionally, and taking themselves unconditionally; all of them flavoured not merely with one grain of salt, but rather endurable only, and sometimes even seductive, when they are overspiced and begin to smell dangerously, especially of "the other world?" That is all of little value when estimated intellectually, and is far from being "science," much less "wisdom"; but, repeated once more, and three times repeated, it is expediency, expediency, expediency, mixed with stupidity, stupidity, stupidity—whether it be the indifference and statuesque coldness towards the heated folly of the emotions, which the Stoics advised and fostered; or the no-more-laughing and no-more-weeping of Spinoza, the destruction of the emotions by their analysis and vivisection, which he recommended so naïvely; or the lowering of the emotions to an innocent mean at which they may be satisfied, the Aristotelianism of morals; or even morality as the enjoyment of the emotions in a voluntary attenuation and spiritualisation by the symbolism of art, perhaps as music, or as love of God, and of mankind for God's sake—

for in religion the passions are once more enfranchised, provided that . . . ; or, finally, even the complaisant and wanton surrender to the emotions, as has been taught by Hafis and Goethe, the bold letting-go of the reins, the spiritual and corporeal *licentia morum* in the exceptional cases of wise old codgers and drunkards, with whom it "no longer has much danger."—This also for the chapter: "Morals as Timidity."

199

Inasmuch as in all ages, as long as mankind has existed, there have also been human herds (family alliances, communities, tribes, peoples, states, churches), and always a great number who obey in proportion to the small number who command—in view, therefore, of the fact that obedience has been most practised and fostered among mankind hitherto, one may reasonably suppose that, generally speaking, the need thereof is now innate in every one, as a kind of *formal conscience* which gives the command: "Thou shalt unconditionally do something, unconditionally refrain from something"; in short, "Thou shalt." This need tries to satisfy itself and to fill its form with a content; according to its strength, impatience, and eagerness, it at once seizes as an omnivorous appetite with little selection, and accepts whatever is shouted into its ear by all sorts of commanders—parents, teachers, laws, class prejudices, or public opinion. The extraordinary limitation of human development, the hesitation, protractedness, frequent retrogression, and turning thereof, is attributable to the fact that the herd-instinct of obedience is transmitted best, and at the cost of the art of command. If one imagine this instinct increasing to its greatest extent, commanders and independent individuals will finally be lacking altogether; or they will suffer inwardly from a bad conscience, and will have to impose a deception on themselves in the first place in order to be able to command: just as if they also were only obeying. This condition of things actually exists in Europe at present—I call it the moral hypocrisy of the commanding class. They know no other way of protecting themselves from their bad conscience than by playing the role of executors of older and higher orders (of predecessors, of the constitution, of justice, of the law, or of God himself), or they even justify themselves by maxims from the current opinions of the herd, as "first servants of their people," or "instruments of the public weal." On the other hand, the gregarious European man nowadays assumes an air as if he were the only kind of man that is allowable; he glorifies his qualities, such as public spirit, kindness, deference, industry, temperance, modesty, indulgence, sympathy, by virtue of which he is gentle, endurable, and useful to the herd, as the peculiarly human virtues. In cases, however, where it is believed that the leader and bellwether cannot be dispensed with, attempt after attempt is made nowadays to replace commanders by the summing together of clever gregarious men: all representative constitutions, for example, are of this origin. In spite of all, what a blessing, what a deliverance from a weight becoming unendurable, is the appearance of an absolute ruler for these gregarious Europeans—of this fact the effect of the appearance of Napoleon was the last great proof: the history of the influence of Napoleon is almost the history of the higher happiness to which the entire century has attained in its worthiest individuals and periods.

200

The man of an age of dissolution which mixes the races with one another, who has the inheritance of a diversified descent in his body—that is to say, contrary, and often not only contrary, instincts and standards of value, which struggle with one another and are seldom at peace—such a man of late culture and broken lights, will, on an average, be a weak man. His fundamental desire is that the war which is *in him* should come to an end; happiness appears to him in the character of a soothing medicine and mode of thought (for instance, Epicurean or Christian); it is above all things the happiness of repose, of undisturbedness, of repletion, of final unity—it is the "Sabbath of Sabbaths," to use the expression of the holy rhetorician, St. Augustine, who was himself such a man.—Should, however, the contrariety and conflict in such natures operate as an *additional* incentive and stimulus to life—and if, on the other hand, in addition to their powerful and irreconcilable instincts, they have also inherited and indoctrinated into them a proper mastery and subtlety for carrying on the conflict with themselves (that is to say, the faculty of self-control and self-deception), there then arise those marvellously incomprehensible, and inexplicable beings, those enigmatical men, predestined for conquering and circumventing others, the finest examples of which are Alcibiades and Cæsar (with whom I should like to associate the *first* of Europeans according to my taste, the Hohenstaufen, Frederick the Second), and amongst artists, perhaps Leonardo da Vinci. They appear precisely in the same periods when that weaker type, with its longing for repose, comes to the front; the two types are complementary to each other, and spring from the same causes.

201

As long as the utility which determines moral estimates is
only gregarious utility, as long as the preservation of the
community is only kept in view, and the immoral is sought
precisely and exclusively in what seems dangerous to the maintenance of the community, there can be no "morality of love
to one's neighbour." Granted even that there is already a little
constant exercise of consideration, sympathy, fairness, gentleness, and mutual assistance, granted that even in this condition
of society all those instincts are already active which are latterly
distinguished by honourable names as "virtues," and eventually almost coincide with the conception "morality": in that
period they do not as yet belong to the domain of moral
valuations—they are still *ultra-moral*. A sympathetic action,
for instance, is neither called good nor bad, moral nor immoral,
in the best period of the Romans; and should it be praised, a
sort of resentful disdain is compatible with this praise, even
at the best, directly the sympathetic action is compared with
one which contributes to the welfare of the whole, to the *res
publica*. After all, "love to our neighbour" is always a secondary matter, partly conventional and arbitrarily manifested in
relation to our *fear of our neighbour*. After the fabric of society seems on the whole established and secured against external
dangers, it is this fear of our neighbour which again creates
new perspectives of moral valuation. Certain strong and dangerous instincts, such as the love of enterprise, foolhardiness,
revengefulness, astuteness, rapacity, and love of power, which
up till then had not only to be honoured from the point of
view of general utility—under other names, of course, than
those here given—but had to be fostered and cultivated (be-

cause they were perpetually required in the common danger against the common enemies), are now felt in their dangerousness to be doubly strong—when the outlets for them are lacking—and are gradually branded as immoral and given over to calumny. The contrary instincts and inclinations now attain to moral honour; the gregarious instinct gradually draws its conclusions. How much or how little dangerousness to the community or to equality is contained in an opinion, a condition, an emotion, a disposition, or an endowment—that is now the moral perspective; here again fear is the mother of morals. It is by the loftiest and strongest instincts, when they break out passionately and carry the individual far above and beyond the average, and the low level of the gregarious conscience, that the self-reliance of the community is destroyed; its belief in itself, its backbone, as it were, breaks; consequently these very instincts will be most branded and defamed. The lofty independent spirituality, the will to stand alone, and even the cogent reason, are felt to be dangers; everything that elevates the individual above the herd, and is a source of fear to the neighbour, is henceforth called *evil*; the tolerant, unassuming, self-adapting, self-equalising disposition, the *mediocrity* of desires, attains to moral distinction and honour. Finally, under very peaceful circumstances, there is always less opportunity and necessity for training the feelings to severity and rigour; and now every form of severity, even in justice, begins to disturb the conscience; a lofty and rigourous nobleness and self-responsibility almost offends, and awakens distrust, "the lamb," and still more "the sheep," wins respect. There is a point of diseased mellowness and effeminacy in the history of society, at which society itself takes the part of him who injures it, the part of the *criminal*, and does so, in fact, seriously and honestly. To punish, appears to it to be somehow unfair—it is certain that the idea of "punishment" and "the obligation to punish" are then painful and alarming to people. "Is it not sufficient if the criminal be rendered *harmless?* Why should we still punish? Punishment itself is terrible!"—with these questions gregarious morality, the morality of fear, draws its ultimate conclusion. If one could at all do away with danger, the cause of fear, one would have done away with this morality at the same time, it would no longer be necessary, it *would not consider itself* any longer necessary!—Whoever examines the conscience of the present-day European, will always elicit the same imperative from its thousand moral folds and hidden recesses, the imperative of the timidity of the herd: "we wish that some time or other there may be *nothing more to fear!"* Some time or other—the will and the way *thereto* is nowadays called "progress" all over Europe.

202

Let us at once say again what we have already said a hundred times, for people's ears nowadays are unwilling to hear such truths—*our* truths. We know well enough how offensively it sounds when any one plainly, and without metaphor, counts man amongst the animals; but it will be accounted to us almost a *crime,* that it is precisely in respect to men of "modern ideas" that we have constantly applied the terms "herd," "herd-instincts," and such like expressions. What avail is it? We cannot do otherwise, for it is precisely here that our new insight is. We have found that in all the principal moral judgments Europe has become unanimous, including likewise the countries where European influence prevails: in Europe people evidently *know* what Socrates thought he did not know, and what the famous serpent of old once promised to teach—they "know" to-day what is good and evil. It must then sound hard and be distasteful to the ear, when we always insist that that which here thinks it knows, that which here glorifies itself with praise and blame, and calls itself good, is the instinct of the herding human animal: the instinct which has come and is ever coming more and more to the front, to preponderance and supremacy over other instincts, according to the increasing physiological approximation and resemblance of which it is the symptom. *Morality in Europe at present is herding-animal morality;* and therefore, as we understand the matter, only one kind of human morality, beside which, before which, and after which many other moralities, and above all *higher* moralities, are or should be possible. Against such a "possibility," against such a "should be," however, this morality defends itself with all its strength; it says obstinately and inexorably: "I am morality itself and nothing else is morality!" Indeed, with the help of a religion which has humoured and flattered the sublimest desires of the herding-animal, things have reached such a point that we always find a more visible expression of this morality even in political and social arrangements: the *democratic* movement is the inheritance of the Christian movement. That its *tempo,* however, is much too slow and sleepy for the more impatient ones, for those who are sick and distracted by the herding-instinct, is indicated by the increasingly furious howling, and always less disguised teeth-gnashing of the anarchist dogs, who are now roving through the highways of European culture. Apparently in opposition to the peacefully industrious democrats and Revolution-ideologues, and still more so to the awkward philosophasters and fraternity-visionaries who call themselves Socialists and want a "free society," those are really at one with them all in their thorough and instinctive hostility to every form of society other than that of the *autonomous* herd (to the extent even of repudiating the notions "master" and "servant"—*ni Dieu ni maître,* says a socialist formula); at one in their tenacious opposition to every special claim, every special right and privilege (this means ultimately opposition to *every* right, for when all are equal, no one needs "rights" any longer); at one in their distrust of punitive justice (as though it were a violation of the weak, unfair to the *necessary* consequences of all former society); but equally at one in their religion of sympathy, in their compassion for all that feels, lives, and suffers (down to the very animals, up even to "God"— the extravagance of "sympathy for God" belongs to a democratic age); altogether at one in the cry and impatience of their sympathy, in their deadly hatred of suffering generally, in their almost feminine incapacity for witnessing it or *allowing* it; at one in their involuntary beglooming and heart-softening, under the spell of which Europe seems to be threatened with a new Buddhism; at one in their belief in the morality of *mutual* sympathy, as though it were morality in itself, the climax, the *attained* climax of mankind, the sole hope of the future, the consolation of the present, the great discharge from all the obligations of the past; altogether at one in their belief in the community as the *deliverer,* in the herd, and therefore in "themselves."

203

We, who hold a different belief—we, who regard the democratic movement, not only as a degenerating form of political organisation, but as equivalent to a degenerating, a waning type of man, as involving his mediocrising and depreciation:

where have *we* to fix our hopes? In *new philosophers*—there is no other alternative: in minds strong and original enough to initiate opposite estimates of value, to transvalue and invert "eternal valuations"; in forerunners, in men of the future, who in the present shall fix the constraints and fasten the knots which will compel millenniums to take *new* paths. To teach man the future of humanity as his *will*, as depending on human will, and to make preparation for vast hazardous enterprises and collective attempts in rearing and educating, in order thereby to put an end to the frightful rule of folly and chance which has hitherto gone by the name of "history" (the folly of the "greatest number" is only its last form)—for that purpose a new type of philosophers and commanders will some time or other be needed, at the very idea of which everything that has existed in the way of occult, terrible, and benevolent beings might look pale and dwarfed. The image of such leaders hovers before *our* eyes:—is it lawful for me to say it aloud, ye free spirits? The conditions which one would partly have to create and partly utilise for their genesis; the presumptive methods and tests by virtue of which a soul should grow up to such an elevation and power as to feel a *constraint* to these tasks; a transvaluation of values, under the new pressure and hammer of which a conscience should be steeled and a heart transformed into brass, so as to bear the weight of such responsibility; and on the other hand the necessity for such leaders, the dreadful danger that they might be lacking, or miscarry and degenerate:—these are *our* real anxieties and glooms, ye know it well, ye free spirits! these are the heavy distant thoughts and storms which sweep across the heaven of *our* life. There are few pains so grievous as to have seen, divined, or experienced how an exceptional man has missed his way and deteriorated; but he who has the rare eye for the universal danger of "man" himself *deteriorating,* he who like us has recognised the extraordinary fortuitousness which has hitherto played its game in respect to the future of mankind—a game in which neither the hand, nor even a "finger of God" has participated!—he who divines the fate that is hidden under the idiotic unwariness and blind confidence of "modern ideas," and still more under the whole of Christo-European morality —suffers from an anguish with which no other is to be compared. He sees at a glance all that could still *be made out of man* through a favourable accumulation and augmentation of human powers and arrangements; he knows with all the knowledge of his conviction how unexhausted man still is for the greatest possibilities, and how often in the past the type man has stood in presence of mysterious decisions and new paths:—he knows still better from his painfulest recollections on what wretched obstacles promising developments of the highest rank have hitherto usually gone to pieces, broken down, sunk, and become contemptible. The *universal degeneracy of mankind* to the level of the "man of the future"—as idealised by the socialistic fools and shallow-pates—this degeneracy and dwarfing of man to an absolutely gregarious animal (or as they call it, to a man of "free society"), this brutalising of man into a pigmy with equal rights and claims, is undoubtedly *possible!* He who has thought out this possibility to its ultimate conclusion knows *another* loathing unknown to the rest of mankind—and perhaps also a new *mission!*

6. We Scholars

204

AT the risk that moralising may also reveal itself here as that which it has always been—namely, resolutely *montrer ses plaies,* according to Balzac—I would venture to protest against an improper and injurious alteration of rank, which quite unnoticed, and as if with the best conscience, threatens nowadays to establish itself in the relations of science and philosophy. I mean to say that one must have the right out of one's own *experience*—experience, as it seems to me, always implies unfortunate experience?—to treat of such an important question of rank, so as not to speak of colour like the blind, or *against* science like women and artists ("Ah! this dreadful science!" sigh their instinct and their shame, "it always *finds things out!*") The declaration of independence of the scientific man, his emancipation from philosophy, is one of the subtler after-effects of democratic organisation and disorganisation: the self-glorification and self-conceitedness of the learned man is now everywhere in full bloom, and in its best springtime—which does not mean to imply that in this case self-praise smells sweetly. Here also the instinct of the populace cries, "Freedom from all masters!" and after science has, with the happiest results, resisted theology, whose "handmaid" it had been too long, it now proposes in its wantonness and indiscretion to lay down laws for philosophy, and in its turn to play the "master" —what am I saying! to play the *philosopher* on its own account. My memory—the memory of a scientific man, if you please!—teems with the naïvetés of insolence which I have

heard about philosophy and philosophers from young naturalists and old physicians (not to mention the most cultured and
most conceited of all learned men, the philologists and schoolmasters, who are both the one and the other by profession).
On one occasion it was the specialist and the Jack Horner who
instinctively stood on the defensive against all synthetic tasks
and capabilities; at another time it was the industrious worker
who had got a scent of *otium* and refined luxuriousness in the
internal economy of the philosopher, and felt himself
aggrieved and belittled thereby. On another occasion it was
the colour-blindness of the utilitarian, who sees nothing in
philosophy but a series of *refuted* systems, and an extravagant
expenditure which "does nobody any good." At another time
the fear of disguised mysticism and of the boundary-adjust-
ment of knowledge became conspicuous, at another time the
disregard of individual philosophers, which had involuntarily
extended to disregard of philosophy generally. In fine, I found
most frequently, behind the proud disdain of philosophy in
young scholars, the evil after-effect of some particular philosopher, to whom on the whole obedience had been foresworn,
without, however, the spell of his scornful estimates of other
philosophers having been got rid of—the result being a
general ill-will to all philosophy. (Such seems to me, for instance, the after-effect of Schopenhauer on the most modern
Germany: by his unintelligent rage against Hegel, he has succeeded in severing the whole of the last generation of Germans
from its connection with German culture, which culture, all
things considered, has been an elevation and a divining refinement of the *historical sense;* but precisely at this point Schopenhauer himself was poor, irreceptive, and un-German to the
extent of ingeniousness.) On the whole, speaking generally,
it may just have been the humanness, all-too-humanness of

[*499*]

the modern philosophers themselves, in short, their con-
temptibleness, which has injured most radically the reverence
for philosophy and opened the doors to the instinct of the
populace. Let it but be acknowledged to what an extent our
modern world diverges from the whole style of the world of
Heraclitus, Plato, Empedocles, and whatever else all the royal
and magnificent anchorites of the spirit were called; and with
what justice an honest man of science *may* feel himself of a
better family and origin, in view of such representatives of
philosophy, who, owing to the fashion of the present day, are
just as much aloft as they are down below—in Germany, for
instance, the two lions of Berlin, the anarchist Eugen Dühring
and the amalgamist Eduard von Hartmann. It is especially the
sight of those hotch-potch philosophers, who call themselves
"realists," or "positivists," which is calculated to implant a
dangerous distrust in the soul of a young and ambitious
scholar: those philosophers, at the best, are themselves but
scholars and specialists, that is very evident! All of them are
persons who have been vanquished and *brought back again*
under the dominion of science, who at one time or another
claimed more from themselves, without having a right to
the "more" and its responsibility—and who now, creditably,
rancorously and vindictively, represent in word and deed,
disbelief in the master-task and supremacy of philosophy.
After all, how could it be otherwise? Science flourishes nowadays and has the good conscience clearly visible on its countenance; while that to which the entire modern philosophy has
gradually sunk, the remnant of philosophy of the present day,
excites distrust and displeasure, if not scorn and pity. Philosophy reduced to a "theory of knowledge," is no more in fact
than a diffident science of epochs and doctrine of forbearance:
a philosophy that never even gets beyond the threshold, and

rigourously *denies* itself the right to enter—that is philosophy in its last throes, an end, an agony, something that awakens pity. How could such a philosophy—*rule!*

205

The dangers that beset the evolution of the philosopher are, in fact, so manifold nowadays, that one might doubt whether this fruit could still come to maturity. The extent and towering structure of the sciences have increased enormously, and therewith also the probability that the philosopher will grow tired even as a learner, or will attach himself somewhere and "specialise": so that he will no longer attain to his elevation, that is to say, to his superspection, his circumspection, and his *despection*. Or he gets aloft too late, when the best of his maturity and strength is past; or when he is impaired, coarsened, and deteriorated, so that his view, his general estimate of things, is no longer of much importance. It is perhaps just the refinement of his intellectual conscience that makes him hesitate and linger on the way; he dreads the temptation to become a dilettante, a millepede, a milleantenna; he knows too well that as a discerner, one who has lost his self-respect no longer commands, no longer *leads;* unless he should aspire to become a great play-actor, a philosophical Cagliostro and spiritual rat-catcher—in short, a misleader. This is in the last instance a question of taste, if it has not really been a question of conscience. To double once more the philosopher's difficulties, there is also the fact that he demands from himself a verdict, a Yea or Nay, not concerning science, but concerning life and the worth of life—he learns unwillingly to believe that it is his right and even his duty to obtain this verdict, and he has to seek his way to the right and the belief only through the most extensive (perhaps disturbing and destroying) experiences, often hesitating, doubting, and dumbfounded. In fact, the philosopher has long been mistaken and confused by the multitude, either with the scientific man and ideal scholar, or with the religiously elevated, desensualised, desecularised visionary and God-intoxicated man; and even yet when one hears anybody praised, because he lives "wisely," or "as a philosopher," it hardly means anything more than "prudently and apart." Wisdom: that seems to the populace to be a kind of flight, a means and artifice for withdrawing successfully from a bad game; but the *genuine* philosopher—does it not seem so to *us*, my friends?—lives "unphilosophically" and "unwisely," above all, *imprudently,* and feels the obligation and burden of a hundred attempts and temptations of life—he risks *himself* constantly, he plays *this* bad game.

206

In relation to the genius, that is to say, a being who either *engenders* or *produces*—both words understood in their fullest sense—the man of learning, the scientific average man, has always something of the old maid about him; for, like her, he is not conversant with the two principal functions of man. To both, of course, to the scholar and to the old maid, one concedes respectability, as if by way of indemnification—in these cases one emphasises the respectability—and yet, in the compulsion of this concession, one has the same admixture of vexation. Let us examine more closely: what is the scientific man? Firstly, a commonplace type of man, with commonplace virtues: that is to say, a non-ruling, non-authoritative, and non-

self-sufficient type of man; he possesses industry, patient adapt-
ableness to rank and file, equability and moderation in
capacity and requirement; he has the instinct for people like
himself, and for that which they require—for instance: the
portion of independence and green meadow without which
there is no rest from labour, the claim to honour and consideration (which first and foremost presupposes recognition and
recognisability), the sunshine of a good name, the perpetual
ratification of his value and usefulness, with which the inward
distrust which lies at the bottom of the heart of all dependent
men and gregarious animals, has again and again to be overcome. The learned man, as is appropriate, has also maladies
and faults of an ignoble kind: he is full of petty envy, and has
a lynx-eye for the weak points in those natures to whose elevations he cannot attain. He is confiding, yet only as one who
lets himself go, but does not *flow;* and precisely before the man
of the great current he stands all the colder and more reserved
—his eye is then like a smooth and irresponsive lake, which
is no longer moved by rapture or sympathy. The worst and
most dangerous thing of which a scholar is capable results from
the instinct of mediocrity of his type, from the Jesuitism of
mediocrity, which labours instinctively for the destruction of
the exceptional man, and endeavours to break—or still better,
to relax—every bent bow. To relax, of course, with consideration, and naturally with an indulgent hand—to *relax* with
confiding sympathy: that is the real art of Jesuitism, which has
always understood how to introduce itself as the religion of
sympathy.

207

However gratefully one may welcome the *objective* spirit—and who has not been sick to death of all subjectivity and its confounded *ipsisimosity!*—in the end, however, one must learn caution even with regard to one's gratitude, and put a stop to the exaggeration with which the unselfing and depersonalising of the spirit has recently been celebrated, as if it were the goal in itself, as if it were salvation and glorification —as is especially accustomed to happen in the pessimist school, which has also in its turn good reasons for paying the highest honours to "disinterested knowledge." The objective man, who no longer curses and scolds like the pessimist, the *ideal* man of learning in whom the scientific instinct blossoms forth fully after a thousand complete and partial failures, is assuredly one of the most costly instruments that exist, but his place is in the hand of one who is more powerful. He is only an instrument; we may say, he is a *mirror*—he is no "purpose in himself." The objective man is in truth a mirror: accustomed to prostration before everything that wants to be known, with such desires only as knowing or "reflecting" imply—he waits until something comes, and then expands himself sensitively, so that even the light footsteps and gliding past of spiritual beings may not be lost on his surface and film. Whatever "personality" he still possesses seems to him accidental, arbitrary, or still oftener, disturbing; so much has he come to regard himself as the passage and reflection of outside forms and events. He calls up the recollection of "himself" with an effort, and not infrequently wrongly; he readily confounds himself with other persons, he makes mistakes with regard to his own needs, and here only is he unrefined and negligent.

Perhaps he is troubled about the health, or the pettiness and confined atmosphere of wife and friend, or the lack of companions and society—indeed, he sets himself to reflect on his suffering, but in vain! His thoughts already rove away to the *more general* case, and tomorrow he knows as little as he knew yesterday how to help himself. He does not now take himself seriously and devote time to himself: he is serene, *not* from lack of trouble, but from lack of capacity for grasping and dealing with *his* trouble. The habitual complaisance with respect to all objects and experiences, the radiant and impartial hospitality with which he receives everything that comes his way, his habit of inconsiderate good-nature, of dangerous indifference as to Yea and Nay: alas! there are enough of cases in which he has to atone for these virtues of his!—and as man generally, he becomes far too easily the *caput mortuum* of such virtues. Should one wish love or hatred from him—I mean love and hatred as God, woman, and animal understand them—he will do what he can, and furnish what he can. But one must not be surprised if it should not be much—if he should show himself just at this point to be false, fragile, questionable, and deteriorated. His love is constrained, his hatred is artificial, and rather *un tour de force,* a slight ostentation and exaggeration. He is only genuine so far as he can be objective; only in his serene totality is he still "nature" and "natural." His mirroring and eternally self-polishing soul no longer knows how to affirm, no longer how to deny; he does not command; neither does he destroy. *"Je ne méprise presque rien"*—he says, with Leibnitz: let us not overlook nor under-value the *presque!* Neither is he a model man; he does not go in advance of any one, nor after, either; he places himself generally too far off to have any reason for espousing the cause of either good or evil. If he has been so long confounded with the *philosopher,* with the Cæsarian trainer and dictator of civilisation, he has had far too much honour, and what is more essential in him has been overlooked—he is an instrument, something of a slave, though certainly the sublimest sort of slave, but nothing in himself—*presque rien!* The objective man is an instrument, a costly, easily injured, easily tarnished, measuring instrument and mirroring apparatus, which is to be taken care of and respected; but he is no goal, no outgoing nor upgoing, no complementary man in whom the *rest* of existence justifies itself, no termination—and still less a commencement, an engendering, or primary cause, nothing hardy, powerful, self-centred, that wants to be master; but rather only a soft, inflated, delicate, movable potter's-form, that must wait for some kind of content and frame to "shape" itself thereto—for the most part a man without frame and content, a "selfless" man. Consequently, also, nothing for women, *in parenthesi.*

208

When a philosopher nowadays makes known that he is not a sceptic—I hope that has been gathered from the foregoing description of the objective spirit?—people all hear it impatiently; they regard him on that account with some apprehension, they would like to ask so many, many questions . . . indeed among timid hearers, of whom there are now so many, he is henceforth said to be dangerous. With his repudiation of scepticism, it seems to them as if they heard some evil-threatening sound in the distance, as if a new kind of explosive were being tried somewhere, a dynamite of the spirit, perhaps a newly discovered Russian *nihiline,* a pessimism *bonae voluntatis,* that not only denies, means denial, but—dreadful thought! *practises* denial. Against this kind of "good will"—a will to the veritable, actual negation of life—there is, as is generally acknowledged nowadays, no better soporific and sedative than scepticism, the mild, pleasing, lulling poppy of scepticism; and Hamlet himself is now prescribed by the doctors of the day as an antidote to the "spirit," and its underground noises. "Are not our ears already full of bad sounds?" say the sceptics, as lovers of repose, and almost as a kind of safety police, "this subterranean Nay is terrible! Be still, ye pessimistic moles!" The sceptic, in effect, that delicate creature, is far too easily frightened; his conscience is schooled so as to start at every Nay, and even at that sharp, decided Yea, and feels something like a bite thereby. Yea! and Nay!—they seem to him opposed to morality; he loves, on the contrary, to make a festival to his virtue by a noble aloofness, while perhaps he says with Montaigne: "What do I know?" Or with Socrates: "I know that I know nothing." Or: "Here I do not trust myself, no door is open to me." Or: "Even if the door were open, why should I enter immediately?" Or: "What is the use of any hasty hypotheses? It might quite well be in good taste to make no hypotheses at all. Are you absolutely obliged to straighten at once what is crooked? to stuff every hole with some kind of oakum? Is there not time enough for that? Has not the time leisure? Oh, ye demons, can ye not at all *wait*? The uncertain also has its charms, the Sphinx, too, is a Circe, and Circe, too, was a philosopher."—Thus does a sceptic console himself; and in truth he needs some consolation. For scepticism is the most spiritual expression of a certain many-sided physiological temperament, which in ordinary language is called nervous debility and sickliness; it arises whenever races or classes which have been long separated, decisively and suddenly blend with one another. In the new generation, which has inherited as it were different standards and valuations in its blood, everything is disquiet, derangement, doubt, and tentative; the best powers operate restrictively, the very virtues prevent each other growing and becoming strong, equilibrium, ballast, and perpendicular stability are lacking in body and soul. That, however, which is most diseased and degenerated in such nondescripts is the *will;* they are no longer familiar with independence of decision, or the courageous feeling of pleasure in willing—they are doubtful of the "freedom of the will" even in their dreams. Our present-day Europe, the scene of a senseless, precipitate attempt at a radical blending of classes, and *consequently* of races, is therefore sceptical in all its heights and depths, sometimes exhibiting the mobile scepticism which springs impatiently and wantonly from branch to branch, sometimes with gloomy aspect, like a cloud overcharged with interrogative signs—and often sick unto death of its will! Paralysis of will; where do we not find this cripple sitting nowadays! And yet how bedecked oftentimes! How seductively ornamented! There are the finest gala dresses and disguises for this disease; and that, for instance, most of what places itself nowadays in the show-cases as "objectiveness," "the scientific spirit," "*l'art pour l'art,*" and "pure voluntary knowledge," is only decked-out scepticism and paralysis of will—I am ready to answer for this diagnosis of the European disease.—The disease of the will is diffused unequally over Europe; it is worst and most varied where civilisation has longest prevailed; it decreases according as "the barbarian" still—or again—asserts his claims under the loose drapery of Western culture. It is therefore in the France of today, as can be readily disclosed and comprehended, that the will is most infirm; and France, which has always had a mas-

terly aptitude for converting even the portentous crises of
its spirit into something charming and seductive, now manifests emphatically its intellectual ascendancy over Europe, by
being the school and exhibition of all the charms of scepticism.
The power to will and to persist, moreover, in a resolution, is
already somewhat stronger in Germany, and again in the
North of Germany it is stronger than in Central Germany; it
is considerably stronger in England, Spain, and Corsica, associated with phlegm in the former and with hard skulls in the
latter—not to mention Italy, which is too young yet to know
what it wants, and must first show whether it can exercise will;
but it is strongest and most surprising of all in that immense
middle empire where Europe as it were flows back to Asia—
namely, in Russia. There the power to will has been long stored
up and accumulated, there the will—uncertain whether to be
negative or affirmative—waits threateningly to be discharged
(to borrow their pet phrase from our physicists). Perhaps not
only Indian wars and complications in Asia would be necessary
to free Europe from its greatest danger, but also internal sub-
version, the shattering of the empire into small states, and
above all the introduction of parliamentary imbecility, together with the obligation of every one to read his newspaper
at breakfast. I do not say this as one who desires it; in my heart
I should rather prefer the contrary—I mean such an increase
in the threatening attitude of Russia, that Europe would have
to make up its mind to become equally threatening—namely,
to acquire one will, by means of a new caste to rule over the
Continent, a persistent, dreadful will of its own, that can set
its aims thousands of years ahead; so that the long spun-out
comedy of its petty-stateism, and its dynastic as well as its
democratic many-willedness, might finally be brought to a

close. The time for petty politics is past; the next century will bring the struggle for the dominion of the world—the *compulsion* to great politics.

209

As to how far the new warlike age on which we Europeans have evidently entered may perhaps favour the growth of another and stronger kind of scepticism, I should like to express myself preliminarily merely by a parable, which the lovers of German history will already understand. That unscrupulous enthusiast for big, handsome grenadiers (who, as King of Prussia, brought into being a military and sceptical genius— and therewith, in reality, the new and now triumphantly emerged type of German), the problematic, crazy father of Frederick the Great, had at one point the very knack and lucky grasp of the genius: he knew what was then lacking in Germany, the want of which was a hundred times more alarming and serious than any lack of culture and social form —his ill-will to the young Frederick resulted from the anxiety of a profound instinct. *Men were lacking;* and he suspected, to his bitterest regret, that his own son was not man enough. There, however, he deceived himself; but who would not have deceived himself in his place? He saw his son lapsed to atheism, to the *esprit,* to the pleasant frivolity of clever Frenchmen—he saw in the background the great bloodsucker, the spider scepticism; he suspected the incurable wretchedness of a heart no longer hard enough either for evil or good, and of a broken will that no longer commands, is no longer *able* to command. Meanwhile, however, there grew up in his son that new kind of harder and more dangerous scepticism—who knows *to what extent* it was encouraged just by his father's hatred and the icy melancholy of a will condemned to solitude? —the scepticism of daring manliness, which is closely related to the genius for war and conquest, and made its first entrance into Germany in the person of the great Frederick. This scepticism despises and nevertheless grasps; it undermines and takes possession; it does not believe, but it does not thereby lose itself; it gives the spirit a dangerous liberty, but it keeps strict guard over the heart. It is the *German* form of scepticism, which, as a continued Fredericianism, risen to the highest spirituality, has kept Europe for a considerable time under the dominion of the German spirit and its critical and historical distrust. Owing to the insuperably strong and tough masculine character of the great German philologists and historical critics (who, rightly estimated, were also all of them artists of destruction and dissolution), a *new* conception of the German spirit gradually established itself—in spite of all Romanticism in music and philosophy—in which the leaning towards masculine scepticism was decidedly prominent: whether, for instance, as fearlessness of gaze, as courage and sternness of the dissecting hand, or as resolute will to dangerous voyages of discovery, to spiritualised North Pole expeditions under barren and dangerous skies. There may be good grounds for it when warm-blooded and superficial humanitarians cross themselves before this spirit, *cet esprit fataliste, ironique, méphisto-phélique,* as Michelet calls it, not without a shudder. But if one would realise how characteristic is this fear of the "man" in the German spirit which awakened Europe out of its "dogmatic slumber," let us call to mind the former conception which had to be overcome by this new one—and that it is not so very long ago that a masculinised woman could dare, with

[*511*]

unbridled presumption, to recommend the Germans to the interest of Europe as gentle, good-hearted, weak-willed, and poetical fools. Finally, let us only understand profoundly enough Napoleon's astonishment when he saw Goethe: it reveals what had been regarded for centuries as the "German spirit." *"Voilà un homme!"*—that was as much as to say: "But this is a *man!* And I only expected to see a German!"

210

Supposing, then, that in the picture of the philosophers of the future, some trait suggests the question whether they must not perhaps be sceptics in the last-mentioned sense, something in them would only be designated thereby—and *not* they themselves. With equal right they might call themselves critics; and assuredly they will be men of experiments. By the name with which I ventured to baptize them, I have already expressly emphasised their attempting and their love of attempting: is this because, as critics in body and soul, they will love to make use of experiments in a new, and perhaps wider and more dangerous sense? In their passion for knowledge, will they have to go further in daring and painful attempts than the sensitive and pampered taste of a democratic century can approve of?—There is no doubt: these coming ones will be least able to dispense with the serious and not unscrupulous qualities which distinguish the critic from the sceptic: I mean the certainty as to standards of worth, the conscious employment of a unity of method, the wary courage, the standing-alone, and the capacity for self-responsibility; indeed, they will avow among themselves a *delight* in denial and dissection, and a certain considerate cruelty, which knows how to handle the knife surely and deftly, even when the heart bleeds. They will be *sterner* (and perhaps not always towards themselves only) than humane people may desire, they will not deal with the "truth" in order that it may "please" them, or "elevate" and "inspire" them—they will rather have little faith in *"truth"* bringing with it such revels for the feelings. They will smile, those rigourous spirits, when any one says in their presence: "that thought elevates me, why should it not be true?" or: "that work enchants me, why should it not be beautiful?" or: "that artist enlarges me, why should he not be great?" Perhaps they will not only have a smile, but a genuine disgust for all that is thus rapturous, idealistic, feminine, and hermaphroditic; and if any one could look into their inmost hearts, he would not easily find therein the intention to reconcile "Christian sentiments" with "antique taste," or even with "modern parliamentarism" (the kind of reconciliation necessarily found even amongst philosophers in our very uncertain and consequently very conciliatory century). Critical discipline, and every habit that conduces to purity and rigour in intellectual matters, will not only be demanded from themselves by these philosophers of the future; they may even make a display thereof as their special adornment—nevertheless they will not want to be called critics on that account. It will seem to them no small indignity to philosophy to have it decreed, as is so welcome nowadays, that "philosophy itself is criticism and critical science—and nothing else whatever!" Though this estimate of philosophy may enjoy the approval of all the Positivists of France and Germany (and possibly it even flattered the heart and taste of *Kant:* let us call to mind the titles of his principal works), our new philosophers will say, notwithstanding, that critics are instruments of the philosopher, and just on that

[*513*]

account, as instruments, they are far from being philosophers themselves! Even the great Chinaman of Königsberg was only a great critic.

211

I insist upon it that people finally cease confounding philosophical workers, and in general scientific men, with philosophers—that precisely here one should strictly give "each his own," and not give those far too much, these far too little. It may be necessary for the education of the real philosopher that he himself should have once stood upon all those steps upon which his servants, the scientific workers of philosophy, remain standing, and *must* remain standing: he himself must perhaps have been critic, and dogmatist, and historian, and besides, poet, and collector, and traveller, and riddle-reader, and moralist, and seer, and "free spirit," and almost everything, in order to traverse the whole range of human values and estimations, and that he may *be able* with a variety of eyes and consciences to look from a height to any distance, from a depth up to any height, from a nook into any expanse. But all these are only preliminary conditions for his task; this task itself demands something else—it requires him *to create values*. The philosophical workers, after the excellent pattern of Kant and Hegel, have to fix and formalise some great existing body of valuations—that is to say, former *determinations of value,* creations of value, which have become prevalent, and are for a time called "truths"—whether in the domain of the *logical*, the *political* (moral), or the *artistic*. It is for these investigators to make whatever has happened and been esteemed hitherto, conspicuous, conceivable, intelligible, and manageable, to shorten everything long, even "time" itself, and to *subjugate* the entire past: an immense and wonderful task, in the carrying out of which all refined pride, all tenacious will, can surely find satisfaction. *The real philosophers, however, are commanders and law-givers;* they say: "Thus *shall* it be!" They determine first the Whither and the Why of mankind, and thereby set aside the previous labour of all philosophical workers, and all subjugators of the past—they grasp at the future with a creative hand, and whatever is and was, becomes for them thereby a means, an instrument, and a hammer. Their "knowing" is *creating,* their creating is a law-giving, their will to truth is—*Will to Power.*—Are there at present such philosophers? Have there ever been such philosophers? *Must* there not be such philosophers some day? . . .

212

It is always more obvious to me that the philosopher, as a man *indispensable* for the morrow and the day after the morrow, has ever found himself, and *has been obliged* to find himself, in contradiction to the day in which he lives; his enemy has always been the ideal of his day. Hitherto all those extraordinary furtherers of humanity whom one calls philosophers—who rarely regarded themselves as lovers of wisdom, but rather as disagreeable fools and dangerous interrogators—have found their mission, their hard, involuntary, imperative mission (in the end however the greatness of their mission), in being the bad conscience of their age. In putting the vivisector's knife to the breast of the very *virtues of their age,* they have betrayed their own secret; it has been for the sake of a *new* greatness of man, a new untrodden path to his aggrandisement. They have always disclosed how much hypocrisy, indolence self-indulgence, and self-neglect, how much falsehood was concealed under the most venerated types of contemporary morality, how much virtue was *outlived;* they have always said: "We must remove hence to where *you* are least at home." In face of a world of "modern ideas," which would like to confine every one in a corner, in a "specialty," a philosopher, if there could be philosophers nowadays, would be compelled to place the greatness of man, the conception of "greatness," precisely in his comprehensiveness and multifariousness, in his all-roundness; he would even determine worth and rank according to the amount and variety of that which a man could bear and take upon himself, according to the *extent* to which a man could stretch his responsibility. Nowadays the taste and virtue of the age weaken and attenuate the will; nothing is so adapted to the spirit of the age as weakness of will: consequently, in the ideal of the philosopher, strength of will, sternness and capacity for prolonged resolution, must specially be included in the conception of "greatness"; with as good a right as the opposite doctrine, with its ideal of a silly, renouncing, humble, selfless humanity, was suited to an opposite age —such as the sixteenth century, which suffered from its accumulated energy of will, and from the wildest torrents and floods of selfishness. In the time of Socrates, among men only of worn-out instincts, old conservative Athenians who let themselves go—"for the sake of happiness," as they said; for the sake of pleasure, as their conduct indicated—and who had continually on their lips the old pompous words to which they had long forfeited the right by the life they led, *irony* was perhaps necessary for greatness of soul, the wicked Socratic assurance of the old physician and plebeian, who cut ruthlessly into his own flesh, as into the flesh and heart of the "noble," with a look that said plainly enough: "Do not dissemble before

me! here——we are equal!" At present, on the contrary, when
throughout Europe the herding animal alone attains to
honours, and dispenses honours, when "equality of right" can
too readily be transformed into equality in wrong: I mean to
say into general war against everything rare, strange, and
privileged, against the higher man, the higher soul, the higher
duty, the higher responsibility, the creative plenipotence and
lordliness——at present it belongs to the conception of "greatness" to be noble, to wish to be apart, to be capable of being
different, to stand alone, to have to live by personal initiative;
and the philosopher will betray something of his own ideal
when he asserts: "He shall be the greatest who can be the most
solitary, the most concealed, the most divergent, the man beyond good and evil, the master of his virtues, and of superabundance of will; precisely this shall be called *greatness:*
as diversified as can be entire, as ample as can be full." And to
ask once more the question: Is greatness *possible*——nowadays?

213

It is difficult to learn what a philosopher is, because it cannot
be taught: one must "know" it by experience——or one should
have the pride *not* to know it. The fact that at present people all
talk of things of which they *cannot* have any experience, is true
more especially and unfortunately as concerns the philosopher
and philosophical matters:——the very few know them, are permitted to know them, and all popular ideas about them are
false. Thus, for instance, the truly philosophical combination
of a bold, exuberant spirituality which runs at *presto* pace, and
a dialectic rigour and necessity which makes no false step, is
unknown to most thinkers and scholars from their own experi-

ence, and therefore, should any one speak of it in their presence, it is incredible to them. They conceive of every necessity as troublesome, as a painful compulsory obedience and state of constraint; thinking itself is regarded by them as something slow and hesitating, almost as a trouble, and often enough as "worthy of the *sweat* of the noble"—but not at all as something easy and divine, closely related to dancing and exuberance! "To think" and to take a matter "seriously," "arduously" —that is one and the same thing to them; such only has been their "experience."—Artists have here perhaps a finer intuition; they who know only too well that precisely when they no longer do anything "arbitrarily," and everything of necessity, their feeling of freedom, of subtlety, of power, of creatively fixing, disposing and shaping, reaches its climax—in short, that necessity and "freedom of will" are then the same thing with them. There is, in fine, a gradation of rank in psychical states, to which the gradation of rank in the problems corresponds; and the highest problems repel ruthlessly every one who ventures too near them, without being predestined for their solution by the loftiness and power of his spirituality. Of what use is it for nimble, everyday intellects, or clumsy, honest mechanics and empiricists to press, in their plebeian ambition, close to such problems, and as it were into this "holy of holies" —as so often happens nowadays! But coarse feet must never tread upon such carpets: this is provided for in the primary law of things; the doors remain closed to those intruders, though they may dash and break their heads thereon! People have always to be born to a high station, or, more definitely, they have to be *bred* for it: a person has only a right to philosophy—taking the word in its higher significance—in virtue of his descent; the ancestors, the "blood," decide here also. Many generations must have prepared the way for the coming of the philosopher; each of his virtues must have been separately acquired, nurtured, transmitted, and embodied; not only the bold, easy, delicate course and current of his thoughts, but above all the readiness for great responsibilities, the majesty of ruling glance and contemning look, the feeling of separation from the multitude with their duties and virtues, the kindly patronage and defence of whatever is misunderstood and calumniated, be it God or devil, the delight and practice of supreme justice, the art of commanding, the amplitude of will, the lingering eye which rarely admires, rarely looks up, rarely loves. . . .

7. Our Virtues

214

OUR Virtues?—It is probable that we, too, have still our virtues, although naturally they are not those sincere and massive virtues on account of which we hold our grandfathers in esteem and also at a little distance from us. We Europeans of the day after tomorrow, we firstlings of the twentieth century —with all our dangerous curiosity, our multifariousness and art of disguising, our mellow and seemingly sweetened cruelty in sense and spirit—we shall presumably, *if* we must have virtues, have those only which have come to agreement with our most secret and heartfelt inclinations, with our most ardent requirements: well, then, let us look for them in our labyrinths! —where, as we know, so many things lose themselves, so many things get quite lost! And is there anything finer than to *search* for one's own virtues? Is it not almost to *believe* in one's own virtues? But this "believing in one's own virtues"—is it not practically the same as what was formerly called one's "good conscience," that long, respectable pigtail of an idea, which our grandfathers used to hang behind their heads, and often enough also behind their understandings? It seems, therefore, that however little we may imagine ourselves to be old-fashioned and grandfatherly respectable in other respects, in one thing we are nevertheless the worthy grandchildren of our grandfathers, we last Europeans with good consciences: we also still wear their pigtail.—Ah! if you only knew how soon, so very soon—it will be different!

215

As in the stellar firmament there are sometimes two suns which determine the path of one planet, and in certain cases suns of different colours shine around a single planet, now with red light, now with green, and then simultaneously illumine and flood it with motley colours: so we modern men, owing to the complicated mechanism of our "firmament," are determined by *different* moralities; our actions shine alternately in different colours, and are seldom unequivocal—and there are often cases, also, in which our actions are *motley-coloured*.

216

To love one's enemies? I think that has been well learned: it takes place thousands of times at present on a large and small scale; indeed, at times the higher and sublimer thing takes place:—we learn to *despise* when we love, and precisely when we love best; all of it, however, unconsciously, without noise, without ostentation, with the shame and secrecy of goodness, which forbids the utterance of the pompous word and the formula of virtue. Morality as attitude—is opposed to our taste nowadays. This is *also* an advance, as it was an advance in our fathers that religion as attitude finally became opposed to their taste, including the enmity and Voltairean bitterness against religion (and all that formerly belonged to freethinker-pantomime). It is the music in our conscience, the dance in our spirit, to which Puritan litanies, moral sermons, and goody-goodness won't chime.

217

Let us be careful in dealing with those who attach great importance to being credited with moral tact and subtlety in moral discernment! They never forgive us if they have once made a mistake *before* us (or even *with regard to* us)—they inevitably become our instinctive calumniators and detractors, even when they still remain our "friends."—Blessed are the forgetful: for they "get the better" even of their blunders.

218

The psychologists of France—and where else are there still psychologists nowadays?—have never yet exhausted their bitter and manifold enjoyment of the *bêtise bourgeoise,* just as though . . . in short, they betray something thereby. Flaubert, for instance, the honest citizen of Rouen, neither saw,

heard, nor tasted anything else in the end; it was his mode of
self-torment and refined cruelty. As this is growing wearisome, I would now recommend for a change something else
for a pleasure—namely, the unconscious astuteness with which
good, fat, honest mediocrity always behaves towards loftier
spirits and the tasks they have to perform, the subtle, barbed,
Jesuitical astuteness, which is a thousand times subtler than the
taste and understanding of the middle-class in its best moments
—subtler even than the understanding of its victims:—a repeated proof that "instinct" is the most intelligent of all kinds
of intelligence which have hitherto been discovered. In short,
you psychologists, study the philosophy of the "rule" in its
struggle with the "exception": there you have a spectacle fit for
Gods and godlike malignity! Or, in plainer words, practise
vivisection on "good people," on the *"homo bonae voluntatis,"*
. . . on *yourselves!*

219

The practice of judging and condemning morally, is the
favourite revenge of the intellectually shallow on those who are
less so; it is also a kind of indemnity for their being badly
endowed by nature; and finally, it is an opportunity for acquiring spirit and *becoming* subtle:—malice spiritualises.
They are glad in their inmost heart that there is a standard
according to which those who are over-endowed with intellectual goods and privileges, are equal to them; they contend for
the "equality of all before God," and almost *need* the belief
in God for this purpose. It is among them that the most powerful antagonists of atheism are found. If any one were to say
to them: "a lofty spirituality is beyond all comparison with

che honesty and respectability of a merely moral man"—it would make them furious; I shall take care not to say so. I would rather flatter them with my theory that lofty spirituality itself exists only as the ultimate product of moral qualities; that it is a synthesis of all qualities attributed to the "merely moral" man, after they have been acquired singly through long training and practice, perhaps during a whole series of generations; that lofty spirituality is precisely the spiritualising of justice, and the beneficent severity which knows that it is authorised to maintain *gradations of rank* in the world, even among things—and not only among men.

220

Now that the praise of the "disinterested person" is so popular one must—probably not without some danger—get an idea of *what* people actually take an interest in, and what are the things generally which fundamentally and profoundly concern ordinary men—including the cultured, even the learned, and perhaps philosophers also, if appearances do not deceive. The fact thereby becomes obvious that the greater part of what interests and charms higher natures, and more refined and fastidious tastes, seems absolutely "uninteresting" to the average man:—if, notwithstanding, he perceive devotion to these interests, he calls it *désintéressé,* and wonders how it is possible to act "disinterestedly." There have been philosophers who could give this popular astonishment a seductive and mystical, other-world expression (perhaps because they did not know the higher nature by experience?), instead of stating the naked and candidly reasonable truth that "disinterested" action is very interesting and "interested" action, provided that . . .

"And love?"—What! Even an action for love's sake shall be "unegoistic"? But you fools—! "And the praise of the self-sacrificer?"—But whoever has really offered sacrifice knows that he wanted and obtained something for it—perhaps something from himself for something from himself; that he relinquished here in order to have more there, perhaps in general to be more, or even feel himself "more." But this is a realm of questions and answers in which a more fastidious spirit does not like to stay: for here truth has to stifle her yawns so much when she is obliged to answer. And after all, truth is a woman; one must not use force with her.

221

"It sometimes happens," said a moralistic pedant and trifle-retailer, "that I honour and respect an unselfish man: not, however, because he is unselfish, but because I think he has a right to be useful to another man at his own expense. In short, the question is always who *he* is, and who *the other* is. For instance, in a person created and destined for command, self-denial and modest retirement, instead of being virtues would be the waste of virtues: so it seems to me. Every system of unegoistic morality which takes itself unconditionally and appeals to every one, not only sins against good taste, but is also an incentive to sins of omission, an *additional* seduction under the mask of philanthropy—and precisely a seduction and injury to the higher, rarer, and more privileged types of men. Moral systems must be compelled first of all to bow before the *gradations of rank;* their presumption must be driven home to their conscience—until they thoroughly understand at last that it is *immoral* to say that "what is right for one is proper for another."—So said my moralistic pedant and *bonhomme.*

Did he perhaps deserve to be laughed at when he thus exhorted systems of morals to practise morality? But one should not be too much in the right if one wishes to have the laughers on *one's own* side; a grain of wrong pertains even to good taste.

222

Wherever sympathy (fellow-suffering) is preached nowadays—and, if I gather rightly, no other religion is any longer preached—let the psychologist have his ears open; through all the vanity, through all the noise which is natural to these preachers (as to all preachers), he will hear a hoarse, groaning, genuine note of *self-contempt*. It belongs to the overshadowing and uglifying of Europe, which has been on the increase for a century (the first symptoms of which are already specified documentarily in a thoughtful letter of Galiani to Madame d'Epinay)—*if it is not really the cause thereof!* The man of "modern ideas," the conceited ape, is excessively dissatisfied with himself—this is perfectly certain. He suffers, and his vanity wants him only "to suffer with his fellows."

223

The hybrid European—a tolerably ugly plebeian, taken all in all—absolutely requires a costume: he needs history as a storeroom of costumes. To be sure, he notices that none of the costumes fit him properly—he changes and changes. Let us look at the nineteenth century with respect to these hasty preferences and changes in its masquerades of style, and also with respect to its moments of desperation on account of "nothing suiting" us. It is in vain to get ourselves up as romantic, or classical, or Christian, or Florentine, or *barocco,* or "national," *in moribus et artibus:* it does not "clothe us"! But the "spirit," especially the "historical spirit," profits even by this desperation: once and again a new sample of the past or of the foreign is tested, put on, taken off, packed up, and above all *studied*—we are the first studious age *in puncto* of "costumes," I mean as concerns morals, articles of belief, artistic tastes, and religions; we are prepared as no other age has ever been for a carnival in the grand style, for the most spiritual festival laughter and arrogance, for the transcendental height of supreme folly and Aristophanic ridicule of the world. Perhaps we are still discovering the domain of our *invention* just here, the domain where even we can still be original, probably as parodists of the world's history and as God's Merry-Andrews,—perhaps, though nothing else of the present have a future, our *laughter* itself may have a future!

224

The *historical sense* (or the capacity for divining quickly the order of rank of the valuations according to which a people, a community, or an individual has lived, the "divining instinct" for the relationships of these valuations, for the relation of the authority of the valuations to the authority of the operating forces),—this historical sense, which we Europeans claim as our specialty, has come to us in the train of the enchanting and mad *semi-barbarity* into which Europe has been plunged by the democratic mingling of classes and races—it is only the nineteenth century that has recognised this faculty as its sixth sense. Owing to this mingling, the past of every form and

mode of life, and of cultures which were formerly closely
contiguous and superimposed on one another, flows forth into
us "modern souls"; our instincts now run back in all directions,
we ourselves are a kind of chaos: in the end, as we have said,
the spirit perceives its advantage therein. By means of our
semi-barbarity in body and in desire, we have secret access
everywhere, such as a noble age never had; we have access
above all to the labyrinth of imperfect civilisations, and to
every form of semi-barbarity that has at any time existed on
earth; and in so far as the most considerable part of human
civilisation hitherto has just been semi-barbarity, the "historical sense" implies almost the sense and instinct for everything,
the taste and tongue for everything: whereby it immediately
proves itself to be an *ignoble* sense. For instance, we enjoy
Homer once more: it is perhaps our happiest acquisition that
we know how to appreciate Homer, whom men of distinguished culture (as the French of the seventeenth century, like
Saint-Evremond, who reproached him for his *esprit vaste,* and
even Voltaire, the last echo of the century) cannot and could
not so easily appropriate—whom they scarcely permitted themselves to enjoy. The very decided Yea and Nay of their palate,
their promptly ready disgust, their hesitating reluctance with
regard to everything strange, their horror of the bad taste even
of lively curiosity, and in general the averseness of every
distinguished and self-sufficing culture to avow a new desire, a
dissatisfaction with its own condition, or an admiration of
what is strange: all this determines and disposes them un-
favourably even towards the best things of the world which
are not their property or *could not* become their prey—and no
faculty is more unintelligible to such men than just this historical sense, with its truckling, plebeian curiosity. The case is
not different with Shakespeare, that marvellous Spanish-

Moorish-Saxon synthesis of taste, over whom an ancient
Athenian of the circle of Æschylus would have half-killed himself with laughter or irritation: but we—accept precisely this
wild motleyness, this medley of the most delicate, the most
coarse, and the most artificial, with a secret confidence and cor-
diality; we enjoy it as a refinement of art reserved expressly for
us, and allow ourselves to be as little disturbed by the repulsive
fumes and the proximity of the English populace in which
Shakespeare's art and taste live, as perhaps on the Chiaja of
Naples, where, with all our senses awake, we go our way,
enchanted and voluntarily, in spite of the drain-odour of the
lower quarters of the town. That as men of the "historical
sense" we have our virtues, is not to be disputed:—we are un-
pretentious, unselfish, modest, brave, habituated to self-control
and self-renunciation, very grateful, very patient, very com-
plaisant—but with all this we are perhaps not very "tasteful."
Let us finally confess it, that what is most difficult for us men
of the "historical sense" to grasp, feel, taste, and love, what
finds us fundamentally prejudiced and almost hostile, is precisely the perfection and ultimate maturity in every culture and
art, the essentially noble in works and men, their moment of
smooth sea and halcyon self-sufficiency, the goldenness and
coldness which all things show that have perfected themselves.
Perhaps our great virtue of the historical sense is in necessary
contrast to *good* taste, at least to the very bad taste; and we can
only evoke in ourselves imperfectly, hesitatingly, and with
compulsion the small, short, and happy godsends and glori-
fications of human life as they shine here and there: those
moments and marvellous experiences when a great power has
voluntarily come to a halt before the boundless and infinite,—
when a superabundance of refined delight has been enjoyed by
a sudden checking and petrifying, by standing firmly and

[528]

planting oneself fixedly on still trembling ground. *Proportionateness* is strange to us, let us confess it to ourselves; our itching is really the itching for the infinite, the immeasurable. Like the rider on his forward panting horse, we let the reins fall before the infinite, we modern men, we semi-barbarians —and are only in *our* highest bliss when we—*are in most danger*.

225

Whether it be hedonism, pessimism, utilitarianism, or eudæmonism, all those modes of thinking which measure the worth of things according to *pleasure* and *pain,* that is, according to accompanying circumstances and secondary considerations, are plausible modes of thought and naïvetés, which every one conscious of *creative* powers and an artist's conscience will look down upon with scorn, though not without sympathy. Sympathy for *you!*—to be sure, that is not sympathy as you understand it: it is not sympathy for social "distress," for "society" with its sick and misfortuned, for the hereditarily vicious and defective who lie on the ground around us; still less is it sympathy for the grumbling, vexed, revolutionary slave-classes who strive after power—they call it "freedom." *Our* sympathy is a loftier and further-sighted sympathy:—we see how *man* dwarfs himself, how *you* dwarf him! and there are moments when we view *your* sympathy with an indescribable anguish, when we resist it,—when we regard your seriousness as more dangerous than any kind of levity. You want, if possible—and there is not a more foolish "if possible"—*to do away with suffering;* and we?—it really seems that *we* would rather have it increased and made worse than it has ever been! Well-being, as you understand it—is certainly not a goal;

[529]

it seems to us an *end;* a condition which at once renders man ludicrous and contemptible—and makes his destruction *desirable!* The discipline of suffering, of *great* suffering—know ye not that it is only *this* discipline that has produced all the elevations of humanity hitherto? The tension of soul in misfortune which communicates to it its energy, its shuddering in view of rack and ruin, its inventiveness and bravery in undergoing, enduring, interpreting, and exploiting misfortune, and whatever depth, mystery, disguise, spirit, artifice, or greatness has been bestowed upon the soul—has it not been bestowed through suffering, through the discipline of great suffering? In man *creature* and *creator* are united: in man there is not only matter, shred, excess, clay, mire, folly, chaos; but there is also the creator, the sculptor, the hardness of the hammer, the divinity of the spectator, and the seventh day—do ye understand this contrast? And that *your* sympathy for the "creature in man" applies to that which has to be fashioned, bruised, forged, stretched, roasted, annealed, refined—to that which must necessarily *suffer,* and *is meant* to suffer? And *our* sympathy—do ye not understand what our *reverse* sympathy applies to, when it resists your sympathy as the worst of all pampering and enervation?—So it is sympathy *against* sympathy!—But to repeat it once more, there are higher problems than the problems of pleasure and pain and sympathy; and all systems of philosophy which deal only with these are naïvetés.

226

We Immoralists.—This world with which *we* are concerned, in which *we* have to fear and love, this almost invisible, inaudible world of delicate command and delicate obedience, a world of "almost" in every respect, captious, insidious, sharp, and tender—yes, it is well protected from clumsy spectators and familiar curiosity! We are woven into a strong net and garment of duties, and *cannot* disengage ourselves—precisely here, we are "men of duty," even we! Occasionally it is true we dance in our "chains" and betwixt our "swords"; it is none the less true that more often we gnash our teeth under the circumstances, and are impatient at the secret hardship of our lot. But do what we will, fools and appearances say of us: "these are men *without* duty,"—we have always fools and appearances against us!

227

Honesty, granting that it is the virtue from which we cannot rid ourselves, we free spirits—well, we will labour at it with all our perversity and love, and not tire of "perfecting" ourselves in *our* virtue, which alone remains: may its glance some day overspread like a gilded, blue, mocking twilight this aging civilisation with its dull gloomy seriousness! And if, nevertheless, our honesty should one day grow weary, and sigh, and stretch its limbs, and find us too hard, and would fain have it pleasanter, easier, and gentler, like an agreeable vice, let us remain *hard,* we latest Stoics, and let us send to its help whatever devilry we have in us:—our disgust at the clumsy and undefined, our *"nitimur in vetitum,"* our love of adventure, our sharpened and fastidious curiosity, our most subtle, disguised, intellectual Will to Power and universal conquest, which rambles and roves avidiously around all the realms of the future—let us go with all our "devils" to the help of our "God"! It is probable that people will misunderstand and mistake us on that account: what does it matter! They will say: "Their 'honesty'—that is their devilry, and nothing else!" What does it matter! And even if they were right—have not all Gods hitherto been such sanctified, re-baptized devils? And after all, what do we know of ourselves? And what the spirit that leads us wants *to be called?* (It is a question of names.) And how many spirits we harbour? Our honesty, we free spirits—let us be careful lest it become our vanity, our ornament and ostentation, our limitation, our stupidity! Every virtue inclines to stupidity, every stupidity to virtue; "stupid to the point of sanctity," they say in Russia,—let us be careful lest out of pure honesty we do not eventually become saints and bores! Is not life a hundred times too short for us—to bore ourselves? One would have to believe in eternal life in order to. . . .

228

I hope to be forgiven for discovering that all moral philosophy hitherto has been tedious and has belonged to the soporific appliances—and that "virtue," in my opinion, has been *more* injured by the *tediousness* of its advocates than by anything else; at the same time, however, I would not wish to overlook their general usefulness. It is desirable that as few people as possible should reflect upon morals, and consequently it is *very* desirable that morals should not some day become interesting! But let us not be afraid! Things still remain today as they have always been: I see no one in Europe who has (or *discloses*) an idea of the fact that philosophising concerning morals might be conducted in a dangerous, captious, and ensnaring manner—that *calamity* might be involved therein.

Observe, for example, the indefatigable, inevitable English utilitarians: how ponderously and respectably they stalk on, stalk along (a Homeric metaphor expresses it better) in the footsteps of Bentham, just as he had already stalked in the footsteps of the respectable Helvétius! (no, he was not a dangerous man, Helvétius, *ce sénateur Pococurante,* to use an expression of Galiani). No new thought, nothing of the nature of a finer turning or better expression of an old thought, not even a proper history of what has been previously thought on the subject: an *impossible* literature, taking it all in all, unless one knows how to leaven it with some mischief. In effect, the old English vice called *cant,* which is *moral Tartuffism,* has insinuated itself also into these moralists (whom one must certainly read with an eye to their motives if one *must* read them), concealed this time under the new form of the scientific spirit; moreover, there is not absent from them a secret struggle with the pangs of conscience, from which a race of former Puritans must naturally suffer, in all their scientific tinkering with morals. (Is not a moralist the opposite of a Puritan? That is to say, as a thinker who regards morality as questionable, as worthy of interrogation, in short, as a problem? Is moralising not—immoral?) In the end, they all want *English* morality to be recognised as authoritative, inasmuch as mankind, or the "general utility," or "the happiness of the greatest number,"—no! the happiness of *England,* will be best served thereby. They would like, by all means, to convince themselves that the striving after *English* happiness, I mean after *comfort* and *fashion* (and in the highest instance, a seat in Parliament), is at the same time the true path of virtue; in fact, that in so far as there has been virtue in the world hitherto, it has just consisted in such striving. Not one of those ponderous, conscience-stricken herding-animals (who undertake to advocate the cause of egoism as conducive to the general welfare) wants to have any knowledge or inkling of the facts that the "general welfare" is no ideal, no goal, no notion that can be at all grasped, but is only a nostrum,—that what is fair to one *may not* at all be fair to another, that the requirement of one morality for all is really a detriment to higher men, in short, that there is a *distinction of rank* between man and man, and consequently between morality and morality. They are an unassuming and fundamentally mediocre species of men, these utilitarian Englishmen, and, as already remarked, in so far as they are tedious, one cannot think highly enough of their utility. One ought even to *encourage* them, as has been partially attempted in the following rhymes:—

> Hail, ye worthies, barrow-wheeling,
> "Longer—better," aye revealing,
>   Stiffer aye in head and knee;
> Unenraptured, never jesting,
> Mediocre everlasting,
>   *Sans genie et sans esprit!*

229

In these later ages, which may be proud of their humanity, there still remains so much fear, so much *superstition* of the fear, of the "cruel wild beast," the mastering of which constitutes the very pride of these humaner ages—that even obvious truths, as if by the agreement of centuries, have long remained unuttered, because they have the appearance of helping the finally slain wild beast back to life again. I perhaps risk something when I allow such a truth to escape; let others capture it again and give it so much "milk of pious sentiment" * to drink, that it will lie down quiet and forgotten, in its old corner.—One ought to learn anew about cruelty, and open one's eyes; one ought at last to learn impatience, in order that such immodest gross errors—as, for instance, have been fostered by ancient and modern philosophers with regard to tragedy—may no longer wander about virtuously and boldly. Almost everything that we call "higher culture" is based upon the spiritualising and intensifying of *cruelty*—this is my thesis; the "wild beast" has not been slain at all, it lives, it flourishes, it has only been—transfigured. That which constitutes the painful delight of tragedy is cruelty; that which operates agreeably in so-called tragic sympathy, and at the basis even of everything sublime, up to the highest and most delicate thrills of metaphysics, obtains its sweetness solely from the intermingled ingredient of cruelty. What the Roman enjoys in the arena, the Christian in the ecstasies of the cross, the Spaniard at the sight of the faggot and stake, or of the bull-fight, the present-day Japanese who presses his way to the tragedy, the workman of the Parisian suburbs who has a homesickness for bloody revolutions, the Wagnerienne who, with unhinged will, "undergoes" the performance of "Tristan and Isolde"—what all these enjoy, and strive with mysterious ardour to drink in, is the philtre of the great Circe "cruelty." Here, to be sure, we must put aside entirely the blundering psychology of former times, which could only teach with regard to cruelty that it originated at the sight of the suffering of *others:* there is an abundant, superabundant enjoyment even in one's own suffering, in causing one's own suffering—and wherever man has allowed himself to be persuaded to self-denial in the *religious* sense, or to self-

---

* An expression from Schiller's *William Tell,* Act IV, Scene 3.

mutilation, as among the Phœnicians and ascetics, or in general, to desensualisation, decarnalisation, and contrition, to Puritanical repentance-spasms, to vivisection of conscience and to Pascal-like *sacrifizia dell' intelleto,* he is secretly allured and impelled forwards by his cruelty, by the dangerous thrill of cruelty *towards himself.*—Finally, let us consider that even the seeker of knowledge operates as an artist and glorifier of cruelty, in that he compels his spirit to perceive *against* its own inclination, and often enough against the wishes of his heart: —he forces it to say Nay, where he would like to affirm, love, and adore; indeed, every instance of taking a thing profoundly and fundamentally, is a violation, an intentional injuring of the fundamental will of the spirit, which instinctively aims at appearance and superficiality,—even in every desire for knowledge there is a drop of cruelty.

230

Perhaps what I have said here about a "fundamental will of the spirit" may not be understood without further details; I may be allowed a word of explanation.—That imperious something which is popularly called "the spirit," wishes to be master internally and externally, and to feel itself master; it has the will of a multiplicity for a simplicity, a binding, taming, imperious, and essentially ruling will. Its requirements and capacities here, are the same as those assigned by physiologists to everything that lives, grows, and multiplies. The power of the spirit to appropriate foreign elements reveals itself in a strong tendency to assimilate the new to the old, to simplify the manifold, to overlook or repudiate the absolutely contradictory; just as it arbitrarily re-underlines, makes prominent

and falsifies for itself certain traits and lines in the foreign elements, in every portion of the "outside world." Its object
thereby is the incorporation of new "experiences," the assort-
ment of new things in the old arrangements—in short, growth;
or more properly, the *feeling* of growth, the feeling of increased power—is its object. This same will has at its service
an apparently opposed impulse of the spirit, a suddenly
adopted preference of ignorance, of arbitrary shutting out, a
closing of windows, an inner denial of this or that, a prohibition to approach, a sort of defensive attitude against much
that is knowable, a contentment with obscurity, with the shut-
ting-in horizon, an acceptance and approval of ignorance: as
that which is all necessary according to the degree of its appro-
priating power, its "digestive power," to speak figuratively
(and in fact "the spirit" resembles a stomach more than anything else). Here also belong an occasional propensity of the
spirit to let itself be deceived (perhaps with a waggish suspicion that it is *not* so and so, but is only allowed to pass as such),
a delight in uncertainty and ambiguity, an exulting enjoyment
of arbitrary, out-of-the-way narrowness and mystery, of the
too-near, of the foreground, of the magnified, the diminished,
the misshapen, the beautified—an enjoyment of the arbitrariness of all these manifestations of power. Finally, in this connection, there is the not unscrupulous readiness of the spirit to
deceive other spirits and dissemble before them—the constant
pressing and straining of a creating, shaping, changeable
power: the spirit enjoys therein its craftiness and its variety of
disguises, it enjoys also its feeling of security therein—it is
precisely by its Protean arts that it is best protected and concealed!—*Counter to* this propensity for appearance, for simplification, for a disguise, for a cloak, in short, for an outside
—for every outside is a cloak—there operates the sublime

tendency of the man of knowledge, which takes, and *insists* on taking things profoundly, variously, and thoroughly; as a kind of cruelty of the intellectual conscience and taste, which every courageous thinker will acknowledge in himself, provided, as it ought to be, that he has sharpened and hardened his eye sufficiently long for introspection, and is accustomed to severe discipline and even severe words. He will say: "There is something cruel in the tendency of my spirit": let the virtuous and amiable try to convince him that it is not so! In fact, it would sound nicer, if, instead of our cruelty, perhaps our "extravagant honesty" were talked about, whispered about and glorified—we free, *very* free spirits—and some day perhaps *such* will actually be our—posthumous glory! Meanwhile—for there is plenty of time until then—we should be at least inclined to deck ourselves out in such florid and fringed moral verbiage; our whole former work has just made us sick of this taste and its sprightly exuberance. They are beautiful, glistening, jingling, festive words: honesty, love of truth, love of wisdom, sacrifice for knowledge, heroism of the truthful—there is something in them that makes one's heart swell with pride. But we anchorites and marmots have long ago persuaded ourselves in all the secrecy of an anchorite's conscience, that this worthy parade of verbiage also belongs to the old false adornment, frippery, and gold-dust of unconscious human vanity, and that even under such flattering colour and repainting, the terrible original text *homo natura* must again be recognised. In effect, to translate man back again into nature; to master the many vain and visionary interpretations and subordinate meanings which have hitherto been scratched and daubed over the eternal original text, *homo natura;* to bring it about that man shall henceforth stand before man as he now, hardened by the discipline of science, stands before the *other* forms of nature, with fearless Œdipus-eyes, and stopped Ulysses-ears, deaf to the enticements of old metaphysical bird-catchers, who have piped to him far too long: "Thou art more! thou art higher! thou hast a different origin!"—this may be a strange and foolish task, but that it is a *task,* who can deny! Why did we choose it, this foolish task? Or, to put the question differently: "Why knowledge at all?" Every one will ask us about this. And thus pressed, we, who have asked ourselves the question a hundred times, have not found, and cannot find any better answer. . . .

231

Learning alters us, it does what all nourishment does that does not merely "conserve"—as the physiologist knows. But at the bottom of our souls, quite "down below," there is certainly something unteachable, a granite of spiritual fate, of predetermined decision and answer to predetermined, chosen questions. In each cardinal problem there speaks an unchangeable "I am this"; a thinker cannot learn anew about man and woman, for instance, but can only learn fully—he can only follow to the end what is "fixed" about them in himself. Occasionally we find certain solutions of problems which make strong beliefs for *us;* perhaps they are henceforth called "convictions." Later on—one sees in them only footsteps to self-knowledge, guide-posts to the problem which we ourselves *are*—or more correctly to the great stupidity which we embody, our spiritual fate, the *unteachable* in us, quite "down below." —In view of this liberal compliment which I have just paid myself, permission will perhaps be more readily allowed me to utter some truths about "woman as she is," provided that it is known at the outset how literally they are merely—*my* truths.

232

Woman wishes to be independent, and therefore she begins to enlighten men about "woman as she is"—*this* is one of the worst developments of the general *uglifying* of Europe. For what must these clumsy attempts of feminine scientificality and self-exposure bring to light! Woman has so much cause for shame; in woman there is so much pedantry, superficiality, schoolmasterliness, petty presumption, unbridledness, and in-discretion concealed—study only woman's behaviour towards children!—which has really been best restrained and domi-nated hitherto by the *fear* of man. Alas, if ever the "eternally tedious in woman"—she has plenty of it!—is allowed to ven-ture forth! if she begins radically and on principle to unlearn her wisdom and art—of charming, of playing, of frightening away sorrow, of alleviating and taking easily; if she forgets her delicate aptitude for agreeable desires! Female voices are already raised, which, by Saint Aristophanes! make one afraid: —with medical explicitness it is stated in a threatening man-ner what woman first and last *requires* from man. Is it not in the very worst taste that woman thus sets herself up to be scientific? Enlightenment hitherto has fortunately been men's affair, men's gift—we remained therewith "among ourselves"; and in the end, in view of all that women write about "woman," we may well have considerable doubt as to whether woman really *desires* enlightenment about herself—and *can* desire it.

If woman does not thereby seek a new *ornament* for herself—
I believe ornamentation belongs to the eternally feminine?
—why, then, she wishes to make herself feared: perhaps she
thereby wishes to get the mastery. But she does not *want* truth
—what does woman care for truth? From the very first nothing is more foreign, more repugnant, or more hostile to woman
than truth—her great art is falsehood, her chief concern is
appearance and beauty. Let us confess it, we men: we honour
and love *this* very art and *this* very instinct in woman: we who
have the hard task, and for our recreation gladly seek the company of beings under whose hands, glances, and delicate follies, our seriousness, our gravity, and profundity appear almost
like follies to us. Finally, I ask the question: Did a woman
herself acknowledge profundity in a woman's mind, or justice
in a woman's heart? And is it not true that on the whole
"woman" has hitherto been most despised by woman herself,
and not at all by us?—We men desire that woman should not
continue to compromise herself by enlightening us; just as it
was man's care and the consideration for woman, when the
church decreed: *mulier taceat in ecclesia.* It was to the benefit
of woman when Napoleon gave the too eloquent Madame de
Staël to understand: *mulier taceat in politicis!*—and in my
opinion, he is a true friend of woman who calls out to women
to-day: *mulier taceat de muliere!*

233

It betrays corruption of the instincts—apart from the fact
that it betrays bad taste—when a woman refers to Madame
Roland, or Madame de Staël, or Monsieur George Sand, as

though something were proved thereby in *favor* of "woman as she is." Among men, these are the three *comical* women as they are—nothing more!—and just the best involuntary *counter-arguments* against feminine emancipation and autonomy.

234

Stupidity in the kitchen; woman as cook; the terrible thoughtlessness with which the feeding of the family and the master of the house is managed! Woman does not understand what food *means,* and she insists on being cook! If woman had been a thinking creature, she should certainly, as cook for thousands of years, have discovered the most important physiological facts, and should likewise have got possession of the healing art! Through bad female cooks—through the entire lack of reason in the kitchen—the development of mankind has been longest retarded and most interfered with: even to-day matters are very little better.—A word to High School girls.

235

There are turns and casts of fancy, there are sentences, little handfuls of words, in which a whole culture, a whole society suddenly crystallises itself. Among these is the incidental remark of Madame de Lambert to her son: *"Mon ami, ne vous permettez jamais que des folies, qui vous feront grand plaisir"* —the motherliest and wisest remark, by the way, that was ever addressed to a son.

236

I have no doubt that every noble woman will oppose what Dante and Goethe believed about woman—the former when he sang, *"ella guardava suso, ed io in lei,"* and the latter when he interpreted it, "the eternally feminine draws us *aloft";* for *this* is just what she believes of the eternally masculine.

237

Seven Apophthegms for Women

How the longest ennui flees,
When a man comes to our knees!

Age, alas! and science staid,
Furnish even weak virtue aid.

Sombre garb and silence meet:
Dress for every dame—discreet.

Whom I thank when in my bliss?
God!—and my good tailoress!

Young, a flower-decked cavern home;
Old, a dragon thence doth roam.

Noble title, leg that's fine,
Man as well: Oh, were *he* mine!

[543]

Speech in brief and sense in mass—
Slippery for the jenny-ass!

237A

Women have hitherto been treated by men like birds, which, losing their way, have come down among them from an elevation: as something delicate, fragile, wild, strange, sweet, and animating—but as something also which must be cooped up to prevent it flying away.

238

To be mistaken in the fundamental problem of "man and woman," to deny here the profoundest antagonism and the necessity for an eternally hostile tension, to dream here perhaps of equal rights, equal training, equal claims and obligations: that is a *typical* sign of shallow-mindedness; and a thinker who has proved himself shallow at this dangerous spot—shallow in instinct!—may generally be regarded as suspicious, nay more, as betrayed, as discovered; he will probably prove too "short" for all fundamental questions of life, future as well as present, and will be unable to descend into *any* of the depths. On the other hand, a man who has depth of spirit as well as of desires, and has also the depth of benevolence which is capable of severity and harshness, and easily confounded with them, can only think of woman as *Orientals* do: he must conceive of her as a possession, as confinable property, as a being predestined for service and accomplishing her mission therein—he must take his stand in this matter upon the immense rationality of Asia, upon the superiority of the instinct of Asia, as the Greeks did formerly; those best heirs and scholars of Asia— who, as is well known, with their *increasing* culture and amplitude of power, from Homer to the time of Pericles, became gradually *stricter* towards woman, in short, more oriental. *How* necessary, *how* logical, even *how* humanely desirable this was, let us consider for ourselves!

239

The weaker sex has in no previous age been treated with so much respect by men as at present—this belongs to the tendency and fundamental taste of democracy, in the same way as disrespectfulness to old age—what wonder is it that abuse should be immediately made of this respect? They want more, they learn to make claims, the tribute of respect is at last felt to be well-nigh galling: rivalry for rights, indeed actual strife itself, would be preferred: in a word, woman is losing modesty. And let us immediately add that she is also losing taste. She is unlearning to *fear* man: but the woman who "unlearns to fear" sacrifices her most womanly instincts. That woman should venture forward when the fear-inspiring quality in man—or more definitely, the *man* in man—is no longer either desired or fully developed, is reasonable enough and also intelligible enough; what is more difficult to understand is that precisely thereby—woman deteriorates. This is what is happening nowadays: let us not deceive ourselves about it! Wherever the industrial spirit has triumphed over the military and aristocratic spirit, woman strives for the economic and legal independence of a clerk: "woman as clerkess" is inscribed on the portal of the modern society which is in course of formation. While she thus appropriates new rights, aspires to be "master," and inscribes "progress" of woman on her flags and banners, the very opposite realises itself with terrible obviousness: *woman retrogrades.* Since the French Revolution the influence of woman in Europe has *declined* in proportion as she has increased her rights and claims; and the "emancipation of woman," in so far as it is desired and demanded by women themselves (and not only by masculine shallowpates), thus proves to be a remarkable symptom of the increased weakening and deadening of the most womanly instincts. There is *stupidity* in this movement, an almost masculine stupidity, of which a well-reared woman—who is always a sensible woman —might be heartily ashamed. To lose the intuition as to the ground upon which she can most surely achieve victory; to neglect exercise in the use of her proper weapons; to let-herself-go before man, perhaps even "to the book," where formerly she kept herself in control and in refined, artful humility; to neutralise with her virtuous audacity man's faith in a *veiled,* fundamentally different ideal in woman, something eternally, necessarily feminine; to emphatically and loquaciously dissuade man from the idea that woman must be preserved, cared for, protected, and indulged, like some delicate, strangely wild, and often pleasant domestic animal; the clumsy and indignant collection of everything of the nature of servitude and bondage which the position of woman in the hitherto existing order of society has entailed and still entails (as though slavery were a counter-argument, and not rather a condition of every higher culture, of every elevation of culture) :— what does all this betoken, if not a disintegration of womanly instincts, a de-feminising? Certainly, there are enough of idiotic friends and corrupters of woman amongst the learned asses of the masculine sex, who advise woman to de-feminise herself in this manner, and to imitate all the stupidities from which "man" in Europe, European "manliness," suffers,—who would like to lower woman to "general culture," indeed even to newspaper reading and meddling with politics. Here and there they wish even to make women into free spirits and literary workers: as though a woman without piety would not be something perfectly obnoxious or ludicrous to a profound and godless man;—almost everywhere her nerves are being ruined by the most morbid and dangerous kind of music (our latest German music), and she is daily being made more hysterical and more incapable of fulfilling her first and last function, that of bearing robust children. They wish to "cultivate" her in general still more, and intend, as they say, to make the "weaker sex" *strong* by culture: as if history did not teach in the most emphatic manner that the "cultivating" of mankind and his weakening—that is to say, the weakening, dissipating, and languishing of his *force of will*—have always kept pace with one another, and that the most powerful and influential women in the world (and lastly, the mother of Napoleon) had just to thank their force of will—and not their schoolmasters!—for their power and ascendency over men. That which inspires respect in woman, and often enough fear also, is her *nature,* which is more "natural" than that of man, her genuine, carnivora-like, cunning flexibility, her tiger-claws beneath the glove, her *naïveté* in egoism, her untrainableness and innate wildness, the incomprehensibleness, extent and deviation of her desires and virtues. . . . That which, in spite of fear, excites one's sympathy for the dangerous and beautiful cat, "woman," is that she seems more afflicted, more vulnerable, more necessitous of love and more condemned to disillusionment than any other creature. Fear and sympathy: it is with these feelings that man has hitherto stood in the presence of woman, always with

[*547*]

one foot already in tragedy, which rends while it delights.—
What? And all that is now to be at an end? And the *disenchant-ment* of woman is in progress? The tediousness of woman is slowly evolving? Oh Europe! Europe! We know the horned animal which was always most attractive to thee, from which danger is ever again threatening thee! Thy old fable might once more become "history"—an immense stupidity might once again overmaster thee and carry thee away! And no God concealed beneath it—no! only an "idea," a "modern idea"! . . .

8. Peoples and Countries

240

I HEARD, once again for the first time, Richard Wagner's overture to the *Mastersingers:* it is a piece of magnificent, gorgeous, heavy, latter-day art, which has the pride to pre-suppose two centuries of music as still living, in order that it may be understood:—it is an honour to Germans that such a pride did not miscalculate! What flavours and forces, what seasons and climes do we not find mingled in it! It impresses us at one time as ancient, at another time as foreign, bitter, and too modern, it is as arbitrary as it is pompously traditional, it is not infrequently roguish, still oftener rough and coarse—it has fire and courage, and at the same time the loose, dun-coloured skin of fruits which ripen too late. It flows broad and full: and suddenly there is a moment of inexplicable hesitation, like a gap that opens between cause and effect, an oppression that makes us dream, almost a nightmare; but already it broadens and widens anew, the old stream of delight—the most manifold delight,—of old and new happiness; including *especially* the joy of the artist in himself, which he refuses to conceal, his astonished, happy cognisance of his mastery of the expedients here employed, the new, newly acquired, imperfectly tested expedients of art which he apparently betrays to us. All in all, however, no beauty, no South, nothing of the delicate southern clearness of the sky, nothing of grace, no dance, hardly a will to logic; a certain clumsiness even, which is also emphasised, as though the artist wished to say to us: "It is part of my intention"; a cumbersome drapery, something arbitrarily barbaric and ceremonious, a flirring of learned and venerable conceits and witticisms; something German in the best and worst sense of the word, something in the German style, manifold, formless, and inexhaustible; a certain German potency and super-plenitude of soul, which is not afraid to hide itself under the *raffinements* of decadence—which, perhaps, feels itself most at ease here; a real, genuine token of the German soul, which is at the same time young and aged, too ripe and yet still too rich in futurity. This kind of music expresses best what I think of the Germans: they belong to the day before yesterday and the day after tomorrow—*they have as yet no today.*

241

We "good Europeans," we also have hours when we allow ourselves a warm-hearted patriotism, a plunge and relapse into old loves and narrow views—I have just given an example of it—hours of national excitement, of patriotic anguish, and all other sorts of old-fashioned floods of sentiment. Duller spirits may perhaps only get done with what confines its operations in us to hours and plays itself out in hours—in a considerable time: some in half a year, others in half a lifetime, according to the speed and strength with which they digest and "change their material." Indeed, I could think of sluggish, hesitating races, which even in our rapidly moving Europe, would require half a century ere they could surmount such atavistic attacks of patriotism and soil-attachment, and return once more to reason, that is to say, to "good Europeanism." And while digressing on this possibility, I happen to become an ear-witness of a conversation between two old patriots—they were evidently both hard of hearing and consequently spoke all the louder. "*He* has as much, and knows as much, philosophy as a peasant or a corps-student," said the one—"he is still innocent. But what does that matter nowadays! It is the age of the masses: they lie on their belly before everything that is massive. And so also *in politicis*. A statesman who rears up for them a new Tower of Babel, some monstrosity of empire and power, they call 'great'—what does it matter that we more prudent and conservative ones do not meanwhile give up the old belief that it is only the great thought that gives greatness to an action or affair. Supposing a statesman were to bring his people into the position of being obliged henceforth to practise 'high politics,' for which they were by nature badly endowed and prepared, so that they would have to sacrifice their old and reliable virtues, out of love to a new and doubtful mediocrity;—supposing a statesman were to condemn his people generally to 'practise politics,' when they have hitherto had something better to do and think about, and when in the depths of their souls they have been unable to free themselves from a prudent loathing of the restlessness, emptiness, and noisy wranglings of the essentially politics-practising nations;—supposing such a statesman were to stimulate the slumbering passions and avidities of his people, were to make a stigma out of their former diffidence and delight in aloofness, an offence out of their exoticism and hidden permanency, were to depreciate their most radical proclivities, subvert their consciences, make their minds narrow, and their tastes 'national'—what! a statesman who should do all this, which his people would have to do penance for throughout their whole future, if they had a future, such a statesman would be *great,* would he?"—"Undoubtedly!" replied the other old patriot vehemently; "otherwise he *could not* have done it! It was mad perhaps to wish such a thing! But perhaps everything great has been just as mad at its commencement!"—"Misuse of words!" cried his interlocutor, contradictorily—"strong! strong! Strong and mad! *Not* great!"—The old men had obviously become heated as they thus shouted their "truths" in each other's faces; but I, in my happiness and apartness, considered how soon a stronger one may become master of the strong; and also that there is a compensation for the intellectual superficialising of a nation— namely, in the deepening of another.

242

Whether we call it "civilisation," or "humanising," or "progress," which now distinguishes the European; whether we call it simply, without praise or blame, by the political formula: the *democratic* movement in Europe—behind all the moral and political foregrounds pointed to by such formulas, an immense *physiological process* goes on, which is ever extending: the process of the assimilation of Europeans; their increasing detachment from the conditions under which, climatically and hereditarily, united races originate; their increasing independence of every definite *milieu,* that for centuries would fain inscribe itself with equal demands on soul and body;—that is to say, the slow emergence of an essentially *super-national* and nomadic species of man, who possesses, physiologically speaking, a maximum of the art and power of adaptation as his typical distinction. This process of the *evolving European,* which can be retarded in its *tempo* by great relapses, but will perhaps just gain and grow thereby in vehemence and depth—the still raging storm and stress of "national sentiment" pertains to it, and also the anarchism which is appearing at present—this process will probably arrive at results on which its naïve propagators and panegyrists, the apostles of "modern ideas," would least care to reckon. The same new conditions under which on an average a levelling and mediocrising of man will take place—a useful, industrious, variously serviceable and clever gregarious man—are in the highest degree suitable to give rise to exceptional men of the most dangerous and attractive qualities. For, while the capacity for adaptation, which is every day trying changing conditions, and begins a new work with every generation, almost with every decade, makes the *powerfulness* of the type impossible; while the collective impression of such future Europeans will probably be that of numerous, talkative, weak-willed, and very handy workmen who *require* a master, a commander, as they require their daily bread; while, therefore, the democratising of Europe will tend to the production of a type prepared for *slavery* in the most subtle sense of the term: the *strong* man will necessarily in individual and exceptional cases, become stronger and richer than he has perhaps ever been before—owing to the unprejudicedness of his schooling, owing to the immense variety of practice, art, and disguise. I meant to say that the democratising of Europe is at the same

time an involuntary arrangement for the rearing of *tyrants*—
taking the word in all its meanings, even in its most spiritual
sense.

243

I hear with pleasure that our sun is moving rapidly towards
the constellation *Hercules:* and I hope that the men on this
earth will do like the sun. And we foremost, we good
Europeans!

244

There was a time when it was customary to call Germans
"deep" by way of distinction; but now that the most successful
type of new Germanism is covetous of quite other honours, and
perhaps misses "smartness" in all that has depth, it is almost
opportune and patriotic to doubt whether we did not formerly
deceive ourselves with that commendation: in short, whether
German depth is not at bottom something different and worse
—and something from which, thank God, we are on the point
of successfully ridding ourselves. Let us try, then, to relearn
with regard to German depth; the only thing necessary
for the purpose is a little vivisection of the German soul.—
The German soul is above all manifold, varied in its source,
aggregated and superimposed, rather than actually built: this
is owing to its origin. A German who would embolden himself
to assert: "Two souls, alas, dwell in my breast," would make a
bad guess at the truth, or, more correctly, he would come far
short of the truth about the number of souls. As a people made
up of the most extraordinary mixing and mingling of races,
perhaps even with a preponderance of the pre-Aryan element,

as the "people of the centre" in every sense of the term, the Germans are more intangible, more ample, more contradictory, more unknown, more incalculable, more surprising, and even more terrifying than other peoples are to themselves:—they escape *definition,* and are thereby alone the despair of the French. It is characteristic of the Germans that the question: "What is German?" never dies out among them. Kotzebue certainly knew his Germans well enough: "we are known," they cried jubilantly to him—but Sand also thought he knew them. Jean Paul knew what he was doing when he declared himself incensed at Fichte's lying but patriotic flatteries and exaggerations,—but it is probable that Goethe thought differently about Germans from Jean Paul, even though he acknowledged him to be right with regard to Fichte. It is a question what Goethe really thought about the Germans?—But about many things around him he never spoke explicitly, and all his life he knew how to keep an astute silence—probably he had good reason for it. It is certain that it was not the "Wars of Independence" that made him look up more joyfully, any more than it was the French Revolution,—the event on account of which he *reconstructed* his "Faust," and indeed the whole problem of "man," was the appearance of Napoleon. There are words of Goethe in which he condemns with impatient severity, as from a foreign land, that which Germans take a pride in: he once defined the famous German turn of mind as "Indulgence towards its own and others' weaknesses." Was he wrong? it is characteristic of Germans that one is seldom entirely wrong about them. The German soul has passages and galleries in it, there are caves, hiding-places, and dungeons therein; its disorder has much of the charm of the mysterious; the German is well acquainted with the by-paths to chaos. And as everything loves its symbol, so the German loves the clouds and all that is ob-

scure, evolving, crepuscular, damp, and shrouded: it seems to
him that everything uncertain, undeveloped, self-displacing,
and growing is "deep." The German himself does not *exist:*
he is *becoming,* he is "developing himself." "Development" is
therefore the essentially German discovery and hit in the great
domain of philosophical formulas,—a ruling idea, which, together with German beer and German music, is labouring
to Germanise all Europe. Foreigners are astonished and attracted by the riddles which the conflicting nature at the basis
of the German soul propounds to them (riddles which Hegel
systematised and Richard Wagner has in the end set to music).
"Good-natured and spiteful"—such a juxtaposition, prepos-
terous in the case of every other people, is unfortunately only
too often justified in Germany: one has only to live for a while
among Swabians to know this! The clumsiness of the German
scholar and his social distastefulness agree alarmingly well
with his physical rope-dancing and nimble boldness, of which
all the Gods have learned to be afraid. If any one wishes to see
the "German soul" demonstrated *ad oculos,* let him only look
at German taste, at German arts and manners: what boorish
indifference to "taste"! How the noblest and the commonest
stand there in juxtaposition! How disorderly and how rich is
the whole constitution of this soul! The German *drags* at his
soul, he drags at everything he experiences. He digests his
events badly; he never gets "done" with them; and German
depth is often only a difficult, hesitating "digestion." And just
as all chronic invalids, all dyspeptics, like what is convenient,
so the German loves "frankness" and "honesty"; it is so *convenient* to be frank and honest!—This confidingness, this
complaisance, this showing-the-cards of German *honesty,* is
probably the most dangerous and most successful disguise
which the German is up to nowadays: it is his proper Mephis-

tophelean art; with this he can "still achieve much"! The German lets himself go, and thereby gazes with faithful, blue, empty German eyes—and other countries immediately confound him with his dressing-gown!—I meant to say that, let "German depth" be what it will—among ourselves alone we perhaps take the liberty to laugh at it—we shall do well to continue henceforth to honour its appearance and good name, and not barter away too cheaply our old reputation as a people of depth for Prussian "smartness," and Berlin wit and sand. It is wise for a people to pose, and *let* itself be regarded, as profound, clumsy, good-natured, honest, and foolish: it might even be—profound to do so! Finally, we should do honour to our name—we are not called the *"tiusche Volk"* (deceptive people) for nothing. . . .

245

The "good old" time is past, it sang itself out in Mozart— how happy are *we* that his *rococo* still speaks to us, that his "good company," his tender enthusiasm, his childish delight in the Chinese and its flourishes, his courtesy of heart, his longing for the elegant, the amorous, the tripping, the tearful, and his belief in the South, can still appeal to *something left* in us! Ah, some time or other it will be over with it!—but who can doubt that it will be over still sooner with the intelligence and taste for Beethoven! For he was only the last echo of a break and transition in style, and *not,* like Mozart, the last echo of a great European taste which had existed for centuries. Beethoven is the intermediate event between an old mellow soul that is constantly breaking down, and a future over-young soul that is always *coming;* there is spread over his music the twilight of eternal loss and eternal extravagant hope,—the same light in which Europe was bathed when it dreamed with Rousseau, when it danced round the Tree of Liberty of the Revolution, and finally almost fell down in adoration before Napoleon. But how rapidly does *this* very sentiment now pale, how difficult nowadays is even the *apprehension* of this sentiment, how strangely does the language of Rousseau, Schiller, Shelley, and Byron sound to our ear, in whom *collectively* the same fate of Europe was able to *speak*, which knew how to *sing* in Beethoven!—Whatever German music came afterwards, belongs to Romanticism, that is to say, to a movement which, historically considered, was still shorter, more fleeting, and more superficial than that great interlude, the transition of Europe from Rousseau to Napoleon, and to the rise of democracy. Weber— but what do *we* care nowadays for "Freischütz" and "Oberon"! Or Marschner's "Hans Heiling" and "Vampyre"! Or even Wagner's "Tannhäuser"! That is extinct, although not yet forgotten music. This whole music of Romanticism, besides, was not noble enough, was not musical enough, to maintain its position anywhere but in the theatre and before the masses; from the beginning it was second-rate music, which was little thought of by genuine musicians. It was different with Felix Mendelssohn, that halcyon master, who, on account of his lighter, purer, happier soul, quickly acquired admiration, and was equally quickly forgotten: as the beautiful *episode* of German music. But with regard to Robert Schumann, who took things seriously, and has been taken seriously from the first— he was the last that founded a school,—do we not now regard it as a satisfaction, a relief, a deliverance, that this very Romanticism of Schumann's has been surmounted? Schumann, fleeing into the "Saxon Switzerland" of his soul, with a half

Werther-like, half Jean-Paul-like nature (assuredly not like Beethoven! assuredly not like Byron!)—his *Manfred* music is a mistake and a misunderstanding to the extent of injustice; Schumann, with his taste, which was fundamentally a *petty* taste (that is to say, a dangerous propensity—doubly dangerous among Germans—for quiet lyricism and intoxication of the feelings), going constantly apart, timidly withdrawing and retiring, a noble weakling who revelled in nothing but anonymous joy and sorrow, from the beginning a sort of girl and *noli me tangere*—this Schumann was already merely a *German* event in music, and no longer a European event, as Beethoven had been, as in a still greater degree Mozart had been; with Schumann German music was threatened with its greatest danger, that of *losing the voice for the soul of Europe* and sinking into a merely national affair.

246

What a torture are books written in German to a reader who has a *third* ear! How indignantly he stands beside the slowly turning swamp of sounds without tune and rhythms without dance, which Germans call a "book"! And even the German who *reads* books! How lazily, how reluctantly, how badly he reads! How many Germans know, and consider it obligatory to know, that there is *art* in every good sentence—art which must be divined, if the sentence is to be understood! If there is a misunderstanding about its *tempo,* for instance, the sentence itself is misunderstood! That one must not be doubtful about the rhythm-determining syllables, that one should feel the breaking of the too-rigid symmetry as intentional and as a charm, that one should lend a fine and patient ear to every *staccato* and every *rubato,* that one should divine the sense in the sequence of the vowels and diphthongs, and how delicately and richly they can be tinted and retinted in the order of their arrangement—who among book-reading Germans is com-plaisant enough to recognise such duties and requirements, and to listen to so much art and intention in language? After all, one just "has no ear for it"; and so the most marked con trasts of style are not heard, and the most delicate artistry is as it were *squandered* on the deaf.—These were my thoughts when I noticed how clumsily and unintuitively two masters in the art of prose-writing have been confounded: one, whose words drop down hesitatingly and coldly, as from the roof of a damp cave—he counts on their dull sound and echo; and another who manipulates his language like a flexible sword, and from his arm down into his toes feels the dangerous bliss of the quivering, over-sharp blade, which wishes to bite, hiss, and cut.

247

How little the German style has to do with harmony and with the ear, is shown by the fact that precisely our good musi-cians themselves write badly. The German does not read aloud, he does not read for the ear, but only with his eyes; he has put his ears away in the drawer for the time. In antiquity when a man read—which was seldom enough—he read something to himself, and in a loud voice; they were surprised when any one read silently, and sought secretly the reason of it. In a loud voice: that is to say, with all the swellings, inflections, and variations of key and changes of *tempo,* in which the ancient *public* world took delight. The laws of the written style were then the same as those of the spoken style; and these laws depended partly on the surprising development and refined requirements of the ear and larynx; partly on the strength, endurance, and power of the ancient lungs. In the ancient sense, a period is above all a physiological whole, inasmuch as it is comprised in one breath. Such periods as occur in Demosthenes and Cicero, swelling twice and sinking twice, and all in one breath, were pleasures to the men of *antiquity,* who knew by their own schooling how to appreciate the virtue therein, the rareness and the difficulty in the deliverance of such a period;—*we* have really no right to the *big* period, we modern men, who are short of breath in every sense! Those ancients, indeed, were all of them dilettanti in speaking, consequently connoisseurs, consequently critics—they thus brought their orators to the highest pitch; in the same manner as in the last century, when all Italian ladies and gentlemen knew how to sing, the virtuosoship of song (and with it also the art of melody) reached its elevation. In Germany, however (until quite recently when a kind of platform eloquence began shyly and awkwardly enough to flutter its young wings), there was properly speaking only one kind of public and *approximately* artistic discourse—that delivered from the pulpit. The preacher was the only one in Germany who knew the weight of a syllable or a word, in what manner a sentence strikes, springs, rushes, flows, and comes to a close; he alone had a conscience in his ears, often enough a bad conscience: for reasons are not lacking why proficiency in oratory should be especially seldom attained by a German, or almost always too late. The masterpiece of German prose is therefore with good reason the masterpiece of its greatest preacher: the *Bible* has hitherto been the best German book. Compared with Luther's

Bible, almost everything else is merely "literature"—something which has not grown in Germany, and therefore has not taken and does not take root in German hearts, as the Bible has done.

248

There are two kinds of geniuses: one which above all engenders and seeks to engender, and another which willingly lets itself be fructified and brings forth. And similarly, among the gifted nations, there are those on whom the woman's problem of pregnancy has devolved, and the secret task of forming, maturing, and perfecting—the Greeks, for instance, were a nation of this kind, and so are the French; and others which have to fructify and become the cause of new modes of life— like the Jews, the Romans, and, in all modesty be it asked: like the Germans?—nations tortured and enraptured by unknown fevers and irresistibly forced out of themselves, amorous and longing for foreign races (for such as "let themselves be fructified"), and withal imperious, like everything conscious of being full of generative force, and consequently empowered "by the grace of God." These two kinds of geniuses seek each other like man and woman; but they also misunderstand each other—like man and woman.

249

Every nation has its own "Tartuffery," and calls that its virtue.—One does not know—cannot know, the best that is in one.

250

What Europe owes to the Jews?—Many things, good and bad, and above all one thing of the nature both of the best and the worst: the grand style in morality, the fearfulness and majesty of infinite demands, of infinite significations, the whole Romanticism and sublimity of moral questionableness —and consequently just the most attractive, ensnaring, and exquisite element in those iridescences and allurements to life, in the aftersheen of which the sky of our European culture, its evening sky, now glows—perhaps glows out. For this, we artists among the spectators and philosophers, are—grateful to the Jews.

251

It must be taken into the bargain, if various clouds and disturbances—in short, slight attacks of stupidity—pass over the spirit of a people that suffers and *wants* to suffer from national nervous fever and political ambition: for instance, among present-day Germans there is alternately the anti-French folly, the anti-Semitic folly, the anti-Polish folly, the Christian-romantic folly, the Wagnerian folly, the Teutonic folly, the Prussian folly (just look at those poor historians, the Sybels and Treitschkes, and their closely bandaged heads), and whatever else these little obscurations of the German spirit and conscience may be called. May it be forgiven me that I, too, when on a short daring sojourn on very infected ground, did not remain wholly exempt from the disease, but like every one else, began to entertain thoughts about matters which did not concern me—the first symptom of political infection. About the Jews, for instance, listen to the following:—I have never yet met a German who was favourably inclined to the Jews; and however decided the repudiation of actual anti-Semitism may be on the part of all prudent and political men, this prudence and policy is not perhaps directed against the nature of the sentiment itself, but only against its dangerous excess, and especially against the distasteful and infamous expression of this excess of sentiment;—on this point we must not deceive ourselves. That Germany has amply *sufficient* Jews, that the German stomach, the German blood, has difficulty (and will long have difficulty) in disposing only of this quantity of "Jew"—as the Italian, the Frenchman, and the Englishman have done by means of a stronger digestion:—that is the un-mistakable declaration and language of a general instinct, to which one must listen and according to which one must act. "Let no more Jews come in! And shut the doors, especially towards the East (also towards Austria)!"—thus commands the instinct of a people whose nature is still feeble and uncer-tain, so that it could be easily wiped out, easily extinguished, by a stronger race. The Jews, however, are beyond all doubt the strongest, toughest, and purest race at present living in Europe; they know how to succeed even under the worst con-ditions (in fact better than under favourable ones), by means of virtues of some sort, which one would like nowadays to label as vices—owing above all to a resolute faith which does not need to be ashamed before "modern ideas"; they alter only, *when* they do alter, in the same way that the Russian Empire makes its conquest—as an empire that has plenty of time and is not of yesterday—namely, according to the principle, "as slowly as possible"! A thinker who has the future of Europe at heart, will, in all his perspectives concerning the future, calculate upon the Jews, as he will calculate upon the Russians, as above all the surest and likeliest factors in the great play and battle of forces. That which is at present called a "nation" in Europe, and is really rather a *res facta* than *nata* (indeed, sometimes confusingly similar to a *res ficta et picta*), is in every case something evolving, young, easily displaced, and not yet a race, much less such a race *aere perennius,* as the Jews are: such "nations" should most carefully avoid all hot-headed rivalry and hostility! It is certain that the Jews, if they desired—or if they were driven to it, as the anti-Semites seem to wish—*could* now have the ascendency, nay, literally the supremacy, over Europe; that they are *not* working and planning for that end is equally certain. Meanwhile, they rather wish and desire, even somewhat importunely, to be insorbed and absorbed by Europe; they long to be finally settled, authorised, and respected somewhere, and wish to put an end to the nomadic life, to the "wandering Jew";—and one should certainly take account of this impulse and tendency, and *make advances* to it (it possibly betokens a mitigation of the Jewish instincts) : for which purpose it would perhaps be useful and fair to banish the anti-Semitic bawlers out of the country. One should make advances with all prudence, and with selection; pretty much as the English nobility do. It stands to reason that the more powerful and strongly marked types of new Germanism could enter into relation with the Jews with the least hesitation, for instance, the nobleman officer from the Prussian border: it would be interesting in many ways to see whether the genius for money and patience (and especially some intellect and intellectuality —sadly lacking in the place referred to) could not in addition be annexed and trained to the hereditary art of commanding and obeying—for both of which the country in question has now a classic reputation. But here it is expedient to break off my festal discourse and my sprightly Teutonomania: for I have already reached my *serious topic,* the "European problem," as I understand it, the rearing of a new ruling caste for Europe.

252

They are not a philosophical race——the English: Bacon represents an *attack* on the philosophical spirit generally, Hobbes, Hume, and Locke, an abasement, and a depreciation of the idea of a "philosopher" for more than a century. It was *against* Hume that Kant uprose and raised himself; it was Locke of whom Schelling *rightly* said, *"Je méprise Locke";* in the struggle against the English mechanical stultification of the world, Hegel and Schopenhauer (along with Goethe) were of one accord; the two hostile brother-geniuses in philosophy, who pushed in different directions towards the opposite poles of German thought, and thereby wronged each other as only brothers will do.——What is lacking in England, and has always been lacking, that half-actor and rhetorician knew well enough, the absurd muddle-head, Carlyle, who sought to conceal under passionate grimaces what he knew about himself: namely, what was *lacking* in Carlyle——real *power* of intellect, real *depth* of intellectual perception, in short, philosophy. It is characteristic of such an unphilosophical race to hold on firmly to Christianity——they *need* its discipline for "moralising" and humanising. The Englishman, more gloomy, sensual, headstrong, and brutal than the German——is for that very reason, as the baser of the two, also the most pious: he has all the *more need* of Christianity. To finer nostrils, this English Christianity itself has still a characteristic English taint of spleen and alcoholic excess, for which, owing to good reasons, it is used as an anti-

[565]

dote—the finer poison to neutralise the coarser: a finer form of poisoning is in fact a step in advance with coarse-mannered people, a step towards spiritualisation. The English coarseness and rustic demureness is still most satisfactorily disguised by Christian pantomime, and by praying and psalm-singing (or, more correctly, it is thereby explained and differently expressed); and for the herd of drunkards and rakes who formerly learned moral grunting under the influence of Methodism (and more recently as the "Salvation Army"), a penitential fit may really be the relatively highest manifestation of "humanity" to which they can be elevated: so much may reasonably be admitted. That, however, which offends even in the humanest Englishman is his lack of music, to speak figuratively (and also literally): he has neither rhythm nor dance in the movements of his soul and body; indeed, not even the desire for rhythm and dance, for "music." Listen to him speaking; look at the most beautiful Englishwoman *walking*—in no country on earth are there more beautiful doves and swans; finally, listen to them singing! But I ask too much. . . .

253

There are truths which are best recognised by mediocre minds, because they are best adapted for them, there are truths which only possess charms and seductive power for mediocre spirits:—one is pushed to this probably unpleasant conclusion, now that the influence of respectable but mediocre Englishmen —I may mention Darwin, John Stuart Mill, and Herbert Spencer—begins to gain the ascendency in the middle-class region of European taste. Indeed, who could doubt that it is a useful thing for *such* minds to have the ascendancy for a time? It would be an error to consider the highly developed and independently soaring minds as specially qualified for determining and collecting many little common facts, and deducing conclusions from them; as exceptions, they are rather from the first in no very favourable position towards those who are "the rules." After all, they have more to do than merely to perceive: —in effect, they have to *be* something new, they have to *signify* something new, they have to *represent* new values! The gulf between knowledge and capacity is perhaps greater, and also more mysterious, than one thinks: the capable man in the grand style, the creator, will possibly have to be an ignorant person;—while on the other hand, for scientific discoveries like those of Darwin, a certain narrowness, aridity, and industrious carefulness (in short something English) may not be unfavourable for arriving at them.—Finally, let it not be forgotten that the English, with their profound mediocrity, brought about once before a general depression of European intelligence. What is called "modern ideas," or "the ideas of the eighteenth century," or "French ideas"—that, consequently, against which the *German* mind rose up with profound disgust—is of English origin, there is no doubt about it. The French were only the apes and actors of these ideas, their best soldiers, and likewise, alas! their first and profoundest *victims;* for owing to the diabolical Anglomania of "modern ideas," the *âme français* has in the end become so thin and emaciated, that at present one recalls its sixteenth and seventeenth centuries, its profound, passionate strength, its inventive excellency, almost with disbelief. One must, however, maintain this verdict of historical justice in a determined manner, and defend it against present prejudices and appearances: the European *noblesse*— of sentiment, taste, and manners, taking the word in every high sense—is the work and invention of *France;* the European ignobleness, the plebeianism of modern ideas—is *England's* work and invention.

254

Even at present France is still the seat of the most intellectual and refined culture of Europe, it is still the high school of taste; but one must know how to find this "France of taste." He who belongs to it keeps himself well concealed:—they may be a small number in whom it lives and is embodied, besides perhaps being men who do not stand upon the strongest legs, in part fatalists, hypochondriacs, invalids, in part persons over-indulged, over-refined, such as have the *ambition* to conceal themselves. They have all something in common: they keep their ears closed in presence of the delirious folly and noisy spouting of the democratic *bourgeois*. In fact, a besotted and brutalised France at present sprawls in the foreground—it recently celebrated a veritable orgy of bad taste, and at the same time of self-admiration, at the funeral of Victor Hugo. There is also something else common to them: a predilection to resist intellectual Germanising—and a still greater inability to do so! In this France of intellect, which is also a France of pessimism, Schopenhauer has perhaps become more at home, and more indigenous than he has ever been in Germany; not to speak of Heinrich Heine, who has long ago been re-incarnated in the more refined and fastidious lyrists of Paris; or of Hegel, who at present, in the form of Taine—the *first* of living historians—exercises an almost tyrannical influence. As regards Richard Wagner, however, the more French music learns to adapt itself to the actual needs of the *âme moderne,* the more will it "Wagnerise"; one can safely predict that beforehand,—it is already taking place sufficiently! There are, however, three things which the French can still boast of with pride as their heritage and possession, and as indelible tokens of their ancient intellectual superiority in Europe, in spite of all voluntary or involuntary Germanising and vulgarising of taste. *Firstly,* the capacity for artistic emotion, for devotion to "form," for which the expression, *l'art pour l'art,* along with numerous others, has been invented:—such capacity has not been lacking in France for three centuries; and owing to its reverence for the "small number," it has again and again made a sort of chamber music of literature possible, which is sought for in vain elsewhere in Europe.—The *second* thing whereby the French can lay claim to a superiority over Europe is their ancient, many-sided, *moralistic* culture, owing to which one finds on an average, even in the petty *romanciers* of the newspapers and chance *boulevardiers de Paris,* a psychological sensitiveness and curiosity, of which, for example, one has no conception (to say nothing of the thing itself!) in Germany. The Germans lack a couple of centuries of the moralistic work requisite thereto, which, as we have said, France has not grudged: those who call the Germans "naïve" on that account give them commendation for a defect. (As the opposite of the German inexperience and innocence *in voluptate psychologica,* which is not too remotely associated with the tediousness of German intercourse,—and as the most successful expression of genuine French curiosity and inventive talent in this domain of delicate thrills, Henri Beyle may be noted; that remarkable anticipatory and forerunning man, who, with a Napoleonic *tempo,* traversed *his* Europe, in fact, several centuries of the European soul, as a surveyor and discoverer thereof:—it has required two generations to *overtake* him one way or other, to divine long afterwards some of the riddles that perplexed and enraptured him—this strange Epicurean and man of interrogation, the last great psychologist of France).—There is yet a *third* claim to superiority: in the French character there is a successful half-way synthesis of the North and South, which makes them comprehend many things, and enjoins upon them other things, which an Englishman can never comprehend. Their temperament, turned alternately to and from the South, in which from time to time the Provençal and Ligurian blood froths over, preserves them from the dreadful, northern gray-in-gray, from sunless conceptual-spectrism and from poverty of blood—our *German* infirmity of taste, for the excessive prevalence of which at the present moment, blood and iron, that is to say "high politics," has with great resolution been prescribed (according to a dangerous healing art, which bids me wait and wait, but not yet hope).—There is also still in France a pre-understanding and ready welcome for those rarer and rarely gratified men, who are too comprehensive to find satisfaction in any kind of fatherlandism, and know how to love the South when in the North and the North when in the South—the born Midlanders, the "good Europeans." For them *Bizet* has made music, this latest genius, who has seen a new beauty and seduction,—who has discovered a piece of the *South in music.*

255

I hold that many precautions should be taken against German music. Suppose a person loves the South as I love it—as a great school of recovery for the most spiritual and the most sensuous ills, as a boundless solar profusion and effulgence which o'erspreads a sovereign existence believing in itself—

[570]

well, such a person will learn to be somewhat on his guard against German music, because, in injuring his taste anew, it will also injure his health anew. Such a Southerner, a Southerner not by origin but by *belief*, if he should dream of the future of music, must also dream of it being freed from the influence of the North, and must have in his ears the prelude to a deeper, mightier, and perhaps more perverse and mysterious music, a super-German music, which does not fade, pale, and die away, as all German music does, at the sight of the blue, wanton sea and the Mediterranean clearness of sky——a super-European music, which holds its own even in presence of the brown sunsets of the desert, whose soul is akin to the palm-tree, and can be at home and can roam with big, beautiful, lonely beasts of prey. . . . I could imagine a music of which the rarest charm would be that it knew nothing more of good and evil; only that here and there perhaps some sailor's homesickness, some golden shadows and tender weaknesses might sweep lightly over it; an art which, from the far distance, would see the colours of a sinking and almost incomprehensible *moral* world fleeing towards it, and would be hospitable enough and profound enough to receive such belated fugitives.

256

Owing to the morbid estrangement which the nationality-craze has induced and still induces among the nations of Europe, owing also to the short-sighted and hasty-handed politicians, who with the help of this craze, are at present in power, and do not suspect to what extent the disintegrating policy they pursue must necessarily be only an interlude policy—owing to all this, and much else that is altogether unmentionable at present, the most unmistakable signs that *Europe wishes to be one,* are now overlooked, or arbitrarily and falsely misinterpreted. With all the more profound and large-minded men of this century, the real general tendency of the mysterious labour of their souls was to prepare the way for that new *synthesis,* and tentatively to anticipate the European of the future; only in their simulations, or in their weaker moments, in old age perhaps, did they belong to the "fatherlands"—they only rested from themselves when they became "patriots." I think of such men as Napoleon, Goethe, Beethoven, Stendhal, Heinrich Heine, Schopenhauer: it must not be taken amiss if I also count Richard Wagner among them, about whom one must not let oneself be deceived by his own misunderstandings (geniuses like him have seldom the right to understand themselves), still less, of course, by the unseemly noise with which he is now resisted and opposed in France: the fact remains, nevertheless, that Richard Wagner and the *later French Romanticism* of the forties, are most closely and intimately related to one another. They are akin, fundamentally akin, in all the heights and depths of their requirements; it is Europe, the *one* Europe, whose soul presses urgently and longingly, outwards and upwards, in their multifarious and boisterous art—whither? into a new light? towards a new sun? But who would attempt to express accurately what all these masters of new modes of speech could not express distinctly? It is certain that the same storm and stress tormented them, that they *sought* in the same manner, these last great seekers! All of them steeped in literature to their eyes and ears—the first artists of universal literary culture—for the most part even themselves writers, poets, intermediaries and blenders of the arts and the senses (Wagner, as musician is reckoned among painters, as poet among musicians, as artist generally among actors); all of them fanatics for *expression* "at any cost"—I specially mention Delacroix, the nearest related to Wagner; all of them great discoverers in the realm of the sublime, also of the loathsome and dreadful, still greater discoverers in effect, in display, in the art of the show-shop; all of them talented far beyond their genius, out and out *virtuosi,* with mysterious accesses to all that seduces, allures, constrains, and upsets; born enemies of logic and of the straight line, hankering after the strange, the exotic, the monstrous, the crooked, and the self-contradictory; as men, Tantaluses of the will, plebeian parvenus, who knew themselves to be incapable of a noble *tempo* or of a *lento* in life and action—think of Balzac, for instance,—unrestrained workers, almost destroying themselves by work; antinomians and rebels in manners, ambitious and insatiable, without equilibrium and enjoyment; all of them finally shattering and sinking down at the Christian cross (and with right and reason, for who of them would have been sufficiently profound and sufficiently original for an *Antichristian* philosophy?);—on the whole, a boldly daring, splendidly overbearing, high-flying, and aloft-up-dragging class of higher men, who had first to teach their century—and it is the century of the *masses* —the conception "higher man." . . . Let the German friends of Richard Wagner advise together as to whether there is any-thing purely German in the Wagnerian art, or whether its dis-tinction does not consist precisely in coming from *super-German* sources and impulses: in which connection it may not be underrated how indispensable Paris was to the development of his type, which the strength of his instincts made him long to visit at the most decisive time—and how the whole style of his proceedings, of his self-apostolate, could only perfect itself in sight of the French socialistic original. On a more subtle comparison it will perhaps be found, to the honour of Richard

Wagner's German nature, that he has acted in everything with more strength, daring, severity, and elevation than a nineteenth-century Frenchman could have done—owing to the circumstance that we Germans are as yet nearer to barbarism than the French;—perhaps even the most remarkable creation of Richard Wagner is not only at present, but for ever inaccessible, incomprehensible, and inimitable to the whole latter-day Latin race: the figure of Siegfried, that *very free* man, who is probably far too free, too hard, too cheerful, too healthy, too *anti-Catholic* for the taste of old and mellow civilised nations. He may even have been a sin against Romanticism, this anti-Latin Siegfried: well, Wagner atoned amply for this sin in his old sad days, when—anticipating a taste which has meanwhile passed into politics—he began, with the religious vehemence peculiar to him, to preach, at least, *the way to Rome,* if not to walk therein.—That these last words may not be misunderstood, I will call to my aid a few powerful rhymes, which will even betray to less delicate ears what I mean—what I mean *counter to* the "last Wagner" and his Parsifal music:—

—Is this our mode?—
From German heart came this vexed ululating?
From German body, this self-lacerating?
Is ours this priestly hand-dilation,
This incense-fuming exaltation?
Is ours this faltering, falling, shambling,
This quite uncertain ding-dong-dangling?
This sly nun-ogling, Ave-hour-bell ringing,
This wholly false enraptured heaven-o'erspringing?
—Is this our mode?—
Think well!—ye still wait for admission—
For what ye hear is *Rome—Rome's faith by intuition!*

9. What Is Noble?

257

EVERY elevation of the type "man," has hitherto been the work of an aristocratic society and so it will always be—a society believing in a long scale of gradations of rank and differences of worth among human beings, and requiring slavery in some form or other. Without the *pathos of distance,* such as grows out of the incarnated difference of classes, out of the constant outlooking and downlooking of the ruling caste on subordinates and instruments, and out of their equally constant practice of obeying and commanding, of keeping down and keeping at a distance—that other more mysterious pathos could never have arisen, the longing for an ever new widening of distance within the soul itself, the formation of ever higher, rarer, further, more extended, more comprehensive states, in short, just the elevation of the type "man," the continued "self-surmounting of man," to use a moral formula in a supermoral sense. To be sure, one must not resign oneself to any humanitarian illusions about the history of the origin of an aristocratic society (that is to say, of the preliminary condition for the elevation of the type "man"): the truth is hard. Let us acknowledge unprejudicedly how every higher civilisation hitherto has *originated!* Men with a still natural nature, barbarians in every terrible sense of the word, men of prey, still in possession of unbroken strength of will and desire for power, threw themselves upon weaker, more moral, more peaceful races (perhaps trading or cattle-rearing communities), or upon old mellow civilisations in which the final vital force was flickering out in brilliant fireworks of wit and depravity. At the commencement, the noble caste was always the barbarian caste: their superiority did not consist first of all in their physical, but in their psychical power—they were more *complete* men (which at every point also implies the same as "more complete beasts").

258

Corruption—as the indication that anarchy threatens to break out among the instincts, and that the foundation of the emotions, called "life," is convulsed—is something radically different according to the organisation in which it manifests itself. When, for instance, an aristocracy like that of France at the beginning of the Revolution, flung away its privileges with sublime disgust and sacrificed itself to an excess of its moral sentiments, it was corruption:—it was really only the closing act of the corruption which had existed for centuries, by virtue of which that aristocracy had abdicated step by step its lordly prerogatives and lowered itself to a *function* of royalty (in the end even to its decoration and parade-dress). The essential thing, however, in a good and healthy aristocracy is that it should *not* regard itself as a function either of the kingship or the commonwealth, but as the *significance* and highest justification thereof—that it should therefore accept with a good conscience the sacrifice of a legion of individuals, who, *for its sake,* must be suppressed and reduced to imperfect men, to slaves and instruments. Its fundamental belief must be precisely that society is *not* allowed to exist for its own sake, but only as a foundation and scaffolding, by means of which a select class of beings may be able to elevate themselves to their higher duties, and in general to a higher *existence:* like those sun-seeking climbing plants in Java—they are called *Sipo Matador,*—which encircle an oak so long and so often with their arms, until at last, high above it, but supported by it, they can unfold their tops in the open light, and exhibit their happiness.

259

To refrain mutually from injury, from violence, from exploitation, and put one's will on a par with that of others: this may result in a certain rough sense in good conduct among individuals when the necessary conditions are given (namely, the actual similarity of the individuals in amount of force and degree of worth, and their co-relation within one organisation). As soon, however, as one wished to take this principle more generally, and if possible even as *the fundamental principle of society,* it would immediately disclose what it really is—namely, a Will to the *denial* of life, a principle of dissolution and decay. Here one must think profoundly to the very basis and resist all sentimental weakness: life itself is *essentially* appropriation, injury, conquest of the strange and weak, suppression, severity, obtrusion of peculiar forms, incorporation, and at the least, putting it mildest, exploitation; —but why should one for ever use precisely these words on which for ages a disparaging purpose has been stamped? Even the organisation within which, as was previously supposed, the individuals treat each other as equal—it takes place in every healthy aristocracy—must itself, if it be a living and not a dying organisation, do all that towards other bodies, which the individuals within it refrain from doing to each other: it will have to be the incarnated Will to Power, it will endeavour to grow, to gain ground, attract to itself and acquire ascendency .——not owing to any morality or immorality, but because it *lives,* and because life *is* precisely Will to Power. On no point, however, is the ordinary consciousness of Europeans more unwilling to be corrected than on this matter; people now rave everywhere, even under the guise of science, about coming conditions of society in which "the exploiting character" is to be absent:——that sounds to my ears as if they promised to invent a mode of life which should refrain from all organic functions. "Exploitation" does not belong to a depraved, or imperfect and primitive society: it belongs to the *nature* of the living being as a primary organic function; it is a consequence of the intrinsic Will to Power, which is precisely the Will to Life.——Granting that as a theory this is a novelty—as a reality it is the *fundamental fact* of all history: let us be so far honest towards ourselves!

260

In a tour through the many finer and coarser moralities which have hitherto prevailed or still prevail on the earth, I found certain traits recurring regularly together, and connected with one another, until finally two primary types revealed themselves to me, and a radical distinction was brought to light. There is *master-morality* and *slave-morality;*——I would at once add, however, that in all higher and mixed civilisations, there are also attempts at the reconciliation of the two moralities; but one finds still oftener the confusion and mutual misunderstanding of them, indeed, sometimes their close juxtaposition ——even in the same man, within one soul. The distinctions of moral values have either originated in a ruling caste, pleasantly conscious of being different from the ruled—or among the ruled class, the slaves and dependents of all sorts. In the first case, when it is the rulers who determine the conception "good," it is the exalted, proud disposition which is regarded as the distinguishing feature, and that which determines the order of rank. The noble type of man separates from himself the beings in whom the opposite of this exalted, proud disposition displays itself: he despises them. Let it at once be noted that in this first kind of morality the antithesis "good" and "bad" means practically the same as "noble" and "despicable"; —the antithesis "good" and *"evil"* is of a different origin. The cowardly, the timid, the insignificant, and those thinking merely of narrow utility are despised; moreover, also, the distrustful, with their constrained glances, the self-abasing, the dog-like kind of men who let themselves be abused, the mendicant flatterers, and above all the liars:—it is a fundamental belief of all aristocrats that the common people are untruthful. "We truthful ones"—the nobility in ancient Greece called themselves. It is obvious that everywhere the designations of moral value were at first applied to *men,* and were only derivatively and at a later period applied to *actions;* it is a gross mistake, therefore, when historians of morals start questions like, "Why have sympathetic actions been praised?" The noble type of man regards *himself* as a determiner of values; he does not require to be approved of; he passes the judgment: "What is injurious to me is injurious in itself"; he knows that it is he himself only who confers honour on things; he is a *creator of values.* He honours whatever he recognises in himself: such morality is self-glorification. In the foreground there is the feeling of plenitude, of power, which seeks to overflow, the happiness of high tension, the consciousness of a wealth which would fain give and bestow:—the noble man also helps the unfortunate, but not—or scarcely—out of pity, but rather from an impulse generated by the super-abundance of power. The noble man honours in himself the powerful one, him also who has power over himself, who knows how to speak and how to keep silence, who takes pleasure in subjecting himself to severity and hardness, and has reverence for all that is severe and hard. "Wotan placed a hard heart in my breast," says an old Scandinavian Saga: it is thus rightly expressed from the soul of a proud Viking. Such a type of man is even proud of *not* being made for sympathy; the hero of the Saga therefore adds warningly: "He who has not a hard heart when young, will never have one." The noble and brave who think thus are the furthest removed from the morality which sees precisely in sympathy, or in acting for the good of others, or in *désintéressement,* the characteristic of the moral; faith in oneself, pride in oneself, a radical enmity and irony towards "selflessness," belong as definitely to noble morality, as do a careless scorn and precaution in presence of sympathy and the "warm heart."—It is the powerful who *know* how to honour, it is their art, their domain for invention. The profound reverence for age and for tradition—all law rests on this double reverence,—the belief and prejudice in favour of ancestors and unfavourable to newcomers, is typical in the morality of the powerful; and if, reversely, men of "modern ideas" believe almost instinctively in "progress" and the "future," and are more and more lacking in respect for old age, the ignoble origin of these "ideas" has complacently betrayed itself thereby. A morality of the ruling class, however, is more especially foreign and irritating to present-day taste in the sternness of its principle that one has duties only to one's equals; that one may act towards beings of a lower rank, towards all that is foreign, just as seems good to one, or "as the

heart desires," and in any case "beyond good and evil": **it is**
here that sympathy and similar sentiments can have a place.
The ability and obligation to exercise prolonged gratitude and
prolonged revenge—both only within the circle of equals,—
artfulness in retaliation, *raffinement* of the idea in friendship,
a certain necessity to have enemies (as outlets for the emotions
of envy, quarrelsomeness, arrogance—in fact, in order to be
a good *friend*) : all these are typical characteristics of the noble
morality, which, as has been pointed out, is not the morality o.
"modern ideas," and is therefore at present difficult to realise,
and also to unearth and disclose.—It is otherwise with the
second type of morality, *slave-morality*. Supposing that the
abused, the oppressed, the suffering, the unemancipated,
the weary, and those uncertain of themselves, should moralise,
what will be the common element in their moral estimates?
Probably a pessimistic suspicion with regard to the entire situation of man will find expression, perhaps a condemnation of
man, together with his situation. The slave has an unfavourable eye for the virtues of the powerful; he has a scepticism
and distrust, a *refinement* of distrust of everything "good"
that is there honoured—he would fain persuade himself that
the very happiness there is not genuine. On the other hand,
those qualities which serve to alleviate the existence of sufferers are brought into prominence and flooded with light; it
is here that sympathy, the kind, helping hand, the warm heart,
patience, diligence, humility, and friendliness attain to honour
for here these are the most useful qualities, and almost the only
means of supporting the burden of existence. Slave-morality is
essentially the morality of utility. Here is the seat of the origin
of the famous antithesis "good" and "evil" :—power and dangerousness are assumed to reside in the evil, a certain dreadfulness, subtlety, and strength, which do not admit of being

[*581*]

despised. According to slave-morality, therefore, the "evil" man arouses fear; according to master-morality, it is precisely the "good" man who arouses fear and seeks to arouse it, while the bad man is regarded as the despicable being. The contrast attains its maximum when, in accordance with the logical consequences of slave-morality, a shade of depreciation—it may be slight and well-intentioned—at last attaches itself to the "good" man of this morality; because, according to the servile mode of thought, the good man must in any case be the *safe* man: he is good-natured, easily deceived, perhaps a little stupid, *un bonhomme*. Everywhere that slave-morality gains the ascendency, language shows a tendency to approximate the significations of the words "good" and "stupid."—At last fundamental difference: the desire for *freedom,* the instinct for happiness and the refinements of the feeling of liberty belong as necessarily to slave-morals and morality, as artifice and enthusiasm in reverence and devotion are the regular symptoms of an aristocratic mode of thinking and estimating. —Hence we can understand without further detail why love *as a passion*—it is our European specialty—must absolutely be of noble origin; as is well known, its invention is due to the Provençal poet-cavaliers, those brilliant, ingenious men of the "*gai saber,*" to whom Europe owes so much, and almost owes itself.

261

Vanity is one of the things which are perhaps most difficult for a noble man to understand: he will be tempted to deny it, where another kind of man thinks he sees it self-evidently. The problem for him is to represent to his mind beings who seek to arouse a good opinion of themselves which they them-

selves do not possess—and consequently also do not "deserve,"
—and who yet *believe* in this good opinion afterwards. This
seems to him on the one hand such bad taste and so self-disre-
spectful, and on the other hand so grotesquely unreasonable,
that he would like to consider vanity an exception, and is
doubtful about it in most cases when it is spoken of. He will
say, for instance: "I may be mistaken about my value, and on
the other hand may nevertheless demand that my value should
be acknowledged by others precisely as I rate it:—that, however, is not vanity (but self-conceit, or, in most cases, that
which is called 'humility,' and also 'modesty')." Or he will
even say: "For many reasons I can delight in the good opinion
of others, perhaps because I love and honour them, and rejoice
in all their joys, perhaps also because their good opinion en-
dorses and strengthens my belief in my own good opinion,
perhaps because the good opinion of others, even in cases
where I do not share it, is useful to me, or gives promise of
usefulness:—all this, however, is not vanity." The man of
noble character must first bring it home forcibly to his mind,
especially with the aid of history, that, from time immemorial,
in all social strata in any way dependent, the ordinary man *was*
only that which he *passed for:*—not being at all accustomed to
fix values, he did not assign even to himself any other value
than that which his master assigned to him (it is the peculiar
right of masters to create values). It may be looked upon as
the result of an extraordinary atavism, that the ordinary man,
even at present, is still always *waiting* for an opinion about
himself, and then instinctively submitting himself to it; yet
by no means only to a "good" opinion, but also to a bad and
unjust one (think, for instance, of the greater part of the self-
appreciations and self-depreciations which believing women
learn from their confessors, and which in general the believing

Christian learns from his Church). In fact, conformably to the slow rise of the democratic social order (and its cause, the blending of the blood of masters and slaves), the originally noble and rare impulse of the masters to assign a value to themselves and to "think well" of themselves, will now be more and more encouraged and extended; but it has at all times an older, ampler, and more radically ingrained propensity opposed to it—and in the phenomenon of "vanity" this older propensity overmasters the younger. The vain person rejoices over *every* good opinion which he hears about himself (quite apart from the point of view of its usefulness, and equally regardless of its truth or falsehood), just as he suffers from every bad opinion: for he subjects himself to both, he *feels* himself subjected to both, by that oldest instinct of subjection which breaks forth in him.—It is "the slave" in the vain man's blood, the remains of the slave's craftiness—and how much of the "slave" is still left in woman, for instance!—which seeks to *seduce* to good opinions of itself; it is the slave, too, who immediately afterwards falls prostrate himself before these opinions, as though he had not called them forth.—And to repeat it again: vanity is an atavism.

262

A *species* originates, and a type becomes established and strong in the long struggle with essentially constant *unfavourable* conditions. On the other hand, it is known by the experience of breeders that species which receive superabundant nourishment, and in general a surplus of protection and care, immediately tend in the most marked way to develop variations, and are fertile in prodigies and monstrosities (also in monstrous vices). Now look at an aristocratic commonwealth, say an ancient Greek *polis,* or Venice, as a voluntary or involuntary contrivance for the purpose of *rearing* human beings; there are there men beside one another, thrown upon their own resources, who want to make their species prevail, chiefly because they *must* prevail, or else run the terrible danger of being exterminated. The favour, the superabundance, the protection are there lacking under which variations are fostered; the species needs itself as species, as something which, precisely by virtue of its hardness, its uniformity, and simplicity of structure, can in general prevail and make itself permanent in constant struggle with its neighbours, or with rebellious or rebellion-threatening vassals. The most varied experience teaches it what are the qualities to which it principally owes the fact that it still exists, in spite of all gods and men, and has hitherto been victorious: these qualities it calls virtues, and these virtues alone it develops to maturity. It does so with severity, indeed it desires severity; every aristocratic morality is intolerant in the education of youth, in the control of women, in the marriage customs, in the relations of old and young, in the penal laws (which have an eye only for the degenerating): it counts intolerance itself among the virtues, under the name of "justice." A type with few, but very marked features, a species of severe, warlike, wisely silent, reserved and reticent men (and as such, with the most delicate sensibility for the charm and *nuances* of society) is thus established, unaffected by the vicissitudes of generations; the constant struggle with uniform *unfavourable* conditions is, as already remarked, the cause of a type becoming stable and hard. Finally, however, a happy state of things results, the enormous tension is relaxed; there are perhaps no more enemies among the neighbouring peoples, and the means of life, even of the enjoyment of life, are present in superabundance. With one stroke the bond and constraint of the old discipline severs: it is no longer regarded as necessary, as a condition of existence—if it would continue, it can only do so as a form of *luxury,* as an archaïsing *taste.* Variations, whether they be deviations (into the higher, finer, and rare), or deteriorations and monstrosities, appear suddenly on the scene in the greatest exuberance and splendour; the individual dares to be individual and detach himself. At this turning-point of history there manifest themselves, side by side, and often mixed and entangled together, a magnificent, manifold, virgin-forest-like up-growth and up-striving, a kind of *tropical tempo* in the rivalry of growth, and an extraordinary decay and self-destruction, owing to the savagely opposing and seemingly exploding egoisms, which strive with one another "for sun and light," and can no longer assign any limit, restraint, or forbearance for themselves by means of the hitherto existing morality. It was this morality itself which piled up the strength so enormously, which bent the bow in so threatening a manner:—it is now "out of date," it is getting "out of date." The dangerous and disquieting point has been reached when the greater, more manifold, more comprehensive life *is lived beyond* the old morality; the "individual" stands out, and is obliged to have recourse to his own law-giving, his own arts and artifices for self-preservation, self-elevation, and self-deliverance. Nothing but new "Whys," nothing but new "Hows," no common formulas any longer, misunderstanding and disregard in league with each other, decay, deterioration, and the loftiest desires frightfully entangled, the genius of the race overflowing from all the cornucopias of good and bad, a portentous simultaneousness of Spring and Autumn, full of new charms and mysteries peculiar to the fresh, still inexhausted, still unwearied corruption. Danger is again present, the mother of morality, great danger; this time shifted into the individual, into the neighbour and friend, into the street, into their own child, into their own heart, into all the most personal and secret recesses of their desires and volitions. What will the moral philosophers who appear at this time have to preach? They discover, these sharp onlookers and loafers, that the end is quickly approaching, that everything around them decays and produces decay, that nothing will endure until the day after tomorrow, except one species of man, the incurably *mediocre*. The mediocre alone have a prospect of continuing and propagating themselves—they will be the men of the future, the sole survivors; "be like them! become mediocre!" is now the only morality which has still a significance, which still obtains a hearing.—But it is difficult to preach this morality of mediocrity! it can never avow what it is and what it desires! it has to talk of moderation and dignity and duty and brotherly love—it will have difficulty *in conceal-ing its irony!*

263

There is an *instinct for rank,* which more than anything else is already the sign of a *high* rank; there is a *delight* in the *nuances* of reverence which leads one to infer noble origin and habits. The refinement, goodness, and loftiness of a soul are put to a perilous test when something passes by that is of the highest rank, but is not yet protected by the awe of authority from obtrusive touches and incivilities: something that goes its way like a living touchstone, undistinguished, undiscovered, and tentative, perhaps voluntarily veiled and disguised. He whose task and practice it is to investigate souls, will avail himself of many varieties of this very art to determine the ultimate value of a soul, the unalterable, innate order of rank to which it belongs: he will test it by its *instinct for reverence*. *Différence engendre haine:* the vulgarity of many a nature spurts up suddenly like dirty water, when any holy vessel, any jewel from closed shrines, any book bearing the marks of great destiny, is brought before it; while on the other hand, there is an involuntary silence, a hesitation of the eye, a cessation of all gestures, by which it is indicated that a soul *feels* the nearness of what is worthiest of respect. The way in which, on the whole, the reverence for the *Bible* has hitherto been maintained in Europe, is perhaps the best example of discipline and refinement of manners which Europe owes to Christianity: books of such profoundness and supreme significance require for their protection an external tyranny of authority, in order to acquire the *period* of thousands of years which is necessary to exhaust and unriddle them. Much has been achieved when the sentiment has been at last instilled into the masses (the shallow-pates and the boobies of every kind) that they are not allowed to touch everything, that there are holy experiences before which they must take off their shoes and keep away the unclean hand—it is almost their highest advance towards humanity. On the contrary, in the so-called cultured classes, the believers in "modern ideas," nothing is perhaps so repulsive as their lack of shame, the easy insolence of eye and hand with which they touch, taste, and finger everything; and it is possible that even yet there is more *relative* nobility of taste, and more tact for reverence among the people, among the lower classes of the people, especially among peasants, than among the newspaper-reading *demimonde* of intellect, the cultured class.

It cannot be effaced from a man's soul what his ancestors have preferably and most constantly done: whether they were perhaps diligent economisers attached to a desk and a cash-box, modest and citizen-like in their desires, modest also in their virtues; or whether they were accustomed to commanding from morning till night, fond of rude pleasures and probably of still ruder duties and responsibilities; or whether, finally, at one time or another, they have sacrificed old privileges of birth and possession, in order to live wholly for their faith—for their "God,"—as men of an inexorable and sensitive conscience, which blushes at every compromise. It is quite impossible for a man *not* to have the qualities and predilections of his parents and ancestors in his constitution, whatever appearances may suggest to the contrary. This is the problem of race. Granted that one knows something of the parents, it is admissible to draw a conclusion about the child: any kind of offensive incontinence, any kind of sordid envy, or of clumsy self-vaunting—the three things which together have constituted the genuine plebeian type in all times—such must pass over to the child, as surely as bad blood; and with the help of the best education and culture one will only succeed in *deceiving* with regard to such heredity.—And what else does education and culture try to do nowadays! In our very democratic, or rather, very plebeian age, "education" and "culture" *must* be essentially the art of deceiving—deceiving with regard to origin, with regard to the inherited plebeianism in body and soul. An educator who nowadays preached truthfulness above everything else, and called out constantly to his pupils: "Be true! Be natural! Show yourselves as you are!"—

even such a virtuous and sincere ass would learn in a short time to have recourse to the *furca* of Horace, *naturam expellere:* with what results? "Plebeianism" *usque recurret.**

265

At the risk of displeasing innocent ears, I submit that egoism belongs to the essence of a noble soul, I mean the unalterable belief that to a being such as "we," other beings must naturally be in subjection, and have to sacrifice themselves. The noble soul accepts the fact of his egoism without question, and also without consciousness of harshness, constraint, or arbitrariness therein, but rather as something that may have its basis in the primary law of things:—if he sought a designation for it he would say: "It is justice itself." He acknowledges under certain circumstances, which made him hesitate at first, that there are other equally privileged ones; as soon as he has settled this question of rank, he moves among those equals and equally privileged ones with the same assurance, as regards modesty and delicate respect, which he enjoys in intercourse with himself—in accordance with an innate heavenly mechanism which all the stars understand. It is an *additional* instance of his egoism, this artfulness and self-limitation in intercourse with his equals—every star is a similar egoist; he honours *himself* in them, and in the rights which he concedes to them, he has no doubt that the exchange of honours and rights, as the *essence* of all intercourse, belongs also to the natural condition of things. The noble soul gives as he takes, prompted by the passionate and sensitive instinct of requital, which is at the

---

* Horace's "Epistles," I. x. 24.

root of his nature. The notion of "favour" has, *inter pares,* neither significance nor good repute; there may be a sublime way of letting gifts as it were light upon one from above, and of drinking them thirstily like dew-drops; but for those arts and displays the noble soul has no aptitude. His egoism hinders him here: in general, he looks "aloft" unwillingly—he looks either *forward,* horizontally and deliberately, or downwards— *he knows that he is on a height.*

266

"One can only truly esteem him who does not *look out for* himself."—Goethe to Rath Schlosser.

267

The Chinese have a proverb which mothers even teach their children: *"Siao-sin"* (*"make thy heart small"*). This is the essentially fundamental tendency in latter-day civilisations. I have no doubt that an ancient Greek, also, would first of all remark the self-dwarfing in us Europeans of today—in this respect alone we should immediately be "distasteful" to him.

268

What, after all, is ignobleness?—Words are vocal symbols for ideas; ideas, however, are more or less definite mental symbols for frequently returning and concurring sensations, for groups of sensations. It is not sufficient to use the same words in order to understand one another: we must also employ the same words for the same kind of internal experiences, we must in the end have experiences *in common*. On this account the people of one nation understand one another better than those belonging to different nations, even when they use the same language; or rather, when people have lived long together under similar conditions (of climate, soil, danger, require- ment, toil) there *originates* therefrom an entity that "under- stands itself"—namely, a nation. In all souls a like number of frequently recurring experiences have gained the upper hand over those occurring more rarely: about these matters people understand one another rapidly and always more rapidly—the history of language is the history of a process of abbreviation; on the basis of this quick comprehension people always unite closer and closer. The greater the danger, the greater is the need of agreeing quickly and readily about what is necessary; not to misunderstand one another in danger—that is what can- not at all be dispensed with in intercourse. Also in all loves and friendships one has the experience that nothing of the kind continues when the discovery has been made that in using the same words, one of the two parties has feelings, thoughts, in- tuitions, wishes, or fears different from those of the other. (The fear of the "eternal misunderstanding": that is the good genius which so often keeps persons of different sexes from too hasty attachments, to which sense and heart prompt them —and *not* some Schopenhauerian "genius of the species"!) Whichever groups of sensations within a soul awaken most readily, begin to speak, and give the word of command—these decide as to the general order of rank of its values, and deter- mine ultimately its list of desirable things. A man's estimates of value betray something of the *structure* of his soul, and wherein it sees its conditions of life, its intrinsic needs. Supposing now that necessity has from all time drawn together only such men as could express similar requirements and similar experiences by similar symbols, it results on the whole that the easy *communicability* of need, which implies ultimately the undergoing only of average and *common* experiences, must have been the most potent of all the forces which have hitherto operated upon mankind. The more similar, the more ordinary people, have always had and are still having the advantage; the more select, more refined, more unique, and difficulty comprehensible, are liable to stand alone; they succumb to accidents in their isolation, and seldom propagate themselves. One must appeal to immense opposing forces, in order to thwart this natural, all-too-natural *progressus in simile,* the evolution of man to the similar, the ordinary, the average, the gregarious—to the *ignoble!*—

269

The more a psychologist—a born, an unavoidable psychologist and soul-diviner—turns his attention to the more select cases and individuals, the greater is his danger of being suffocated by sympathy: he *needs* sternness and cheerfulness more than any other man. For the corruption, the ruination of higher men, of the more unusually constituted souls, is in fact, the rule: it is dreadful to have such a rule always before one's eyes. The manifold torment of the psychologist who has discovered this ruination, who discovers once, and then discovers *almost* repeatedly throughout all history, this universal inner "desperateness" of higher men, this eternal "too late!" in every sense —may perhaps one day be the cause of his turning with bitterness against his own lot, and of his making an attempt at self-destruction—of his "going to ruin" himself. One may perceive in almost every psychologist a tell-tale inclination for delightful intercourse with commonplace and well-ordered men: the fact is thereby disclosed that he always requires healing, that he needs a sort of flight and forgetfulness, away from what his insight and incisiveness—from what his "business"—has laid upon his conscience. The fear of his memory is peculiar to him. He is easily silenced by the judgment of others; he hears with unmoved countenance how people honour, admire, love, and glorify, where he has *perceived*—or he even conceals his silence by expressly assenting to some plausible opinion. Perhaps the paradox of his situation becomes so dreadful that, precisely where he has learned *great sympathy,* together with *great contempt,* the multitude, the educated, and the visionaries, have on their part learned great reverence—reverence for "great men" and marvellous animals, for the sake of whom one blesses and honours the fatherland, the earth, the dignity of mankind, and one's own self, to whom one points the young, and in view of whom one educates them. And who knows but in all great instances hitherto just the same happened: that the multitude worshipped a God, and that the "God" was only a poor sacrificial animal! *Success* has always been the greatest liar—and the "work" itself is a success; the great statesman, the conqueror, the discoverer, are disguised in their creations until they are unrecognisable; the "work" of the artist, of the philosopher, only invents him who has created it, is *reputed* to have created it; the "great men," as they are reverenced, are poor little fictions composed afterwards; in the world of historical values spurious coinage *prevails.* Those great poets, for example, such as Byron, Musset, Poe, Leopardi, Kleist, Gogol (I do not venture to mention much greater names, but I have them in my mind), as they now appear, and were perhaps obliged to be: men of the moment, enthusiastic, sensuous, and childish, light-minded and impulsive in their trust and distrust; with souls in which usually some flaw has to be concealed; often taking revenge with their works for an internal defilement, often seeking forgetfulness in their soaring from a too true memory, often lost in the mud and almost in love with it, until they become like the Will-o'-the-Wisps around the swamps, and *pretend to be* stars—the people then call them idealists,— often struggling with protracted disgust, with an ever-reappearing phantom of disbelief, which makes them cold, and obliges them to languish for *gloria* and devour "faith as it is" out of the hands of intoxicated adulators:—what a *torment* these great artists are and the so-called higher men in general, to him who has once found them out! It is thus conceivable that it is just from woman—who is clairvoyant in the world of suffering, and also unfortunately eager to help and save to an extent far beyond her powers—that *they* have learned so readily those outbreaks of boundless devoted *sympathy,* which the multitude, above all the reverent multitude, do not understand, and overwhelm with prying and self-gratifying interpretations. This sympathising invariably deceives itself as to its power; woman would like to believe that love can do *everything*—it is the *superstition* peculiar to her. Alas, he who knows the heart finds out how poor, helpless, pretentious, and blundering even the best and deepest love is—he finds that it rather *destroys* than saves!—It is possible that under the holy fable and travesty of the life of Jesus there is hidden one of the most painful cases of the martyrdom of *knowledge about love:* the martyrdom of the most innocent and most craving heart, that never had enough of any human love, that *demanded* love, that demanded inexorably and frantically to be loved and nothing else, with terrible outbursts against those who refused him their love; the story of a poor soul insatiated and insatiable in love, that had to invent hell to send thither those who *would not* love him——and that at last, enlightened about human love, had to invent a God who is entire love, entire *capacity* for love——who takes pity on human love, because it is so paltry, so ignorant! He who has such sentiments, he who has such *knowledge* about love—*seeks* for death!—But why should one deal with such painful matters? Provided, of course, that one is not obliged to do so.

270

The intellectual haughtiness and loathing of every man who has suffered deeply—it almost determines the order of rank *how* deeply men can suffer—the chilling certainty, with which he is thoroughly imbued and coloured, that by virtue of his suffering he *knows more* than the shrewdest and wisest can ever know, that he has been familiar with, and "at home" in, many distant, dreadful worlds of which *"you* know nothing"! —this silent intellectual haughtiness of the sufferer, this pride of the elect of knowledge, of the "initiated," of the almost sacrificed, finds all forms of disguise necessary to protect itself from contact with officious and sympathising hands, and in general from all that is not its equal in suffering. Profound suffering makes noble: it separates.—One of the most refined forms of disguise is Epicurism, along with a certain ostentatious boldness of taste, which takes suffering lightly, and puts itself on the defensive against all that is sorrowful and profound. They are "gay men" who make use of gaiety, because they are misunderstood on account of it—they *wish* to be mis-understood. There are "scientific minds" who make use of science, because it gives a gay appearance, and because scien-tificalness leads to the conclusion that a person is superficial—they *wish* to mislead to a false conclusion. There are free inso-lent minds which would fain conceal and deny that they are broken, proud, incurable hearts (the cynicism of Hamlet—the case of Galiani); and occasionally folly itself is the mask of an unfortunate *over-assured* knowledge.—From which it follows that it is the part of a more refined humanity to have reverence "for the mask," and not to make use of psychology and curi-osity in the wrong place.

271

That which separates two men most profoundly is a dif-ferent sense and grade of purity. What does it matter about all their honesty and reciprocal usefulness, what does it matter about all their mutual good-will: the fact still remains—they "cannot smell each other!" The highest instinct for purity places him who is affected with it in the most extraordinary and dangerous isolation, as a saint: for it is just holiness—the highest spiritualisation of the instinct in question. Any kind of cognisance of an indescribable excess in the joy of the bath, any kind of ardour or thirst which perpetually impels the soul out of night into the morning, and out of gloom, out of "afflic-tion" into clearness, brightness, depth, and refinement:—just as much as such a tendency *distinguishes*—it is a noble tendency—it also *separates*.—The pity of the saint is pity for the *filth* of the human, all-too-human. And there are grades and heights where pity itself is regarded by him as impurity, as filth.

272

Signs of nobility: never to think of lowering our duties to the rank of duties for everybody; to be unwilling to renounce or to share our responsibilities; to count our prerogatives, and the exercise of them, among our *duties*.

273

A man who strives after great things, looks upon every one whom he encounters on his way either as a means of advance, or a delay and hindrance—or as a temporary resting-place. His peculiar lofty *bounty* to his fellow-men is only possible when he attains his elevation and dominates. Impatience, and the consciousness of being always condemned to comedy up to that time—for even strife is a comedy, and conceals the end, as every means does—spoil all intercourse for him; this kind of man is acquainted with solitude, and what is most poisonous in it.

274

The Problem of those who Wait.—Happy chances are necessary, and many incalculable elements, in order that a higher man in whom the solution of a problem is dormant may yet take action, or "break forth," as one might say—at the right moment. On an average it *does not* happen; and in all

corners of the earth there are waiting ones sitting who hardly
know to what extent they are waiting, and still less that they
wait in vain. Occasionally, too, the waking call comes too late
—the chance which gives "permission" to take action—when
their best youth, and strength for action have been used up in
sitting still; and how many a one, just as he "sprang up," has
found with horror that his limbs are benumbed and his spirits
are now too heavy! "It is too late," he has said to himself—and
has become self-distrustful and henceforth for ever useless.—
In the domain of genius, may not the "Raphael without hands"
(taking the expression in its widest sense) perhaps not be the
exception, but the rule?—Perhaps genius is by no means so
rare: but rather the five hundred *hands* which it requires in
order to tyrannise over the καιρός "the right time"—in order
to take chance by the forelock!

275

He who does not *wish* to see the height of a man, looks all
the more sharply at what is low in him, and in the foreground
—and thereby betrays himself.

276

In all kinds of injury and loss the lower and coarser soul is
better off than the nobler soul: the dangers of the latter must
be greater, the probability that it will come to grief and perish
is in fact immense, considering the multiplicity of the conditions of its existence.—In a lizard a finger grows again which
has been lost; not so in man.—

[*599*]

277

It is too bad! Always the old story! When a man has finished building his house, he finds that he had learned unawares something which he *ought* absolutely to have known before he—began to build. The eternal, fatal "Too late!" The melancholia of everything *completed!*—

278

—Wanderer, who art thou? I see thee follow thy path without scorn, without love, with unfathomable eyes, wet and sad as a plummet which has returned to the light insatiated out of every depth—what did it seek down there?—with a bosom that never sighs, with lips that conceal their loathing, with a hand which only slowly grasps: who art thou? what hast thou done? Rest thee here: this place has hospitality for every one —refresh thyself! And whoever thou art, what is it that now pleases thee? What will serve to refresh thee? Only name it, whatever I have I offer thee! "To refresh me? To refresh me? Oh, thou prying one, what sayest thou! But give me, I pray thee——" What? what? Speak out! "Another mask! A second mask!"

279

Men of profound sadness betray themselves when they are happy: they have a mode of seizing upon happiness as though they would choke and strangle it, out of jealousy—ah, they know only too well that it will flee from them!

280

"Bad! Bad! What? Does he not—go back?" Yes! But you misunderstand him when you complain about it. He goes back like every one who is about to make a great spring.

281

—"Will people believe it of me? But I insist that they believe it of me: I have always thought very unsatisfactorily of myself and about myself, only in very rare cases, only compulsorily, always without delight in 'the subject,' ready to digress from 'myself,' and always without faith in the result, owing to an unconquerable distrust of the *possibility* of self-knowledge, which has led me so far as to feel a *contradictio in adjecto* even in the idea of 'direct knowledge' which theorists allow themselves:—this matter of fact is almost the most certain thing I know about myself. There must be a sort of repugnance in me to *believe* anything definite about myself.—Is there perhaps some enigma therein? Probably; but fortunately nothing for my own teeth.—Perhaps it betrays the species to which I belong?—but not to myself, as is sufficiently agreeable to me."

282

—"But what has happened to you?"—"I do not know," he said, hesitatingly; "perhaps the Harpies have flown over my table."—It sometimes happens nowadays that a gentle, sober, retiring man becomes suddenly mad, breaks the plates, upsets the table, shrieks, raves, and shocks everybody—and finally withdraws, ashamed, and raging at himself—whither? for what purpose? To famish apart? To suffocate with his memories?——To him who has the desires of a lofty and dainty soul, and only seldom finds his table laid and his food prepared, the danger will always be great—nowadays, however, it is extraordinarily so. Thrown into the midst of a noisy and plebeian age, with which he does not like to eat out of the same dish, he may readily perish of hunger and thirst—or, should he nevertheless finally "fall to," of sudden nausea.— We have probably all sat at tables to which we did not belong; and precisely the most spiritual of us, who are most difficult to nourish, know the dangerous *dyspepsia* which originates from a sudden insight and disillusionment about our food and our messmates—the *after-dinner nausea*.

283

If one wishes to praise at all, it is a delicate and at the same time a noble self-control, to praise only where one *does not* agree—otherwise in fact one would praise oneself, which is contrary to good taste:—a self-control, to be sure, which offers excellent opportunity and provocation to constant *misunderstanding*. To be able to allow oneself this veritable luxury of taste and morality, one must not live among intellectual imbeciles, but rather among men whose misunderstandings and mistakes amuse by their refinement—or one will have to pay dearly for it!—"He praises me, *therefore* he acknowledges me to be right"—this asinine method of inference spoils half of the life of us recluses, for it brings the asses into our neighbourhood and friendship.

284

To live in a vast and proud tranquillity; always beyond . . . To have, or not to have, one's emotions, one's For and Against, according to choice; to lower oneself to them for hours; to *seat* oneself on them as upon horses, and often as upon asses:—for one must know how to make use of their stupidity as well as of their fire. To conserve one's three hundred foregrounds; also one's black spectacles: for there are circumstances when nobody must look into our eyes, still less into our "motives." And to choose for company that roguish and cheerful vice, politeness. And to remain master of one's four virtues, courage, insight, sympathy, and solitude. For solitude is a virtue with us, as a sublime bent and bias to purity, which divines that in the contact of man and man—"in society" —it must be unavoidably impure. All society makes one somehow, somewhere, or sometime—"commonplace."

285

The greatest events and thoughts—the greatest thoughts, however, are the greatest events—are longest in being comprehended: the generations which are contemporary with them do not *experience* such events—they live past them. Something happens there as in the realm of stars. The light of the furthest stars is longest in reaching man; and before it has arrived man *denies*—that there are stars there. "How many centuries does a mind require to be understood?—that is also a standard, one also makes a gradation of rank and an etiquette therewith, such as is necessary for mind and for star.

286

' Here is the prospect free, the mind exalted." *—But there
is a reverse kind of man, who is also upon a height, and ha:
also a free prospect—but looks *downwards*.

287

—What is noble? What does the word "noble" still mean
for us nowadays? How does the noble man betray himself,
how is he recognised under this heavy overcast sky of the com-
mencing plebeianism, by which everything is rendered opaque
and leaden?—It is not his actions which establish his claim—
actions are always ambiguous, always inscrutable; neither is it
his "works." One finds nowadays among artists and scholars
plenty of those who betray by their works that a profound
longing for nobleness impels them; but this very *need of*
nobleness is radically different from the needs of the noble
soul itself, and is in fact the eloquent and dangerous sign of
the lack thereof. It is not the works, but the *belief* which is
here decisive and determines the order of rank—to employ
once more an old religious formula with a new and deeper
meaning,—it is some fundamental certainty which a noble
soul has about itself, something which is not to be sought, is
not to be found, and perhaps, also, is not to be lost.—*The
noble soul has reverence for itself.*—

---

* Goethe's "Faust," Part II., Act V. The words of Dr. Marianus.

288

There are men who are unavoidably intellectual, let them turn and twist themselves as they will, and hold their hands before their treacherous eyes—as though the hand were not a betrayer; it always comes out at last that they have something which they hide—namely, intellect. One of the subtlest means of deceiving, at least as long as possible, and of successfully representing oneself to be stupider than one really is—which in everyday life is often as desirable as an umbrella,—is called *enthusiasm,* including what belongs to it, for instance, virtue. For as Galiani said, who was obliged to know it: *vertu est enthousiasme.*

289

In the writings of a recluse one always hears something of the echo of the wilderness, something of the murmuring tones and timid vigilance of solitude; in his strongest words, even in his cry itself, there sounds a new and more dangerous kind of silence, of concealment. He who has sat day and night, from year's end to year's end, alone with his soul in familiar discord and discourse, he who has become a cave-bear, or a treasure-seeker, or a treasure-guardian and dragon in his cave —it may be a labyrinth, but can also be a gold-mine—his ideas themselves eventually acquire a twilight-colour of their own, and an odour, as much of the depth as of the mould, something uncommunicative and repulsive, which blows chilly upon every passer-by. The recluse does not believe that a philosopher— supposing that a philosopher has always in the first place been

[605]

a recluse—ever expressed his actual and ultimate opinions in books: are not books written precisely to hide what is in us?—indeed, he will doubt whether a philosopher *can* have "ultimate and actual" opinions at all; whether behind every cave in him there is not, and must necessarily be, a still deeper cave: an ampler, stranger, richer world beyond the surface, an abyss behind every bottom, beneath every "foundation." Every philosophy is a foreground philosophy—this is a recluse's verdict. "There is something arbitrary in the fact that the *philosopher* came to a stand here, took a retrospect and looked around; that he *here* laid his spade aside and did not dig any deeper—there is also something suspicious in it." Every philosophy also *conceals* a philosophy; every opinion is also a *lurking-place,* every word is also a *mask.*

290

Every deep thinker is more afraid of being understood than of being misunderstood. The latter perhaps wounds his vanity; but the former wounds his heart, his sympathy, which always says: "Ah, why would *you* also have as hard a time of it as I have?"

291

Man, a *complex,* mendacious, artful, and inscrutable animal, uncanny to the other animals by his artifice and sagacity, rather than by his strength, has invented the good conscience in order finally to enjoy his soul as something *simple;* and the whole of morality is a long, audacious falsification, by virtue of which generally enjoyment at the sight of the soul becomes possible. From this point of view there is perhaps much more in the conception of "art" than is generally believed.

292

A philosopher: that is a man who constantly experiences, sees, hears, suspects, hopes, and dreams extraordinary things; who is struck by his own thoughts as if they came from the outside, from above and below, as a species of events and lightning-flashes *peculiar to him;* who is perhaps himself a storm pregnant with new lightnings; a portentous man, around whom there is always rumbling and mumbling and gaping and something uncanny going on. A philosopher: alas, a being who often runs away from himself, is often afraid of himself —but whose curiosity always makes him "come to himself" again.

293

A man who says: "I like that, I take it for my own, and mean to guard and protect it from every one"; a man who can conduct a case, carry out a resolution, remain true to an opinion, keep hold of a woman, punish and overthrow insolence; a man who has his indignation and his sword, and to whom the weak, the suffering, the oppressed, and even the animals willingly submit and naturally belong; in short, a man who is a *master* by nature—when such a man has sympathy, well! *that* sympathy has value! But of what account is the sympathy of those who suffer! Or of those even who preach sympathy! There is nowadays, throughout almost the whole of Europe, a sickly irritability and sensitiveness towards pain, and also a repulsive irrestrainableness in complaining, an effeminising, which, with the aid of religion and philosophical nonsense, seeks to deck itself out as something superior—there is a regular cult of suffering. The *unmanliness* of that which is called "sympathy" by such groups of visionaries, is always, I believe, the first thing that strikes the eye.—One must resolutely and radically taboc this latest form of bad taste; and finally I wish people to put the good amulet, *"gai saber"* ("gay science," in ordinary language), on heart and neck, as a protection against it.

294

The Olympian Vice.—Despite the philosopher who, as a genuine Englishman, tried to bring laughter into bad repute in all thinking minds—"Laughing is a bad infirmity of human nature, which every thinking mind will strive to overcome" (Hobbes),—I would even allow myself to rank philosophers according to the quality of their laughing—up to those who are capable of *golden* laughter. And supposing that gods also philosophise, which I am strongly inclined to believe, owing to many reasons—I have no doubt that they also know how to laugh thereby in an overmanlike and new fashion—and at the expense of all serious things! Gods are fond of ridicule: it seems that they cannot refrain from laughter even in holy matters.

295

The genius of the heart, as that great mysterious one possesses it, the tempter-god and born rat-catcher of consciences, whose voice can descend into the nether-world of every soul, who neither speaks a word nor casts a glance in which there may not be some motive or touch of allurement, to whose perfection it pertains that he knows how to appear,—not as he is, but in a guise which acts as an *additional* constraint on his followers to press ever closer to him, to follow him more cordially and thoroughly;—the genius of the heart, which imposes silence and attention on everything loud and self-conceited, which smooths rough souls and makes them taste a new longing—to lie placid as a mirror, that the deep heavens may be reflected in them;—the genius of the heart, which teaches the clumsy and too hasty hand to hesitate, and to grasp more delicately; which scents the hidden and forgotten treasure, the drop of goodness and sweet spirituality under thick dark ice, and is a divining-rod for every grain of gold, long buried and imprisoned in mud and sand; the genius of the heart, from contact with which every one goes away richer; not favoured or surprised, not as though gratified and oppressed by the good things of others; but richer in himself, newer than before, broken up, blown upon, and sounded by a thawing wind; more uncertain, perhaps, more delicate, more fragile, more bruised, but full of hopes which as yet lack names, full of a new will and current, full of a new ill-will and counter-current . . . but what am I doing, my friends? Of whom am I talking to you? Have I forgotten myself so far that I have not even told you his name? Unless it be that you have already divined of your own accord who this questionable God and spirit is, that wishes to be *praised* in such a manner? For, as it happens to every one who from childhood onward has always been on his legs, and in foreign lands, I have also encountered on my path many strange and dangerous spirits; above all, however, and again and again, the one of whom I have just spoken: in fact, no less a personage than the god

Dionysus, the great equivocator and tempter, to whom, as you know, I once offered in all secrecy and reverence my first-fruits —the last, as it seems to me, who has offered a *sacrifice* to him, for I have found no one who could understand what I was then doing. In the meantime, however, I have learned much, far too much, about the philosophy of this god, and, as I said, from mouth to mouth—I, the last disciple and initiate of the god Dionysus: and perhaps I might at last begin to give you, my friends, as far as I am allowed, a little taste of this philosophy? In a hushed voice, as is but seemly: for it has to do with much that is secret, new, strange, wonderful, and uncanny. The very fact that Dionysus is a philosopher, and that therefore gods also philosophise, seems to me a novelty which is not unensnaring, and might perhaps arouse suspicion precisely amongst philosophers;—amongst you, my friends, there is less to be said against it, except that it comes too late and not at the right time; for, as it has been disclosed to me, you are loth nowadays to believe in God and gods. It may happen, too, that in the frankness of my story I must go further than is agreeable to the strict usages of your ears? Certainly the god in question went further, very much further, in such dialogues, and was always many paces ahead of me. . . . Indeed, if it were allowed, I should have to give him, according to human usage, fine ceremonious titles of lustre and merit, I should have to extol his courage as investigator and discoverer, his fearless honesty, truthfulness, and love of wisdom. But such a God does not know what to do with all that respectable trumpery and pomp. "Keep that," he would say, "for thyself and those like thee, and whoever else require it! I—have no reason to cover my nakedness!" One suspects that this kind of divinity and philosopher perhaps lacks shame?—He once said:

[*610*]

"Under certain circumstances I love mankind"—and referred thereby to Ariadne, who was present; "in my opinion man is an agreeable, brave, inventive animal, that has not his equal upon earth, he makes his way even through all labyrinths. I like man, and often think how I can still further advance him, and make him stronger, more evil, and more profound."— "Stronger, more evil, and more profound?" I asked in horror. "Yes," he said again, "stronger, more evil, and more profound; also more beautiful"—and thereby the tempter-god smiled with his halcyon smile, as though he had just paid some charming compliment. One here sees at once that it is not only shame that this divinity lacks;—and in general there are good grounds for supposing that in some things the gods could all of them come to us men for instruction. We men are—more human.—

296

Alas! what are you, after all, my written and painted thoughts! Not long ago you were so variegated, young and malicious, so full of thorns and secret spices, that you made me sneeze and laugh—and now? You have already doffed your novelty, and some of you, I fear, are ready to become truths, so immortal do they look, so pathetically honest, so tedious! And was it ever otherwise? What then do we write and paint, we mandarins with Chinese brush, we immortalisers of things which *lend* themselves to writing, what are we alone capable of painting? Alas, only that which is just about to fade and begins to lose its odour! Alas, only exhausted and departing storms and belated yellow sentiments! Alas, only birds strayed and fatigued by flight, which now let themselves be captured with the hand—with *our* hand! We immortalise what cannot live and fly much longer, things only which are exhausted and mellow! And it is only for your *afternoon,* you, my written and painted thoughts, for which alone I have colours, many colours, perhaps, many variegated softenings, and fifty yellows and browns and greens and reds;—but nobody will divine thereby how ye looked in your morning, you sudden sparks and marvels of my solitude, you, my old, beloved—*evil* thoughts!

From the Heights

TRANSLATED BY L. A. MAGNUS

1

MIDDAY of Life! Oh, season of delight!
My summer's park!
Uneaseful joy to look, to lurk, to hark:—
I peer for friends, am ready day and night,—
Where linger ye, my friends? The time is right!

2

Is not the glacier's grey today for you
Rose-garlanded?
The brooklet seeks you; wind, cloud, with longing thread
And thrust themselves yet higher to the blue,
To spy for you from farthest eagle's view.

3

My table was spread out for you on high:—
        Who dwelleth so
Star-near, so near the grisly pit below?—
My realm—what realm hath wider boundary?
My honey—who hath sipped its fragrancy?

4

Friends, ye are there! Woe me,—yet I am not
        He whom ye seek?
Ye stare and stop—better your wrath could speak!
I am not I? Hand, gait, face, changed? And what
I am, to you my friends, now am I not?

5

Am I an other? Strange am I to Me?
        Yet from Me sprung?
A wrestler, by himself too oft self-wrung?
Hindering too oft my own self's potency,
Wounded and hampered by self-victory?

6

I sought where-so the wind blow keenest. There I learned
        to dwell
Where no man dwells, on lonesome ice-lorn fell,
And unlearned Man and God and curse and prayer?
Became a ghost haunting the glaciers bare?

[*613*]

7

Ye, my old friends! Look! Ye turn pale, filled o'er
        With love and fear!
Go! Yet not in wrath. Ye could ne'er live here.
Here in the farthest realm of ice and scaur,
A huntsman must one be, like chamois soar.

8

An evil huntsman was I? See how taut
        My bow was bent!
Strongest was he by whom such bolt were sent—
Woe now! That arrow is with peril fraught,
Perilous as none.—Have yon safe home ye sought!

9

Ye go! Thou didst endure enough, oh, heart;—
        Strong was thy hope;
Unto new friends thy portals widely ope,
Let old ones be. Bid memory depart!
Wast thou young then, now—better young thou art!

10

What linked us once together, one hope's tie—
        (Who now doth con
Those lines, now fading, Love once wrote thereon?)—
Is like a parchment, which the hand is shy
To touch—like crackling leaves, all seared, all dry.

[*614*]

11

Oh! Friends no more! They are—what name for those?—
    Friends' phantom-flight
Knocking at my heart's window-pane at night,
Gazing on me, that speaks "We were" and goes,—
Oh, withered words once fragrant as the rose!

12

Pinings of youth that might not understand!
    For which I pined,
Which I deemed changed with me, kin of my kind:
But they grew old, and thus were doomed and banned:
None but new kith are native of my land!

13

Midday of life! My second youth's delight!
    My summer's park!
Unrestful joy to long, to lurk, to hark!
I peer for friends!—am ready day and night,
For my new friends. Come! Come! The time is right!

14

This song is done,—the sweet sad cry of rue
    Sang out its end;
A wizard wrought it, he the timely friend,
The midday friend,—no, do not ask me who;
At mid-day 'twas, when one became as two.

15

We keep our Feast of Feasts, sure of our bourne,
    Our aims self-same:
The Guest of Guests, friend Zarathustra, came!
The world now laughs, the grisly veil was torn,
And Light and Dark were one that wedding-morn.

THE GENEALOGY OF MORALS

Translated by HORACE B. SAMUEL, M.A.

EDITOR'S NOTE

In 1887, with the view of amplifying and completing certain new doctrines which he had merely sketched in *Beyond Good and Evil* (see especially Aphorism 260), Nietzsche published *The Genealogy of Morals*. This work is perhaps the least aphoristic, in form, of all Nietzsche's productions. For analytical power, more especially in those parts where Nietzsche examines the ascetic ideal, *The Genealogy of Morals* is unequalled by any other of his works; and, in the light which it throws upon the attitude of the ecclesiast to the man of resentment and misfortune, it is one of the most valuable contributions to sacerdotal psychology.

CONTENTS

PREFACE

1

WE are unknown, we knowers, ourselves to ourselves: this has its own good reason. We have never searched for ourselves —how should it then come to pass, that we should ever *find* ourselves? Rightly has it been said: "Where your treasure is, there will your heart be also." *Our* treasure is there, where stand the hives of our knowledge. It is to those hives that we are always striving; as born creatures of flight, and as the honey-gatherers of the spirit, we care really in our hearts only for one thing—to bring something "home to the hive!"

As far as the rest of life with its so-called "experiences" is concerned, which of us has even sufficient serious interest? or sufficient time? In our dealings with such points of life, we are, I fear, never properly to the point; to be precise, our heart is not there, and certainly not our ear. Rather like one who, delighting in a divine distraction, or sunken in the seas of his own soul, in whose ear the clock has just thundered with all its force its twelve strokes of noon, suddenly wakes up, and asks himself, "What has in point of fact just struck?" so do we at times rub afterwards, as it were, our puzzled ears, and ask in complete astonishment and complete embarrassment, "Through what have we in point of fact just lived?" further, "who are we in point of fact?" and count, *after they have struck,* as I have explained, all the twelve throbbing beats of the clock of our experience, of our life, of our being—ah!—and count wrong in the endeavour. Of necessity we remain strangers to ourselves, we understand ourselves not, in ourselves we are bound to be mistaken, for of us holds good to all eternity the motto, "Each one is the farthest away from himself"—as far as ourselves are concerned we are not "knowers."

2

My thoughts concerning the *genealogy* of our moral prejudices—for they constitute the issue in this polemic—have their first, bald, and provisional expression in that collection of aphorisms entitled *Human, all-too-Human, a Book for Free Minds,* the writing of which was begun in Sorrento, during a winter which allowed me to gaze over the broad and dangerous territory through which my mind had up to that time wandered. This took place in the winter of 1876-77; the thoughts themselves are older.

They were in their substance already the same thoughts which I take up again in the following treatises:—we hope that they have derived benefit from the long interval, that they have grown riper, clearer, stronger, more complete. The fact, however, that I still cling to them even now, that in the meanwhile they have always held faster by each other, have, in fact, grown out of their original shape and into each other, all this strengthens in my mind the joyous confidence that they must have been originally neither separate, disconnected, capricious nor sporadic phenomena, but have sprung from a common root, from a fundamental *"fiat"* of knowledge, whose empire reached to the soul's depth, and that ever grew more definite in its voice, and more definite in its demands. That is

the only state of affairs that is proper in the case of a philosopher.

We have no right to be *"disconnected"*; we must neither err
"disconnectedly" nor strike the truth "disconnectedly." Rather
with the necessity with which a tree bears its fruit, so do our
thoughts, our values, our Yes's and No's and If's and
Whether's, grow connected and interrelated, mutual witnesses
of *one* will, *one* health, *one* kingdom, *one* sun—as to whether
they are to *your* taste, these fruits of ours?—But what matters
that to the trees? What matters that to us, us the philosophers?

3

Owing to a scrupulosity peculiar to myself, which I confess
reluctantly,—it concerns indeed *morality,*—a scrupulosity,
which manifests itself in my life at such an early period, with
so much spontaneity, with so chronic a persistence and so keen
an opposition to environment, epoch, precedent, and ancestry
that I should have been almost entitled to style it my *"a priori"*
—my curiosity and my suspicion felt themselves betimes bound
to halt at the question, of what in point of actual fact was the
origin of our "Good" and of our "Evil." Indeed, at the boyish
age of thirteen the problem of the origin of Evil already
haunted me: at an age "when games and God divide one's
heart," I devoted to that problem my first childish attempt at
the literary game, my first philosophic essay—and as regards
my infantile solution of the problem, well, I gave quite properly the honour to God, and made him the *father* of evil. Did
my own *"a priori"* demand that precise solution from me?
that new, immoral, or at least "amoral" *"a priori"* and that
"categorical imperative" which was its voice (but, oh! how

[*623*]

hostile to the Kantian article, and how pregnant with problems!), to which since then I have given more and more attention, and indeed what is more than attention. Fortunately I soon learned to separate theological from moral prejudices, and I gave up looking for a *supernatural* origin of evil. A certain amount of historical and philological education, to say nothing of an innate faculty of psychological discrimination *par excellence* succeeded in transforming almost immediately my original problem into the following one:——Under what conditions did Man invent for himself those judgments of values, "Good" and "Evil"? *And what intrinsic value do they possess in themselves?* Have they up to the present hindered or advanced human well-being? Are they a symptom of the distress, impoverishment, and degeneration of Human Life? Or, conversely, is it in them that is manifested the fullness, the strength, and the will of Life, its courage, its self-confidence, its future? On this point I found and hazarded in my mind the most diverse answers, I established distinctions in periods, peoples, and castes, I became a specialist in my problem, and from my answers grew new questions, new investigations, new conjectures, new probabilities; until at last I had a land of my own and a soil of my own, a whole secret world growing and flowering, like hidden gardens of whose existence no one could have an inkling—oh, how happy are we, we finders of knowledge, provided that we know how to keep silent sufficiently long.

4

My first impulse to publish some of my hypotheses concerning the origin of morality I owe to a clear, well-written, and even precocious little book, in which a perverse and

vicious kind of moral philosophy (your real *English* kind)
was definitely presented to me for the first time; and this attracted me—with that magnetic attraction, inherent in that
which is diametrically opposed and antithetical to one's own
ideas. The title of the book was *The Origin of the Moral Emotions;* its author, Dr. Paul Rée; the year of its appearance, 1877.
I may almost say that I have never read anything in which
every single dogma and conclusion has called forth from me
so emphatic a negation as did that book; albeit a negation un-
tainted by either pique or intolerance. I referred accordingly
both in season and out of season in the previous works, at
which I was then working, to the arguments of that book, not
to refute them—for what have I got to do with mere refutations—but substituting, as is natural to a positive mind, for an
improbable theory one which is more probable, and occasionally no doubt for one philosophic error another. In that
early period I gave, as I have said, the first public expression
to those theories of origin to which these essays are devoted,
but with a clumsiness which I was the last to conceal from
myself, for I was as yet cramped, being still without a special
language for these special subjects, still frequently liable to
relapse and to vacillation. To go into details, compare what I
say in *Human, all-too-Human,* part i., about the parallel early
history of Good and Evil, Aph. 45 (namely, their origin from
the castes of the aristocrats and the slaves); similarly, Aph.
136 et seq., concerning the birth and value of ascetic morality;
similarly, Aphs. 96, 99, vol. ii., Aph. 89, concerning the
Morality of Custom, that far older and more original kind of
morality which is *toto cœlo* different from the altruistic ethics
(in which Dr. Rée, like all the English moral philosophers,
sees the ethical "Thing-in-itself"); finally, Aph. 92. Similarly,
Aph. 26 in *Human, all-too-Human,* part ii., and Aph. 112, the

Dawn of Day, concerning the origin of Justice as a balance between persons of approximately equal power (equilibrium as
the hypothesis of all contract, consequently of all law);
similarly, concerning the origin of Punishment, *Human, all-
too-Human,* part ii., Aphs. 22, 23, in regard to which the
deterrent object is neither essential nor original (as Dr. Rée
thinks:—rather is it that this object is only imported, under
certain definite conditions, and always as something extra
and additional).

5

In reality I had set my heart at that time on something
much more important than the nature of the theories of
myself or others concerning the origin of morality (or, more
precisely, the real function from my view of these theories was
to point an end to which they were one among many means).
The issue for me was the value of morality, and on that subject I had to place myself in a state of abstraction, in which I
was almost alone with my great teacher Schopenhauer, to
whom that book, with all its passion and inherent contradiction (for that book also was a polemic), turned for present
help as though he were still alive. The issue was, strangely
enough, the value of the "unegoistic" instincts, the instincts
of pity, self-denial, and self-sacrifice which Schopenhauer had
so persistently painted in golden colours, deified and etherealised, that eventually they appeared to him, as it were, high and
dry, as "intrinsic values in themselves," on the strength of
which he uttered both to Life and to himself his own negation.
But against *these very* instincts there voiced itself in my soul a
more and more fundamental mistrust, a scepticism that dug

ever deeper and deeper: and in this very instinct I saw the *great* danger of mankind, its most sublime temptation and seduction—seduction to what? to nothingness?—in these very instincts I saw the beginning of the end, stability, the exhaustion that gazes backwards, the will turning *against* Life, the last illness announcing itself with its own mincing melancholy: I realised that the morality of pity which spread wider and wider, and whose grip infected even philosophers with its disease, was the most sinister symptom of our modern European civilisation; I realised that it was the route along which that civilisation slid on its way to—a new Buddhism?—a European Buddhism?—*Nihilism?* This exaggerated estimation in which modern philosophers have held pity, is quite a new phenomenon: up to that time philosophers were absolutely unanimous as to the *worthlessness* of pity. I need only mention Plato, Spinoza, La Rochefoucauld, and Kant—four minds as mutually different as is possible, but united on one point; their contempt of pity.

6

This problem of the value of pity and of the pity-morality (I am an opponent of the modern infamous emasculation of our emotions) seems at the first blush a mere isolated problem, a note of interrogation for itself; he, however, who once halts at this problem, and learns how to put questions, will experience what I experienced:—a new and immense vista unfolds itself before him, a sense of potentiality seizes him like a vertigo, every species of doubt, mistrust, and fear springs up, the belief in morality, nay, in all morality, totters,—finally a new demand voices itself. Let us speak out this *new demand:* we need a *critique* of moral values, *the value of these values* is for the first time to be called into question—and for this purpose a knowledge is necessary of the conditions and circumstances out of which these values grew, and under which they experienced their evolution and their distortion (morality as a result, as a symptom, as a mask, as Tartuffism, as disease, as a misunderstanding; but also morality as a cause, as a remedy, as a stimulant, as a fetter, as a drug), especially as such a knowledge has neither existed up to the present time nor is even now generally desired. The value of these "values" was taken for granted as an indisputable fact, which was beyond all question. No one has, up to the present, exhibited the faintest doubt or hesitation in judging the "good man" to be of a higher value than the "evil man," of a higher value with regard specifically to human progress, utility, and prosperity generally, not forgetting the future. What? Suppose the converse were the truth! What? Suppose there lurked in the "good man" a symptom of retrogression, such as a danger, a temptation, a poison, a *narcotic*, by means of which the present *battened on the future!* More comfortable and less risky perhaps than its opposite, but also pettier, meaner! So that morality would really be saddled with the guilt, if the *maximum potentiality of the power and splendour* of the human species were never to be attained? So that really morality would be the danger of dangers?

7

Enough, that after this vista had disclosed itself to me, I myself had reason to search for learned, bold, and industrious colleagues (I am doing it even to this very day). It means traversing with new clamorous questions, and at the same time

with new eyes, the immense, distant, and completely unexplored land of morality—of a morality which has actually
existed and been actually lived! and is this not practically
equivalent to first *discovering* that land? If, in this context, I
thought, amongst others, of the aforesaid Dr. Rée, I did so
because I had no doubt that from the very nature of his questions he would be compelled to have recourse to a truer method,
in order to obtain his answer. Have I deceived myself on that
score? I wished at all events to give a better direction of vision
to an eye of such keenness and such impartiality. I wished to
direct him to the real *history of morality,* and to warn him,
while there was yet time, against a world of English theories
that culminated *in the blue vacuum of heaven.* Other colours,
of course, rise immediately to one's mind as being a hundred
times more potent than blue for a genealogy of morals:—for
instance, *grey,* by which I mean authentic facts capable of
definite proof and having actually existed, or, to put it shortly,
the whole of that long hieroglyphic script (which is so hard
to decipher) about the past history of human morals. This
script was unknown to Dr. Rée; but he had read Darwin:—
and so in his philosophy the Darwinian beast and that pink of
modernity, the demure weakling and dilettante, who "bites no
longer," shake hands politely in a fashion, that is at least instructive, the latter exhibiting a certain facial expression of
refined and good-humoured indolence, tinged with a touch of
pessimism and exhaustion; as if it really did not pay to take all
these things—I mean moral problems—so seriously. I, on the
other hand, think that there are no subjects which *pay* better
for being taken seriously; part of this payment is, that perhaps eventually they admit of being taken *gaily.* This gaiety,
indeed, or, to use my own language, this *joyful wisdom,* is a
payment; a payment for a protracted, brave, laborious, and

burrowing seriousness, which, it goes without saying, is the attribute of but a few. But on that day on which we say from the fullness of our hearts, "Forward! our old morality too is fit material *for Comedy,*" we shall have discovered a new plot, and a new possibility for the Dionysian drama entitled *The Soul's Fate*—and he will speedily utilise it, one can wager safely, he, the great ancient eternal dramatist of the comedy of our existence.

8

If this writing be obscure to any individual, and jar on his ears, I do not think that it is necessarily I who am to blame. It is clear enough, on the hypothesis which I presuppose, namely, that the reader has first read my previous writings and has not grudged them a certain amount of trouble: it is not, indeed, a simple matter to get really at their essence. Take, for instance, my *Zarathustra;* I allow no one to pass muster as knowing that book, unless every single word therein has at some time wrought in him a profound wound, and at some time exercised on him a profound enchantment: then and not till then can he enjoy the privilege of participating reverently in the halcyon element, from which that work is born, in its sunny brilliance, its distance, its spaciousness, its certainty. In other cases the aphoristic form produces difficulty, but this is only because this form is treated *too casually.* An aphorism properly coined and cast into its final mould is far from being "deciphered" as soon as it has been read; on the contrary, it is then that it first requires *to be expounded*—of course for that purpose an art of exposition is necessary. The third essay in this book provides an example of what is offered, of what in such cases I call exposition: an aphorism is prefixed to that essay, the essay itself is its commentary. Certainly one *quality* which nowadays has been best forgotten—and that is why it will take some time yet for my writings to become readable—is essential in order to practise reading as an art—a quality for the exercise of which it is necessary to be a cow, and under *no circumstances* a modern man!—*rumination*.

SILS-MARIA, UPPER ENGADINE,
    July, 1887.

"Good and Evil," "Good and Bad"

1

THOSE English psychologists, who up to the present are the only philosophers who are to be thanked for any endeavour to get as far as a history of the origin of morality—these men, I say, offer us in their own personalities no paltry problem;—they even have, if I am to be quite frank about it, in the capacity of living riddles, an advantage over their books—*they themselves are interesting!* These English psychologists—what do they really mean? We always find them voluntarily or involuntarily at the same task of pushing to the front the *partie honteuse* of our inner world, and looking for the efficient, governing, and decisive principle in that precise quarter where the intellectual self-respect of the race would be the most reluctant to find it (for example, in the *vis inertiæ* of habit, or in forgetfulness, or in a blind and fortuitous mechanism and association of ideas, or in some factor that is purely passive, reflex, molecular, or fundamentally stupid)—what is the real motive power which always impels these psychologists in precisely *this* direction? Is it an instinct for human disparagement somewhat sinister, vulgar, and malignant, or perhaps in-

[*632*]

comprehensible even to itself? or perhaps a touch of pessimistic jealousy, the mistrust of disillusioned idealists who have become gloomy, poisoned, and bitter? or a petty subconscious enmity and rancour against Christianity (and Plato), that has conceivably never crossed the threshold of consciousness? or just a vicious taste for those elements of life which are bizarre, painfully paradoxical, mystical, and illogical? or, as a final alternative, a dash of each of these motives—a little vulgarity, a little gloominess, a little anti-Christianity, a little craving for the necessary piquancy?

But I am told that it is simply a case of old frigid and tedious frogs crawling and hopping around men and inside men, as if they were as thoroughly at home there, as they would be in a *swamp*.

I am opposed to this statement, nay, I do not believe it; and if, in the impossibility of knowledge, one is permitted to wish, so do I wish from my heart that just the converse metaphor should apply, and that these analysts with their psychological microscopes should be, at bottom, brave, proud, and magnanimous animals who know how to bridle both their hearts and their smarts, and have specifically trained themselves to sacrifice what is desirable to what is true, *any* truth in fact, even the simple, bitter, ugly, repulsive, unchristian, and immoral truths—for there are truths of that description.

2

All honour, then, to the noble spirits who would fain dominate these historians of morality. But it is certainly a pity that they lack the *historical sense* itself, that they themselves are quite deserted by all the beneficent spirits of history. The whole train of their thought runs, as was always the way of old-fashioned philosophers, on *thoroughly* unhistorical lines: there is no doubt on this point. The crass ineptitude of their genealogy of morals is immediately apparent when the question arises of ascertaining the origin of the idea and judgment of "good." "Man had originally," so speaks their decree, "praised and called 'good' altruistic acts from the standpoint of those on whom they were conferred, that is, those to whom they were *useful;* subsequently the origin of this praise was *forgotten,* and altruistic acts, simply because, as a sheer matter of habit, they were praised as good, came also to be felt as good —as though they contained in themselves some intrinsic goodness." The thing is obvious:—this initial derivation contains already all the typical and idiosyncratic traits of the English psychologists—we have "utility," "forgetting," "habit," and finally "error," the whole assemblage forming the basis of a system of values, on which the higher man has up to the present prided himself as though it were a kind of privilege of man in general. This pride *must* be brought low, this system of values *must* lose its values: is that attained?

Now the first argument that comes ready to my hand is that the real homestead of the concept "good" is sought and located in the wrong place: the judgment "good" did *not* originate among those to whom goodness was shown. Much rather has it been the good themselves, that is, the aristocratic, the powerful, the high-stationed, the high-minded, who have felt that they themselves were good, and that their actions were good, that is to say of the first order, in contradistinction to all the low, the low-minded, the vulgar, and the plebeian. It was out of this pathos of distance that they first arrogated the right to create values for their own profit, and to coin the names of such values: what had they to do with utility? The standpoint of utility is as alien and as inapplicable as it could possibly be, when we have to deal with so volcanic an effervescence of supreme values, creating and demarcating as they do a hierarchy within themselves: it is at this juncture that one arrives at an appreciation of the contrast to that tepid temperature, which is the presupposition on which every combination of worldly wisdom and every calculation of practical expediency is always based—and not for one occasional, not for one exceptional instance, but chronically. The pathos of nobility and distance, as I have said, the chronic and despotic *esprit de corps* and fundamental instinct of a higher dominant race coming into association with a meaner race, an "under race," this is the origin of the antithesis of good and bad.

(The masters' right of giving names goes so far that it is permissible to look upon language itself as the expression of the power of the masters: they say "this *is* that, and that," they seal finally every object and every event with a sound, and thereby at the same time take possession of it.) It is because of this origin that the word "good" is far from having any necessary connection with altruistic acts, in accordance with the superstitious belief of these moral philosophers. On the contrary, it is on the occasion of the *decay* of aristocratic values, that the antitheses between "egoistic" and "altruistic" press more and more heavily on the human conscience—it is, to use my own language, the *herd instinct* which finds in this antithesis an expression in many ways. And even then it takes a considerable time for this instinct to become sufficiently dominant, for the valuation to be inextricably dependent on this antithesis (as is the case in contemporary Europe); for today the prejudice is predominant, which, acting even now with all the intensity of an obsession and brain disease, holds that "moral," "altruistic," and *"désintéressé"* are concepts of equal value.

3

In the second place, quite apart from the fact that this hypothesis as to the genesis of the value "good" cannot be historically upheld, it suffers from an inherent psychological contradiction. The utility of altruistic conduct has presumably been the origin of its being praised, and this origin has become *forgotten:*—But in what conceivable way is this forgetting *possible?* Has perchance the utility of such conduct ceased at some given moment? The contrary is the case. This utility has rather been experienced every day at all times, and is consequently a feature that obtains a new and regular emphasis with every fresh day; it follows that, so far from vanishing from the consciousness, so far indeed from being forgotten, it must necessarily become impressed on the consciousness with ever-increasing distinctness. How much more logical is that contrary theory (it is not the truer for that) which is represented, for instance, by Herbert Spencer, who places the concept "good" as essentially similar to the concept "useful," "purposive," so that in the judgments "good" and "bad" mankind is simply summarising and investing with a sanction its *unforgotten* and *unforgettable experiences* concerning the "useful-purposive" and the "mischievous-non-purposive." According to this theory, "good" is the attribute of that which has previously shown itself useful; and so is able to claim to be considered "valuable in the highest degree," "valuable in itself."

This method of explanation is also, as I have said, wrong, but at any rate the explanation itself is coherent, and psychologically tenable.

4

The guide-post which first put me on the *right* track was this question—what is the true etymological significance of the various symbols for the idea "good" which have been coined in the various languages? I then found that they all led back to *the same evolution of the same idea*—that everywhere "aristocrat," "noble" (in the social sense), is the root idea, out of which have necessarily developed "good" in the sense of "with aristocratic soul," "noble," in the sense of "with a soul of high calibre," "with a privileged soul"—a development which invariably runs parallel with that other evolution by which "vulgar," "plebeian," "low," are made to change finally into "bad." The most eloquent proof of this last contention is the German word *"schlecht"* itself: this word is identical with *"schlicht"*—(compare *"schlechtweg"* and *"schlechterdings"*)—which, originally and as yet without any sinister innuendo, simply denoted the plebeian man in contrast to the aristocratic man. It is at the sufficiently late period of the Thirty Years' War that this sense becomes changed to the sense now current. From the standpoint of the Genealogy of Morals this discovery seems to be substantial: the lateness of it is to be attributed to the retarding influence exercised in the modern world by democratic prejudice in the sphere of all questions of origin. This extends, as will shortly be shown, even to the province of natural science and physiology, which *prima facie* is the most objective. The extent of the mischief

which is caused by this prejudice (once it is free of all tram-
mels except those of its own malice), particularly to Ethics and
History, is shown by the notorious case of Buckle: it was in
Buckle that that *plebeianism* of the modern spirit, which is
of English origin, broke out once again from its malignant soil
with all the violence of a slimy volcano, and with that salted,
rampant, and vulgar eloquence with which up to the present
time all volcanoes have spoken.

5

With regard to *our* problem, which can justly be called an
intimate problem, and which elects to appeal to only a limited
number of ears: it is of no small interest to ascertain that in
those words and roots which denote "good" we catch glimpses
of that arch-trait, on the strength of which the aristocrats feel
themselves to be beings of a higher order than their fellows.
Indeed, they call themselves in perhaps the most frequent instances simply after their superiority in power (*e.g.* "the
powerful," "the lords," "the commanders"), or after the most
obvious sign of their superiority, as for example "the rich,"
"the possessors" (that is the meaning of *arya;* and the Iranian
and Slav languages correspond). But they also call themselves
after some *characteristic idiosyncrasy;* and this is the case which
now concerns us. They name themselves, for instance, "the
truthful": this is first done by the Greek nobility whose mouthpiece is found in Theognis, the Megarian poet. The word
ἐσθλός, which is coined for the purpose, signifies etymologi-
cally "one who *is*," who has reality, who is real, who is true;
and then with a subjective twist, the "true," as the "truthful":
at this stage in the evolution of the idea, it becomes the motto

and party cry of the nobility, and quite completes the transition
to the meaning "noble," so as to place outside the pale the
lying, vulgar man, as Theognis conceives and portrays him—
till finally the word after the decay of the nobility is left to
delineate psychological *noblesse,* and becomes as it were ripe
and mellow. In the word κακός as in δειλὸς (the plebeian in
contrast to the ἀγαθός) the cowardice is emphasized. This
affords perhaps an inkling on what lines the etymological
origin of the very ambiguous ἀγαθός is to be investigated. In
the Latin *malus* (which I place side by side with μέλας)
the vulgar man can be distinguished as the dark-coloured, and
above all as the black-haired (*"hic niger est"*), as the pre-
Aryan inhabitants of the Italian soil, whose complexion
formed the clearest feature of distinction from the dominant
blonds, namely, the Aryan conquering race:—at any rate
Gaelic has afforded me the exact analogue—*Fin* (for instance.
in the name *Fin-Gal*), the distinctive word of the nobility,
finally—good, noble, clean, but originally the blond-haired
man in contrast to the dark black-haired aboriginals. The Celts,
if I may make a parenthetic statement, were throughout a
blond race; and it is wrong to connect, as Virchow still con-
nects, those traces of an essentially dark-haired population
which are to be seen on the more elaborate ethnographical maps
of Germany with any Celtic ancestry or with any admixture of
Celtic blood: in this context it is rather the *pre-Aryan* population of Germany which surges up to these districts. (The same
is true substantially of the whole of Europe: in point of fact,
the subject race has finally again obtained the upper hand, in
complexion and the shortness of the skull, and perhaps in the
intellectual and social qualities. Who can guarantee that
modern democracy, still more modern anarchy, and indeed that
tendency to the "Commune," the most primitive form of

society, which is now common to all the Socialists in Europe, does not in its real essence signify a monstrous reversion—and that the conquering and *master* race—the Aryan race, is not also becoming inferior physiologically?) I believe that I can explain the Latin *bonus* as the "warrior": my hypothesis is that I am right in deriving *bonus* from an older *duonus* (compare *bellum-duellum = duen-lum,* in which the word *duonus* appears to me to be contained). *Bonus* accordingly as the man of discord, of variance, "entzweiung" (*duo*), as the warrior: one sees what in ancient Rome "the good" meant for a man. Must not our actual German word *gut* mean *"the godlike,* the man of godlike race"? and be identical with the national name (originally the nobles' name) of the *Goths?*

The grounds for this supposition do not appertain to this work.

6

Above all, there is no exception (though there are opportunities for exceptions) to this rule, that the idea of political superiority always resolves itself into the idea of psychological superiority, in those cases where the highest caste is at the same time the *priestly* caste, and in accordance with its general characteristics confers on itself the privilege of a title which alludes specifically to its priestly function. It is in these cases, for instances, that "clean" and "unclean" confront each other for the first time as badges of class distinction; here again there develops a "good" and a "bad," in a sense which has ceased to be merely social. Moreover, care should be taken not to take these ideas of "clean" and "unclean" too seriously, too broadly, or too symbolically: all the ideas of ancient man have, on the contrary, got to be understood in their initial stages, in a sense which is, to an almost inconceivable extent, crude, coarse, physical, and narrow, and above all essentially *unsymbolical*. The "clean man" is originally only a man who washes himself, who abstains from certain foods which are conducive to skin diseases, who does not sleep with the unclean women of the lower classes, who has a horror of blood—not more, not much more! On the other hand, the very nature of a priestly aristocracy shows the reason why just at such an early juncture there should ensure a really dangerous sharpening and intensification of opposed values: it is, in fact, through these opposed values that gulfs are cleft in the social plane, which a veritable Achilles of free thought would shudder to cross. There is from the outset a certain *diseased taint* in such sacerdotal aristocracies, and in the habits which prevail in such societies—habits which, *averse* as they are to action, constitute a compound of introspection and explosive emotionalism, as a result of which there appears that introspective morbidity and neurasthenia, which adheres almost inevitably to all priests at all times: with regard, however, to the remedy which they themselves have invented for this disease—the philosopher has no option but to state, that it has proved itself in its effects a hundred times more dangerous than the disease, from which it should have been the deliverer. Humanity itself is still diseased from the effects of the naïvetés of this priestly cure. Take, for instance, certain kinds of diet (abstention from flesh), fasts, sexual continence, flight into the wilderness (a kind of Weir-Mitchell isolation, though of course without that system of excessive feeding and fattening which is the most efficient antidote to all the hysteria of the ascetic ideal); consider too the whole metaphysic of the priests, with its war on the senses, its enervation, its hair-splitting; consider its self-hypnotism on the fakir and Brahman principles (it uses Brahman as a glass disc and obses-

sion), and that climax which we can understand only too well
of an unusual satiety with its panacea of *nothingness* (or God:
—the demand for a *unio mystica* with God is the demand of
the Buddhist for nothingness, Nirvana—and nothing else!).
In sacerdotal societies *every* element is on a more dangerous
scale, not merely cures and remedies, but also pride, revenge,
cunning, exaltation, love, ambition, virtue, morbidity:—further, it can fairly be stated that it is on the soil of this *essentially
dangerous* form of human society, the sacerdotal form, that
man really becomes for the first time an *interesting animal*,
that it is in this form that the soul of man has in a higher sense
attained *depths* and become *evil*—and those are the two fundamental forms of the superiority which up to the present man
has exhibited over every other animal.

7

The reader will have already surmised with what ease the
priestly mode of valuation can branch off from the knightly
aristocratic mode, and then develop into the very antithesis of
the latter: special impetus is given to this opposition, by every
occasion when the castes of the priests and warriors confront
each other with mutual jealousy and cannot agree over the
prize. The knightly-aristocratic "values" are based on a careful
cult of the physical, on a flowering, rich, and even effervescing
healthiness, that goes considerably beyond what is necessary
for maintaining life, on war, adventure, the chase, the dance,
the tourney—on everything, in fact, which is contained in
strong, free, and joyous action. The priestly-aristocratic mode
of valuation is—we have seen—based on other hypotheses: it
is bad enough for this class when it is a question of war! Yet

the priests are, as is notorious, *the worst enemies*—why? Because they are the weakest. Their weakness causes their hate to expand into a monstrous and sinister shape, a shape which is most crafty and most poisonous. The really great haters in the history of the world have always been priests, who are also the cleverest haters—in comparison with the cleverness of priestly revenge, every other piece of cleverness is practically negligible. Human history would be too fatuous for anything were it not for the cleverness imported into it by the weak—take at once the most important instance. All the world's efforts against the "aristocrats," the "mighty," the "masters," the "holders of power," are negligible by comparison with what has been accomplished against those classes by *the Jews*—the Jews, that priestly nation which eventually realised that the one method of effecting satisfaction on its enemies and tyrants was by means of a radical transvaluation of values, which was at the same time an act of the *cleverest revenge*. Yet the method was only appropriate to a nation of priests, to a nation of the most jealously nursed priestly revengefulness. It was the Jews who, in opposition to the aristocratic equation (good = aristocratic = beautiful = happy = loved by the gods), dared with a terrifying logic to suggest the contrary equation, and indeed to maintain with the teeth of the most profound hatred (the hatred of weakness) this contrary equation, namely, "the wretched are alone the good; the poor, the weak, the lowly, are alone the good; the suffering, the needy, the sick, the loathsome, are the only ones who are pious, the only ones who are blessed, for them alone is salvation—but you, on the other hand, you aristocrats, you men of power, you are to all eternity the evil, the horrible, the covetous, the insatiate, the godless; eternally also shall you be the unblessed, the cursed, the damned!" We know who it was who reaped the heritage of this Jewish transvaluation. In the context of the monstrous and inordinately fateful initiative which the Jews have exhibited in connection with this most fundamental of all declarations of war, I remember the passage which came to my pen on another occasion (*Beyond Good and Evil*, Aph. 195)—that it was, in fact, with the Jews that the *revolt of the slaves* begins in the sphere *of morals;* that revolt which has behind it a history of two millennia, and which at the present day has only moved out of our sight, because it—has achieved victory.

8

But you understand this not? You have no eyes for a force which has taken two thousand years to achieve victory?—There is nothing wonderful in this: all *lengthy* processes are hard to see and to realise. But *this* is what took place: from the trunk of that tree of revenge and hate, Jewish hate,—that most profound and sublime hate, which creates ideals and changes old values to new creations, the like of which has never been on earth,—there grew a phenomenon which was equally incomparable, *a new love,* the most profound and sublime of all kinds of love;—and from what other trunk could it have grown? But beware of supposing that this love has soared on its upward growth, as in any way a real negation of that thirst for revenge, as an antithesis to the Jewish hate! No, the contrary is the truth! This love grew out of that hate, as its crown, as its triumphant crown, circling wider and wider amid the clarity and fullness of the sun, and pursuing in the very kingdom of light and height its goal of hatred, its victory, its spoil, its strategy, with the same intensity with which the roots of that tree of hate sank into everything which was deep and evil with increasing stability and increasing desire. This Jesus of Nazareth, the incarnate gospel of love, this "Redeemer" bring-ing salvation and victory to the poor, the sick, the sinful—was he not really temptation in its most sinister and irresistible form, temptation to take the tortuous path to those very *Jewish* values and those very Jewish ideals? Has not Israel really obtained the final goal of its sublime revenge, by the tortuous paths of this "Redeemer," for all that he might pose as Israel's adversary and Israel's destroyer? Is it not due to the black magic of a really *great* policy of revenge, of a far-seeing, burrowing revenge, both acting and calculating with slowness, that Israel himself must repudiate before all the world the actual instrument of his own revenge and nail it to the cross, so that all the world—that is, all the enemies of Israel—could nibble without suspicion at this very bait? Could, moreover, any human mind with all its elaborate ingenuity invent a bait that was more truly *dangerous?* Anything that was even equiva-lent in the power of its seductive, intoxicating, defiling, and corrupting influence to that symbol of the holy cross, to that awful paradox of a "god on the cross," to that mystery of the unthinkable, supreme, and utter horror of the self-crucifixion of a god for the *salvation of man?* It is at least certain that *sub hoc signo* Israel, with its revenge and transvaluation of all values, has up to the present always triumphed again over all other ideals, over all more aristocratic ideals.

9

"But why do you talk of nobler ideals? Let us submit to the facts; that the people have triumphed—or the slaves, or the populace, or the herd, or whatever name you care to give them

—if this has happened through the Jews, so be it! In that case no nation ever had a greater mission in the world's history. The 'masters' have been done away with; the morality of the vulgar man has triumphed. This triumph may also be called a blood-poisoning (it has mutually fused the races)—I do not dispute it; but there is no doubt but that this intoxication has succeeded. The 'redemption' of the human race (that is, from the masters) is progressing swimmingly; everything is obviously becoming Judaised, or Christianised, or vulgarised (what is there in the words?). It seems impossible to stop the course of this poisoning through the whole body politic of mankind —but its *tempo* and pace may from the present time be slower, more delicate, quieter, more discreet—there is time enough. In view of this context has the Church nowadays any necessary purpose? Has it, in fact, a right to live? Or could man get on without it? *Quæritur*. It seems that it fetters and retards this tendency, instead of accelerating it. Well, even that might be its utility. The Church certainly is a crude and boorish institution, that is repugnant to an intelligence with any pretence at delicacy, to a really modern taste. Should it not at any rate learn to be somewhat more subtle? It alienates nowadays, more than it allures. Which of us would, forsooth, be a freethinker if there were no Church? It is the Church which repels us, *not* its poison—apart from the Church we like the poison." This is the epilogue of a freethinker to my discourse, of an honourable animal (as he has given abundant proof), and a democrat to boot; he had up to that time listened to me, and could not endure my silence, but for me, indeed, with regard to this topic there is much on which to be silent.

10

The revolt of the slaves in morals begins in the very principle of *resentment* becoming creative and giving birth to values—a resentment experienced by creatures who, deprived as they are of the proper outlet of action, are forced to find their compensation in an imaginary revenge. While every aristocratic morality springs from a triumphant affirmation of its own demands, the slave morality says "no" from the very outset to what is "outside itself," "different from itself," and "not itself": and this "no" is its creative deed. This volte-face of the valuing standpoint—this *inevitable* gravitation to the objective instead of back to the subjective—is typical of "resentment": the slave-morality requires as the condition of its existence an external and objective world, to employ physiological terminology, it requires objective stimuli to be capable of action at all—its action is fundamentally a reaction. The contrary is the case when we come to the aristocrat's system of values: it acts and grows spontaneously, it merely seeks its antithesis in order to pronounce a more grateful and exultant "yes" to its own self;—its negative conception, "low," "vulgar," "bad," is merely a pale late-born foil in comparison with its positive and fundamental conception (saturated as it is with life and passion), of "we aristocrats, we good ones, we beautiful ones, we happy ones."

When the aristocratic morality goes astray and commits sacrilege on reality, this is limited to that particular sphere with which it is *not* sufficiently acquainted—a sphere, in fact, from the real knowledge of which it disdainfully defends itself. It misjudges, in some cases, the sphere which it despises, the sphere of the common vulgar man and the low people: on the other hand, due weight should be given to the consideration that in any case the mood of contempt, of disdain, of superciliousness, even on the supposition that it *falsely* portrays the object of its contempt, will always be far removed from that degree of falsity which will always characterise the attacks—in effigy, of course—of the vindictive hatred and revengefulness of the weak in onslaughts on their enemies. In point of fact, there is in contempt too strong an admixture of nonchalance, of casualness, of boredom, of impatience, even of personal exultation, for it to be capable of distorting its victim into a real caricature or a real monstrosity. Attention again should be paid to the almost benevolent *nuances* which, for instance, the Greek nobility imports into all the words by which it distinguishes the common people from itself; note how continuously a kind of pity, care, and consideration imparts its honeyed *flavour*, until at last almost all the words which are applied to the vulgar man survive finally as expressions for "unhappy," "worthy of pity" (compare δειλός, δείλαιος, πονηρός, μοχθηρός; the latter two names really denoting the vulgar man as labour-slave and beast of burden) —and how, conversely, "bad," "low," "unhappy" have never ceased to ring in the Greek ear with a tone in which "unhappy" is the predominant note: this is a heritage of the old noble aristocratic morality, which remains true to itself even in contempt (let philologists remember the sense in which ὀϊζυρός, ἄνολβος, τλήμων, δυστυχεῖν, ξυμφορά used to be employed). The "well-born" simply *felt* themselves the "happy"; they did not have to manufacture their happiness artificially through looking at their enemies, or in cases to talk and lie themselves into happiness (as is the custom with all resentful men); and similarly, complete men as they were, exuberant with strength, and consequently *necessarily* energetic, they were too wise to dissociate happiness from action—activity becomes in their minds necessarily counted as happiness (that is the etymology of εὖ πράττειν)—all in sharp contrast to the "happiness" of the weak and the oppressed, with their festering venom and malignity, among whom happiness appears essentially as a narcotic, a deadening, a quietude, a peace, a "Sabbath," an enervation of the mind and relaxation of the limbs,—in short, a purely *passive* phenomenon. While the aristocratic man lived in confidence and openness with himself (γενναῖος, "noble-born," emphasises the nuance "sincere," and perhaps also "naïf"), the resentful man, on the other hand, is neither sincere nor naïf, nor honest and candid with himself. His soul *squints;* his mind loves hidden crannies, tortuous paths and backdoors, everything secret appeals to him as *his* word, *his* safety, *his* balm; he is past master in silence, in not forgetting, in waiting, in provisional self-depreciation and self-abasement. A race of such *resentful* men will of necessity eventually prove more *prudent* than any aristocratic race, it will honour prudence on quite a distinct scale, as, in fact, a paramount condition of existence, while prudence among aristocratic men is apt to be tinged with a delicate flavour of luxury and refinement; so among them it plays nothing like so integral a part as that complete certainty of function of the governing *unconscious* instincts, or as indeed a certain lack of prudence, such as a vehement and valiant charge, whether against danger or the enemy, or as those ecstatic bursts of rage, love, reverence, gratitude, by which at all times noble souls have recognised each other. When the resentment of the aristocratic man manifests itself, it fulfils and exhausts itself in an immediate reaction, and consequently instills no *venom*: on the other hand, it never manifests itself at all in countless instances, when in the case of the feeble and weak it would be inevitable. An inability to take seriously for any length of time their enemies, their disasters, their *misdeeds*—that is the sign of the full strong natures who possess a superfluity of moulding plastic force, that heals completely and produces forgetfulness: a good example of this in the modern world is Mirabeau, who had no memory for any insults and meannesses which were practised on him, and who was only incapable of forgiving because he forgot. Such a man indeed shakes off with a shrug many a worm which would have buried itself in another; it is only in characters like these that we see the possibility (supposing, of course, that there is such a possibility in the world) of the real "*love* of one's enemies." What respect for his enemies is found, forsooth, in an aristocratic man—and such a reverence is already a bridge to love! He insists on having his enemy to himself as his distinction. He tolerates no other enemy but a man in whose character there is nothing to despise and *much* to honour! On the other hand, imagine the "enemy" as the resentful man conceives him—and it is here exactly that we see his work, his creativeness; he has conceived "the evil enemy," the "evil one," and indeed that is the root idea from which he now evolves as a contrasting and corresponding figure a "good one," himself—his very self!

11

The method of this man is quite contrary to that of the aristocratic man, who conceives the root idea "good" spontaneously and straight away, that is to say, out of himself, and from that material then creates for himself a concept of "bad"! This "bad" of aristocratic origin and that "evil" out of the cauldron of unsatisfied hatred—the former an imitation, an "extra," an additional nuance; the latter, on the other hand, the original, the beginning, the essential act in the conception of a slave-morality—these two words "bad" and "evil," how great a difference do they mark, in spite of the fact that they have an identical contrary in the idea "good." But the idea "good" is *not* the same: much rather let the question be asked, "Who is really evil according to the meaning of the morality of resentment?" In all sternness let it be answered thus:— *just* the good man of the other morality, just the aristocrat, the powerful one, the one who rules, but who is distorted by the venomous eye of resentfulness, into a new colour, a new signification, a new appearance. This particular point we would be the last to deny: the man who learned to know those "good" ones only as enemies, learned at the same time not to know them only as *"evil enemies,"* and the same men who *inter pares* were kept so rigorously in bounds through convention, respect, custom, and gratitude, though much more through mutual vigilance and jealousy *inter pares,* these men who in their relations with each other find so many new ways of manifesting consideration, self-control, delicacy, loyalty, pride, and friendship, these men are in reference to what is outside their circle (where the foreign element, a *foreign* country, begins), not much better than beasts of prey, which have been let loose. They enjoy there freedom from all social control, they feel that in the wilderness they can give vent with impunity to that tension which is produced by enclosure and imprisonment in the peace of society, they *revert* to the innocence of the beast-of-prey conscience, like jubilant monsters, who perhaps come from a ghostly bout of murder, arson, rape, and torture, with bravado and a moral equanimity, as though merely some wild student's prank had been played, perfectly convinced that the poets have now an ample theme to sing and celebrate. It is impossible not to recognise at the core of all these aristocratic races the beast of prey; the magnificent *blond brute,* avidly rampant for spoil and victory; this hidden core needed an outlet from time to time, the beast must get loose again, must return into the wilderness—the Roman, Arabic, German, and Japanese nobility, the Homeric heroes, the Scandinavian Vikings, are all alike in this need. It is the aristocratic races who have left the idea "Barbarian" on all the tracks in which they have marched; nay, a consciousness of this very barbarianism, and even a pride in it, manifests itself even in their highest civilisation (for example, when Pericles says to his Athenians in that celebrated funeral oration, "Our audacity has forced a way over every land and sea, rearing everywhere imperishable memorials of itself for *good* and for *evil"*). This audacity of aristocratic races, mad, absurd, and spasmodic as may be its expression; the incalculable and fantastic nature of their enterprises,—Pericles sets in special relief and glory the ϱαϑυμία of the Athenians, their nonchalance and contempt for safety, body, life, and comfort, their awful joy and intense delight in all destruction, in all the ecstasies of victory and cruelty,—all these features become crystallised, for those who suffered thereby in the picture of the "barbarian," of the "evil enemy," perhaps of the "Goth" and of the "Vandal." The profound, icy mistrust which the German provokes, as soon as he arrives at power,—even at the present time,—is always still an aftermath of that inextinguishable horror with which for whole centuries Europe has regarded the wrath of the blond Teuton beast (although between the old Germans and ourselves there exists scarcely a psychological, let alone a physical, relationship). I have once called attention to the embarrassment of Hesiod, when he conceived the series of social ages, and endeavoured to express them in gold, silver, and bronze. He could only dispose of the contradiction, with which he was confronted, by the Homeric world, an age magnificent indeed, but at the same time so awful and so violent, by making two ages out of one, which he henceforth placed one behind the other—first, the age of the heroes and demigods, as that world had remained in the memories of the aristocratic families, who found therein their own ancestors; secondly, the bronze age, as that corresponding age appeared to the descendants of the oppressed, spoiled, ill-treated, exiled, enslaved; namely, as an age of bronze, as I have said, hard, cold, terrible, without feelings and without conscience, crushing everything, and bespattering everything with blood. Granted the truth of the theory now believed to be true, that the very *essence of all civilisation* is to *train* out of man, the beast of prey, a tame and civilised animal, a domesticated animal, it follows indubitably that we must regard as the real *tools of civilisation* all those instincts of reaction and resentment, by the help of which the aristocratic races, together with their ideals, were finally degraded and overpowered; though that has not yet come to be synonymous with saying that the bearers of those tools also *represented* the civilisation. It is rather the contrary that is not only probable—nay, it is *palpable* today; these bearers of vindictive instincts that have to be bottled up, these descendants of all European and non-European slavery, especially of the pre-Aryan population—these people, I say, represent the *decline* of humanity! These "tools of civilisation" are a disgrace to humanity, and constitute in reality more of an argument against civilisation, more of a reason why civilisation should be suspected. One may be perfectly justified in being always afraid of the blonde beast that lies at the core of all aristocratic races, and in being on one's guard: but who would not a

[*653*]

hundred times prefer to be afraid, when one at the same time
admires, than to be immune from fear, at the cost of being
perpetually obsessed with the loathsome spectacle of the distorted, the dwarfed, the stunted, the envenomed? And is that
not our fate? What produces today our repulsion towards
"man"?—for we *suffer* from "man," there is no doubt about
it. It is not fear; it is rather that we have nothing more to fear
from men; it is that the worm "man" is in the foreground
and pullulates; it is that the "tame man," the wretched mediocre and unedifying creature, has learned to consider himself
a goal and a pinnacle, an inner meaning, an historic principle,
a "higher man"; yes, it is that he has a certain right so to consider himself, in so far as he feels that in contrast to that excess
of deformity, disease, exhaustion, and effeteness whose odour
is beginning to pollute present-day Europe, he at any rate has
achieved a relative success, he at any rate still says "yes" to life.

12

I cannot refrain at this juncture from uttering a sigh and
one last hope. What is it precisely which I find intolerable?
That which I alone cannot get rid of, which makes me choke
and faint? Bad air! Bad air! That something misbegotten
comes near me; that I must inhale the odour of the entrails of
a misbegotten soul!—That excepted, what can one not endure
in the way of need, privation, bad weather, sickness, toil, solitude? In point of fact, one manages to get over everything,
born as one is to a burrowing and battling existence; one
always returns once again to the light, one always lives again
one's golden hour of victory—and then one stands as one was
born, unbreakable, tense, ready for something more difficult,

for something more distant, like a bow stretched but the tauter by every strain. But from time to time do ye grant me—assuming that "beyond good and evil" there are goddesses who can grant—one glimpse, grant me but one glimpse only, of something perfect, fully realised, happy, mighty, triumphant, of something that still gives cause for fear! A glimpse of a man that justifies the existence of man, a glimpse of an incarnate human happiness that realises and redeems, for the sake of which one may hold fast to *the belief in man!* For the position is this: in the dwarfing and levelling of the European man lurks *our* greatest peril, for it is this outlook which fatigues— we see today nothing which wishes to be greater, we surmise that the process is always still backwards, still backwards towards something more attenuated, more inoffensive, more cunning, more comfortable, more mediocre, more indifferent, more Chinese, more Christian—man, there is no doubt about it, grows always "better"—the destiny of Europe lies even in this—that in losing the fear of man, we have also lost the hope in man, yea, the will to be man. The sight of man now fatigues. —What is present-day Nihilism if it is not *that?*—We are tired of *man.*

13

But let us come back to it; the problem of *another* origin of the good—of the good, as the resentful man has thought it out —demands its solution. It is not surprising that the lambs should bear a grudge against the great birds of prey, but that is no reason for blaming the great birds of prey for taking the little lambs. And when the lambs say among themselves, "Those birds of prey are evil, and he who is as far removed

from being a bird of prey, who is rather its opposite, a lamb,—
is he not good?" then there is nothing to cavil at in the setting
up of this ideal, though it may also be that the birds of prey
will regard it a little sneeringly, and perchance say to themselves, "*We* bear no grudge against them, these good lambs,
we even like them: nothing is tastier than a tender lamb."
To require of strength that it should *not* express itself as
strength, that it should not be a wish to overpower, a wish to
overthrow, a wish to become master, a thirst for enemies and
antagonisms and triumphs, is just as absurd as to require of
weakness that it should express itself as strength. A quantum
of force is just such a quantum of movement, will, action—
rather it is nothing else than just those very phenomena of
moving, willing, acting, and can only appear otherwise in the
misleading errors of language (and the fundamental fallacies
of reason which have become petrified therein), which understands, and understands wrongly, all working as conditioned
by a worker, by a "subject." And just exactly as the people separate the lightning from its flash, and interpret the latter as a
thing done, as the working of a subject which is called lightning, so also does the popular morality separate strength from
the expression of strength, as though behind the strong man
there existed some indifferent neutral *substratum,* which enjoyed a *caprice and option* as to whether or not it should express strength. But there is no such *substratum,* there is no
"being" behind doing, working, becoming; "the doer" is a
mere appanage to the action. The action is everything. In point
of fact, the people duplicate the doing, when they make the
lightning lighten, that is a "doing-doing"; they make the same
phenomenon first a cause, and then, secondly, the effect of that
cause The scientists fail to improve matters when they say,

"Force moves, force causes," and so on. Our whole science is still, in spite of all its coldness, of all its freedom from passion, a dupe of the tricks of language, and has never succeeded in getting rid of that superstitious changeling "the subject" (the atom, to give another instance, is such a changeling, just as the Kantian "Thing-in-itself"). What wonder, if the suppressed and stealthily simmering passions of revenge and hatred exploit for their own advantage their belief, and indeed hold no belief with a more steadfast enthusiasm than this—"that the strong has the *option* of being weak, and the bird of prey of being a lamb." Thereby do they win for themselves the right of attributing to the birds of prey the *responsibility* for being birds of prey: when the oppressed, downtrodden, and overpowered say to themselves with the vindictive guile of weakness, "Let us be otherwise than the evil, namely, good! and good is every one who does not oppress, who hurts no one, who does not attack, who does not pay back, who hands over revenge to God, who holds himself, as we do, in hiding; who goes out of the way of evil, and demands, in short, little from life; like ourselves the patient, the meek, the just,"—yet all this, in its cold and unprejudiced interpretation, means nothing more than "once for all, the weak are weak; it is good to do *nothing for which we are not strong enough*"; but this dismal state of affairs, this prudence of the lowest order, which even insects possess (which in a great danger are fain to sham death so as to avoid doing "too much"), has, thanks to the counterfeiting and self-deception of weakness, come to masquerade in the pomp of an ascetic, mute, and expectant virtue, just as though the *very* weakness of the weak—that is, forsooth, its *being*, its working, its whole unique inevitable inseparable reality—were a voluntary result, something wished, chosen, a deed, an act of *merit*. This kind of man finds the belief in a neutral, free-choosing "subject" *necessary* from an instinct of self-preservation, of self-assertion, in which every lie is fain to sanctify itself. The subject (or, to use popular language, the *soul*) has perhaps proved itself the best dogma in the world simply because it rendered possible to the horde of mortal, weak, and oppressed individuals of every kind, that most sublime specimen of self-deception, the interpretation of weakness as freedom, of being this, or being that, as *merit*.

14

Will any one look a little into—right into—the mystery of how *ideals* are *manufactured* in this world? Who has the courage to do it? Come!

Here we have a vista opened into these grimy workshops. Wait just a moment, dear Mr. Inquisitive and Foolhardy; your eye must first grow accustomed to this false changing light— Yes! Enough! Now speak! What is happening below down yonder? Speak out! Tell what you see, man of the most dangerous curiosity—for now *I* am the listener.

"I see nothing, I hear the more. It is a cautious, spiteful, gentle whispering and muttering together in all the corners and crannies. It seems to me that they are lying; a sugary softness adheres to every sound. Weakness is turned to *merit*, there is no doubt about it—it is just as you say."

Further!

"And the impotence which requites not, is turned to 'goodness,' craven baseness to meekness, submission to those whom one hates, to obedience (namely, obedience to one of whom they say that he ordered this submission—they call him God).

The inoffensive character of the weak, the very cowardice in which he is rich, his standing at the door, his forced necessity of waiting, gain here fine names, such as 'patience,' which is also called 'virtue'; not being able to avenge one's self, is called not wishing to avenge one's self, perhaps even forgiveness (for *they* know not what they do—we alone know what they do). They also talk of the 'love of their enemies' and sweat thereby."

Further!

"They are miserable, there is no doubt about it, all these whisperers and counterfeiters in the corners, although they try to get warm by crouching close to each other, but they tell me that their misery is a favour and distinction given to them by God, just as one beats the dogs one likes best; that perhaps this misery is also a preparation, a probation, a training; that perhaps it is still more something which will one day be compensated and paid back with a tremendous interest in gold, nay in happiness. This they call 'Blessedness.' "

Further!

"They are now giving me to understand, that not only are they better men than the mighty, the lords of the earth, whose spittle they have got to lick (*not* out of fear, not at all out of fear! But because God ordains that one should honour all authority)—not only are they better men, but that they also have a 'better time,' at any rate, will one day have a 'better time.' But enough! Enough! I can endure it no longer. Bad air! Bad air! These workshops *where ideals are manufactured* —verily they reek with the crassest lies."

Nay. Just one minute! You are saying nothing about the masterpieces of these virtuosos of black magic, who can produce whiteness, milk, and innocence out of any black you like: have you not noticed what a pitch of refinement is attained by their *chef d'œuvre,* their most audacious, subtle, ingenious, and lying artist-trick? Take care! These cellar-beasts, full of revenge and hate—what do they make, forsooth, out of their revenge and hate? Do you hear these words? Would you suspect, if you trusted only their words, that you are among men of resentment and nothing else?

"I understand, I prick my ears up again (ah! ah! ah! and I hold my nose). Now do I hear for the first time that which they have said so often: 'We good, *we are the righteous'*— what they demand they call not revenge but 'the triumph of *righteousness';* what they hate is not their enemy, no, they hate 'unrighteousness,' 'godlessness'; what they believe in and hope is not the hope of revenge, the intoxication of sweet revenge (—'sweeter than honey,' did Homer call it?), but the victory of God, of the *righteous God* over the 'godless'; what is left for them to love in this world is not their brothers in hate, but their 'brothers in love,' as they say, all the good and righteous on the earth."

And how do they name that which serves them as a solace against all the troubles of life—their phantasmagoria of their anticipated future blessedness?

"How? Do I hear right? They call it 'the last judgment,' the advent of *their* kingdom, 'the kingdom of God'—but *in the meanwhile* they live 'in faith,' 'in love,' 'in hope.' "

Enough! Enough!

15

In the faith in what? In the love for what? In the hope of what? These weaklings!—they also, forsooth, wish to be strong some time; there is no doubt about it, some time *their* kingdom also must come—"the kingdom of God" is their name for it, as has been mentioned:—they are so meek in everything! Yet in order to experience *that* kingdom it is necessary to live long, to live beyond death,—yes, *eternal* life is necessary so that one can make up for ever for that earthly life "in faith," "in love," "in hope." Make up for what? Make up by what? Dante, as it seems to me, made a crass mistake when with awe-inspiring ingenuity he placed that inscription over the gate of his hell, "Me too made eternal love": at any rate the following inscription would have a much better right to stand over the gate of the Christian Paradise and its "eternal blessedness"—"Me too made eternal hate"—granted of course that a truth may rightly stand over the gate to a lie! For what is the blessedness of that Paradise? Possibly we could quickly surmise it; but it is better that it should be explicitly attested by an authority who in such matters is not to be disparaged, Thomas Aquinas, the great teacher and saint. *"Beati in regno celesti,"* says he, as gently as a lamb, *"videbunt pœnas damnatorum, ut beatitudo illis magis complaceat."* Or if we wish to hear a stronger tone, a word from the mouth of a triumphant father of the Church, who warned his disciples against the cruel ecstasies of the public spectacles—But why? Faith offers us much more,—says he, *de Spectac.,* c. 29 ss.,—something much stronger; thanks to the redemption, joys of quite another kind stand at our disposal; instead of athletes we have our martyrs; we wish for blood, well, we have the blood of Christ—but what then awaits us on the day of his return, of his triumph? And then does he proceed, does this enraptured visionary: *"at enim supersunt alia spectacula, ille ultimus et perpetuus judicii dies, ille nationibus insperatus, ille derisus, cum tanta sæculi vetustas et tot ejus nativitates uno igne haurientur. Quæ tunc spectaculi latitudo! Quid admirer!*

quid rideam! Ubi gaudeam! Ubi exultem, spectans tot et tantos reges, qui in cœlum recepti nuntiabantur, cum ipso Jove et ipsis suis testibus in imis tenebris congemescentes! Item præsides" (the provisional governors) *"persecutores dominici nominis sævioribus quam ipsi flammis sævierunt insultantibus contra Christianos liquescentes! Quos præterea sapientes illos philosophos coram discipulis suis una conflagrantibus erubescentes, quibus nihil ad deum pertinere suadebant, quibus animas aut nullas aut non in pristina corpora redituras affirmabant! Etiam poetas non ad Rhadamanti nec ad Minois, sed ad inopinati Christi tribunal palpitantes! Tunc magis tragædi audiendi, magis scilicet vocales"* (with louder tones and more violent shrieks) *"in sua propria calamitate; tunc histriones cognoscendi, solutiores multo per ignem; tunc spectandus auriga in flammea rota totus rubens, tunc xystici contemplandi non in gymnasiis, sed in igne jaculati, nisi quod ne tunc quidem illos velim vivos, ut qui malim ad eos potius conspectum insatiabilem conferre, qui in dominum sævierunt. Hic est illes, dicam fabri aut quæstuariæ filius"* (as is shown by the whole of the following, and in particular by this well-known description of the mother of Jesus from the Talmud, Tertullian is henceforth referring to the Jews), *"sabbati destructor, Samarites et dæmonium habens. Hic est quem a Juda redemistis, hic est ille arundine et colaphis diverberatus, sputamentis de decoratus, felle et aceto potatus. Hic est, quem clam discentes subripuerunt, ut resurrexisse dicatur vel hortulanus detraxit, ne lactucæ suæ frequentia commeantium læderentur. Ut talia spectes, ut talibus exultes, quis tibi prætor aut consul aut sacerdos de sua liberalitate præstabit? Et tamen hæc jam habemus quodammodo per fidem spiritu imaginante repræsentata. Ceterum qualia illa sunt, quæ nec oculus vidit nec auris audivit*

[662]

nec in cor hominis ascenderunt?" (I Cor. ii. 9.) *"Credo circo et utraque caved"* (first and fourth row, or, according to others, the comic and the tragic stage) *"et omni studio gratiora."* **Per fidem**: so stands it written.

16

Let us come to a conclusion. The two *opposing values,* "good and bad," "good and evil," have fought a dreadful, thousand-year fight in the world, and though indubitably the second value has been for a long time in the preponderance, there are not wanting places where the fortune of the fight is still indecisive. It can almost be said that in the meanwhile the fight reaches a higher and higher level, and that in the meanwhile it has become more and more intense, and always more and more psychological; so that nowadays there is perhaps no more decisive mark of the *higher nature,* of the more psychological nature, than to be in that sense self-contradictory, and to be actually still a battleground for those two opposites. The symbol of this fight, written in a writing which has remained worthy of perusal throughout the course of history up to the present time, is called "Rome against Judæa, Judæa against Rome." Hitherto there has been no greater event *than* that fight, the putting of *that* question, *that* deadly antagonism. Rome found in the Jew the incarnation of the unnatural, as though it were its diametrically opposed monstrosity, and in Rome the Jew was held to be *convicted of hatred* of the whole human race: and rightly so, in so far as it is right to link the well-being and the future of the human race to the unconditional mastery of the aristocratic values, of the Roman values.

What, conversely, did the Jews feel against Rome? One can surmise it from a thousand symptoms, but it is sufficient to carry one's mind back to the Johannian Apocalypse, that most obscene of all the written outbursts, which has revenge on its conscience. (One should also appraise at its full value the profound logic of the Christian instinct, when over this very book of hate it wrote the name of the Disciple of Love, that self-same disciple to whom it attributed that impassioned and ecstatic Gospel—therein lurks a portion of truth, however much literary forging may have been necessary for this purpose.) The Romans were the strong and aristocratic; a nation stronger and more aristocratic has never existed in the world, has never even been dreamed of; every relic of them, every inscription enraptures, granted that one can divine *what* it is that writes the inscription. The Jews, conversely, were that priestly nation of resentment *par excellence,* possessed by a unique genius for popular morals: just compare with the Jews the nations with analogous gifts, such as the Chinese or the Germans, so as to realise afterwards what is first rate, and what is fifth rate.

Which of them has been provisionally victorious, Rome or Judæa? but there is not a shadow of doubt; just consider to whom in Rome itself nowadays you bow down, as though before the quintessence of all the highest values—and not only in Rome, but almost over half the world, everywhere where man has been tamed or is about to be tamed—to *three Jews,* as we know, and *one Jewess* (to Jesus of Nazareth, to Peter the fisher, to Paul the tentmaker, and to the mother of the aforesaid Jesus, named Mary). This is very remarkable: Rome is undoubtedly defeated. At any rate there took place in the Renaissance a brilliantly sinister revival of the classical ideal, of the aristocratic valuation of all things: Rome herself, like a man waking up from a trance, stirred beneath the burden of the new Judaised Rome that had been built over her, which presented the appearance of an œcumenical synagogue and was called the "Church": but immediately Judæa triumphed again, thanks to that fundamentally popular (German and English) movement of revenge, which is called the Reformation, and taking also into account its inevitable corollary, the restoration of the Church—the restoration also of the ancient graveyard peace of classical Rome. Judæa proved yet once more victorious over the classical ideal in the French Revolution, and in a sense which was even more crucial and even more profound: the last political aristocracy that existed in Europe, that of the *French* seventeenth and eighteenth centuries, broke into pieces beneath the instincts of a resentful populace—never had the world heard a greater jubilation, a more uproarious enthusiasm: indeed, there took place in the midst of it the most monstrous and unexpected phenomenon; the ancient ideal *itself* swept before the eyes and conscience of humanity with all its life and with unheard-of splendour, and in opposition to resentment's lying war-cry of *the prerogative of the most,* in opposition to the will to lowliness, abasement, and equalisation, the will to a retrogression and twilight of humanity, there rang out once again, stronger, simpler, more penetrating than ever, the terrible and enchanting counter-war-cry of *the prerogative of the few!* Like a final sign-post to other ways, there appeared Napoleon, the most unique and violent anachronism that ever existed, and in him the incarnate problem *of the aristocratic ideal in itself*—consider well what a problem it is:—Napoleon, that synthesis of Monster and Superman.

17

Was it therewith over? Was that greatest of all antitheses of ideals thereby relegated *ad acta* for all time? Or only postponed, postponed for a long time? May there not take place at some time or other a much more awful, much more carefully prepared flaring up of the old conflagration? Further! Should not one wish *that* consummation with all one's strength?—will it one's self? demand it one's self? He who at this juncture begins, like my readers, to reflect, to think further, will have difficulty in coming quickly to a conclusion,—ground enough for me to come myself to a conclusion, taking it for granted that for some time past what I mean has been sufficiently clear, what I exactly *mean* by that dangerous motto which is inscribed on the body of my last book: *Beyond Good and Evil*—at any rate that is not the same as "Beyond Good and Bad."

NOTE.—I avail myself of the opportunity offered by this treatise to express, openly and formally, a wish which up to the present has only been expressed in occasional conversations with scholars, namely, that some Faculty of philosophy should, by means of a series of prize essays, gain the glory of having promoted the further study of the *history of morals*—perhaps this book may serve to give a forcible impetus in such a direction. With regard to a possibility of this character, the following question deserves consideration. It merits quite as much the attention of philologists and historians as of actual professional philosophers.

"What indication of the history of the evolution of the moral ideas is afforded by philology, and especially by etymological investigation?"

On the other hand, it is, of course, equally necessary to induce physiologists and doctors to be interested in these problems (*of the value* of the *valuations* which have prevailed up to the present): in this connection the professional philosophers may be trusted to act as the spokesmen and intermediaries in these particular instances, after, of course, they have quite succeeded in transforming the relationship between philosophy and physiology and medicine, which is originally one of coldness and suspicion, into the most friendly and fruitful reciprocity. In point of fact, all tables of values, all the "thou shalts" known to history and ethnology, need primarily a *physiological,* at any rate in preference to a psychological, elucidation and interpretation; all equally require a critique from medical science. The question, "What is the *value* of this or that table of 'values' and morality?" will be asked from the most varied standpoints. For instance, the question of "valuable *for what*" can never be analysed with sufficient nicety. That, for instance, which would evidently have value with regard to promoting in a race the greatest possible powers of endurance (or with regard to increasing its adaptability to a specific climate, or with regard to the preservation of the greatest number) would have nothing like the same value, if it were a question of evolving a stronger species. In gauging values, the good of the majority and the good of the minority are opposed standpoints: we leave it to the naïveté of English biologists to regard the former standpoint as *intrinsically* superior. *All* the sciences have now to pave the way for the future task of the philosopher; this task being understood to mean, that he must solve the problem of *value,* that he has to fix the *hierarchy of values.*

"Guilt," "Bad Conscience," and the Like

1

THE breeding of an animal that *can promise*—is not this just that very paradox of a task which nature has set itself in regard to man? Is not this the very problem of man? The fact that this problem has been to a great extent solved, must appear all the more phenomenal to one who can estimate at its full value that force of *forgetfulness* which works in opposition to it. Forgetfulness is no mere *vis inertiæ,* as the superficial believe, rather is it a power of obstruction, active and, in the strictest sense of the word, positive—a power responsible for the fact that what we have lived, experienced, taken into ourselves, no more enters into consciousness during the process of digestion (it might be called psychic absorption) than all the whole manifold process by which our physical nutrition, the so-called "incorporation," is carried on. The temporary shutting of the doors and windows of consciousness, the relief from the clamant alarums and excursions, with which our subconscious world of servant organs works in mutual co-operation and antagonism; a little quietude, a little *tabula rasa* of the consciousness, so as to make room again for the new, and above all for the more noble functions and functionaries, room for government, foresight, predetermination (for our organism is on an oligarchic model)—this is the utility, as I have said, of the active forgetfulness, which is a very sentinel and nurse of psychic order, repose, etiquette; and this shows at once why it is that there can exist no happiness, no gladness, no hope, no pride, no real *present,* without forgetfulness. The man in whom this preventative apparatus is damaged and discarded, is to be compared to a dyspeptic, and it is something more than a comparison—he can "get rid of" nothing. But this very animal who finds it necessary to be forgetful, in whom, in fact, forgetfulness represents a force and a form of *robust* health, has reared for himself an opposition-power, a memory, with whose help forgetfulness is, in certain instances, kept in check —in the cases, namely, where promises have to be made;—so that it is by no means a mere passive inability to get rid of a once indented impression, not merely the indigestion occasioned by a once pledged word, which one cannot dispose of, but an *active* refusal to get rid of it, a continuing and a wish to continue what has once been willed, an actual *memory of the will;* so that between the original "I will," "I shall do," and the actual discharge of the will, its *act,* we can easily interpose a world of new strange phenomena, circumstances, veritable volitions, without the snapping of this long chain of the will. But what is the underlying hypothesis of all this? How thoroughly, in order to be able to regulate the future in this way, must man have first learnt to distinguish between necessitated and accidental phenomena, to think casually, to see the distant as present and to anticipate it, to fix with certainty what is the end, and what is the means to that end; above all, to reckon, to have power to calculate—how thoroughly must man have first become *calculable, disciplined, necessitated* even for himself and his own conception of himself, that, like a man entering a promise, he could guarantee himself *as a future.*

2

This is simply the long history of the origin of *responsibility.* That task of breeding an animal which can make promises, includes, as we have already grasped, as its condition and preliminary, the more immediate task of first *making* man to a certain extent, necessitated, uniform, like among his like, regular, and consequently calculable. The immense work of what I have called, "morality of custom" * (cp. *Dawn of Day,* Aphs. 9, 14, and 16), the actual work of man on himself during the longest period of the human race, his whole prehistoric work, finds its meaning, its great justification (in spite of all its innate hardness, despotism, stupidity, and idiocy) in this fact: man, with the help of the morality of customs and of social strait-waistcoats, was *made* genuinely calculable. If, however, we place ourselves at the end of this colossal process, at the point where the tree finally matures its fruits, when society and its morality of custom finally bring to light that to which it was only the means, then do we find as the ripest fruit on its tree the *sovereign individual,* that resembles only himself, that has got loose from the morality of custom, the autonomous "supermoral" individual (for "autonomous" and "moral" are mutually exclusive terms),—in short, the man of the personal, long, and independent will, *competent to*

---

* The German is: "Sittlichkeit der Sitte." H. B. S.

promise,—and we find in him a proud consciousness (vibrating in every fibre), of *what* has been at last achieved and become vivified in him, a genuine consciousness of power and freedom, a feeling of human perfection in general. And this man who has grown to freedom, who is really *competent* to promise, this lord of the *free* will, this sovereign—how is it possible for him not to know how great is his superiority over everything incapable of binding itself by promises, or of being its own security, how great is the trust, the awe, the reverence that he awakes—he "deserves" all three—not to know that with this mastery over himself he is necessarily also given the mastery over circumstances, over nature, over all creatures with shorter wills, less reliable characters? The "free" man, the owner of a long unbreakable will, finds in this possession his *standard of value:* looking out from himself upon the others, he honours or he despises, and just as necessarily as he honours his peers, the strong and the reliable (those who can bind themselves by promises),—that is, every one who promises like a sovereign, with difficulty, rarely and slowly, who is sparing with his trusts but confers *honour* by the very fact of trusting, who gives his word as something that can be relied on, because he knows himself strong enough to keep it even in the teeth of disasters, even in the "teeth of fate,"—so with equal necessity will he have the heel of his foot ready for the lean and empty jackasses, who promise when they have no business to do so, and his rod of chastisement ready for the liar, who already breaks his word at the very minute when it is on his lips. The proud knowledge of the extraordinary privilege of *responsibility,* the consciousness of this rare freedom, of this power over himself and over fate, has sunk right down to his innermost depths, and has become an instinct, a dominating instinct—what name will he give to it, to this dominating instinct, if he needs to have a word for it? But there is no doubt about it—the sovereign man calls it his *conscience*.

3

His conscience?—One apprehends at once that the idea "conscience," which is here seen in its supreme manifestation, supreme in fact to almost the point of strangeness, should already have behind it a long history and evolution. The ability to guarantee one's self with all due pride, and also at the same time to *say yes* to one's self—that is, as has been said, a ripe fruit, but also a *late* fruit:—How long must needs this fruit hang sour and bitter on the tree! And for an even longer period there was not a glimpse of such a fruit to be had—no one had taken it on himself to promise it, although everything on the tree was quite ready for it, and everything was maturing for that very consummation. "How is a memory to be made for the man-animal? How is an impression to be so deeply fixed upon this ephemeral understanding, half dense, and half silly, upon this incarnate forgetfulness, that it will be permanently present?" As one may imagine, this primeval problem was not solved by exactly gentle answers and gentle means; perhaps there is nothing more awful and more sinister in the early history of man than his *system of mnemonics*. "Something is burnt in so as to remain in his memory: only that which never stops *hurting* remains in his memory." This is an axiom of the oldest (unfortunately also the longest) psychology in the world. It might even be said that wherever solemnity, seriousness, mystery, and gloomy colours are now found in the life of the men and of nations of the world, there is some *survival* of that horror which was once the universal concomitant of all promises, pledges, and obligations. The past, the past with all its length, depth, and hardness, wafts to us its breath, and bubbles up in us again, when we become "serious." When man thinks it necessary to make for himself a memory, he never accomplishes it without blood, tortures and sacrifice; the most dreadful sacrifices and forfeitures (among them the sacrifice of the first-born), the most loathsome mutilation (for instance, castration), the most cruel rituals of all the religious cults (for all religions are really at bottom systems of cruelty)—all these things originate from that instinct which found in pain its most potent mnemonic. In a certain sense the whole of asceticism is to be ascribed to this: certain ideas have got to be made inextinguishable, omnipresent, "fixed," with the object of hypnotising the whole nervous and intellectual system through these "fixed ideas"— and the ascetic methods and modes of life are the means of freeing those ideas from the competition of all other ideas so as to make them "unforgettable." The worse memory man had, the ghastlier the signs presented by his customs; the severity of the penal laws affords in particular a gauge of the extent of man's difficulty in conquering forgetfulness, and in keeping a few primal postulates of social intercourse ever present to the minds of those who were the slaves of every momentary emotion and every momentary desire. We Germans do certainly not regard ourselves as an especially cruel and hard-hearted nation, still less as an especially casual and happy-go-lucky one; but one has only to look at our old penal ordinances in order to realise what a lot of trouble it takes in the world to evolve a "nation of thinkers" (I mean: *the* European nation which exhibits at this very day the maximum of reliability, seriousness, bad taste, and positiveness, which has on the strength of these qualities a right to train every kind of European mandarin). These Germans employed terrible means to make for themselves a memory, to enable them to master their rooted plebeian instincts and the brutal crudity of those instincts: think of the old German punishments, for instance, stoning (as far back as the legend, the millstone falls on the head of the guilty man), breaking on the wheel (the most original invention and speciality of the German genius in the sphere of punishment), dart-throwing, tearing, or trampling by horses ("quartering"), boiling the criminal in oil or wine (still prevalent in the fourteenth and fifteenth centuries), the highly popular flaying ("slicing into strips"), cutting the flesh out of the breast; think also of the evil-doer being besmeared with honey, and then exposed to the flies in a blazing sun. It was by the help of such images and precedents that man eventually kept in his memory five or six "I will nots" with regard to which he had already given his *promise,* so as to be able to enjoy the advantages of society—and verily with the help of this kind of memory man eventually attained "reason"! Alas! reason, seriousness, mastery over the emotions, all these gloomy, dismal things which are called reflection, all these privileges and pageantries of humanity: how dear is the price that they have exacted! How much blood and cruelty is the foundation of all "good things"!

4

But how is it that that other melancholy object, the consciousness of sin, the whole "bad conscience," came into the world? And it is here that we turn back to our genealogists of morals. For the second time I say—or have I not said it yet?—

that they are worth nothing. Just their own five-spans-long limited modern experience; no knowledge of the past, and no wish to know it; still less a historic instinct, a power of "second sight" (which is what is really required in this case)—and despite this to go in for the history of morals. It stands to reason that this must needs produce results which are removed from the truth by something more than a respectful distance.

Have these current genealogists of morals ever allowed themselves to have even the vaguest notion, for instance, that the cardinal moral idea of "ought" * originates from the very material idea of "owe"? Or that punishment developed as a *retaliation* absolutely independently of any preliminary hypothesis of the freedom or determination of the will?—And this to such an extent, that a *high* degree of civilisation was always first necessary for the animal man to begin to make those much more primitive distinctions of "intentional," "negligent," "accidental," "responsible," and their contraries, and apply them in the assessing of punishment. That idea—"the wrong-doer deserves punishment *because* he might have acted otherwise," in spite of the fact that it is nowadays so cheap, obvious, natural, and inevitable, and that it has had to serve as an illustration of the way in which the sentiment of justice appeared on earth, is in point of fact an exceedingly late, and even refined form of human judgment and inference; the placing of this idea back at the beginning of the world is simply a clumsy violation of the principles of primitive psychology. Throughout the longest period of human history punishment was *never* based on the responsibility of the evil-doer for his action, and was consequently *not* based

---

* The German word "schuld" means both debt and guilt. Cp. the English "owe" and "ought," by which I occasionally render the double meaning.— H. B. S.

on the hypothesis that only the guilty should be punished;— on the contrary, punishment was inflicted in those days for the same reason that parents punish their children even nowadays, out of anger at an injury that they have suffered, an anger which vents itself mechanically on the author of the injury— but this anger is kept in bounds and modified through the idea that every injury has somewhere or other its *equivalent* price, and can really be paid off, even though it be by means of pain to the author. Whence is it that this ancient deeprooted and now perhaps ineradicable idea has drawn its strength, this idea of an equivalency between injury and pain? I have already revealed its origin, in the contractual relationship between *creditor* and *ower,* that is as old as the existence of legal rights at all, and in its turn points back to the primary forms of purchase, sale, barter, and trade.

5

The realisation of these contractual relations excites, of course (as would be already expected from our previous observations), a great deal of suspicion and opposition towards the primitive society which made or sanctioned them. In this society promises will be made; in this society the object is to provide the promiser with a memory; in this society, so may we suspect, there will be full scope for hardness, cruelty, and pain: the "ower," in order to induce credit in his promise of repayment, in order to give a guarantee of the earnestness and sanctity of his promise, in order to drill into his own conscience the duty, the solemn duty, of repayment, will, by virtue of a contract with his creditor to meet the contingency of his not paying, pledge something that he still possesses, something that he still has in his power, for instance, his life or his wife, or his freedom or his body (or under certain religious conditions even his salvation, his soul's welfare, even his peace in the grave; so in Egypt, where the corpse of the ower found even in the grave no rest from the creditor—of course, from the Egyptian standpoint, this peace was a matter of particular importance). But especially has the creditor the power of inflicting on the body of the ower all kinds of pain and torture— the power, for instance, of cutting off from it an amount that appeared proportionate to the greatness of the debt;—this point of view resulted in the universal prevalence at an early date of precise schemes of valuation, frequently horrible in the minuteness and meticulosity of their application, *legally* sanctioned schemes of valuation for individual limbs and parts of the body. I consider it as already a progress, as a proof of a freer, less petty, and more *Roman* conception of law, when the Roman Code of the Twelve Tables decreed that it was immaterial how much or how little the creditors in such a contingency cut off, *"si plus minusve secuerunt, ne fraude esto."* Let us make the logic of the whole of this equalisation process clear; it is strange enough. The equivalence consists in this: instead of an advantage directly compensatory of his injury (that is, instead of an equalisation in money, lands, or some kind of chattel), the creditor is granted by way of repayment and compensation a certain *sensation of satisfaction*—the satisfaction of being able to vent, without any trouble, his power on one who is powerless, the delight *"de faire le mal pour le plaisir de la faire,"* the joy in sheer violence: and this joy will be relished in proportion to the lowness and humbleness of the creditor in the social scale, and is quite apt to have the effect of the most delicious dainty, and even seem the foretaste of a higher social position. Thanks to the punishment of the

"ower," the creditor participates in the rights of the masters.
At last he too, for once in a way, attains the edifying consciousness of being able to despise and ill-treat a creature—as an
"inferior"—or at any rate of *seeing* him being despised and
ill-treated, in case the actual power of punishment, the administration of punishment, has already become transferred to
the "authorities." The compensation consequently consists in
a claim on cruelty and a right to draw thereon.

6

It is then in *this* sphere of the law of contract that we find
the cradle of the whole moral world of the ideas of "guilt,"
"conscience," "duty," the "sacredness of duty,"—their commencement, like the commencement of all great things in the
world, is thoroughly and continuously saturated with blood.
And should we not add that this world has never really lost a
certain savour of blood and torture (not even in old Kant:
the categorical imperative reeks of cruelty). It was in this
sphere likewise that there first became formed that sinister and
perhaps now indissoluble association of the ideas of "guilt"
and "suffering." To put the question yet again, why can suffering be a compensation for "owing"?—Because the *infliction* of suffering produces the highest degree of happiness,
because the injured party will get in exchange for his loss
(including his vexation at his loss) an extraordinary counter-
pleasure: the *infliction* of suffering—a real *feast,* something
that, as I have said, was all the more appreciated the greater
the paradox created by the rank and social status of the creditor. These observations are purely conjectural; for, apart from
the painful nature of the task, it is hard to plumb such pro-

found depths: the clumsy introduction of the idea of "revenge" as a connecting-link simply hides and obscures the
view instead of rendering it clearer (revenge itself simply
leads back again to the identical problem—"How can the infliction of suffering be a satisfaction?"). In my opinion it is
repugnant to the delicacy, and still more to the hypocrisy of
tame domestic animals (that is, modern men; that is, ourselves) to realise with all their energy the extent to which
cruelty constituted the great joy and delight of ancient man,
was an ingredient which seasoned nearly all his pleasures, and
conversely the extent of the naïveté and innocence with which
he manifested his need for cruelty, when he actually made as
a matter of principle "disinterested malice" (or, to use Spinoza's expression, the *sympathia malevolens*) into a *normal*
characteristic of man—as consequently something to which
the conscience says a hearty *yes*. The more profound observer
has perhaps already had sufficient opportunity for noticing
this most ancient and radical joy and delight of mankind; in
Beyond Good and Evil, Aph. 188 (and even earlier, in *The
Dawn of Day,* Aphs. 18, 77, 113), I have cautiously indicated
the continually growing spiritualisation and "deification" of
cruelty, which pervades the whole history of the higher civilisation (and in the larger sense even constitutes it). At any
rate the time is not so long past when it was impossible to
conceive of royal weddings and national festivals on a grand
scale, without executions, tortures, or perhaps an *auto-da-fé,*
or similarly to conceive of an aristocratic household, without
a creature to serve as a butt for the cruel and malicious baiting
of the inmates. (The reader will perhaps remember Don
Quixote at the court of the Duchess: we read nowadays the
whole of *Don Quixote* with a bitter taste in the mouth, almost
with a sensation of torture, a fact which would appear very

[*679*]

strange and very incomprehensible to the author and his contemporaries—they read it with the best conscience in the world
as the gayest of books; they almost died with laughing at it.)
The sight of suffering does one good, the infliction of suffering
does one more good—this is a hard maxim, but none the less
a fundamental maxim, old, powerful, and "human, all-too-
human"; one, moreover, to which perhaps even the apes as
well would subscribe: for it is said that in inventing bizarre
cruelties they are giving abundant proof of their future humanity, to which, as it were, they are playing the prelude.
Without cruelty, no feast: so teaches the oldest and longest
history of man—and in punishment too is there so much of
the *festive*.

7

Entertaining, as I do, these thoughts, I am, let me say in
parenthesis, fundamentally opposed to helping our pessimists
to new water for the discordant and groaning mills of their
disgust with life; on the contrary, it should be shown specifically that, at the time when mankind was not yet ashamed of
its cruelty, life in the world was brighter than it is nowadays
when there are pessimists. The darkening of the heavens over
man has always increased in proportion to the growth of man's
shame *before man*. The tired pessimistic outlook, the mistrust
of the riddle of life, the icy negation of disgusted ennui, all
those are not the signs of the *most evil* age of the human race:
much rather do they come first to the light of day, as the
swamp-flowers, which they are, when the swamp to which they
belong, comes into existence—I mean the diseased refinement
and moralisation, thanks to which the "animal man" has at

last learned to be ashamed of all his instincts. On the road to angel-hood (not to use in this context a harder word) man has developed that dyspeptic stomach and coated tongue, which have made not only the joy and innocence of the animal repulsive to him, but also life itself:—so that sometimes he stands with stopped nostrils before his own self, and, like Pope Innocent the Third, makes a black list of his own horrors ("unclean generation, loathsome nutrition when in the maternal body, badness of the matter out of which man develops, awful stench, secretion of saliva, urine, and excrement"). Nowadays, when suffering is always trotted out as the first argument *against* existence, as its most sinister query, it is well to remember the times when men judged on converse principles because they could not dispense with the *infliction* of suffering, and saw therein a magic of the first order, a veritable bait of seduction to life.

Perhaps in those days (this is to solace the weaklings) pain did not hurt so much as it does nowadays: any physician who has treated Negroes (granted that these are taken as representative of the prehistoric man) suffering from severe internal inflammations which would bring a European, even though he had the soundest constitution, almost to despair, would be in a position to come to this conclusion. Pain has *not* the same effect with Negroes. (The curve of human sensibilities to pain seems indeed to sink in an extraordinary and almost sudden fashion, as soon as one has passed the upper ten thousand or ten millions of over-civilised humanity, and I personally have no doubt that, by comparison with one painful night passed by one single hysterical chit of a cultured woman, the suffering of all the animals taken together who have been put to the question of the knife, so as to give scientific answers, are simply negligible.) We may perhaps be allowed to admit the possibility of the craving for cruelty not necessarily having become really extinct: it only requires, in view of the fact that pain hurts more nowadays, a certain sublimation and subtilisation, it must especially be translated to the imaginative and psychic plane, and be adorned with such smug euphemisms, that even the most fastidious and hypocritical conscience could never grow suspicious of their real nature ("Tragic pity" is one of these euphemisms: another is *les nostalgies de la croix*). What really raises one's indignation against suffering is not suffering intrinsically, but the senselessness of suffering; such a *senselessness,* however, existed neither in Christianity, which interpreted suffering into a whole mysterious salvation-apparatus, nor in the beliefs of the naïve ancient man, who only knew how to find a meaning in suffering from the stand-point of the spectator, or the inflictor of the suffering. In order to get the secret, undiscovered, and unwitnessed suffering out of the world it was almost compulsory to invent gods and a hierarchy of intermediate beings, in short, something which wanders even among secret places, sees even in the dark, and makes a point of never missing an interesting and painful spectacle. It was with the help of such inventions that life got to learn the *tour de force,* which has become part of its stock-in-trade, the *tour de force* of self-justification, of the justifica-tion of evil; nowadays this would perhaps require other auxil-iary devices (for instance, life as a riddle, life as a problem of knowledge). "Every evil is justified in the sight of which a god finds edification," so rang the logic of primitive sentiment —and, indeed, was it only of primitive? The gods conceived as friends of spectacles of cruelty—oh, how far does this primeval conception extend even nowadays into our European civilisation! One would perhaps like in this context to consult Luther and Calvin. It is at any rate certain that even the Greeks knew no more piquant seasoning for the happiness of their gods than the joys of cruelty. What, do you think, was the mood with which Homer makes his gods look down upon the fates of men? What final meaning have at bottom the Trojan War and similar tragic horrors? It is impossible to entertain any doubt on the point: they were intended as festival games for the gods, and, in so far as the poet is of a more godlike breed than other men, as festival games also for the poets. It was in just this spirit and no other, that at a later date the moral philosophers of Greece conceived the eyes of God as still looking down on the moral struggle, the heroism, and the self-torture of the virtuous; the Heracles of duty was on a stage, and was conscious of the fact; virtue without witnesses was something quite unthinkable for this nation of actors. Must not that philosophic invention, so audacious and so fatal, which was then absolutely new to Europe, the invention of "free will," of the absolute spontaneity of man in good and evil, simply have been made for the specific purpose of justifying the idea, that the interest of the gods in humanity and human virtue was *inexhaustible?*

There would never on the stage of this free-will world be a dearth of really new, really novel and exciting situations, plots, catastrophes. A world thought out on completely deterministic lines would be easily guessed by the gods, and would consequently soon bore them—sufficient reason for these *friends of the gods,* the philosophers, not to ascribe to their gods such a deterministic world. The whole of ancient humanity is full of delicate consideration for the spectator, being as it is a world of thorough publicity and theatricality, which could not conceive of happiness without spectacles and festivals.—And, as has already been said, even in great *punishment* there is so much which is festive.

8

The feeling of "ought," of personal obligation (to take up again the train of our inquiry), has had, as we saw, its origin in the oldest and most original personal relationship that there is, the relationship between buyer and seller, creditor and owner: here it was that individual confronted individual, and that individual *matched himself against* individual. There has not yet been found a grade of civilisation so low, as not to manifest some trace of this relationship. Making prices, assessing values, thinking out equivalents, exchanging—all this pre-occupied the primal thoughts of man to such an extent that in a certain sense it constituted *thinking* itself: it was here that was trained the oldest form of sagacity, it was here in this sphere that we can perhaps trace the first commencement of man's pride, of his feeling of superiority over other animals. Perhaps our word "Mensch" (manas) still expresses just something of *this* self-pride: man denoted himself as the being who measures values, who values and measures, as the "assessing" animal *par excellence*. Sale and purchase, together with their psychological concomitants, are older than the origins of any form of social organisation and union: it is rather from the most rudimentary form of individual right that the budding consciousness of exchange, commerce, debt, right, obligation, compensation was first transferred to the rudest and most elementary of the social complexes (in their relation to similar complexes), the habit of comparing force with force, together with that of measuring, of calculating. His eye was now focussed to this perspective; and with that ponderous consistency characteristic of ancient thought, which, though set in motion with difficulty, yet proceeds inflexibly along the line on which it has started, man soon arrived at the great generalisation, "everything has its price, *all* can be paid for," the oldest and most naïve moral canon of *justice,* the beginning of all "kindness," of all "equity," of all "good will," of all "objectivity" in the world. Justice in this initial phase is the good will among people of about equal power to come to terms with each other, to come to an understanding again by means of a settlement, and with regard to the less powerful, to *compel* them to agree among themselves to a settlement.

9

Measured always by the standard of antiquity (this antiquity, moreover, is present or again possible at all periods), the community stands to its members in that important and radical relationship of creditor to his "owers." Man lives in a community, man enjoys the advantages of a community (and what advantages! we occasionally underestimate them nowadays), man lives protected, spared, in peace and trust, secure from certain injuries and enmities, to which the man outside the community, the "peaceless" man, is exposed,—a German understands the original meaning of "Elend" (*êlend*),—secure because he has entered into pledges and obligations to the community in respect of these very injuries and enmities. What happens *when this is not the case?* The community, the defrauded creditor, will get itself paid, as well as it can, one can reckon on that. In this case the question of the direct damage done by the offender is quite subsidiary: quite apart from this the criminal * is above all a breaker, a breaker of word

---

* *German:* "Verbrecher."—H. B. S.

and covenant *to the whole,* as regards all the advantages and amenities of the communal life in which up to that time he had participated. The criminal is an "ower" who not only fails to repay the advances and advantages that have been given to him, but even sets out to attack his creditor: consequently he is in the future not only, as is fair, deprived of all these advantages and amenities—he is in addition reminded of the *importance* of those advantages. The wrath of the injured creditor, of the community, puts him back in the wild and outlawed status from which he was previously protected: the community repudiates him—and now every kind of enmity can vent itself on him. Punishment is in this stage of civilisation simply the copy, the mimic, of the normal treatment of the hated, disdained, and conquered enemy, who is not only deprived of every right and protection but of every mercy; so we have the martial law and triumphant festival of the *væ victis!* in all its mercilessness and cruelty. This shows why war itself (counting the sacrificial cult of war) has produced all the forms under which punishment has manifested itself in history.

10

As it grows more powerful, the community tends to take the offences of the individual less seriously, because they are now regarded as being much less revolutionary and dangerous to the corporate existence: the evil-doer is no more outlawed and put outside the pale, the common wrath can no longer vent itself upon him with its old licence,—on the contrary, from this very time it is against this wrath, and particularly against the wrath of those directly injured, that the evil-doer is carefully shielded and protected by the community. As, in fact, the penal law develops, the following characteristics become more and more clearly marked: compromise with the wrath of those directly affected by the misdeed; a consequent endeavour to localise the matter and to prevent a further, or indeed a general spread of the disturbance; attempts to find equivalents and to settle the whole matter (*compositio*); above all, the will, which manifests itself with increasing definiteness, to treat every offence as in a certain degree capable of *being paid off*, and consequently, at any rate up to a certain point, to *isolate* the offender from his act. As the power and the self-consciousness of a community increases, so proportionately does the penal law become mitigated; conversely every weakening and jeopardising of the community revives the harshest forms of that law. The creditor has always grown more humane proportionately as he has grown more rich; finally the amount of injury he can endure without really suffering becomes the criterion of his wealth. It is possible to conceive of a society blessed with so great a *consciousness of its own power* as to indulge in the most aristocratic luxury of letting its wrong-doers go *scot-free*.—"What do my parasites matter to me?" might society say. "Let them live and flourish! I am strong enough for it."—The justice which began with the maxim, "Everything can be paid off, everything must be paid off," ends with connivance at the escape of those who cannot pay to escape—it ends, like every good thing on earth, by *destroying itself*.—The self-destruction of Justice! we know the pretty name it calls itself—*Grace!* it remains, as is obvious, the privilege of the strongest, better still, their super-law.

11

A deprecatory word here against the attempts, that have lately been made, to find the origin of justice on quite another basis—namely, on that of *resentment*. Let me whisper a word in the ear of the psychologists, if they would fain study revenge itself at close quarters: this plant blooms its prettiest at present among Anarchists and anti-Semites, a hidden flower, as it has ever been, like the violet, though, forsooth, with another perfume. And as like must necessarily emanate from like, it will not be a matter for surprise that it is just in such circles that we see the birth of endeavours (it is their old birthplace—compare above, First Essay, paragraph 14), to sanctify *revenge* under the name of *justice* (as though Justice were at bottom merely a development of the consciousness of injury), and thus with the rehabilitation of revenge to reinstate generally and collectively all the *reactive* emotions. I object to this last point least of all. It even seems *meritorious* when regarded from the standpoint of the whole problem of biology (from which standpoint the value of these emotions has up to the present been underestimated). And that to which I alone call attention, is the circumstance that it is the spirit of revenge itself, from which develops this new nuance of scientific equity (for the benefit of hate, envy, mistrust, jealousy, suspicion, rancour, revenge). This scientific "equity" stops immediately and makes way for the accents of deadly enmity and prejudice, so soon as another group of emotions comes on the scene, which in my opinion are of a much higher biological value than these reactions, and consequently have a paramount claim to the valuation and appreciation of *science:* I mean the really *active*

emotions, such as personal and material ambition, and so forth.
(E. Dühring, *Value of Life; Course of Philosophy,* and
passim.) So much against this tendency in general: but as for
the particular maxim of Dühring's, that the home of Justice
is to be found in the sphere of the reactive feelings, our love
of truth compels us drastically to invert his own proposition
and to oppose to him this other maxim: the *last* sphere conquered by the spirit of justice is the sphere of the feeling of
reaction! When it really comes about that the just man remains
just even as regards his injurer (and not merely cold, moderate,
reserved, indifferent: being just is always a *positive* state);
when, in spite of the strong provocation of personal insult,
contempt, and calumny, the lofty and clear objectivity of the
just and judging eye (whose glance is as profound as it is
gentle) is untroubled, why then we have a piece of perfection,
a past master of the world—something, in fact, which it
would not be wise to expect, and which should not at any rate
be too easily *believed.* Speaking generally, there is no doubt
but that even the justest individual only requires a little dose
of hostility, malice, or innuendo to drive the blood into his
brain and the fairness *from* it. The active man, the attacking,
aggressive man is always a hundred degrees nearer to justice
than the man who merely reacts; he certainly has no need
to adopt the tactics, necessary in the case of the reacting man, of
making false and biassed valuations of his object. It is, in point
of fact, for this reason that the aggressive man has at all times
enjoyed the stronger, bolder, more aristocratic, and also *freer*
outlook, the *better* conscience. On the other hand, we already
surmise who it really is that has on his conscience the invention
of the "bad conscience,"—the resentful man! Finally, let man
look at himself in history. In what sphere up to the present has

the whole administration of law, the actual need of law, found its earthly home? Perchance in the sphere of the reacting man? Not for a minute: rather in that of the active, strong, spontaneous, aggressive man? I deliberately defy the above-mentioned agitator (who himself makes this self-confession, "the creed of revenge has run through all my works and endeavours like the red thread of Justice") and say that judged historically, law in the world represents the very war *against* the reactive feelings, the very war waged on those feelings by the powers of activity and aggression, which devote some of their strength to damming and keeping within bounds this effervescence of hysterical reactivity, and to forcing it to some compromise. Everywhere where justice is practised and justice is maintained, it is to be observed that the stronger power, when confronted with the weaker powers which are inferior to it (whether they be groups, or individuals), searches for weapons to put an end to the senseless fury of resentment, while it carries on its object, partly by taking the victim of resentment out of the clutches of revenge, partly by substituting for revenge a campaign of its own against the enemies of peace and order, partly by finding, suggesting, and occasionally enforcing settlements, partly by standardising certain equivalents for injuries, to which equivalents the element of resentment is henceforth finally referred. The most drastic measure, however, taken and effectuated by the supreme power, to combat the preponderance of the feelings of spite and vindictiveness—it takes this measure as soon as it is at all strong enough to do so—is the foundation of *law,* the imperative declaration of what in its eyes is to be regarded as just and lawful, and what unjust and unlawful: and while, after the foundation of law, the supreme power treats the aggressive and arbitrary acts of individuals, or of whole groups, as a violation of law, and a revolt against itself, it distracts the feelings of its subjects from the immediate injury inflicted by such a violation, and thus eventually attains the very opposite result to that always desired by revenge, which sees and recognises nothing but the standpoint of the injured party. From henceforth the eye becomes trained to a more and more *impersonal* valuation of the deed, even the eye of the injured party himself (though this is in the final stage of all, as has been previously remarked)—on this principle "right" and "wrong" first manifest themselves after the foundation of law (and *not,* as Dühring maintains, only after the act of violation). To talk of intrinsic right and intrinsic wrong is absolutely nonsensical; intrinsically, an injury, an oppression, an exploitation, an annihilation can be nothing wrong, inasmuch as life is *essentially* (that is, in its cardinal functions) something which functions by injuring, oppressing, exploiting, and annihilating, and is absolutely inconceivable without such a character. It is necessary to make an even more serious confession:—viewed from the most advanced biological standpoint, conditions of legality can be only *exceptional conditions,* in that they are partial restrictions of the real life-will, which makes for power, and in that they are subordinated to the life-will's general end as particular means, that is, as means to create *larger* units of strength. A legal organisation, conceived of as sovereign and universal, not as a weapon in a fight of complexes of power, but as a weapon *against* fighting, generally something after the style of Dühring's communistic model of treating every will as equal with every other will, would be a principle *hostile to life,* a destroyer and dissolver of man, an outrage on the future of man, a symptom of fatigue, a secret cut to Nothingness.—

[*691*]

12

A word more on the origin and end of punishment—two problems which are or ought to be kept distinct, but which unfortunately are usually lumped into one. And what tactics have our moral genealogists employed up to the present in these cases? Their inveterate naïveté. They find out some "end" in the punishment, for instance, revenge and deterrence, and then in all their innocence set this end at the beginning, as the *causa fiendi* of the punishment, and—they have done the trick. But the patching up of a history of the origin of law is the last use to which the "End in Law" * ought to be put. Perhaps there is no more pregnant principle for any kind of history than the following, which, difficult though it is to master, *should* none the less be *mastered* in every detail.—The origin of the existence of a thing and its final utility, its practical application and incorporation in a system of ends, are *toto cælo* opposed to each other—everything, anything, which exists and which prevails anywhere, will always be put to new purposes by a force superior to itself, will be commandeered afresh, will be turned and transformed to new uses; all "happening" in the organic world consists of *overpowering* and dominating, and again all overpowering and domination is a new interpretation and adjustment, which must necessarily obscure or absolutely extinguish the subsisting "meaning" and "end." The most perfect comprehension of the utility of any physiological organ (or also of a legal institution, social custom, political habit, form in art or in religious worship) does not for a minute imply any simultaneous comprehension of its

---

* An allusion to *Der Zweck im Recht,* by the great German jurist, Professor Ihering.

origin: this may seem uncomfortable and unpalatable to the older men,—for it has been the immemorial belief that under-standing the final cause or the utility of a thing, a form, an institution, means also understanding the reason for its origin: to give an example of this logic, the eye was made to see, the hand was made to grasp. So even punishment was conceived as invented with a view to punishing. But all ends and all utilities are only *signs* that a Will to Power has mastered a less power-ful force, has impressed thereon out of its own self the mean-ing of a function; and the whole history of a "Thing," an organ, a custom, can on the same principle be regarded as a continuous "sign-chain" of perpetually new interpretations and adjustments, whose causes, so far from needing to have even a mutual connection, sometimes follow and alternate with each other absolutely haphazardly. Similarly, the evolution of a "Thing," of a custom, is anything but its *progressus* to an end, still less a logical and direct *progressus* attained with the minimum expenditure of energy and cost: it is rather the succession of processes of subjugation, more or less profound, more or less mutually independent, which operate on the thing itself; it is, further, the resistance which in each case in-variably displayed this subjugation, the Protean wriggles by way of defence and reaction, and, further, the results of suc-cessful counter-efforts. The form is fluid, but the meaning is even more so—even inside every individual organism the case is the same: with every genuine growth of the whole, the "function" of the individual organs becomes shifted,—in cer-tain cases a partial perishing of these organs, a diminution of their numbers (for instance, through annihilation of the con-necting members), can be a symptom of growing strength and perfection. What I mean is this: even partial *loss of utility,* decay, and degeneration, loss of function and purpose, in a

[*693*]

word, death, appertain to the conditions of the genuine *progressus;* which always appears in the shape of a will and way to *greater* power, and is always realised at the expense of innumerable smaller powers. The magnitude of a "progress" is gauged by the greatness of the sacrifice that it requires: humanity as a mass sacrificed to the prosperity of the one *stronger* species of Man—that *would be* a progress. I emphasise all the more this cardinal characteristic of the historic method, for the reason that in its essence it runs counter to predominant instincts and prevailing taste, which must prefer to put up with absolute casualness, even with the mechanical senselessness of all phenomena, than with the theory of a power-will, in exhaustive play throughout all phenomena. The democratic idiosyncrasy against everything which rules and wishes to rule, the modern *misarchism* (to coin a bad word for a bad thing), has gradually but so thoroughly transformed itself into the guise of intellectualism, the most abstract intellectualism, that even nowadays it penetrates and *has the right* to penetrate step by step into the most exact and apparently the most objective sciences: this tendency has, in fact, in my view already dominated the whole of physiology and biology, and to their detriment, as is obvious, in so far as it has spirited away a radical idea, the idea of true *activity*. The tyranny of this idiosyncrasy, however, results in the theory of "adaptation" being pushed forward into the van of the argument, exploited; adaptation—that means to say, a second-class activity, a mere capacity for "reacting"; in fact, life itself has been defined (by Herbert Spencer) as an increasingly effective internal adaptation to external circumstances. This definition, however, fails to realise the real essence of life, its will to power. It fails to appreciate the paramount superiority enjoyed by those plastic forces of spontaneity, aggression, and encroachment with their new interpretations and tendencies, to the operation of which adaptation is only a natural corollary: consequently the sovereign office of the highest functionaries in the organism itself (among which the life-will appears as an active and formative principle) is repudiated. One remembers Huxley's reproach to Spencer of his "administrative Nihilism": but it is a case of something much *more* than "administration."

13

To return to our subject, namely *punishment,* we must make consequently a double distinction: first, the relatively permanent *element,* the custom, the act, the "drama," a certain rigid sequence of methods of procedure; on the other hand, the fluid element, the meaning, the end, the expectation which is attached to the operation of such procedure. At this point we immediately assume, *per analogiam* (in accordance with the theory of the historic method, which we have elaborated above), that the procedure itself is something older and earlier than its utilisation in punishment, that this utilisation was *introduced* and interpreted into the procedure (which had existed for a long time, but whose employment had another meaning), in short, that the case is *different* from that hitherto supposed by our *naïf* genealogists of morals and of law, who thought that the procedure was *invented* for the purpose of punishment, in the same way that the hand had been previously thought to have been invented for the purpose of grasping. With regard to the other element in *punishment,* its fluid element, its meaning, the idea of punishment in a very late stage of civilisation (for instance, contemporary

Europe) is not content with manifesting merely one meaning, but manifests a whole synthesis "of meanings." The past general history of punishment, the history of its employment for the most diverse ends, crystallises eventually into a kind of unity, which is difficult to analyse into its parts, and which, it is necessary to emphasise, absolutely defies definition. (It is nowadays impossible to say definitely *the precise reason* for punishment: all ideas, in which a whole process is promiscuously comprehended, elude definition; it is only that which has no history, which can be defined.) At an earlier stage, on the contrary, that synthesis of meanings appears much less rigid and much more elastic; we can realise how in each individual case the elements of the synthesis change their value and their position, so that now one element and now another stands out and predominates over the others, nay, in certain cases one element (perhaps the end of deterrence) seems to eliminate all the rest. At any rate, so as to give some idea of the uncertain, supplementary, and accidental nature of the meaning of punishment and of the manner in which one identical procedure can be employed and adapted for the most diametrically opposed objects, I will at this point give a scheme that has suggested itself to me, a scheme itself based on comparatively small and accidental material.—Punishment, as rendering the criminal harmless and incapable of further injury.—Punishment, as compensation for the injury sustained by the injured party, in any form whatsoever (including the form of sentimental compensation).—Punishment, as an isolation of that which disturbs the equilibrium, so as to prevent the further spreading of the disturbance.—Punishment as a means of inspiring fear of those who determine and execute the punishment.—Punishment as a kind of compensation for advantages which the wrong-doer has up to that time enjoyed (for example, when he is utilised as a slave in the mines).—Punishment, as the elimination of an element of decay (sometimes of a whole branch, as according to the Chinese laws, consequently as a means to the purification of the race, or the preservation of a social type).—Punishment as a festival, as the violent oppression and humiliation of an enemy that has at last been subdued.—Punishment as a mnemonic, whether for him who suffers the punishment—the so-called "correction," or for the witnesses of its administration.—Punishment, as the payment of a fee stipulated for by the power which protects the evil-doer from the excesses of revenge.—Punishment, as a compromise with the natural phenomenon of revenge, in so far as revenge is still maintained and claimed as a privilege by the stronger races.—Punishment as a declaration and measure of war against an enemy of peace, of law, of order, of authority, who is fought by society with the weapons which war provides, as a spirit dangerous to the community, as a breaker of the contract on which the community is based, as a rebel, a traitor, and a breaker of the peace.

14

This list is certainly not complete; it is obvious that punishment is overloaded with utilities of all kinds. This makes it all the more permissible to eliminate one *supposed* utility, which passes, at any rate in the popular mind, for its most essential utility, and which is just what even now provides the strongest support for that faith in punishment which is nowadays for many reasons tottering. Punishment is supposed to have the value of exciting in the guilty the consciousness of guilt; in punishment is sought the proper *instrumentum* of that psychic reaction which becomes known as a "bad conscience," "re-morse." But this theory is even, from the point of view of the present, a violation of reality and psychology: and how much more so is the case when we have to deal with the longest period of man's history, his primitive history! Genuine re-morse is certainly extremely rare among wrong-doers and the victims of punishment; prisons and houses of correction are not *the* soil on which this worm of remorse pullulates for choice—this is the unanimous opinion of all conscientious observers, who in many cases arrive at such a judgment with enough reluctance and against their own personal wishes. Speaking generally, punishment hardens and numbs, it pro-duces concentration, it sharpens the consciousness of aliena-tion, it strengthens the power of resistance. When it happens that it breaks the man's energy and brings about a piteous prostration and abjectness, such a result is certainly even less salutary than the average effect of punishment, which is char-acterised by a harsh and sinister doggedness. The thought of those *prehistoric* millennia brings us to the unhesitating con-clusion, that it was simply through punishment that the evo-lution of the consciousness of guilt was most forcibly retarded —at any rate in the victims of the punishing power. In par-ticular, let us not underestimate the extent to which, by the very sight of the judicial and executive procedure, the wrong-doer is himself prevented from feeling that his deed, the character of his act, is *intrinsically* reprehensible: for he sees clearly the same kind of acts practised in the service of justice, and then called good, and practised with a good conscience; acts such as espionage, trickery, bribery, trapping, the whole intriguing and insidious art of the policeman and the informer—the whole system, in fact, manifested in the different kinds of punishment (a system not excused by passion, but based on principle), of robbing, oppressing, insulting, imprisoning, racking, murdering.—All this he sees treated by his judges, not as acts meriting censure and condemnation *in themselves,* but only in a particular context and application. It was *not* on this soil that grew the "bad conscience," that most sinister and interesting plant of our earthly vegetation—in point of fact, throughout a most lengthy period, no suggestion of having to do with a "guilty man" manifested itself in the consciousness of the man who judged and punished. One had merely to deal with an author of an injury, an irresponsible piece of fate. And the man himself, on whom the punishment subsequently fell like a piece of fate, was occasioned no more of an "inner pain" than would be occasioned by the sudden approach of some uncalculated event, some terrible natural catastrophe, a rushing, crushing avalanche against which there is no resistance.

15

This truth came insidiously enough to the consciousness of Spinoza (to the disgust of his commentators, who (like Kuno Fischer, for instance) give themselves no end of *trouble* to misunderstand him on this point), when one afternoon (as he sat raking up who knows what memory) he indulged in the question of what was really left for him personally of the celebrated *Morsus conscientiæ*—Spinoza, who had relegated "good and evil" to the sphere of human imagination, and indignantly defended the honour of his "free" God against those blasphemers who affirmed that God did everything *sub ratione boni* ("but this was tantamount to subordinating God to fate, and would really be the greatest of all absurdities"). For Spinoza the world had returned again to that innocence in which it lay before the discovery of the bad conscience: what, then, had happened to the *morsus conscientiæ?* "The antithesis of *gaudium,*" said he at last to himself,—"A sadness accompanied by the recollection of a past event which has turned out contrary to all expectation" (*Eth*. iii., Propos. XVIII. Schol. i. ii.). Evil-doers have throughout thousands of years felt when overtaken by punishment *exactly like Spinoza,* on the subject of their "offence": "here is something which went wrong contrary to my anticipation," *not* "I ought not to have done this."—They submitted themselves to punishment, just as one submits one's self to a disease, to a misfortune, or to death, with that stubborn and resigned fatalism which gives the Russians, for instance, even nowadays, the advantage over us Westerners, in the handling of life. If at that period there was a critique of action, the criterion was prudence: the real *effect* of punishment is unquestionably chiefly to be found in a sharpening of the sense of prudence, in a lengthening of the memory, in a will to adopt more of a policy of caution, suspicion, and secrecy; in the recognition that there are many things which are unquestionably beyond one's capacity; in a kind of improvement in self-criticism. The broad effects which can be obtained by punishment in man and beast, are the increase of fear, the sharpening of the sense of cunning, the mastery of the desires: so it is that punishment *tames* man, but does not make him "better"—it would be more correct even to go so far as to assert the contrary ("Injury makes a man cunning," says a popular proverb: so far as it makes him cunning, it makes him also bad. Fortunately, it often enough makes him stupid).

[*700*]

16

At this juncture I cannot avoid trying to give a tentative and provisional expression to my own hypothesis concerning the origin of the bad conscience: it is difficult to make it fully appreciated, and it requires continuous meditation, attention, and digestion. I regard the bad conscience as the serious illness which man was bound to contract under the stress of the most radical change which he has ever experienced—that change, when he found himself finally imprisoned within the pale of society and of peace.

Just like the plight of the water-animals, when they were compelled either to become land-animals or to perish, so was the plight of these half-animals, perfectly adapted as they were to the savage life of war, prowling, and adventure—suddenly all their instincts were rendered worthless and "switched off." Henceforward they had to walk on their feet—"carry themselves," whereas heretofore they had been carried by the water: a terrible heaviness oppressed them. They found themselves clumsy in obeying the simplest directions, confronted with this new and unknown world they had no longer their old guides—the regulative instincts that had led them unconsciously to safety—they were reduced, were those unhappy creatures, to thinking, inferring, calculating, putting together causes and results, reduced to that poorest and most erratic organ of theirs, their "consciousness." I do not believe there was ever in the world such a feeling of misery, such a leaden discomfort—further, those old instincts had not immediately ceased their demands! Only it was difficult and rarely possible to gratify them: speaking broadly, they were compelled to satisfy themselves by new and, as it were, hole-and-corner methods. All instincts which do not find a vent without, *turn inwards*—this is what I mean by the growing "internalisation" of man: consequently we have the first growth in man, of what subsequently was called his soul. The whole inner world, originally as thin as if it had been stretched between two layers of skin, burst apart and expanded proportionately, and obtained depth, breadth, and height, when man's external outlet became *obstructed*. These terrible bulwarks, with which the social organisation protected itself against the old instincts of freedom (punishments belong pre-eminently to these bulwarks), brought it about that all those instincts of wild, free, prowling man became turned backwards *against man himself*. Enmity, cruelty, the delight in persecution, in surprises, change, destruction—the turning all these instincts against their own possessors: this is the origin of the "bad conscience." It was man, who, lacking external enemies and obstacles, and imprisoned as he was in the oppressive narrowness and monotony of custom, in his own impatience lacerated, persecuted, gnawed, frightened, and ill-treated himself; it was this animal in the hands of the tamer, which beat itself against the bars of its cage; it was this being who, pining and yearning for that desert home of which it had been deprived, was compelled to create out of its own self, an adventure, a torture-chamber, a hazardous and perilous desert—it was this fool, this homesick and desperate prisoner—who invented the "bad conscience." But thereby he introduced that most grave and sinister illness, from which mankind has not yet recovered, the suffering of man from the disease called man, as the result of a violent breaking from his animal past, the result, as it were, of a spasmodic plunge into a new environment and new conditions of existence, the result of a declaration of war against the old instincts, which up to that time had been the staple of his power, his joy, his formidableness. Let us immediately add that this fact of an animal ego turning against itself, taking part against itself, produced in the world so novel, profound, unheard-of, problematic, inconsistent, and *pregnant* a phenomenon, that the aspect of the world was radically altered thereby. In sooth, only divine spectators could have appreciated the drama that then began, and whose end baffles conjecture as yet—a drama too subtle, too wonderful, too paradoxical to warrant its undergoing a nonsensical and unheeded performance on some random grotesque planet! Henceforth man is to be counted as one of the most unexpected and sensational lucky shots in the game of the "big baby" of Heracleitus, whether he be called Zeus or Chance—he awakens on his behalf the interest, excitement, hope, almost the confidence, of his being the harbinger and forerunner of something, of man being no end, but only a stage, an interlude, a bridge, a great promise.

17

It is primarily involved in this hypothesis of the origin of the bad conscience, that that alteration was no gradual and no voluntary alteration, and that it did not manifest itself as an organic adaptation to new conditions, but as a break, a jump, a necessity, an inevitable fate, against which there was no resistance and never a spark of resentment. And secondarily, that the fitting of a hitherto unchecked and amorphous population into a fixed form, starting as it had done in an act of violence, could only be accomplished by acts of violence and nothing else—that the oldest "State" appeared consequently as a ghastly tyranny, a grinding ruthless piece of machinery, which went on working, till this raw material of a semi-animal populace was not only thoroughly kneaded and elastic, but also *moulded*. I used the word "State"; my meaning is self-evident, namely, a herd of blonde beasts of prey, a race of conquerors and masters, which with all its war-like organisation and all its organising power pounces with its terrible claws on a population, in numbers possibly tremendously superior, but as yet formless, as yet nomad. Such is the origin of the "State." That fantastic theory that makes it begin with a contract is, I think, disposed of. He who can command, he who is a master by "nature," he who comes on the scene forceful in deed and gesture—what has he to do with contracts? Such beings defy calculation, they come like fate, without cause, reason, notice, excuse, they are there as the lightning is there, too terrible, too sudden, too convincing, too "different," to be personally even hated. Their work is an instinctive creating and impressing of forms, they are the most involuntary, unconscious artists that there are:—their appearance produces instantaneously a scheme of sovereignty which is *live,* in which the functions are partitioned and apportioned, in which above all no part is received or finds a place, until pregnant with a "meaning" in regard to the whole. They are ignorant of the meaning of guilt, responsibility, consideration, are these born organisers; in them predominates that terrible artist-egoism, that gleams like brass, and that knows itself justified to all eternity, in its work, even as a mother in her child. It is not in *them* that there grew the bad conscience, that is elementary—but it would not have grown *without them,* repulsive growth as it was, it would be missing, had not a tremendous quantity of freedom been expelled from the world by the stress of their hammer-strokes, their artist violence, or been at any rate made invisible and, as it were, *latent.* This *instinct of freedom* forced into being latent—it is already clear—this instinct of freedom forced back, trodden back, imprisoned within itself, and finally only able to find vent and relief in itself; this, only this, is the beginning of the "bad conscience."

18

Beware of thinking lightly of this phenomenon, by reason of its initial painful ugliness. At bottom it is the same active force which is at work on a more grandiose scale in those potent artists and organisers, and builds states, where here, internally, on a smaller and pettier scale and with a retrogressive tendency, makes itself a bad conscience in the "labyrinth of the breast," to use Goethe's phrase, and which builds negative ideals; it is, I repeat, that identical *instinct of freedom* (to use my own language, the will to power) : only the material, on which this force with all its constructive and tyrannous nature is let loose, is here man himself, his whole old animal self—and *not* as in the case of that more grandiose and sensational phenomenon, the *other* man, *other* men. This secret self-tyranny, this cruelty of the artist, this delight in giving a form to one's self as a piece of difficult, refractory, and suffering material, in burning in a will, a critique, a contradiction, a contempt, a negation; this sinister and ghastly labour of love on the part of a soul, whose will is cloven in two within itself, which makes itself suffer from delight in the infliction of suffering; this wholly *active* bad conscience has finally (as one already anticipates)—true fountainhead as it is of idealism and imagination—produced an abundance of novel and amazing beauty and affirmation, and perhaps has really been the first to give birth to beauty at all. What would beauty be, forsooth, if its contradiction had not first been presented to consciousness, if the ugly had not first said to itself, "I am ugly"? At any rate, after this hint the problem of how far idealism and beauty can be traced in such opposite ideas as *"selflessness," self-denial, self-sacrifice,* becomes less problematical; and indubitably in future we shall certainly know the real and original character of the *delight* experienced by the self-less, the self-denying, the self-sacrificing: this delight is a phase of cruelty.—So much provisionally for the origin of "altruism" as a *moral* value, and the marking out the ground from which this value has grown: it is only the bad conscience, only the will for self-abuse, that provides the necessary conditions for the existence of altruism as a *value.*

19

Undoubtedly the bad conscience is an illness, but an illness as pregnancy is an illness. If we search out the conditions under which this illness reaches its most terrible and sublime zenith, we shall see what really first brought about its entry into the world. But to do this we must take a long breath, and we must first of all go back once again to an earlier point of view. The relation at civil law of the ower to his creditor (which has already been discussed in detail), has been interpreted once again (and indeed in a manner which historically is exceedingly remarkable and suspicious) into a relationship, which is perhaps more incomprehensible to us moderns than to any other era; that is, into the relationship of the *existing* generation to its *ancestors.* Within the original tribal association—we are talking of primitive times—each living generation recognises a legal obligation towards the earlier generation, and particularly towards the earliest, which founded the family (and this is something much more than a mere sentimental obligation, the existence of which, during the longest period of man's history, is by no means indisputable). There prevails in them the conviction that it is only thanks to sacrifices and efforts of their ancestors, that the race *persists* at all—and that this has to be *paid back* to them by sacrifices and services. Thus is recognized the *owing* of a debt, which accumulates continually by reason of these ancestors never ceasing in their subsequent life as potent spirits to secure by their power new privileges and advantages to the race. Gratis, perchance? But there is no gratis for that raw and "mean-souled" age. What return can be made?—Sacrifice (at first, nourishment, in its crudest sense), festivals, temples, tributes of veneration, above all, obedience—since all customs are, *qua* works of the ancestors, equally their precepts and commands—are the ancestors ever given enough? This suspicion remains and grows: from time to time it extorts a great wholesale ransom, something monstrous in the way of repayment of the creditor (the notorious sacrifice of the first-born, for example, blood, human blood in any case). The *fear* of ancestors and their power, the consciousness of owing debts to them, necessarily increases, according to this kind of logic, in the exact proportion that the race itself increases, that the race itself becomes more victorious, more independent, more honoured, more feared. This, and not the contrary, is the fact. Each step towards race decay, all disastrous events, all symptoms of degeneration, of approaching disintegration, always *diminish* the fear of the founders' spirit, and whittle away the idea of his sagacity, providence, and potent presence. Conceive this crude kind of logic carried to its climax: it follows that the ancestors of the *most powerful* races must, through the growing fear that they exercise on the imaginations, grow themselves into monstrous dimensions, and become relegated to the gloom of a divine mystery that transcends imagination—the ancestor becomes at last necessarily transfigured into a *god*. Perhaps this is the very origin of the gods, that is, an origin from *fear!* And those who feel bound to add, "but from piety also," will have difficulty in maintaining this theory, with regard to the primeval and longest period of the human race. And, of course, this is even more the case as regards the *middle* period, the formative period of the aristocratic races—the aristocratic races which have given back with interest to their founders, the ancestors (heroes, gods), all those qualities which in the meanwhile have appeared in themselves, that is, the aristocratic qualities. We will later on glance again at the ennobling and promotion of the gods (which, of course, is totally distinct from their "sanctification") : let us now provisionally follow to its end the course of the whole of this development of the conscious· ness of "owing."

20

According to the teaching of history, the consciousness of owing debts to the deity by no means came to an end with the decay of the clan organisation of society; just as mankind has inherited the ideas of "good" and "bad" from the race-nobility (together with its fundamental tendency towards establishing social distinctions), so with the heritage of the racial and tribal gods it has also inherited the incubus of debts as yet unpaid and the desire to discharge them. The transition is effected by those large populations of slaves and bondsmen, who, whether through compulsion or through submission and *"mimicry,"* have accommodated themselves to the religion of their masters; through this channel these inherited tendencies inundate the world. The feeling of owing a debt to the deity has grown continuously for several centuries, always in the same proportion in which the idea of God and the consciousness of God have grown and become exalted among mankind. (The whole history of ethnic fights, victories, reconciliations, amalgamations, everything, in fact, which precedes the eventual classing of all the social elements in each great race-synthesis, are mirrored in the hotch-potch genealogy of their gods, in the legends of their fights, victories, and reconciliations. Progress towards universal empires invariably means progress towards universal deities; despotism. with its subjugation of the independent nobility, always paves the way for some system or other of monotheism.) The appearance of the Christian god, as the record god up to this time, has for that very reason brought equally into the world the record amount of guilt consciousness. Granted that we have gradually started on the *reverse* movement, there is no little probability in the deduction, based on the continuous decay in the belief in the Christian god, to the effect that there also already exists a considerable decay in the human consciousness of owing (ought); in fact, we cannot shut our eyes to the prospect of the complete and eventual triumph of atheism freeing mankind from all this feeling of obligation to their origin, their *causa prima*. Atheism and a kind of second innocence complement and supplement each other.

21

So much for my rough and preliminary sketch of the inter-relation of the ideas "ought" (owe) and "duty" with the postulates of religion. I have intentionally shelved up to the present the actual moralisation of these ideas (their being pushed back into the conscience, or more precisely the inter-weaving of the *bad* conscience with the idea of God), and at the end of the last paragraph used language to the effect that this moralisation did not exist, and that consequently these ideas had necessarily come to an end, by reason of what had happened to their hypothesis, the credence in our "creditor," in God. The actual facts differ terribly from this theory. It is with the moralisation of the ideas "ought" and "duty," and with their being pushed back into the *bad* conscience, that comes the first actual attempt to *reverse* the direction of the development we have just described, or at any rate to arrest its evolution; it is just at this juncture that the very hope of an eventual redemption *has to* put itself once for all into the prison of pessimism, it is at this juncture that the eye *has to* recoil and rebound in despair from off an adamantine impossi-bility, it is at this juncture that the ideas "guilt" and "duty" have to turn backwards—turn backwards against *whom?* There is no doubt about it; primarily against the "ower," in whom the bad conscience now establishes itself, eats, extends, and grows like a polypus throughout its length and breadth, all with such virulence, that at last, with the impossibility of paying the debt, there becomes conceived the idea of the im-possibility of paying the penalty, the thought of its inexpia-bility (the idea of "eternal punishment")—finally, too, it turns against the "creditor," whether found in the *causa prima* of man, the origin of the human race, its sire, who henceforth becomes burdened with a curse ("Adam," "original sin," "de-termination of the will"), or in Nature from whose womb man springs, and on whom the responsibility for the principle of evil is now cast ("Diabolisation of Nature"), or in existence generally, on this logic an absolute *white elephant,* with which mankind is landed (the Nihilistic flight from life, the demand for Nothingness, or for the opposite of existence, for some other existence, Buddhism and the like)—till suddenly we stand before that paradoxical and awful expedient, through which a tortured humanity has found a temporary alleviation, that stroke of genius called Christianity:—God personally immolating himself for the debt of man, God paying himself personally out of a pound of his own flesh, God as the one being who can deliver man from what man had become unable to deliver himself—the creditor playing scapegoat for his debtor, from *love* (can you believe it?), from love of his debtor! . . .

<hr>

22

The reader will already have conjectured what took place on the stage and *behind the scenes* of this drama. That will for self-torture, that inverted cruelty of the animal man, who, turned subjective and scared into introspection (encaged as he was in "the State," as part of his taming process), invented the bad conscience so as to hurt himself, after the *natural* outlet for this will to hurt, became blocked—in other words, this man of the bad conscience exploited the religious hypothesis so as to carry his martyrdom to the ghastliest pitch of agonised intensity. Owing something to *God:* this thought becomes his instrument of torture. He apprehends in God the most extreme antitheses that he can find to his own characteristic and ineradicable animal instincts, he himself gives a new interpretation to these animal instincts as being against what he "owes" to God (as enmity, rebellion, and revolt against the "Lord," the "Father," the "Sire," the "Beginning of the world"), he places himself between the horns of the dilemma, "God" and "Devil." Every negation which he is inclined to utter to himself, to the nature, naturalness, and reality of his being, he whips into an ejaculation of "yes," uttering it as something existing, living, efficient, as being God, as the holiness of God, the judgment of God, as the hangmanship of God, as transcendence, as eternity, as unending torment, as hell, as infinity of punishment and guilt. This is a kind of madness of the will in the sphere of psychological cruelty which is absolutely unparalleled:——man's *will* to find himself guilty and blameworthy to the point of inexpiability, his *will* to think of himself as punished, without the punishment ever being able to balance the guilt, his *will* to infect and to poison the fundamental basis of the universe with the problem of punishment and guilt, in order to cut off once and for all any escape out of this labyrinth of "fixed ideas," his will for rearing an ideal—that of the "holy God"——face to face with which he can have tangible proof of his own unworthiness. Alas for this mad melancholy beast man! What phantasies invade it, what paroxysms of perversity, hysterical senselessness, and *mental bestiality* break out immediately, at the very slightest check on its being the beast of action! All this is excessively interesting, but at the same time tainted with a black, gloomy, enervating melancholy, so that a forcible veto must be invoked against looking too long into these abysses. Here is *disease,* undubitably, the most ghastly disease that has as yet played havoc among men: and he who can still hear (but man turns now deaf ears to such sounds), how in this night of torment and nonsense there has rung out the cry of *love,* the cry of the most passionate ecstasy, of redemption in *love,* he turns away gripped by an invincible horror——in man there is so much that is ghastly—too long has the world been a mad-house.

23

Let this suffice once for all concerning the origin of the "holy God." The fact that *in itself* the conception of gods is not bound to lead necessarily to this degradation of the imagination (a temporary representation of whose vagaries we felt bound to give), the fact that there exist *nobler* methods of utilising the invention of gods than in this self-crucifixion and self-degradation of man, in which the last two thousand years of Europe have been past masters—these facts can fortunately be still perceived from every glance that we cast at the Grecian gods, these mirrors of noble and grandiose men, in which the *animal* in man felt itself deified, and did *not* devour itself in subjective frenzy. These Greeks long utilised their gods as simple buffers against the "bad conscience"—so that they could continue to enjoy their freedom of soul: this, of course, is diametrically opposed to Christianity's theory of its god. They went *very far* on this principle, did these splendid and lion-hearted children; and there is no lesser authority than that of the Homeric Zeus for making them realise occasionally that they are taking life too casually. "Wonderful," says he on one occasion—it has to do with the case of Ægistheus, a *very* bad case indeed—

"Wonderful how they grumble, the mortals against the im mortals
   Only from us, they presume, *comes evil,* but in their folly,
Fashion they, spite of fate, the doom of their own disaster."

Yet the reader will note and observe that this Olympian spectator and judge is far from being angry with them and thinking evil of them on this score. "How *foolish* they are," so thinks he of the misdeeds of mortals—and "folly," "imprudence," "a little brain disturbance," and nothing more, are what the Greeks, even of the strongest, bravest period, have admitted to be the ground of much that is evil and fatal.—Folly, *not* sin, do you understand? . . . But even this brain disturbance was a problem—"Come, how is it even possible? How could it have really got in brains like ours, the brains of men of aristocratic ancestry, of men of fortune, of men of good natural endowments, of men of the best society, of men of nobility and virtue?" This was the question that for century on century the aristocratic Greek put to himself when confronted with every (to him incomprehensible) outrage and sacrilege with which one of his peers had polluted himself. "It must be that a *god* had infatuated him," he would say at last, nodding his head.— This solution is *typical* of the Greeks, . . . accordingly the gods in those times subserved the functions of justifying man to a certain extent even in evil—in those days they took upon themselves not the punishment, but, what is *more noble,* the guilt.

24

I conclude with three queries, as you will see. "Is an ideal actually set up here, or is one pulled down?" I am perhaps asked. . . . But have ye sufficiently asked yourselves how dear a payment has the setting up of *every* ideal in the world exacted? To achieve that consummation how much truth must always be traduced and misunderstood, how many lies must be sanctified, how much conscience has got to be disturbed, how many pounds of "God" have got to be sacrificed every time?

To enable a sanctuary to be set up *a sanctuary has got to be destroyed:* that is a law—show me an instance where it has not been fulfilled! . . . We modern men, we inherit the immemorial tradition of vivisecting the conscience, and practising cruelty to our animal selves. That is the sphere of our most protracted training, perhaps of our artistic prowess, at any rate of our dilettantism and our perverted taste. Man has for too long regarded his natural proclivities with an "evil eye," so that eventually they have become in his system affiliated with a bad conscience. A converse endeavour would be intrinsically feasible—but who is strong enough to attempt it? —namely, to affiliate to the "bad conscience" all those *unnatural* proclivities, all those transcendental aspirations, contrary to sense, instinct, nature, and animalism—in short, all past and present ideals, which are all ideals opposed to life, and traducing the world. To whom is one to turn nowadays with *such* hopes and pretensions?—It is just the *good* men that we should thus bring about our ears; and in addition, as stands to reason, the indolent, the hedgers, the vain, the hysterical, the tired. . . . What is more offensive or more thoroughly calculated to alienate, than giving any hint of the exalted severity with which we treat ourselves? And again how conciliatory, how full of love does all the world show itself towards us so soon as we do as all the world does, and "let ourselves go" like all the world. For such a consummation we need spirits of *different* calibre than seems really feasible in this age; spirits rendered potent through wars and victories, to whom conquest, adventure, danger, even pain, have become a need; for such a consummation we need habituation to sharp, rare air, to winter wanderings, to literal and metaphorical ice and mountains; we even need a kind of sublime malice, a supreme and most self-conscious insolence of knowledge, which is the appanage of great health; we need (to summarise the awful truth) just this *great health!*

Is this even feasible today? . ∴ . But some day, in a stronger age than this rotting and introspective present, must he in sooth come to us, even the *redeemer* of great love and scorn, the creative spirit, rebounding by the impetus of his own force back again away from every transcendental plane and dimension, he whose solitude is misunderstood by the people, as though it were a flight *from* reality;—while actually it is only his diving, burrowing, and penetrating *into* reality, so that when he comes again to the light he can at once bring about by these means the *redemption* of this reality; its redemption from the curse which the old ideal has laid upon it. This man of the future, who in this wise will redeem us from the old ideal, as he will from that ideal's necessary corollary of great nausea, will to nothingness, and Nihilism; this tocsin of noon and of the great verdict, which renders the will again free, who gives back to the world its goal and to man his hope, this Antichrist and Antinihilist, this conqueror of God and of Nothingness—*he must one day come.*

25

But what am I talking of? Enough! Enough? At this juncture I have only one proper course, silence: otherwise I trespass on a domain open alone to one who is younger than I, one stronger, more *"future"* than I—open alone to *Zarathustra, Zarathustra the godless.*

What Is the Meaning of Ascetic Ideals?

"Careless, mocking, forceful—so does wisdom wish us: she is a woman, and never loves any one but a warrior."

Thus Spake Zarathustra.

1

WHAT is the meaning of ascetic ideals? In artists, nothing, or too much; in philosophers and scholars, a kind of "flair" and instinct for the conditions most favourable to advanced intellectualism; in women, at best an *additional* seductive fascination, a little *morbidezza* on a fine piece of flesh, the angelhood of a fat, pretty animal; in physiological failures and whiners (in the *majority* of mortals), an attempt to pose as "too good" for this world, a holy form of debauchery, their chief weapon in the battle with lingering pain and ennui; in priests, the actual priestly faith, their best engine of power, and also the supreme authority for power; in saints, finally a pretext for hibernation, their *novissima gloriæ cupido,* their peace in nothingness ("God"), their form of madness.

[*717*]

But in the very fact that the ascetic ideal has meant so much to man, lies expressed the fundamental feature of man's will, his *horror vacui: he needs a goal*—and he will sooner will nothingness than not will at all.—Am I not understood?—Have I not been understood?—"Certainly not, sir?"—Well, let us begin at the beginning.

2

What is the meaning of ascetic ideals? Or, to take an individual case in regard to which I have often been consulted, what is the meaning, for example, of an artist like Richard Wagner paying homage to chastity in his old age? He had always done so, of course, in a certain sense, but it was not till quite the end, that he did so in an ascetic sense. What is the meaning of this "change of attitude," this radical revolution in his attitude—for that was what it was? Wagner veered thereby straight round into his own opposite. What is the meaning of an artist veering round into his own opposite? At this point (granted that we do not mind stopping a little over this question), we immediately call to mind the best, strongest, gayest, and boldest period, that there perhaps ever was in Wagner's life: that was the period when he was genuinely and deeply occupied with the idea of "Luther's Wedding." Who knows what chance is responsible for our now having the *Meistersingers* instead of this wedding music? And how much in the latter is perhaps just an echo of the former? But there is no doubt but that the theme would have dealt with the praise of chastity. And certainly it would also have dealt with the praise of sensuality, and even so, it would seem quite in order, and even so, it would have been equally Wagnerian. For there is no necessary antithesis between chastity and sensuality: every good marriage, every authentic heart-felt love transcends this antithesis. Wagner would, it seems to me, have done well to have brought this *pleasing* reality home once again to his Germans, by means of a bold and graceful "Luther Comedy," for there were and are among the Germans many revilers of sensuality; and perhaps Luther's greatest merit lies just in the fact of his having had the courage of his *sensuality* (it used to be called, prettily enough, "evangelistic freedom"). But even in those cases where that antithesis between chastity and sensuality does exist, there has fortunately been for some time no necessity for it to be in any way a tragic antithesis. This should, at any rate, be the case with all beings who are sound in mind and body, who are far from reckoning their delicate balance between "animal" and "angel," as being on the face of it one of the principles opposed to existence—the most subtle and brilliant spirits, such as Goethe, such as Hafiz, have even seen in this a *further* charm of life. Such "conflicts" actually allure one to life. On the other hand, it is only too clear that when once these ruined swine are reduced to worshipping chastity— and there are such swine—they only see and worship in it the antithesis to themselves, the antithesis to ruined swine. Oh, what a tragic grunting and eagerness! You can just think of it —they worship that painful and superfluous contrast, which Richard Wagner in his latter days undoubtedly wished to set to music, and to place on the stage! *"For what purpose, forsooth?"* as we may reasonably ask. What did the swine matter to him; what do they matter to us?

3

At this point it is impossible to beg the further question of what he really had to do with that manly (ah, so unmanly) country bumpkin, that poor devil and natural, Parsifal, whom he eventually made a Catholic by such fraudulent devices. What? Was this Parsifal really meant *seriously?* One might be tempted to suppose the contrary, even to wish it—that the Wagnerian Parsifal was meant joyously, like a concluding play of a trilogy or satyric drama, in which Wagner the tragedian wished to take farewell of us, of himself, above all of *tragedy,* and to do so in a manner that should be quite fitting and worthy, that is, with an excess of the most extreme and flippant parody of the tragic itself, of the ghastly earthly seriousness and earthly woe of old—a parody of that *most crude phase* in the unnaturalness of the ascetic ideal, that had at length been overcome. That, as I have said, would have been quite worthy of a great tragedian; who like every artist first attains the supreme pinnacle of his greatness when he can look *down into himself* and his art, when he can *laugh* at himself. Is Wagner's Parsifal his secret laugh of superiority over himself, the triumph of that supreme artistic freedom and artistic transcendency which he has at length attained? We might, I repeat, wish it were so, for what can Parsifal, *taken seriously,* amount to? Is it really necessary to see in it (according to an expression once used against me) the product of an insane hate of knowledge, mind, and flesh? A curse on flesh and spirit in one breath of hate? An apostasy and reversion to the morbid Christian and obscurantist ideals? And finally a self-negation and self-elimination on the part of an artist, who till then had devoted all the strength of his will to the contrary, namely, the *highest* artistic expression of soul and body. And not only his art; of his life as well. Just remember with what enthusiasm Wagner followed in the footsteps of Feuerbach. Feuerbach's motto of "healthy sensuality" rang in the ears of Wagner during the thirties and forties of the century, as it did in the ears of many Germans (they dubbed themselves *"Young* Germans"), like the word of redemption. Did he eventually *change his mind* on the subject? For it seems at any rate that he eventually wished to *change his teaching* on that subject . . . and not only is that the case with the Parsifal trumpets on the stage: in the melancholy, cramped, and embarrassed lucubrations of his later years, there are a hundred places in which there are manifestations of a secret wish and will, a despondent, uncertain, unavowed will to preach actual retrogression, conversion, Christianity, mediævalism, and to say to his disciples, "All is vanity! Seek salvation elsewhere!" Even the "blood of the Redeemer" is once invoked.

4

Let me speak out my mind in a case like this, which has many painful elements—and it is a typical case: it is certainly best to separate an artist from his work so completely that he cannot be taken as seriously as his work. He is after all merely the presupposition of his work, the womb, the soil, in certain cases the dung and manure, on which and out of which it grows—and consequently, in most cases, something that must be forgotten if the work itself is to be enjoyed. The insight into the *origin* of a work is a matter for psychologists and vivisectors, but never either in the present or the future for the

æsthetes, the artists. The author and creator of Parsifal was as
little spared the necessity of sinking and living himself into
the terrible depths and foundations of mediæval soul-contrasts,
the necessity of a malignant abstraction from all intellectual
elevation, severity, and discipline, the necessity of a kind of
mental *perversity* (if the reader will pardon me such a word),
as little as a pregnant woman is spared the horrors and marvels
of pregnancy, which, as I have said, must be forgotten if the
child is to be enjoyed. We must guard ourselves against the
confusion, into which an artist himself would fall only too
easily (to employ the English terminology) out of psychological "contiguity"; as though the artist himself actually *were* the
object which he is able to represent, imagine, and express. In
point of fact, the position is that even if he conceived he were
such an object, he would certainly not represent, conceive,
express it. Homer would not have created an Achilles, nor
Goethe a Faust, if Homer had been an Achilles or if Goethe
had been a Faust. A complete and perfect artist is to all eternity
separated from the "real," from the actual; on the other hand,
it will be appreciated that he can at times get tired to the point
of despair of this eternal "unreality" and falseness of his
innermost being—and that he then sometimes attempts to
trespass on to the most forbidden ground, on reality, and
attempts to have real *existence*. With what success? The success will be guessed—it is the *typical velleity* of the artist; the
same velleity to which Wagner fell a victim in his old age, and
for which he had to pay so dearly and so fatally (he lost
thereby his most valuable friends). But after all, quite apart
from this velleity, who would not wish emphatically for Wagner's own sake that he had taken farewell of us and of his art
in a *different* manner, not with a *Parsifal,* but in more victori-

ous, more self-confident, more Wagnerian style—a style less
misleading, a style less ambiguous with regard to his whole
meaning, less Schopenhauerian, less Nihilistic? . . .

5

What, then, is the meaning of ascetic ideals? In the case of
an artist we are getting to understand their meaning: *Nothing
at all* . . . or so much that it is as good as nothing at all. Indeed, what is the use of them? Our artists have for a long time
past not taken up a sufficiently independent attitude, either in
the world or against it, to warrant their valuations and the
changes in these valuations exciting interest. At all times they
have played the valet of some morality, philosophy, or religion,
quite apart from the fact that unfortunately they have often
enough been the inordinately supple courtiers of their clients
and patrons, and the inquisitive toadies of the powers that are
existing, or even of the new powers to come. To put it at the
lowest, they always need a rampart, a support, an already constituted authority: artists never stand by themselves, standing
alone is opposed to their deepest instincts. So, for example,
did *Richard Wagner* take, "when the time had come," the
philosopher Schopenhauer for his covering man in front, for
his rampart. Who would consider it even thinkable, that he
would have had the *courage* for an ascetic ideal, without the
support afforded him by the philosophy of Schopenhauer,
without the authority of Schopenhauer, which *dominated*
Europe in the seventies? (This is without consideration of the
question whether an artist without the milk * of an orthodoxy

---

* An allusion to the celebrated monologue in *William Tell.*

would have been possible at all.) This brings us to the more serious question: What is the meaning of a real *philosopher* paying homage to the ascetic ideal, a really self-dependent intellect like Schopenhauer, a man and knight with a glance of bronze, who has the courage to be himself, who knows how to stand alone without first waiting for men who cover him in front, and the nods of his superiors? Let us now consider at once the remarkable attitude of Schopenhauer towards *art*, an attitude which has even a fascination for certain types. For that is obviously the reason why Richard Wagner *all at once* went over to Schopenhauer (persuaded thereto, as one knows, by a poet, Herwegh), went over so completely that there ensued the cleavage of a complete theoretic contradiction between his earlier and his later æsthetic faiths—the earlier, for example, being expressed in *Opera and Drama*, the later in the writings which he published from 1870 onwards. In particular, Wagner from that time onwards (and this is the volte-face which alienates us the most) had no scruples about changing his judgment concerning the value and position of music itself. What did he care if up to that time he had made of music a means, a medium, a "woman," that in order to thrive needed an end, a man—that is, the drama? He suddenly realised that *more* could be effected by the novelty of the Schopenhauerian theory in *majorem musicæ gloriam*—that is to say, by means of the *sovereignty* of music, as Schopenhauer understood it; music abstracted from and opposed to all the other arts, music as the independent art-in-itself, *not* like the other arts, affording reflections of the phenomenal world, but rather the language of the will itself, speaking straight out of the "abyss" as its most personal, original, and direct manifestation. This extraordinary rise in the value of music (a rise which seemed to grow out of the Schopenhauerian philosophy) was at once accompanied by an unprecedented rise in the estimation in which the *musician* himself was held: he became now an oracle, a priest, nay, more than a priest, a kind of mouthpiece for the "intrinsic essence of things," a telephone from the other world—from henceforward he talked not only music, did this ventriloquist of God, he talked metaphysic; what wonder that one day he eventually talked *ascetic ideals!*

6

Schopenhauer has made use of the Kantian treatment of the æsthetic problem—though he certainly did not regard it with the Kantian eyes. Kant thought that he showed honour to art when he favoured and placed in the foreground those of the predicates of the beautiful, which constitute the honour of knowledge: impersonality and universality. This is not the place to discuss whether this was not a complete mistake; all that I wish to emphasise is that Kant, just like other philosophers, instead of envisaging the æsthetic problem from the standpoint of the experiences of the artist (the creator), has only considered art and beauty from the standpoint of the spectator, and has thereby imperceptibly imported the spectator himself into the idea of the "beautiful"! But if only the philosophers of the beautiful had sufficient knowledge of this "spectator"!—Knowledge of him as a great fact of personality, as a great experience, as a wealth of strong and most individual events, desires, surprises, and raptures in the sphere of beauty! But, as I feared, the contrary was always the case. And so we get from our philosophers, from the very beginning, definitions on which the lack of a subtler personal experience squats like a fat worm of crass error, as it does on Kant's famous definition of the beautiful. "That is beautiful," says Kant, "which pleases without interesting." Without interesting! Compare this definition with this other one, made by a real "spectator" and "artist"—by Stendhal, who once called the beautiful *une promesse de bonheur*. Here, at any rate, the one point which Kant makes prominent in the æsthetic position is repudiated and eliminated—*le désintéressement*. Who is right, Kant or Stendhal? When, forsooth, our æsthetes never get tired of throwing into the scales in Kant's favour the fact that under the magic of beauty men can look at even naked female statues "without interest," we can certainly laugh a little at their expense:—in regard to this ticklish point the experiences of *artists* are more "interesting," and at any rate Pygmalion was not necessarily an "unæsthetic man." Let us think all the better of the innocence of our æsthetes, reflected as it is in such arguments; let us, for instance, count to Kant's honour the country-parson naïveté of his doctrine concerning the peculiar character of the sense of touch! And here we come back to Schopenhauer, who stood in much closer neighbourhood to the arts than did Kant, and yet never escaped outside the pale of the Kantian definition; how was that? The circumstance is marvellous enough: he interprets the expression, "without interest," in the most personal fashion, out of an experience which must in his case have been part and parcel of his regular routine. On few subjects does Schopenhauer speak with such certainty as on the working of æsthetic contemplation: he says of it that it simply counteracts sexual interest, like lupulin and camphor; he never gets tired of glorifying this escape from the "Life-will" as the great advantage and utility of the æsthetic state. In fact, one is tempted to ask if his fundamental conception of Will and Idea, the thought that there can only exist freedom from the "will" by means of "idea," did not originate in a generalisation from this sexual experience. (In all questions concerning the Schopenhauerian philosophy, one should, by the bye, never lose sight of the consideration that it is the conception of a youth of twenty-six, so that it participates not only in what is peculiar to Schopenhauer's life, but in what is peculiar to that special period of his life.) Let us listen, for instance, to one of the most expressive among the countless passages which he has written in honour of the æsthetic state (*World as Will and Idea,* i. 231); let us listen to the tone, the suffering, the happiness, the gratitude, with which such words are uttered: "This is the painless state which Epicurus praised as the highest good and as the state of the gods; we are during that moment freed from the vile pressure of the will, we celebrate the Sabbath of the will's hard labour, the wheel of Ixion stands still." What vehemence of language! What images of anguish and protracted revulsion! How almost pathological is that temporal antithesis between "that moment" and everything else, the "wheel of Ixion," "the hard labour of the will," "the vile pressure of the will." But granted that Schopenhauer was a hundred times right for himself personally, how does that help our insight into the nature of the beautiful? Schopenhauer has described one effect of the beautiful,—the calming of the will,—but is this effect really normal? As has been mentioned, Stendhal, an equally sensual but more happily constituted nature than Schopenhauer, gives prominence to another effect of the "beautiful." "The beautiful *promises* happiness." To him it is just the *excitement* of the will (the "interest") by the beauty that seems the essential fact. And does not Schopenhauer ultimately lay himself open to the objection, that he is quite wrong in regarding himself as a Kantian on this point, that he has absolutely failed to understand in a Kantian sense the Kantian definition of the beautiful—that the beautiful pleased him as well by means of an interest, by means, in fact, of the strongest and most personal interest of all, that of the victim of torture who escapes from his torture?—And to come back again to our first question, "What is the *meaning* of a philosopher paying homage to ascetic ideals?" We get now, at any rate, a first hint; he wishes to *escape from a torture*.

7

Let us beware of making dismal faces at the word "torture" —there is certainly in this case enough to deduct, enough to discount—there is even something to laugh at. For we must certainly not underestimate the fact that Schopenhauer, who in practice treated sexuality as a personal enemy (including its tool, woman, that *"instrumentum diaboli"*), needed enemies to keep him in a good humour; that he loved grim, bitter, blackish-green words; that he raged for the sake of raging, out of passion; that he would have grown ill, would have become a pessimist (for he was not a pessimist, however much he wished to be), without his enemies, without Hegel, woman, sensuality, and the whole "will for existence" "keeping on." Without them Schopenhauer would not have "kept on," that is a safe wager; he would have run away: but his enemies held him fast, his enemies always enticed him back again to existence, his wrath was just as theirs was to the ancient Cynics, his balm, his recreation, his recompense, his *remedium* against disgust, his *happiness*. So much with regard to what is most personal in the case of Schopenhauer; on the other hand, there is still much which is typical in him—and only now we come back to our problem. It is an accepted and indisputable fact, so long as there are philosophers in the world, and wherever philosophers have existed (from India to England, to take the opposite poles of philosophic ability), that there exists a real irritation and rancour on the part of philosophers towards sensuality. Schopenhauer is merely the most eloquent, and if one has the ear for it, also the most fascinating and enchanting outburst. There similarly exists a real philosophic bias and affection for the whole ascetic ideal; there should be no illusions on this score. Both these feelings, as has been said, belong to the type; if a philosopher lacks both of them, then he is—you may be certain of it—never anything but a "pseudo." What does this *mean?* For this state of affairs must first be interpreted: in itself it stands there stupid to all eternity, like any "Thing-in-itself." Every animal, including *la bête philosophe,* strives instinctively after an *optimum* of favourable conditions, under which he can let his whole strength have play, and achieves his maximum consciousness of power; with equal instinctiveness, and with a fine perceptive flair which is superior to any reason, every animal shudders mortally at every kind of disturbance and hindrance which obstructs or could obstruct his way to that *optimum* (it is not his way to happiness of which I am talking, but his way to power, to action, the most powerful action, and in point of fact in many cases his way to unhappiness). Similarly, the philosopher shudders mortally at *marriage,* together with all that could persuade him to it—marriage as a fatal hindrance on the way to the *optimum.* Up to the present what great philosophers have been married? Heracleitus, Plato, Descartes, Spinoza, Leibnitz, Kant, Schopenhauer—they were not married, and, further, one cannot *imagine* them as married. A married philosopher belongs to *comedy,* that is my rule; as for that exception of a Socrates—the malicious Socrates married himself, it seems, *ironice,* just to prove this very rule. Every philosopher would say, as Buddha said, when the birth of a son was announced to him: "Râhoula has been born to me, a fetter has been forged for me" (Râhoula means here "a little demon"); there must come an hour of reflection to every "free spirit" (granted that he has had previously an hour of thoughtlessness), just as one came once to the same Buddha: "Narrowly cramped," he reflected, "is life in the house; it is a place of uncleanness; freedom is found in leaving the house." Because he thought like this, he left the house. So many bridges to *independence* are shown in the ascetic ideal, that the philosopher cannot refrain from exultation and clapping of hands when he hears the history of all those resolute ones, who on one day uttered a nay to all servitude and went into some *desert;* even granting that they were only strong asses, and the absolute opposite of strong minds. What, then, does the ascetic ideal mean in a philosopher? This is my answer—it will have been guessed long ago: when he sees this ideal the philosopher smiles be-cause he sees therein an *optimum* of the conditions of the highest and boldest intellectuality; he does not thereby deny "existence," he rather affirms thereby *his* existence and *only* his existence, and this perhaps to the point of not being far off the blasphemous wish, *pereat mundus, fiat philosophia, fiat philosophus, fiam!* . . .

8

These philosophers, you see, are by no means uncorrupted witnesses and judges of the *value* of the ascetic ideal. They think *of themselves*—what is the "saint" to them? They think of that which to them personally is most indispensable; of freedom from compulsion, disturbance, noise; freedom from business, duties, cares; of a clear head; of the dance, spring, and flight of thoughts; of good air—rare, clear, free, dry, as is the air on the heights, in which every animal creature becomes more intellectual and gains wings; they think of peace in every cellar; all the hounds neatly chained; no baying of enmity and uncouth rancour; no remorse of wounded ambition; quiet and submissive internal organs, busy as mills, but unnoticed; the heart alien, transcendent, future, posthumous —to summarise, they mean by the ascetic ideal the joyous asceticism of a deified and newly fledged animal, sweeping over life rather than resting. We know what are the three great catch-words of the ascetic ideal: poverty, humility, chastity; and now just look closely at the life of all the great fruitful inventive spirits—you will always find again and again these three qualities up to a certain extent. *Not* for a minute, as is self-evident, as though, perchance, they were part of their virtues— what has this type of man to do with virtues—but as the most essential and natural conditions of their *best* existence, their *finest* fruitfulness. In this connection it is quite possible that their predominant intellectualism had first to curb an unruly and irritable pride, or an insolent sensualism, or that it had all its work cut out to maintain its wish for the "desert" against perhaps an inclination to luxury and dilettantism, or similarly against an extravagant liberality of heart and hand. But their intellect did effect all this, simply because it was the *dominant* instinct, which carried through its orders in the case of all the other instincts. It effects it still; if it ceased to do so, it would simply not be dominant. But there is not one iota of "virtue" in all this. Further, the *desert,* of which I just spoke, in which the strong, independent, and well-equipped spirits retreat into their hermitage—oh, how different is it from the cultured

classes' dream of a desert! In certain cases, in fact, the cultured
classes themselves are the desert. And it is certain that all the
actors of the intellect would not endure this desert for a minute. It is nothing like romantic and Syrian enough for them,
nothing like enough of a stage desert! Here as well there are
plenty of asses, but at this point the resemblance ceases. But
a desert nowadays is something like this—perhaps a deliberate obscurity; a getting-out-of the way of one's self; a fear of
noise, admiration, papers, influence; a little office, a daily task,
something that hides rather than brings to light; sometimes
associating with harmless, cheerful beasts and fowls, the sight
of which refreshes; a mountain for company, but not a dead
one, one with *eyes* (that is, with lakes); in certain cases even
a room in a crowded hotel where one can reckon on not being
recognised, and on being able to talk with impunity to every
one: here is the desert—oh, it is lonely enough, believe me!
I grant that when Heracleitus retreated to the courts and clois-
ters of the colossal temple of Artemis, that "wilderness" was
worthier; why do we *lack* such temples? (perchance we do not
lack them: I just think of my splendid study in the *Piazza di
San Marco,* in spring, of course, and in the morning, between
ten and twelve). But that which Heracleitus shunned is still
just what we too avoid nowadays: the noise and democratic
babble of the Ephesians, their politics, their news from the
"empire" (I mean, of course, Persia), their market-trade in
"the things of today"—for there is one thing from which we
philosophers especially need a rest—from the things of "today." We honour the silent, the cold, the noble, the far, the
past, everything, in fact, at the sight of which the soul is not
bound to brace itself up and defend itself—something with
which one can speak without *speaking aloud.* Just listen now
to the tone a spirit has when it speaks; every spirit has its own

tone and loves its own tone. That thing yonder, for instance, is bound to be an agitator, that is, a hollow head, a hollow mug: whatever may go into him, everything comes back from him dull and thick, heavy with the echo of the great void. That spirit yonder nearly always speaks hoarse: has he, perchance, *thought* himself hoarse? It may be so—ask the physiologists—but he who thinks in *words,* thinks as a speaker and not as a thinker (it shows that he does not think of objects or think objectively, but only of his relations with objects—that, in point of fact, he only thinks of himself and his audience). This third one speaks aggressively, he comes too near our body, his breath blows on us—we shut our mouth involuntarily, although he speaks to us through a book: the tone of his style supplies the reason—he has no time, he has small faith in himself, he finds expression now or never. But a spirit who is sure of himself speaks softly; he seeks secrecy, he lets himself be awaited. A philosopher is recognised by the fact that he shuns three brilliant and noisy things—fame, princes, and women: which is not to say that they do not come to him. He shuns every glaring light: therefore he shuns his time and its "daylight." Therein he is as a shadow; the deeper sinks the sun, the greater grows the shadow. As for his humility, he endures, as he endures darkness, a certain dependence and obscurity: further, he is afraid of the shock of lightning, he shudders at the insecurity of a tree which is too isolated and too exposed, on which every storm vents its temper, every temper its storm. His "maternal" instinct, his secret love for that which grows in him, guides him into states where he is relieved from the necessity of taking care of *himself,* in the same way in which the *"mother"* instinct in woman has thoroughly maintained up to the present woman's dependent position. After all, they demand little enough, do these philosophers, their favourite motto is, "He who possesses is possessed." All this is *not*, as I must say again and again, to be attributed to a virtue, to a meritorious wish for moderation and simplicity; but because their supreme lord so demands of them, demands wisely and inexorably; their lord who is eager only for one thing, for which alone he musters, and for which alone he hoards everything—time, strength, love, interest. This kind of man likes not to be disturbed by enmity, he likes not to be disturbed by friendship, it is a type which forgets or despises easily. It strikes him as bad form to play the martyr, "to *suffer* for truth"—he leaves all that to the ambitious and to the stage-heroes of the intellect, and to all those, in fact, who have time enough for such luxuries (they themselves, the philosophers, have something *to do* for truth). They make a sparing use of big words; they are said to be adverse to the word "truth" itself: it has a "high falutin' " ring. Finally, as far as the chastity of philosophers is concerned, the fruitfulness of this type of mind is manifestly in another sphere than that of children; perchance in some other sphere, too, they have the survival of their name, their little immortality (philosophers in ancient India would express themselves with still greater boldness: "Of what use is posterity to him whose soul is the world?"). In this attitude there is not a trace of chastity, by reason of any ascetic scruple or hatred of the flesh, any more than it is chastity for an athlete or a jockey to abstain from women; it is rather the will of the dominant instinct, at any rate, during the period of their advanced philosophic pregnancy. Every artist knows the harm done by sexual intercourse on occasions of great mental strain and preparation; as far as the strongest artists and those with the surest instincts are concerned, this is not necessarily a case of experience—hard experience—but it is simply

their "maternal" instinct which, in order to benefit the growing work, disposes recklessly (beyond all its normal stocks
and supplies) of the *vigour* of its *animal* life; the greater
power then *absorbs* the lesser. Let us now apply this interpretation to gauge correctly the case of Schopenhauer, which we
have already mentioned: in his case, the sight of the beautiful
acted manifestly like a resolving irritant on the chief power of
his nature (the power of contemplation and of intense penetra-
tion); so that this strength exploded and became suddenly
master of his consciousness. But this by no means excludes
the possibility of that particular sweetness and fullness, which
is peculiar to the æsthetic state, springing directly from the
ingredient of sensuality (just as that "idealism" which is
peculiar to girls at puberty originates in the same source)—it
may be, consequently, that sensuality is not removed by the
approach of the æsthetic state, as Schopenhauer believed, but
merely becomes transfigured, and ceases to enter into the consciousness as sexual excitement. (I shall return once again to
this point in connection with the more delicate problems of
the *physiology of the æsthetic,* a subject which up to the present has been singularly untouched and unelucidated.)

9

A certain asceticism, a grimly gay whole-hearted renunciation, is, as we have seen, one of the most favourable conditions
for the highest intellectualism, and, consequently, for the
most natural corollaries of such intellectualism: we shall therefore be proof against any surprise at the philosophers in particular always treating the ascetic ideal with a certain amount

or predilection. A serious historical investigation shows the bond between the ascetic ideal and philosophy to be still much tighter and still much stronger. It may be said that it was only in the *leading strings* of this ideal that philosophy really learned to make its first steps and baby paces—alas how clumsily, alas how crossly, alas how ready to tumble down and lie on its stomach was this shy little darling of a brat with its bandy legs! The early history of philosophy is like that of all good things;—for a long time they had not the courage to be themselves, they kept always looking round to see if no one would come to their help; further, they were afraid of all who looked at them. Just enumerate in order the particular tendencies and virtues of the philosopher—his tendency to doubt, his tendency to deny, his tendency to wait (to be "ephectic"), his tendency to analyse, search, explore, dare, his tendency to compare and to equalise, his will to be neutral and objective, his will for everything which is *"sine ira et studio"*: has it yet been realised that for quite a lengthy period these tendencies went counter to the first claims of morality and conscience? (To say nothing at all of *Reason,* which even Luther chose to call *Frau Klüglin,** the sly whore.*) Has it been yet appreciated that a philosopher, in the event of his *arriving* at self-consciousness, must needs feel himself an incarnate *"nitimur in vetitum,"*—and consequently *guard* himself against "his own sensations," against self-consciousness? It is, I repeat, just the same with all good things, on which we now pride ourselves; even judged by the standard of the ancient Greeks, our whole modern life, in so far as it is not weakness, but power and the consciousness of power, appears pure "Hybris" and godlessness: for the things which are the very reverse of

* Mistress Sly.—Tr.

those which we honour today, have had for a long time conscience on their side, and God as their guardian. "Hybris" is our whole attitude to nature nowadays, our violation of nature with the help of machinery, and all the unscrupulous ingenuity of our scientists and engineers. "Hybris" is our attitude to God, that is, to some alleged teleological and ethical spider behind the meshes of the great trap of the causal web. Like Charles the Bold in his war with Louis the Eleventh, we may say, *"je combats l'universelle araignée"*; "Hybris" is our attitude to ourselves—for we experiment with ourselves in a way that we would not allow with any animal, and with pleasure and curiosity open our soul in our living body: what matters now to us the "salvation" of the soul? We heal ourselves afterwards: being ill is instructive, we doubt it not, even more instructive than being well—inoculators of disease seem to us today even more necessary than any medicine-men and "saviours." There is no doubt we do violence to ourselves nowadays, we crackers of the soul's kernel, we incarnate riddles, who are ever asking riddles, as though life were naught else than the cracking of a nut; and even thereby must we necessarily become day by day more and more worthy to be asked questions and *worthy* to ask them, even thereby do we perchance also become worthier to—live?

. . . All good things were once bad things; from every original sin has grown an original virtue. Marriage, for example, seemed for a long time a sin against the rights of the community; a man formerly paid a fine for the insolence of claiming one woman to himself (to this phase belongs, for instance, the *jus primæ noctis,* to-day still in Cambodia the privilege of the priest, that guardian of the "good old customs").

The soft, benevolent, yielding, sympathetic feelings—eventually valued so highly that they almost became "intrinsic values," were for a very long time actually despised by their possessors: gentleness was then a subject for shame, just as hardness is now (compare *Beyond Good and Evil,* Aph. 260). The submission to *law*: oh, with what qualms of conscience was it that the noble races throughout the world renounced the *vendetta* and gave the law power over themselves! Law was long a *vetitum,* a blasphemy, an innovation; it was introduced with force *like* a force, to which men only submitted with a sense of personal shame. Every tiny step forward in the world was formerly made at the cost of mental and physical torture. Nowadays the whole of this point of view—"that not only stepping forward, nay, stepping at all, movement, change, all needed their countless martyrs," rings in our ears quite strangely. I have put it forward in the *Dawn of Day,* Aph. 18. "Nothing is purchased more dearly," says the same book a little later, "than the modicum of human reason and freedom which is now our pride. But that pride is the reason why it is now almost impossible for us to feel in sympathy with those immense periods of the 'Morality of Custom,' which lie at the beginning of the 'world's history,' constituting as they do the real decisive historical principle which has fixed the character of humanity; those periods, I repeat, when throughout the world suffering passed for virtue, cruelty for virtue, deceit for virtue, revenge for virtue, repudiation of the reason for virtue; and when, conversely, well-being passed current for danger, the desire for knowledge for danger, pity for danger, peace for danger, being pitied for shame, work for shame, madness for divinity, and *change* for immorality and incarnate corruption!"

10

There is in the same book, Aph. 12, an explanation of the *burden* of unpopularity under which the earliest race of contemplative men had to live—despised almost as widely as they were first feared! Contemplation first appeared on earth in a disguised shape, in an ambiguous form, with an evil heart and often with an uneasy head: there is no doubt about it. The inactive, brooding, unwarlike element in the instincts of contemplative men long invested them with a cloud of suspicion: the only way to combat this was to excite a definite *fear*. And the old Brahmans, for example, knew to a nicety how to do this! The oldest philosophers were well versed in giving to their very existence and appearance, meaning, firmness, background, by reason whereof men learned to *fear* them; considered more precisely, they did this from an even more fundamental need, the need of inspiring in themselves fear and self-reverence. For they found even in their own souls all the valuations turned *against* themselves; they had to fight down every kind of suspicion and antagonism against "the philosophic element in themselves." Being men of a terrible age, they did this with terrible means: cruelty to themselves, ingenious self-mortification—this was the chief method of these ambitious hermits and intellectual revolutionaries, who were obliged to force down the gods and the traditions of their own soul, so as to enable themselves to *believe* in their own revolution. I remember the famous story of the King Vicvamitra, who, as the result of a thousand years of self-martyrdom, reached such a consciousness of power and such a confidence in himself that he undertook to build a *new heaven*: the sinister symbol of the oldest and newest history of philosophy in the whole world. Every one who has ever built anywhere a *"new heaven"* first found the power thereto in his *own hell*. . . . Let us compress the facts into a short formula. The philosophic spirit had, in order to be *possible* to any extent at all, to masquerade and disguise itself as one of the *previously fixed* types of the contemplative man, to disguise itself as priest, wizard, soothsayer, as a religious man generally: the *ascetic ideal* has for a long time served the philosopher as a superficial form, as a condition which enabled him to exist. . . . To be able to be a philosopher he had to exemplify the ideal; to exemplify it, he was bound to *believe* in it. The peculiarly etherealised abstraction of philosophers, with their negation of the world, their enmity to life, their disbelief in the senses, which has been maintained up to the most recent time, and has almost thereby come to be accepted as the ideal *philosophic attitude*—this abstraction is the result of those enforced conditions under which philosophy came into existence, and continued to exist; inasmuch as for quite a very long time philosophy would have been *absolutely impossible* in the world without an ascetic cloak and dress, without an ascetic self-misunderstanding. Expressed plainly and palpably, the *ascetic priest* has taken the repulsive and sinister form of the caterpillar, beneath which and behind which alone philosophy could live and slink about. . . .

Has all that really changed? Has that flamboyant and dangerous winged creature, that "spirit" which that caterpillar concealed within itself, has it, I say, thanks to a sunnier, warmer, lighter world, really and finally flung off its hood and escaped into the light? Can we today point to enough pride, enough daring, enough courage, enough self-confidence, enough mental will, enough will for responsibility, enough freedom of the will, to enable the philosopher to *be* now in the world really—*possible?*

11

And now, after we have caught sight of the *ascetic priest,* let us tackle our problem. What is the meaning of the ascetic ideal? It now first becomes serious—vitally serious. We are now confronted with the *real representatives of the serious.* "What is the meaning of all seriousness?" This even more radical question is perchance already on the tip of our tongue: a question, fairly, for physiologists, but which we for the time being skip. In that ideal the ascetic priest finds not only his faith, but also his will, his power, his interest. His *right* to existence stands and falls with that ideal. What wonder that we here run up against a terrible opponent (on the supposition, of course, that we are the opponents of that ideal), an opponent fighting for his life against those who repudiate that ideal! . . . On the other hand, it is from the outset improbable that such a biased attitude towards our problem will do him any particular good; the ascetic priest himself will scarcely prove the happiest champion of his own ideal (on the same principle on which a woman usually fails when she wishes to champion "woman")—let alone proving the most objective critic and judge of the controversy now raised. We shall therefore—so much is already obvious—rather have actually to help him to defend himself properly against ourselves, than we shall have to fear being too well beaten by him. The idea, which is the subject of this dispute, is the *value* of our life from the standpoint of the ascetic priests: this life, then (together with the whole of which it is a part, "Nature," "the world," the whole sphere of becoming and passing away), is placed by them in relation to an existence of quite another character, which it excludes and to which it is opposed, unless it *deny* its own self: in this case, the case of an ascetic life, life is taken as a bridge to another existence. The ascetic treats life as a maze, in which one must walk backwards till one comes to the place where it starts; or he treats it as an error which one may, nay *must*, refute by action: for he *demands* that he should be followed; he enforces, where he can, *his* valuation of existence. What does this mean? Such a monstrous valuation is not an exceptional case, or a curiosity recorded in human history: it is one of the most general and persistent facts that there are. The reading from the vantage of a distant star of the capital letters of our earthly life, would perchance lead to the conclusion that the earth was the especially *ascetic planet,* a den of discontented, arrogant, and repulsive creatures, who never got rid of a deep disgust of themselves, of the world, of all life, and did themselves as much hurt as possible out of pleasure in hurting—presumably their one and only pleasure. Let us consider how regularly, how universally, how practically at every single period the ascetic priest puts in his appearance: he belongs to no particular race; he thrives everywhere; he grows out of all classes. Not that he perhaps bred this valuation by heredity and propagated it—the contrary is the case. It must be a necessity of the first order which makes this species, *hostile,* as it is, to *life,* always grow again and always thrive again.—*Life* itself must certainly *have an interest* in the continuance of such a type of self-contradiction. For an ascetic life is a self-contradiction: here rules resentment without parallel, the resentment of an insatiate instinct and ambition, that would be master, not over some element in life, but over life itself, over life's deepest, strongest, innermost conditions; here is an attempt made to utilise power to dam the sources of power; here does the green eye of jealousy turn even against physiological well-being, especially against the expression of such well-being, beauty, joy; while a sense of pleasure is experienced and *sought* in abortion, in decay, in pain, in misfortune, in ugliness, in voluntary punishment, in the exercising, flagellation, and sacrifice of the self. All this is in the highest degree paradoxical: we are here confronted with a rift that *wills* itself to be a rift, which *enjoys* itself in this very *suffering,* and even becomes more and more certain of itself, more and more triumphant, in proportion as its own presupposition, physiological vitality, *decreases.* "The triumph just in the supreme agony": under this extravagant emblem did the ascetic ideal fight from of old; in this mystery of seduction, in this picture of rapture and torture, it recognised its brightest light, its salvation, its final victory. *Crux, nux, lux*—it has all these three in one.

12

Granted that such an incarnate will for contradiction and unnaturalness is induced to *philosophise;* on what will it vent its pet caprice? On that which has been felt with the greatest certainty to be true, to be real; it will look for *error* in those very places where the life instinct fixes truth with the greatest positiveness. It will, for instance, after the example of the ascetics of the Vedanta Philosophy, reduce matter to an illusion, and similarly treat pain, multiplicity, the whole logical contrast of *"Subject"* and *"Object"*—errors, nothing but errors! To renounce the belief in one's own ego, to deny to one's self one's own "reality"—what a triumph! and here already we have a much higher kind of triumph, which is not merely a triumph over the senses, over the palpable, but an infliction of violence and cruelty on *reason;* and this ecstasy culminates in the ascetic self-contempt, the ascetic scorn of one's own reason making this decree: *there is* a domain of truth and of life, but reason is specially *excluded* therefrom. . . . By the bye, even in the Kantian idea of "the intelligible character of things" there remains a trace of that schism, so dear to the heart of the ascetic, that schism which likes to turn reason against reason; in fact, "intelligible character" means in Kant a kind of quality in things of which the intellect comprehends so much, that for it, the intellect, it is *absolutely incomprehensible.* After all, let us, in our character of knowers, not be ungrateful towards such determined reversals of the ordinary perspectives and values, with which the mind had for too long raged against itself with an apparently futile sacrilege! In the same way the very seeing of another vista, the very *wishing* to see another vista, is no little training and preparation of the intellect for its eternal *"Objectivity"*—objectivity being understood not as "contemplation without interest" (for that is inconceivable and nonsensical), but as the ability to have the pros and cons *in one's power* and to switch them on and off, so as to get to know how to utilise, for the advancement of knowledge, the *difference* in the perspective and in the emotional interpretations. But let us, forsooth, my philosophic colleagues, henceforward guard ourselves more carefully against this mythology of dangerous ancient ideas, which has set up a "pure, will-less, painless, timeless subject of knowledge"; let us guard ourselves from the tentacles of such contradictory ideas as "pure reason," "absolute spirituality," "knowledge-in-itself":—in these theories an eye that cannot be

[744]

thought of is required to think, an eye which *ex hypothesi* has no direction at all, an eye in which the active and interpreting functions are cramped, are absent; those functions, I say, by means of which "abstract" seeing first became seeing some thing; in these theories consequently the absurd and the non sensical is always demanded of the eye. There is only a seeing from a perspective, only a "knowing" from a perspective, and the *more* emotions we express over a thing, the *more* eyes, different eyes, we train on the same thing, the more complete will be our "idea" of that thing, our "objectivity." But the elimination of the will altogether, the switching off of the emotions all and sundry, granted that we could do so, what! would not that be called intellectual *castration?*

13

But let us turn back. Such a self-contradiction, as apparently manifests itself among the ascetics, "Life turned against Life," is—so much is absolutely obvious—from the physiological and not now from the psychological standpoint, simply nonsense. It can only be an *apparent* contradiction; it must be a kind of provisional expression, an explanation, a formula, an adjustment, a psychological misunderstanding of something, whose real nature could not be understood for a long time, and whose *real essence* could not be described; a mere word jammed into an old *gap* of human knowledge. To put briefly the facts against its being real: *the ascetic ideal springs from the prophylactic and self-preservative instincts which mark a decadent life,* which seeks by every means in its power to maintain its position and fight for its existence; it points to a partial physiological depression and exhaustion, against which the most profound and intact life-instincts fight ceaselessly with new weapons and discoveries. The ascetic ideal is such a weapon: its position is consequently exactly the reverse of that which the worshippers of the ideal imagine—life struggles in it and through it with death and *against* death; the ascetic ideal is a dodge for the *preservation* of life. An important fact is brought out in the extent to which, as history teaches, this ideal could rule and exercise power over man, especially in all those places where the civilisation and taming of man was completed: that fact is, the diseased state of man up to the present, at any rate, of the man who has been tamed, the physiological struggle of man with death (more precisely, with the disgust with life, with exhaustion, with the wish for the "end"). The ascetic priest is the incarnate wish for an existence of another kind, an existence on another plane,—he is, in fact, the highest point of this wish, its official ecstasy and passion: but it is the very *power* of this wish which is the fetter that binds him here; it is just that which makes him into a tool that must labour to create more favourable conditions for earthly existence, for existence on the human plane—it is with this very *power* that he keeps the whole herd of failures, distortions, abortions, unfortunates, *sufferers from themselves* of every kind, fast to existence, while he as the herdsman goes instinctively on in front. You understand me already: this ascetic priest, this apparent enemy of life, this denier—he actually belongs to the really great *conservative* and *affirmative* forces of life. . . . What does it come from, this diseased state? For man is more diseased, more uncertain, more changeable, more unstable than any other animal, there is no doubt of it—he is *the* diseased animal: what does it spring from? Certainly he has also dared, innovated, braved more, challenged fate more than all the other animals put together; he, the great experimenter with himself, the unsatisfied, the insatiate, who struggles for the supreme mastery with beast, Nature, and gods, he, the as yet ever uncompelled, the ever future, who finds no more any rest from his own aggressive strength, goaded inexorably on by the spur of the future dug into the flesh of the present:—how should not so brave and rich an animal also be the most endangered, the animal with the longest and deepest sickness among all sick animals? . . . Man is sick of it, oft enough there are whole epidemics of this satiety (as about 1348, the time of the Dance of Death): but even this very nausea, this tiredness, this disgust with himself, all this is discharged from him with such force that it is immediately made into a new fetter. His "nay," which he utters to life, brings to light as though by magic an abundance of graceful "yeas"; even when he *wounds* himself, this master of destruction, of self-destruction, it is subsequently the wound itself that forces him to live.

14

The more normal is this sickliness in man—and we cannot dispute this normality—the higher honour should be paid to the rare cases of psychical and physical powerfulness, the *windfalls* of humanity, and the more strictly should the sound be guarded from that worst of air, the air of the sick-room. Is that done? The sick are the greatest danger for the healthy; it is not from the strongest that harm comes to the strong, but from the weakest. Is that known? Broadly considered, it is not for a minute the fear of man, whose diminution should be wished for; for this fear forces the strong to be strong, to be at times terrible—it preserves in its integrity the sound type of man. What is to be feared, what does work with a fatality found in no other fate, is not the great fear of, but the great *nausea* with, man; and equally so the great pity for man. Supposing that both these things were one day to espouse each other, then inevitably the maximum of monstrousness would immediately come into the world—the "last will" of man, his will for nothingness, Nihilism. And, in sooth, the way is well paved thereto. He who not only has his nose to smell with, but also has eyes and ears, he sniffs almost wherever he goes today an air something like that of a mad-house, the air of a hospital —I am speaking, as stands to reason, of the cultured areas of mankind, of every kind of "Europe" that there is in fact in the world. The *sick* are the great danger of man, *not* the evil, *not* the "beasts of prey." They who are from the outset botched, oppressed, broken, those are they, the weakest are they, who most undermine the life beneath the feet of man, who instil the most dangerous venom and scepticism into our trust in life, in man, in ourselves. Where shall we escape from it, from that covert look (from which we carry away a deep sadness), from that averted look of him who is misborn from the beginning, that look which betrays what such a man says to himself—that look which is a groan? "Would that I were something else," so groans this look, "but there is no hope. I am what I am: how could I get away from myself? And, verily—*I am sick of myself!*" On such a soil of self-contempt, a veritable swamp soil, grows that weed, that poisonous growth, and all so tiny, so hidden, so ignoble, so sugary. Here teem the worms of revenge and vindictiveness; here the air reeks of things secret and unmentionable; here is ever spun the net of the most malignant conspiracy—the conspiracy of the sufferers against the sound and the victorious; here is the sight of the victorious *hated*. And what lying so as not to acknowledge this hate as hate! What a show of big words and attitudes, what an art of "righteous" calumniation! These abortions! what a noble eloquence gushes from their lips! What an amount of sugary, slimy, humble submission oozes in their eyes! What do they really want? At any rate to *represent* right-eousness, love, wisdom, superiority, that is the ambition of these "lowest ones," these sick ones! And how clever does such an ambition make them! You cannot, in fact, but admire the counterfeiter dexterity with which the stamp of virtue, even the ring, the golden ring of virtue, is here imitated. They have taken a lease of virtue absolutely for themselves, have these weaklings and wretched invalids, there is no doubt of it; "We alone are the good, the righteous," so do they speak, "we alone are the *homines bonæ voluntatis.*" They stalk about in our midst as living reproaches, as warnings to us—as though health, fitness, strength, pride, the sensation of power, were really vicious things in themselves, for which one would have some day to do penance, bitter penance. Oh, how they them-selves are ready in their hearts to *exact* penance, how they thirst after being *hangmen!*

Among them is an abundance of revengeful ones disguised as judges, who ever mouth the word righteousness like a ven-omous spittle—with mouth, I say, always pursed, always ready to spit at everything, which does not wear a discontented look, but is of good cheer as it goes on its way. Among them, again, is that most loathsome species of the vain, the lying abortions, who make a point of representing "beautiful souls," and per-chance of bringing to the market as "purity of heart" their distorted sensualism swathed in verses and other bandages; the species of "self-comforters" and masturbators of their own souls. The sick man's will to represent *some* form or other of superiority, his instinct for crooked paths, which lead to a tyranny over the healthy—where can it not be found, this will to power of the very weakest? The sick woman especially: no one surpasses her in refinements for ruling, oppressing, tyrannising. The sick woman, moreover, spares nothing living, nothing dead; she grubs up against the most buried things (the Bogos say, "Woman is a hyena"). Look into the background of every family, of every body, of every community: everywhere the fight of the sick against the healthy—a silent fight for the most part with minute poisoned powders, with pin-pricks, with spiteful grimaces of patience, but also at times with that diseased pharisaism of *pure* pantomime, which plays for the choice rôle of "righteous indignation." Right into the hallowed chambers of knowledge can it make itself heard, can this hoarse yelping of sick hounds, this rabid lying and frenzy of such "noble" Pharisees (I remind readers, who have ears, once more of that Berlin apostle of revenge, Eugen Dühring, who makes most disreputable and revolting use in all present-day Germany of moral refuse; Dühring, the paramount moral blusterer that there is today, even among his own kidney, the Anti-Semites). They are all men of resentment, are these physiological distortions and worm-riddled objects, a whole quivering kingdom of burrowing revenge, indefatigable and insatiable in its outbursts against the happy, and equally so in disguises for revenge, in pretexts for revenge: when will they really reach their final, fondest, most sublime triumph of revenge? At that time, doubtless, when they succeed in pushing their own misery, in fact, all misery, *into the consciousness* of the happy; so that the latter begin one day to be ashamed of their happiness, and perchance say to themselves when they meet, "It is a shame to be happy; *there is too much misery!*"

. . . But there could not possibly be a greater and more fatal misunderstanding than that of the happy, the fit, the strong in body and soul, beginning in this way to doubt their right to happiness. Away with this "perverse world"! Away with this shameful soddenness of sentiment! Preventing the sick making the healthy sick—for that is what such a soddenness comes to—this ought to be our supreme object in the world— but for this it is above all essential that the healthy should remain *separated* from the sick, that they should even guard themselves from the look of the sick, that they should not even associate with the sick. Or may it, perchance, be their mission to be nurses or doctors? But they could not mistake and disown *their* mission more grossly—the higher *must* not degrade itself to be the tool of the lower, the pathos of distance must to all eternity keep their missions also separate. The right of the happy to existence, the right of bells with a full tone over the discordant cracked bells, is verily a thousand times greater: they alone are the *sureties* of the future, they alone are *bound* to man's future. What they can, what they must do, that can the sick never do, should never do! but if *they are* to be enabled to do what *only* they must do, how can they possibly be free to play the doctor, the comforter, the "Saviour" of the sick? . . . And therefore good air! good air! and away, at any rate, from the neighbourhood of all the madhouses and hospitals of civilisation! And therefore good company, *our own* company, or solitude, if it must be so! but away, at any rate, from the evil fumes of internal corruption and the secret worm-eaten state of the sick! that, forsooth, my friends, we may defend ourselves, at any rate for still a time, against the two worst plagues that could have been reserved for us—against the *great nausea with man!* against the *great pity for man!*

15

If you have understood in all their depths—and I demand that you should *grasp them profoundly* and understand them profoundly—the reasons for the impossibility of its being the business of the healthy to nurse the sick, to make the sick healthy, it follows that you have grasped this further necessity —the necessity of doctors and nurses *who themselves are sick*. And now we have and hold with both our hands the essence of the ascetic priest. The ascetic priest must be accepted by us as the predestined saviour, herdsman, and champion of the sick herd: thereby do we first understand his awful historic mission. The *lordship over sufferers* is his kingdom, to that points his instinct, in that he finds his own special art, his master-skill, his kind of happiness. He must himself be sick, he must be kith and kin to the sick and the abortions so as to understand them, so as to arrive at an understanding with them; but he must also be strong, even more master of himself than of others, impregnable, forsooth, in his will for power, so as to acquire the trust and the awe of the weak, so that he can be their hold, bulwark, prop, compulsion, overseer, tyrant, god. He has to protect them, protect his herds—*against* whom? Against the healthy, doubtless also against the envy towards the healthy. He must be the natural adversary and scorner of every rough, stormy, reinless, hard, violently-predatory health and power. The priest is the first form of the more delicate animal that scorns more easily than it hates. He will not be spared the waging of war with the beasts of prey, a war of guile (of "spirit") rather than of force, as is self-evident—he will in certain cases find it necessary to conjure up out of himself, or at any rate to represent practically a new type of the beast of prey—a new animal monstrosity in which the polar bear, the supple, cold, crouching panther, and, not least important, the fox, are joined together in a trinity as fascinating as it is fear-some. If necessity exacts it, then will he come on the scene with bearish seriousness, venerable, wise, cold, full of treach-erous superiority, as the herald and mouthpiece of mysterious powers, sometimes going among even the other kind of beasts of prey, determined as he is to sow on their soil, wherever he can, suffering, discord, self-contradiction, and only too sure of his art, always to be lord of *sufferers* at all times. He brings with him, doubtless, salve and balsam; but before he can play the physician he must first wound; so, while he soothes the pain which the wound makes, *he at the same time poisons the wound*. Well versed is he in this above all things, is this wizard and wild beast tamer, in whose vicinity everything healthy must needs become ill, and everything ill must needs become tame. He protects, in sooth, his sick herd well enough, does this strange herdsman; he protects them also against them-selves, against the sparks (even in the centre of the herd) of wickedness, knavery, malice, and all the other ills that the plaguey and the sick are heir to; he fights with cunning, hard-ness, and stealth against anarchy and against the ever immi-nent break-up inside the herd, where *resentment,* that most dangerous blasting-stuff and explosive, ever accumulates and accumulates. Getting rid of this blasting-stuff in such a way that it does not blow up the herd and the herdsman, that is his real feat, his supreme utility; if you wish to comprise in the shortest formula the value of the priestly life, it would be correct to say the priest is the *diverter of the course of resent-ment*. Every sufferer, in fact, searches instinctively for a cause of his suffering; to put it more exactly, a doer,—to put it still more precisely, a sentient *responsible* doer,—in brief, something living, on which, either actually or in *effigy,* he can on any pretext vent his emotions. For the venting of emotions is the sufferer's greatest attempt at alleviation, that is to say, *stupefaction,* his mechanically desired narcotic against pain of any kind. It is in this phenomenon alone that is found, according to my judgment, the real physiological cause of resentment, revenge, and their family is to be found--that is, in a demand for the *deadening of pain through emotion*: this cause is generally, but in my view very erroneously, looked for in the defensive parry of a bare protective principle of reaction, of a "reflex movement" in the case of any sudden hurt and danger, after the manner that a decapitated frog still moves in order to get away from a corrosive acid. But the difference is fundamental. In one case the object is to prevent being hurt any more; in the other case the object is to *deaden* a racking, insidious, nearly unbearable pain by a more violent emotion of any kind whatsoever, and at any rate for the time being to drive it out of the consciousness—for this purpose an emotion is needed, as wild an emotion as possible, and to excite that emotion some excuse or other is needed. "It must be somebody's fault that I feel bad"—this kind of reasoning is peculiar to all invalids, and is but the more pronounced, the more ignorant they remain of the real cause of their feeling bad, the physiological cause (the cause may lie in a disease of the *nervous sympathicus,* or in an excessive secretion of bile, or in a want of sulphate and phosphate of potash in the blood, or in pressure in the bowels which stops the circulation of the blood, or in degeneration of the ovaries, and so forth). All sufferers have an awful resourcefulness and ingenuity in finding excuses for painful emotions; they even enjoy their jealousy, their broodings over base actions and apparent injuries, they burrow through the intestines of their past and present in their search for obscure mysteries, wherein they will be at liberty to wallow in a torturing suspicion and get drunk on the venom of their own malice—they tear open the oldest wounds, they make themselves bleed from the scars which have long been healed, tney make evil-doers out of friends, wife, child, and everything which is nearest to them. "I suffer: it must be somebody's fault"—so thinks every sick sheep. But his herdsman, the ascetic priest, says to him, "Quite so, my sheep, it must be the fault of some one; but thou thyself art that same one, it is all the fault of thyself alone—*it is the fault of thyself alone against thyself*": that is bold enough, false enough, but one thing is at least attained; thereby, as I have said, the course of resentment is—*diverted*.

16

You can see now what the remedial instinct of life has at least *tried* to effect, according to my conception, through the ascetic priest, and the purpose for which he had to employ a temporary tyranny of such paradoxical and anomalous ideas as "guilt," "sin," "sinfulness," "corruption," "damnation." What was done was to make the sick *harmless* up to a certain point, to destroy the incurable by means of themselves, to turn the milder cases severely on to themselves, to give their resentment a backward direction ("man needs but one thing"), and to *exploit* similarly the bad instincts of all sufferers with a view to self-discipline, self-surveillance, self-mastery. It is obvious that there can be no question at all in the case of a "medication" of this kind, a mere emotional medication, of any real *healing* of the sick in the physiological sense; it cannot even for a moment be asserted that in this connection the instinct of life has taken healing as its goal and purpose. On the one hand, a kind of congestion and organisation of the sick (the word "Church" is the most popular name for it); on the other, a kind of provisional safeguarding of the comparatively healthy, the more perfect specimens, the cleavage of a *rift* between healthy and sick—for a long time that was all! and it was much! it was *very* much!

I am proceeding, as you see, in this essay, from an hypothesis which, as far as such readers as I want are concerned, does not require to be proved; the hypothesis that "sinfulness" in man is not an actual fact, but rather merely the interpretation of a fact, of a physiological discomfort,—a discomfort seen through a moral religious perspective which is no longer binding upon us. The fact, therefore, that any one feels "guilty," "sinful," is certainly not yet any proof that he is right in feeling so, any more than any one is healthy simply because he feels healthy. Remember the celebrated witch-ordeals: in those days the most acute and humane judges had no doubt but that in these cases they were confronted with guilt,—the "witches" *themselves had no doubt on the point,*—and yet the guilt was lacking. Let me elaborate this hypothesis: I do not for a minute accept the very "pain in the soul" as a real fact, but only as an explanation (a casual explanation) of facts that could not hitherto be precisely formulated; I regard it therefore as something as yet absolutely in the air and devoid of scientific cogency—just a nice fat word in the place of a lean note of interrogation. When any one fails to get rid of his "pain in the soul," the cause is, speaking crudely, to be found *not* in his "soul" but more probably in his stomach (speaking crudely, I repeat, but by no means wishing thereby that you should listen to me or understand me in a crude spirit). A strong and well-constituted man digests his experiences (deeds and misdeeds all included) just as he digests his meats, even when he has some tough morsels to swallow. If he fails to "relieve himself" of an experience, this kind of indigestion is quite as much physiological as the other indigestion—and indeed, in more ways than one, simply one of the results of the other. You can adopt such a theory, and yet *entre nous* be nevertheless the strongest opponent of all materialism.

17

But is he really a *physician,* this ascetic priest? We already understand why we are scarcely allowed to call him a physician, however much he likes to feel a "saviour" and let himself be worshipped as a saviour.* It is only the actual suffering, the discomfort of the sufferer, which he combats, not its cause, not the actual state of sickness—this needs must constitute our most radical objection to priestly medication. But just once put yourself into that point of view, of which the priests have a monopoly, you will find it hard to exhaust your amazement. at what from that standpoint he has completely seen, sought, and found. The *mitigation* of suffering, every kind of "consoling"—all this manifests itself as his very genius: with what ingenuity has he interpreted his mission of consoler, with what aplomb and audacity has he chosen weapons necessary for the part. Christianity in particular should be dubbed a great treasure-chamber of ingenious consolations,—such a store of refreshing, soothing, deadening drugs has it accumulated within itself; so many of the most dangerous and daring expedients has it hazarded; with such subtlety, refinement, Oriental re-

---

* In the German text "Heiland." This has the double meaning of "healer" and "saviour."—H. B. S.

finement, has it divined what emotional stimulants can conquer, at any rate for a time, the deep depression, the leaden fatigue, the black melancholy of physiological cripples—for, speaking generally, all religions are mainly concerned with fighting a certain fatigue and heaviness that has infected everything. You can regard it as *prima facie* probable that in certain places in the world there was almost bound to prevail from time to time among large masses of the population a *sense of physiological depression,* which, however, owing to their lack of physiological knowledge, did not appear to their consciousness as such, so that consequently its "cause" and its *cure* can only be sought and essayed in the science of moral psychology (this, in fact, is my most general formula for what is generally called a *"religion"*). Such a feeling of depression can have the most diverse origins; it may be the result of the crossing of too heterogeneous races (or of classes—genealogical and racial differences are also brought out in the classes: the European "Weltschmerz," the "Pessimism" of the nineteenth century, is really the result of an absurd and sudden class-mixture); it may be brought about by a mistaken emigration—a race falling into a climate for which its power of adaptation is insufficient (the case of the Indians in India); it may be the effect of old age and fatigue (the Parisian pessimism from 1850 onwards); it may be a wrong diet (the alcoholism of the Middle Ages, the nonsense of vegetarianism—which, however, have in their favour the authority of Sir Christopher in Shakespeare); it may be blood-deterioration, malaria, syphilis, and the like (German depression after the Thirty Years' War, which infected half Germany with evil diseases, and thereby paved the way for German servility, for German pusillanimity). In such a case there is invariably recourse to a *war* on a grand scale with the feeling of depression; let us inform ourselves briefly on its most important practices and phases (I leave on one side, as stands to reason, the actual *philosophic* war against the feeling of depression which is usually simultaneous—it is interesting enough, but too absurd, too practically negligible, too full of cobwebs, too much of a hole-and-corner affair, especially when pain is proved to be a mistake, on the *naïf* hypothesis that pain must needs *vanish* when the mistake underlying it is recognised—but behold! it does anything but vanish . . .). That dominant depression is *primarily fought* by weapons which reduce the consciousness of life itself to the lowest degree. Wherever possible, no more wishes, no more wants; shun everything which produces emotion, which produces "blood" (eating no salt, the fakir hygiene); no love; no hate; equanimity; no revenge; no getting rich; no work; begging! as far as possible, no woman, or as little woman as possible; as far as the intellect is concerned, Pascal's principle, *"il faut s'abêtir."* To put the result in ethical and psychological language, "self-annihilation," "sanctification"; to put it in physiological language, "hypnotism"—the attempt to find some approximate human equivalent for what *hibernation* is for certain animals, for what *æstivation* is for many tropical plants, a minimum of assimilation and metabolism in which life just manages to subsist without really coming into the consciousness. An amazing amount of human energy has been devoted to this object—perhaps uselessly? There cannot be the slightest doubt but that such *sportsmen* of "saintliness," in whom at times nearly every nation has abounded, have really found a genuine relief from that which they have combated with such a rigorous *training*—in countless cases they really escaped by the help of their system of hypnotism *away* from deep physiological depression; their method is consequently counted among the most universal ethnological facts. Similarly it is improper to consider such a plan for starving the physical element and the desires, as in itself a symptom of insanity (as a clumsy species of roast-beef-eating "freethinkers" and Sir Christophers are fain to do); all the more certain is it that their method can and does pave the way to all kinds of mental disturbances, for instance, "inner lights" (as far as the case of Hesychasts of Mount Athos), auditory and visual hallucinations, voluptuous ecstasies and effervescences of sensualism (the history of St. Theresa). The explanation of such events given by the victims is always the acme of fanatical falsehood; this is self-evident. Note well, however, the tone of implicit gratitude that rings in the very *will* for an explanation of such a character. The supreme state, salvation itself, that final goal of universal hypnosis and peace, is always regarded by them as the mystery of mysteries, which even the most supreme symbols are inadequate to express; it is regarded as an entry and homecoming to the essence of things, as a liberation from all illusions, as "knowledge," as "truth," as "being," as an escape from every end, every wish, every action, as something even beyond Good and Evil.

"Good and Evil," quoth the Buddhists, "both are fetters. The perfect man is master of them both."

"The done and the undone," quoth the disciple of the Vedanta, "do him no hurt; the good and the evil he shakes from off him, sage that he is; his kingdom suffers no more from any act; good and evil, he goes beyond them both."—An absolutely Indian conception, as much Brahmanist as Buddhist. Neither in the Indian nor in the Christian doctrine is this "Redemption" regarded as attainable by means of virtue and moral improvement, however high they may place the value of the hypnotic efficiency of virtue: keep clear on this point—

indeed it simply corresponds with the facts. The fact that they remained *true* on this point is perhaps to be regarded as the best specimen of realism in the three great religions, absolutely soaked as they are with morality, with this one exception. "For those who know, there is no duty." "Redemption is not attained by the acquisition of virtues; for redemption consists in being one with Brahman, who is incapable of acquiring any perfection; and equally little does it consist in the *giving up of faults,* for the Brahman, unity with whom is what constitutes redemption, is eternally pure" (these passages are from the Commentaries of the Cankara, quoted from the first real European *expert* of the Indian philosophy, my friend Paul Deussen). We wish, therefore, to pay honour to the idea of "redemption" in the great religions, but it is somewhat hard to remain serious in view of the appreciation meted out to the *deep sleep* by these exhausted pessimists who are too tired even to dream—to the deep sleep considered, that is, as already a fusing into Brahman, as the attainment of the *unio mystica* with God. "When he has completely gone to sleep," says on this point the oldest and most venerable "script," "and come to perfect rest, so that he sees no more any vision, then, oh dear one, is he united with Being, he has entered into his own self —encircled by the Self with its absolute knowledge, he has no more any consciousness of that which is without or of that which is within. Day and night cross not these bridges, nor age, nor death, nor suffering, nor good deeds, nor evil deeds." "In deep sleep," say similarly the believers in this deepest of the three great religions, "does the soul lift itself from out this body of ours, enters the supreme light and stands out therein in its true shape: therein is it the supreme spirit itself, which travels about, while it jests and plays and enjoys itself, whether with women, or chariots, or friends; there do its thoughts turn no more back to this appanage of a body, to which the 'prâna' (the vital breath) is harnessed like a beast of burden to the cart." None the less we will take care to realise (as we did when discussing "redemption") that in spite of all its pomps of Oriental extravagance this simply expresses the same criticism on life as did the clear, cold, Greekly cold, but yet suffering Epicurus. The hypnotic sensation of nothingness, the peace of deepest sleep, anæsthesia in short—that is what passes with the sufferers and the absolutely depressed for, forsooth, their supreme good, their value of values; that is what *must* be treasured by them as something positive, be felt by them as the essence of *the* Positive (according to the same logic of the feelings, nothingness is in all pessimistic religions called God).

13

Such a hypnotic deadening of sensibility and susceptibility to pain, which presupposes somewhat rare powers, especially courage, contempt of opinion, intellectual stoicism, is less frequent than another and certainly easier *training* which is tried against states of depression. I mean *mechanical activity*. It is indisputable that a suffering existence can be thereby considerably alleviated. This fact is called today by the somewhat ignoble title of the "Blessing of work." The alleviation consists in the attention of the sufferer being absolutely diverted from suffering, in the incessant monopoly of the consciousness by action, so that consequently there is little room left for suffering—for narrow is it, this chamber of human consciousness! Mechanical activity and its corollaries, such as absolute regularity, punctilious unreasoning obedience, the chronic routine of life, the complete occupation of time, a certain liberty to be impersonal, nay, a training in "impersonality," self-forgetfulness, *"incuria sui"*—with what thoroughness and expert subtlety have all these methods been exploited by the ascetic priest in his war with pain!

When he has to tackle sufferers of the lower orders, slaves, or prisoners (or women, who for the most part are a compound of labour-slave and prisoner), all he has to do is to juggle a little with the names, and to rechristen, so as to make them see henceforth a benefit, a comparative happiness, in objects which they hated—the slave's discontent with his lot was at any rate *not* invented by the priests. An even more popular means of fighting depression is the ordaining of a *little joy,* which is easily accessible and can be made into a rule; this medication is frequently used in conjunction with the former ones. The most frequent form in which joy is prescribed as a cure is the joy in *producing* joy (such as doing good, giving presents, alleviating, helping, exhorting, comforting, praising, treating with distinction); together with the prescription of "love your neighbour." The ascetic priest prescribes, though in the most cautious doses, what is practically a stimulation of the strongest and most life-assertive impulse —the Will for Power. The happiness involved in the "smallest superiority" which is the concomitant of all benefiting, helping, extolling, making one's self useful, is the most ample consolation, of which, if they are well-advised, physiological distortions avail themselves: in other cases they hurt each other, and naturally in obedience to the same radical instinct. An investigation of the origin of Christianity in the Roman world shows that co-operative unions for poverty, sickness, and burial sprang up in the lowest stratum of contemporary society, amid which the chief antidote against depression, the little joy experienced in mutual benefits, was deliberately fostered. Perchance this was then a novelty, a real discovery? This conjuring up of the will for co-operation, for family organisation, for communal life, for "*Cœnacula*," necessarily brought the Will for Power, which had been already infinitesimally stimulated, to a new and much fuller manifestation. The herd organisation is a genuine advance and triumph in the fight with depression. With the growth of the community there matures even to individuals a new interest, which often enough takes him out of the more personal element in his discontent, his aversion to himself, the "*despectus sui*" of Geulincx. All sick and diseased people strive instinctively after a herd-organisation, out of a desire to shake off their sense of oppressive discomfort and weakness; the ascetic priest divines this instinct and promotes it; wherever a herd exists it is the instinct of weakness which has wished for the herd, and the cleverness of the priests which has organised it, for, mark this: by an equally natural necessity the strong strive as much for *isolation* as the weak for *union:* when the former bind themselves it is only with a view to an aggressive joint action and joint satisfaction of their Will for Power, much against the wishes of their individual consciences; the latter, on the contrary, range themselves together with positive *delight* in such a muster—their instincts are as much gratified thereby as the instincts of the "born master" (that is, the solitary beast-of-prey species of man) are disturbed and wounded to the quick by organisation. There is always lurking beneath every oligarchy—such is the universal lesson of history—the desire for tyranny. Every oligarchy is continually quivering with the tension of the effort required by each individual to keep mastering this desire. (Such, *e.g.*, was the Greek; Plato shows it in a hundred places, Plato, who knew his contemporaries—and *himself*.)

The methods employed by the ascetic priest, which we have already learned to know—stifling of all vitality, mechanical energy, the little joy, and especially the method of "love your neighbour" herd-organisation, the awaking of the communal consciousness of power, to such a pitch that the individual's disgust with himself becomes eclipsed by his delight in the thriving of the community—these are, according to modern standards, the "innocent" methods employed in the fight with depression; let us turn now to the more interesting topic of the "guilty" methods. The guilty methods spell one thing: to produce *emotional excess*—which is used as the most efficacious anæsthetic against their depressing state of protracted pain; this is why priestly ingenuity has proved quite inexhaustible in thinking out this one question: *"By what means* can you produce an emotional excess?" This sounds harsh: it is manifest that it would sound nicer and would grate on one's ears less, if I were to say, forsooth: "The ascetic priest made use at all times of the enthusiasm contained in all strong emotions." But what is the good of still soothing the delicate ears of our modern effeminates? What is the good *on our side* of budging one single inch before their verbal Pecksniffianism? For us psychologists to do that would be at once *practical Pecksniffianism,* apart from the fact of its nauseating us. The *good taste* (others might say, the righteousness) of a psychologist nowadays consists, if at all, in combating the shamefully moralised language with which all modern judgments on men and things are smeared. For, do not deceive yourself: what constitutes the chief characteristic of modern souls and of modern books is not the lying, but the *innocence* which is part

and parcel of their intellectual dishonesty. The inevitable running up against this "innocence" everywhere constitutes the
most distasteful feature of the somewhat dangerous business
which a modern psychologist has to undertake: it is a part of
our great danger—it is a road which perhaps leads us straight
to the great nausea—I know quite well the purpose which all
modern books will and can serve (granted that they last,
which I am not afraid of, and granted equally that there is to
be at some future day a generation with a more rigid, more
severe, and *healthier* taste)—the *function* which all modernity generally will serve with posterity: that of an emetic,—
and this by reason of its moral sugariness and falsity, its ingrained feminism, which it is pleased to call "Idealism," and
at any rate believes to be idealism. Our cultured men of today, our "good" men, do not lie—that is true; but it does *not*
redound to their honour! The real lie, the genuine, determined,
"honest" lie (on whose value you can listen to Plato) would
prove too tough and strong an article for them by a long way;
it would be asking them to do what people have been forbidden
to ask them to do, to open their eyes to their own selves, and to
learn to distinguish between "true" and "false" in their own
selves. The dishonest lie alone suits them: everything which
fools a good man is perfectly incapable of any other attitude to
anything than that of a dishonourable liar, an absolute liar,
but none the less an innocent liar, a blue-eyed liar, a virtuous
liar. These "good men," they are all now tainted with morality
through and through, and as far as honour is concerned they
are disgraced and corrupted for all eternity. Which of them
could stand a further truth "about man"? or, put more tangibly,
which of them could put up with a true biography? One or two
instances: Lord Byron composed a most personal autobiography, but Thomas Moore was "too good" for it; he burnt his

friend's papers. Dr. Gwinner, Schopenhauer's executor, is said to have done the same; for Schopenhauer as well wrote much about himself, and perhaps also *against* himself (εἰς ἑαυτόν). The virtuous American Thayer, Beethoven's biographer, suddenly stopped his work: he had come to a certain point in that honourable and simple life, and could stand it no longer. Moral: What sensible man nowadays writes one honest word about himself? He must already belong to the Order of Holy Foolhardiness. We are promised an autobiography of Richard Wagner; who doubts but that it would be a *clever* autobiography? Think, forsooth, of the grotesque horror which the Catholic priest Janssen aroused in Germany with his inconceivably square and harmless pictures of the German Reformation; what wouldn't people do if some real psychologist were to tell us about a genuine Luther, tell us, not with the moralist simplicity of a country priest or the sweet and cautious modesty of a Protestant historian, but say with the fearlessness of a Taine, that springs from force of character and not from a prudent toleration of force. (The Germans, by the bye, have already produced the classic specimen of this toleration—they may well be allowed to reckon him as one of their own, in Leopold Ranke, that born classical advocate of every *causa fortior,* that cleverest of all the clever opportunists.)

20

But you will soon understand me.—Putting it shortly, there is reason enough, is there not, for us psychologists nowadays never to get away from a certain mistrust of our *own selves?* Probably even we ourselves are still "too good" for our work; probably, whatever contempt we feel for this popular craze for morality, we ourselves are perhaps none the less its victims, prey, and slaves; probably it infects even *us*. Of what was that diplomat warning us, when he said to his colleagues: "Let us especially mistrust our first impulses, gentlemen! *they are almost always good*"? So should nowadays every psychologist talk to his colleagues. And thus we get back to our problem, which in point of fact does require from us a certain severity, a certain mistrust especially against "first impulses." *The ascetic ideal in the service of projected emotional excess:*—he who remembers the previous essay will already partially anticipate the essential meaning compressed into these above ten words. The thorough unswitching of the human soul, the plunging of it into terror, frost, ardour, rapture, so as to free it, as through some lightning shock, from all the smallness and pettiness of unhappiness, depression, and discomfort: what ways lead to *this* goal? And which of these ways does so most safely? . . . At bottom all great emotions have this power, provided that they find a sudden outlet—emotions such as rage, fear, lust, revenge, hope, triumph, despair, cruelty; and, in sooth, the ascetic priest has had no scruples in taking into his service the whole pack of hounds that rage in the human kennel, unleashing now these and now those, with the same constant object of waking man out of his protracted melancholy, of chasing away, at any rate for a time, his dull pain, his shrinking misery, but always under the sanction of a religious interpretation and justification. This emotional excess has subsequently to be *paid for,* this is self-evident—it makes the ill more ill—and therefore this kind of remedy for pain is according to modern standards a "guilty" kind.

The dictates of fairness, however, require that we should all the more emphasise the fact that this remedy is applied with a *good conscience,* that the ascetic priest has prescribed it in the most implicit belief in its utility and indispensability;—often enough almost collapsing in the presence of the pain which he created;—that we should similarly emphasise the fact that the violent physiological revenges of such excesses, even pei-haps the mental disturbances, are not absolutely inconsistent with the general tenor of this kind of remedy; this remedy, which, as we have shown previously, is *not* for the purpose of healing diseases, but of fighting the unhappiness of that de-pression, the alleviation and deadening of which was its object. The object was consequently achieved. The keynote by which the ascetic priest was enabled to get every kind of agonising and ecstatic music to play on the fibres of the human soul—was, as every one knows, the exploitation of the feeling of *"guilt."* I have already indicated in the previous essay the origin of this feeling—as a piece of animal psychology and nothing else: we were thus confronted with the feeling of "guilt," in its crude state, as it were. It was first in the hands of the priest, real artist that he was in the feeling of guilt, that it took shape—oh, what a shape!

"Sin"—for that is the name of the new priestly version of the animal "bad-conscience" (the inverted cruelty)—has up to the present been the greatest event in the history of the dis-eased soul; in "sin" we find the most perilous and fatal master-piece of religious interpretation. Imagine man, suffering from himself, some way or other but at any rate physiologically, per-haps like an animal shut up in a cage, not clear as to the why and the wherefore! imagine him in his desire for reasons—reasons bring relief—in his desire again for remedies, nar-cotics at last, consulting one, who knows even the occult—and see, lo and behold, he gets a hint from his wizard, the ascetic priest, his *first* hint on the "cause" of his trouble: he must search for it *in himself,* in his guiltiness, in a piece of the past, he must understand his very suffering as a *state of punishment.* He has heard, he has understood, has the unfortunate: he is now in the plight of a hen round which a line has been drawn. He never gets out of the circle of lines. The sick man has been turned into "the sinner"——and now for a few thousand years we never get away from the sight of this new invalid, of "a sinner"——shall we ever get away from it?——wherever we just look, everywhere the hypnotic gaze of the sinner always moving in one direction (in the direction of guilt, the *only* cause of suffering); everywhere the evil conscience, this *"greuliche Thier,"* * to use Luther's language; everywhere rumination over the past, a distorted view of action, the gaze of the "green-eyed monster" turned on all action; everywhere the wilful misunderstanding of suffering, its transvaluation into feelings of guilt, fear of retribution; everywhere the scourge, the hair shirt, the starving body, contrition; everywhere the sinner breaking himself on the ghastly wheel of a restless and morbidly eager conscience; everywhere mute pain, extreme fear, the agony of a tortured heart, the spasms of an unknown happiness, the shriek for "redemption." In point of fact, thanks to this system of procedure, the old depression, dullness, and fatigue were absolutely conquered, life itself became *very* interesting again, awake, eternally awake, sleepless, glowing, burnt away, exhausted and yet not tired——such was the figure cut by man, "the sinner," who was initiated into these mysteries. This grand old wizard of an ascetic priest fighting with depression——he had clearly triumphed, *his* kingdom had come: men no longer grumbled at pain, men *panted* after pain: *"More pain!* More pain!" So for centuries on end

* "Horrible beast."

shrieked the demand of his acolytes and initiates. Every emotional excess which hurt; everything which broke, overthrew,
crushed, transported, ravished; the mystery of torture-cham-
bers, the ingenuity of hell itself—all this was now discovered,
divined, exploited, all this was at the service of the wizard, all
this served to promote the triumph of his ideal, the ascetic
ideal. *"My kingdom is not of this world,"* quoth he, both at the
beginning and at the end: had he still the right to talk like
that?—Goethe has maintained that there are only thirty-six
tragic situations: we would infer from that, did we not know
otherwise, that Goethe was no ascetic priest. He—knows more.

21

So far as all *this* kind of priestly medicine-mongering, the
"guilty" kind, is concerned, every word of criticism is superfluous. As for the suggestion that emotional excess of the type,
which in these cases the ascetic priest is fain to order to his
sick patients (under the most sacred euphemism, as is obvious, and equally impregnated with the sanctity of his purpose), has ever really been of use to any sick man, who,
forsooth, would feel inclined to maintain a proposition of
that character? At any rate, some understanding should be
come to as to the expression "be of use." If you only wish to
express that such a system of treatment has *reformed* man, I
do not gainsay it: I merely add that "reformed" conveys to my
mind much as "tamed," "weakened," "discouraged," "refined," "daintified," "emasculated" (and thus it means almost
as much as injured). But when you have to deal principally
with sick, depressed, and oppressed creatures, such a system,
even granted that it makes the ill "better," under any circum-

stances also makes them more *ill:* ask the mad-doctors the invariable result of a methodical application of penance-torture, contritions, and salvation ecstasies. Similarly ask history. In every body politic where the ascetic priest has established this treatment of the sick, disease has on every occasion spread with sinister speed throughout its length and breadth. What was always the "result"? A shattered nervous system, in addition to the existing malady, and this in the greatest as in the smallest, in the individuals as in masses. We find, in consequence of the penance and redemption-training, awful epileptic epidemics, the greatest known to history, such as the St. Vitus and St. John dances of the Middle Ages; we find, as another phase of its after-effect, frightful mutilations and chronic depressions, by means of which the temperament of a nation or a city (Geneva, Bâle) is turned once for all into its opposite;—this *training,* again, is responsible for the witch-hysteria, a phenomenon analogous to somnambulism (eight great epidemic outbursts of this only between 1564 and 1605);—we find similarly in its train those delirious death-cravings of large masses, whose awful "shriek," *"evviva la morte!"* was heard over the whole of Europe, now interrupted by voluptuous variations and anon by a rage for destruction, just as the same emotional sequence with the same intermittencies and sudden changes is now universally observed in every case where the ascetic doctrine of sin scores once more a great success (religious neurosis *appears* as a manifestation of the devil, there is no doubt of it. What is it? *Quæritur*). Speaking generally, the ascetic ideal and its sublime-moral cult, this most ingenious, reckless, and perilous systematisation of all methods of emotional excess, is writ large in a dreadful and unforgettable fashion on the whole history of man, and unfortunately not only on history. I was scarcely able to put forward any other element which attacked the *health* and race efficiency of Europeans with more destructive power than did this ideal; it can be dubbed, without exaggeration, *the real fatality* in the history of the health of the European man. At the most you can merely draw a comparison with the specifically German influence. I mean the alcohol poisoning of Europe, which up to the present has kept pace exactly with the political and racial predominance of the Germans (where they inoculated their blood, there too did they inoculate their vice). Third in the series comes syphilis—*magno sed proximo intervallo.*

22

The ascetic priest has, wherever he has obtained the mastery, corrupted the health of the soul, he has consequently also corrupted *taste in artibus et litteris*—he corrupts it still. "Consequently?" I hope I shall be granted this "consequently"; at any rate, I am not going to prove it first. One solitary indication, it concerns the arch-book of Christian literature, their real model, their "book-in-itself." In the very midst of the Graeco-Roman splendour, which was also a splendour of books, face to face with an ancient world of writings which had not yet fallen into decay and ruin, at a time when certain books were still to be read, to possess which we would give nowadays half our literature in exchange, at that time the simplicity and vanity of Christian agitators (they are generally called Fathers of the Church) dared to declare: "We too have our classical literature, *we do not need that of the Greeks*"—and meanwhile they proudly pointed to their books of legends, their letters of apostles, and their apologetic tractlets, just in the same way that today the English "Salvation Army" wages its fight against Shakespeare and other "heathens" with an analogous literature. You already guess it, I do not like the "New Testament"; it almost upsets me that I stand so isolated in my taste so far as concerns this valued, this over-valued Scripture; the taste of two thousand years is *against* me; but what boots it! "Here I stand! I cannot help myself" *—I have the courage of my bad taste. The *Old* Testament—yes, that is something quite different, all honour to the Old Testament! I find therein great men, an heroic landscape, and one of the rarest phenomena in the world, the incomparable naïveté *of the strong heart;* further still, I find a people. In the New, on the contrary, just a hostel of petty sects, pure rococo of the soul, twisting angles and fancy touches, nothing but conventicle air, not to forget an occasional whiff of bucolic sweetness which appertains to the epoch (*and* the Roman province) and is less Jewish than Hellenistic. Meekness and braggadocio cheek by jowl; an emotional garrulousness that almost deafens; passionate hysteria, but no passion; painful pantomime; here manifestly every one lacked good breeding. How dare any one make so much fuss about their little failings as do these pious little fellows! No one cares a straw about it—let alone God. Finally they actually wish to have "the crown of eternal life," do all these little provincials! In return for what, in sooth? For what end? It is impossible to carry insolence any further. An immortal Peter! who could stand *him!* They have an ambition which makes one laugh: the *thing* dishes up cut and dried his most personal life, his melancholies, and common-or-garden troubles, as though the Universe itself were under an

---

* "Here I stand! I cannot help myself. God help me! Amen"—were Luther's words before the Reichstag at Worms.—H. B. S.

obligation to bother itself about them, for it never gets tired of wrapping up God Himself in the petty misery in which its troubles are involved. And how about the atrocious form of this chronic hobnobbing with God? This Jewish, and not merely Jewish, slobbering and clawing importunacy towards God!—There exist little despised "heathen nations" in East Africa, from whom these first Christians could have learned something worth learning, a little tact in worshipping; these nations do not allow themselves to say aloud the name of their God. This seems to me delicate enough, it is certain that it is *too* delicate, and not only for primitive Christians; to take a contrast, just recollect Luther, the most "eloquent" and insolent peasant whom Germany has had, think of the Lutherian tone, in which he felt quite the most in his element during his *tête-à-têtes* with God. Luther's opposition to the mediæval saints of the Church (in particular, against "that devil's hog, the Pope"), was, there is no doubt, at bottom the opposition of a boor, who was offended at the *good etiquette* of the Church, that worship-etiquette of the sacerdotal code, which only admits to the holy of holies the initiated and the silent, and shuts the door against the boors. These definitely were not to be allowed a hearing in this planet—but Luther the peasant simply wished it otherwise; as it was, it was not German enough for him. He personally wished himself to talk direct, to talk personally, to talk "straight from the shoulder" with his God. Well, he's done it. The ascetic ideal, you will guess, was at no time and in no place, a school of good taste, still less of good manners—at the best it was a school for sacerdotal manners: that is, it contains in itself something which was a deadly enemy to all good manners. Lack of measure, opposition to measure it is itself a *"non plus ultra."*

The ascetic ideal has corrupted not only health and taste, there are also third, fourth, fifth, and sixth things which it has corrupted——I shall take care not to go through the catalogue (when should I get to the end?). I have here to expose not what this ideal effected; but rather only what it *means*, on what it is based, what lies lurking behind it and under it, that of which it is the provisional expression, an obscure expression bristling with queries and misunderstandings. And with *this* object only in view I presumed "not to spare" my readers a glance at the awfulness of its results, a glance at its fatal results; I did this to prepare them for the final and most awful aspect presented to me by the question of the significance of that ideal. What is the significance of the *power* of that ideal, the monstrousness of its power? Why is it given such an amount of scope? Why is not a better resistance offered against it? The ascetic ideal expresses one will: where is the opposition will, in which an *opposition ideal* expresses itself? The ascetic ideal has an aim——this goal is, putting it generally, that all the other interests of human life should, measured by its standard, appear petty and narrow; it explains epochs, nations, men, in reference to this one end; it forbids any other interpretation, any other end; it repudiates, denies, affirms, confirms, only in the sense of its own interpretation (and was there ever a more thoroughly elaborated system of interpretation?); it subjects itself to no power, rather does it believe in its own precedence over every power——it believes that nothing powerful exists in the world that has not first got to receive from "it" a meaning, a right to exist, a value, as being an instrument in its work, a way and means to its end, to one end.

Where is the *counterpart* of this complete system of will, end, and interpretation? Why is the counterpart lacking? Where is the other "one aim"? But I am told it is not lacking, that not only has it fought a long and fortunate fight with that ideal, but that further it has already won the mastery over that ideal in all essentials: let our whole modern *science* attest this—that modern science, which, like the genuine reality-philosophy which it is, manifestly believes in itself alone, manifestly has the courage to be itself, the will to be itself, and has got on well enough without God, another world, and negative virtues.

With all their noisy agitator-babble, however, they effect nothing with me; these trumpeters of reality are bad musicians, their voices do not come from the deeps with sufficient audibility, they are *not* the mouthpiece for the abyss of scientific knowledge—for to-day scientific knowledge is an abyss—the word "science," in such trumpeter-mouths, is a prostitution, an abuse, an impertinence. The truth is just the opposite from what is maintained in the ascetic theory. Science has today absolutely *no* belief in itself, let alone in an ideal superior to itself, and wherever science still consists of passion, love, ardour, suffering, it is not the opposition to that ascetic ideal, but rather the *incarnation of its latest and noblest form*. Does that ring strange? There are enough brave and decent working people, even among the learned men of today, who like their little corner, and who, just because they are pleased so to do, become at times indecently loud with their demand, that people today should be quite content, especially in science—for in science there is so much useful work to do. I do not deny it—there is nothing I should like less than to spoil the delight of these honest workers in their handiwork; for I rejoice in their work. But the fact of science requiring hard work, the fact of its having contented workers, is absolutely no proof of science as a whole having today one end, one will, one ideal, one passion for a great faith; the contrary, as I have said, is the case. When science is not the latest manifestation of the ascetic ideal—but these are cases of such rarity, selectness, and exquisiteness, as to preclude the general judgment being affected thereby—science is a *hiding-place* for every kind of cowardice, disbelief, remorse, *despectio sui,* bad conscience—it is the very *anxiety* that springs from having no ideal, the suffering from the *lack* of a great love, the discontent with an enforced moderation. Oh, what does all science not cover today? How much, at any rate, does it not try to cover? The diligence of our best scholars, their senseless industry, their burning the candle of their brain at both ends—their very mastery in their handiwork—how often is the real meaning of all that to prevent themselves continuing to see a certain thing? Science as a self-anæsthetic: *do you know that?* You wound them—every one who consorts with scholars experiences this —you wound them sometimes to the quick through just a harmless word; when you think you are paying them a compliment you embitter them beyond all bounds, simply because you didn't have the *finesse* to infer the real kind of customers you had to tackle, the *sufferer* kind (who won't own up even to themselves what they really are), the dazed and unconscious kind who have only one fear—*coming to consciousness.*

24

And now look at the other side, at those rare cases, of which I spoke, the most supreme idealists to be found nowadays among philosophers and scholars. Have we, perchance, found in them the sought-for *opponents* of the ascetic ideal, its *anti-*

idealists? In fact, they *believe* themselves to be such, these "unbelievers" (for they are all of them that) : it seems that this idea is their last remnant of faith, the idea of being opponents of this ideal, so earnest are they on this subject, so passionate in word and gesture;—but does it follow that what they believe must necessarily be *true?* We "knowers" have grown by degrees suspicious of all kinds of believers, our suspicion has step by step habituated us to draw just the opposite conclusions to what people have drawn before; that is to say, wherever the strength of a belief is particularly prominent to draw the conclusion of the difficulty of proving what is believed, the conclusion of its actual *improbability.* We do not again deny that "faith produces salvation": *for that very reason* we do deny that faith *proves* anything,—a strong faith, which produces happiness, causes suspicion of the object of that faith, it does not establish its "truth," it does establish a certain probability of—*illusion.* What is now the position in these cases? These solitaries and deniers of today; these fanatics in one thing, in their claim to intellectual cleanness; these hard, stern, continent, heroic spirits, who constitute the glory of our time; all these pale atheists, anti-Christians, immoralists, Nihilists; these sceptics, "ephectics," and "hectics" of the intellect (in a certain sense they are the latter, both collectively and individually); these supreme idealists of knowledge, in whom alone nowadays the intellectual conscience dwells and is alive —in point of fact they believe themselves as far away as possible from the ascetic ideal, do these "free, very free spirits": and yet, if I may reveal what they themselves cannot see—for they stand too near themselves: this ideal is simply *their* ideal, they represent it nowadays and perhaps no one else, they themselves are its most spiritualised product, its most advanced picket of skirmishers and scouts, its most insidious, delicate and elusive form of seduction.—If I am in any way a reader of riddles, then I will be one with this sentence: for some time past there have been no *free spirits; for they still believe in truth.* When the Christian Crusaders in the East came into collision with that invincible order of assassins, that order of free spirits *par excellence,* whose lowest grade lives in a state of discipline such as no order of monks has ever attained, then in some way or other they managed to get an inkling of that symbol and tally-word, that was reserved for the highest grade alone as their *secretum,* "Nothing is true, everything is allowed,"—in sooth, *that* was *freedom* of thought, thereby was *taking leave* of the very belief in truth. Has indeed any European, any Christian freethinker, ever yet wandered into this proposition and its labyrinthine *conse-quences?* Does he know *from experience* the Minotauros of this den?—I doubt it—nay, I know otherwise. Nothing is more really alien to these "monofanatics," these *so-called* "free spirits," than freedom and unfettering in that sense; in no respect are they more closely tied. the absolute fanaticism of their belief in truth is unparalleled. I know all this perhaps too much from experience at close quarters—that dignified philosophic abstinence to which a belief like that binds its adherents, that stoicism of the intellect, which eventually vetoes negation as rigidly as it does affirmation, that *wish* for standing still in front of the actual, the *factum brutum,* that fatalism in "*petits faits*" (*ce petit fatalisme,* as I call it), in which French Science now attempts a kind of moral superiority over German, this renunciation of interpretation generally (that is, of forcing, doctoring, abridging, omitting, suppress-ing, inventing, falsifying, and all the other *essential* attributes of interpretation)—all this, considered broadly, expresses the asceticism of virtue, quite as efficiently as does any repu-

diation of the senses (it is at bottom only a *modus* of that repudiation). But what forces it into that unqualified will for
truth is the faith *in the ascetic ideal itself,* even though it take
the form of its unconscious imperatives,—make no mistake
about it, it is the faith, I repeat, in a *metaphysical* value, an
intrinsic value of truth, of a character which is only warranted
and guaranteed in this ideal (it stands and falls with that
ideal). Judged strictly, there does not exist a science without
its "hypotheses," the thought of such a science is inconceivable,
illogical: a philosophy, a faith, must always exist first to enable
science to gain thereby a direction, a meaning, a limit and
method, a *right* to existence. (He who holds a contrary opinion
on the subject—he, for example, who takes it upon himself
to establish philosophy "upon a strictly scientific basis"—has
first got to "turn upside-down" not only philosophy but also
truth itself—the gravest insult which could possibly be offered
to two such respectable females!) Yes, there is no doubt about
it—and here I quote my *Joyful Wisdom,* cp. Book V. Aph.
344: "The man who is truthful in that daring and extreme
fashion, which is the presupposition of the faith in science,
asserts thereby a different world from that of life, nature, and
history; and in so far as he asserts the existence of that different
world, come, must he not similarly repudiate its counterpart,
this world, *our* world? The belief on which our faith in science
is based has remained to this day a metaphysical belief—even
we knowers of today, we godless foes of metaphysics, we, too,
take our fire from that conflagration which was kindled by a
thousand-year-old faith, from that Christian belief, which was
also Plato's belief, the belief that God is truth, that truth is
divine. . . . But what if this belief becomes more and more
incredible, what if nothing proves itself to be divine, unless it
be error, blindness, lies—what if God Himself proved Him-

self to be our *oldest lie?"*—It is necessary to stop at this point and to consider the situation carefully. Science itself now *needs* a justification (which is not for a minute to say that there is such a justification). Turn in this context to the most ancient and the most modern philosophers: they all fail to realise the extent of the need of a justification on the part of the Will for Truth—here is a gap in every philosophy—what is it caused by? Because up to the present the ascetic ideal dominated all philosophy, because Truth was fixed as Being, as God, as the Supreme Court of Appeal, because Truth was not allowed to be a problem. Do you understand this "allowed"? From the minute that the belief in the God of the ascetic ideal is repudiated, there exists *a new problem:* the problem of the value of truth. The Will for Truth needed a critique—let us define by these words our own task—the value of truth is tentatively *to be called in question.* . . . (If this seems too laconically expressed, I recommend the reader to peruse again that passage from the *Joyful Wisdom* which bears the title, "How far we also are still pious," Aph. 344, and best of all the whole fifth book of that work, as well as the Preface to *The Dawn of Day.*)

25

No! You can't get round me with science, when I search for the natural antagonists of the ascetic ideal, when I put the question: *"Where* is the opposed will in which the *opponent ideal* expresses itself?" Science is not, by a long way, independent enough to fulfil this function; in every department science needs an ideal value, a power which creates values, and in whose *service* it *can believe* in itself—science itself never creates values. Its relation to the ascetic ideal is not in itself antagonistic; speaking roughly, it rather represents the progressive force in the inner evolution of that ideal. Tested more exactly, its opposition and antagonism are concerned not with the ideal itself, but only with that ideal's outworks, its outer garb, its masquerade, with its temporary hardening, stiffening, and dogmatising—it makes the life in the ideal free once more, while it repudiates its superficial elements. These two phenomena, science and the ascetic ideal, both rest on the same basis—I have already made this clear—the basis, I say, of the same over-appreciation of truth (more accurately the same belief in the *impossibility* of valuing and of criticising truth), and consequently they are *necessarily* allies, so that, in the event of their being attacked, they must always be attacked and called into question together. A valuation of the ascetic ideal inevitably entails a valuation of science as well; lose no time in seeing this clearly, and be sharp to catch it! (*Art,* I am speaking provisionally, for I will treat it on some other occasion in greater detail,—art, I repeat, in which lying is sanctified and the *will for deception* has good conscience on its side, is much more fundamentally opposed to the ascetic ideal than is science: Plato's instinct felt this—Plato, the greatest enemy of art which Europe has produced up to the present. Plato *versus* Homer, that is the complete, the true antagonism—on the one side, the wholehearted "transcendental," the great defamer of life; on the other, its involuntary panegyrist, the *golden* nature. An artistic subservience to the service of the ascetic ideal is consequently the most absolute artistic *corruption* that there can be, though unfortunately it is one of the most frequent phases, for nothing is more corruptible than an artist.) Considered physiologically, moreover, science rests on the same basis as does the ascetic ideal: a certain *impoverish-*

ment of life is the presupposition of the latter as of the former —add frigidity of the emotions, slackening of the *tempo,* the substitution of dialectic for instinct, *seriousness* impressed on mien and gesture (seriousness, that most unmistakable sign of strenuous metabolism, of struggling, toiling life). Consider the periods in a nation in which the learned man comes into prominence; they are the periods of exhaustion, often of sunset, of decay—the effervescing strength, the confidence in life, the confidence in the future are no more. The preponderance of the mandarins never signifies any good, any more than does the advent of democracy, or arbitration instead of war, equal rights for women, the religion of pity, and all the other symptoms of declining life. (Science handled as a problem! what is the meaning of science?—upon this point the Preface to the *Birth of Tragedy.*) No! this "modern science"—mark you this well—is at times the *best* ally for the ascetic ideal, and for the very reason that it is the ally which is most unconscious, most automatic, most secret, and most subterranean! They have been playing into each other's hands up to the present, have these "poor in spirit" and the scientific opponents of that ideal (take care, by the bye, not to think that these opponents are the antithesis of this ideal, that they are the *rich* in spirit—that they are *not;* I have called them the *hectic* in spirit). As for these celebrated *victories* of science; there is no doubt that they are victories—but victories over what? There was not for a single minute any victory among their list over the ascetic ideal, rather was it made stronger, that is to say, more elusive, more abstract, more insidious, from the fact that a wall, an outwork, that had got built on to the main fortress and disfigured its appearance, should from time to time be ruthlessly destroyed and broken down by science. Does any one seriously suggest that the downfall of the theological

[784]

astronomy signified the downfall of that ideal?—Has, perchance, man grown *less in need* of a transcendental solution of
his riddle of existence, because since that time his existence has
become more random, casual, and superfluous in the *visible*
order of the universe? Has there not been since the time of
Copernicus an unbroken progress in the self-belittling of man
and his *will* for belittling himself? Alas, his belief in his
dignity, his uniqueness, his irreplaceableness in the scheme of
existence, is gone—he has become animal, literal, unqualified,
and unmitigated animal, he who in his earlier belief was
almost God ("child of God," "demi-God"). Since Copernicus
man seems to have fallen on to a steep plane—he rolls faster
and faster away from the centre—whither? into nothingness?
into the "thrilling sensation of his own nothingness"?—Well!
this would be the straight way—to the *old* ideal?—*All* science
(and by no means only astronomy, with regard to the humiliating and deteriorating effect of which Kant has made a remarkable confession, "it annihilates my own importance"), all
science, natural as much as *unnatural*—by unnatural I mean
the self-critique of reason—nowadays sets out to talk man out
of his present opinion of himself, as though that opinion had
been nothing but a bizarre piece of conceit; you might go so
far as to say that science finds its peculiar pride, its peculiar
bitter form of stoical ataraxia, in preserving man's *contempt of
himself,* that state which it took so much trouble to bring
about, as man's final and most serious claim to self-appreciation
(rightly so, in point of fact, for he who despises is always "one
who has not forgotten how to appreciate"). But does all this
involve any real effort to *counteract* the ascetic ideal? Is it
really seriously suggested that Kant's *victory* over the theological dogmatism about "God," "Soul," "Freedom," "Immortality," has damaged that ideal in any way (as the theologians

have imagined to be the case for a long time past)?—And in this connection it does not concern us for a single minute, if Kant himself intended any such consummation. It is certain that from the time of Kant every type of transcendentalist is playing a winning game—they are emancipated from the theologians; what luck!—he has revealed to them that secret art, by which they can now pursue their "heart's desire" on their own responsibility, and with all the respectability of science. Similarly, who can grumble at the agnostics, reverers, as they are, of the unknown and the absolute mystery, if they now worship *their very query* as God? (Xaver Doudan talks somewhere of the *ravages* which *l'habitude d'admirer l'inintelligible au lieu de rester tout simplement dans l'inconnu* has produced—the ancients, he thinks, must have been exempt from those ravages.) Supposing that everything, "known" to man, fails to satisfy his desires, and on the contrary contradicts and horrifies them, what a divine way out of all this to be able to look for the responsibility, not in the "desiring" but in "knowing"!—"There is no knowledge. *Consequently*—there is a God"; what a novel *elegantia syllogismi!* what a triumph for the ascetic ideal!

26

Or, perchance, does the whole of modern history show in its demeanour greater confidence in life, greater confidence in its ideals? Its loftiest pretension is now to be a *mirror;* it repudiates all teleology; it will have no more "proving"; it disdains to play the judge, and thereby shows its good taste—it asserts as little as it denies, it fixes, it "describes." All this is to a high degree ascetic, but at the same time it is to a much

greater degree *nihilistic;* make no mistake about this! You see
in the historian a gloomy, hard, but determined gaze,—an eye
that *looks out* as an isolated North Pole explorer looks out
(perhaps so as not to look within, so as not to look back?)—
there is snow—here is life silenced, the last crows which caw
here are called "whither?" "Vanity," "Nada"—here nothing
more flourishes and grows, at the most the metapolitics of St.
Petersburg and the "pity" of Tolstoi. But as for that other
school of historians a perhaps still more "modern" school, a
voluptuous and lascivious school which ogles life and the
ascetic ideal with equal fervour, which uses the word "artist"
as a glove, and has nowadays established a "corner" for itself,
in all the praise given to contemplation; oh, what a thirst do
these sweet intellectuals excite even for ascetics and winter
landscapes! Nay! The devil take these "contemplative" folk!
How much liefer would I wander with those historical Nihilists through the gloomiest, grey, cold mist!—nay, I shall not
mind listening (supposing I have to choose) to one who is
completely unhistorical and anti-historical (a man, like
Dühring for instance, over whose periods a hitherto shy and
unavowed species of "beautiful souls" has grown intoxicated
in contemporary Germany, *the species anarchistica* within the
educated proletariat). The "contemplative" are a hundred
times worse—I never knew anything which produced such
intense nausea as one of those "objective" *chairs,** one of those
scented mannikins-about-town of history, a thing half-priest,
half-satyr (Renan *parfum*), which betrays by the high, shrill
falsetto of his applause what he lacks and where he lacks it,
who betrays where in this case the Fates have plied their ghastly
shears, alas! in too surgeon-like a fashion! This is distasteful

---

* *E.g.* Lectureships.

to me, and irritates my patience; let him keep patient at such
sights who has nothing to lose thereby,—such a sight enrages
me, such spectators embitter me against the "play," even more
than does the play itself (history itself, you understand);
Anacreontic moods imperceptibly come over me. This Nature,
who gave to the steer its horn, to the lion its χάσμ' ὀδόντων,
for what purpose did Nature give me my foot?—To kick, by
St. Anacreon, and not merely to run away! To trample on all
the worm-eaten "chairs," the cowardly contemplators, the
lascivious eunuchs of history, the flirters with ascetic ideals,
the righteous hypocrites of impotence! All reverence on my
part to the ascetic ideal, *in so far as it is honourable!* So long
as it believes in itself and plays no pranks on us! But I like
not all these coquettish bugs who have an insatiate ambition to
smell of the infinite, until eventually the infinite smells of
bugs; I like not the whited sepulchres with their stagey repro-
duction of life; I like not the tired and the used up who wrap
themselves in wisdom and look "objective"; I like not the
agitators dressed up as heroes, who hide their dummy-heads
behind the stalking-horse of an ideal; I like not the ambitious
artists who would fain play the ascetic and the priest, and are
at bottom nothing but tragic clowns; I like not, again, these
newest speculators in idealism, the Anti-Semites, who nowadays roll their eyes in the patent Christian-Aryan-man-of-
honour fashion, and by an abuse of moralist attitudes and agitation dodges, so cheap as to exhaust any patience, strive to
excite all the blockhead elements in the populace (the invariable success of *every* kind of intellectual charlatanism in
present-day Germany hangs together with the almost indisputable and already quite palpable desolation of the German
mind, whose cause I look for in a too exclusive diet, of papers,
politics, beer, and Wagnerian music, not forgetting the con-

dition precedent of this diet, the national exclusiveness and
vanity, the strong but narrow principle, "Germany, Germany
above everything," * and finally the *paralysis agitans* of "modern ideas"). Europe nowadays is, above all, wealthy and ingenious in means of excitement: it apparently has no more
crying necessity than *stimulantia* and alcohol. Hence the enormous counterfeiting of ideals, those most fiery spirits of the
mind; hence too the repulsive, evil-smelling, perjured, pseudo-
alcoholic air everywhere. I should like to know how many
cargoes of imitation idealism, of hero-costumes and high
falutin' clap-trap, how many casks of sweetened pity liqueur
(Firm: *la religion de la souffrance*), how many crutches of
righteous indignation for the help of these flat-footed intellects, how many *comedians* of the Christian moral ideal would
need today to be exported from Europe, to enable its air to
smell pure again. It is obvious that, in regard to this over-
production, a new *trade* possibility lies open; it is obvious that
there is a new business to be done in little ideal idols and
obedient "idealists"—don't pass over this tip! Who has sufficient courage? We have *in our hands* the possibility of
idealising the whole earth. But what am I talking about courage? we only need one thing here—a hand, a free, a very free
hand.

27

Enough! enough! let us leave these curiosities and com-
plexities of the modern spirit, which excite as much laughter
as disgust. *Our* problem can certainly do without them, the
problem of the *meaning* of the ascetic ideal—what has it got

* An illusion to the well-known patriotic song.—H. B. S.

to do with yesterday or today? those things shall be handled by me more thoroughly and severely in another connection (under the title "A Contribution to the History of European Nihilism," I refer for this to a work which I am preparing: *The Will to Power, an Attempt at a Transvaluation of All Values*). The only reason why I come to allude to it here is this: the ascetic ideal has at times, even in the most intellectual sphere, only one real kind of enemies and *damagers:* these are the comedians of this ideal—for they awake mistrust. Everywhere otherwise, where the mind is at work seriously, powerfully, and without counterfeiting, it dispenses altogether now with an ideal (the popular expression for this abstinence is "Atheism")—*with the exception of the will for truth.* But this will, this *remnant* of an ideal, is, if you will believe me, that ideal itself in its severest and cleverest formulation, esoteric through and through, stripped of all outworks, and consequently not so much its remnant as its *kernel.* Unqualified honest atheism (and its air only do we breathe, we, the most intellectual men of this age) is *not* opposed to that ideal, to the extent that it appears to be; it is rather one of the final phases of its evolution, one of its syllogisms and pieces of inherent logic—it is the awe-inspiring *catastrophe* of a two-thousand-year training in truth, which finally forbids itself *the lie of the belief in God.* (The same course of development in India—quite independently, and consequently of some demonstrative value—the same ideal driving to the same conclusion the decisive point reached five hundred years before the European era, or more precisely at the time of Buddha—it started in the Sankhyam philosophy, and then this was popularised through Buddha, and made into a religion.)

What, I put the question with all strictness, has really *triumphed* over the Christian God? The answer stands in my

Joyful Wisdom, Aph. 357: "the Christian morality itself, the idea of truth, taken as it was with increasing seriousness, the confessor-subtlety of the Christian conscience translated and sublimated into the scientific conscience into intellectual clean-ness at any price. Regarding Nature as though it were a proof of the goodness and guardianship of God; interpreting history in honour of a divine reason, as a constant proof of a moral order of the world and a moral teleology; explaining our own personal experiences, as pious men have for long enough ex-plained them, as though every arrangement, every nod, every single thing were invented and sent out of love for the salvation of the soul; all this is now done away with, all this has the conscience *against* it, and is regarded by every subtler con-science as disreputable, dishonourable, as lying, feminism, weakness, cowardice—by means of this severity, if by means of anything at all, are we, in sooth, *good Europeans* and heirs of Europe's longest and bravest self-mastery." . . . All great things go to ruin by reason of themselves, by reason of an act of self-dissolution: so wills the law of life, the law of *neces-sary* "self-mastery" even in the essence of life—ever is the law-giver finally exposed to the cry, *"patere legem quam ipse tulisti";* in thus wise did Christianity *go to ruin as a dogma,* through its own morality; in thus wise must Christianity go again to ruin today as a morality—we are standing on the threshold of this event. After Christian truthfulness has drawn one conclusion after the other, it finally draws its *strongest conclusion,* its conclusion *against* itself; this, however, hap-pens, when it puts the question, *"what is the meaning of every will for truth?"* And here again do I touch on my problem, on our problem, my *unknown* friends (for as yet I *know* of no friends): what sense has our whole being, if it does not mean that in our own selves that will for truth has come to its own consciousness *as a problem?*—By reason of this attainment of self-consciousness on the part of the will for truth, morality from henceforward—there is no doubt about it—goes *to pieces:* this is that great hundred-act play that is reserved for the next two centuries of Europe, the most terrible, the most mysterious, and perhaps also the most hopeful of all plays.

28

If you except the ascetic ideal, man, the *animal* man had no meaning. His existence on earth contained no end; "What is the purpose of man at all?" was a question without an answer; the *will* for man and the world was lacking; behind every great human destiny rang as a refrain a still greater "Vanity!" The ascetic ideal simply means this: that something *was lacking,* that a tremendous *void* encircled man—he did not know how to justify himself, to explain himself, to affirm himself, he *suffered* from the problem of his own meaning. He suffered also in other ways, he was in the main a *diseased* animal; but his problem was not suffering itself, but the lack of an answer to that crying question, *"To what purpose* do we suffer?" Man, the bravest animal and the one most inured to suffering, does *not* repudiate suffering in itself: he *wills* it, he even seeks it out, provided that he is shown a meaning for it, a *purpose* of suffering. *Not* suffering, but the senselessness of suffering was the curse which till then lay spread over humanity—*and the ascetic ideal gave it a meaning!* It was up till then the only meaning; but any meaning is better than no meaning; the ascetic ideal was in that connection the *"faute de mieux"* par *excellence* that existed at that time. In that ideal suffering *found an explanation;* the tremendous gap seemed filled; the

door to all suicidal Nihilism was closed. The explanation—
there is no doubt about it—brought in its train new suffering,
deeper, more penetrating, more venomous, gnawing more
brutally into life: it brought all suffering under the perspective
of *guilt;* but in spite of all that—man was *saved* thereby, he
had a *meaning,* and from henceforth was no more like a leaf
in the wind, a shuttle-cock of chance, of nonsense, he could
now "will" something—absolutely immaterial to what end,
to what purpose, with what means he wished: *the will itself
was saved.* It is absolutely impossible to disguise *what* in point
of fact is made clear by every complete will that has taken its
direction from the ascetic ideal: this hate of the human, and
even more of the animal, and more still of the material, this
horror of the senses, of reason itself, this fear of happiness
and beauty, this desire to get right away from all illusion,
change, growth, death, wishing and even desiring—all this
means—let us have the courage to grasp it—a will for Nothingness, a will opposed to life, a repudiation of the most
fundamental conditions of life, but it is and remains *a will!*—
and to say at the end that which I said at the beginning—man
will wish *Nothingness* rather than not wish *at all.*

Peoples and Countries

TRANSLATED BY J. M. KENNEDY

(The following twenty-seven fragments were intended by Nietzsche to form a supplement to Chapter VIII of *Beyond Good and Evil*, dealing with Peoples and Countries.)

1

THE Europeans now imagine themselves as representing, in the main, the highest types of men on earth.

2

A characteristic of Europeans: inconsistency between word and deed; the Oriental is true to himself in daily life. How the European has established colonies is explained by his nature, which resembles that of a beast of prey.

This inconsistency is explained by the fact that Christianity has abandoned the class from which it sprang.

This is the difference between us and the Hellenes: their morals grew up among the governing castes. Thucydides' morals are the same as those that exploded everywhere with Plato.

Attempts towards honesty at the Renaissance, for example: always for the benefit of the arts. Michael Angelo's conception of God as the "Tyrant of the World" was an honest one.

[794]

3

I rate Michael Angelo higher than Raphael, because, through all the Christian clouds and prejudices of his time, he saw the ideal of a culture *nobler* than the Christo-Raphaelite: whilst Raphael truly and modestly glorified only the values handed down to him, and did not carry within himself any inquiring, yearning instincts. Michael Angelo, on the other hand, saw and felt the problem of the law-giver of new values: the problem of the conqueror made perfect, who first had to subdue the "hero within himself," the man exalted to his highest pedestal, master even of his pity, who mercilessly shatters and annihilates everything that does not bear his own stamp, shining in Olympian divinity. Michael Angelo was naturally only at certain moments so high and so far beyond his age and Christian Europe; for the most part he adopted a condescending attitude towards the eternal feminine in Christianity; it would seem, indeed, that in the end he broke down before her, and gave up the idea of his most inspired hours. It was ..n ideal which only a man in the strongest and highest vigour of life could bear; but not a man advanced in years! Indeed, he would have had to demolish Christianity with his ideal! But he was not thinker and philosopher enough for that. Perhaps Leonardo da Vinci alone of those artists had a really super-Christian outlook. He knows the East, the "land of dawn," within himself as well as without himself. There is something super-European and silent in him: a characteristic of every one who has seen too wide a circle of things good and bad.

4

How much we have learned and learned anew in fifty years! The whole Romantic School with its belief in "the people" is refuted! No Homeric poetry as "popular" poetry! No deification of the great powers of Nature! No deduction from language-relationship to race-relationship! No "intellectual contemplations" of the supernatural! No truth enshrouded in religion!

The problem of truthfulness is quite a new one. I am astonished. From this standpoint we regard such natures as Bismarck as culpable out of carelessness, such as Richard Wagner out of want of modesty; we would condemn Plato for his *pia fraus,* Kant for the derivation of his Categorical Imperative, his own belief certainly not having come to him from this source.

Finally, even doubt turns against itself: doubt in doubt. And the question as to the *value* of truthfulness and its extent lies *there.*

5

What I observe with pleasure in the German is his Mephistophelian nature; but, to tell the truth, one must have a higher conception of Mephistopheles than Goethe had, who found it necessary to *diminish* his Mephistopheles in order to magnify his "inner Faust." The true German Mephistopheles is much more dangerous, bold, wicked, and cunning, and *consequently* more open-hearted: remember the nature of Frederick the Great, or of that much greater Frederick, the Hohenstaufen, Frederick II.

The real German Mephistopheles crosses the Alps, and believes that everything there belongs to him. Then he recovers himself, like Winckelmann, like Mozart. He looks upon Faust and Hamlet as caricatures, invented to be laughed at, and upon Luther also. Goethe had his good *German* moments, when he laughed inwardly at all these things. But then he fell back again into his cloudy moods.

6

Perhaps the Germans have only grown up in a wrong climate! There is something in them that might be Hellenic!—something that is awakened when they are brought into touch with the South—Winckelmann, Goethe, Mozart. We should not forget, however, that we are still young. Luther is still our last event; our last book is still the Bible. The Germans have never yet "moralised." Also, the very food of the Germans was their doom: its consequence, Philistinism.

7

The Germans are a dangerous people: they are experts at inventing intoxicants. Gothic, rococo (according to Semper), the historical sense and exoticism, Hegel, Richard Wagner—Leibnitz, too (dangerous at the present day)—(they even idealised the serving soul as the virtue of scholars and soldiers, also as the simple mind). The Germans may well be the most composite people on earth.

"The people of the Middle," the inventors of porcelain, and of a kind of Chinese breed of Privy Councillor.

8

The smallness and baseness of the German soul were not and are not consequences of the system of small states; for it is well known that the inhabitants of much smaller states were proud and independent: and it is not a large state *per se* that makes souls freer and more manly. The man whose soul obeys the slavish command: "Thou shalt and must kneel!" in whose body there is an involuntary bowing and scraping to tiles, orders, gracious glances from above—well, such a man in an "Empire" will only bow all the more deeply and lick the dust more fervently in the presence of the greater sovereign than in the presence of the lesser: this cannot be doubted. We can still see in the lower classes of Italians that aristocratic self-sufficiency; manly discipline and self-confidence still form a part of the long history of their country: these are virtues which once manifested themselves before their eyes. A poor Venetian gondolier makes a far better figure than a Privy Councillor from Berlin, and is even a better man in the end—any one can see this. Just ask the women.

9

Most artists, even some of the greatest (including the historians) have up to the present belonged to the serving classes (whether they serve people of high position or princes or women or "the masses"), not to speak of their dependence upon the Church and upon moral law. Thus Rubens portrayed the nobility of his age; but only according to *their* vague conception of taste, not according to his own measure of beauty—

on the whole, therefore, against his own taste. Van Dyck was nobler in this respect: who in all those whom he painted added a certain amount of what he himself most highly valued: he did not descend from himself, but rather lifted up others to himself when he "rendered."

The slavish humility of the artist to his public (as Sebastian Bach has testified in undying and outrageous words in the dedication of his High Mass) is perhaps more difficult to perceive in music; but it is all the more deeply engrained. A hearing would be refused me if I endeavoured to impart my views on this subject. Chopin possesses distinction, like Van Dyck. The disposition of Beethoven is that of a proud peasant; of Haydn, that of a proud servant. Mendelssohn, too, possesses distinction—like Goethe, in the most natural way in the world.

10

We could at any time have counted on the fingers of one hand those German learned men who possessed wit: the remainder have understanding, and a few of them, happily, that famous "childlike character" which divines. . . . It is our privilege: with this "divination" German science has discovered some things which we can hardly conceive of, and which, after all, do not exist, perhaps. It is only the Jews among the Germans who do not "divine" like them.

11

As Frenchmen reflect the politeness and *esprit* of French society, so do Germans reflect something of the deep, pen-sive earnestness of their mystics and musicians, and also of their silly childishness. The Italian exhibits a great deal of republican distinction and art, and can show himself to be noble and proud without vanity.

12

A larger number of the higher and better-endowed men will, I hope, have in the end so much self-restraint as to be able to get rid of their bad taste for affectation and sentimental darkness, and to turn against Richard Wagner as much as against Schopenhauer. These two Germans are leading us to ruin; they flatter our dangerous qualities. A stronger future is prepared for us in Goethe, Beethoven, and Bismarck than in these racial aberrations. We have had no philosophers yet.

13

The peasant is the commonest type of noblesse, for he is dependent upon himself most of all. Peasant blood is still the best blood in Germany—for example, Luther, Niebuhr, Bismarck.

Bismarck a Slav. Let any one look upon the face of Germans. Everything that had manly, exuberant blood in it went abroad. Over the smug populace remaining, the slave-souled people, there came an improvement from abroad, especially by a mixture of Slavonic blood.

The Brandenburg nobility and the Prussian nobility in general (and the peasant of certain North German districts), comprise at present the most manly natures in Germany.

That the manliest men shall rule: this is only the natural order of things.

14

The future of German culture rests with the sons of the Prussian officers.

15

There has always been a want of wit in Germany, and mediocre heads attain there to the highest honours, because even they are rare. What is most highly prized is diligence and perseverance and a certain cold-blooded, critical outlook, and, for the sake of such Qualities, German scholarship and the German military system have become paramount in Europe.

16

Parliaments may be very useful to a strong and versatile statesman: he has something there to rely upon (every such thing must, however, be able to resist!)—upon which he can throw a great deal of responsibility. On the whole, however, I could wish that the counting mania and the superstitious belief in majorities were not established in Germany, as with the Latin races, and that one could finally invent something new even in politics! It is senseless and dangerous to let the custom of universal suffrage—which is still but a short time under cultivation, and could easily be uprooted—take a deeper root: whilst, of course, its introduction was merely an expedient to steer clear of temporary difficulties.

[801]

17

Can any one interest himself in this German Empire? Where is the new thought? Is it only a new combination of power? All the worse, if it does not know its own mind. Peace and *laisser aller* are not types of politics for which I have any respect. Ruling, and helping the highest thoughts to victory— the only things that can make me interested in Germany. England's small-mindedness is the great danger now on earth. I observe more inclination towards greatness in the feelings of the Russian Nihilists than in those of the English Utilitarians. We require an intergrowth of the German and Slav races, and we require, too, the cleverest financiers, the Jews, for us to become masters of the world.

(*a*) The sense of reality.

(*b*) A giving-up of the English principle of the people's right of representation. We require the representation of the great interests.

(*c*) We require an unconditional union with Russia, together with a mutual plan of action which shall not permit any English schemata to obtain the mastery in Russia. No American future!

(*d*) A national system of politics is untenable, and embarrassment by Christian views is a very great evil. In Europe all sensible people are sceptics, whether they say so or not.

18

I see over and beyond all these national wars, new "empires," and whatever else lies in the foreground. What I am concerned with—for I see it preparing itself slowly and hesitatingly—is the United Europe. It was the only real work, the one impulse in the souls, of all the broad-minded and deep thinking men of this century—this preparation of a new syn- thesis, and the tentative effort to anticipate the future of "the European." Only in their weaker moments, or when they grew old, did they fall back again into the national narrowness of the "Fatherlanders"—then they were once more "patriots." I am thinking of men like Napoleon, Heinrich Heine, Goethe, Beethoven, Stendhal, Schopenhauer. Perhaps Richard Wag- ner likewise belongs to their number, concerning whom, as a successful type of German obscurity, nothing can be said without some such "perhaps."

But to the help of such minds as feel the need of a new unity there comes a great explanatory economic fact: the small States of Europe—I refer to all our present kingdoms and "empires"—will in a short time become economically unten- able, owing to the mad, uncontrolled struggle for the posses- sion of local and international trade. Money is even now compelling European nations to amalgamate into one Power. In order, however, that Europe may enter into the battle for the mastery of the world with good prospects of victory (it is easy to perceive against whom this battle will be waged), she must probably "come to an understanding" with England. The English colonies are needed for this struggle, just as much as modern Germany, to play her new rôle of broker and mid- dleman, requires the colonial possessions of Holland. For no one any longer believes that England alone is strong enough to continue to act her old part for fifty years more; the impos- sibility of shutting out *homines novi* from the government will ruin her, and her continual change of political parties is a fatal obstacle to the carrying out of any tasks which require to be spread out over a long period of time. A man must today be a soldier first and foremost that he may not afterwards lose his credit as a merchant. Enough; here, as in other matters, the coming century will be found following in the footsteps of Napoleon—the first man, and the man of greatest initiative and advanced views, of modern times. For the tasks of the next century, the methods of popular representation and parliaments are the most inappropriate imaginable.

19

The condition of Europe in the next century will once again lead to the breeding of manly virtues, because men will live in continual danger. Universal military service is already the curious antidote which we possess for the effeminacy of democratic ideas, and it has grown up out of the struggle of the nations. (Nation—men who speak one language and read the same newspapers. These men now call themselves "nations," and would far too readily trace their descent from the same source and through the same history; which, however, even with the assistance of the most malignant lying in the past, they have not succeeded in doing.)

20

What quagmires and mendacity must there be about if it is possible, in the modern European hotch-potch, to raise questions of "race"! (It being premised that the origin of such writers is not in Horneo and Borneo.)

21

Maxim: To associate with no man who takes any part in the mendacious race swindle.

22

With the freedom of travel now existing, groups of men of the same kindred can join together and establish communal habits and customs. The overcoming of "nations."

23

To make Europe a centre of culture, national stupidities should not make us blind to the fact that in the higher regions there is already a continuous reciprocal dependence. France and German philosophy. Richard Wagner and Paris (1830-50). Goethe and Greece. All things are impelled towards a synthesis of the European past in the highest types of mind.

24

Mankind has still much before it—how, generally speaking, could the ideal be taken from the past? Perhaps merely in relation to the present, which latter is possibly a lower region.

25

This is our distrust, which recurs again and again; our care, which never lets us sleep; our question, which no one listens to or wishes to listen to; our Sphinx, near which there is more than one precipice: we believe that the men of present-day Europe are deceived in regard to the things which we love best, and a pitiless demon (no, not pitiless, only indifferent and puerile)—plays with our hearts and their enthusiasm, as it may perhaps have already played with everything that lived and loved; I believe that everything which we Europeans of today are in the habit of admiring as the values of all these respected things called "humanity," "mankind," "sympathy," "pity," may be of some value as the debilitation and moderating of certain powerful and dangerous primitive impulses. Nevertheless, in the long run all these things are nothing else than the belittlement of the entire type "man," his mediocrisation, if in such a desperate situation I may make use of such a desperate expression. I think that the *commedia umana* for an epicurean spectator-god must consist in this: that the Europeans, by virtue of their growing morality, believe in all their innocence and vanity that they are rising higher and higher, whereas the truth is that they are sinking lower and lower— *i.e.,* through the cultivation of all the virtues which are useful to a herd, and through the repression of the other and contrary virtues which give rise to a new, higher, stronger, masterful race of men—the first-named virtues merely develop the herd-animal in man and stabilitate the animal "man," for until now man has been "the animal as yet unstabilitated."

26

GENIUS AND EPOCH.—Heroism is no form of selfishness, for one is shipwrecked by it. . . . The direction of power is often conditioned by the state of the period in which the great man happens to be born; and this fact brings about the superstition that he is the expression of his time. But this same power could be applied in several different ways; and between him and his time there is always this difference: that public opinion always worships the herd instinct,—*i.e.*, the instinct of the weak,—while he, the strong man, fights for strong ideals.

27

The fate now overhanging Europe is simply this: that it is exactly her strongest sons that come rarely and late to the spring-time of their existence; that, as a rule, when they are already in their early youth they perish, saddened, disgusted, darkened in mind, just because they have already, with the entire passion of their strength, drained to the dregs the cup of disillusionment, which in our days means the cup of knowledge, and they would not have been the strongest had they not also been the most disillusioned. For that is the test of their power—they must first of all rise out of the illness of their epoch to reach their own health. A late spring-time is their mark of distinction; also, let us add, late merriment, late folly, the late exuberance of joy! For this is the danger of today: everything that we loved when we were young has betrayed us. Our last love—the love which makes us acknowledge her, our love for Truth—let us take care that she, too, does not betray us!

ECCE HOMO

Translated by CLIFTON P. FADIMAN

1

In view of the fact that before long I must confront my fellow-men with the very greatest demand that has ever yet been made upon them, it seems to me indispensable to declare here who and what I am. As a matter of fact, this should be pretty well known already, for I have not allowed myself to be "without witness." But the disparity between the greatness of my task and the smallness of my contemporaries is made plain by the fact that people have neither heard me nor seen me. I live on my own credit—perhaps it is only a prejudice to suppose that I am living at all. All I have to do is to speak to any one of the "scholars" who visit the Ober-Engadine in the summer, in order to convince myself that I am *not* alive. . . . Under these circumstances, it is a duty—and one against which my customary reserve, and still more the pride of my instincts, rebel—to say: *"Listen! for I am such and such a person. For Heaven's sake do not confuse me with any one else!"*

2

For instance, I am in no way a bugbear, a moral monster. It is true that my nature is in direct contrast to the sort of man who has hitherto been honored as virtuous. But between ourselves, it seems to me that this is precisely a reason for pride. I am a disciple of the philosopher Dionysus, and I would sooner be a satyr than a saint. But I merely ask that you read this book! Perhaps I have here succeeded in expressing this contrast in a cheerful and sympathetic manner. Perhaps the work may have no other purpose.

The very last thing I should promise to accomplish would be to "improve" mankind. I set up no new idols; I only want old idols to learn what it means to have feet of clay. To overthrow idols (the name I give to ideals) is very much more like my business. In proportion as we have invented an ideal world we have deprived reality of its value, its meaning, and its truth. . . . The "true world" and the "apparent world"—in plain English, the fictitious world and reality. . . . Hitherto the *lie* of the ideal has been the curse of reality; by means of it man's most basic instincts have become mendacious and false; so much so that those values have come to be worshiped which are most exactly antagonistic to the ones which would ensure man's prosperity, his future, and his great right to that future.

3

He who can breathe in the air of my writings knows that it is the air of the heights, that it is bracing. A man must be formed for it, otherwise there is no little danger of chill. The ice is near, the loneliness is terrible—but how quiet everything is in the sunshine! how freely one breathes! how much, one feels, lies beneath one! Philosophy, as I have understood and experienced it hitherto, is a voluntary retirement into a region of ice and mountain-peaks—the search for all that is strange and questionable in existence, everything upon which, hitherto, morality has set its ban. Through long experience, derived from such wanderings in the forbidden land, I learned to look at the causes of mankind's moralising and idealising in a manner very different from that which may seem ordinarily desirable. The secret history of philosophers, the psychology of their great names, was revealed to me. How much truth can a mind endure? How much truth will it dare? These questions became for me more and more the essential criterion. Error (the belief in the ideal) is not blindness; error is cowardice. . . . Every conquest, all progress in knowledge, is the result of courage, of hardness towards one's self, of cleanliness towards one's self. I do not refute ideals; I merely draw on my gloves in their presence. . . . *Nitimur in vetitum:* by this sign I shall conquer; for that which has hitherto been most stringently forbidden has always been the Truth.

4

Among my writings, my *Zarathustra* holds a special place. With it, I gave my fellow-men the greatest gift that has ever been bestowed upon them. This book, whose voice resounds across the ages, is not only the loftiest book in the world, the veritable book of mountain air—the whole phenomenon, mankind, lies at an incalculable distance beneath it—but it is also the deepest book, born of the inmost fullness of truth; an inexhaustible well, into which no pitcher descends without rising again laden with gold and goodness. No "prophet" speaks here, no horrible hybrids of sickness and the Will to Power, called by men founders of religions. If a man would not do terrible wrong to his own wisdom, he must above all

[*813*]

give proper heed to the tones—the halcyon tones—that come from *Zarathustra:*

"The most silent words are harbingers of the storm; thoughts that come on dove's feet lead the world.

"The figs fall from the trees; they are good and sweet; and, in falling, the red skins of them break. A north wind am I to ripe figs.

"Thus, like figs, do these doctrines fall for you, my friends: imbibe now their juice and their sweet substance! It is autumn all around, and clear sky, and afternoon." *

No fanatic speaks to you here; this is not a "sermon"; no faith is demanded. From out an infinite fullness of light and depth of joy, drop by drop, my words issue—the tempo of these discourses is slow and measured. Such things are only for the most elect; it is an unparalleled privilege to be a listener here; not every one who likes can have ears to hear *Zarathustra.* Then shall we not say of *Zarathustra,* that he is a *seducer?* . . . But what, indeed, does he himself say, the first time he returns to his solitude? Just the opposite of what any "Sage," "Saint," "Redeemer," or other decadent would say. . . . Not only his words, but he himself is different from them.

"I now go alone, my disciples! Ye also now go away, and alone! So will I have it.

"Verily, I advise you: depart from me, and guard yourselves against *Zarathustra!* And better still: be ashamed of him! Perhaps he hath deceived you.

"The man of knowledge must be able not only to love his enemies, but also to hate his friends.

* See page 90.

"One requiteth a teacher badly if one remain merely a scholar. And why will ye not pluck at my wreath?

"Ye venerate me; but what if your veneration should some day collapse? Take heed lest a statue crush you!

"Ye say, ye believe in *Zarathustra?* But of what account is *Zarathustra?* Ye are my believers: but of what account are all believers?

"Ye had not yet sought yourselves: then did ye find me. So do all believers; therefore all belief is of so little account.

"Now do I bid you lose me and find yourselves; and only when ye have all denied me, will I return unto you." *

FRIEDRICH NIETZSCHE.

---

* Commons' Trans., Mod. Lib. Ed., pp. 82-83.

ON this perfect day, when everything is ripening, and not only the grapes are getting brown, a ray of sunshine fell across my life: I looked behind me, I looked before me, and never did I see so many good things all at once. Not in vain have I buried my four-and-fortieth year today; I had the *right* to bury it—what was vital in it has been saved and is immortal. The first book of the *Transvaluation of all Values, The Songs of Zarathustra, The Twilight of the Idols,* my attempt to philosophise with the hammer—all are the gifts of this year, even of its last quarter—*How could I help being thankful to the whole of my life?*

And so I am going to tell myself the story of that life.

Why I Am So Wise

1

THE happiness of my existence, its unique character perhaps, lies in its fatefulness: expressing it in the form of a riddle, as my own father I am already dead, as my own mother I still live and grow old. This double origin, taken as it were from the highest and lowest rungs of the ladder of life, at once a decadence and a beginning, this, if anything, explains that neutrality, that freedom from partisanship with regard to the general problem of life, which perhaps distinguishes me. I am more sensitive to the first indications of ascent and descent than any man that has yet lived. In this domain I am a master *par excellence*—I know both sides, for I am both sides. My father died in his thirty-sixth year: he was delicate, lovable, and morbid, like one fated for but a short life—a gracious reminder of life rather than life itself. In the same year that his life declined mine also declined: in my thirty-sixth year my vitality reached its lowest point—I still lived, but I could not see three paces before me. At that time—it was the year 1879—I resigned my professorship at Basel, lived through the summer like a shadow in St. Moritz, and spent the following winter, the most sunless of my life, like a shadow in Naumburg. I was then at my lowest ebb. *The Wanderer and His Shadow* was the product of this period. There is no doubt that

I was familiar with shadows then. The following winter, my first winter in Genoa, brought with it that sweetness and spirituality which is almost inseparable from extreme poverty of blood and muscle, in the shape of *The Dawn of Day*. The perfect brightness and cheerfulness, the intellectual exuberance even, that this work reflects, coincide, in my case, not only with the most profound bodily weakness, but also with an excess of suffering. In the midst of the agony caused by a seventy-two hour headache and violent attacks of nausea, I was possessed of extraordinary dialectical clearness, and in utter cold blood I then thought out things, for which, in my more healthy moments, I am not enough of a climber, not subtle enough, not cold enough. My readers may know to what extent I consider dialectic a symptom of decadence, as, for example, in the most famous case of all—that of Socrates. All the morbid disturbances of the intellect, even that semistupor which follows fever, are to this day strangers to me; and to inform myself concerning their nature and frequency, I had to resort to learned works. My circulation is slow. No one has ever been able to detect fever in me. A doctor who treated me for some time as a nerve patient finally declared: "No! there's nothing the matter with *your* nerves; I myself am the nervous one." They have been unable to discover any local degeneration in me, or any organic stomach trouble, however much I may have suffered from profound weakness of the gastric system as the result of general exhaustion. Even my eye trouble, which at times approached dangerously near blindness, was only an effect and not a cause; for, with every improvement of my general bodily health came a corresponding increase in my power of vision. An all too long series of years meant recovery to me. But, sad to say, it also meant relapse, breakdown, periods of decadence. After this, need I say that I am experienced in questions of decadence? I know them inside and out. Even that filigree art of prehension and comprehension in general, that feeling for nuances, that psychology of "seeing what is around the corner," and whatever else I may be able to do, was first learned then, and is the specific gift of that period during which everything in me was subtilized—observation itself, together with all the organs of observation. To view healthier concepts and values from the standpoint of the sick, and conversely to view the secret work of the instinct of decadence out of the abundance and self-confidence of a rich life—this has been my principal experience, what I have been longest trained in. If in anything at all, it was in this that I became a master. Today my hand is skilful; it has the knack of reversing perspectives: the first reason perhaps why a *Transvaluation of all Values* has been possible to me alone.

2

Agreed that I am a decadent, I am also the very reverse. Among other things there is this proof: I always instinctively select the proper remedy in preference to harmful ones; whereas the decadent, as such, invariably chooses those remedies which are bad for him. As a whole I was healthy, but in certain details I was a decadent. The energy with which I forced myself to absolute solitude, and to an alienation from my customary habits of life; the self-discipline that forbade me to be pampered, waited on, and doctored—all this betrays the absolute certainty of my instincts in regard to what at that time was most needful to me. I placed myself in my own hands, I restored myself to health: to do this, the first condition of success, as every physiologist will admit, is that the man be basically sound. A typically morbid nature cannot become healthy at all, much less by his own efforts. On the other hand, to an intrinsically sound nature, illness may even act as a powerful stimulus to life, to an abundance of life. It is thus that I now regard my long period of illness: it seemed then as if I had discovered life afresh, my own self included. I tasted all good and even trifling things in a way in which others could not very well taste them—out of my Will to Health and to Life I made my philosophy. . . . For I wish this to be understood; it was during those years of most low-ered vitality that I ceased from being a pessimist: the instinct of self-recovery forbade a philosophy of poverty and despera-tion. Now, how are we to recognize Nature's most excellent human products? They are recognized by the fact that an excellent man of this sort gladdens our senses; he is carved from a single block, which is hard, sweet, and fragrant. He enjoys only what is good for him; his pleasure, his desire, ceases when the limits of what is good for him are overstepped. He divines remedies against injuries; he knows how to turn serious accidents to his own advantage; whatever does not kill him makes him stronger. He instinctively gathers his material from all he sees, hears, and experiences. He is a selective prin-ciple; he rejects much. He is always in his own company, whether his intercourse be with books, men or natural scenery; he honors the things he chooses, the things he acknowledges, the things he trusts. He reacts slowly to all kinds of stimuli, with that tardiness which long caution and deliberate pride have bred in him—he tests the approaching stimulus; he would not think of going toward it. He believes in neither "ill-fortune" nor "guilt"; he can digest himself and others;

he knows how to forget—he is strong enough to make every·
thing turn to his own advantage.

Lo then! I am the very reverse of a decadent, for he whom
I have just described is none other than myself.

3

This double series of experiences, this means of access to
two worlds that seem so far asunder, finds an exact reflection
in my own nature—I have an alter ego: I have a "second"
sight, as well as a first. Perhaps I even have a third sight. The
very nature of my origin allowed me an outlook transcending
merely local, merely national and limited horizons; it cost me
no effort to be a "good European." On the other hand, I am
perhaps more German than modern Germans—mere Imperial
Germans—can possibly be—I, the last anti-political German.
And yet my ancestors were Polish noblemen: it is owing to
them that I have so much race instinct in my blood—who
knows? perhaps even the *liberum veto*.[1] When I think of how
often I have been accosted as a Pole when traveling, even by
Poles themselves, and how seldom I have been taken for a
German, it seems to me as if I belonged to those who have but
a sprinkling of German in them. But my mother, Franziska
Oehler, is at any rate something very German; as is also my
paternal grandmother, Erdmuthe Krause. The latter spent the
whole of her youth in good old Weimar, not without coming
into contact with Goethe's circle. Her brother, Krause, Professor of Theology in Königsberg, was called to the post of
General Superintendent at Weimar after Herder's death. It is

---

[1] The right of any Polish noble deputy to veto entirely any bill by casting
his individual negative vote.—Tr.

not unlikely that her mother, my great-grandmother, appears
in young Goethe's diary under the name of "Muthgen." The
husband of her second marriage was Superintendent Nietzsche
of Eilenburg. On the 10th of October, 1813, the year of the
great war, when Napoleon with his general staff entered Eilenburg, she gave birth to a son. As a Saxon, she was a great
admirer of Napoleon, and perhaps I too am so still. My father,
born in 1813, died in 1849. Before taking over the pastorship
of the parish of Röcken, not far from Lützen, he had lived
for some years at the Castle of Altenburg, where he had charge
of the education of the four princesses. His pupils are the
Queen of Hanover, the Grand-Duchess Constantine, the
Grand-Duchess of Oldenburg, and the Princess Theresa of
Saxe-Altenburg. He was full of pious respect for the Prussian
King, Frederick William the Fourth, from whom he obtained
his living at Röcken; the events of 1848 caused him great
sorrow. As I was born on the 15th of October, the birthday
of the king above mentioned, I naturally received the Hohen-
zollern names of Frederick William. There was at all events
one advantage in the choice of this day: my birthday throughout my entire childhood was a public holiday. I regard it as a
great privilege to have had such a father: it even seems to me
that this exhausts all that I can claim in the matter of privileges—life, the great yea to life, excepted. What I owe to him
above all is this, that I do not need any special intention, but
merely patience, in order to enter involuntarily into a world
of higher and finer things. There I am at home, there alone
does my profoundest passion have free play. The fact that I
almost paid for this privilege with my life, certainly does not
make it a bad bargain. In order to understand even a little of
my *Zarathustra,* perhaps a man must be situated much as I
am myself—with one foot beyond life.

4

I have never understood the art of arousing antagonism (and for this, too, I may thank my incomparable father), even when it seemed to me most worth while to do so. However unchristian it may seem, I do not even bear any ill-feeling towards myself. Examine my life as you may, you will find but seldom—perhaps indeed only once—any trace of some one's having shown me ill-will; but you might perhaps discover too many traces of *good*-will. . . . My experiences even with those with whom every other man's relations have been disastrous, speak without exception in their favor; I tame every bear, I can make even clowns behave well. During the seven years in which I taught Greek to the upper class of the College at Basel, I never had occasion to administer a punishment; even the laziest youths were diligent in my class. Accident has always found me ready for it; I must be unprepared in order to keep my self-command. I could take any instrument, even if it be as out of tune as only the instrument "man" can possibly be and—except when I was ill—I could always succeed in coaxing from it something worth hearing. And how often have I not been told by the "instruments" themselves, that they had never before heard such utterances. . . . Perhaps the most charming expression of this feeling was that of young Heinrich von Stein, who died at such an unpardonably early age, and who, after having considerately secured permission, once appeared in Sils-Maria for a three days' stay, explaining to every one there that he had *not* come because of the Engadine. This excellent person, who with all the impetuous simplicity of a young Prussian nobleman, had waded deep into the

Wagnerian swamp (and into that of Dühringism [2] besides!),
seemed during these three days almost transformed by a hurricane of freedom, like one who has been suddenly raised to
his full height and given wings. Again and again I told him
that this was merely the result of the bracing air; everybody
felt the same—one could not stand 6000 feet above Bayreuth
without feeling it—but he would not believe me. . . . All
this notwithstanding, if I have been the victim of many a small
or even great offense, it was not "will," least of all *ill*-will, that
caused it; rather, as I have already indicated, it was good-will
that gave me cause to complain, that good-will which is responsible for no small amount of mischief in my life. My experience gave me a right to feel suspicious in regard to all so-called
"unselfish" tendencies, in regard to the whole of "neighborly
love" which is ever ready and waiting with deeds or with
advice. It seems to me that they are signs of weakness, examples of the inability to withstand an incitement—it is only
among decadents that this *pity* is called a virtue. What I reproach the pitiful with is, that they are too ready to forget
modesty, reverence, and the delicacy of feeling which knows
how to keep at a distance; they forget that this sentimental pity
stinks of the mob, and that it is but a step removed from bad
manners—that pitiful hands may be thrust with destructive
results into a great destiny, into a wounded isolation, and into
the privileges that go with great guilt. The overcoming of pity
I reckon among the noble virtues. In the "Temptation of
Zarathustra" I have imagined a case, in which he hears a great
cry of distress, in which pity swoops down upon him like a
last sin, seeking to make him break faith with himself. To
remain master over one's self in such circumstances, to keep

---

[2] Eugen Dühring was a contemporary German philosopher and political
economist.—Tr.

the sublimity of one's mission free from the many ignoble and
more short-sighted impulses which so-called unselfish actions
excite—this is the test, the last test perhaps, which a Zarathustra has to undergo—the real proof of his power.

5

In yet another respect I am simply my father over again,
and as it were the continuation of his life after an all-too-early
death. Like every man who has never been able to meet his
equal, and to whom the notion of "retaliation" is just as incomprehensible as the notion of "equal rights," I have forbidden myself all measures of security or protection—and also,
naturally, of defense and "justification"—in all cases where
I have encountered foolishness, whether trifling or *very great*.
My form of retaliation is this: as soon as possible I follow up
my encounter with stupidity with a piece of cleverness; by this
means perhaps one may still overtake it. To use an image: I
swallow a pot of jam in order to get rid of a sour taste. . . .
Just let anybody give me offense—I shall "retaliate," he may
be assured of That: before long I shall find an opportunity of
expressing my thanks to the "offender" (among other things
even for the offense)—or of *asking* him for something, which
can be more courteous even than giving. It also seems to me
that the rudest word, the rudest letter, is more good-natured,
more honest, than silence. Those who keep silent are almost
always lacking in delicacy and refinement of heart; silence is
an objection; to swallow a grievance necessarily produces a
bad temper—it even upsets the stomach. All silent people are
dyspeptic. You may note that I do not care to see rudeness
undervalued; it is by far the most *humane* form of contradic-

tion, and, amid modern effeminacy, it is one of our first virtues. If one is sufficiently rich for it, it may even be a joy to be
wrong. A god descending to this earth could do nothing
but wrong—for to take upon one's self *guilt,* not punishment,
is the first sign of divinity.

6

Freedom from resentment and the understanding of resentment—who knows after all how greatly I am indebted to
my long illness for these things? The problem is not exactly
simple: a man must have experienced through both his
strength and his weakness. It we are to bear any grudge against
illness and weakness, it is the fact that along with it there
decays the very instinct of recovery, which is the instinct of
defense and of war in man. He does not know how to get rid
of anything, how to finish anything, how to cast anything
behind him. Everything wounds him. People and things ob-
trude too closely, all experiences strike too deep, memory is a
festering sore. Illness is a sort of resentment in itself. Against
it the invalid has only one great remedy—I call it *Russian
fatalism,* that unrebellious fatalism with which the Russian
soldier, when a campaign becomes unbearable, finally lies
down in the snow. To accept nothing more—to cease entirely
from reacting. . . . The high sagacity of this fatalism, which
is not always mere courage in the face of death, but which in
the most dangerous circumstances may work toward self-preservation, is tantamount to a reduction of activity in the vital
functions, the slowing down of which is like a sort of will to
hibernate. A few steps farther in this direction we have the
fakir, who will sleep for weeks in a tomb. . . . Since one

would be used up too quickly if one reacted, one no longer reacts at all: this is the principle. And nothing consumes a man more quickly than the emotion of resentment. Mortification, morbid susceptibility, the inability to revenge oneself, the desire, the thirst for revenge, the concoction of every kind of poison—for an exhausted man this is surely the most injurious manner of reacting. It involves a rapid using up of nervous energy, an abnormal increase of harmful secretions, as, for instance, that of bile into the stomach. Resentment should above all be forbidden the sick man—it is *his* special danger: unfortunately, however, it is also his most natural propensity. This was perfectly understood by that profound physiologist Buddha. His "religion," which it would be better to call a system of hygiene, to avoid confounding it with so wretched a thing as Christianity, depended for its effect upon the triumph over resentment: to free the soul from it—that was the first step towards recovery. "Not through hostility does hostility end; through friendship does hostility end": this stands at the beginning of Buddha's teaching—this is not the voice of morality, but of physiology. Resentment born of weakness is harmful to no one more than to the weak man himself—conversely, with a fundamentally rich nature, resentment is a superfluous feeling, which, if one remains master of it, is almost a proof of riches. Those readers who know the earnestness with which my philosophy wages war against the feelings of revenge and rancor, even to the extent of attacking the doctrine of "free will" (my conflict with Christianity is only a particular instance of it), will understand why I wish to emphasize my own personal attitude and the certainty of my practical instincts precisely in this matter. In my decadent period, I forbade myself these feelings, because they were harmful; but as soon as my life had recovered enough riches and pride,

I still forbade myself them, but now because they were *beneath* me. That "Russian fatalism" of which I spoke manifested itself in me in such a way that for years I clung tenaciously to almost unbearable conditions, places, habitations, and companions, once chance had placed them in my way—it was better than changing them, than feeling that they could be changed, than revolting against them. . . . He who disturbed this fatalism, who tried by force to awaken me, seemed to me then a mortal enemy—in fact, there was danger of death each time this was done. To think of one's self as a destiny, not to wish one's self "different"—this, in such circumstances, is the very highest wisdom.

7

But war is another thing. I am essentially a warrior. To attack is instinctive with me. To *be able to be* an enemy, to *be* an enemy—this, perhaps, presupposes a strong nature; in any case it is bound up with all strong natures. They need resistance, accordingly they seek for it: the pathos of aggression belongs of necessity to strength as much as the feelings of revenge and rancor belong to weakness. Woman, for instance, is revengeful; her weakness involves this passion, just as it involves her susceptibility to others' distress. The strength of the aggressor is in a manner determined by the opposition he needs; every increase of strength betrays itself by a search for a more formidable opponent—or problem: for a philosopher who is combative will challenge even problems to a duel. The task is not to overcome opponents in general, but only those against whom one must pit all one's strength, skill, and swordsmanship—opponents who are one's equals. . . . To be the equal of the enemy—this is the first condition of an honorable duel. Where one despises, one *cannot* wage war. Where one commands, where one sees something *beneath* one, one *ought* not to wage war. My war tactics are comprised in four principles: First, I attack only things that are triumphant—if necessary I wait until they become so. Secondly, I attack only those things against which I find no allies, against which I stand alone—against which I compromise only myself. . . . I have never publicly taken a single step which did not compromise me: that is *my* criterion of the proper mode of action. Thirdly, I never attack persons—I make use of a personality merely as a powerful magnifying-glass, by means of which I render a general, but elusive and hardly tangible, evil more visible. In this way I attacked David Strauss, or more exactly the successful reception given to a senile book by the cultured classes of Germany—thereby catching this culture red-handed. In this way I attacked Wagner, or more exactly the falsity or mongrel instincts of our "culture" which confounds superrefinement with abundance, and decadence with greatness. Fourthly, I attack only those things from which all personal differences are excluded, in which any background of disagreeable experiences is lacking. Indeed, attacking is to me a proof of good-will and, in certain circumstances, of gratitude. By means of it, I honor a thing, I distinguish a thing; it is all the same to me whether I associate my name with that of an institution or a person, whether I am *against* or *for* either. If I wage war against Christianity, I do so because I have met with no fatalities and difficulties from that quarter—the most earnest Christians have always been favorably disposed to me. I, personally, the severest opponent of Christianity, am far from holding the individual responsible for what is the inevitable outcome of long ages.

[*829*]

8

May I venture to indicate one last trait of my nature, which has caused me no little difficulty in my intercourse with men? I am gifted with an utterly uncanny instinct of cleanliness; so that I can ascertain physiologically—that is to say, smell—the proximity, I may say, the inmost core, the "entrails" of every human soul. . . . This sensitiveness has psychological antennæ, with which I feel and handle every secret: the hidden filth at the base of many a human character which may be the result of base blood, but which may be superficially overlaid by education, is revealed to me at the first glance. If my observation has been correct, such people, unbearable to my sense of cleanliness, also become conscious, on their part, of the cautiousness resulting from my loathing: and this does not make them any more fragrant. . . . A rigid attitude of cleanliness towards myself is the first condition of my existence; I would die in unclean surroundings—and so I have always accustomed myself to swim, bathe, and splash about, as it were, incessantly in water, in any kind of perfectly transparent and shining element. That is why social intercourse is no small trial to my patience; my humanity does not consist in the fact that I sympathize with the feelings of my fellows, but that I can endure that very sympathy. . . . My humanity is a continual self-mastery. But I need solitude—that is to say, recovery, return to myself, the breathing of free, light, bracing air. . . . The whole of my *Zarathustra* is a dithyramb of solitude, or, rightly understood, of purity. Fortunately, it is not one of "pure foolery"![3] He who has an eye for color will call them diamonds.

---

[3] A reference to Wagner's *Parsifal.*—Tr.

The loathing of mankind, of the rabble, was always my greatest danger. . . . Would you hearken to the words in which Zarathustra speaks concerning deliverance from loathing?

"What hath happened unto me? How have I freed myself from loathing? Who hath rejuvenated mine eye? How have I flown to the height, where no rabble any longer sit at the wells?

"Did my loathing itself create for me wings and fountain-divining powers? Verily to the loftiest height had I to fly, to find again the well of delight!

"Oh, I have found it, my brethren! Here, on the loftiest height bubbleth up for me the well of delight. And there is a life at whose waters none of the rabble drink with me!

"Almost too violently dost thou flow for me, thou fountain of delight! And often emptiest thou the goblet again in wanting to fill it!

"And yet must I learn to approach thee more modestly: far too violently doth my heart still flow towards thee:—

"My heart, on which my summer burneth, my short, hot, melancholy, over-happy summer: how my summer heart longeth for thy coolness!

"Past, the lingering distress of my spring! Past, the wickedness of my snowflakes in June! Summer have I become entirely, and summer-noontide!

"A summer on the loftiest height, with cold fountains and blissful stillness: oh, come, my friends, that the stillness may become more blissful!

"For this is our height and our home: too high and steep do we here dwell for all uncleanly ones and their thirst.

"Cast but your pure eyes into the well of my delight, my friends! How could it become turbid thereby! It shall laugh back to you with *its* purity.

"On the tree of the future build we our nest; eagles shall bring us lone ones food in their beaks!

"Verily, no food of which the impure could be fellow-partakers! Fire would they think they devoured and burn their mouths!

"Verily, no abodes do we here keep ready for the impure! An ice-cave to their bodies would our happiness be, and to their spirits!

"And as strong winds will we live above them, neighbors to the eagles, neighbors to the snow, neighbors to the sun: thus live the strong winds.

"And like a wind will I one day blow amongst them, and with my spirit, take the breath from their spirit: thus willeth my future.

"Verily, a strong wind is Zarathustra to all low places; and this counsel counseleth he to his enemies and to whatever spitteth and speweth: 'Take care not to spit *against* the wind!' " 4

---

4 Commons' Trans., Modern Library Edition, pp. 105-106.

Why I Am So Clever

1

Why do I know more than other people? Why, in general, am I so clever? I have never pondered over questions that are not really questions. I have never wasted my strength. I have no experience, for instance, of actual religious difficulties. I am quite unfamiliar with the feeling of "sinfulness." Similarly I lack a reliable criterion for determining a prick of conscience: from what one hears, a prick of conscience does not seem to me anything very worthy of veneration. . . . I dislike to leave an action of mine in the lurch; I prefer to omit utterly the bad result, the consequences, from any problem involving values. In the face of evil consequences it is too easy to lose the proper standpoint from which to view an action. A prick of conscience seems to me a sort of "evil eye." Something that has failed should be all the more honored just because it has failed—this agrees much better with my morality.—"God," "the immortality of the soul," "salvation," a "beyond"—these are mere notions, to which I paid no attention, on which I never wasted any time, even as a child—though perhaps I was never enough of a child for that—I am quite unacquainted with atheism as a result, and still less as an event: with me it is instinctive. I am too inquisitive, too

[*833*]

skeptical, too arrogant, to let myself be satisfied with an obvious and crass solution of things. God is such an obvious and crass solution; a solution which is a sheer indelicacy to us thinkers—at bottom He is really nothing but a coarse *commandment* against us: ye shall not think! . . . I am much more interested in another question—on which the "salvation of humanity" depends much more than upon any piece of theological curiosity: the question of nutrition. For ordinary purposes, it may be formulated thus: "How precisely must *thou* nourish thyself in order to attain to thy maximum of power, or *vertu* in the Renaissance style—of virtue free from moralism?" Here my experiences have been the worst possible; I am surprised that it took me so long to become aware of this question and to derive "understanding" from my experiences. Only the utter worthlessness of our German culture—its "idealism"—can to some extent explain how it was that precisely in this matter I was so backward that my ignorance was almost saintly. For this "culture" from first to last teaches one to lose sight of realities and instead to hunt after thoroughly problematic, so-called ideal goals, as, for instance, "classical culture"—as if we were not doomed from the start in our endeavor to unite "classical" and "German" in one concept! It is even a little comical—just try to picture a "classically cultured" citizen of Leipzig!—Indeed, I confess that up to a very mature age, my food was quite bad—expressed in moral terms, it was "impersonal," "selfless," "altruistic," to the glory of cooks and other fellow-Christians. For example, it was the Leipzig cookery, together with my first study of Schopenhauer (1865), that made me gravely renounce my "Will to Live." To become a malnutritient and to spoil one's stomach in the process—this problem seemed to me to be admirably solved by the above-mentioned cookery. (It is said that the year 1866 introduced changes into this department.) But as to German cookery in general—what has it not got on its conscience! Soup *before* the meal (still called *alla tedesca* in the sixteenth century Venetian cook-books; meat cooked till the flavor is gone, vegetables cooked with fat and flour; the degeneration of pastries into paper-weights! Add to this the utterly bestial post-prandial habits of the *ancients,* not merely of the ancient Germans, and you will begin to understand where German intellect had its origin—in a disordered intestinal tract. . . . German intellect is indigestion; it can assimilate nothing. But even English, which, as against German, and indeed French, diet, seems to me to be a "return to Nature"—that is to say, to cannibalism—is basically repugnant to my own instincts. It seems to me that it gives the intellect heavy feet, Englishwomen's feet. . . . The best cooking is that of Piedmont. Alcohol does not agree with me; one glass of wine or beer a day is enough to turn life into a valley of tears for me;—in Munich live my antipodes. Admitting that I came to understand this rationally rather late, yet I had *experienced* it as a mere child. As a boy I believed that wine-drinking and tobacco-smoking were at first but youthful vanities, and later simply bad habits. Perhaps the wine of Naumburg was partly responsible for this harsh judgment. To believe that wine was exhilarating, I should have had to be a Christian—in other words, I should have had to believe in what, for me, is an absurdity. Strangely enough, whereas small largely diluted quantities of alcohol depressed me, great quantities made me act almost like a sailor on shore leave. Even as a boy I showed my bravado in this respect. To compose and transcribe a long Latin essay in one night, ambitious of emulating with my pen the austerity and terseness of my model, Sallust, and to sprinkle the exercise with a few strong hot toddies—this procedure, while I was a pupil at the venerable old school of Pforta, did not disagree in the least with my physiology, nor perhaps with that of Sallust—however badly it may have agreed with dignified Pforta. Later on, towards the middle of my life, I grew more and more decisive in my opposition to spirituous drinks: I, an opponent of vegetarianism from experience—like Richard Wagner, who reconverted me—cannot with sufficient earnestness advise all more *spiritual* natures to abstain absolutely from alcohol. Water answers the same purpose. . . . I prefer those places where there are of the world about the concept "Truth"—with me spirit moves numerous opportunities of drinking from running brooks as at Nice, Turin, Sils, where water follows me wherever I turn. *In vino veritas:* it seems that here too I disagree with the rest on the face of the waters. . . . Here are a few more bits of advice taken from my morality. A heavy meal is digested more easily than one that is too meager. The first condition of a good digestion is that the stomach should be active as a whole. Therefore a man ought to know the size of his stomach. For the same reasons I advise against all those interminable meals, which I call interrupted sacrificial feasts, and which are to be had at any *table d'hôte*. Nothing between meals, no coffee— coffee makes one gloomy. Tea is advisable only in the morning —in small quantities, but very strong. It may be very harmful, and indispose you for the whole day, if it is the least bit too weak. Here each one has his own standard, often between the narrowest and most delicate limits. In a very enervating climate it is inadvisable to begin the day with tea: an hour before, it is a good thing to have a cup of thick cocoa, free from oil. Remain seated as little as possible; trust no thought that is not born in the open, to the accompaniment of free bodily motion

—nor one in which your very muscles do not celebrate a feast. All prejudices may be traced back to the intestines. A seden· tary life, as I have already said elsewhere, is the real sin against the Holy Ghost.

2

The question of nutrition is closely related to that of local· ity and climate. None of us can live anywhere; and he who has great tasks to perform, which demand all his energy, has, in this respect, a very limited choice. The influence of climate upon the bodily functions, affecting their retardation or ac· celeration, is so great, that a blunder in the choice of locality and climate may not merely alienate a man from his duty, but may withhold it from him altogether, so that he never comes face to face with it. Animal vigor never preponderates in him to the extent that it lets him attain that exuberant freedom in which he may say to himself: I, alone, can do that. . . . The slightest torpidity of the intestines, once it has become a habit, is quite sufficient to turn a genius into something mediocre, something "German"; the climate of Germany, alone, is more than enough to discourage the strongest and most heroic in· testines. Upon the tempo of the body's functions closely de· pend the agility or the slowness of the spirit's feet; indeed spirit itself is only a form of these bodily functions. Enumerate the places in which men of great intellect have been and are still found; where wit, subtlety, and malice are a part of happi· ness; where genius is almost necessarily at home: all of them have an unusually dry atmosphere. Paris, Provence, Florence, Jerusalem, Athens—these names prove this: that genius is de· pendent on dry air, on clear skies—in other words, on rapid organic functions, on the possibility of continuously securing for one's self great and even enormous quantities of energy. I have a case in mind where a man of significant and independent mentality became a narrow, craven specialist, and a crank, simply because he had no feeling for climate. I myself might have come to the same end, if illness had not forced me to reason, and to reflect upon reason realistically. Now long practice has taught me to read the effects of climatic and meteorological influences, from self-observation, as though from a very delicate and reliable instrument, so that I can calculate the change in the degree of atmospheric moisture by means of this physiological self-observation, even on so short a journey as that from Turin to Milan; accordingly I think with horror of the ghastly fact that my whole life, up to the last ten years—the most dangerous years—has always been spent in the wrong places, places that should have been precisely forbidden to me. Naumburg, Pforta, Thuringia in general, Leipzig, Basel, Venice—so many disastrous places for my constitution. If I have not a single happy memory of my childhood and youth, it would be foolish to account for this by so-called "moral" causes—as, for instance, the incontestable lack of sufficient companionship; for this lack is present today as it was before and it does not prevent me from being cheerful and brave. But it was ignorance of physiology—that confounded "Idealism"—that was the real curse of my life, the superfluous and stupid element in it; from which nothing good could develop, for which there can be no settlement and no compensation. The consequences of this "Idealism" explain all the blunders, the great aberrations of instinct, and the "modest specializations" which diverted me from my life-task; as, for instance, the fact that I became a philologist—why not at least a doctor or anything else that might have opened my eyes? During my stay at Basel, my whole intellectual routine, including my daily schedule, was an utterly senseless abuse of extraordinary powers, without any sort of compensation for the strength I spent, without even a thought of its exhaustion and the problem of replacement. I lacked that subtle egoism, the protection that an imperative instinct gives; I regarded all men as my equals, I was "disinterested," I forgot my distance from others—in short, I was in a condition for which I can never forgive myself. When I had almost reached the end, simply because I had almost reached it, I began to reflect upon the basic absurdity of my life—"Idealism." It was *illness* that first brought me to reason.

3

The choice of nutrition; the choice of climate and locality; the third thing in which one must not on any account make a blunder, concerns the method of *recuperation* or *recreation.* Here, again, according to the extent to which a spirit is *sui generis,* the limits of what is permitted—that is, beneficial to him—become more and more narrow. In my case, *reading* in general is one of my methods of recuperation; consequently it is a part of that which enables me to escape from myself, to wander in strange sciences and strange souls—of that, about which I am no longer in earnest. Indeed, reading allows me to recover from *my* earnestness. When I am deep in work, no books are to be seen near me; I carefully guard against allowing any one to speak or even to think in my presence. For that is what reading amounts to. . . . Has any one ever actually noticed, that, during that profound tension to which the state of pregnancy condemns the mind, and fundamentally, the whole organism, accident and every kind of external stimulus acts too vigorously and penetrates too deeply? One must avoid accident and external stimuli as far as possible: a sort of self-circumvallation is one of the first instinctive precautions of spiritual pregnancy. Shall I permit a strange thought to climb secretly over the wall? For that is just what reading would mean. . . . The periods of work and productivity are followed by periods of recuperation: to me, ye pleasant, intellectual, intelligent books! Shall it be a German book? . . . I must go back six months to catch myself with a book in my hand. What was it? An excellent study by Victor Brochard, *Les Sceptiques Grecques,* in reading which my Laertiana [1] was of great help to me. The skeptics!—the only *honorable* types among that double-faced, aye, quintuple-faced race, the philosophers! . . . Otherwise I almost always take refuge in the same books, few in number, books exactly fitting my needs. Perhaps it is not in my nature to read much, or variously: a library makes me ill. Neither is it my nature to love much or many kinds of things. Suspicion, even hostility towards new books is nearer to my instinct than "toleration," *largeur de cœur,* and other forms of "neighborly love." . . . Ultimately it is to a few old French authors that I return again and again; I believe only in French culture, and regard everything else in Europe which calls itself "culture" as pure misunderstanding. It is hardly necessary to speak of the German variety. . . . The few instances of higher culture I have encountered in Germany were all French in their origin, above all, Madame Cosima Wagner, who had by far the most superior judgment in matters of taste that I have ever heard. Even if I do not read, but literally love Pascal, as the most instructive sacrifice to Christianity, killing himself slowly, first in body, then in mind in accord with the logic of this most horrible form of inhuman

---

[1] The reference here is to a prize essay, *De fontibus Diogenis Laertii,* written when Nietzsche was twenty-three.—Tr.

cruelty; even if I have something of Montaigne's malice in my soul, and—who knows?—perhaps in my body, too; even if my artist's taste endeavors to protect the names of Molière, Corneille, and Racine, not without bitterness, against a wild genius like Shakespeare—all this does not prevent me from regarding even the modern Frenchmen as charming companions also. I can imagine no century in history in which a netful of more inquisitive and at the same time more subtle psychologists could be drawn up together than in present-day Paris. I will name a few at random—for their number is by no means small—Paul Bourget, Pierre Loti, Gyp, Meilhac, Anatole France, Jules Lemaître; or, singling out one of strong race, a genuine Latin, of whom I am particularly fond, Guy de Maupassant. Between ourselves, I prefer this generation even to its great masters, all of whom were corrupted by German philosophy (Taine, for instance, by Hegel, whom he has to thank for his misunderstanding of great men and great ages). Wherever Germany penetrates, she corrupts culture. It was the war which first "redeemed" the spirit of France. . . . Stendhal is one of the happiest accidents of my life—for everything epochal in that life came to me by accident, never by recommendation—Stendhal is quite priceless, with his anticipatory psychologist's eye; with his grasp of facts, reminiscent of the greatest of all masters of facts (*ex ungue Napoleoneum*); and, last, but not least, as an honest atheist—a specimen both rare and difficult to discover in France—all honor to Prosper Mérimée! . . . Perhaps I am even envious of Stendhal? He robbed me of the best atheistic joke I of all people could have made: "God's only excuse is that He does not exist." . . . I myself have said somewhere—What hitherto has been the greatest objection to Life?—God. . . .

4

It was Heinrich Heine who gave me the highest conception of a lyrical poet. I search vainly through the kingdoms of all the ages for anything to equal his sweet and passionate music. He possessed that divine wickedness, without which I cannot conceive of perfection; I value men and races, according to the necessity they have to imagine a god partaking of the nature of the satyr. And how masterfully he handles German! Some day men will declare of Heine and myself that we were by far the greatest of all artists in the German language; that we out-stripped incalculably all that pure Germans could do with this language. I must be profoundly related to Byron's *Manfred:* I discovered all his abysses in my own soul—at thirteen I was ripe for this book. Words fail me, I have merely a glance of contempt for those who dare to mention *Faust* in the presence of *Manfred*. The Germans are *incapable* of a conception of greatness—witness Schumann! Angry at this cloying Saxon, I once composed a counter-overture to *Manfred,* of which Hans von Bülow declared he had never seen the like before on paper: it was a sheer violation of Euterpe. Seeking for my highest formula for Shakespeare, I invariably find only this: he conceived the type of Cæsar. Such things a man cannot guess —he either is the thing, or he is not. The great poet draws only from his own experience—to such an extent that later he can no longer endure his own work. . . . After glancing at my *Zarathustra,* I pace to and fro in my room for a half hour, unable to control an unbearable fit of sobbing. I know of no more heart-rending reading than Shakespeare: what he must have suffered to be so much in need of playing the clown! Is Hamlet *understood?* Not doubt but certainty drives one mad.

. . . But to feel this, one must be profound, abysmal, a philosopher. . . . We all fear the truth. . . . And, to make a
confession: I feel instinctively certain that Lord Bacon is the
originator, the self-torturer, of this most appalling literature:
what do I care about the wretched gabble of American fools
and half-wits? But the power for the greatest realism in vision
is not only compatible with the greatest realism in deeds, with
the monstrous, with crime—*it actually presupposes the latter*.
. . . We hardly know enough about Lord Bacon—the first
realist in the highest sense of the word—to be sure of everything he did, everything he willed, and everything he experienced in himself. . . . To the devil with the critics! Suppose
I had christened my *Zarathustra* with a name not my own—
with Richard Wagner's, for instance—the insight of two thousand years would not have sufficed to guess that the author of
Human, all-too-Human was the visionary of *Zarathustra*.

5

In speaking of the recreations of my life, I must express a
word or two of gratitude for the one which has afforded me by
far the greatest and heartiest refreshment. This was undoubtedly my intimate relationship with Richard Wagner. I pass
over my other relationships with men quite lightly; but at no
price would I have my life deprived of those days at Tribschen
—days of confidence, of cheerfulness, of sublime flashes, and
of profound moments. I know not what Wagner may have
been for others; but no cloud ever obscured *our* sky. And this
brings me back again to France—I have no quarrel with
Wagnerites, and *hoc genus omne,* who think to honor Wagner
by believing him to be like themselves; for such people I have

[*843*]

only a contemptuous curl of my lip. With my nature, so alien
to everything Teutonic that the mere presence of a German retards my digestion, my first contact with Wagner was also the
first moment in my life in which I breathed freely: I felt him,
I honored him, as a foreigner, as the antithesis of and incarnate protest against all "German virtues." We who as children breathed the marshy atmosphere of the fifties, are necessarily pessimists with regard to the idea "German"; we can be
nothing else but revolutionaries—we can give our assent to no
state of affairs in which a hypocrite is at the top. It is a matter
of indifference to me whether this hypocrite acts in different
colors to-day, whether he dresses in scarlet or dons the uniform
of a hussar.[2] Very good, then! Wagner, too, was a revolutionary—he fled from the Germans. . . . The artist has no
home in Europe except in Paris; that subtlety of all the five
senses which is the condition of Wagner's art, that sensitivity
to the nuance, to psychological morbidity—these are to be
found only in Paris. Nowhere else is there this passion for
problems of form, this seriousness about the *mise-en-scène,*
which is the Parisian seriousness *par excellence.* In Germany
one can have no notion of the tremendous ambition that lives
in the soul of a Parisian artist. The German is good-natured.
Wagner was by no means good-natured. . . . But I have
already said enough on the subject of Wagner's attachments
(see *Beyond Good and Evil,* Aphorism 269), and about those
to whom he is most closely related. He is one of the late French
romanticists, that high-soaring and heaven-aspiring band of
artists, like Delacroix and Berlioz, who are essentially sick and
incurable, pure fanatics of *expression,* virtuosos through and
through. . . . Who was the first intelligent follower of

---

[2] This was the favorite uniform of the ex-Kaiser.—Tr.

[*844*]

Wagner? Charles Baudelaire, the same man who was the first to understand Delacroix—that typical decadent, in whom a whole generation of artists has recognized itself; he was perhaps the last of them too. . . . What is it that I have never forgiven Wagner? The fact that he condescended to the Germans—that he became a German Imperialist. . . . Wherever Germany spreads, she corrupts culture.

6

All things considered, I could never have survived my youth without Wagnerian music. For I seemed condemned to the society of Germans. If a man wishes to rid himself of a feeling of unbearable oppression, he may have to take to hashish. Well, I had to take to Wagner. Wagner is the counter-poison to everything essentially German—he is a poison, I do not deny it. From the moment that *Tristan* was arranged for the piano—my compliments, Herr von Bülow!—I was a Wagnerite. I deemed Wagner's previous works beneath me—they were too common, too "German." . . . But to this day I am still looking for a work to equal *Tristan* in dangerous fascination, that gruesome yet sweet quality of infinity; I seek among all the arts in vain. All the bizarreries of Leonardo da Vinci lose their charm with the first note of *Tristan*. It is absolutely Wagner's *non plus ultra;* the *Mastersingers* and the *Ring* were mere relaxation to him. To become more healthy—this is a step backwards for a nature like Wagner's. I regard it as a first-class bit of good luck to have lived at the right time, and to have lived precisely among Germans, in order to be ripe for this work: so strongly in me works the curiosity of the psychologist. The world must be a poor thing for him who has never been unhealthy enough for this "voluptuousness of Hell": it is allowable, it is even imperative, that one here employ a mystic formula. I suppose I know better than any one else the prodigies of which Wagner was capable, the fifty worlds of strange ecstasies to reach which no one but he had wings strong enough; and as I am today sufficiently powerful to turn even the most dubious and dangerous things to my own advantage, and thus to grow more powerful, I name Wagner as the greatest benefactor of my life. The bond which unites us is the fact that we have suffered greater agony, even at each other's hands, than most men of this century are able to bear; and this will associate our names forever. For, just as Wagner is merely a misunderstanding among Germans, so surely am I, and ever will be. You must first have two centuries of psychological and artistic discipline, my dear countrymen! . . . But you can never turn back the hands of the clock.

7

To the most exceptional of my readers I should like to say just a word as to what I really demand of music. It should be cheerful and yet profound, like an October afternoon. It should be unique, wanton, and tender, and like a dainty, sweet woman in roguishness and grace. . . . I shall never admit that a German *can* understand what music is. Those musicians, the greatest of them, who are called German, are all foreigners, Slavs, Croats, Italians, Dutchmen—or Jews; or else, like Heinrich Schütz, Bach, and Handel, they are Germans of a strong race, a type now extinct. I myself have still enough of the Pole in me to let all other music go, if only Chopin is left to me. For three reasons I would except Wagner's *Siegfried Idyll*, and perhaps also a few things of Liszt, who excelled all other musicians in the noble accent of his orchestration; and finally everything that has come from beyond the Alps—*this side* of the Alps. I would not know how to dispense with Rossini, and still less with my Southern counterpart in music, my Venetian maestro, Pietro Gasti. And when I say beyond the Alps, I really mean only Venice. Seeking to find another word for music, I inevitably come back to Venice. I do not know how to make a distinction between tears and music. I do not know how to think of joy, or of the south, without a shudder of fear.

> On the bridge I stood
> But lately, in the dark night.
> From far away came the sound of singing;
> In golden drops it rolled away
> Over the glittering rim.
>
> Gondolas, lights, music
> Drunk, swam far out in the darkness. . . .
> My soul, a stringed instrument,
> Invisibly moved,
> Sang a gondola song secretly,
> Gleaming in bright happiness.
> —Did any hearken?

8

In all these things—the choice of food, locality, climate, and recreation—the instinct of self-preservation dominates, expressing itself with least ambiguity in the form of an instinct of self-defense. To limit what one hears and sees, to detach one's self from many things—this is elementary prudence, the first proof that a man is not an accident but a necessity. The customary word for this instinct of self-defense is *taste*. It is imperative not only to say "no" where "yes" would indicate "disinterestedness," but even to say "no" *as seldom as possible*. One must separate from anything that forces one to repeat "no," again and again. The reason for this is that all expenditures of defensive energy, however slight, involve enormous and absolutely superfluous losses when they become regular and habitual. Our greatest expenditure of energy is comprised of these small frequent discharges of it. To preserve one's self intact, to hold things at a distance—do not deceive yourselves on this point!—is an expenditure of energy and one directed towards purely negative ends. The mere constant necessity of being on his guard may weaken a man so much that he can no longer defend himself. Suppose I were to step out of my house, and, instead of the quiet and aristocratic city of Turin, I were to find a German provincial town; my instinct would have to pull itself together to repel everything that would invade it from this downtrodden, cowardly world. Or suppose I found a German metropolis—that structure of vice in which nothing grows, but where every single thing, good or bad, is imported. Would I not have to become a hedgehog? [3] But to have quills amounts to a squandering of strength; a two-fold luxury, for, if we chose, we could dispense with them and open our hands instead. . . .

Another form of prudence and self-defense consists in reacting as seldom as possible, and in detaching one's self from those circumstances and conditions which condemn one, as it were, to suspend one's "liberty" and initiative, and become a

[3] The reference, of course, is to Schopenhauer's well-known simile likening men to porcupines whose gregarious tendency drives them together, and whose quills drive them apart again.—Tr.

mere bundle of reactions. A good type of this is furnished by intercourse with books. The scholar who actually does little else than welter in a sea of books—the average philologist may handle two hundred a day—finally loses completely the ability to think for himself. He cannot think unless he has a book in his hands. When he thinks, he responds to a stimulus (a thought he has read)—and finally all he does is react. The scholar devotes all his energy to affirming or denying or criticizing matter which has already been thought out—he no longer thinks himself. . . . In him the instinct of self-defense has decayed, otherwise he would defend himself against books. The scholar is a decadent. With my own eyes I have seen gifted, richly-endowed, free-spirited natures already "read to pieces" at thirty—nothing but matches that have to be struck before they can emit any sparks—or "thoughts." To read a book early in the morning, at daybreak, in the vigor and dawn of one's strength—this is sheer viciousness!

9

At this point I can no longer evade a direct answer to the question, *how one becomes what one is*. And here I touch upon the master stroke of the art of self-preservation—*selfishness*. . . . If we assume that one's life-task—the determination and the fate of one's life-task—appreciably surpasses the average measure, nothing would be more dangerous than to come face to face with one's self by the side of this life-task. The fact that one becomes what one is, presupposes that one has not the remotest suspicion of what one is. From this standpoint a unique meaning and value is given to even the blunders of one's life, the temporary deviations and aberrations, the hesitations, the timidities, the earnestness wasted upon tasks remote from the central one. In these matters there is opportunity for great wisdom, perhaps even the highest wisdom; in circumstances, where *nosce teipsum* would be the passport to ruin, the forgetting of one's self, the misunderstanding, the belittling, the narrowing and the mediocratizing of one's self, amount to reason itself. In moral terms: to love one's neighbor and to live for others and for other things *may* be the means of protection for the maintenance of the most rigorous egoism. This is the exceptional case in which I, contrary to my custom and conviction, take the side of the "selfless" tendencies, for here they are engaged in the service of selfishness and self-discipline. The whole surface of consciousness—for consciousness *is* a surface—must be kept free of any of the great imperatives. Beware even of every striking word, of every striking gesture! They all lead to the dangerous possibility that the instinct may "understand itself" too soon. Meanwhile the organizing "idea," destined to mastery, continues to grow in the depths—it begins to command, it leads you slowly back from your deviations and aberrations, it makes ready individual qualities and capacities, which will some day make themselves felt as indispensable to the whole of your task—gradually it cultivates all the serviceable faculties before it ever whispers a word concerning the dominant task, the "goal," the "purpose," and the "meaning." Viewed from this angle, my life is simply amazing. For the task of *transvaluing values,* more abilities were necessary perhaps than could ever be found combined in one individual; and above all, opposed abilities which must yet not be mutually inimical and destructive. An order of rank among capacities; distance; the art of separating without creating hostility; to confuse nothing; to reconcile nothing; to be tremendously various and yet to be the reverse of chaos—all this was the first condition, the long secret work and artistry of my instinct. Its superior guardian-ship manifested itself so powerfully that at no time did I have any intimation of what was growing within me—until sud-denly all my capacities were ripe, and one day burst forth in full perfection. I can recall no instance of my ever having exerted myself, there is no evidence of *struggle* in my life; I am the reverse of a heroic nature. To "will" something, to "strive" after something, to have a "purpose" or a "desire" in my mind—I know none of these things from experience. At this very moment I look out upon my future—a *broad* future! —as upon a calm sea: no longing disturbs its serenity. I have not the slightest wish that anything should be different than it is: I myself do not wish to be different. . . . I have always been this way. I have never had a desire. A man who, after his forty-fourth year, can say that he has never troubled himself about *honors, women,* or *money!*—not that they were lacking to me. . . . It was in this way, for example, that one day I became a University Professor—such an idea had never even entered my head, for I was hardly twenty-four. In the same way, two years before, I had one day become a philologist, in the sense that my *first* philological work,[4] my start in every way, was requested by my master, Ritschl, for publication in his *Rheinisches Museum.* (Ritschl—I say it in all reverence— was the only genial scholar I have ever known. He possessed that engaging depravity which distinguishes us Thuringians, and which can make even a German sympathetic—even to arrive at truth we prefer roundabout ways. These words should not be taken as a deprecation in any sense of my Thuringian co-dweller, the intelligent Leopold von Ranke. . . .)

---

[4] The reference here is to Nietzsche's essay on Diogenes Laertius. See note on p. 840.—Tr.

10

The question will be raised why I should actually have related all these trivial and, judged according to ordinary standards, insignificant details. I would seem to be hurting my own cause, more particularly if I am destined to assume great tasks. I reply that these trivial details—diet, locality, climate, recreation, the whole casuistry of self-love—are inconceivably more important than everything men have hitherto considered essential. It is just here that we must begin to learn afresh. All the things men have valued with such earnestness heretofore are not even realities; they are mere fantasies, or, more strictly speaking, *lies* arising from the evil instincts of diseased and, in the deepest sense, harmful natures—all the concepts, "God," "soul," "virtue," "sin," "Beyond," "truth," "eternal life." . . . And yet men sought in them for the greatness of human nature, its "divinity." . . . All questions of politics, of the social order, of education, have been falsified from top to bottom, because the most harmful men have been taken for great men, and because people were taught to despise the "details," more properly, the fundamentals of life. If I now compare myself with those creatures who have hitherto been honored as the first among men, the difference becomes obvious. I do not consider these so-called "first" men as human beings—for me they are the excrement of mankind, the products of disease and the instinct of revenge: they are so many monsters, rotten, utterly incurable, avenging themselves on life. . . . I would be their very opposite. It is my privilege to be extremely sensitive to any sign of healthy instincts. There is not a morbid trait in me; even in times of serious illness I have never become morbid; you will look in vain for a trace of fanaticism in my nature. No one can point out a single moment of my life in which I have assumed either an arrogant or a pathetic attitude. Pathetic attitudes do not belong to greatness; he who needs attitudes is false. . . . Beware of all picturesque men! Life came most easily to me when it demanded the greatest labor from me. Whoever could have seen me during the seventy days of this autumn, when, without interruption, with a sense of responsibility to posterity, I performed so much work of the highest type—work no man did before or will do after me—would have noticed no sign of tension in me, but on the contrary exuberant freshness and gayety. Never have my meals been more enjoyable, never has my sleep been better. I know of no other manner of dealing with great tasks than as *play:* this, as a sign of greatness, is an essential pre-requisite. The slightest constraint, a gloomy appearance, any hard accent in the voice—all these things are objections to a man, but how much more to his work! . . . One must have no nerves. . . . Even to *suffer* from solitude is an objection —the only thing I have always suffered from is "multitude," the infinite variety of my own soul. At the absurdly tender age of seven, I already knew that no human speech would ever reach me: did any one ever see me disconsolate therefor? To-day I still possess the same affability towards everybody, I am even full of consideration for the humblest: in all this there is not an ounce of arrogance or contempt. He whom I despise divines the fact that I despise him; my mere existence angers those who have bad blood in their veins. My formula for great-ness in man is *amor fati:* that a man should wish to have noth-ing altered, either in the future, the past, or for all eternity. Not only must he endure necessity, and on no account conceal it—all idealism is falsehood in the face of necessity—but he must *love* it. . . .

[*853*]

Why I Write Such Excellent Books

1

I AM one thing, my writings are another. Here, before I speak of the books themselves, I shall touch upon the question of the understanding and misunderstanding they have received. I shall do this with no more thoroughness than is necessary; for the time has by no means come for this question. My time has not yet come either; some people are born posthumously. At some time or other a need will be felt for institutions in which men will live and teach, as I understand living and teaching; perhaps, too, that day will witness the endowment of chairs for the interpretation of *Zarathustra.* But it would be an utter contradiction of myself to expect to find any welcome for my truth today: the fact that today no one listens to me, that no one knows how to receive what I have to offer, is not only comprehensible but quite proper. I do not wish to be mistaken for another—consequently I must not mistake myself. Let me say again that I can point to few instances of ill-will in my life: and as for literary ill-will, I can mention hardly a single example of it. On the other hand, I have met with far too much *pure foolishness!* . . . It seems to me that to take up one of my books is one of the highest distinctions a man can confer on himself—even assuming that he removed his shoes beforehand, not to mention his boots. . . . When

on one occasion Dr. Heinrich von Stein complained frankly
that he could not understand a word of my *Zarathustra,* I said
to him that this was just as it should be: to have understood six
sentences in that book—that is to say, to have lived them—
raises a man to a higher plane among mortals than "modern"
men can attain. With this feeling of distance, how could I even
wish to be read by the "moderns" whom I know! My triumph
is the very reverse of Schopenhauer's—I say *"Non* legor, *non*
legar."* Not that I should like to deprecate the amusement I
have frequently derived from the innocence with which my
works have been contradicted. As late as last summer, at a
time when I was trying, perhaps by means of my weighty, all-
too-weighty, literature, to throw the rest of literature off its
balance, one of the professors in the University of Berlin
kindly gave me to understand that I ought really to use a different form: no one could read that sort of thing. Finally, it
was not Germany, but Switzerland, that presented me with the
two most extreme cases. An essay on *Beyond Good and Evil,*
by Dr. V. Widmann, in the *Bund,* headed "Nietzsche's Dangerous Book," and a general account of all my works, by Herr
Karl Spitteler, also in the *Bund,* were high points in my life—
I shall not say of what. . . . For example, the latter treated
my *Zarathustra* as *"advanced exercises in style,"* and expressed
the hope that later on I might give a thought to content also;
Dr. Widmann expressed the respect he felt for the courage
I showed in my endeavors to renounce all decent feelings.
Thanks to a little trick of fate, every sentence in these criticisms seemed, with a consistency that I could not but admire,
to be an inverted truth. In fact it seemed that all one had to
do was to "transvalue all values," and, in the most remarkable
manner, one hit the nail on the head with regard to me, instead
of striking my head with the nail. . . . I am all the more

anxious therefore to arrive at an explanation. After all, no one can draw more out of things, books included, than he already knows. A man has ears only for such things to which experience has given him access. Let us take an extreme case: suppose a book speaks only of experiences which lie entirely outside the range of general or even exceptional knowledge—suppose it to be the *first* expression of an entirely new series of experiences. In this case nothing it contains will really be heard at all, and, by an acoustic delusion, people will assume that where nothing is heard there is nothing to hear. . . . This, at any rate, has been my ordinary experience, and indicates, if you will, its originality. He who thought he had understood something in my work, had interpreted something in it according to his own image—not infrequently the very opposite of myself, an "idealist," for instance. He who understood nothing in my work, denied me any consideration at all. The word "Superman," designating a type of man whose appearance would be a piece of the greatest good fortune, a type opposed to "modern" men, to "good" men, to Christians and other nihilists—a word which in the mouth of *Zarathustra*, the destroyer of morality, becomes profoundly significant—this word is understood almost everywhere, and with perfect innocence, to correspond to those values of which *Zarathustra* is a flat repudiation—he was considered as an "ideal" type, a higher kind of man, half "saint," half "genius." . . . Other learned cattle have suspected me of Darwinism on account of this word: even the "hero worship" of that great unconscious and involuntary swindler, Carlyle—a worship I repudiated with malice—was recognized in my doctrine. If I had intimated to some one that he would do better to seek for the Superman in a Cæsar Borgia than in a Parsifal, he would not have believed his ears. I will have to be forgiven my complete lack of curiosity with regard to criticisms of my books, more particularly newspaper criticisms. My friends and publishers know this, and never speak to me of things like this. In one particular case, I once saw all the sins that had been committed against a single book—it was *Beyond Good and Evil;* I could tell you a nice story about it. Is it possible that the *National-Zeitung*—a Prussian paper (I mention this for the sake of my foreign readers—for my own part, I beg to state, I read only the *Journal des Débats*)—should seriously regard the book as a "sign of the times," as a genuine example of Junkerism, for which the *Kreuz-Zeitung* [1] had not sufficient courage?

2

This is true only of Germans: for everywhere else I have readers—all of them exceptional intelligences, natures tested and tried, reared in high offices, amid superior duties; I have even real geniuses among my readers. In Vienna, in St. Petersburg, in Stockholm, in Copenhagen, in Paris, and New York —I have been discovered everywhere: except in Europe's flatland—Germany. . . . And, to tell the truth, I rejoice much more over those who do not read me, over those who have never even heard either of my name or of the word philosophy. But wherever I go, here in Turin, for instance, every face brightens and relaxes at the sight of me. A thing that has flattered me more than anything else hitherto is the fact that old market-women cannot rest until they have picked out the sweetest of their grapes for me. To this extent must a man be a philosopher. . . . It is not in vain that the Poles are called

---

[1] The organ of the Junker party.—Tr.

the Frenchmen of the Slavic peoples. A charming Russian lady will never for a moment mistake my origin. I am not successful at being pompous, the best I can do is to appear embarrassed. . . . I can think in German, I can feel in German—I can do most things; but *that* is beyond my powers. . . . My old master, Ritschl, even used to observe that I conceived my very philological treatises like a Parisian novelist—that I made them absurdly thrilling. In Paris itself people are surprised at *"toutes mes audaces et finesses"*—to use Taine's expression—I fear that even in the highest forms of the dithyramb my work will be seasoned with that salt which never becomes insipid, which never becomes "German"—I mean wit. . . . I can do nought else. God help me! Amen.—We all know, some of us even from experience, what a "long-ears" is. Well, then, I dare to assert that I have the smallest of all ears. This interests women not a little—it seems to me they feel that I understand them better. . . . I am the anti-ass *par excellence,* and on this account alone a monster in the world's history—in Greek, and not only in Greek, I am the *Antichrist.*

3

I know quite well my privileges as a writer: in one or two instances it has even been made apparent to me how very much the habitual reading of my works "spoils" a man's taste. Other books simply cannot be endured, least of all books of philosophy. It is an incomparable distinction to enter this noble and subtle world—to do so one must certainly not be a German; it is, in short, a distinction one must have deserved. He, however, who is akin to me in grandeur of will experiences genuine raptures of understanding in my books: for I descend from heights into which no bird has ever soared; I know abysses into which no foot has ever slipped. I have been told that once begun it is impossible to relinquish a book of mine—that I disturb even the night's rest. . . . There is no prouder or at the same time more subtle sort of books: occasionally they attain the highest point possible to humans, cynicism; to master them a man must have the most delicate fingers as well as the boldest fists. Any spiritual weakness is fatal to them—even any dyspepsia: a man must have no nerves, but he must have a cheerful belly. Not only the poverty and limitation of a man's soul is fatal to them, but also, and to a much greater degree, cowardice, uncleanliness, and secret intestinal revengefulness; a word from me is enough to drive all the evil instincts into a face. Among my acquaintances I have a number of experimental subjects, who offer me the opportunity of seeing all the different, instructively different, reactions to my works. Those who will have nothing to do with the contents of my books, my so-called friends, for example, are quite "impersonal": they congratulate me on the appearance of another work, and also on the progress indicated by a greater cheerfulness of tone. . . . The thoroughly vicious spirits, the "beautiful souls," the false from top to toe, have not the slightest notion as to how to receive my books—consequently, with the beautiful consistency of all beautiful souls, they scorn my work as beneath their notice. The cattle among my acquaintances, the mere Germans, give me to understand, if you please, that they are not always of my opinion, although occasionally, etc., etc. . . . I have even heard this sort of thing said about *Zarathustra*. "Feminism," in mankind as in man, is also a barrier to my writings; with it, no one shall ever enter this labyrinth of fearless knowledge. A man must never have spared himself, he must have been vigorous in his habits, in order to be good-humored and gay among so many hard truths. In picturing the perfect reader, I always imagine a monster of courage and curiosity, as well as of suppleness, cunning, and prudence—a born adventurer and explorer. After all, I cannot do better than use *Zarathustra* to indicate to whom I address myself fundamentally: to whom alone does he wish to reveal his riddle?

"Unto you, daring explorers and experimenters, and unto all who have ever embarked beneath cunning sails upon terrible seas;

"Unto you who revel in riddles and in twilight, whose souls are lured by flutes unto every treacherous abyss:

"For ye care not to grope your way along a thread with craven fingers; and where ye are able to *guess*, ye hate to *argue.*"

4

I would now like to make a few general observations about my *art of style.* To communicate a state, an inner tension of pathos by means of signs, including the tempo of these signs —this is the meaning of every style; and since the multiplicity of inner states in me is enormous, I am capable of many kinds of style—in short, of the most varied art of style that any man has ever had at his disposal. Any style is *good* which really communicates an inner state, which does not blunder over the signs, over the tempo of the signs, or over *gestures*—all rhetoric is merely the art of gesture. In this respect my instinct is infallible. A good style, *per se,* is nonsense, mere idealism, like "beauty in itself," for instance, or "goodness in itself," or "the thing-in-itself." This assumes that there are ears to hear, that there are men who are capable and worthy of a like pathos, that there is no lack of those to whom one may communicate one's self. In the meantime my *Zarathustra*, for instance, is still looking for such people—alas! he will have to seek a long while yet! A man must be worthy to know him. . . . And, until that time comes, there will be no one who will understand the art I have lavished on the book. No one has ever had more novel, original, and purposely created art-forms to squander. It remained to be proved that such things were possible in the German language; formerly, I myself would have been utterly skeptical. Before my time people did not know what could be done with the German language— what could be done with language in general. The art of grand rhythm, or grand style in phrasing, for the expression of the tremendous fluctuations of sublime and superhuman passion, was first discovered by me: with a dithyramb such as "The Seven Seals," at the end of the third part of *Zarathustra*, I soared a thousand miles above all that had hitherto been called poetry.

5

The fact that my works bespeak a psychologist who has not his peer, is probably the first discovery a good reader will make —that is to say, a reader such as I deserve, one who reads me as the good old philologists used to read their Horace. Those very propositions everybody—not to mention fashionable philosophers, moralists and other empty-headed and cabbage-brained people—agree on, seem to me merely naïve blunders: as, for example, the belief that "altruistic" and "egoistic" are antithetical, when the "ego" itself is nothing but a "refined swindle," an "ideal." . . . Actions are neither egoistic nor altruistic: both concepts are psychological nonsense. Or the proposition that "man pursues happiness"; or that "happiness is the reward of virtue." . . . Or that "pleasure and pain are opposites." . . . Morality, the Circe of mankind, has falsified everything psychological, from beginning to end; it has demoralized everything, even to the terrible nonsense of making love "altruistic." A man must be firm, he must stand securely on his two legs,—otherwise he cannot love at all. Indeed the girls know this only too well: they don't care a straw for unselfish, purely objective men. . . . May I venture to suggest, by the way, that I know women? That is part of my Dionysian patrimony. Who knows? Perhaps I am the first psychologist of the eternal feminine. They all like me. . . . That's an old story; save, of course, the abortions among them, the "emancipated" ones, unable to have children. Fortunately I am not willing to let myself be torn to pieces! The perfect woman tears you to pieces when she loves you: I know these amiable Mænads. . . . What a dangerous, creeping, subterranean little beast of prey! And so agreeable at the same time! . . . A little woman, bent on revenge, would annihilate Destiny itself. Woman is indescribably more wicked than man, and cleverer also. In a woman goodness is already a sign of *degeneration*. All so-called "beautiful souls" have their origin in some physiological trouble—but I say no more, lest I become medicynical. The struggle for equal rights is definitely a symptom of disease; every doctor knows this. The more womanly a woman is, the more she fights tooth and nail against rights in general: the natural order of things, the eternal war between the sexes, assigns to her by far the foremost rank. Have people listened to my definition of love? It is the only one worthy of a philosopher. Love's methods are war; love's basis is the mortal hatred between the sexes. Have you heard my answer to the question how a woman can be cured, "re-deemed"?— Give her a child! A woman needs children, man is always only a means; thus spake Zarathustra. "The emancipation of women,"—this is the instinctive hatred of degenerate—that is, barren—women for those who are healthy: the battle against "man" is always only a means, a pretext, a tactical move. In their efforts to rise to the "Ideal Woman *per se*," to the "Higher Woman," to the "Ideal Woman," all they really wish to do is to lower the general level of women: and there are no more certain means to this end than university education, trousers, and the rights of voting like cattle. Fundamentally, the emancipated are the anarchists in the world of the "eternal feminine," the misbegotten whose most deep-rooted instinct is revenge. A whole species of the most malicious "idealism"—which, by the bye, also appears in men, in Henrik Ibsen for instance, that typical old maid—has as its object to poison the clear conscience, the natural element in sexual love. . . . And in order to leave no doubt as to my opinion, which in this matter is as honest as it is severe, I will tell you one more clause out of my moral code against vice— with the word "vice" I combat every kind of unnatural practice, or, if you prefer fine words, idealism. The clause reads: "The preaching of chastity is a public incitement to unnatural practices. Every depreciation of the sexual life, every sullying of it with the concept 'impure,' is the essential crime against Life—is the essential sin against Life's Holy Ghost."

6

That you may get some notion of myself as a psychologist, I shall abstract the following curious piece of psychological analysis from my book *Beyond Good and Evil.* In passing, I may state that I forbid any speculation as to the person described in this passage. "The genius of the heart, as that great mysterious one possesses it, the tempter-god and born rat-catcher of consciences, whose voice can descend into the nether-world of every soul, who neither speaks a word nor casts a glance, in which there may not be some motive or touch of allurement, to whose perfection it pertains that he knows how to appear,—not as he is, but in a guise which acts as an additional constraint on his followers to press ever closer to him, to follow him more cordially and thoroughly;—the genius of the heart, which imposes silence and attention on everything loud and self-conceited, which smooths rough souls and makes them taste a new longing—to lie placid as a mirror, that the deep heavens may be reflected in them;—the genius of the heart which teaches the clumsy and too hasty hand to hesitate and to grasp more delicately; which scents the hidden and forgotten treasure, the drop of goodness and sweet spirituality, under thick dark ice, and is a divining rod for every grain of gold, long buried and imprisoned in mud and sand;—the genius of the heart, from contact with which every one goes away richer; not favored, or surprised, not as though gratified and oppressed by the good things of others; but richer in himself, newer than before, broken up, blown upon, and sounded by a thawing wind; more uncertain, perhaps, more delicate, more fragile, more bruised, but full of hopes which as yet lack names, full of a new will and current, full of a new ill-will and counter-current." . . . [2]

---

[2] *Beyond Good and Evil,* Modern Library Edition, pp. 608-609.

"*The Birth of Tragedy*"

1

To do justice to *The Birth of Tragedy* (1872) certain things will have to be forgotten. Its very errors produced a great effect, and account for the fascination it contained. By these errors I mean my treatment of Wagnerism, as if the latter were the symptom of an ascending tendency. On that account alone, this essay was an event in Wagner's life: from that time on the greatest hopes were associated with his name. In connection with *Parsifal*, people to this very day sometimes remind me that the responsibility is essentially mine, for the prevalent opinion, that this movement is of great value to culture. I often found that people quoted the book as "The Rebirth of Tragedy from the Spirit of Music": they were on the lookout only for a new formula for Wagner's art, aims, and mission—and thus the fundamental importance hidden in the book was quite overlooked. "Hellenism and Pessimism" would have been a less ambiguous title. It would have indicated that the book contains the first attempt to show how the Greeks succeeded in disposing of pessimism—how they overcame it. . . . Tragedy is the very proof of the fact that the Greeks were not pessimists: Schopenhauer was mistaken here as he was in everything else. Viewed impartially, *The Birth of Tragedy* came at a most inopportune time. No one would dream that it was begun amid the thunder of the battle of Wörth. I thought out these problems on cold September nights beneath the walls of Metz, while serving as a hospital nurse; one would much sooner believe it to have been written fifty years before. It is quite indifferent to politics—"un-German," people would say nowadays—there is a strong smell of Hegel about it; only a few of the formulæ are pervaded with that bitter odor of corpses peculiar to Schopenhauer. An idea—the opposition of the Dionysian and the Apollonian conceptions—is translated into metaphysics; history itself is treated as the development of this idea; in tragedy this opposition merges into a higher unity; from this standpoint things which had previously never been juxtaposed are suddenly brought face to face, with the result that they illuminate and clarify each other (Opera and Revolution, for instance). . . . The two distinct innovations in the book are, first, the comprehension of the *Dionysian* phenomenon among the Greeks—for the first time, it offers a psychological analysis of this phenomenon, viewing it as the single basis of all Greek art. The second innovation lies in the interpretation of Socratism—Socrates being recognized for the first time as the instrument of Greek decline, as the type of decadence. "Reason" *versus* Instinct. "Reason" at any rate, as a dangerous, life-undermining force. The whole book is marked by a profoundly hostile silence concerning Christianity: the latter is neither Apollonian nor Dionysian; it denies all esthetic values—the only values recognized by *The Birth of Tragedy*. In the deepest sense, it is nihilistic, whereas in the Dionysian symbol, the most extreme limits of affirmation are reached. Only once is the Christian priesthood alluded to as a "malignant sort of dwarfs," as "subterraneans."

2

This, my first effort, was remarkable beyond measure. I had revealed to my inmost experience the only symbolic image that history offers,—and so I was the first to comprehend the wonderful phenomenon of the Dionysian. At the same time, by recognizing Socrates as a decadent, I proved quite unequivocally that the sureness of my psychological grasp would encounter but small danger at the hands of any sort of moral idiosyncrasy: to view morality itself as a symptom of decadence is an innovation, a unique event of the first order in the history of knowledge. How high my dual concept enabled me to rise above the pitiful empty gabble about Optimism and Pessimism! I was the first to see the essential opposition: the degenerate instinct which turns upon life with a subterranean desire for vengeance (Christianity, Schopenhauer's philosophy, in a sense even Plato's philosophy—in short, the whole of idealism in its typical forms), as opposed to a formula of the most extreme life-affirmation, born of abundance, of superabundance—a yea-saying free of reserve, an affirmation of suffering itself, of guilt, of all that is questionable and strange in existence. . . . This last, most joyful, exuberant, exultant yea to life, is not only the highest of all insights, but it is also the profoundest, the one most strongly confirmed and supported by truth and science. We must neglect nothing; we must dispense with nothing. Those elements of existence which Christians and other nihilists reject, take infinitely higher rank in the hierarchy of values, than those which the instinct of decadence approves of. To understand this requires courage and, its prime condition, a superfluity of strength: for a man can approach truth only in so far as his courage and his strength will permit him to do so. Knowledge and the affirmation of reality are as necessary to the strong man as cowardice and the retreat from reality (the "ideal") are necessary to the weak inspired by weakness. . . . These latter are not free to "know"; decadents depend on lies; it is one of their methods of self-preservation. He who not only understands the word "Dionysian," but understands *himself* in terms of it, has no need of any refutation of Plato, or Christianity, or Schopenhauer—for his nose scents *decomposition*.

3

In *The Twilight of the Idols* (Aph. 5, part 10) I finally discussed how far these doctrines enabled me to discover the idea of "tragedy," the conclusive recognition of the psychology of tragedy. . . . "The yea-saying to life, even to its strangest and most difficult problems: the will to life rejoicing at its own inexhaustibleness in the sacrifice of its highest types—" this is what I called Dionysian, this is what I meant as the bridge to the psychology of the tragic poet. "Not to relieve one's self of terror and pity, not to purge one's self of dangerous emotion by a vehement discharge (this was Aristotle's misunderstanding of it) but rather, far beyond pity and terror, to be the eternal joy of Becoming itself—that joy which also involves the joy of destruction." . . . In this sense I have the right to regard myself as the first *tragic philosopher*—that is to say, the extreme antithesis and antipodes of a pessimistic philosopher. Before me there was no such translation of the Dionysian phenomenon into philosophic pathos: tragic wisdom was lacking; I have sought vainly for signs of it even among the great Greek philosophers—those belonging to the

two centuries before Socrates. I still retained a doubt about
Heraclitus, in whose presence, in general, I felt warmer and
more at ease than anywhere else. The yea-saying to the flux
and destruction of all things, the decisive element in any Dionysian philosophy; the yea-saying to contradiction and strife,
the idea of Becoming, together with the radical rejection even
of the concept *Being*—these things, at all events, force me to
recognize him who has hitherto had the closest affinity to my
thought. The doctrine of "Eternal Recurrence"—that is, of
the absolute and eternal cyclical repetition of all things—this
doctrine of Zarathustra's might also have been taught by Heraclitus. At least, the Stoics, who derived nearly all their fundamental ideas from Heraclitus, show traces of it.

4

A great hope is voiced in *The Birth of Tragedy*. After all,
there is absolutely no reason for me to renounce the hope of a
Dionysian future of music. Let us anticipate a century; let us
assume the success of my onslaught on two thousand years of
opposition to Nature, of the degradation of humanity. That
new party of life-affirmers, which will take into its hands the
greatest of all tasks, the elevation of mankind, as well as the
relentless destruction of everything degenerate and parasitical,
will reëstablish *superabundance of life* on earth out of which
the Dionysian state must rise once more. I predict a new age
of tragedy: the highest art of life-affirmation, tragedy, will be
reborn when mankind is conscious, but *without any feeling
of suffering,* that it has behind it the hardest but most necessary of wars. . . . A psychologist might add that what I
heard in Wagnerian music during my early years had practi-

cally nothing to do with Wagner; that when I described Dionysian music, I simply described what I myself had heard—that my instinct compelled me to translate and transfigure everything in terms of the new ardor I bore within me. A proof of this, as strong as any proof can be, is my essay, *Wagner in Bayreuth:* every psychological passage that is significant is concerned only with me—you need not hesitate to substitute my name or that of "Zarathustra" wherever the text gives the name of Wagner. The whole picture of the *dithyrambic* artist is a picture of the already existing author of *Zarathustra,* drawn with an abysmal depth and not for a moment even touching the real Wagner. Wagner himself had an inkling of this; he did not recognize himself in the essay.—In the meantime "the idea of Bayreuth" had been transformed into something that will be no riddle to those who know my *Zarathustra* —that is to say, into that Great Noontide when the chosen among the chosen consecrate themselves to the greatest of all tasks. Who can tell? Perhaps it is the vision of a feast I may yet live to see. . . . The pathos of the first few pages is universal history; the look discussed on page 105,[1] is the actual look of *Zarathustra;* Wagner, Bayreuth, the whole of this contemptible little German business, is a cloud upon which is reflected an infinite Fata Morgana of the future. Speaking psychologically, all the significant traits of my own nature are presented as belonging to Wagner—the juxtaposition of the most lucid and fateful forces, a Will to Power such as no man has yet possessed, reckless spiritual courage, an unlimited capacity to learn without any corresponding diminution of capacity for action. Everything in the essay is prophetic: the

---

[1] This page number and those which follow refer to *Thoughts out of Season,* Part I, in the complete edition of Nietzsche's Works. The Macmillan Company, New York.—Tr.

approaching resurrection of the Greek spirit, the necessity for counter-Alexanders, who will retie the Gordian knot of Greek culture, after it has been cut. Hearken to the world-historic accent with which on page 180 I introduce the concept of the "sense for the tragic": the essay contains nothing but world-historic accents. This is the strangest possible kind of "objectivity": my absolute certainty in regard to what I *am*, projects itself into any accidental reality—the truth about myself is voiced from out a fearful depth. On pages 174 and 175 the style of *Zarathustra* is described and foretold with incisive certainty, and no more magnificent expression will ever be found than that on pages 144-147 for the event for which *Zarathustra* stands—the tremendous purification and consecration of mankind.

"*Thoughts Out of Season*"

1

THE four essays composing the *Thoughts out of Season* are thoroughly warlike in tone. They prove that I was no John-o'-dreams, that I can find joy in drawing the sword—and perhaps, also, that I have a perilously supple wrist. The first attack (1873) was directed against German culture, for which even at that time I had the most thorough contempt. It was without sense, without substance, without aim; it was simply "public opinion." There can be no more vicious misunderstanding than to assume that Germany's great military success proved anything in favor of German culture—and still less the triumph of this culture over that of France. The second *Thought Out of Season* (1874) throws light on the dangerous, life-corroding, and life-poisoning element in our scientific pursuits: Life is diseased, thanks to this dehumanized piece of clock-work and mechanism, thanks to the "impersonality" of the workman, and to the false economy of the "division of labor." The end, namely, culture, is lost sight of: modern scientific activity as a means to it produces barbarism. In this treatise, the "historical sense," on which our century prides itself, is for the first time recognized as a disease, as a typical sign of decay. In the third and fourth *Thoughts* as signposts pointing to a higher concept of culture, to a reëstablishment of the idea of culture, two pictures of the most vigorous self-love and self-discipline are presented, two essentially un-modern types, full of sovereign contempt for everything around them—"Empire," "Culture," "Christianity," "Bismarck," and "Success"—these were Schopenhauer and Wagner, *or,* in a word, Nietzsche. . . .

2

Of these four attacks the first met with extraordinary success. The storm it evoked was in every way splendid. I had touched the vulnerable spot of a victorious nation—I told it that its victory was not an event in the history of culture, but, perhaps, something quite different. The reply came from all sides, and certainly not only from old friends of David Strauss, whom I had made ridiculous as the type of a complacent German Culture-Philistine—in short, as the author of that Main Street Gospel, called *The Old and the New Faith.* (The term "Culture-Philistine" entered the language of Germany after the appearance of my book.) These old friends from Württemburg and Swabia felt that their local pride was grossly insulted by my rather comic view of their prize exhibits, their bird of Paradise. Their replies were as obvious and gross as I could possibly have desired. But the Prussian replies were more clever: they had more "Prussian blue" in them. The rudest attitude was that of a Leipzig paper, the infamous *Grenzboten:* I had some trouble in preventing my enraged friends in Basel from taking action against it. Only a few old gentlemen took my side unconditionally, and for very confused and partly unaccountable reasons. Among them was

Ewald of Göttingen, who made it clear that my attack had
been quite fatal for Strauss. There was also the old Hegelian,
Bruno Bauer, whom thenceforward I could reckon among my
most attentive readers. In his later years he liked to point to
me, when, for instance, he wanted to give Herr von Treitschke,
the Prussian Historiographer, a hint as to where he could get
information about the idea "Culture," of which he (Herr
von T.) had completely lost sight. The longest and most
thoughtful notice of the book and its author was written by
an old pupil of the philosopher von Baader, a certain Professor Hoffman of Wörzburg. The essays made him forecast a
great destiny for me, namely, that of bringing about a sort
of crisis and decisive turning-point in the problem of atheism.
In me he recognized the latter's most instinctive and radical
exponent. It was atheism that had attracted me to Schopenhauer. What received by far the most attention, and excited
the most bitterness, was an extraordinarily vigorous and bold
appreciation of my work by the ordinarily mild Carl Hillebrand, the last *humane* German who knew how to wield a pen.
His article appeared in the *Augsburger Zeitung;* it can be read
today, in a more cautious and modified form, among his collected essays. In it my work was represented as an event, a
turning-point, as the first sign of an awakening, as the happiest of auguries, as a genuine revival of German earnestness
and of German spiritual passion. Hillebrand was full of the
greatest respect for the form of the book, its mature taste, its
perfect tact in discriminating between persons and principles:
he characterized it as the best polemical work the language had
yet produced,—the best performance in the art of polemics,
which is ordinarily so dangerous and so ill-advised, especially
for Germans. He not only affirmed unreservedly, but emphasized, what I had dared to say about the deterioration of lan-

guage in Germany (nowadays writers pose as Purists though they can hardly construct a sentence); sharing my contempt for the "leading authors" of this nation, he concluded by expressing his admiration for my courage—that "greatest courage of all which dares to bring accusation against the very favorites of a people." . . . The after-effects of this essay of mine have been quite invaluable to me in my life. No one has ever tried to meddle with me since. People are silent. Germany treats me with gloomy caution: for years I have been accustomed to such absolute freedom of speech, as no one nowadays, least of all in the "Empire," is at liberty to claim. My paradise is "in the shadow of my sword." Actually I had put into practice one of Stendhal's maxims: he counsels one to make one's entrance into society by a duel. And how well I had chosen my opponent!—the foremost freethinker of Germany. As a matter of fact, it was a quite novel kind of free thought that found expression in my book: to this day nothing is stranger and less akin to me than the whole of that European and American species known as *libres penseurs*. Incorrigible blockheads and clowns of "modern ideas" that they are, I feel much more profoundly at variance with them than with any one of their adversaries. They also wish to "improve" mankind, after their own fashion—that is to say, in their own image; against what I stand for and desire (provided they understood it) they would wage implacable war; all of them still believe in an "ideal." . . . I am the first *Immoralist*.

3

I should not like to affirm that the two essays in the *Thoughts Out of Season,* dealing with Schopenhauer and Wagner, conduce particularly to an understanding of them or their psychological problems. The statement, however, admits of a few exceptions. Thus, for instance, my deep and sure instinct had already indicated the fundamental element in Wagner's nature as a theatrical talent of which all his methods and goals are simply the normal consequences. At bottom, I wanted this essay to be something quite removed from a mere psychological exercise: a unique problem in education, a new conception of self-discipline and self-defense carried to the point of hardness, a road to greatness and to world-historic tasks—these all demanded utterance. Roughly speaking, I seized two famous and, previously, quite vague types by the forelock, just as one seizes opportunities, simply in order to express myself, to have a few more formulas, symbols, language-counters at my disposal. Indeed this is finally indicated with uncanny sagacity, on page 183 [1] of *Schopenhauer as Educator*. Plato made use of Socrates in the same way—that is to say, as a means of expressing his own ideas. Now that, from some distance, I can look back upon the circumstances to which these essays bear witness, I cannot deny that at bottom they refer solely to me. The essay *Wagner in Bayreuth* is a vision of my own future; conversely, *Schopenhauer as Educator* is the record of my most personal history and development. But above all things there is the promise I made to myself! What I am today, the position I now hold—a height from which I no longer speak with words but with thunderbolts—oh, how far I was from all this when I wrote the book! But I sighted land—I did not deceive myself for one moment as to the route, the sea, the danger—*and* success! The great tranquillity of that promise, a happy prospect of a future which was not to

---

[1] Macmillan Edition.

remain mere expectation! Every word has been lived, pro
foundly and personally; it is not lacking in painful things;
there are words in it which are literally running with blood.
But a wind of great freedom blows through all of it; its very
wounds do not constitute an objection. As to my notion of a
philosopher,—that is, a terrible explosive imperiling all
things; as to how I separate my idea of the philosopher by
miles from the idea which can admit even a Kant, not to speak
of the academic "ruminators" and other professors of philosophy—on all these things the essay gives invaluable information, even granting that at bottom, it is not "Schopenhauer as
Educator," but his opposite, "Nietzsche as Educator," who is
speaking. In view of the fact that, at the time, my trade was
that of a scholar, and perhaps, also, that I *understood* my trade,
the austere piece of scholar psychology which suddenly appears
in the essay is not without significance: it expresses the feeling
of distance, my profound confidence in my real life-task, as
opposed to mere means, interludes, and accessories. It is my
wisdom to have been many things, and in many places, in
order to become one thing and to attain one result. And so,
during one period, I was even destined to be a scholar.

"*Human, All-Too-Human*"

WITH ITS TWO SEQUELS

1

Human, all-too-Human, with its two sequels, marks a crisis. It is called a book for *free* spirits: almost every sentence in it expresses a victory—it enabled me to purge myself of everything which was alien to my nature. Idealism is alien to me: the title of the book implies: "Where ye see ideal things I see—things human, alas! all-too-human!" . . . I know men better. The words "free spirit" can be understood only as meaning a spirit that has become free, that has regained possession of itself. The book marks a complete change of tone and accent; it will be thought clever, cool, and in places hard and scornful. A certain noble and refined spirituality seems to be engaged in a continual struggle with a torrent of passion. This lends some significance to the fact that it was really the hundredth anniversary of Voltaire's death that, in a way, furnished an excuse for publishing the book as early as 1878. For Voltaire, as opposed to all those who wrote after him, was preëminently an intellectual aristocrat—which is precisely what I am also. To place Voltaire's name on one of my writings—this was really a step forward—towards me. Examining the book more closely, you discover a relentless spirit ac-

[*878*]

quainted with all the secret hiding-places of the ideal—its strongholds and its last refuge. Torch in hand (and its light is by no means a flickering one), I illuminate this underworld with a penetrating gleam. It is war, but war without powder or smoke, without any warlike gestures, without pathos and contorted limbs—for these things in themselves would still be "idealism." One error after the other is calmly laid upon ice; the ideal is not refuted—it freezes. Here, for instance, "genius" freezes; round the corner the "saint" freezes; under a thick icicle the "hero" freezes; and in conclusion "faith," so-called "conviction" and also "pity" are considerably cooled —and throughout the book the "thing in itself" is freezing.

2

I began the volume in the middle of the first Bayreuth festival; a deep sense of estrangement from my surroundings was one of its first conditions. Any one who has an idea of the kind of visions which even at that time had flitted across my path, can imagine how I felt when one day I woke up in Bayreuth. It was just as if I had been dreaming. Where was I? I could recognize nothing; I hardly recognized Wagner. I searched my memory—in vain. Tribschen—remote island of the blessed: not a hint of any resemblance! The incomparable days when we laid the corner-stone, the small homogeneous group who celebrated them, who were filled with the most delicate sensitiveness: of this not a trace! *What had happened?* Wagner had been translated into German! The Wagnerite had triumphed over Wagner!—*German* art! the German master! German beer! . . . Those of us who know only too well to what refined artists, to what cosmopolitanism of taste Wag-

ner's art can alone appeal, were beside ourselves at the sight
of Wagner bedecked with German virtues. I think I know
the Wagnerite, I have experienced three generations of him,
from Brendel of blessed memory, who confounded Wagner
with Hegel, to the "idealists" of the Bayreuth press, who confound Wagner with themselves. I have heard all sorts of
confessions about Wagner, from "beautiful souls." My kingdom for one intelligent word! That crowd was enough to
make your hair stand on end! Nohl, Pohl, and *Kohl*,[1] and an
infinite number of people like them. Not a single abortion
was missing—not even the anti-Semite. Poor Wagner! To
what pass had he come? If only he had fallen among swine!
But among Germans! Some day, for the edification of posterity, they ought really to have a genuine Bayreuthian stuffed,
or, better still, preserved in spirit,—for that is exactly what is
lacking,—with this inscription below: "A specimen of the
spirit on which the 'German Empire' was founded." . . .
But enough! Suddenly in the midst of everything, I left for a
few weeks, despite the fact that a charming Parisian lady
sought to console me; I excused myself to Wagner quite simply with a fatalistic telegram. In a little place called Klingen-
brunn, hidden deep in the Böhmerwald, I bore my melancholy
and my contempt of Germans about with me like a disease—
and, from time to time, under the general title of "The Plough-
share," I wrote a few sentences in my notebook, all vigorous
psychological observations which quite possibly reappeared
in *Human, all-too-Human*.

---

[1] Nohl and Pohl were actually music critics of the time; Kohl is a colloquial-
ism meaning nonsense, twaddle.—Tr.

That sudden change in me was not merely a breach with Wagner—I was suffering from a general aberration of my instincts, of which any single blunder, whether it be Wagner or my professorship at Basel, was only a symptom. A fit of impatience overcame me; I saw that it was high time for a little introspection. At once it became appallingly clear to me how much time I had already wasted—how useless, how willful my whole existence as a philologist appeared by the side of my life-task. I was ashamed of this false modesty. . . . Ten years were behind me, during which I had received absolutely no spiritual nourishment, during which I had acquired no useful knowledge, but had forgotten countless things in the pursuit of a hotch-potch of dry-as-dust scholarship. To plow through old Greek metricians, meticulously, half-blind—that was what I had come to! . . . Moved to pity I saw myself quite thin, emaciated: realities were utterly lacking from my stock of knowledge, and the devil only knew what the "idealities" were worth! A positively burning thirst possessed me: thenceforth my studies were entirely in the fields of physiology, medicine, and natural science—I even returned to the actual study of history only when compelled to do so by my life-task. It was then, too, that I first perceived the relation between an occupation chosen against one's instincts, a so-called vocation, which is the last thing to which one is "called," and that necessity for stilling a feeling of emptiness and hunger, through the medium of a narcotic art—Wagner's, for instance. After careful observation, I have discovered that a large number of young men suffer from the same trouble: one unnatural practice leads directly to another. In Germany, or

more exactly, in the Empire, only too many are condemned
to make their choice of profession too early, and then to pine
away under an inescapable burden. . . . Such men require
Wagner as an opiate,—they forget themselves, they escape
from themselves for a moment. . . . What am I saying!—
for five or six hours!

4

At this time my instinct decided absolutely against any
further yielding or misunderstanding of myself. Any kind of
life, the most unfavorable conditions, illness, poverty—anything seemed to me preferable to that unworthy "selfishness"
into which I had at first fallen due to my ignorance and youth,
and in which I had afterward remained out of sheer inertia,
otherwise known as a "sense of duty." And now, in a way I
cannot sufficiently admire, and precisely at the right time, I was
aided by that evil heritage which I derive from the paternal
side,—fundamentally, a predisposition to an early death. Illness gave me my freedom gradually; it spared me any sort of
sudden break, any sort of violent or impetuous move. At that
time I suffered no loss of good-will; on the contrary, I acquired more. Illness likewise gave me the right to a complete
reversal of my mode of life; it not only allowed, it actually
ordered me to forget; it enforced the necessity of repose, of
idleness, of waiting, of patience. . . . And all that meant
thinking! . . . The state of my eyes was enough to stop all
bookwormishness, or, in plain English, philology: I was delivered from books; for years I read nothing—the greatest
boon I have ever conferred upon myself! That essential self,
which had been buried, as it were, which had lost its voice

under the pressure of being forced to listen to other selves continually (which is what reading means!), awakened slowly, timidly, doubtfully—but at last it *spoke again*. Never have I been so happy as during the sickest and most painful periods of my life. One need merely examine *The Dawn of Day,* or, perhaps, *The Wanderer and His Shadow,* to realize what this "return to myself" meant: it was itself the highest kind of recovery! . . . The other purely physical one was a simple consequence of it.

5

Human, all-too-Human, this monument of vigorous self-discipline, which put an abrupt end to all the humbug of superiority, "idealism," "beautiful feelings," and other effeminacies I had absorbed, was given its main outlines at Sorrento; it was concluded and put into final shape during a winter at Basel, under conditions far less favorable than those in Sorrento. As a matter of fact, it is Peter Gast, at that time a student at the University of Basel, and extremely devoted to me, who is responsible for the book. With my aching head wrapped in bandages, I dictated while he wrote and corrected—actually, he was the real composer, whereas I was merely the author. When I finally received the completed book,—to the great surprise of the serious invalid I then was,—I sent, among others, two copies to Bayreuth. By a wonderful stroke of ironical intelligence on the part of chance, I received at exactly the same time a splendid copy of the *Parsifal* text, with the following inscription from Wagner's pen: "To his dear friend Friedrich Nietzsche, from Richard Wagner, Ecclesiastical Councillor." At this crossing of the two books I seemed to hear an ominous note. Did it not sound as if two *swords* had crossed? In any case we felt it as such; for each of us remained silent. At about this time appeared the first Bayreuth Pamphlets: and I then understood why it was high time for me to act as I had done. Incredible! Wagner had become pious.

6

What I thought of myself at that time (1876), the terrific assurance with which I assumed my life-task together with all that was world-historic in it, is well exhibited throughout the book, but especially in one very expressive passage. This is so despite the fact that, with my instinctive cunning, I again avoided the little word "I,"—this time, however, illuminating with world-historic glory not Schopenhauer or Wagner, but one of my friends, the excellent Dr. Paul Rée—fortunately much too subtle a creature to be deceived (others were less so). Among my readers I have some hopeless cases, the typical German professor, for instance, who can always be recognized by the fact that the passage mentioned compels him to consider the whole book as a sort of advanced Réealism. As a matter of fact it contradicts five or six of my friend's propositions: in proof, one may read the introduction to *The Genealogy of Morals*. The passage above referred to reads: "What, then, is the main conclusion to which one of the boldest and coldest of thinkers, the author of the book *On the Origin of Moral Sensations* (read Nietzsche, the first Immoralist), has arrived by means of his incisive and decisive analysis of human actions? 'The moral man,' he says, 'is no nearer to the intelligible world than is the physical man—for there is no intelligible world.' This proposition, hardened and sharpened under the hammer-blow of historical knowledge (read *The Transvalua-*

tion of all Values), may perhaps at some future time—1890!
—serve as the ax which will be applied to the root of the
'metaphysical need' of man—whether more as a blessing than
a curse to mankind, who shall predict?—But in any case it is
a proposition involving the most weighty consequences, at
once fruitful and terrible, facing the world with that Janus-
face possessed by all great knowledge." [2]

---

[2] *Human, all-too-Human*, Aph. 37.

"*The Dawn of Day: Thoughts About Morality as Prejudice*"

1

WITH this book I started my campaign against morality. Not that there is the slightest smell of powder about it—indeed you will find quite other and much more pleasant smells in it, if your nostrils are at all sensitive. No heavy artillery, no light artillery—if the effect of the book be negative, its methods are not so—methods from which the effect follows like a conclusion, *not* like a cannon-shot. The reader may leave the book with a feeling of timid caution in regard to everything which has hitherto received honor and even worship under the name of morality; but this does not contradict the fact that there is not one negative word in the whole book, no attacks, no malice—rather does it lie in the sun, smooth and happy, like a marine animal basking between two rocks. In fact, I was this marine animal: almost every sentence in the book was thought out, or rather *caught,* among that mass of rocks near Genoa, where I lived alone, and exchanged secrets with the ocean. Even now, when I chance to look through the book, almost every sentence seems to me like a hook with which I again draw from the depths some incomparable thing; its whole skin quivers with delicate shudders of recollection.

This book is not deficient in that art of neatly securing things which usually whisk away quickly and silently, moments which I call divine lizards.—It secures them not with the cruelty of that young Greek god who simply transfixed the poor little lizard; but still it too uses something pointed—a pen. "There are so many dawns still to spread their light"—this Indian maxim is written over the threshold of this book. Where shall its maker look for that new morning, that still undiscovered delicate red, with which another day—ah! a whole series of days, a whole world of new days!—shall begin? In a *Transvaluation of all Values,* in an emancipation from all moral values, in a yea-saying, confidence in all that has formerly been forbidden, despised, and damned. This yea-saying book sends out its light, its love, its tenderness, over all things evil, it gives them back their "soul," their serene conscience, their high right and privilege of existence. Morality is not assailed, it is simply no longer considered. This book concludes with the word "or?"—and it is the only book that so concludes.

2

My life-task is to prepare for humanity a moment of supreme self-consciousness, a Great Noontide when it will gaze both backwards and forwards, when it will emerge from the tyranny of accident and the priesthood, and for the first time pose the question of the Why and Wherefore of humanity as a whole. This life-task is a necessary result of the view that mankind does *not* follow the right road of its own accord, that it is by no means divinely ruled, but rather, that it is precisely under the cover of its most sacred values that the tendency to negation, corruption, and decadence has exerted such seductive power. The question as to the origin of moral values is therefore a question of primary importance to me because it determines the future of mankind. We are asked to believe that at bottom everything is in the best hands, that a book, the Bible, gives us the definite assurance of a divine guidance and wisdom overlooking man's destiny. Translated back into reality, what we have is this, namely, the will to stifle the terrible truth which maintains the very opposite, which is that up to now man has been in the *worst* hands, that he has been ruled by the misfits, the physiologically botched, the men of cunning and revengefulness, the so-called "saints"—those slanderers of the world and traducers of humanity. A decisive proof of the fact that the priest (including those priests in disguise, philosophers) has become master, not only within a limited religious community, but everywhere, and that the morality of decadence, the will to nothingness, has passed as morality *per se,* is to be found in this: that altruism is considered an absolute value, but egoism meets with hostility everywhere. He who disagrees with me on this point, I regard as infected. But all the world disagrees with me. For a physiologist such an opposition of values would leave no room for doubt. If the smallest organ within the body neglects, however slightly, to exercise with complete assurance its self-preservative powers, its recuperative claims, and its "egoism," the whole system will degenerate. The physiologist insists that these decayed parts be cut out; he denies all fellow-feeling for such parts; he pities them not at all. But what the priest wants is precisely the degeneration of the whole of mankind; hence he preserves the decayed elements—this is the price of his rule over humanity. What meaning have those lies, those ancillary concepts of morality, "Soul," "Spirit," "Free Will," "God," if their aim be not that of the physiological ruin of mankind? When one is no longer serious about self-preservation and the increase of bodily energy, *i.e., of life;* when anemia is made an ideal and the contempt of the body is construed as "the salvation of the soul," what can all this be if not a recipe for decadence? Loss of ballast, resistance offered to natural instincts, in a word, "selflessness,"—this is what has hitherto been called morality. With *The Dawn of Day* I first took up the struggle against the morality of self-renunciation.

"Joyful Wisdom: La Gaya Scienza"

The Dawn of Day is a yea-saying book, profound but clear and gracious in style. This is true also and in the highest degree of *La Gaya Scienza:* in almost every sentence of this book profundity and high spirits are delicately combined. A verse which expresses my gratitude for the most wonderful January in my experience—the whole book is its gift—sufficiently reveals from what depths "wisdom" has emerged to become "joyful":

> Der du mit dem Flammenspeere
> Meine Seele Eis zertheilt,
> Das sie brausend nun zum Meere
> Ihrer höchsten Hoffnung eilt;
> Heller stets und stets gesunder,
> Frei im liebevollsten Musz—
> Also preist sie deine Wunder,
> Schönster Januarius! [1]

Who can have any doubt as to what "supreme hope" means here, once he has caught the gleam of the jeweled beauty of Zarathustra's first words at the close of the fourth book? Or

---

[1] "You melt the ice around my heart with your flaming spear; with a roar it hastens to empty itself into the sea of its supreme hope; it is ever brighter, ever purer: thus, O beautiful January, does it praise the marvels you accomplish."

once he has read the granite-like sentences at the end of the third book, where there is the first formulation of a destiny for all ages? The songs of Prince Free-as-a-Bird, written for the most part in Sicily, remind one quite forcibly of that Provençal notion of *"La Gaya Scienza,"* of that union of *singer, knight, and free spirit,* which distinguishes that wonderfully early culture of the Provençals from all ambiguous cultures. The last poem, "To the Mistral,"—an exuberant dance song in which, if you please, morality is freely trodden on,—is a perfect Provençalism.

"*Thus Spake Zarathustra: A Book for All and None*"

1

I WOULD now like to tell you the history of my *Zarathustra*. Its fundamental conception, the idea of *Eternal Recurrence,* the highest formula of affirmation that can ever be attained, belongs to August, 1881. I made a hasty note of it on a sheet of paper, with the postscript: "Six thousand feet beyond man and time." That day I was walking through the woods beside Lake Silvaplana; I halted not far from Surlei, beside a huge, towering, pyramidal rock. It was there that the idea came to me. If I count back two months previous to this day, I can discover a warning sign in the form of an abrupt and profoundly decisive change in my tastes—more especially in music. Perhaps the whole of *Zarathustra* may be classified as music—I am sure that one of the conditions of its production was a renaissance in me of the art of hearing. In Recoaro, a little mountain watering-place near Vicenza, where I spent the spring of 1881, I, together with my friend and maestro, Peter Gast (another who had been reborn), discovered that the phœnix bird of music hovered over us, decked in more beautiful and brilliant plumage than it had ever before exhibited. If, therefore, I reckon from that day to the sudden birth of the book, amid the most unlikely circumstances, in February, 1883,—its last part, from which I quoted a few lines in my preface, was finished exactly during the hallowed hour of Richard Wagner's death in Venice,—it would appear that the period of gestation was eighteen months. This period of exactly eighteen months might suggest, at least to Buddhists, that I am in reality a female elephant. The interval was devoted to the *Gaya Scienza,* which has a hundred indications of the approach of something unparalleled; its conclusion shows the beginning of *Zarathustra,* since it presents *Zarathustra's* fundamental thought in the last aphorism but one of the fourth book. To this interval also belongs that *Hymn to Life* (for a mixed choir and orchestra), the score of which was published in Leipzig two years ago by E. W. Fritsch. Perhaps it is no small indication of my spiritual state during this year, when the essentially yea-saying pathos, which I call the tragic pathos, filled my soul to the brim. Some day people will sing it to my memory. As there seems to be some misunderstanding current, I should like to emphasize the point that the text is not by me; it was the astounding inspiration of a young Russian lady, Miss Lou von Salome, with whom I was then very friendly. He who can in any way derive some meaning from the last words of the poem will understand why I preferred and admired it: there is greatness in them. Pain cannot rank as an objection to life: "No matter if thou hast no happiness left to give me! Thou hast thy Sorrow still."

In this passage it may be that my music also rises to greatness. (The last note of the oboe should be C-sharp, not C. The latter is a misprint.) During the following winter, I was living not far from Genoa on that pleasant peaceful Gulf of Rapallo, which cuts inland between Chiavari and Cape Porto Fino. I was not in the best of health; the winter was cold and exceptionally rainy; and my small *albergo* was so close to shore that the noise of a rough sea rendered sleep impossible. These circumstances were the very reverse of favorable; and yet, despite them, and as if in proof of my theory that everything decisive arises as the result of opposition, it was during this very winter and amid these unfavorable circumstances that my *Zarathustra* was born. In the morning I used to start out in a southerly direction on the glorious road to Zoagli, which rises up through a forest of pines and gives one a view far out to sea. In the afternoon, whenever my health permitted, I would walk around the whole bay from Santa Margherita to beyond Porto Fino. This spot and the country around it is the more firmly enshrined in my affections because it was so dearly loved by the Emperor Frederick III. In the fall of 1886 I happened to be there again when he was revisiting this small forgotten world of happiness for the last time. It was on these two roads that all *Zarathustra,* and particularly Zarathustra himself as a type, came to me—perhaps I should rather say—*invaded me.*

2

In order to understand the Zarathustra-type, you must first be quite clear as to its prime physiological condition, a condition I choose to call *great healthiness.* I cannot make this idea any plainer or more personal than I have done already in one of the last aphorisms (No. 382) of the fifth book of the *Gaya Scienza:* "We new, nameless, and unfathomable beings," so runs the passage, "premature births of a future still unproved—we need new means towards our new goal; we need a new healthiness, a stronger, keener, harder, bolder, and merrier healthiness than any that has been seen up to this time. He whose soul longs to experience the whole range of previous values and desires to circumnavigate this ideal 'Mediterranean Sea'; who, from the adventures of his own profound experience, would know how it feels to be a conqueror and discoverer of the ideal;—and who would likewise know how it feels to be an artist, saint, legislator, sage, scholar, pietist, and godlike anchorite of old;—such a man requires one thing preëminently, and that is, *great healthiness*—healthiness which is not a mere static possession, but which he is constantly acquiring and must acquire, because he is continually sacrificing it, and must so sacrifice it! And now, therefore, after having been long on the way, we Argonauts of the ideal, our courage perhaps greater than our prudence, often shipwrecked and bruised, but, as I say, healthier than people would like to admit, dangerously healthy, recovering health again and again— it would seem as if our trouble were to be rewarded, as if we saw before us that undiscovered country, whose frontiers no one has yet seen, a land lying beyond all other known lands and hiding-places of the ideal, a world so overflowing with beauty, strangeness, doubt, terror, and divinity, that both our curiosity and our lust for possession are wrought to a pitch of extreme excitement. Nothing on earth can satisfy us. Alas! how with such vistas before us and with our conscience and consciousness full of such burning desire, can we still be content with *the man of the present day?* This is bad enough; but, further, it is inevitable that we should regard his highest aims and hopes with but a mock seriousness, or perhaps give them no further consideration. Another ideal hovers before our eyes, a wonderful, seductive, perilous ideal, which we should be unwilling to urge upon any one, because we cannot so easily admit any one's *right to it*. It is an ideal of a spirit who plays innocently (that is to say, involuntarily, out of his supera-

bundance of power) with everything that has hitherto been
called holy, good, inviolable, divine; a spirit to whom the
highest popular standards would be a mere danger, a decay,
an abasement, or at the very least, a relaxation, a blindness,
and a temporary forgetfulness of self: the ideal of a humanly
superhuman well-being and good-will, which often enough
may seem unhuman—when, for example, it confronts all mankind's former seriousness and solemnities as their most lifelike
and unconscious parody in gesture, speech, accent, look, morality, and duty—but with which, nevertheless, *great seriousness*
perhaps first arises, the first note of interrogation is affixed,
the soul's destiny changes, the hour hand moves, and tragedy
begins."

3

Can any one at the end of this nineteenth century possibly
have any distinct notion of what poets of a more vigorous
period meant by inspiration? If not, I should like to describe
it. Provided one has the slightest remnant of superstition left,
one can hardly reject completely the idea that one is the mere
incarnation, or mouthpiece, or medium of some almighty
power. The notion of revelation describes the condition quite
simply; by which I mean that something profoundly convulsive and disturbing suddenly becomes visible and audible with
indescribable definiteness and exactness. One hears—one does
not seek; one takes—one does not ask who gives: a thought
flashes out like lightning, inevitably without hesitation—I
have never had any choice about it. There is an ecstasy whose
terrific tension is sometimes released by a flood of tears, during which one's progress varies from involuntary impetuosity

to involuntary slowness. There is the feeling that one is utterly out of hand, with the most distinct consciousness of an infinitude of shuddering thrills that pass through one from head to foot;—there is a profound happiness in which the most painful and gloomy feelings are not discordant in effect, but are required as necessary colors in this overflow of light. There is an instinct for rhythmic relations which embraces an entire world of forms (length, the need for a widely extended rhythm, is almost a measure of the force of inspiration, a sort of counterpart to its pressure and tension). Everything occurs quite without volition, as if in an eruption of freedom, independence, power and divinity. The spontaneity of the images and similes is most remarkable; one loses all perception of what is imagery and simile; everything offers itself as the most immediate, exact, and simple means of expression. If I may recall a phrase of Zarathustra's, it actually seems as if the things themselves came to one, and offered themselves as similes. ("Here do all things come caressingly to thy discourse and flatter thee, for they would fain ride upon thy back. On every simile thou ridest here to every truth. Here fly open before thee all the speech and word shrines of existence, here all existence would become speech, here all Becoming would learn of thee how to speak.") This is *my* experience of inspiration. I have no doubt that I should have to go back millenniums to find another who could say to me: "It is mine also!"

4

For a few weeks afterwards I lay ill in Genoa. Then followed a depressing spring in Rome, where I escaped with my life. It was not a pleasant experience. This city, which I did not choose myself and which is of all places the most unsuited to the author of *Zarathustra,* weighed heavily upon my spirit. I tried to leave it. I wanted to go to Aquila—Rome's complete antithesis, and founded in a spirit of enmity towards that city, just as I too shall found a city some day, in commemoration of an atheist and anti-ecclesiast, a man after my own heart, the great Hohenstaufen, Emperor Frederick II. But Destiny said no: I had to return again to Rome. Finally I had to be content with the Piazza Barberini, after I had exhausted myself in the search for an antichristian quarter. I fear that on one occasion, to avoid bad smells as much as possible, I actually inquired at the Palazzo del Quirinale whether they did not have a quiet room for a philosopher. In a *loggia* high above the Piazza over- looking Rome, with the plash of fountains far below, sound- ing in my ears, the loneliest of all songs was composed—"The Night-Song." About this time I was continually obsessed by a melody of ineffable sadness, whose refrain I recognized in the words, "dead through immortality." . . . In the summer, on my return to the sacred spot where the first thought of *Zarathustra* had flashed like lightning across my mind, I con- ceived the second part. Ten days sufficed. Neither for the sec- ond, the first, nor the third part, have I required a day longer. The following winter, beneath the halcyon sky of Nice, which then for the first time filled me with its brilliant light, I found the third *Zarathustra*—and so completed the work. The whole composition had taken scarcely a year. Many hidden corners and heights in the country round Nice are hallowed for me by unforgettable moments. That decisive section, "Old and New Tables," was composed during the arduous ascent from the station to Eza, that wonderful Moorish eyrie. When my crea- tive energy flowed most freely, my muscular activity was al- ways greatest. The body is inspired: let us leave the "soul" out of consideration. I might often have been seen dancing; I used to walk through the hills for seven or eight hours on end without a hint of fatigue. I slept well, laughed a good deal—I was perfectly vigorous and patient.

5

Excluding these ten-day work periods, the years during the production of *Zarathustra,* but especially thereafter, were for me years of unparalleled misery. It is a dear price that a man pays for being immortal: he must die many times over during his life. There is a thing that I call the rancor of greatness: everything great, whether it be a work or a deed, once it is completed, turns immediately against its author. The very fact that he is its author now makes him weak. Henceforth he can no longer endure his deed. He cannot face it squarely. To have done something one could never have willed, something to which the knot of human destiny is bound—and to carry this about! It almost crushes one! The rancor of greatness! And there is another thing—the uncanny silence that prevails. Solitude has seven skins; nothing can penetrate it. You go among men; you greet friends: but it is only a new wilderness you encounter—their faces are blank, or at best merely expressive of a sort of revolt. I experienced this latter reaction, in varying degrees of intensity, from almost every one who came near me; it would seem that nothing inflicts a deeper wound than suddenly to make one's distance felt. Those noble natures are scarce who cannot live without reverence. A third thing is the absurd sensitivity of the skin to small pin-pricks, a sort of helplessness in the presence of all small things. This seems to me an inevitable condition resulting from that appalling expenditure of defensive energy, which is the prerequisite of every *creative* act, of every act born of a man's most intimate and personal being. Thus the small defensive forces are, as it were, suspended, and they receive no fresh supply of energy. I even dare suggest that one's digestive processes are impeded, that one has a greater tendency to inertia, and that one is much too open to sensations of cold and suspicion, suspicion that in many cases is merely a blunder in etiology. On one such occasion I became conscious of the proximity of a herd of cows, some time before I could possibly have seen it with my eyes, simply owing to a return in me of milder and more benevolent sentiments: *they* communicated warmth to me. . . .

6

This work is utterly unique. Let us leave the poets out of consideration: it may be that nothing has yet been produced out of such a superabundance of strength. My concept "Dionysian" here became the *highest* deed; measured by it all other human deeds seem poor and limited. The fact that a Goethe or a Shakespeare would not have been able to breathe for a moment in this terrific atmosphere of passion and elevation; the fact that compared with Zarathustra, Dante is no more than a believer, and not one who *creates* truth for the first time—a world-ruling spirit, a *Destiny;* the fact that the Vedic poets were priests and not even fit to unfasten Zarathustra's sandal —all this is of no great importance; it gives no idea of the distance, of the azure solitude, wherein this work dwells. Zarathustra has an eternal right to say: "I draw circles around me and holy boundaries. Ever fewer are they that mount with me to ever loftier heights. I build me a mountain range of ever holier mountains." All the spirit and goodness of every great soul combined could not create one of Zarathustra's discourses. The ladder of his ascent and descent is of boundless length; he has seen further, willed further, and *gone* further than any other man. He contradicts himself in every word, this most yea-saying of all spirits. Yet in him all oppositions are resolved into a new unity. The loftiest and the basest powers of human nature, the sweetest, the lightest, and the most terrible, stream from one source with an eternal certainty. Before him, no one knew what was height, or depth; still less did they know what was truth. There is not a single moment in this revelation of truth which had been anticipated or divined by even the greatest among men. Before *Zarathustra* there was no wisdom, no examination of the soul, no art of speech: the most familiar, the most ordinary things now utter unheard-of words. The sentence quivers with passion. Eloquence has become music. Lightning-bolts are hurled towards undreamed-of futures. The hitherto most powerful use of parables is timid child's play beside this return of language to the nature of imagery. See how Zarathustra descends from the mountain! How graciously he speaks to all! See how tenderly he treats his adversaries, the priests, how he suffers with them from themselves! Here, at every moment, man is surpassed, and the concept "Superman" becomes the greatest reality—everything that has hitherto been called great in man lies far beneath, immeasurably distant. The halcyonic temper, the light feet, the omnipresence of wickedness and exuberance and everything typical of Zarathustra, was never before thought to be bound up with the essence of greatness. In precisely these spatial limits and this accessibility to opposites Zarathustra feels himself *the highest of all living things:* and when you hear how he defines himself, you will give up trying to find his equal.

"The soul which hath the longest ladder and can go deepest
down,

"The most comprehensive soul, which can run and stray
and rove furthest in itself, the most necessary soul, which out
of joy flingeth itself into chance;—

"The soul in Being which plungeth into Becoming; the
possessing soul, which *seeketh* to attain desire and longing;—

"The soul fleeing from itself, which overtaketh itself in the
widest circuit;—the wisest soul unto which folly speaketh
most sweetly:—

"The soul most self-loving, in which all things have their
current and counter-current, their ebb and their flow." [1]

But this is the very essence of Dionysus. Another consideration leads to this same idea. The psychological problem the
Zarathustra-type presents is this: how can he, who to an unprecedented extent says no, and *acts* no, in reference to all to
which man has hitherto said yes, nevertheless remain the
opposite of a no-saying spirit? How can he who bears destiny's
heaviest burden, whose life-task is a fatality, yet be the lightest and the most transcendental of spirits—for Zarathustra
is a dancer? how can he who has the hardest and most terrible
insight into reality, and who has thought the most "abysmal
thoughts," nevertheless find in these things no objections to
existence, or to its eternal recurrence?—how is it that on the
contrary he finds reasons for *being himself* the everlasting
Yea to all things, "the tremendous and unlimited saying of
Yea and Amen"? . . . "Into every abyss do I bear the bene-
diction of my yea to Life." . . . *But this again is the very
essence of Dionysus.*

---

[*] Modern Library Edition, p. 233.

7

What language will such a spirit speak, when he communes with himself? The language of the *dithyramb*. I am the inventor of the dithyramb. Hearken unto the manner in which Zarathustra speaks to his soul *Before Sunrise* (iii. 48). Before I came such emerald joys, such divine tenderness, had found no voice. Even the profoundest melancholy of such a Dionysus becomes a dithyramb. I take as an example "The Night-Song" —the immortal lament of one who, because of his superabundance of light and power, because of his solar nature, is condemned never to love:

" 'Tis night: now do all gushing fountains speak louder. And my soul also is a gushing fountain.

" 'Tis night: now only do all songs of the loving ones awake. And my soul also is the song of a loving one.

"Something unappeased, unappeasable, is within me; it longeth to find expression. A craving for love is within me, which speaketh itself the language of love.

"Light am I: ah, that I were night! But it is my lonesomeness, to be begirt with light!

"Ah, that I were dark and nightly! How would I suck at the breasts of light!

"And you yourselves would I bless, ye twinkling starlets and glow-worms aloft!—and would rejoice in the gifts of your light.

"But I live in mine own light, I drink again into myself the flames that break forth from me.

"I know not the happiness of the receiver; and oft have I dreamed that stealing must be more blessed than receiving.

"It is my poverty that my hand never ceaseth bestowing;

't is mine envy that I see waiting eyes and brightened nights of longing.

"Oh, the misery of all bestowers! Oh, the darkening of my sun! Oh, the craving to crave! Oh, the violent hunger in satiety!

"They take from me; but do I yet touch their soul? There is a gap 'twixt giving and receiving; and the smallest gap hath finally to be bridged over.

"A hunger ariseth out of my beauty: I should like to injure those I illumine; I should like to rob those I have gifted:— thus do I hunger for wickedness.

"Withdrawing my hand when another hand already stretch-eth out to it; hesitating like the cascade, which hesitateth even in its leap:—thus do I hunger for wickedness.

"Such revenge doth mine abundance think of: such mis-chief welleth out of my lonesomeness.

"My happiness in bestowing died in bestowing. My virtue became weary of itself by its abundance!

"He who ever bestoweth is in danger of losing his shame; to him who ever dispenseth the hand and heart become cal-lous by very dispensing.

"Mine eye no longer overfloweth for the shame of suppli-ants; my hand hath become too hard for the trembling of filled hands.

"Whence have gone the tears of mine eye, and the down of my heart? Oh, the lonesomeness of all bestowers! Oh, the silence of all shining ones!

"Many suns circle in desert space: to all that is dark do they speak with their light—but to me they are silent.

"Oh, this is the hostility of light to the shining one: unpity-ingly does it pursue its course.

"Unfair to the shining one in its innermost heart, cold to the suns:—thus traveleth every sun.

"Like a storm do the suns pursue their courses: that is their traveling. Their inexorable will do they follow: that is their coldness.

"Oh, ye only is it, ye dark, nightly ones, that extract warmth from the shining ones! Oh, ye only drink milk and refreshment from the light udders!

"Ah, there is ice around me, my hand burneth with the ice! Ah, there is thirst in me; it panteth after your thirst!

" 'Tis night: alas, that I have to be light! And thirst for the nightly! And lonesomeness!

" 'Tis night: now doth my longing break forth in me as a fountain—for speech do I long.

" 'Tis night: now do all gushing fountains speak louder: and my soul also is a gushing fountain.

" 'Tis night: now do all songs of loving ones awake. And my soul also is the song of a loving one."

8

Such things have never been written, never been felt, never been *suffered:* such suffering can be borne only by a God, Dionysus. The reply to such a dithyramb on the sun's solitude in light would be Ariadne. . . . Who beside me knows who Ariadne is! No one hitherto has found any clue to such riddles; I even doubt whether any one ever saw a riddle here. One day Zarathustra severely determines his life-task—and it is also mine. Let no one misunderstand its meaning. It is a yea-saying to the point of justifying, to the point of redeeming all past things.

"I walk amongst men as the fragments of the future: that future which I contemplate.

"And it is all my poetization and aspiration to compose and collect into unity what is fragment and riddle and fearful chance.

"And how could I endure to be a man, if man were not also the composer, and riddle reader, and redeemer of chance!

"To redeem what is past, and to transform every 'It was' into 'Thus would I have it'!—that alone do I call redemption!" [2]

In another passage he defines as strictly as possible exactly what "man" can be to him—not the object of love nor yet of pity—Zarathustra has mastered even his loathing of man: man is to him something inchoate, raw material, an ugly stone in need of the sculptor.

"No longer willing, no longer valuing, and no longer creating! Oh, that that great debility may ever be far from me!

"And also in discerning do I feel only my will's procreation and evolving delight; and if there be innocence in my knowledge, it is because there is will to procreation in it.

"Away from God and gods did this will allure me; what would there be to create if there were—gods!

"But to man doth it ever impel me anew, my fervent creative will; thus impelleth it the hammer to the stone.

"Ah, ye men, within the stone slumbereth an image for me, the image of my visions! Ah, that it should slumber in the hardest, ugliest stone!

"*Now rageth my hammer ruthlessly against its prison.* From the stone fly the fragments: what's that to me?

---

[2] See page 153.

"I will complete it: for a shadow came unto me—the stillest and lightest of all things once came unto me!

"The beauty of the Superman came unto me as a shadow. Ah, my brethren! Of what account are—the gods to me!" [3]

One last observation, suggested by the italicized line. To the Dionysian life-task belongs the hardness of the hammer, and one of its prime conditions is a definite *joy even in destruction.* The command, "Harden yourselves!" and the deep conviction that *all creators are hard,* is the essential sign of a Dionysian nature.

---

[3] See pages 92-93.

"*Beyond Good and Evil: The Prelude to a Philosophy of the Future*"

1

MY work for the years that followed was prescribed as distinctly as possible. Now that the yea-saying part of my life-task was achieved, there came the turn of the negative portion, which was to deny both in word and in deed: the transvaluation of all previous values, the great war,—the evocation of the day of the final decision. Now I had to look about me slowly for my peers, for those who, out of strength, would assist me in the work of destruction. Thenceforth all my writings are so much bait: perhaps I understand angling as well as any one? If nothing was *caught,* I was not to blame. *There were simply no fish.*

2

In all essential points, this book (1886) is a criticism of *modernity,* including modern science, modern art, even modern politics, along with some indications as to a contrasting type which would be as little like modern man as possible, a noble, a yea-saying type. In this latter sense the book as a *school for gentlemen*—the term here being used with a much more spiritual and radical significance than it has ever had before. Even to endure the idea one must be physically courageous, one must never have learned fear. All those things on which the age prides itself are felt as conflicting with the type mentioned; they are looked upon almost in the light of bad manners. Among these things are our far-famed "objectivity," "sympathy with all that suffers," "the historical sense," with its servility before foreign tastes, its lying-in-the-dust before *petits faits,* and finally the science mania,—if you consider the fact that this book follows *Zarathustra,* you may perhaps guess to what dietetic régime it owes its life. The eye which has been vigorously compelled to see things at a great distance,—*Zarathustra* is even more far-sighted than the Tsar,—is here forced, on the contrary, to focus sharply on that which is close at hand, our own age and environment. In all the aphorisms and especially in the form, the reader will find the same *voluntary* rejection of those instincts which made a *Zarathustra* possible. Refinement in form, in aims, and in the art of keeping silent, are emphasized; psychology is handled with a deliberate hardness and cruelty,—the book manages to get along without a single good-natured word. . . . All this is invigorating. Who can conceive the kind of recreation made necessary by such an expenditure of goodness as is to be found in *Zarathustra?* Theologically speaking—pay close attention for I seldom speak as a theologian—it was God Himself who, at the end of His day's work, coiled Himself up in the form of a serpent at the foot of the tree of knowledge. It was thus that He recovered from being a God. . . . He had made everything too beautiful. . . . The devil is simply God's moment of idleness at the end of that seventh day.

"*The Genealogy of Morals: A Polemic*"

THE three essays which make up this genealogy are, as regards expression, aim, and the technique of the unexpected, perhaps the most curious things that have ever been written. Dionysus, as you know, is also the god of darkness. In each case the beginning is calculated to lead one astray; it is cool, scientific, even ironical, intentionally thrust to the fore, intentionally reticent. Gradually the atmosphere becomes less calm; there is an occasional flash of lightning; exceedingly unpleasant truths emphasize their appearance with a dull, rumbling sound from out remote distances—until finally a fierce tempo is attained in which everything strains forward with terrible intensity. At the end, in each case, amid fearful thunderclaps, a new truth becomes visible through heavy clouds. The truth of the first essay is the psychology of Christianity: the birth of Christianity out of the spirit of resentment, not, as is supposed, out of the "Spirit"—essentially a counter-movement, a great rebellion against domination by noble values. This second essay deals with the psychology of conscience: this is not, as is supposed, "the voice of God in man"; it is the instinct of cruelty, turning in upon itself after it can no longer release itself outwardly. Cruelty is here revealed, for the first time, as one of the oldest and most indispensable elements in the foundation of culture. The third essay is a reply to the question as to the origin of the terrific power of the ascetic ideal, of the priest ideal, despite the fact that this ideal is essentially harmful, that it is the will to annihilation and decadence. Reply: it was powerful not because God was active behind the priests, as is supposed, but because it was a *faute de mieux*—hitherto it has been the only ideal; it has had no competition. "For man would rather aspire to nothingness than not aspire at all." The main trouble was that before *Zarathustra,* a counter-ideal was lacking. You have understood my meaning. Three decisive psychological overtures preceding a *Transvaluation of all Values.*—This book contains the first psychology of the priest.

"*The Twilight of the Idols: How to Philosophize with the Hammer*"

1

THIS work of not quite one hundred and fifty pages, with its cheerful and fateful tone, like a laughing demon, the work of so few days that I hesitate to give their number—is altogether an exception among books: there is no work more rich in substance, more independent, more subversive—more wicked. Should any one care to get a brief idea of how everything, before my time, was standing on its head, he might begin by reading this book. What is called "Idols" on the title page is quite simply everything that has hitherto been called truth. *The Twilight of the Idols*—in plain English, the old truth is nearing its end.

2

There is no reality, no "ideality," that has not been touched upon in this book (touched! what a cautious euphemism!). Not merely those idols which are eternal, but those that are most recent—and consequently, most senile: modern ideas, for instance. A strong wind blows among the trees and everywhere fruit—truths—fall to earth. There is a surplus as of an overfruitful autumn here: you trip over truths; you even crush some to death, there are too many of them. But those things that you grasp are no longer questionable; they have the stamp of decisiveness. I alone possess a yardstick for "truth"; I am the sole arbiter. It would seem as if a second consciousness had arisen in me, as if the "will" in me had cast a light upon the downward path along which it has been running for ages. *The downward path*—that was what they called the road to "Truth." All dark impulse—"obscurest aspiration"—is at an end; the *"good man"* is precisely he who is least aware of the "true way." [1] And, speaking quite seriously, no one before me knew the true way, the way upwards: only after my time could men once again find hopes, life-tasks, and paths leading to culture—of which *I am the joyful herald*. It is on this account that I am also a fatality.

3

Immediately after completing this work, and without losing a single day, I attacked the formidable task of the *Transvaluation* with a supreme feeling of pride which nothing could equal; and, sure at every moment of my immortality, I engraved sign after sign upon brass tablets with the certainty of Fate. The Preface was born on September 3, 1888. When, after finishing it, I emerged into the morning air, I was greeted by the most beautiful day the Upper Engadine had ever disclosed to me—clear, glowing with color, and including all

---

[1] A good man through obscurest aspiration,
Has still an instinct of the one true way.
            —Prologue to *Faust,* Bayard Taylor's Trans

the contrasts and all the intermediary gradations between ice and the south. Owing to a delay caused by floods, I did not leave Sils-Maria until the 20th of September, so that I was finally the only visitor in this wonderful spot, on which my gratitude bestows the gift of an immortal name. After a journey full of incident, including one narrow escape from death in the waters of Lake Como, which was flooded when I reached it in the dead of night,—I arrived at Turin on the afternoon of the 21st. Turin, the only suitable place for me, and from that time on, my home. I took the same lodgings I had occupied in the spring, Via Carlo Alberto 6, III, opposite the mighty Palazzo Carignano, in which Vittorio Emanuele was born; I had a view of the Piazza Carlo Alberto and of the hill-country beyond it. Without hesitating, without letting myself be diverted for a moment, I returned to my work; only the last quarter still remained to be written. On the 30th of September, a great triumph; the seventh day; divine idleness on the banks of the Po. The same day, I wrote the Preface to *The Twilight of the Idols,* the correction of the proofs of which was a recreation for me during the month of September. I never experienced such an autumn; nor ever imagined that such things could be possible—a Claude Lorrain extended to infinity, every day of an equal unlimited perfection.

"*The Case of Wagner: A Musician's Problem*"

1

To do justice to this essay a man ought to suffer from the fate
of music as from an open wound.—From what do I suffer
when I suffer from the fate of music? From this, that music
has been deprived of its world-transfiguring, yea-saying character—that it is decadent music and no longer the flute of
Dionysus. Suppose, however, that a man feels the cause of
music to be his own cause, the expression of his own passion;
in that case he will find this essay exceptionally mild and
courteous. To be cheerful amid such circumstances, and with
others to make good-natured fun of one's self,—*ridendo
dicere severum,*[1] when the *verum dicere* would justify any degree of hardness,—is humanity itself. Who can doubt that I,
as an old artillery-man, had it in my power to train my *heavy*
guns on Wagner?—Everything decisive in this matter I kept
to myself——I have loved Wagner.—But after all, an attack
upon a more than usually subtle "unknown person" whom another would not have divined so easily, is a significant part of
my life-task. Oh, I still have quite a few other "unknown per-

---

[1] The motto of *The Case of Wagner.*—Tr.

sons" to unmask besides a Cagliostro of Music! Especially, I have to direct an attack against the German people, who, in spiritual matters, grow constantly more indolent, poorer in instincts, and more *honest;* who, with enviable appetite, persist in nourishing themselves with contradictions, and gulp down "Faith" together with science, Christian love together with anti-Semitism, and the will to power (to the "Empire"), together with the gospel of humility—all this without the slightest sign of indigestion! They take no sides amid all these contradictions! What stomachic neutrality! What "selflessness"! What a sense of justice there is in the German palate, which grants equal rights to all,—which finds everything delicious! The Germans are undoubtedly idealists. On my last visit to Germany, I found German taste engaged in granting equal right to Wagner and the *Trumpeter of Säkkingen;* and I myself saw how Leipzig tried to honor one of the most genuine and most German of musicians—(using German in the old sense of the word)—a man who was no mere German of the Empire, the master Heinrich Schütz, by founding a Liszt Society, with the aim of cultivating and spreading artful (*listige* [2]) Church music. The Germans are undoubtedly idealists. . . .

2

But here nothing shall prevent me from being rude, and telling the Germans a few unpleasant truths: who else is there to do it? I am speaking of their laxity in historical matters. Not only have the German historians completely lost that *broad*

---

[2] The pun, of course, is not transferable.—Tr.

view of cultural progress and cultural values; not only are they all political (or Church) puppets; but this broad view itself is banned by them. First and foremost a man must be "German," he must belong to *the* race"; only then can he decide upon all historical values and lack of values—only then can he establish them. . . . "I am a German," constitutes an argument, "Deutschland über Alles," a principle; the Germans represent the "moral order of the universe" in history; in their relation to the Roman Empire, they are standard-bearers of freedom; in their relation to the eighteenth century, they are the restorers of morality, of the "Categorical Imperative." There is such a thing as history interpreted according to Imperial Germany; there is, I fear, even anti-Semitic history—there is also court history, for which Herr von Treitschke is not ashamed of himself. Recently an idiotic opinion, a theory of Vischer the Swabian esthete, since happily deceased, made the rounds of the German newspapers as a "truth" to which every German *must perforce assent*. Here it is: "The Renaissance *and* the Reformation must be taken together to constitute a whole—the esthetic rebirth and the moral rebirth." Such sentences exhaust my patience, and I feel a desire, I even feel it my duty, to tell the Germans, once for all, what they already have on their conscience. *Every great crime against culture committed during the last four hundred years lies on their conscience!* . . . And always for the same reason, because of their fundamental cowardice in the face of reality, which is also cowardice in the face of truth; because of the falsehood which has become almost instinctive with them—because of "idealism." The Germans deprived Europe of the fruits, the whole meaning of her last period of greatness—the Renaissance; and this at a moment when a higher order of values, when values that were noble, that said yea to life, that assured a future, had achieved a victory over the opposing values of degeneration, *in the very hearts of their supporters!* Then Luther, that fatal monk, not only restored the Church, but, what was a thousand times worse, restored Christianity the very moment that it lay prostrate. Christianity, the *Denial of the Will to Live,* became a religion! Luther was an impossible monk who, on the basis of his "impossibility," attacked the Church, and consequently restored it! Catholics would have good reason to celebrate feasts in honor of Luther, and to produce festival plays in his honor. Luther and the "moral rebirth"! To the devil with all psychology! There is no doubt about it—the Germans are idealists. On two separate occasions when, by terrific boldness and self-control, an upright, unequivocal, and perfectly scientific attitude of mind had been attained, the Germans knew how to find a secret path back to the old "ideal," reconciliations between truth and the "ideal," and, at bottom, formulæ for a right to reject science and reinstate falsehood. Leibniz and Kant—these two great drag-chains upon the intellectual honesty of Europe! Finally, when there appeared on the bridge spanning two centuries of decadence, a superior force of genius and will strong enough to weld Europe into a political and economic unit, that it might rule the world, the Germans, with their Wars of Independence, robbed Europe of the meaning, the marvelous meaning, of Napoleon's life. And with this they incurred the responsibility for everything that resulted, everything that exists today—the sickliness and stupidity that opposes culture, the neurosis called Nationalism, from which Europe suffers, this eternal subdivision of Europe into petty states, accompanied by petty politics: they have robbed Europe itself of its meaning and intelligence, —they have led it into a blind alley. Is there any one but I

[*918*]

who knows a way out of this blind alley? Any one who knows
of a common task great enough to reunite the peoples of
Europe?

3

And after all, why should I not utter my suspicions? In my
case, too, the Germans will attempt to make a great destiny
give birth merely to a mouse. They have compromised themselves with me up to the present; I doubt whether things will
get better in the future. Oh, how I should like to prove a false
prophet here! My natural readers and listeners are already
Russians, Scandinavians, and Frenchmen—will they always be
the same? In the history of knowledge, Germans are represented only by doubtful names, they have produced only *"unconscious"* swindlers (the word applies to Fichte, Schelling,
Schopenhauer, Hegel, and Schleiermacher, as well as to Kant
or Leibniz; they were all mere *Schleiermachers*).[3] The Germans must not have the honor of associating with theirs the
first upright intellect in their history of intellect, an intellect in
which truth prevailed over a swindle lasting four thousand
years. "German intellect" is bad air for me: I breathe with
difficulty in the neighborhood of this psychological uncleanliness that has now become instinctive—an uncleanliness
which in every word and gesture betrays a German. They have
never endured a seventeenth century of vigorous self-examination, as have the French,—a La Rochefoucauld, a Descartes, are
a hundred times more upright than the first among Germans—
who till now have had no psychologists. But psychology is
practically the standard of measurement for the cleanliness or

---

[3] *Schleiermacher* = a maker of veils.—Tr.

uncleanliness of a race. . . . And if a man is not clean, how can he be deep? The Germans are like women, you can never fathom their depths—they have none, and that ends it. They cannot even be called shallow. What is called "deep" in Germany, is precisely this instinctive uncleanliness toward one's self, of which I have just spoken: they *will* not be clear in regard to their own natures. Might I not suggest the word "German" as an international epithet to indicate this psychological depravity?—At this moment, for instance, the German Emperor is declaring it to be his Christian duty to free the slaves in Africa; among us good Europeans, this would simply be called "German." . . . Have the Germans ever produced even a book that had depth? They have no notion what constitutes depth. I have known scholars who considered Kant deep. At the Prussian Court I fear that Herr von Treitschke is regarded as deep. And when I have chanced to praise Stendhal as a deep psychologist, I have often been compelled, among German university professors, to spell out his name for them.

4

And why should I not proceed to the end? I love to make a clean breast of things. It is even part of my ambition to be considered as a despiser of Germans *par excellence*. At the age of twenty-six I had already expressed my suspicions of the German character (see my *Thoughts out of Season,* third part). The Germans are impossible for me. When I try to think of a man who runs counter to all my instincts, the result is always a German. My first test of a man, is, whether he has a feeling for distance in him; whether he sees rank, gradation, and order everywhere between man and man; whether he makes distinctions; for this is what constitutes a gentleman. Otherwise he belongs irrevocably to that open-hearted, alas! quite good-natured species, *la canaille!* But the Germans are *canaille*—for, alas! they are so good-natured! A man debases himself by consorting with Germans: the German places every one on an equal footing. If I except my intercourse with a few artists, and especially with Richard Wagner, I may say that I have not spent one pleasant hour with Germans. If the profoundest spirit of the ages were to appear among Germans, some savior of the Capitol would be sure to declare that his own unbeautiful soul was at least as great. I cannot endure this race with which a man is always in bad company, which has no feeling for nuances (and alas! I am a nuance), which has no *esprit* in its feet, and cannot even walk! For the Germans have no feet at all, they merely have legs. The Germans have no idea of how vulgar they are—which is itself the very acme of vulgarity,—they are not once ashamed of being merely Germans. They will have their say in everything, they regard themselves as fit to decide everything; I fear that they have even decided about me. . . . My whole life is essentially a proof of this. In vain have I sought among them for a sign of tact and delicacy towards myself. Among Jews I did indeed find it, but never among Germans. My instinct is to be mild and benevolent to all,—I have the right not to draw distinctions,—but this does not prevent me from keeping my eyes open. I except no one, least of all my friends,—I can only hope that this has not prejudiced my reputation for humanity towards them. There are five or six things which I have always held as points of honor. Nevertheless, the truth remains that for many years I have regarded almost every letter I received as a piece of cynicism. For there is more cynicism in an attitude of good-will towards me than in any sort of hatred. I tell every one of my friends frankly that he has never thought it worth the trouble to *study* any of my writings: I can guess, from some slight indications, that they are not even familiar with their contents. And as concerns my *Zarathustra,* which of my friends would have seen more in it than a piece of inexcusable, though fortunately quite harmless, arrogance? Ten years have elapsed, and no one has yet felt himself in duty bound to defend my name against the absurd silence under which it lies buried. It was a foreigner, a Dane, who first showed sufficient keenness of instinct and courage to do this, and who grew indignant at my so-called friends. At what German university today would such lectures on my philosophy be possible, as those which Dr. Brandes delivered last spring in Copenhagen, thus proving once more his right to be called a psychologist? I myself have never suffered from all this; what is *necessary* does not offend me. *Amor fati* is the essence of my nature. This, however, does not prevent a love of irony, even world-historic irony. And, accordingly, about two years before hurling the annihilating thunderbolt of the *Transvaluation,* which will send the whole earth into convulsions, I sent my *Case of Wagner* out into the world. The Germans were to immortalize themselves once more by completely misunderstanding me—there is still time for it. And have they done so? Admirably, my dear Germans! Allow me to congratulate you. . . .

Why I Am a Fatality

1

I KNOW my destiny. Some day my name will be bound up with the recollection of something terrific—of a crisis quite unprecedented, of the most profound clash of consciences, and the decisive condemnation of all that theretofore had been believed, required, and hallowed. I am not a man, I am dynamite. And with all this there is nothing in me to suggest the founder of a religion. Religions are the business of the mob; after coming in contact with a religious man, I always have to wash my hands. . . . I want no "believers"; I think I am too full of malice even to believe in myself; I never address myself to the masses. I have a terrific fear that some day I shall be pronounced "holy." You can easily guess why I publish this book beforehand—it is to prevent people from wronging me. I do not wish to be a saint; I would much rather be a clown. Perhaps I am a clown. And despite this—or rather not despite this (for there has never been anything falser than a saint)— I am the voice of truth. But my truth is terrible: for hitherto *lies* have been called truth. *The Transvaluation of all Values:* that is my formula for mankind's act of highest self-recognition, which in me has become flesh and genius. My destiny ordains that I should be the first decent human being, that I should feel myself opposed to the falsehood of ages. I was the first to discover truth, by sensing falsehood as falsehood. I smelled it as such. . . . My genius resides in my nostrils. I contradict as no one has contradicted before, and nevertheless I am the reverse of a negative spirit. I am a joyful herald, unparalleled in history; I am acquainted with tasks of a grandeur formerly inconceivable. Hope is reborn with me. Thus, I am necessarily a Man of Destiny. For when Truth engages in struggle with the falsehood of ages, we must expect shocks and a series of earthquakes, with a rearrangement of hills and valleys, such as has never yet been dreamed of. The concept "politics" is thus raised bodily into the realm of spiritual warfare. All the mighty forms of the old society are blown into space—for they all rest on falsehood: there will be wars, whose like have never been seen on earth before. Politics on a grand scale will date from me.

2

Do you desire a formula for such a destiny become incarnate? It is contained in my *Zarathustra:*

"And he who would be a creator in good and evil must first be a destroyer, and break values into pieces.

"Thus the greatest evil belongeth unto the greatest good: but this is the creative good."

I am by far the most terrible man that has ever existed; but this does not negate the fact that I shall be the most beneficent. I know the joy of *annihilation* to a degree commensurate with my power to annihilate. In both cases I obey my Dionysian nature, which cannot separate the negative deed from yeasaying. I am the first immoralist, and thus I am the essential destroyer.

[*924*]

3

I have not been asked, as I should have been, precisely what the name of Zarathustra meant in my mouth, in the mouth of the first immoralist; for what constitutes the historical uniqueness of this Persian is the fact that he was the exact opposite. Zarathustra was the first to see in the struggle between good and evil the essential wheel in the working of things. The translation of morality into metaphysics, as force, first cause, end-in-itself, is his work. But the very question already suggests its own manner. Zarathustra created this most fateful of all errors—morality; consequently, he must be the first to recognize it as an error. Not only because he has had longer and greater experience of the subject than any other thinker,—all history is indeed the experimental refutation of the theory of the so-called moral order of the world,—what is more important is that Zarathustra is more truthful than any other thinker. His teaching and his alone defines truthfulness as the highest virtue—that is to say, as the reverse of the cowardice of the "idealist" who flees at the sight of reality. Zarathustra has more boldness in him than all other thinkers put together. To tell the truth and to shoot straight: those are the Persian virtues. Do you understand? . . . The defeat of morality by itself, through truthfulness, the moralist's defeat of himself in his opposite—in me—that is what the name Zarathustra means in my mouth.

4

At bottom there are two negations included in the term Immoralist. First I deny the type of man who formerly passed as the highest—the *good,* the *benevolent,* the *charitable;* and, on the other hand, I deny that kind of morality which has become recognized and dominant as morality-in-itself—the morality of decadence, or, to use a cruder term, Christian morality. I would agree to consider the second of these negations as the more decisive, for, generally speaking, the over-evaluation of goodness and kindness seems to me already a consequence of decadence, a symptom of weakness, incompatible with an ascending, yea-saying life. Negation and annihilation are conditions of the yea-saying attitude. Let me pause for a moment at the problem of the psychology of the good man. In order to evaluate any type of man, we must calculate the cost of his maintenance, we must know the conditions of his existence. The condition of the existence of the *good* is falsehood: or, expressed differently, the unwillingness to see how reality is actually constituted; a reality which is not always provocative of beneficent instincts, and which is still less pleased at the continual intrusion of careless, good-natured hands. To consider distress of all kinds as an objection, as something to be destroyed, is sheer idiocy; generally speaking, it is actually harmful in its consequences, a fatal stupidity— almost as mad as the desire to abolish bad weather, out of pity for the poor, perhaps. In the great economy of the universe, the terrors of reality (in the passions, in the desires, in the will to power) are incalculably more essential than that form of petty happiness, so-called "goodness"; it is sheer indulgence to grant the latter any place at all, since it is bound up with a falsification of the instincts. I shall have a good opportunity of showing the ghastly consequences to history, of optimism, this misshapen offspring of the *homines optimi.* Zarathustra, the first to see that the optimist is just as degenerate as the pessimist, and perhaps more harmful, says: *"Good men never speak the truth. False shores and false harbors were ye taught by the good. In the lies of the good were ye born and bred. Through the good everything hath become false and crooked from the very roots."* Fortunately the world is not built merely upon those instincts in which the good-natured herd-animal would find his paltry happiness. To demand that everybody become a "good man," a gregarious animal, a blue-eyed, benevolent, "beautiful soul," or—as Herbert Spencer wished—an altruist, would mean robbing existence of its greatest character, castrating mankind and reducing it to a wretched Mongolism. *And this has been attempted! It is this that men call morality.* In this sense Zarathustra calls "the good" now "the last men," and again "the beginning of the end"; and above all, he considers them *the most harmful kind of men,* because they secure their existence at the cost of Truth and at the cost of the Future.

"The good—they cannot create; they are ever the beginning of the end.

"They crucify him who writeth new values on new tables; they sacrifice *unto themselves* the future; they crucify the whole future of humanity!

"The good—they are ever the beginning of the end.

"And whatever harm the slanderers of the world may do, *the harm of the good is the most calamitous of all harm."*

5

Zarathustra, the first psychologist of the good man, is consequently the friend of the evil man. When a degenerate man arises to the highest rank, he must do so only at the cost of the reverse type—at the cost of the strong man who is certain of life. When the herd-animal shines with the bright rays of the purest virtue, the exceptional man must be degraded to the rank of the evil. When falsehood insists at all costs on claiming the word "truth" as its world-outlook, the really truthful man must be sought out among those of worst repute. Zarathustra is quite unequivocal here; he says that it was precisely the knowledge of the good, of the "best," that caused his horror of men. And it was out of this feeling of repulsion that he grew the wings with which to soar into distant futures. He does not conceal the fact that this type of man, a relatively superhuman type, is superhuman particularly as compared with the "good" man, and that the good and the just would call his superman the *devil*.

"Ye higher men, on whom my gaze now falls, this is the doubt that ye wake in my breast, and this is my secret laughter: methinks ye would call my Superman—the devil! So strange are ye in your souls to all that is great, that the Superman would be terrible in your eyes for his goodness."

It is from this and no other passage, that one must set out to understand the goal that Zarathustra wants—the kind of man that he conceives, conceives reality *as it is;* he is strong enough for this—he is not estranged or removed from it, he is himself the reality, in him can be found all the doubt and terror of reality: *only thus can man have greatness.*

6

But I have chosen the title of Immoralist as a mark of distinction in still another sense; I am very proud to possess this name that elevates me above all mankind. No one hitherto has felt Christian morality beneath him; to do that one must have height, far vision, and an abysmal psychological depth, previously utterly unheard of. Up to the present Christian morality has been the Circe of all thinkers—they stood at her service. What man, before me, had descended into the caves from which the poisonous fumes of this ideal—of this slandering of the world—burst forth? What man before me had even dared to suspect that they were caves? What one of the philosophers preceding me was a real psychologist, and not its very reverse, a "superior swindler," an "Idealist"? Before me there was no psychology. To be the first may be a curse; in any case, it is a destiny: *for as the first one also can despise*. My danger is the loathing of mankind.

7

Have you understood me? What defines me, what places me apart from the rest of humanity, is the fact that I *unmasked* Christian morality. For this reason I needed a word which would contain the idea of a universal challenge. Not to have seen these things before seemed to me to be the sign of the greatest uncleanliness mankind has on its conscience, to be self-deception become instinctive, to be the fundamental will to close one's eyes to every phenomenon, every cause, every reality; in fact, it was a psychological deception that amounted

to crime. Blindness in the face of Christianity is the essential
crime—it is the crime *against* life. Ages and peoples, the first
as well as the last, philosophers and old women, with the
exception of five or six moments in history (and of myself, the
seventh), are all equally guilty. Christian morality is the most
pernicious form of the will to falsehood, the real Circe of
humanity, that has corrupted it. It is not error as error which
infuriates me here; it is not the age-long lack of "good-will,"
of discipline, of decency, and of spiritual courage, which betrays itself in the triumph of Christian morality; it is the
absence of nature, it is the perfectly ghastly fact that what was
unnatural received the highest honors as morality, and remained suspended over man as the law of the Categorical Imperative. Imagine blundering in this way, *not* as an individual,
not as a people, but as mankind! To teach the contempt of the
primal life-instincts; to set up fraudulently a "soul," a "spirit,"
in order to overthrow the body; to teach man to find impurity
in the prerequisite of life—in sex; to look for the principle of
evil in the profound need for expansion—that is to say, in
vigorous self-love (the term itself is slanderous); and conversely to see a higher moral value—but what am I saying?—
I mean the *moral value per se,* in the typical signs of decay, in
the antagonism of the instincts in "selflessness," in the loss of
ballast, in "objectivity" and in "neighbor love." What! is
humanity itself in a state of decadence? Has it always been so?
One thing is established, that ye have been taught only the
values of decadence as the highest values. The morality of
self-renunciation is essentially the morality of degeneration;
the fact, "I am going to the dogs," is translated into the imperative, "Ye shall all go to the dogs"—and not only into the
imperative. This morality of self-renunciation, the only kind

of morality that has been taught hitherto, betrays the will to nothingness—it is a basic denial of life. There still remains the possibility that it is not mankind that is degenerating, but only that parasitical kind of man—the priest, who, by means of morality has lied himself into his position of determiner of values, who has divined in Christian morality his road to power. And, in fact, this is my opinion. The teachers and leaders of mankind—including the theologians—have been, every one of them, decadents: hence their transvaluation of all values into a hostility to life; hence morality. Here is a *definition of morality:* Morality is the idiosyncrasy of decadents, actuated by a desire *to avenge themselves successfully upon life.* I attach great value to this definition.

8

Have you understood me? I have not uttered a single word which I had not already said five years ago through the mouth of Zarathustra. The unmasking of Christian morality is a unique event, a real catastrophe. He who throws light upon it is a *force majeure,* a fatality; he breaks the history of mankind in two. Man lives either before or after him. The lightning truth struck precisely that which heretofore had stood highest: he who understands what was then destroyed should look to see whether he still holds anything in his hands. Everything which until then was called truth, is now recognized as the most harmful, spiteful, and concealed form of falsehood; the sacred pretext, the "improvement" of man, is recognized as a ruse to drain life of its blood. Morality as *Vampirism.* . . . He who unmasks morality simultaneously unmasks the worthlessness of the values in which men believe or have believed; he sees nothing worthy of honor in the most venerated men—even in the type of men that has been pronounced holy; he sees in them only the most fatal kind of abortions, fatal, *because they fascinate*. The concept "God" was invented as the counter-concept to life—everything harmful, poisonous, slanderous, and all deadly hostility to life, all bound together in one horrible unit. The concepts "beyond" and "true world" were invented in order to depreciate the only word that exists —in order to leave no goal, no significance, no task, to our earthly reality. The concepts "soul," "spirit," and last of all the concept "immortal soul," were invented to despise the body, to make it sick and "holy," to inspire a terrible levity towards all those things in life which deserve to be treated seriously, questions of nutrition, housing, intellectual diet, care of the sick, cleanliness, and weather. Instead of health, we find the "salvation of the soul"—in other words, a *folie circulaire* fluctuating between the convulsions of penitence and the hysteria of redemption. The concept "sin," together with the instrument of torture appertaining to it, the concept of "free will," was invented in order to mislead our instincts, to render the mistrust of them man's second nature! In the concepts "selflessness" and "self-denial," the actual symptoms of decadence are revealed. The allurement of the harmful, the inability to discover one's real needs, and finally self-destruction, are converted into values, into the "duty," the "holiness," and the "divinity" of man. Finally—most frightful of all—the notion of the *good* man comes to mean everything which is weak, ill, misshapen, and suffering from itself, everything which should be obliterated. The law of selection is thwarted, an ideal is made in opposition to the proud, fortunate man, to the yea-saying man, to him who is certain of the future, to him who guarantees the future—this man is henceforth called *evil*. And all this was believed in as *morality!*—*Ecrasez l'infâme!*

9

Have you understood me? *Dionysus* versus *Christ.* . . .

An Attempt at Self-Criticism
(1886)

1
___

WHATEVER may lie at the bottom of this doubtful book is a question of the first rank and interest; moreover it is a deeply personal question—in proof thereof note the time in which it originated, and *despite* which it originated, the exciting period of the Franco-German war of 1870-71. While the thunder of the battle of Wörth was rolling over Europe, the ruminator and riddle-lover, who was to be the father of this book, sat somewhere in a corner of the Alps, lost in riddles and ruminations, consequently very much concerned and at the same time unconcerned; and he wrote down his meditations on the *Greeks*—the kernel of the curious and difficult book, to which this belated prologue (or epilogue) is devoted. A few weeks passed and he found himself under the walls of Metz, his mind not yet free of questions concerning the alleged "cheerfulness" of the Greeks and of Greek art; till at last, in that month of greatest suspense, when peace was being debated at Versailles, he too attained to peace with himself, and slowly convalescing from a disease brought home from the field, made up his mind definitely regarding the "Birth of Tragedy from the Spirit of Music." Music? Music—and Tragedy? Greeks—and tragic music? Greeks and the Art-products of pessimism? A race of men, well-fashioned, beautiful, envied, life-inspiring, like no other race hitherto, the Greeks—indeed? Were the Greeks *in need* of tragedy? Yea—of art? Wherefore—Greek art? . . .

We can thus guess the great question that arose concerning the value of existence. Is pessimism *necessarily* the sign of decline, of decay, of failure, of exhausted and debilitated instincts?—as was the case with the Indians, as is, to all appearance, the case with us "modern" men and Europeans? Is there a pessimism of *strength?* Is there an intellectual predilection for what is hard, awful, evil, problematical in existence— a tendency that is the result of well-being, exuberant health, a *fullness* of existence? Is there perhaps suffering involved in that very overfullness? A seductive keen-eyed boldness which *yearns* for the terrible, as for the enemy, the worthy enemy, against whom it may measure its strength, from whom it would learn what "fear" is? What does *tragic* myth mean to the Greeks of the best, the strongest, the bravest era? And the prodigious phenomenon of the Dionysian? And that which was born of the Dionysian, tragedy? And again: that of which tragedy died, the Socratism of morality, the dialectic complacency and cheerfulness of the theoretical man? Might not this very Socratism be a sign of decline, of fatigue, of disease, of anarchical disintegrating instincts? And the "Greek cheerfulness" of the later Hellenism, might that not be merely a glowing sunset? Is the Epicurean will *counter* to pessimism merely a precaution of the sufferer? And science itself, our science—aye, considered as a symptom of life, what does all science really signify? Whither, worse still, *whence*—all science? Well? Is scientism perhaps only a fear and an evasion of pessimism? A subtle defense against—*truth?* Morally speaking, something like falsehood and cowardice? And, un-morally speaking, an artifice? O Socrates, Socrates, was this perhaps *thy* secret? Oh, mysterious ironist, was this perhaps thine—irony? . . .

2

What I then began to deal with was a thing terrible and dangerous, a problem with horns, not necessarily a bull, but in any case a *new* problem. Today I should say it was the *problem of science* itself—science glimpsed for the first time as problematic, as questionable. But the book, the outlet for my youthful ardors and suspicions—what an *impossible* book must needs be the result of a task so unfit for a youth. Constructed out of mere precocious, immature personal ex-periences, all of which lay close to the threshold of the com-municable, seen from the standpoint of *art*—for the problem of science cannot be discerned on the groundwork of science, a book perhaps for artists (that is, an exceptional kind of artists, for whom one must seek and does not even care to seek . . .), with the analytical and retrospective tendencies that accompany such artists, full of psychological innovations and artists' secrets, with an artist's metaphysics in the back-ground, a work of youth, full of youthful spirit and youthful melancholy, independent, defiantly self-sufficient even when it seems to bow to some authority and self-veneration; in short, a firstling-work, in every bad sense of the term; in spite of its old problem, filled with every fault of youth, above all with youth's prolixity and youth's "storm and stress": on the other hand, in view of the success it had (especially with the great artist to whom it addressed itself, as it were, in a duologue, Richard Wagner), it was a *demonstrated* book, I mean a book which, at any rate, sufficed "for the best of its time." On this account, it should be treated with some consideration and re serve; yet I shall not altogether conceal how unpleasant are the feelings it awakens in me, how after sixteen years it stands a total stranger before me,—before an eye which is more mature and a hundred times more fastidious, but which has by no means grown colder, an eye that has lost none of its interest in that very problem attacked for the first time by this daring book,—*to view science through the eyes of the artist, and art through the eyes of life.* . . .

3

Let me repeat that today the book appears impossible to me,—I consider it badly written, heavy, painful, full of a straining after images, maudlin, sugared at times to the point of effeminacy, uneven in tempo, devoid of the will to logical clarity, utterly convinced and therefore contemptuous of demonstration, distrustful even of the *propriety* of demonstra- tion, viewing itself as a book for initiates, as "music" for those who are baptized in the name of Music, as a book for those who are united from the beginning of things by common and rare experiences in art, as a countersign for blood-relations *in artibus*,—a haughty and fantastic book, which from the very first page withdraws even more from the *profanum vulgus* of the "cultured" than from the "people," but which also, as its effect has shown and still shows, knows quite well how to seek out fellow-enthusiasts and lure them into new byways and dancing-grounds. Here, at any rate—this much was acknowl·

edged with curiosity as well as with aversion—here spoke a *strange* voice, the disciple of a still "unknown God," who for the time being had concealed himself under the scholar's hood, under the German's gravity and discomfort in the face of dialectic, even under the bad manners of the Wagnerian; here was a spirit with strange and still nameless needs, a memory bristling with questions, experiences and obscurities, beside which stood the name Dionysus like still another question mark; here spoke—people said to themselves with suspicion— something akin to a mystic and almost mænadic soul, which, undecided whether it should reveal or conceal itself, stammers uncontrolled, with difficulty as in a strange tongue. It should have *sung*, this "new soul"—not spoken! What a pity that I did not dare to utter my thoughts as a poet! Perhaps I could have done so! Or at least as a philologist: for even today almost everything in this domain remains to be discovered and disinterred by the philologist! Above all was the problem, *that* here there *is* a problem before us,—and that, as long as we have no answer to the question "What is Dionysian?" the Greeks must remain, now as ever, wholly unknown and unintelligible. . . .

4

Yes, what is Dionysian? In this book an answer is found,— for here speaks a "knowing one," the votary and disciple of his god. Perhaps to-day I should speak with more caution and less eloquence of a psychological question so difficult as that of the origin of Greek tragedy. A fundamental question is the relation of the Greek to pain, his degree of sensitivity—did it remain constant? or did it vary?—did his ever-increasing *longing for beauty,* for festivals, merriment, new cults, really grow out of want, privation, melancholy, pain? For even if this were true—and Pericles (or Thucydides) intimates as much in the great Funeral Oration—how shall we account for the opposite longing, that preceded it, the *longing for the ugly,* the Old Hellene's stout, resolute will to pessimism, to tragic myth, to a conception of all that is terrible, evil, mysterious, destructive, fatal, at the basis of existence? Whence then must tragedy have sprung? Perhaps from *joy,* from strength, from exuberant health, from overfullness. And what then, physiologically speaking, is the significance of that madness, the Dionysian madness, out of which grew comic as well as tragic art? What? Is it possible that madness is not necessarily a symptom of de-generation, of decline, of a decadent culture? Perhaps this is a question for alienists—there are neuroses of *health?* Of folk-youth and folk-youthfulness? What does that synthesis of god and goat in the satyr mean? What personal experience, what compulsion, made the Greek conceive the Dionysian reveler and primitive man as a satyr? And as regards the origin of the tragic chorus: perhaps there were endemic ecstasies in these periods when the Greek body flourished and the Greek soul overflowed with life? Visions, perhaps, and hallucinations, which gripped entire communities, entire cult-assemblies? What if the Greeks in the very wealth of their youth had the will *to be* tragic and were pessimists? What if it was madness itself, to use a word of Plato's, which conferred the *greatest* blessings upon Hellas? And what if, on the other hand and conversely, at the very moment of their dissolution and weak-ness, the Greeks became increasingly more optimistic, more superficial, more histrionic, also more ardent for logic and the logicizing of the world,—consequently at the same time more "cheerful" and more "scientific"? Yes, despite all "modern ideas" and democratic prejudices, may not the triumph of *optimism,* the domination of *common sense,* the practical and theoretical *utilitarianism* (like democracy itself, with which it is synchronous)—may not all these be symptomatic of declining vigor, of approaching age, of bodily fatigue? And *not,* in any sense,—pessimism? Was Epicurus an optimist—because a *sufferer?* . . . We can now see the load of weighty questions with which this book has burdened itself—let us not fail to add the weightiest question of all! Viewed through the eyes of *life,* what is the meaning of—morality? . . .

5

Even in the foreword to Richard Wagner, art—and *not* morality—is set down as the properly *metaphysical* activity of man; in the book itself there recurs time and again the piquant proposition that the existence of the world is *justified* only as an esthetic phenomenon. In fact, the entire book recognizes only an artist-thought and an artist-afterthought behind all occurrences,—a "God," if you wish, but assuredly only a quite thoughtless and unmoral artist-God, who, in creation as in destruction, in good as in evil, desires to become conscious of his own equable joy and mastery; who, in creating worlds, frees himself from the *anguish* of fullness and *overfullness,* from the *suffering* of the contradictions concentrated within him. The world is conceived as the continuous redemption of God, as the ever-changing, ever-new vision of the most suffering, most discordant, most contradictory being, who can redeem himself only in *appearance.* You may call it arbitrary, idle, fantastic, if you will,—but the point is, that this entire artist-metaphysics already betrays a spirit, which is determined some day, at all hazards, to make a stand against the *moral* interpretation and significance of life. Here, for the first time perhaps, a pessimism "Beyond Good and Evil" announces itself; here form and expression are given to that "perverseness of disposition" against which Schopenhauer never tired of hurling thunderbolts;—here is a philosophy which, with derogatory intent, dares to place morality itself in the world of phenomena, and not only among "phenomena" (in the sense of the idealistic *terminus technicus*), but among the "illusions," as appearance, semblance, error, interpretation, rationalization, art. Perhaps the depth of this *anti-moralistic* tendency may be best estimated from the guarded and hostile silence with which Christianity is treated throughout the book,—Christianity, considered as the most extravagant burlesque of the moral theme to which mankind has hitherto been obliged to listen. In fact, there is no greater antithesis to the purely esthetic world-interpretation and justification taught in this book, than the Christian dogma, which is *only* moral, which wishes to be only moral, and which, with its absolute standards (for instance, the truthfulness of God), relegates—that is, disowns, convicts, condemns—art, *all* art, to the realm of *falsehood*. Behind such a mode of thought and evaluation, which, if at all genuine, must be hostile to art, I could always feel something *hostile to life,* the wrathful, vindictive negation of the will to life: for all life rests on appearance, art, illusion, the human vision, the necessity of perspective and error. From the beginning, Christianity was, essentially and thoroughly, the nausea and surfeit of Life for Life, which merely disguised, concealed and decked itself out under the belief in "another" or "better" life. The hatred of the "world," the condemnation of emotion, the fear of beauty and sensuality, a beyond, invented to slander this world all the more, at bottom a longing for Nothingness, for the end, for rest, for the "Sabbath of Sabbaths"—all this, together with the unconditional insistence of Christianity on the recognition *only* of moral values, has always appeared to me as the most dangerous and ominous of all possible forms of a "will to perish"; at the very least, as the symptom of a most fatal disease, of the profoundest weariness, faint-heartedness, exhaustion, anemia—for judged by morality (especially Christian, that is, absolute morality) life *must* constantly and inevitably be the loser, because life is something essentially unmoral,—indeed, bowed down under the weight of contempt and the everlasting No, life *must* finally be felt as unworthy of desire, as in itself unworthy. Morality itself— what?—may not morality be a "will to negate life," a secret instinct for annihilation, a principle of decay, of depreciation, of slander, the beginning of the end? And, accordingly, the danger of dangers? . . . It was *against* morality, therefore, that my instinct, an instinct defending life, turned in this provocative book, inventing for itself a fundamental counter-dogma and counter-evaluation of life, one purely artistic and *anti-Christian*. What should I call it? As a philologist and man of words I baptized it, not without some impertinence,—for who could be sure of the proper name of the Antichrist?—with the name of a Greek god: I called it *Dionysian*.

6

Can you now see the problem I dared suggest in this early work? How I now regret that at that time I did not have the courage (immodesty?) to allow myself an *individual* language for such individual contemplations and attempts—that I painfully sought to express, in Kant's and Schopenhauer's terms, strange and new values, which were fundamentally opposed to the spirit, as well as the taste, of Kant and Schopenhauer! What, for example, were Schopenhauer's views on tragedy? "What gives"—he says in *The World as Will and Idea,* II. 495—"to all tragedy that singular swing towards elevation, is the awakening of the knowledge that the world, that life, cannot satisfy us thoroughly, and consequently is *not worthy* of our attachment. In this consists the tragic spirit: it therefore leads to *resignation."* Oh, how different was the voice of Dionysus! How alien to me then was this very resignationism! But there is something far worse in this book, which I now regret even more than I regret having obscured and spoiled Dionysian anticipations with Schopenhauerian formulæ: to wit, that, in general, I *spoiled* the grand *Hellenic problem,* as I saw it, by an admixture of modern ideas! That I entertained hopes, when there was no hope, when everything pointed but too plainly to an approaching end! That, on the basis of our latter-day German music, I began to make up stories about the "Teutonic spirit" as if it were on the point of discovering and returning to itself—aye, and that I did this just when the German spirit which not long before had still had the will to lead and master Europe, testamentarily and conclusively *resigned,* and, under the pompous pretense of founding an empire, effected its transition to mediocrity, democracy, and "modern ideas." In fact, I have since learned to regard this "Teutonic spirit" without either hope or pity, just as I regard our contemporary *German music,* which is romantic through and through, the most un-Grecian of all art-forms, and moreover a first-class nerve-destroyer, doubly dangerous for a people that likes drinking and honors obscurity as a virtue—dangerous in its twofold capacity of an intoxicating and stupefying narcotic. Of course, apart from all precipitate hopes and faulty applica-

tions to matters specially modern, with which I then spoiled
my first book, the great Dionysian problem there suggested,
persists, even with reference to music: how shall we conceive
of a music, which is no longer, like the German, of Romantic
origin, but of *Dionysian.* . . .

7

——But, my dear Sir, if *your* book is not Romanticism, what
in Heaven's name is? Can a deep hatred of the present, of
"reality" and "modern ideas," be more emphasized than it is
in your artist-metaphysics?——which would rather believe in
Nothing, or in the devil, than in the "Now"? Is there not a
fundamental bass growl of wrath and destructive joy beneath
all your contrapuntal vocal art and aural seduction? Does not
the book contain a mad determination to oppose all that is
"now," a will not very far removed from practical nihilism
which seems to say: "Let nothing be true, sooner than have
you right, and *your* truth prevail!" Listen to yourself, my dear
Sir Pessimist and art-defier, listen with open ears, to a single
select passage of your own book, that not ineloquent dragon-
slayer passage, which may have a seductive Pied Piper appeal
to young ears and hearts. What? Is not that the romanticism
of 1830 *par excellence,* masked as the pessimism of 1850?
After which, of course, the usual romanticist finale at once
strikes up——rupture, collapse, return and prostration before
an old belief, before *the* old God. . . . What? is not your
pessimist book itself a piece of anti-Hellenism, an example of
Romanticism, something "equally intoxicating and stupefying," a narcotic at all events, aye, a piece of music, of *German*
music? Hearken to this:

"Let us imagine a rising generation with this bold vision, this heroic desire for the magnificent; let us imagine the valiant step of these dragon-slayers, the proud daring with which they turn their backs on all the effeminate doctrines of optimism, that they may 'live resolutely,' wholly and fully. *Would it not be necessary* for the tragic man of this culture, with his self-discipline of seriousness and terror, to desire a new art, *the art of metaphysical comfort,* namely, tragedy—to claim it as Helen, and exclaim with Faust:

"Und sollt ich nicht, sehnsüchtigster Gewalt.
Ins Leben ziehn die einzigste Gestalt?" [1]

"Would it not be *necessary?*" . . . No, thrice no! ye young romanticists: it would *not* be necessary! But it is very probable, that things may *end* thus, that *ye* may end thus, namely "comforted," to use my term, in spite of all self-discipline of seriousness and terror; metaphysically comforted, in short, as Romanticists are wont to end, as *Christians.* . . . No! ye should first of all learn the art of earthly comfort, ye should learn to *laugh,* my young friends, if ye wish to remain.pessimists: if so, you will perhaps, as laughing ones, eventually send all metaphysical comfortism to the devil—and metaphysics first of all! Or, in the language of that Dionysian ogre, called *Zarathustra:*

"Lift up your hearts, my brethren, high, higher! And do not forget your legs! Lift up also your legs, ye good dancers, and better still if ye stand upon your heads!

"This crown of the laughter, this rose-garland crown: I myself have put on this crown; I myself have consecrated my

---

[1] And shall not I, by mightiest desire,
In living forms that sole fair form acquire?
                              —*Faust,* Swanwick's Trans.

laughter. No one else have I found today potent enough for this.

"Zarathustra the dancer, Zarathustra the light one, who beckoneth with his pinions, one ready for flight, beckoning unto all birds, ready and prepared, a blissfully light-spirited one:—

"Zarathustra the soothsayer, Zarathustra the sooth-laugher, no impatient one, no absolute one, one who loveth leaps and side-leaps: I myself have put on this crown!

"This crown of the laughter, this rose-garland crown: to you, my brethren, do I cast this crown! Laughing have I consecrated; ye higher men, *learn,* I pray you—to laugh!" [2]

---

[2] *Thus Spake Zarathustra,* lxxiii. 17, 18, and 20.
Modern Library Edition.

Sils-Maria, Oberengadin, August, 1886.

THE BIRTH OF TRAGEDY
FROM THE SPIRIT OF MUSIC

Translated by CLIFTON P. FADIMAN

FOREWORD TO
RICHARD WAGNER

IN order to keep at a distance all the possible scruples, excitements, and misunderstandings to which the thoughts gathered in this essay will give occasion, considering the peculiar character of our esthetic publicity; and also that I may be able to write the introductory remarks with the same contemplative joy, whose reflection (the result of good and elevating hours) it bears on every page; that I may do this, I picture the moment when you, my much respected friend, will receive this essay; perhaps, after an evening walk in the winter snow, you will behold the unbound Prometheus on the title-page, read my name, and be at once convinced that, whatever this essay may contain, the author has something serious and impressive to say, and, moreover, that in all his meditations he communed with you as with one present and so could write only what befitted that presence. Thus you will be reminded that I collected myself for these thoughts just when your magnificent dissertation on Beethoven originated, amid the horrors and sublimities of the war which had just then broken out. But it would be a mistake for any to suppose that this collection merely opposes esthetic revelry to patriotic excitement, gay dilettanteism to gallant earnestness. Upon a real perusal of this essay, such a reader, rather to his surprise, will discover how serious is the German problem we must deal with, which we properly place, as the critical consideration, in the very center of German hopes. Perhaps, however, this same class of readers will be shocked at seeing an esthetic problem taken so seriously, especially if they see in art nothing but a merry diversion, an easily dispensed-with tinkling accompaniment to the "seriousness of existence": as if no one had any idea of the meaning of the opposition implied. These earnest ones may be informed of my conviction that art is the highest task and the proper metaphysical activity of this life, as it is understood by the man, to whom, as my noble champion on this same path, I now dedicate this essay.

Basel, *end of the year*, 1871.

The Birth of Tragedy

1

WE shall do a great deal for the science of esthetics, once we perceive not merely by logical inference, but with the immediate certainty of intuition, that the continuous development of art is bound up with the *Apollonian* and *Dionysian* duality: just as procreation depends on the duality of the sexes, involving perpetual strife with only periodically intervening reconciliations. The terms Dionysian and Apollonian we borrow from the Greeks, who disclose to the discerning mind the profound mysteries of their view of art, not, to be sure, in concepts, but in the impressively clear figures of their gods. Through Apollo and Dionysus, the two art-deities of the Greeks, we come to recognize that in the Greek world there existed a sharp opposition, in origin and aims, between the Apollonian art of sculpture, and the non-plastic, Dionysian, art of music. These two distinct tendencies run parallel to each other, for the most part openly at variance; and they continually incite each other to new and more powerful births, which perpetuate an antagonism, only superficially reconciled by the common term "Art"; till at last, by a metaphysical miracle of the Hellenic will, they appear coupled with each other, and through this coupling eventually generate the art-product, equally Dionysian and Apollonian, of Attic tragedy.

In order to grasp these two tendencies, let us first conceive of them as the separate art-worlds of *dreams* and *drunkenness*. These physiological phenomena present a contrast analogous to that existing between the Apollonian and the Dionysian. It was in dreams, says Lucretius, that the glorious divine figures first appeared to the souls of men; in dreams the great shaper beheld the splendid corporeal structure of superhuman beings; and the Hellenic poet, if questioned about the mysteries of poetic inspiration, would likewise have suggested dreams and he might have given an explanation like that of Hans Sachs in the *Mastersingers:*

> *"Mein Freund, das grad' ist Dichters Werk,*
> *dess er sein Träumen deut' and merk'.*
> *Glaubt mir, des Menschen wahrster Wahn*
> *wird ihm im Traume aufgethan:*
> *all' Dichtkunst und Poëterei*
> *ist nichts als Wahrtraum-Deuterei."* [1]

The beautiful appearance of the dream-worlds, in creating which every man is a perfect artist, is the prerequisite of all plastic art, and in fact, as we shall see, of an important part of poetry also. In our dreams we delight in the immediate apprehension of form; all forms speak to us; none are unimportant, none are superfluous. But, when this dream-reality is most intense, we also have, glimmering through it, the sensation of its appearance: at least this is my experience, as to whose frequency, aye, normality, I could adduce many proofs, in addition to the sayings of the poets. Indeed, the man of philosophic

---

[1] "My friend, that is exactly the poet's task, to mark his dreams and to attach meanings to them. Believe me, man's most profound illusions are revealed to him in dreams; and all versifying and poetizing is nothing but an interpretation of them."

mind has a presentiment that underneath this reality in which we live and have our being, is concealed another and quite different reality, which, like the first, is an appearance; and Schopenhauer actually indicates as the criterion of philosophical ability the occasional ability to view men and things as mere phantoms or dream-pictures. Thus the esthetically sensitive man stands in the same relation to the reality of dreams as the philosopher does to the reality of existence; he is a close and willing observer, for these pictures afford him an interpretation of life, and it is by these processes that he trains himself for life. And it is not only the agreeable and friendly pictures that he experiences in himself with such perfect understanding: but the serious, the troubled, the sad, the gloomy, the sudden restraints, the tricks of fate, the uneasy presentiments, in short, the whole Divine Comedy of life, and the Inferno, also pass before him, not like mere shadows on the wall—for in these scenes he lives and suffers—and yet not without that fleeting sensation of appearance. And perhaps many will, like myself, recall that amid the dangers and terrors of dream-life they would at times, cry out in self-encouragement, and not without success. "It is only a dream! I will dream on!" I have likewise heard of persons capable of continuing one and the same dream for three and even more successive nights: facts which indicate clearly that our innermost beings, our common subconscious experiences, express themselves in dreams because they must do so and because they take profound delight in so doing.

This joyful necessity of the dream-experience has been embodied by the Greeks in their Apollo: for Apollo, the god of all plastic energies, is at the same time the soothsaying god. He, who (as the etymology of the name indicates) is the "shining one," the deity of light, is also ruler over the fair appearance of the inner world of fantasy. The higher truth, the perfection of these states in contrast to the incompletely intelligible everyday world, this deep consciousness of nature, healing and helping in sleep and dreams, is at the same time the symbolical analogue of the soothsaying faculty and of the arts generally, which make life possible and worth living. But we must also include in our picture of Apollo that delicate boundary, which the dream-picture must not overstep—lest it act pathologically (in which case appearance would impose upon us as pure reality). We must keep in mind that measured restraint, that freedom from the wilder emotions, that philosophical calm of the sculptor-god. His eye must be "sunlike," as befits his origin; even when his glance is angry and distempered, the sacredness of his beautiful appearance must still be there. And so, in one sense, we might apply to Apollo the words of Schopenhauer when he speaks of the man wrapped in the veil of Mâyâ:[2] *Welt als Wille und Vorstellung,* I. p. 416: "Just as in a stormy sea, unbounded in every direction, rising and falling with howling mountainous waves, a sailor sits in a boat and trusts in his frail barque: so in the midst of a world of sorrows the individual sits quietly, supported by and trusting in his *principium individuationis.*" In fact, we might say of Apollo, that in him the unshaken faith in this *principium* and the calm repose of the man wrapped therein receive their sublimest expression; and we might consider Apollo himself as the glorious divine image of the *principium individuationis,* whose gestures and expression tell us of all the joy and wisdom of "appearance," together with its beauty.

In the same work Schopenhauer has depicted for us the terrible *awe* which seizes upon man, when he is suddenly

---

[2] Cf. *World as Will and Idea,* I. 455 ff., trans. by Haldane and Kemp.

unable to account for the cognitive forms of a phenomenon, when the principle of reason, in some one of its manifestations, seems to admit of an exception. If we add to this awe the blissful ecstasy which rises from the innermost depths of man, aye, of nature, at this very collapse of the *principium individuationis,* we shall gain an insight into the nature of the *Dionysian,* which is brought home to us most intimately perhaps by the analogy of *drunkenness.* It is either under the influence of the narcotic draught, which we hear of in the songs of all primitive men and peoples, or with the potent coming of spring penetrating all nature with joy, that these Dionysian emotions awake, which, as they intensify, cause the subjective to vanish into complete self-forgetfulness. So also in the German Middle Ages singing and dancing crowds, ever increasing in number, were whirled from place to place under this same Dionysian impulse. In these dancers of St. John and St. Vitus, we rediscover the Bacchic choruses of the Greeks, with their early history in Asia Minor, as far back as Babylon and the orgiastic Sacæa. There are some, who, from obtuseness, or lack of experience, will deprecate such phenomena as "folk-diseases," with contempt or pity born of the consciousness of their own "healthy-mindedness." But, of course, such poor wretches can not imagine how anemic and ghastly their so-called "healthy-mindedness" seems in contrast to the glowing life of the Dionysian revellers rushing past them.

Under the charm of the Dionysian not only is the union between man and man reaffirmed, but Nature which has become estranged, hostile, or subjugated, celebrates once more her reconciliation with her prodigal son, man. Freely earth proffers her gifts, and peacefully the beasts of prey approach from desert and mountain. The chariot of Dionysus is bedecked with flowers and garlands; panthers and tigers pass beneath his yoke. Transform Beethoven's "Hymn to Joy" into a painting; let your imagination conceive the multitudes bowing to the dust, awestruck—then you will be able to appreciate the Dionysian. Now the slave is free; now all the stubborn, hostile barriers, which necessity, caprice or "shameless fashion" have erected between man and man, are broken down. Now, with the gospel of universal harmony, each one feels himself not only united, reconciled, blended with his neighbor, but as one with him; he feels as if the veil of Mâyâ had been torn aside and were now merely fluttering in tatters before the mysterious Primordial Unity. In song and in dance man expresses himself as a member of a higher community; he has forgotten how to walk and speak; he is about to take a dancing flight into the air. His very gestures bespeak enchantment. Just as the animals now talk, just as the earth yields milk and honey, so from him emanate supernatural sounds. He feels himself a god, he himself now walks about enchanted, in ecstasy, like to the gods whom he saw walking about in his dreams. He is no longer an artist, he has become a work of art: in these paroxysms of intoxication the artistic power of all nature reveals itself to the highest gratification of the Primordial Unity. The noblest clay, the most costly marble, man, is here kneaded and cut, and to the sound of the chisel strokes of the Dionysian world-artist rings out the cry of the Eleusinian mysteries: "Do ye bow in the dust, O millions? Do you divine your creator, O world?"

2

Thus far we have considered the Apollonian and its antithesis, the Dionysian, as artistic energies which burst forth from nature herself, *without the mediation of the human artist;*

energies in which nature's art-impulses are satisfied in the
most immediate and direct way: first, on the one hand, in the
pictorial world of dreams, whose completeness is not dependent upon the intellectual attitude or the artistic culture of any
single being; and, on the other hand, as drunken reality, which
likewise does not heed the single unit, but even seeks to destroy the individual and redeem him by a mystic feeling of
Oneness. With reference to these immediate art-states of
nature, every artist is an "imitator," that is to say, either an
Apollonian artist in dreams, or a Dionysian artist in ecstasies,
or finally—as for example in Greek tragedy—at once artist
in both dreams and ecstasies: so we may perhaps picture him
sinking down in his Dionysian drunkenness and mystical self-
abnegation, alone, and apart from the singing revelers, and
we may imagine how now, through Apollonian dream-inspiration, his own state, *i.e.,* his oneness with the primal nature of
the universe, is revealed to him in a *symbolical dream-picture.*

So much for these general premises and contrasts. Let us
now approach the *Greeks* in order to learn how highly these
art-impulses of nature were developed in them. Thus we shall
be in a position to understand and appreciate more deeply that
relation of the Greek artist to his archetypes, which, according to the Aristotelian expression, is "the imitation of nature."
In spite of all the dream-literature and the numerous dream-
anecdotes of the Greeks, we can speak only conjecturally,
though with reasonable assurance, of their *dreams.* If we consider the incredibly precise and unerring plastic power of their
eyes, together with their vivid, frank delight in colors, we can
hardly refrain (to the shame of all those born later) from
assuming even for their dreams a certain logic of line and
contour, colors and groups, a certain pictorial sequence reminding us of their finest bas-reliefs, whose perfection would

[*957*]

certainly justify us, if a comparison were possible, in designating the dreaming Greeks as Homers and Homer as a dreaming Greek: in a deeper sense than that in which modern man, speaking of his dreams, ventures to compare himself with Shakespeare.

On the other hand, there is no conjecture as to the immense gap which separates the *Dionysian Greek* from the Dionysian barbarian. From all quarters of the Ancient World,—to say nothing here of the modern,—from Rome to Babylon, we can point to the existence of Dionysian festivals, types which bear, at best, the same relation to the Greek festivals as the bearded satyr, who borrowed his name and attributes from the goat, does to Dionysus himself. In nearly every case these festivals centered in extravagant sexual licentiousness, whose waves overwhelmed all family life and its venerable traditions; the most savage natural instincts were unleashed, including even that horrible mixture of sensuality and cruelty which has always seemed to me to be the genuine "witches' brew." For some time, however, it would appear that the Greeks were perfectly insulated and guarded against the feverish excitements of these festivals by the figure of Apollo himself rising here in full pride, who could not have held out the Gorgon's head to any power more dangerous than this grotesquely uncouth Dionysian. It is in Doric art that this majestically-rejecting attitude of Apollo is eternized. The opposition between Apollo and Dionysus became more hazardous and even impossible, when, from the deepest roots of the Hellenic nature, similar impulses finally burst forth and made a path for themselves: the Delphic god, by a seasonably effected reconciliation, now contented himself with taking the destructive weapons from the hands of his powerful antagonist. This reconciliation is the most important moment in the history of the Greek cult: wherever we turn we note the revolutions resulting from this event. The two antagonists were reconciled; the boundary lines thenceforth to be observed by each were sharply defined, and there was to be a periodical exchange of gifts of esteem. At bottom, however, the chasm was not bridged over. But if we observe how, under the pressure of this treaty of peace, the Dionysian power revealed itself, we shall now recognize in the Dionysian orgies of the Greeks, as compared with the Babylonian Sacæa with their reversion of man to the tiger and the ape, the significance of festivals of world-redemption and days of transfiguration. It is with them that nature for the first time attains her artistic jubilee; it is with them that the destruction of the *principium individuationis* for the first time becomes an artistic phenomenon. The horrible "witches' brew" of sensuality and cruelty becomes ineffective: only the curious blending and duality in the emotions of the Dionysian revelers remind us—as medicines remind us of deadly poisons —of the phenomenon that pain begets joy, that ecstasy may wring sounds of agony from us. At the very climax of joy there sounds a cry of horror or a yearning lamentation for an irretrievable loss. In these Greek festivals, nature seems to reveal a sentimental trait; it is as if she were heaving a sigh at her dismemberment into individuals. The song and pantomime of such dually-minded revelers was something new and unheard-of for the Homeric-Grecian world: and the Dionysian *music* in particular excited awe and terror. If music, as it would seem, had been known previously as an Apollonian art, it was so, strictly speaking, only as the wave-beat of rhythm, whose formative power was developed for the representation of Apollonian states. The music of Apollo was Doric architectonics in tones, but in tones that were merely suggestive, such as those of the cithara. The very element which forms the essence of Dionysian music (and hence of music in general) is carefully excluded as un-Apollonian: namely, the emotional power of the tone, the uniform flow of the melos, and the utterly incomparable world of harmony. In the Dionysian dithyramb man is incited to the greatest exaltation of all his symbolic faculties; something never before experienced struggles for utterance—the annihilation of the veil of Mâyâ, Oneness as the soul of the race, and of nature itself. The essence of nature is now to be expressed symbolically; we need a new world of symbols; for once the entire symbolism of the body is called into play, not the mere symbolism of the lips, face, and speech, but the whole pantomime of dancing, forcing every member into rhythmic movement. Thereupon the other symbolic powers suddenly press forward, particularly those of music, in rhythmics, dynamics, and harmony. To grasp this collective release of all the symbolic powers, man must have already attained that height of self-abnegation which wills to express itself symbolically through all these powers: and so the dithyrambic votary of Dionysus is understood only by his peers! With what astonishment must the Apollonian Greek have beheld him! With an astonishment that was all the greater the more it was mingled with the shuddering suspicion that all this was actually not so very alien to him after all, in fact, that it was only his Apollonian consciousness which, like a veil, hid this Dionysian world from his vision.

3

To understand this, it becomes necessary to level the artistic structure of the *Apollonian culture,* as it were, stone by stone, till the foundations on which it rests become visible. First of all we see the glorious *Olympian* figures of the gods, standing on the gables of this structure. Their deeds, pictured in brilliant reliefs, adorn its friezes. We must not be misled by the fact that Apollo stands side by side with the others as an individual deity, without any claim to priority of rank. For the same impulse which embodied itself in Apollo gave birth in general to this entire Olympian world, and so in this sense Apollo is its father. What terrific need was it that could produce such an illustrious company of Olympian beings?

He who approaches these Olympians with another religion in his heart, seeking among them for moral elevation, even for sanctity, for disincarnate spirituality, for charity and benevolence, will soon be forced to turn his back on them, discouraged and disappointed. For there is nothing here that suggests asceticism, spirituality, or duty. We hear nothing but the accents of an exuberant, triumphant life, in which all things, whether good or bad, are deified. And so the spectator may stand quite bewildered before this fantastic superfluity of life, asking himself what magic potion these mad glad men could have imbibed to make life so enjoyable that, wherever they turned, their eyes beheld the smile of Helen, the ideal picture of their own existence, "floating in sweet sensuality." But to this spectator, who has his back already turned, we must perforce cry: "Go not away, but stay and hear what Greek folk-wisdom has to say of this very life, which with such inexplicable gayety unfolds itself before your eyes. There is an ancient story that King Midas hunted in the forest a long time for the wise *Silenus,* the companion of Dionysus, without capturing him. When Silenus at last fell into his hands, the king asked what was the best and most desirable of all things for man. Fixed and immovable, the demigod said not a word; till at last, urged by the king, he gave a shrill laugh and broke out into these words: 'Oh, wretched ephemeral race, children of chance and misery, why do ye compel me to tell you what it were most expedient for you not to hear? What is best of all is beyond your reach forever: not to be born, not to *be*, to be *nothing*. But the second best for you—is quickly to die.' "

How is the Olympian world of deities related to this folk-wisdom? Even as the rapturous vision of the tortured martyr to his suffering.

Now it is as if the Olympian magic mountain had opened before us and revealed its roots to us. The Greek knew and felt the terror and horror of existence. That he might endure this terror at all, he had to interpose between himself and life the radiant dream-birth of the Olympians. That overwhelming dismay in the face of the titanic powers of nature, the Moira enthroned inexorably over all knowledge, the vulture of the great lover of mankind, Prometheus, the terrible fate of the wise Œdipus, the family curse of the Atridæ which drove Orestes to matricide: in short, that entire philosophy of the sylvan god, with its mythical exemplars, which caused the downfall of the melancholy Etruscans—all this was again and again overcome by the Greeks with the aid of the Olympian *middle world* of art; or at any rate it was veiled and withdrawn from sight. It was out of the direst necessity to live that the Greeks created these gods. Perhaps we may picture the process to ourselves somewhat as follows: out of the original Titan thearchy of terror the Olympian thearchy of joy gradually evolved through the Apollonian impulse towards beauty, just as roses bud from thorny bushes. How else could this people, so sensitive, so vehement in its desires, so singularly constituted for *suffering*, how could they have endured existence, if it had not been revealed to them in their gods, surrounded with a higher glory? The same impulse which calls art into being, as the complement and consummation of existence, seducing one to a continuation of life, was also the cause of the Olympian world which the Hellenic "will" made use of as a transfiguring mirror. Thus do the gods justify the life of man, in that they themselves live it—the only satisfactory Theodicy! Existence under the bright sunshine of such gods is regarded as desirable in itself, and the real *grief* of the Homeric men is caused by parting from it, especially by early parting: so that now, reversing the wisdom of Silenus, we might say of the Greeks that "to die early is worst of all for them, the next worst—some day to die at all." Once heard, it will ring out again; forget not the lament of the short-lived Achilles, mourning the leaflike change and vicissitude of the race of men and the decline of the heroic age. It is not unworthy of the greatest hero to long for a continuation of life, aye, even though he live as a slave. At the Apollonian stage of development, the "will" longs so vehemently for this existence, the Homeric man feels himself so completely at one with it, that lamentation itself becomes a song of praise.

Here we should note that this harmony which is contemplated with such longing by modern man, in fact, this oneness of man with nature (to express which Schiller introduced the technical term "naïve"), is by no means a simple condition, resulting naturally, and as if inevitably. It is not a condition which, like a terrestrial paradise, *must* necessarily be found at the gate of every culture. Only a romantic age could believe this, an age which conceived of the artist in terms of Rousseau's *Emile* and imagined that in Homer it had found such an artist Emile, reared in Nature's bosom. Wherever we meet with the "naïve" in art, we recognize the highest effect of the Apollonian culture, which in the first place has always to overthrow some Titanic empire and slay monsters, and which, through its potent dazzling representations and its pleasurable illusions, must have triumphed over a terrible depth of world-contemplation and a most keen sensitivity to suffering. But how seldom do we attain to the naïve—that complete absorption in the beauty of appearance! And hence how inexpressibly sublime is *Homer,* who, as individual being, bears the same relation to this Apollonian folk-culture as the individual dream-artist does to the dream-faculty of the people and of Nature in general. The Homeric "naïveté" can be understood only as the complete victory of the Apollonian illusion: an illusion similar to those which Nature so frequently employs to achieve her own ends. The true goal is veiled by a phantasm: and while we stretch out our hands for the latter, Nature attains the former by means of your illusion. In the Greeks the "will" wished to contemplate itself in the transfiguration of genius and the world of art; in order to glorify themselves, its creatures had to feel themselves worthy of glory; they had to behold themselves again in a higher sphere, without this perfect world of contemplation acting as a command or a reproach. Such is the sphere of beauty, in which they saw their mirrored images, the Olympians. With this mirroring of beauty the Hellenic will combated its artistically correlative talent for suffering and for the wisdom of suffering: and, as a monument of its victory, we have Homer, the naïve artist.

4

Now the dream-analogy may throw some light on the problem of the naïve artist. Let us imagine the dreamer: in the midst of the illusion of the dream-world and without disturbing it, he calls out to himself: "It is a dream, I will dream on."

What must we infer? That he experiences a deep inner joy in dream-contemplation; on the other hand, to be at all able to dream with this inner joy in contemplation, he must have completely lost sight of the waking reality and its ominous obtrusiveness. Guided by the dream-reading Apollo, we may interpret all these phenomena to ourselves somewhat in this way. Though it is certain that of the two halves of our existence, the waking and the dreaming states, the former appeals to us as infinitely preferable, important, excellent and worthy of being lived, indeed, as that which alone is lived: yet, in relation to that mysterious substratum of our nature of which we are the phenomena, I should, paradoxical as it may seem, maintain the very opposite estimate of the value of dream life. For the more clearly I perceive in Nature those omnipotent art impulses, and in them an ardent longing for release, for redemption through release, the more I feel myself impelled to the metaphysical assumption that the Truly-Existent and Primal Unity, eternally suffering and divided against itself, has need of the rapturous vision, the joyful appearance, for its continuous salvation: which appearance we, completely wrapped up in it and composed of it, are compelled to apprehend as the True Non-Being,—*i.e.*, as a perpetual becoming in time, space and causality,—in other words, as empiric reality. If, for the moment, we do not consider the question of our own "reality," if we conceive of our empirical existence, and that of the world in general, as a continuously manifested representation of the Primal Unity, we shall then have to look upon the dream as an *appearance of appearance*, hence as a still higher appeasement of the primordial desire for appearance. And that is why the innermost heart of Nature feels that ineffable joy in the naïve artist and the naïve work of art, which is likewise only "an appearance of appearance." In a symbolic painting, *Raphael,* himself one of these immortal "naïve" ones, has represented for us this devolution of appearance to appearance, the primitive process of the naïve artist and of Apollonian culture. In his "Transfiguration," the lower half of the picture, with the possessed boy, the despairing bearers, the bewildered, terrified disciples, shows us the reflection of suffering, primal and eternal, the sole basis of the world: the "appearance" here is the counter-appearance of eternal contradiction, the father of things. From this appearance now arises, like ambrosial vapor, a new visionary world of appearances, invisible to those wrapped in the first appearance—a radiant floating in purest bliss, a serene contemplation beaming from wide-open eyes. Here we have presented, in the most sublime artistic symbolism, that Apollonian world of beauty and its substratum, the terrible wisdom of Silenus; and intuitively we comprehend their necessary interdependence. Apollo, however, again appears to us as the apotheosis of the *principium individuationis,* in which alone is consummated the perpetually attained goal of the Primal Unity, its redemption through appearance. With his sublime gestures, he shows us how necessary is the entire world of suffering, that by means of it the individual may be impelled to realize the redeeming vision, and then, sunk in contemplation of it, sit quietly in his tossing barque, amid the waves.

If we at all conceive of it as imperative and mandatory, this apotheosis of individuation knows but one law—the individual, *i.e.,* the delimiting of the boundaries of the individual, *measure* in the Hellenic sense. Apollo, as ethical deity, exacts measure of his disciples, and, that to this end, he requires self-knowledge. And so, side by side with the esthetic necessity for beauty, there occur the demands "know thyself" and "nothing overmuch"; consequently pride and excess are regarded as the truly inimical demons of the non-Apollonian sphere, hence as characteristics of the pre-Apollonian age— that of the Titans; and of the extra-Apollonian world—that of the barbarians. Because of his Titan-like love for man, Prometheus must be torn to pieces by vultures; because of his excessive wisdom, which could solve the riddle of the Sphinx, Œdipus must be plunged into a bewildering vortex of crime. Thus did the Delphic god interpret the Greek past.

Similarly the effects wrought by the *Dionysian* seemed "titan-like" and "barbaric" to the Apollonian Greek: while at the same time he could not conceal from himself that he too was inwardly related to these overthrown Titans and heroes. Indeed, he had to recognize even more than this: despite all its beauty and moderation, his entire existence rested on a hidden substratum of suffering and of knowledge, which was again revealed to him by the Dionysian. And lo! Apollo could not live without Dionysus! The "titanic" and the "barbaric" were in the last analysis as necessary as the Apollonian.

And now let us take this artistically limited world, based on appearance and moderation; let us imagine how into it there penetrated, in tones ever more bewitching and alluring, the ecstatic sound of the Dionysian festival; let us remember that in these strains all of Nature's excess in joy, sorrow, and knowledge become audible, even in piercing shrieks; and finally, let us ask ourselves what significance remains to the psalmodizing artist of Apollo, with his phantom harp-sound, once it is compared with this demonic folk-song! The muses of the arts of "appearance" paled before an art which, in its intoxication, spoke the truth. The wisdom of Silenus cried "Woe! woe!" to the serene Olympians. The individual, with all his restraint and proportion, succumbed to the self-oblivion of the Dionysian state, forgetting the precepts of Apollo. Excess revealed itself as truth. Contradiction, the bliss born of pain, spoke out from the very heart of Nature. And so, wherever the Dionysian prevailed, the Apollonian was checked and destroyed. But, on the other hand, it is equally certain that, wherever the first Dionysian onslaught was successfully withstood, the authority and majesty of the Delphic god exhibited itself as more rigid and menacing than ever. For to me the *Doric* state and Doric art are explicable only as a permanent citadel of the Apollonian. For an art so defiantly prim, and so encompassed with bulwarks, a training so warlike and rigorous, a political structure so cruel and relentless, could endure for any length of time only by incessant opposition to the titanic-barbaric nature of the Dionysian.

Up to this point we have simply enlarged upon the observation made at the beginning of this essay: that the Dionysian and the Apollonian, in new births ever following and mutually augmenting one another, controlled the Hellenic genius; that from out the age of "bronze," with its wars of the Titans and its rigorous folk-philosophy, the Homeric world developed under the sway of the Apollonian impulse to beauty; that this "naïve" splendor was again overwhelmed by the influx of the Dionysian; and that against this new power the Apollonian rose to the austere majesty of Doric art and the Doric view of the world. If, then, amid the strife of these two hostile principles, the older Hellenic history thus falls into four great periods of art, we are now impelled to inquire after the *final goal* of these developments and processes, lest perchance we should regard the last-attained period, the period of Doric art, as the climax and aim of these artistic impulses. And here the sublime and celebrated art of *Attic tragedy* and the dramatic dithyramb presents itself as the common goal of both these tendencies, whose mysterious union, after many and long precursory struggles, found glorious consummation in this child,—at once Antigone and Cassandra.

5

We now approach the real goal of our investigation, which is directed towards acquiring a knowledge of the Dionysian-Apollonian genius and its art-product, or at least an anticipatory understanding of its mysterious union. Here we shall first of all inquire after the first evidence in Greece of that new germ which subsequently developed into tragedy and the dramatic dithyramb. The ancients themselves give us a symbolic answer, when they place the faces of *Homer* and *Archilochus* as the forefathers and torchbearers of Greek poetry side by side on gems, sculptures, etc., with a sure feeling that consideration should be given only to these two thoroughly original compeers, from whom a stream of fire flows over the whole of later Greek history. Homer, the aged self-absorbed dreamer, the type of the Apollonian naïve artist, now beholds with astonishment the passionate genius of the war-like votary of the muses, Archilochus, passing through life with fury and violence; and modern esthetics, by way of interpretation, can only add that here the first "objective" artist confronts the first "subjective" artist. But this interpretation helps us but little, because we know the subjective artist only as the poor artist, and throughout the entire range of art we demand specially and first of all the conquest of the Subjective, the release from the ego and the silencing of the individual will and desire; indeed, we find it impossible to believe in any truly artistic production, however insignificant, if it is without objectivity, without pure, detached contemplation. Hence our esthetic must first solve the problem of how the "lyrist" is possible as an artist—he who, according to the experience of all ages, is continually saying "I" and running through the entire chromatic scale of his passions and desires. Compared with Homer, this very Archilochus appalls us by his cries of hatred and scorn, by his drunken outbursts of desire. Therefore is not he, who has been called the first subjective artist, essentially the non-artist? But in this case, how explain the reverence which was shown to him—the poet—in very remarkable utterances by the Delphic oracle itself, the center of "objective" art?

Schiller has thrown some light on the poetic process by a psychological observation, inexplicable to himself, yet apparently valid. He admits that before the act of creation he did not perhaps have before him or within him any series of images accompanied by an ordered thought-relationship; but his condition was rather that of a *musical mood*. ("With me the perception has at first no clear and definite object; this is formed later. A certain musical mood of mind precedes, and only after this ensues the poetical idea.") Let us add to this the natural and most important phenomenon of all ancient lyric poetry, *the union,* indeed, the *identity,* of the *lyrist with the musician,*—compared with which our modern lyric poetry appears like the statue of a god without a head,—with this in mind we may now, on the basis of our metaphysics of esthetics set forth above, explain the lyrist to ourselves in this manner: In the first place, as Dionysian artist he has identified himself with the Primal Unity, its pain and contradiction. Assuming that music has been correctly termed a repetition and a recast of the world, we may say that he produces the copy of this Primal Unity as music. Now, however, under the Apollonian dream-inspiration, this music reveals itself to him again as a *symbolic dream-picture*. The inchoate, intangible reflection of the primordial pain in music, with its redemption in appearance, now produces a second mirroring as a specific symbol or example. The artist has already surrendered his subjectivity in the Dionysian process. The picture which now shows him his identity with the heart of the world, is a dream-scene, which embodies the primordial contradiction and primordial pain, together with the primordial joy, of appearance. The "I" of the lyrist therefore sounds from the depth of his being: its "subjectivity," in the sense of the modern esthetes, is pure imagination. When Archilochus, the first Greek lyrist, proclaims to the daughters of Lycambes both his mad love and his contempt, it is not his passion alone which dances before us in orgiastic frenzy; but we see Dionysus and the Mænads, we see the drunken reveler Archilochus sunk down in slumber —as Euripides depicts it in the *Bacchæ*, the sleep on the high mountain pasture, in the noonday sun. And now Apollo approaches and touches him with the laurel. Then the Dionyso-musical enchantment of the sleeper seems to emit picture sparks, lyrical poems, which in their highest form are called tragedies and dramatic dithyrambs.

The plastic artist, as also the epic poet, who is related to him, is sunk in the pure contemplation of images. The Dionysian musician is, without any images, himself pure primordial pain and its primordial reëchoing. The lyric genius is conscious of a world of pictures and symbols—growing out of his state of mystical self-abnegation and oneness. This state has a coloring, a causality and a velocity quite different from that of the world of the plastic artist and the epic poet. For the latter lives in these pictures, and only in them, with joyful satisfaction. He never grows tired of contemplating lovingly even their minutest traits. Even the picture of the angry Achilles is only a picture to him, whose angry expression he enjoys with the dream-joy in appearance. Thus, by this mirror of appearance, he is protected against being united and blended with his figures. In direct contrast to this, the pictures of the *lyrist* are nothing but *his very* self and, as it were, only different projections of himself, by force of which he, as the moving center of this world, may say "I": only of course this self is not the same as that of the waking, empirically real man, but the only truly existent and eternal self resting at the basis of things, and with the help of whose images, the lyric genius can penetrate to this very basis.

Now let us suppose that among these images he also beholds *himself* as non-genius, *i.e.,* his subject, the whole throng of subjective passions and agitations directed to a definite object which appears real to him. It may now seem as if the lyric genius and the allied non-genius were one, as if the former had of its own accord spoken that little word "I." But this identity is but superficial and it will no longer be able to lead us astray, as it certainly led astray those who designated the lyrist as the subjective poet. For, as a matter of fact, Archilochus, the passionately inflamed, loving and hating man, is but a vision of the genius, who by this time is no longer merely Archilochus, but a world-genius expressing his primordial pain symbolically in the likeness of the man Archilochus: while the subjectively willing and desiring man, Archilochus, can never at any time be a poet. It is by no means necessary, however, that the lyrist should see nothing but the phenomenon of the man Archilochus before him as a reflection of eternal being; and tragedy shows how far the visionary world of the lyrist may be removed from this phenomenon, which, of course, is intimately related to it.

Schopenhauer, who did not conceal from himself the difficulty the lyrist presents in the philosophical contemplation of art, thought he had found a solution, with which, however, I am not in entire accord. (Actually, it was in his profound metaphysics of music that he alone held in his hands the means whereby this difficulty might be definitely removed: as I believe I have removed it here in his spirit and to his honor). In contrast to our view, he describes the peculiar nature of song as follows [3] (*Welt als Wille und Vorstellung*, I. 295):

"It is the subject of will, *i.e.*, his own volition, which the consciousness of the singer feels; often as a released and satisfied desire (joy), but still oftener as a restricted desire (grief), always as an emotion, a passion, a moved frame of mind. Besides this, however, and along with it, by the sight of surrounding nature, the singer becomes conscious of himself as the subject of pure will-less knowing, whose unbroken, blissful peace now appears, in contrast to the stress of desire, which is always restricted and always needy. The feeling of this contrast, this alternation, is really what the lyric as a whole expresses and what principally constitutes the lyrical state of mind. In it pure knowing comes to us as it were to deliver us from desire and its strain; we follow, but only for an instant; desire, the remembrance of our own personal ends, tears us anew from peaceful contemplation; yet ever again the next beautiful surrounding in which the pure will-less knowledge presents itself to us, allures us away from desire. Therefore, in the lyric and the lyrical mood, desire (the personal interest of the ends) and pure perception of the surrounding presented are wonderfully mingled with each other; connections between them are sought for and imagined; the subjective dis-

---

[3] *World as Will and Idea*, I. 322, 6th ed. of Haldane and Kemp's Trans.

position, the affection of the will, imparts its own hue to the perceived surrounding, and conversely, the surroundings communicate the reflex of their color to the will. The true lyric is the expression of the whole of this mingled and divided state of mind."

Who could fail to recognize in this description that lyric poetry is here characterized as an incompletely attained art, which arrives at its goal infrequently and only as it were by leaps? Indeed, it is described as a semi-art, whose essence is said to consist in this, that desire and pure contemplation, *i.e.,* the unesthetic and the esthetic condition, are wonderfully mingled with each other. It follows that Schopenhauer still classifies the arts as subjective or objective, using the antithesis as if it were a criterion of value. But it is our contention, on the contrary, that this antithesis between the subjective and the objective is especially irrelevant in esthetics, since the subject, the desiring individual furthering his own egoistic ends, can be conceived of only as the antagonist, not as the origin of art. In so far as the subject is the artist, however, he has already been released from his individual will, and has become as it were the medium through which the one truly existent Subject celebrates his release in appearance. For, above all, to our humiliation *and* exaltation, one thing must be clear to us. The entire comedy of art is neither performed for our betterment or education nor are we the true authors of this art-world. On the contrary, we may assume that we are merely pictures and artistic projections for the true author, and that we have our highest dignity in our significance as works of art—for it is only as an *esthetic phenomenon* that existence and the world are eternally *justified*—while of course our consciousness of our own significance hardly differs from that which the soldiers painted on canvas have of the battle represented on it. Thus all our knowledge of art is basically quite illusory, because as knowing beings we are not one and identical with that Being who, as the sole author and spectator of this comedy of art, prepares a perpetual entertainment for himself. Only in so far as the genius in the act of artistic creation coalesces with this primordial artist of the world, does he catch sight of the eternal essence of art; for in this state he is, in a marvelous manner, like the weird picture of the fairy-tale which can turn its eyes at will and behold itself; he is now at once subject and object, at once poet, actor, and spectator.

6

In connection with Archilochus, scholarly research has discovered that he introduced the *folk-song* into literature, and, on account of this, deserved, according to the general estimate of the Greeks, his unique position beside Homer. But what is the folk-song in contrast to the wholly Apollonian epos? What else but the *perpetuum vestigium* of a union of the Apollonian and the Dionysian? Its enormous diffusion among all peoples, further re-enforced by ever-new births, is testimony to the power of this artistic dual impulse of Nature: which leaves its vestiges in the folk-song just as the orgiastic movements of a people perpetuate themselves in its music. Indeed, it might also be historically demonstrable that every period rich in folk-songs has been most violently stirred by Dionysian currents, which we must always consider the substratum and prerequisite of the folk-song.

First of all, however, we must conceive the folk-song as the musical mirror of the world, as the original melody, now seeking for itself a parallel dream-phenomenon and expressing it in poetry. *Melody is therefore primary and universal,* and so may admit of several objectifications in several texts. Likewise, in the naïve estimation of the people, it is regarded as by far the more important and essential element. Melody generates the poem out of itself by a continuous process. *The strophic form of the folk-song* points to the same thing; a phenomenon which I had always beheld with astonishment, until at last I found this explanation. Any one who in accordance with this theory examines a collection of folk-songs, such as *Des Knaben Wunderhorn,* will find innumerable instances of the way the continuously generating melody scatters picture sparks all around, which in their variegation, their abrupt change, their mad precipitation, manifest a power quite unknown to the epic and its steady flow. From the standpoint of the epos, this unequal and irregular pictorial world of lyric poetry is definitely to be condemned: and it certainly has been thus condemned by the solemn epic rhapsodists of the Apollonian festivals in the age of Terpander.

Accordingly, we observe that in the poetry of the folk-song, language is strained to its utmost that it may *imitate music;* and hence with Archilochus begins a new world of poetry, which is basically opposed to the Homeric. And in saying this we have indicated the only possible relation between poetry and music, between word and tone: the word, the picture, the concept here seeks an expression analogous to music and now feels in itself the power of music. In this sense we may discriminate between two main currents in the history of the language of the Greek people, according to whether their language imitated the world of image and phenomenon, or the world of music. One need only reflect more deeply on the linguistic difference with regard to color, syntactical structure, and vocabulary in Homer and Pindar, in order to understand the significance of this contrast; indeed, it becomes palpably clear that in the period between Homer and Pindar there must have sounded out the *orgiastic flute tones of Olympus,* which, even in Aristotle's time, when music was infinitely more developed, transported people to drunken ecstasy, and which, in their primitive state of development, undoubtedly incited to imitation all the poetic means of expression of contemporaneous man. I here call attention to a familiar phenomenon of our own times, against which our esthetic raises many objections. We again and again have occasion to observe that a Beethoven symphony compels its individual auditors to use figurative speech in describing it, no matter how fantastically variegated and even contradictory may be the composition and make-up of the different pictorial world produced by a piece of music. To exercise its poor wit on such compositions, and to overlook a phenomenon which is certainly worth explaining, is quite in keeping with this esthetic. Indeed, even when the tone-poet expresses his composition in pictures, when for instance he designates a certain symphony as the "pastoral" symphony, or a passage in it as the "scene by the brook," or another as the "merry gathering of rustics," these too are only symbolical representations born of music—and not perhaps the imitated objects of music—representations which can teach us nothing whatsoever concerning the *Dionysian* content of music, and which indeed have no distinctive value of their own beside other pictorial expressions. We have now to transfer this process of a discharge of music in pictures to some fresh, youthful, linguistically creative people, in order to get a notion of how the strophic faculty of speech is stimulated by this new principle of the imitation of music.

If, therefore, we may regard lyric poetry as the fulguration of music in images and concepts, we should now ask: "In what form does music *appear* in the mirror of symbolism and conception?" *It appears as will,* taking the term in Schopenhauer's sense, *i.e.,* as the antithesis of the esthetic, purely contemplative, and passive frame of mind. Here, however, we must make as sharp a distinction as possible between the concept of essence and the concept of phenomenon; for music, according to its essence, cannot possibly be will. To be will it would have to be wholly banished from the realm of art—for the will is the unesthetic-in-itself. Yet though *essentially* it is not will, *phenomenally* it *appears* as will. For in order to express the phenomenon of music in images, the lyrist needs all the agitations of passion, from the whisper of mere inclination to the roar of madness. Impelled to speak of music in Apollonian symbols, he conceives of all nature, and himself therein, only as eternal Will, Desire, Longing. But in so far as he interprets music by means of images, he himself rests in the quiet calm of Apollonian contemplation, though everything around him which he beholds through the medium of music may be confused and violent. Indeed, when he beholds himself through this same medium, his own image appears to him as an unsatisfied feeling: his own willing, longing, moaning, rejoicing, are to him symbols by which he interprets music. This is the phenomenon of the lyrist: as Apollonian genius he interprets music through the image of the will, while he himself, completely released from the desire of the will, is the pure, undimmed eye of day.

Our whole discussion insists that lyric poetry is dependent on the spirit of music just as music itself in its absolute sovereignty does not need the picture and the concept, but merely *endures* them as accompaniments. The poems of the lyrist can express nothing which did not already lie hidden in the vast universality and absoluteness of the music which compelled him to figurative speech. Language can never adequately render the cosmic symbolism of music, because music stands in symbolic relation to the primordial contradiction and primordial pain in the heart of the Primal Unity, and therefore symbolizes a sphere which is beyond and before all phenomena. Rather are all phenomena, compared with it, merely symbols: hence *language,* as the organ and symbol of phenomena, can never, by any means, disclose the innermost heart of music; language, in its attempt to imitate it, can only be in superficial contact with music; while the deepest significance of the latter cannot with all the eloquence of lyric poetry be brought one step nearer to us.

7

We must now avail ourselves of all the principles of art hitherto considered, in order to find our way through the labyrinth, as we must call it, of *the origin of Greek tragedy.* I do not think I am unreasonable in saying that the problem of this origin has as yet not even been seriously stated, not to say solved, however often the ragged tatters of ancient tradition are sewn together in various combinations and torn apart again. This tradition tells us quite unequivocally, *that tragedy arose from the tragic chorus,* and was originally only chorus and nothing but chorus; and hence we feel it our duty to look into the heart of this tragic chorus as being the real protodrama. We shall not let ourselves be at all satisfied with that current art-lingo which makes the chorus the "ideal spectator," or has it represent the people in contrast to the aristocratic elements of the scene. This latter explanation has a sublime sound to many a politician. It insists that the immutable moral law was embodied by the democratic Athenians in the popular chorus, which always wins out over the passionate excesses and extravagances of kings. This theory may be ever so forcibly suggested by one of Aristotle's observations; still, it has no influence on the original formation of tragedy, inasmuch as the entire antithesis of king and people, and, in general, the whole politico-social sphere, is excluded from the purely religious origins of tragedy. With this in mind, and remembering the well-known classical form of the chorus in Æschylus and Sophocles, we should even deem it blasphemy to speak here of the anticipation of a "constitutional popular representation." From this blasphemy, however, others have not shrunk. The ancient governments knew of no constitutional representation of the people *in praxi,* and it is to be hoped that they did not "anticipate" it in their tragedy either.

Much more famous than this political interpretation of the chorus is the theory of A. W. Schlegel, who advises us to regard the chorus, in a manner, as the essence and extract of the crowd of spectators,—as the "ideal spectator." This view, when compared with the historical tradition that originally tragedy was only chorus, reveals itself for what it is,—a crude, unscientific, yet brilliant generalization, which, however, acquires that brilliancy only through its epigrammatic form of expression, the deep Germanic bias in favor of anything called "ideal," and our momentary astonishment. For we are certainly astonished the moment we compare our familiar theatrical public with this chorus, and ask ourselves whether it could ever be possible to idealize something analogous to the Greek tragic chorus out of such a public. We tacitly deny this, and now wonder as much at the boldness of Schlegel's assertion as at the totally different nature of the Greek public. For hitherto we had always believed that the true spectator, whoever he may be, must always remain conscious that he was viewing a work of art, and not an empirical reality. But the tragic chorus of the Greeks is forced to recognize *real beings* in the figures of the drama. The chorus of the Oceanides really believes that it sees before it the Titan Prometheus, and considers itself as real as the god of the scene. And are we to designate as the highest and purest type of spectator, one who, like the Oceanides, regards Prometheus as real and present in body? Is it characteristic of the ideal spectator to run on to the stage and free the god from his torments? We had always believed in an esthetic public, we had considered the individual spectator the better qualified the more he was capable of viewing a work of art as art, that is, esthetically. But now Schlegel tells us that the perfect ideal spectator does not at all allow the world of the drama to act on him *esthetically,* but corporeally and empirically. Oh, these Greeks! we sighed; they upset all our esthetics! . . . But once accustomed to it, we have repeated Schlegel's saying whenever the chorus came up for discussion.

Now, the tradition which is quite explicit here, speaks against Schlegel. The chorus as such, without the stage,—the primitive form of tragedy,—and the chorus of ideal spectators do not go together. What kind of art would that be in which the spectator does not enter as a separate concept? What kind of art is that whose true form is identical with the "spectator as such"? The spectator without the play is nonsense. We fear that the birth of tragedy is to be explained neither by the high esteem for the moral intelligence of the multitude nor by the concept of the spectator minus the play. We must regard the problem as too deep to be even touched by such superficial generalizing.

An infinitely more valuable insight into the significance of

the chorus had already been displayed by Schiller in the celebrated Preface to his *Bride of Messina,* where he regards the
chorus as a living barrier which tragedy constructs round herself to cut off her contact with the world of reality, and to
preserve her ideal domain and her poetical freedom.

With this, his chief weapon, Schiller combats the ordinary
conception of the natural, the illusion usually demanded in
dramatic poetry. Although it is true that the stage day is merely
artificial, the architecture only symbolical, and the metrical
language purely ideal in character, nevertheless an erroneous
view still prevails in the main: that we should not excuse these
conventions merely on the ground that they constitute a poetical license. Now in reality these "conventions" form the essence of all poetry. The introduction of the chorus, says Schiller, is the decisive step by which open and honorable war is
declared against all naturalism in art. It would seem that to
denigrate this view of the matter our would-be superior age
has coined the disdainful catchword "pseudo-idealism." I
fear, however, that we, on the other hand, with our present
adoration of the natural and the real, have reached the opposite
pole of all idealism, namely, in the region of wax-work cabi-
nets. There is an art in these too, as certain novels much in
vogue at present evidence: but let us not disturb ourselves at
the claim that by any such art the Schiller-Goethian "pseudo-
idealism" has been vanquished.

It is indeed an "ideal" domain, as Schiller correctly perceived, in which the Greek satyr chorus, the chorus of primitive tragedy, was wont to dwell. It is a domain raised high
above the actual path of mortals. For this chorus the Greek
built up the scaffolding of a fictitious *natural state* and on it
placed fictitious *natural beings.* On this foundation tragedy
developed and so, of course, it could dispense from the begin-

ning with a painful portrayal of reality. Yet it is no arbitrary world placed by whim between heaven and earth; rather is it a world with the same reality and credibility that Olympus with its dwellers possessed for the believing Hellene. The satyr, as the Dionysian chorist, lives in a religiously acknowl-edged reality under the sanction of the myth and the cult. That tragedy should begin with him, that he should be the voice of the Dionysian tragic wisdom, is just as strange a phenomenon as the general derivation of tragedy from the chorus.

Perhaps we shall have a point of departure for our inquiry, if I put forward the proposition that the satyr, the fictitious natural being, bears the same relation to the man of culture that Dionysian music does to civilization. Concerning this lat-ter, Richard Wagner says that it is neutralized by music just as lamplight is neutralized by the light of day. Similarly, I believe, the Greek man of culture felt himself neutralized in the presence of the satyric chorus: and this is the most imme-diate effect of the Dionysian tragedy, that the state and society, and, in general, the gulfs between man and man give way to an overwhelming feeling of unity leading back to the very heart of nature. The metaphysical comfort—with which, as I have here intimated, every true tragedy leaves us—that, in spite of the flux of phenomena, life at bottom is indestructibly power-ful and pleasurable, appears with objective clarity as the satyr chorus, the chorus of natural beings, who as it were live inerad-icably behind every civilization, and who, despite the ceaseless change of generations and the history of nations, remain the same to all eternity.

With this chorus the deep-minded Hellene consoles him-self, he who is so singularly constituted for the most sensitive and grievous suffering, he who with a piercing glance has penetrated into the very heart of the terrible destructive processes of so-called universal history, as also into the cruelty of nature, and who is in danger of longing for a Buddhistic negation of the will. Art saves him, and through art life saves him —for herself.

For we must realize that in the ecstasy of the Dionysian state, with its annihilation of the ordinary bounds and limits of existence, there is contained a *lethargic* element, in which are submerged all past personal experiences. It is this gulf of oblivion that separates the world of everyday from the world of Dionysian reality. But as soon as we become conscious again of this everyday reality, we feel it as nauseating and repulsive; and an ascetic will-negating mood is the fruit of these states. In this sense the Dionysian man resembles Hamlet: both have for once penetrated into the true nature of things,—they have *perceived,* but it is irksome for them to act; for their action cannot change the eternal nature of things; the time is out of joint and they regard it as shameful or ridiculous that they should be required to set it right. Knowledge kills action, action requires the veil of illusion—it is this lesson which Hamlet teaches, and not the idle wisdom of John-o'-Dreams who from too much reflection, from a surplus of possibilities, never arrives at action at all. Not reflection, no!—true knowledge, insight into the terrible truth, preponderate over all motives inciting to action, in Hamlet as well as in the Dionysian man. There is no longer any use in comfort; his longing goes beyond a world after death, beyond the gods themselves; existence with its glittering reflection in the gods or in an immortal beyond is abjured. In the consciousness of the truth once perceived, man now sees everywhere only the terror or the absurdity of existence; now he can understand the symbolism of Ophelia's fate; now he can realize the wisdom of the sylvan god Silenus: and he is filled with loathing.

But at this juncture, when the will is most imperiled, *art* approaches, as a redeeming and healing enchantress; she alone may transform these horrible reflections on the terror and absurdity of existence into representations with which man may live. These are the representation of the *sublime* as the artistic conquest of the awful, and of the *comic* as the artistic release from the nausea of the absurd. The satyric chorus of the dithyramb is the saving device of Greek art; the paroxysms described above exhaust themselves in the intermediary world of these Dionysian votaries.

8

The satyr, like the idyllic shepherd of our more recent time, is the offspring of a longing for the Primitive and the Natural; but how firmly and fearlessly the Greek embraced the man of the woods, and how timorously and mawkishly modern man dallied with the flattering picture of a sentimental, flute-playing, soft-mannered shepherd! Nature, as yet unchanged by knowledge, maintaining impregnable barriers to culture—that is what the Greek saw in his satyr, which nevertheless was not on this account to be confused with the primitive cave-man. On the contrary, the satyr was the archetype of man, the embodiment of his highest and intensest emotions, the ecstatic reveler enraptured by the proximity of his god, the sympathetic companion in whom is repeated the suffering of the god, wisdom's harbinger speaking from the very heart of nature, emblem of the sexual omnipotence of nature, which the Greek was wont to contemplate with reverence and wonder. The satyr was something sublime and godlike: it was inevitable that he should appear so, especially to the sad downcast glance of the Dionysian man. Our counterfeit tricked-up shepherd would have repulsed the Dionysian; but on the naked and magnificent characters of nature his eye dwelt with rapt satisfaction. Here the illusion of culture was cast off from the archetype of man; here the true man, the bearded satyr, revealed himself, shouting joyfully to his god. Face to face with him the man of culture shrank to a specious caricature. Schiller is right also with regard to these beginnings of tragic art: the chorus is a living bulwark against the onslaught of reality, because it—the satyr chorus—portrays existence more truthfully, more essentially, more perfectly than the cultured man who ordinarily considers himself as the sole reality. The sphere of poetry does not lie outside the world, like some chimera of the poetic imagination; it seeks to be the very opposite, the unvarnished expression of truth, and for this very reason it must reject the false finery of that supposed reality of the cultured man. The contrast between this intrinsic truth of nature and the falsehood of culture, which poses as the only reality, is similar to that existing between the eternal heart of things, the thing in itself, and the collective world of phenomena. And just as tragedy, with its metaphysical comfort, points to the eternal life of this kernel of existence, and to the perpetual dissolution of phenomena, so the symbolism of the satyr chorus already expresses figuratively this primal relation between the thing in itself and the phenomenon. The idyllic shepherd of the modern man is but a copy of the sum of the culture—illusions which he calls nature; the Dionysian Greek desires truth and nature in their most potent form—and so he sees himself metamorphosed into the satyr.

The reveling throng of the votaries of Dionysus rejoice

under the influence of such moods and perceptions, the power of which transforms them before their own eyes, so that they imagine they behold themselves as recreated genii of nature, as satyrs. The latter constitution of the tragic chorus is the artistic imitation of this natural phenomenon, which of course necessitated a separation of the Dionysian spectators from the enchanted Dionysians. However, we must always remember that the public of the Attic tragedy rediscovered itself in the chorus of the orchestra, that there was at bottom no opposition of public and chorus: for all was but one great sublime chorus of dancing and singing satyrs, or of such as allowed themselves to be represented by these satyrs. Schlegel's observation in this sense reveals a deeper significance. The chorus *is* the "ideal spectator" [4] in so far as it is the only *beholder*,[5] the beholder of the visionary world of the scene. A public of spectators, as we know it, was unknown to the Greeks. In their theaters the terraced structure of the theatron rising in concentric arcs enabled every one to *overlook,* in an actual sense, the entire world of culture around him, and in an overabundance of contemplation to imagine himself one of the chorus. According to this view, then, we may call the chorus in its primitive stage in early tragedy a self-mirroring of the Dionysian man: a phenomenon which is most clearly exemplified by the process of the actor, who, if he be truly gifted, sees hovering almost tangibly before his eyes the character he is to represent. The satyr chorus is above all a vision of the Dionysian throng, just as the world of the stage is, in turn, a vision of the satyr chorus. The power of this vision is great enough to render the eye dull and insensible to the impression of "reality," to the presence of the cultured men occupying the

---

[4] Zuschauer.
[5] Schauer.

tiers of seats on every side. The form of the Greek theater
reminds one of a lonesome mountain-valley. The architecture
of the scene is a luminous cloud-picture and the Bacchants
swarming on the mountains behold this picture from the
heights,—the splendid encirclement in the midst of which is
visible the image of Dionysus.

Brought in contact with our learned notions of the elementary artistic processes, this artistic proto-phenomenon, here
introduced as an explanation of the tragic chorus, is almost
shocking: yet nothing can be more certain than that the poet
is a poet only in so far as he sees himself surrounded by forms
which live and act before him, and into whose innermost
being he penetrates. By reason of a peculiar defect in our
modern critical faculty, we are inclined to consider the esthetic
proto-phenomenon too complexly, too abstractly. For the true
poet a metaphor is not a figure of speech, but a vicarious image
which actually hovers before him in place of a concept. To him
a character is not an aggregate composed of a number of particular traits, but an organic person pressing himself upon his
attention, and differing from the similar vision of the painter
only in the continuousness of its life and action. Why does
Homer describe much more vividly [6] than all the other poets?
Because he contemplates [7] much more. We talk so abstractly
about poetry, because we are all bad poets. At bottom the
esthetic phenomenon is simple: if a man merely has the faculty
of seeing perpetual vitality around him, of living continually
surrounded by hosts of spirits, he will be a poet. If he but feels
the impulse to transform himself and to speak from out the
bodies and souls of others, he will be a dramatist.

The Dionysian excitement is able to inspire a whole mass

---

[6] Anschaulicher.
[7] Anschaut.

of men with this artistic faculty of seeing themselves surrounded by such a host of spirits with whom they know themselves to be essentially one. This process of the tragic chorus is the *dramatic* proto-phenomenon: to see yourself transformed before your own eyes, and then to act as if you had actually taken possession of another body and another character. This process stands at the beginning of the development of the drama. Here we have something different from the rhapsodist, who does not unite with his images, but, like the painter, merely views them contemplatively, with detachment. Here we actually have the individual surrendering himself by the fact of his entrance into an alien nature. Moreover, this phenomenon is epidemic in its manifestation: a whole throng experiences this metamorphosis. Hence it is that the dithyramb is essentially different from every other variety of choric song. The virgins, who, laurel branches in hand, solemnly make their way to the temple of Apollo singing a processional hymn, remain what they are and retain their civic names: but the dithyrambic chorus is a chorus of transformed beings, whose civic past and social position are totally forgotten. They have become the timeless servants of their god, living apart from all the life of the community. Every other kind of choric lyric of the Hellenes is nothing but an enormous intensification of the Apollonian unit-singer: while in the dithyramb we have a community of unconscious actors, who mutually regard themselves as transformed among one another.

This enchantment is the prerequisite for all dramatic art. Under its spell the Dionysian reveler sees himself as a satyr, *and as satyr he in turn beholds the god,* that is, in his transformation he sees a new vision outside him as the Apollonian consummation of his own state. With this new vision the drama completes itself.

According to this view, we must understand Greek tragedy as the Dionysian chorus, disburdening itself again and again in an Apollonian image-world. The choric parts, therefore, with which tragedy is interlaced, are in a sense the maternal womb of the entire so-called dialogue, that is, of the whole stage-world, of the drama proper. In several successive outbursts this primal basis of tragedy releases this vision of the drama, which is a dream-phenomenon throughout, and, as such, epic in character: on the other hand, however, as the objectification of a Dionysian state, it represents not the Apollonian redemption in appearance, but, conversely, the dissolution of the individual and his unification with primordial existence. And so the drama becomes the Apollonian embodiment of Dionysian perceptions and influences, and therefore separates itself by a tremendous gap from the epic.

The *chorus* of the Greek tragedy, the symbol of the collectively excited Dionysian throng, thus finds its full explanation in our conception. Accustomed as we were to the function performed by our modern stage chorus, especially an operatic one, we could never comprehend why the tragic chorus of the Greeks should be older, more primitive, indeed, more important than the "action" proper—as has been so plainly declared by the voice of tradition; whereas, furthermore, we could not reconcile with this traditional primacy and primitiveness the fact that the chorus was composed only of humble, attendant beings—indeed, in the beginning, only of goatlike satyrs; and, finally, there remained the riddle of the orchestra before the scene. We have at last realized that the scene, together with the action, was fundamentally and originally thought of only as a *vision*, that the only reality is just the chorus, which of itself generates the vision and celebrates it with the entire symbolism of dancing, music, and speech. In the vision, this

chorus beholds its lord and master Dionysus, and so it is forever a chorus that *serves;* it seems how he, the god, suffers and
glorifies himself, and therefore does not itself *act*. But though
its attitude towards the god is throughout the attitude of min-
istration, this is nevertheless the highest, that is, the Dionysian, expression of *Nature,* and therefore, like Nature herself
in a state of transport, the chorus utters oracles and wise sayings: as *fellow-sufferer* it is at the same time the *sage* who proclaims truth from out the heart of Nature. Thus, then, originates the fantastic figure, seemingly so discordant, of the wise
and inspired satyr, who is at the same time "the dumb man"
in contrast to the god: who is the image of Nature and her
strongest impulses, the very symbol of Nature, and at the same
time the *proclaimer* of her art and vision: musician, poet,
dancer, and visionary united in one person.

In accordance with this view, and with tradition, *Dionysus,*
the proper stage-hero and focus of vision, is in the remotest
period of tragedy not at first actually present, but is only so
imagined, which means that tragedy is originally only "chorus"
and not "drama." Later on the attempt is made to present the
god as real and to display the visionary figure together with its
aura of splendor before the eyes of all; here the "drama," in
the narrow sense of the term, begins. The dithyrambic chorus
is now assigned the task of exciting the minds of the audience
to such a pitch of Dionysian frenzy, that, when the tragic hero
appears on the stage, they do not see in him an unshapely man
wearing a mask, but they see a visionary figure, born as it were
of their own ecstasy. Picture Admetus, sunk in profound meditation about his lately departed wife, Alcestis, and quite consuming himself in fancied contemplation. Suddenly the veiled
figure of a woman, resembling her in form and gait, is led
towards him. Picture his sudden trembling anxiety, his excited

comparisons, his instinctive conviction—and we shall have a sensation comparable to that with which the dionysiacally excited spectator saw approaching on the stage, the god with whose sufferings he has already become identified. Involuntarily, he transferred the whole image of the god, fluttering magically before his soul, to this masked figure and resolved its reality as it were into a phantasmal unreality. This is the Apollonian dream-state, in which the world of day is veiled, and a new world, clearer, more intelligible, more vivid and yet more shadowy than the old, is, by a perpetual transformation, born and reborn before our eyes. Accordingly we recognize in tragedy a complete stylistic opposition: the language, color, flexibility and movement of the dialogue fall apart into two entirely separate realms of expression, into the Dionysian lyrics of the chorus on the one hand, and the Apollonian dream-world of the scene on the other. The Apollonian appearances, in which Dionysus objectifies himself, are no longer "ein ewiges Meer, ein wechselnd Weben, ein glühend Leben," [8] as is the music of the chorus. They are no longer those forces merely felt, but not condensed into a picture, by which the inspired votary of Dionysus divines the proximity of his god. Now the clearness and firmness of epic form speak to him from the scene; now Dionysus no longer speaks through forces, but as an epic hero, almost with the tongue of Homer.

9

Whatever rises to the surface in the dialogue of the Apollonian part of Greek tragedy, appears simple, transparent,

---

[8] An eternal sea, A weaving, flowing, Life, all glowing. *Faust*, Bayard Taylor's Trans.

beautiful. In this sense the dialogue is a reflection of the
Hellene, whose nature reveals itself in the dance, because in
the dance while the greatest energy is merely potential, it
nevertheless betrays itself in the flexibility and exuberance of
movement. The language of the Sophoclean heroes, for instance, surprises us so much by its Apollonian precision and
clarity, that we at once think we see into the innermost recesses
of their being, not a little astounded that the way thereto is so
short. But let us, for the moment, disregard the character of
the hero which rises to the surface and grows visible—and
which at bottom is nothing but the light-picture cast on a dark
wall, that is, appearance through and through. Instead, let us
enter into the myth which is projected in these bright mirror·
ings. We shall suddenly experience a phenomenon which has
an inverse relation to one familiar in optics. When, after trying
hard to look straight at the sun, we turn away blinded, we have
dark-colored spots before our eyes as restoratives, so to speak;
while, reversing the colors, those light-picture phenomena of
the Sophoclean hero,—in short, the Apollonian of the mask,
—are the inevitable consequences of a glance into the secret
and terrible things of nature. They are shining spots intended
to heal the eye which dire night has seared. Only in this sense
can we hope to grasp the true meaning of the serious and
significant idea of "Greek cheerfulness"; while no matter
where we turn at the present time we encounter the false
notion that this cheerfulness results from a state of unendan·
gered comfort.

The most sorrowful figure of the Greek stage, the unfortunate Œdipus, is conceived by Sophocles as the type of the
noble man who despite his wisdom is fated to error and misery,
but who nevertheless, through his extraordinary sufferings,

ultimately exerts a magical, healing effect on all around him, which continues even after his death. The noble man does not sin; this is what the profound poet would tell us. All laws, all natural order, yea, the moral world itself, may be destroyed through his action, but through this very action there is brought into play a higher magic circle of influences which build up a new world on the ruins of the old. This is what the poet, in so far as he is at the same time a religious thinker, wishes to tell us: as poet, he first of all discloses to us a wonderfully complicated legal mystery, which slowly, link by link, the judge to his own destruction unravels. The truly Hellenic delight in this dialectical resolution is so great that a touch of surpassing cheerfulness is thereby communicated to the whole play. This touch everywhere softens the edge of the horrible presuppositions of the plot. In the *Œdipus at Colonus* we find this same cheerfulness, only infinitely transfigured. In contrast to the aged king, burdened with an excess of misery, whose relation to all that befalls him is solely that of a sufferer, we have here a supramundane cheerfulness, descending from a divine sphere and making us feel that in his purely passive attitude the hero achieves his highest activity, whose influence extends far beyond his life, while his earlier conscious thought and striving led him only to passivity. Thus, the legal knot of the Œdipus fable, which to mortal eyes appears impossibly complicated, is slowly unraveled—and at this divine counterpart of dialectic we are filled with a profound human joy. If this explanation does justice to the poet, it may still be asked whether the content of the myth is thereby exhausted; and here it becomes evident that the entire conception of the poet is nothing but the light-picture which, after our glance into the abyss, healing nature holds up to our eyes. Œdipus, murderer of his father, husband of his mother, solver of the riddle of the Sphinx! What is the significance of the mysterious triad of these deeds of destiny? There is, especially in Persia, a primitive popular belief that a wise Magian can be born only of incest. With the riddle-solving and mother-marrying Œdipus in mind, we must immediately interpret this to the effect that wherever by some prophetic and magical power the boundary of the present and future, the inflexible law of individuation and, in general, the intrinsic spell of nature, are broken, an extraordinary counter-naturalness—in this case, incest—must have preceded as a cause; for how else could one force nature to surrender her secrets but by victoriously opposing her by means of the Unnatural? This is the secret which I see involved in the awful triad of the destiny of Œdipus; the very man who solves the riddle of nature—that doubly-constituted Sphinx— must also, as the murderer of his father and husband of his mother, break the holiest laws of nature. Indeed, it seems as if the myth were trying to whisper into our ears the fact that wisdom, especially Dionysian wisdom, is an unnatural abomination; that whoever, through his own knowledge, plunges nature into an abyss of annihilation, must also expect to experience the dissolution of nature in himself. "The sharpness of wisdom turns upon the sage: wisdom is a crime against nature": such are the terrible expressions the myth cries out to us. But the Hellenic poet, like a sunbeam, touches the sublime and terrible Memnonian statue of the myth, and suddenly it begins to sound—in Sophoclean melodies.

Let me now contrast the glory of passivity with the glory of activity which illuminates the *Prometheus* of Æschylus. What Æschylus the thinker had to tell us here, but which as a poet he only allows us to surmise through his symbolic picture, the

youthful Goethe has known how to reveal to us in the bold
words of his Prometheus:—

> "Hier sitz' ich, forme Menschen
> Nach meinem Bilde,
> Ein Geschlecht, das mir gleich sei,
> Zu leiden, zu weinen,
> Zu geniessen und zu freuen sich,
> Und dein nicht zu achten,
> Wie ich!" [9]

Man, rising to the level of the Titans, acquires his culture
by himself, and compels the gods to ally themselves with him,
because in his self-sufficient wisdom he holds in his hands their
existence and their limitations. The most wonderful thing,
however, in this Prometheus fable, which according to its
fundamental conception is an essential hymn of impiety, is the
profound Æschylean yearning for *justice*. The infinite tragedy
of the bold "individual" on the one hand, and the divine
necessity and premonition of a twilight of the gods on the
other, the force in these two worlds of suffering operating to
produce reconciliation, metaphysical oneness—all this strongly
suggests the central and main position of the Æschylean view
of the world, which sees Moira as eternal justice enthroned
over gods and men. Lest we be surprised at the astounding
boldness with which Æschylus weighs the Olympian world in
his scales of justice, we must always keep in mind that the

---

[9] "Here I sit, forming mankind
In my own image,
A race resembling me—
To sorrow, to weep,
To taste, to have pleasure,
And to have no need of thee,
Even as I!"

thinking Greek had an immovably firm substratum of meta
physical thought in his mysteries, and that all his fits or skepti
cism could be vented upon the Olympians. When he thought of
these deities, the Greek artist in particular had an obscure feel
ing of *mutual* dependency: and it is precisely in the Prome
theus of Æschylus that this feeling is symbolized. The Titanic
artist discovered in himself a bold confidence in his ability to
create men and at least destroy the gods. He might do this by
his superior wisdom, for which, to be sure, he had to atone by
eternal suffering. The splendid "I can" of the great genius,
bought cheaply even at the price of eternal suffering, the stern
pride of the artist: this is the essence and soul of Æschylean
poetry, while Sophocles in his Œdipus strikes up as prelude the
triumphal chant of the *saint*. But even this interpretation
which Æschylus has given to the myth does not reveal the
astounding depth of its terror. As a matter of fact, the artist's
delight in unfolding, the gayety of artistic creation bidding
defiance to all calamity, is actually a shining stellar and nebular
image reflected in a black sea of sadness. The story of Prome
theus is an original possession of the entire Aryan race, and is
documentary evidence of its capacity for the profoundly tragic.
Indeed, it is not entirely improbable that this myth has the
same characteristic significance for the Aryan genius that the
myth of the fall of man has for the Semitic, and that the two
are related like brother and sister. The presupposition of the
Promethean myth is the transcendent value which a naïve
humanity attaches to *fire* as the true palladium of every rising
culture. That man, however, should not receive this fire only
as a gift from heaven, in the form of the igniting lightning
or the warming sunshine, but should, on the contrary, be able
to control it at will—this appeared to the reflective primitive
man as sacrilege, as robbery of the divine nature. And thus

the first philosophical problem at once causes a painful, irreconcilable antagonism between man and God, and puts as it were a mass of rock at the gate of every culture. The best and highest that men can acquire they must obtain by a crime, and then they must in turn endure its consequences, namely, the whole flood of sufferings and sorrows with which the offended divinities *must* requite the nobly aspiring race of man. It is a bitter thought, which, by the *dignity* it confers on crime, contrasts strangely with the Semitic myth of the fall of man, in which curiosity, deception, weakness in the face of temptation, wantonness,—in short, a whole series of preëminently feminine passions,—were regarded as the origin of evil. What distinguishes the Aryan conception is the sublime view of *active sin* as the essential Promethean virtue, and the discovery of the ethical basis of pessimistic tragedy in the *justification* of human evil—of human guilt as well as of the suffering incurred thereby. The pain implicit in the very structure of things—which the contemplative Aryan is not disposed to explain away—the antagonism in the heart of the world, manifests itself to him as a medley of different worlds, for instance, a Divine and a human world, both of which are in the right individually, but which, because they exist separately side by side, must suffer for that very individuation. In the heroic effort towards universality made by the individual, in his attempt to penetrate beyond the bounds of individuation and become himself the *one* world-being, he experiences in himself the primordial contradiction concealed in the essence of things, that is, he trespasses and he suffers. Accordingly crime [10] is understood by the Aryans to be masculine, sin [11] by the Semites to be feminine; just as the original crime is com-

---

[10] *Der* Frevel.
[11] *Die* Sünde.

mitted by man, the original sin by woman. Besides, as the witches' chorus says:

"Wir nehmen das nicht so genau:
Mit tausend Schritten macht's die Frau;
Doch wie sie auch sich eilen kann
Mit einem Sprunge macht's der Mann." [12]

He who understands this innermost core of the Prometheus myth—namely, the necessity for crime imposed on the titanically striving individual—will at once feel the un-Apollonian element in this pessimistic representation. For Apollo seeks to calm individual beings precisely by drawing boundary lines between them, and by again and again, with his requirements of self-knowledge and self-control, recalling these bounds to us as the holiest laws of the universe. However, in order that this Apollonian tendency might not congeal the form to Egyptian rigidity and coldness, in order that the effort to prescribe to the individual wave its path and compass might not ruin the motion of the entire lake, the high tide of the Dionysian tendency destroyed from time to time all those little circles in which the one-sided Apollonian "will" sought to confine the Hellenic world. The suddenly swelling Dionysian tide then takes the separate little wave-mountains of individuals on its back, just as the brother of Prometheus, the Titan Atlas, does with the earth. This Titanic impulse, to become as it were the Atlas of all individuals, and on broad shoulders to bear them higher and higher, farther and farther, is what the

---

[12] We do not measure with such care:
Woman in thousand steps is there,
But howsoe'er she hasten may,
Man in one leap has cleared the way.
Faust, Bayard Taylor's Trans.

Promethean and the Dionysian have in common. In this respect the Æschylean Prometheus is a Dionysian mark, while, in the aforementioned profound yearning for justice, Æschylus betrays to the intelligent eye his paternal descent from Apollo, the god of individuation, the god who sets the boundaries of justice. And so the double personality of the Æschylean Prometheus, his conjoint Dionysian and Apollonian nature, might be thus expressed in an abstract formula: "Whatever exists is alike just and unjust, and in both cases equally justified."

"Das ist deine Welt! Das heisst eine Welt!" [13]

10

The tradition is undisputed that Greek tragedy in its earliest form had for its sole theme the sufferings of Dionysus, and that for a long time the only stage-hero was simply Dionysus himself. With equal confidence, however, we can assert that, until Euripides, Dionysus never once ceased to be the tragic hero; that in fact all the celebrated figures of the Greek Stage —Prometheus, Œdipus, etc.—are but masks of this original hero, Dionysus. There is godhead behind all these masks; and that is the one essential cause of the typical "ideality," so often wondered at, of these celebrated characters. I know not who it was maintained that all individuals as such are comic and consequently untragic: whence we might infer that the Greeks in general *could* not endure individuals on the tragic stage. And they really seem to have felt this: as, in general, we may note in the Platonic distinction, so deeply rooted in the Hellenic nature, of the "idea" in contrast to the "eidolon," or

---

[13] There is thy world, and what a world!—*Faust.*

image. Using Plato's terms we should have to speak of the tragic figures of the Hellenic stage somewhat as follows: the one truly real Dionysus appears in a variety of forms, in the mask of a fighting hero and entangled, as it were, in the net of the individual will. In the latter case the visible god talks and acts so as to resemble an erring, striving, suffering individual. That, generally speaking, he *appears* with such epic precision and clarity is the work of the dream-reading Apollo, who through this symbolic appearance indicates to the chorus its Dionysian state. In reality, however, and behind this appearance, the hero is the suffering Dionysus of the mysteries, the god experiencing in himself the agonies of individuation, of whom wonderful myths tell that as a boy he was torn to pieces by the Titans and has been worshiped in this state as Zagreus: whereby is intimated that this dismemberment, the properly Dionysian *suffering,* is like a transformation into air, water, earth, and fire, that we are therefore to regard the state of individuation as the origin and prime cause of all suffering, as something objectionable in itself. From the smile of this Dionysus sprang the Olympian gods, from his tears sprang man. In this existence as a dismembered god, Dionysus possesses the dual nature of a cruel barbarized demon and a mild, gentle-hearted ruler. But the hope of the epopts looked towards a new birth of Dionysus, which we must now in anticipation conceive as the end of individuation. It was for this coming third Dionysus that the epopts' stormy hymns of joy resounded. And it is this hope alone that casts a gleam of joy upon the features of a world torn asunder and shattered into individuals: as is symbolized in the myth of Demeter, sunk in eternal sorrow, who *rejoices* again only when told that she may *once more* give birth to Dionysus. This view of things already provides us with all the elements of a profound and pessimistic contemplation of the world, together with the *mystery doctrine of tragedy:* the fundamental knowledge of the oneness of everything existent, the conception of individuation as the prime cause of evil, and of art as the joyous hope that the bonds of individuation may be broken in augury of a restored oneness.

We have already pointed out that the Homeric epos is the poem of Olympian culture, in which this culture has sung its own song of victory over the terrors of the war of the Titans. Under the predominating influence of tragic poetry, these Homeric myths are now born anew; and this metempsychosis reveals that in the meantime the Olympian culture also has been conquered by a still deeper view of things. The insolent Titan Prometheus has announced to his Olympian tormentor that some day the greatest danger will menace his rule, unless Zeus ally with him in time. In Æschylus we perceive the terrified Zeus, fearful of his end, allying himself with the Titan. Thus, the former age of the Titans is once more recovered from Tartarus and brought to the light of day. The philosophy of wild and naked nature beholds with the frank, undissembling gaze of truth the myths of the Homeric world as they dance past: they turn pale, they tremble under the piercing glance of this goddess—till the powerful fist of the Dionysian artist forces them into the service of the new deity. Dionysian truth takes over the entire domain of myth as the symbolism of *its* knowledge. This it makes known partly in the public cult of tragedy and partly in the secret celebration of the dramatic mysteries, but always in the old mythical garb. What power was it that freed Prometheus from his vultures and transformed the myth into a vehicle of Dionysian wisdom? It is the Heracleian power of music: which, having reached its highest manifestation in tragedy, can invest myths with a new and most profound significance. This we have

already characterized as the most powerful function of music.
For it is the fate of every myth to creep by degrees into the
narrow limits of some alleged historical reality, and to be
treated by some later generation as a unique fact with historical
claims: and the Greeks were already fairly on the way to re-
stamp the whole of their mythical juvenile dream sagaciously
and arbitrarily into a historico-pragmatical *juvenile history.*
For this is the way in which religions are wont to die out: when
under the stern, intelligent eyes of an orthodox dogmatism,
the mythical premises of a religion are systematized as a sum
total of historical events; when one begins apprehensively to
defend the credibility of the myths, while at the same time
one opposes any continuation of their natural vitality and
growth; when, accordingly, the feeling for myth perishes, and
its place is taken by the claim of religion to historical foundations. This dying myth was now seized by the new-born genius
of Dionysian music; and in these hands it flourished yet again,
with colors such as it had never yet displayed, with a fragrance
that awakened a longing anticipation of a metaphysical world.
After this final effulgence it collapses, its leaves wither, and
soon the mocking Lucians of antiquity catch at the discolored
and faded flowers carried away by the four winds. Through
tragedy the myth attains its most vital content, its most expressive form; it rises once more like a wounded hero, and its
whole excess of strength, together with the philosophic calm
of the dying, burns in its eyes with a last powerful gleam.

What didst thou mean, O impious Euripides, in seeking once
more to subdue this dying one to your service? Under thy
ruthless hands it died: and then thou madest use of counterfeit, masked myth, which like the ape of Heracles could but
trick itself out in the old finery. And as myth died in thy hands,
so too died the genius of music; though thou didst greedily

plunder all the gardens of music—thou didst attain but a counterfeit, masked music. And as thou hast forsaken Dionysus, Apollo hath also forsaken thee; rouse up all the passions from their haunts and conjure them into thy circle, sharpen and whet thy sophistical dialectic for the speeches of thy heroes —thy very heroes have but counterfeit, masked passions, and utter but counterfeit, masked words.

11

Greek tragedy met an end different from that of her older sister arts: she died by suicide, in consequence of an irreconcilable conflict. Accordingly she died tragically, while all the others passed away calmly and beautifully at a ripe old age. If it be consonant with a happy natural state to take leave of life easily, leaving behind a fair posterity, the closing period of these older arts exhibits such a happy natural state: slowly they sink from sight, and before their dying eyes already stand their fairer progeny, who impatiently, with a bold gesture, lift up their heads. But when Greek tragedy died, there rose everywhere the deep feeling of an immense void. Just as the Greek sailors in the time of Tiberius once heard upon a lonesome island the thrilling cry, "Great Pan is dead": so now through the Hellenic world there sounded the grievous lament: "Tragedy is dead! Poetry itself has perished with her! Away with you, ye pale, stunted epigones! Away to Hades, that ye may for once eat your fill of the crumbs of your former masters!"

And when after this death a new Art blossomed forth which revered tragedy as her ancestress and mistress, it was observed with horror that she did indeed bear the features of her mother, but that they were the very features the latter had exhibited in her long death-struggle. It was Euripides who fought this death-struggle of tragedy; the later art is known as the *New Attic Comedy*. In it the degenerate form of tragedy lived on as a monument of its painful and violent death.

This connection helps to explain the passionate attachment that the poets of the New Comedy felt for Euripides; so that we are no longer surprised at the wish of Philemon, who would have let himself be hanged at once, merely that he might visit Euripides in the lower world: if he could only be certain that the deceased still had possession of his reason. But if we desire, as briefly as possible, and without claiming to say anything exhaustive, to characterize what Euripides has in common with Menander and Philemon, and what appealed to them so strongly as worthy of imitation, it is sufficient to say that Euripides brought the *spectator* upon the stage. He who has perceived the material out of which the Promethean tragic writers prior to Euripides formed their heroes, and how remote from their purpose it was to bring the true mask of reality on the stage, will also be able to explain the utterly opposite tendency of Euripides. Through him the average man forced his way from the spectators' benches on to the stage itself; the mirror in which formerly only grand and bold traits were represented now showed the painful fidelity that conscientiously reproduces even the abortive outlines of nature. Odysseus, the typical Hellene of the older art, now sank, in the hands of the new poets, to the figure of the Græculus, who, as the good-naturedly cunning house-slave, henceforth occupies the center of dramatic interest. What Euripides claims credit for in Aristophanes' *Frogs,* namely, that his household medicines have freed tragic art from its pompous corpulency, is apparent above all in his tragic heroes. The spectator now actually saw and heard his double on the Euripidean stage, and rejoiced that he could talk so well. But this joy was not all: you could even learn of Euripides how to speak. He prides himself upon this in his contest with Æschylus: from him the people have learned how to observe, debate, and draw conclusions according to the rules of art and with the cleverest sophistries. In general, through this revolution of the popular speech, he had made the New Comedy possible. For henceforth it was no longer a secret, how—and with what wise maxims—the commonplace was to express itself on the stage. Civic mediocrity, on which Euripides built all his political hopes, was now given a voice, while heretofore the demigod in tragedy and the drunken satyr, or demiman, in comedy, had detcrmined the character of the language. And so the Aristophanean Euripides prides himself on having portrayed the common, familiar, everyday life and activities of the people, about which all are qualified to pass judgment. If now the entire populace philosophizes, manages land and goods and conducts law-suits with unheard-of circumspection, the glory is all his, together with the splendid results of the wisdom with which he has inoculated the rabble.

It was to a populace thus prepared and illuminated that that New Comedy could now address itself, of which Euripides had become as it were the chorus-master; only that this time the chorus of spectators had to be trained. As soon as this chorus was trained to sing in the Euripidean key, there arose that drama which resembles a game of chess—the New Comedy, with its perpetual triumphs of cunning and artfulness. But Euripides—the chorus-master—was still praised continually: indeed, people would have killed themselves in order to learn still more from him, if they had not known that tragic poets were quite as dead as tragedy. But with that death the

Hellene had given up his belief in immortality; not only his belief in an ideal past, but also his belief in an ideal future. The words of the well-known epitaph, "frivolous and capricious as an old man," also suit senile Hellenism. The passing moment, wit, levity, and caprice are its highest deities; the fifth estate, that of the slaves, now comes into power, at least in sentiment: and if we may still speak at all of "Greek cheerfulness," it is the cheerfulness of the slave who has nothing of consequence to be responsible for, nothing great to strive for, and who cannot value anything in the past or future higher than the present. It was this semblance of "Greek cheerfulness" which so aroused the deep-minded and formidable natures of the first four centuries of the Christian era: this womanish flight from seriousness and terror, this craven satisfaction with easy enjoyment, seemed to them not only contemptible, but a specifically anti-Christian sentiment. And to influence of that sentiment we must ascribe the fact that the conception of Greek antiquity, which endured for centuries, preserved with almost unconquerable persistency that feverish hue of cheerfulness—as if there had never been a Sixth Century with its birth of tragedy, its Mysteries, its Pythagoras and Heraclitus, as if the very art-works of that great period did not at all exist, though these phenomena can hardly be explained as having originated in any such senile and slavish love of existence and cheerfulness, and though they indicate as the source of their being an altogether different conception of the world.

The assertion made above, that Euripides brought the spectator on the stage that he might better qualify him to pass judgment on the drama, makes it appear as if the old or tragic art had always been in a false relation to the spectator; and one might be tempted to extol as an advance over Sophocles the radical tendency of Euripides to produce a proper relation between art-work and public. But "public," after all, is only a word. In no sense is it a homogeneous and constant quantity. Why should the artist be bound to accommodate himself to a power whose strength lies merely in numbers? And if, by virtue of his endowments and aspirations, he should feel himself superior to every one of these spectators, how should he feel greater respect for the collective expression of all these subordinate capacities than for the relatively highest-endowed individual spectator? In truth, if ever a Greek artist throughout a long life treated his public with arrogance and self-sufficiency, it was Euripides. When the rabble threw themselves at his feet, he openly and with sublime defiance attacked his own tendency, the very tendency with which he had won over the masses. If this genius had had the slightest respect for the noise the mob makes, he would have broken down long before the middle of his career beneath the heavy blows of his own failures. These considerations make it clear that our formula —namely, that Euripides brought the spectator on the stage in order to make him truly competent to pass judgment—was but a provisional one, and that therefore we must penetrate more deeply to understand his tendency. Conversely, it is known beyond any question that Æschylus and Sophocles during the whole of their lives, and indeed, long after their deaths, were in complete possession of the people's favor, and that therefore in the case of these fore-runners of Euripides there was never any question of a false relation between art-work and public. What was it then that thus forcibly drove this artist, so richly endowed, so constantly impelled to production, from the path warmed by the sun of the greatest names in poetry and covered by the cloudless heaven of popular favor? What strange consideration for the spectator led him to oppose the spectator? How could he, out of too great a respect for his public—despise his public?

Euripides—and this is the solution of the riddle just propounded—undoubtedly felt himself, as a poet, superior to the masses in general; but to two of his spectators he did not feel superior. He brought the masses upon the stage; and these two spectators he revered as the only competent judges and masters of his art. Complying with their directions and admonitions, he transferred the entire world of sentiments, passions, and experiences, hitherto present at every festival representation as the invisible chorus on the spectators' benches, into the souls of his stage-heroes. He yielded to their demands, too, when for these new characters he sought out a new language and a new accent. Only in their voices could he hear any conclusive verdict on his work, and also the cheering promise of triumph when he found himself as usual condemned by the public judgment.

Of these two spectators, one is—Euripides himself, Euripides *as thinker*, not as poet. It might be said of him, as of Lessing, that his copious fund of *critical* talent, if it did not create, at least constantly stimulated a corresponding and productive *artistic* impulse. With this faculty, with all the clarity and dexterity of his critical temper, Euripides had sat in the theater and striven to recognize in the masterpieces of his great predecessors, as in faded paintings, feature after feature, line after line. And here he had experienced something which any one initiated in the deeper secrets of Æschylean tragedy might have foretold. He observed something incommensurable in every feature and in every line of the tragedy, a certain deceptive distinctness and at the same time a mysterious depth, almost an infinitude, of background. Even the clearest figure always had a comet's tail attached to it, which seemed to suggest the uncertain, the nebulous. A similar twilight shrouded the structure of the drama, especially the element of the function of the chorus. And how dubious remained the solution of the ethical problems! How questionable the treatment of the myths! How unequal the distribution of good and bad fortune! In the very language of the Old Tragedy there was much that was objectionable to him, or at least puzzling; especially he encountered too much pomp for simple affairs, too many tropes and monstrous expressions to suit the plainness of the characters. So he sat in the theater, pondering uneasily, and as a spectator he confessed to himself that he did not understand his great predecessors. If, however, it was his opinion that the understanding was the essential root of all enjoyment and creation, he must inquire, he must look about to see whether any one else had the same opinion, and whether they also felt this incommensurability. But most people, and among them the finest individuals, answered him only with a distrustful smile; while none could explain why the great masters were still in the right despite his scruples and objections. And in this state of torment, he found *that other spectator,* who did not comprehend tragedy, and therefore did not esteem it. Allied with him, in solitary state, he could now venture to begin the terrific struggle against the art of Æschylus and Sophocles— not as a polemist, but as a dramatic poet, who would oppose *his own* conception of tragedy to the traditional one.

12

Before we name this other spectator, let us pause here a moment in order to recall to our minds our own previously described impression of the discordant and incommensurable elements in the genius of Æschylean tragedy. Let us think of our own surprise at the *chorus* and the *tragic hero* of that tragedy, neither of which we could reconcile with our own customs any more than with tradition—till we rediscovered this duality itself as the origin and essence of Greek tragedy, as the expression of two interwoven artistic impulses, *the Apollonian and the Dionysian.*

To separate this primitive and all-powerful Dionysian element from tragedy, and to construct a new and purified form on the basis of an un-Dionysian art, morality, and conception of the world—this is the tendency of Euripides as it is now clearly revealed to us.

In the evening of his life, Euripides himself composed a myth in which he urgently propounded to his contemporaries the question as to the value and significance of this tendency. Is the Dionysian entitled to exist at all? Should it not be forcibly uprooted from Hellenic soil? Certainly, the poet tells us, if it were only possible: but the god Dionysus is too powerful; his most intelligent adversary—like Pentheus in the *Bacchæ*—is unwittingly enchanted by him, and in this enchantment runs to meet his fate. The judgment of the two old prophets, Cadmus and Tiresias, seems also to be the judgment of the aged poet: that the reflection of the wisest individuals does not overthrow old popular traditions, nor the perpetually self-propagating worship of Dionysus; that in fact it is to our interest to display at the very least a diplomatically cautious concern in the presence of such strange forces: although there is always the possibility that the god may take offense at such lukewarm participation, and eventually transform the diplomat—in this case Cadmus—into a dragon. This is what we are told by a poet who opposed Dionysus with heroic valor throughout a long life—and who finally ended his career with a glorification of his adversary, and with suicide, like one staggering from giddiness, who, to escape the horrible vertigo he can no longer endure, casts himself from a tower. This tragedy—the *Bacchæ*—is a protest against the practicability of his own tendency; but alas, it has already been put into practice! The surprising thing had happened: when the poet recanted, his tendency had already conquered. Dionysus had already been scared from the tragic stage; he had been scared by a demonic power speaking through Euripides. For even Euripides was, in a sense, only a mask: the deity that spoke through him was neither Dionysus nor Apollo. It was an altogether new-born demon. And it was called *Socrates*. Thus we have a new antithesis—the Dionysian and the Socratic; and on that antithesis the art of Greek tragedy was wrecked. In vain does Euripides seek to comfort us by his recantation. It avails not: the most magnificent temple lies in ruins. Of what use is the lamentation of the destroyer, of what use his confession that it was the most beautiful of all temples? And even if Euripides has been punished by being changed into a dragon by the art-critics of all ages—who could be content with so miserable a compensation?

Let us now examine this *Socratic* tendency with which Euripides combated and vanquished Æschylean tragedy.

We must first ask ourselves, what could be the aim of the Euripidean design, which, in its most ideal form, would wish to base drama exclusively on the un-Dionysian? What other form of drama still remained, if it was not to be born of the womb of music, in the mysterious twilight of the Dionysian? Only *the dramatized epos:* in which Apollonian domain of art the *tragic* effect is of course unattainable. For it is not bound up with the subject-matter of the events represented; indeed, I maintain that it would have been impossible for Goethe in his projected *Nausikaa* to have rendered tragically effective the suicide of the idyllic being, the scene which was to have completed the fifth act. So extraordinary is the power of the epic-Apollonian representation, that before our very eyes it transforms the most terrible things by the joy in appearance and in redemption through appearance. The poet of the dramatized epos cannot blend completely with his pictures any more than the epic rhapsodist can. He is still just the calm, unmoved embodiment of Contemplation whose wide eyes see the picture *before* them. The actor in this dramatized epos still remains fundamentally a rhapsodist: the consecration of the inner dream lies on all his actions, so that he is never wholly an actor.

How, then, is the Euripidean play related to this ideal of the Apollonian drama? Just as the younger rhapsodist is related to the solemn rhapsodist of the old time. In the Platonic *Ion,* the former describes his own nature as follows: "When I am saying anything sad, my eyes fill with tears; when, however, I am saying something awful and terrible, then my hair stands on end with fright and my heart beats quickly." Here we no longer remark anything of the epic absorption in appearance, or of the dispassionate coolness of the true actor, who precisely in his highest activity is wholly appearance and joy in appearance. Euripides is that actor whose heart beats, whose hair stands on end; as Socratic thinker he designs the plan, as passionate actor he executes it. Neither in the designing nor in the execution is he a pure artist. And so the Euripidean drama is a thing both cool and fiery, equally capable of freezing and burning. It is impossible for it to attain the Apollonian effect of the epos, while, on the other hand, it has alienated itself as much as possible from Dionysian elements. Now, in order to develop at all, it requires new stimulants, which can no longer lie within the sphere of the two unique art-impulses, the Apollonian and the Dionysian. These stimulants are cool, paradoxical *thoughts,* replacing Apollonian intuitions—and fiery *passions,* replacing Dionysian ecstasies; and, it may be added, thoughts and passions copied very realistically and in no sense suffused with the atmosphere of art.

Accordingly, having perceived this much, that Euripides did not succeed in establishing the drama exclusively on an Apollonian basis, but rather that his un-Dionysian inclinations deviated into a naturalistic and inartistic tendency, we should now be able to get a nearer view of the character of *esthetic Socratism,* whose supreme law reads about as follows: "To be beautiful everything must be intelligible," as the counterpart to the Socratic identity: "Knowledge is virtue." With this canon in his hands, Euripides measures all the separate elements of the drama—language, characters, dramaturgic structure, and choric music—and corrects them according to his principle. The poetic deficiency and degeneration, which we are so often wont to impute to Euripides in comparison with Sophocles, is for the most part the product of this penetrating critical process, this daring intelligibility. The Euripidean *prologue* may serve as an example of the results of this rationalistic method. Nothing could be more antithetical to the technique of our own stage than the prologue in the drama of Euripides. For a single person to appear at the outset of the play telling us who he is, what precedes the action, what has happened so far, even what will happen in the course of the play, would be condemned by a modern playwright as a willful, inexcusable abandonment of the effect of suspense. We know everything that is going to happen; who cares to wait till it actually does happen?—considering, moreover, that here we do not by any means have the exciting relation of a prophetic dream to a reality taking place later on. But Euripides' speculations took a different turn. The effect of tragedy never depended on epic suspense, on a fascinating uncertainty as to what is to happen now and afterwards: but rather on the great rhetorical-lyric scenes in which the passion and dialectic of the chief hero swelled to a broad and mighty stream. Everything was directed toward pathos, not action: and whatever was not directed toward pathos was considered objectionable. But what interferes most with the hearer's pleasurable satisfaction in such scenes is a missing link, a gap in the texture of the previous history. So long as the spectator has to divine the meaning of this or that person, or the presuppositions of this or that conflict of views and inclinations, his complete absorption in the activities and sufferings of the chief characters is impossible, as is likewise breathless fellow-feeling and fellow-fearing. The Æschylean-Sophoclean tragedy employed the most ingenious devices in the initial scenes to place in the spectator's hands, as if by chance, all the threads necessary for a complete understanding: a trait whereby that noble artistry is approved, which as it were masks the *inevitably* formal element, and makes it appear something accidental. Notwithstanding this, Euripides thought he observed that during these first scenes the spectator was so peculiarly anxious to make out the problem of the previous history, that the poetic beauties and pathos of the exposition were lost to him. Accordingly he put the prologue even before the exposition, and placed it in the mouth of a person who could be trusted: some deity had often as it were to guarantee the particulars of the tragedy to the public, to remove every doubt as to the reality of the myth, just as did Descartes who could prove the reality of the empirical world only by appealing to the truthfulness of God and His inability to utter falsehood. Euripides makes use of this same divine truthfulness once more at the close of his drama, in order to reassure the public as to the future of his heroes; this is the task of the notorious *deus ex machina*. Between this epic retrospect and epic prospect, is placed the dramatico-lyric present, the "drama" as such.

Thus Euripides as a poet is essentially an echo of his own conscious knowledge; and it is precisely on this account that he occupies such a notable position in the history of Greek art. With reference to his critical-productive activity, he must often have felt that he ought to make objective in drama the words at the beginning of the essay of Anaxagoras: "In the beginning all things were mixed together; then came the understanding and created order." Anaxagoras with his "nous" is said to have appeared among philosophers as the only sober person amid a crowd of drunken ones. Euripides may also have conceived his relation to the other tragic poets under a similar figure. As long as the sole ruler and disposer of the universe, the *nous,* remained excluded from artistic activity, things were all mixed together in a primeval chaos. This was what Euripides was obliged to think; and so, as the first "sober" one among them, he was bound to condemn the "drunken" poets. Sophocles said of Æschylus that he did what was right, though he did it unconsciously. This would surely never have been the opinion of Euripides. He would have said, on the contrary, that Æschylus, *because* he created unconsciously, did what was *wrong*. Similarly the divine Plato for the most part speaks but ironically of the creative faculty of the poet, in so far as it is not conscious insight, and places it on a par with the gift of the soothsayer and dream-interpreter. The intimation is that the poet is incapable of composing until he has become unconscious and bereft of reason. Like Plato, Euripides undertook to show to the world the reverse of the "unintelligent" poet; his esthetic principle that "to be beautiful everything must be known" is, as I have said, the parallel to the Socratic, "to be good everything must be known." So that we may consider Euripides as the poet of esthetic Socratism. But Socrates was that *second spectator* who did not comprehend and therefore did not esteem the Old Tragedy; in alliance with him Euripides dared to be the herald of a new art. If it was this then, that destroyed the older tragedy in general, it follows that esthetic Socratism was the fatal principle; but in so far as the struggle is directed against the *Dionysian element* in the older tragedy, we may recognize in Socrates the opponent of Dionysus. He is the new Orpheus rebelling against Dionysus, and although he is destined to be torn to pieces by the Mænads of the Athenian court, yet he puts to flight the overpowerful god himself. The latter, you will recall, fleeing from Lycurgus, the King of Edoni, sought refuge in the depths of the ocean—or, in this case, in the mystical flood of a secret cult which gradually overran the earth.

13

That Socrates was closely related to the tendency of Euripides did not escape the notice of contemporaneous antiquity. The most eloquent expression of this felicitous insight was the story current in Athens that Socrates used to help Euripides in poetizing. Whenever an occasion arose to enumerate the popular agitators of the day, the adherents of the "good old times" would mention both names in the same breath. To the influence of Socrates and Euripides they attributed the fact that the old Marathonian stalwart capacity of body and soul was being sacrificed more and more to a dubious enlightenment that involved the progressive degeneration of the physical and mental powers. It is in this tone, half indignant, half contemptuous, that Aristophanic comedy is wont to speak of both of them—to the consternation of modern men, who are quite willing to give up Euripides, but who cannot help being amazed that Socrates should appear in the comedies of Aristophanes as the first and leading *sophist,* as the mirror and epitome of all sophistical tendencies. The result of their bewilderment is that they give themselves the unique consolation of putting Aristophanes himself in the pillory, as a dissolute, lying Alcibiades of poetry. Without here defending the profound insight of Aristophanes against such attacks, I shall now continue to show, by means of the sentiments of the time, the close connection between Socrates and Euripides. With this in view, we must remember particularly that Socrates, as an opponent of tragic art, refrained from patronizing tragedy, but that he appeared among the spectators only when a new play of Euripides was to be performed. Most famous of all, however, is the juxtaposition of the two names by the Delphic oracle, which designated Socrates as the wisest of men, but at the same time decided that the second prize in the contest of wisdom belonged to Euripides.

Sophocles was named third in order of rank; he who could pride himself that, as compared with Æschylus, he did what was right, and moreover did so because he *knew* what the right was. Evidently it is merely the degree of clearness of this *knowledge* which distinguishes these three men in common as the three "knowing ones" of their time.

[*1018*]

The most decisive word, however, for this new and un-precedented value set upon knowledge and insight was spoken by Socrates when he found that he was the only one who acknowledged to himself that he *knew nothing;* for in his critical peregrinations through Athens, he called on the great-est statesmen, orators, poets, and artists, and everywhere he discovered the conceit of knowledge. To his astonishment he perceived that all these celebrities were without a proper and sure insight, even with regard to their own professions, and that they practiced them only by instinct. "Only by instinct": with this phrase we touch upon the heart and core of the Socratic tendency. With it Socratism condemns existing art as well as existing ethics. Wherever Socratism turns its search-ing eyes it sees lack of insight, it sees the force of illusion; and from this lack it infers the essential perversity and objection-ableness of existing conditions. From this point onwards, Socrates conceives it as his duty to correct existence; and, with an air of irreverence and superiority, as the precursor of an altogether different culture, art, and morality, he enters single-handed into a world, to touch whose very hem would give us the greatest happiness.

For an extraordinary hesitancy always seizes upon us with regard to Socrates. Again and again we are impelled to ascer-tain the sense and purpose of the most puzzling phenomenon of antiquity. Who is this that dares single-handed to disown the Greek genius, which, as Homer, Pindar, and Æschylus, as Phidias, as Pericles, as Pythia and Dionysus, as the deepest abyss and the highest height, compels our wondering admira-tion? What demonic power is this which dares spill this magic draught in the dust? What demigod is this to whom the chorus of spirits of the noblest of mankind must call out. "Weh!

Weh! Du hast sie zerstört, die schöne Welt, mit mächtiger Faust; sie stürzt, sie zerfällt!" [14]

We are offered a key to the character of Socrates by the wonderful phenomenon which he calls his dæmon. In exceptional circumstances, when his gigantic intellect begins to fail him, he receives a secure support in the utterances of a divine voice which manifests itself at such moments. This voice, whenever it comes, always *dissuades*. In this utterly abnormal nature instinctive wisdom only appears in order to *hinder* here and there the progress of conscious perception. Whereas in all productive men it is instinct that is the creatively affirmative force, and consciousness that acts critically and dissuasively; with Socrates it is instinct that becomes critic, and consciousness that becomes creator—a perfect monstrosity *per defectum!* And we do indeed observe here a monstrous *defectus* of all mystical aptitude so that Socrates might be called the typical *non-mystic,* in whom, through a superfœtation, the logical nature is developed, to the same excessive degree as instinctive wisdom is developed in the mystic. Unlike his instinct, however, the logic of Socrates was absolutely prevented from turning against itself; in its unimpeded flow it manifests a native power such as we meet with, to our awe and surprise, only among the very greatest instinctive forces. Any one who has experienced even a breath of the divine naïveté and security of the Socratic way of life in the Platonic writings, will also feel that the enormous driving-wheel of logical Socratism is in motion, as it were, *behind* Socrates, and that it must be viewed through Socrates

---

[14] Woe! Woe!
    Thou hast it destroyed,
    The beautiful world;
    With powerful fist;
    In ruin 'tis hurled!

Faust, Bayard Taylor's Trans.

as through a shadow. And that he himself had a premonition of this relationship is apparent from the dignified seriousness with which he everywhere, even before his judges, insists on his divine calling. It is really as impossible to refute him here as to approve of his instinct-disintegrating influence. In view of this indissoluble conflict, when he had at last been brought before the forum of the Greek state, there was only one kind of punishment demanded, namely, exile. He might have been sped across the borders as something thoroughly enigmatical, inexplicable, and impossible to characterize, and so posterity would never have been justified in charging the Athenians with an ignominious deed. But that the sentence of death, and not mere exile, was pronounced upon him, seems to have been the work of Socrates himself, who encountered the decree with perfect awareness and without the natural fear of death. He met his death with the calmness with which, according to Plato's description, he, last of the revelers, leaves the Symposium at dawn to begin a new day; while his sleepy fellow-banqueters remain behind on the couches and the floor, to dream of Socrates, the true eroticist. *The dying Socrates* became the new ideal of the noble Greek youths,—an ideal they had never yet beheld,—and above all, the typical Hellenic youth, Plato, prostrated himself before this scene with all the burning devotion of his visionary soul.

14

Let us now imagine the one great Cyclops eye of Socrates fixed on tragedy, an eye in which the fine frenzy of artistic enthusiasm had never glowed. To this eye was denied the pleasure of gazing into the Dionysian abysses. For what was it bound to see in the "sublime and greatly lauded" tragic art, as Plato called it? A thing devoid of sense, full of causes apparently without effects, and effects apparently without causes; the whole, moreover, so motley and diversified that though it could not but be repugnant to a thoughtful mind, it was a dangerous incentive for sensitive and irritable souls. We know what was the only kind of poetry he understood: the *Æsopian fable:* and this he favored no doubt with the good-natured acquiescence with which the good honest Gellert sings the praise of poetry in the fable of the bee and the hen:—

> "Du siehst an mir, wozu si nutzt,
> Dem, der nicht viel Verstand besitzt,
> Die Wahrheit durch ein Bild zu sagen." [15]

But it seemed to Socrates that tragic art did not even "tell the truth": not to mention the fact that it addressed itself to him who has "no great understanding." Consequently, it did not recommend itself to the philosopher: a twofold reason for shunning it. Like Plato, he reckoned it among the seductive arts which portray only the agreeable, not the useful; and hence he required of his disciples abstinence and strict separation from such unphilosophical temptations, with such success that the youthful tragic poet Plato first of all burned his poems that he might become a student of Socrates. But where unconquerable natural tendencies struggled against the Socratic maxims, their power, together with the momentum of his mighty character, was still enough to force poetry itself into new and hitherto unknown channels.

An instance of this is the aforesaid Plato, Plato who in condemning tragedy and art in general certainly did not lag be-

---

[15] Through me, you may observe how useful it is to tell the truth to those of no great understanding, by means of a parable.

hind the naïve cynicism of his master, was nevertheless by sheer artistic necessity constrained to create an art-form which is essentially related to those very forms of art which he repudiated. Plato's main objection to the old art—that it is the imitation of a phantom,[16] and hence belongs to a sphere still lower than the empiric world—could not at all be directed against the new art: and so we find Plato endeavoring to go beyond reality and to represent the idea which underlies this pseudo-reality. But Plato, the thinker, thereby arrived by a roundabout road at the very point where he had always been at home as poet, and from which Sophocles and all the older artists had solemnly protested against that objection. If tragedy had absorbed into itself all the earlier varieties of art, the same might also be said in an unusual sense of the Platonic dialogue, which, a mixture of all the then existent forms and styles, hovers midway between narrative, lyric and drama, between prose and poetry, and so has also broken loose from the older strict law of unity of linguistic form. This tendency was carried still farther by the *Cynic* writers, who in the greatest stylistic medley, oscillating between prose and metrical forms, realized also the literary picture of the "raving Socrates" whom they were wont to represent in real life. The Platonic dialogue was a sort of boat in which the shipwrecked ancient poetry was rescued with all her children: crowded into a narrow space and timidly submissive to the single pilot, Socrates, they now launched forth into a new world, which never tired of looking at the fantastic spectacle of this procession. The fact is that Plato has given to all posterity the prototype of a new art-form, the prototype of the *novel*: which may be described as an infinitely developed Æsop fable, in which poetry holds the

---

[16] Scheinbild.

same rank with reference to dialectic philosophy as this same philosophy held for many centuries with reference to theology: that is to say, the rank of *ancilla*. This was the new position into which Plato, under the pressure of the dæmon-inspired Socrates, forced poetry.

Here *philosophic thought* overgrows art and compels it to cling close to the trunk of dialectic. The *Apollonian* tendency has withdrawn into the shell of logical schematism; just as we noticed something analogous in the case of Euripides (and moreover a transformation of the *Dionysian* into the naturalistic emotion). Socrates, the dialectical hero of the Platonic drama, reminds us of the kindred nature of the Euripidean hero, who must defend his actions with arguments and counter-arguments, and who thereby so often incurs the danger of forfeiting our tragic pity; for who could mistake the *optimistic* element in the essence of dialectics, which celebrates a triumph with every conclusion, and can breathe only in cool clearness and consciousness: the optimistic element, which, having once forced its way into tragedy must gradually pass its Dionysian bounds, and necessarily impel it to self-destruction—even to the death-leap into the bourgeois drama. Let us but realize the consequences of the Socratic maxims: "Virtue is knowledge; man sins only from ignorance; he who is virtuous is happy." In these three fundamental forms of optimism lies the death of tragedy. For the virtuous hero must now be a dialectician; there must now be a necessary, visible connection between virtue and knowledge, between belief and morality. The transcendental justice of Æschylus is now degraded to the superficial and audacious principle of "poetic justice" with its customary *deus ex machina*.

In the light of this new Socratic-optimistic stage-world, what becomes of the *chorus* and, in general, of the entire

Dionyso-musical substratum of tragedy? The chorus is something accidental, a readily dispensed-with vestige of the origin of tragedy; while, as a matter of fact, we have seen that the chorus can be understood only as the *cause* of tragedy, and of the tragic in general. This perplexity in regard to the chorus already manifests itself in Sophocles—an important indication that even with him the Dionysian basis of tragedy is already beginning to break down. He no longer dares to entrust to the chorus the main share of the effect, but he limits its sphere to such an extent that it now appears almost coördinate with the actors, just as if it were elevated from the orchestra into the scene: whereby of course its character is completely destroyed, notwithstanding that Aristotle countenances this very theory of the chorus. This alteration in the position of the chorus, which Sophocles at any rate recommended by his practice, and, according to tradition, even by a treatise, is the first step towards its destruction, the phases of which follow one another with alarming rapidity in Euripides, Agathon, and the New Comedy. Optimistic dialectic drives *music* out of tragedy with the scourge of its syllogisms: that is, it destroys the essence of tragedy, which can be interpreted only as a manifestation and illustration of Dionysian states, as the visible symbolizing of music, as the dream-world of Dionysian ecstasy.

If, therefore, we must assume an anti-Dionysian tendency operating even before Socrates, which merely received in him a uniquely great expression, we must not draw back before the question as to what such a phenomenon as that of Socrates indicates: whom in view of the Platonic dialogues we are certainly not entitled to regard as a purely disintegrating, negative force. And though there can be no doubt that the most immediate effect of the Socratic impulse tended to the dissolution of Dionysian tragedy, yet a profound experience in Socrates' own life impels us to ask whether there is *necessarily* only an antagonistic relation between Socratism and art, and whether the birth of an "artistic Socrates" is in general a contradiction in terms.

For that despotic logician had now and then with respect to art the feeling of a gap, a void, a feeling of misgiving, of a possibly neglected duty. As he tells his friends in prison, there often came to him one and the same dream-apparition, which kept constantly repeating to him: "Socrates, practice music." Up to his very last days he comforts himself with the statement that his philosophizing is the highest form of art; he finds it hard to believe that a deity should remind him of the "common, popular music." Finally, when in prison and in order that he may thoroughly unburden his conscience, he consents to practice also this music for which he has but little respect. And in this mood he composes a poem on Apollo and turns a few Æsopian fables into verse. It was something akin to the demonic warning voice which urged him to these practices; it was due to his Apollonian insight that, like a barbaric king, he did not understand the noble image of a god and was in danger of sinning against a deity—through his lack of understanding. The voice of the Socratic dream-vision is the only sign of doubt as to the limits of logic. "Perhaps"—thus he must have asked himself—"what is not intelligible to me is not therefore unintelligible? Perhaps there is a realm of wisdom from which the logician is shut out? Perhaps art is even a necessary correlative of, and supplement to, science?"

15

With reference to these last weighty questions we must now explain how the influence of Socrates (extending to the present moment, indeed, to all futurity) has spread over posterity like an ever-increasing shadow in the evening sun, and how this influence again and again involves a regeneration of *art*—yea, of art already in the most metaphysical, broadest and profoundest sense—and how its own eternity is also a warrant for the eternity of art.

Before this could be perceived, before the intrinsic dependence of every art on the Greeks, from Homer to Socrates, was conclusively demonstrated, we had to have the same experience with regard to these Greeks as the Athenians had with regard to Socrates. Nearly every age and stage of culture has at some time or other sought with deep irritation to free itself from the Greeks, because in their presence everything self-achieved, sincerely admired and apparently quite original, seemed suddenly to lose life and color, to shrink to an abortive copy, even to caricature. And so time after time hearty resentment breaks forth against this presumptuous little nation, which for all time dared to designate everything not native as "barbaric." Who are they, one asks, who, though they have nothing to show but an ephemeral historical splendor, ridiculously restricted institutions, a dubious excellence in their customs, and the stigma attaching to ugly vices, yet lay claim to the dignity and preëminence among peoples to which genius is entitled among the masses? What a pity we have not been fortunate enough to find the cup of hemlock with which we might very simply rid ourselves of such a character: for all the poison which envy, calumny, and rankling resentment created within themselves have not been able to destroy that self-sufficient grandeur! And so one feels ashamed and afraid in the presence of the Greeks, unless one prizes truth above all things; unless one dares acknowledge to one's self this truth, that the Greeks, as charioteers, hold the reins of our own and every other culture, but that almost always chariot and horses are of too poor material and hardly up to the glory of their guides. Unless we acknowledge this, who will deem it sport to run such a team into an abyss which they themselves could clear with the leap of Achilles?

In order to endow Socrates with the dignity of such a leading position, it is enough to recognize in him a type unheard of before him, the type of the *theoretical man*. Our next task will be to obtain an insight into the meaning and purpose of this theoretical man. Like the artist, the theorist finds an infinite satisfaction in the present, and, like the former also, this satisfaction protects him from the practical ethics of pessimism with its lynx eyes shining only in the dark. Whenever the truth is unveiled, the artist will always cling with rapt gaze to whatever still remains veiled after the unveiling; but the theoretical man gets his enjoyment and satisfaction out of the cast-off veil. He finds his highest pleasure in the process of a continuously successful unveiling effected through his own unaided efforts. There would have been no science if it had been concerned only with that *one* naked goddess and nothing else. For then its disciples would have felt like those who wished to dig a hole straight through the earth: each one of them perceives that with his utmost lifelong efforts he can excavate but a very small portion of the enormous depth, and this is filled up again before his eyes by the labors of his successor, so that a third man seems to be doing a sensible thing in selecting a new spot for his attempts at tunneling. Now suppose some one shows conclusively that the antipodal goal cannot be attained thus directly. Who will then still care to toil on in the old depths, unless in the meantime he has learned to content himself with finding precious stones or discovering natural laws? For this reason Lessing, the most honest of theoretical men, boldly said that he cared more for the search after truth than for truth itself: in saying which, he revealed the fundamental secret of science, to the astonishment, and indeed, to the anger of scientists. Well, to be sure, beside this detached perception there stands, with an air of great frankness, if not presumption, a profound *illusion* which first came to birth in the person of Socrates. This illusion consists in the imperturbable belief that, with the clue of logic, thinking can reach to the nethermost depths of being, and that thinking can not only perceive being but even modify it. This sublime metaphysical illusion is added as an instinct to science and again and again leads the latter to its limits, where it must change into *art; which is really the end to be attained by this mechanism.*

If we now look at Socrates in the light of this idea, he appears to us as the first who could not only live, but—what is far greater—also die by the guidance of this instinct of science: and hence the picture of the *dying Socrates,* as the man raised above the fear of death by knowledge and reason, is the sign above the entrance-gate of science reminding every one of its mission, namely, to make existence seem intelligible, and therefore justified: for which purpose, if arguments are not enough, *myth* also must be used, which I have just indicated as the necessary consequence, as the very goal of science.

He who once sees clearly how, after Socrates, the mystagogue of science, one philosophical school succeeds another, like wave upon wave;—how an entirely unforeseen universal development of the thirst for knowledge throughout the cultured world (together with the feeling that the acquisition of knowledge was the specific task of every one highly gifted) led science on to the high sea from which since then it has never been entirely driven. He who sees how through the universality of this movement a common net of thought was for the first time stretched over the entire globe, with prospects, moreover, of conformity to law in an entire solar system;—He who realizes all this, together with the amazingly high pyramid of our contemporary knowledge, cannot fail to see in Socrates the turning-point and vortex of so-called universal history. For if one were to imagine the whole incalculable sum of energy which has been used up by that universal tendency,—used *not* in the service of knowledge, but for the practical, *i.e.,* egotistical ends of individuals and peoples—then probably the instinctive love of life would be so much weakened in general wars of destruction and continual migrations of peoples, that, owing to the practice of suicide, the individual would perhaps feel the last remnant of a sense of duty, similar to that of the Fiji Islander who, as son, strangles his parents and, as friend, his friend: and thus a practical pessimism might even give rise to a horrible ethics of general slaughter out of pity—which, as a matter of fact, exists and has existed wherever art in one form or another, especially as science and religion, has not appeared as a remedy for and preventive of that pestilential breath.

As against this practical pessimism, Socrates is the prototype of the theoretical optimist who with his belief in the explicability of the nature of things, attributes to knowledge and perception the power of a universal panacea, and in error sees evil in itself. To penetrate into the depths and to distinguish true perception from error and illusion seemed to the Socratic man the noblest and even the only truly human calling: just as from the time of Socrates onwards the mechanism of making concepts, judgments, and inferences was prized above all other activities as the highest talent and the most admirable gift of nature. Even the sublimest moral acts, the stirrings of pity, of self-sacrifice, of heroism, and that tranquillity of soul, so difficult of attainment, which the Apollonian Greek called Euphrosyne were, by Socrates, and his like-minded successors up to today, derived from the dialectic of knowledge and accordingly were designated as teachable. Any one who has experienced in himself the joy of a Socratic perception, and felt how, in constantly widening circles, it seeks to embrace the entire world of phenomena, will thenceforth find no stimulus urging him to existence more forcible than the desire to complete that conquest, to draw the net impenetrably close. To such a temper the Platonic Socrates then appears as the teacher of an entirely new form of "Greek cheerfulness" and vital happiness, which seeks to express itself in action, and will, for the most part, find that expression in maieutic and pedagogic influences on noble youths, with a view to the ultimate production of genius.

But now science, stimulated by its powerful illusion, hastens irresistibly to its limits, on which its optimism, hidden in the essence of logic, is wrecked. For the periphery of the circle of science has an infinite number of points, and while there is still no telling how this circle can ever be completely measured, yet the noble and gifted man, even before the middle of his career, inevitably comes in contact with those extreme points of the periphery where he stares into the unfathomable. When to his dismay he here sees how logic coils round itself at these limits and finally bites its own tail—then the new form of perception rises to view, namely *tragic perception,* which, in order even to be endured, requires art as protection and remedy.

With eyes strengthened and refreshed by the sight of the

Greeks, let us look upon the highest spheres of the world around us. We behold the eagerness of the insatiate optimistic knowledge, of which Socrates is the typical representative, transformed into tragic resignation and the need for art: while, to be sure, this same avidity, in its lower stages, must exhibit itself as inimical to art, and must especially have an inward detestation of Dionyso-tragic art, as was exemplified in the opposition of Socratism to Æschylean tragedy.

Here then, in a mood of agitation, we knock at the gates of the present and the future: will that "transforming" lead to ever-new configurations of genius, and especially of the *music-practicing* Socrates? Will the net of art which is spread over the whole of existence, whether under the name of religion or of science, be knit ever more closely and delicately, or is it destined to be torn to shreds under the restlessly barbaric activity and whirl which calls itself "the present"? Anxious, yet not despairing, we stand apart for a brief space, like spectators who are permitted to be witnesses of these tremendous struggles and transitions. Alas! It is the magic effect of these struggles that he who beholds them must also participate in them!

16

By this elaborate historical example we have sought to make it clear that just as surely as tragedy perishes with the evanescence of the spirit of music, so sure is it that only from this spirit can it be reborn. In order to qualify the singularity of this assertion, and, on the other hand, to disclose the origin of this insight, we must now confront clearly the analogous phenomena of our own time; we must enter into the midst of those struggles, which, as I have just said, are being waged in the

highest spheres of our contemporary world between the insatiate optimistic perception and the tragic need of art. In my
examination I shall leave out of account all those other
antagonistic tendencies which at all times oppose art, especially
tragedy, and which now are again extending their triumphant
sway to such an extent that of the theatrical arts only the farce
and the ballet, for example, put forth their blossoms, which
perhaps not every one cares to smell, in rather rich luxuriance.
I will speak only of the *most noted opposition* to the tragic
world-conception—and by this I mean optimistic science in its
most essential form with its ancestor Socrates at its head. A
little later on I shall also name those forces which seem to me
to guarantee a *rebirth of tragedy*—and perhaps other blessed
hopes for the German genius!

Before we plunge into the midst of these struggles, let us
array ourselves in the armor of the knowledge we have already
acquired. In contrast to all those who are intent on deriving
the arts from one exclusive principle, as the necessary vital
source of every work of art, I shall keep my eyes fixed on the
two artistic deities of the Greeks, Apollo and Dionysus, and
recognize in them the living and conspicuous representatives
of *two* worlds of art differing in their intrinsic essence and in
their highest aims. I see Apollo as the transfiguring genius of
the *principium individuationis* through which alone the redemption in appearance is truly to be obtained; while by the
mystical triumphant cry of Dionysus the spell of individuation
is broken, and the way lies open to the Mothers of Being,[17]
to the innermost heart of things. This extraordinary antithesis,
which stretches like a yawning gulf between plastic art as the
Apollonian, and music as the Dionysian art, has revealed itself

---

[17] Cf. *Faust,* Part 2. Act 1.

to only one of the great thinkers, to such an extent that, even without this clue to the symbolism of the Hellenic divinities, he conceded to music a character different from, and an origin anterior to, all the other arts, because, unlike them, it is not a copy of the phenomenon, but an immediate copy of the will itself, and therefore represents *the metaphysical of everything physical in the world,* the thing-in-itself of every phenomenon. (Schopenhauer, *Welt als Wille und Vorstellung,* I. 310.) [18] To this most important perception of esthetics (with which, in the most serious sense, esthetics properly begins), Richard Wagner, by way of confirmation of its eternal truth, affixed his seal, when he asserted in his *Beethoven* that music must be evaluated according to esthetic principles quite different from those which apply to all plastic arts, and not, in general, according to the category of beauty: although an erroneous esthetics, inspired by a mistaken and degenerate art, has, by virtue of the concept of beauty obtaining in the plastic domain, accustomed itself to demand of music an effect similar to that produced by works of plastic art, namely, the arousing of *delight in beautiful forms.* Upon perceiving this extraordinary antithesis, I felt a strong necessity to approach the essence of Greek tragedy and, with it, the profoundest revelation of the Hellenic genius: for I at last thought that I possessed a charm to enable me—far beyond the phraseology of our usual esthetics—to represent vividly to my mind the fundamental problem of tragedy: whereby I was granted such a surprising and unusual insight into the Hellenic character that it necessarily seemed to me as if our classical-Hellenic science that bears itself so proudly had thus far contrived to subsist mainly on phantasmagoria and externals.

---

[18] *World as Will and Idea,* I. p. 338—6th Ed. in trans. by Haldane & Kemp.

Perhaps we may lead up to this fundamental problem by asking: what esthetic effect results when the essentially separate art-forces, the Apollonian and the Dionysian, enter into simultaneous activity? Or more briefly: how is music related to image and concept? Schopenhauer, whom Richard Wagner, with special reference to this point, praises for an unsurpassable clearness and perspicuity of exposition, expresses himself most thoroughly on the subject in the following passage which I shall cite here at full length [19] (*Welt als Wille und Vorstellung*, I. p. 309): "According to all this, we may regard the phenomenal world, or nature, and music as two different expressions of the same thing,[20] which is therefore itself the only medium of their analogy, so that a knowledge of it is demanded in order to understand that analogy. Music, therefore, if regarded as an expression of the world, is in the highest degree a universal language, which is related indeed to the universality of concepts, much as they are related to the particular things. Its universality, however, is by no means that empty universality of abstraction, but quite of a different kind, and is united with thorough and distinct definiteness. In this respect it resembles geometrical figures and numbers, which are the universal forms of all possible objects of experience and applicable to them all *a priori,* and yet are not abstract but perceptible and thoroughly determinate. All possible efforts, excitements and manifestations of will, all that goes on in the heart of man and that reason includes in the wide, negative concept of feeling, may be expressed by the infinite number of possible melodies, but always in the universal, in the mere form, without the material, always according to the thing-initself, not the phenomenon, the inmost soul, as it were, of the

---

[19] *World as Will and Idea,* I. p. 239—6th Ed., trans. by Haldane & Kemp.
[20] That is, "the will" as understood by Schopenhauer.

phenomenon without the body. This deep relation which music has to the true nature of all things also explains the fact that suitable music played to any scene, action, event, or surrounding seems to disclose to us its most secret meaning, and appears as the most accurate and distinct commentary upon it. This is so truly the case, that whoever gives himself up entirely to the impression of a symphony, seems to see all the possible events of life and the world take place in himself, yet if he reflects, he can find no likeness between the music and the things that passed before his mind. For, as we have said, music is distinguished from all the other arts by the fact that it is not a copy of the phenomenon, or, more accurately, the adequate objectivity of the will, but is the direct copy of the will itself, and therefore exhibits itself as the metaphysical to everything physical in the world, and as the thing-in-itself to every phenomenon. We might, therefore, just as well call the world embodied music as embodied will; and this is the reason why music makes every picture, and indeed every scene of real life and of the world, at once appear with higher significance, certainly all the more, in proportion as its melody is analogous to the inner spirit of the given phenomenon. It rests upon this that we are able to set a poem to music as a song, or a perceptible representation as a pantomime, or both as an opera. Such particular pictures of human life, set to the universal language of music, are never bound to it or correspond to it with stringent necessity; but they stand to it only in the relation of an example chosen at will to a general concept. In the determinateness of the real, they represent that which music expresses in the universality of mere form. For melodies are to a certain extent, like general concepts, an abstraction from the actual. This actual world, then, the world of particular things, affords the object of perception, the special and individual, the particular case, both to the universality of the concepts and to the universality of the melodies. But these two universalities are in a certain respect opposed to each other; for the concepts contain particulars only as the first forms abstracted from perception, as it were, the separated shell of things; thus they are, strictly speaking, *abstracta:* music, on the other hand, gives the inmost kernel which precedes all forms, or the heart of things. This relation may be very well expressed in the language of the schoolmen, by saying, the concepts are the *universalia post rem,* but music gives the *universalia ante rem,* and the real world the *universalia in re.* But that in general a relation is possible between a composition and a perceptible representation rests, as we have said, upon the fact that both are simply different expressions of the same inner being of the world. When now, in the particular case, such a relation is actually given, that is to say, when the composer has been able to express in the universal language of music the emotions of will which constitute the heart of an event, then the melody of the song, the music of the opera, is expressive. But the analogy discovered by the composer between the two must have proceeded from the direct knowledge of the nature of the world unknown to his reason, and must not be an imitation produced with conscious intention by means of conceptions, otherwise the music does not express the inner nature of the will itself, but merely gives an inadequate imitation of its phenomenon. All specially imitative music does this."

According to the doctrine of Schopenhauer, therefore, we may understand music as the immediate language of the will, and we feel our fancy stimulated to give form to this invisible and yet so actively stirred spirit-world which speaks to us, and we feel prompted to embody it in an analogous example. On the other hand, image and concept, under the influence of a truly corresponding music, acquire a higher significance. Dionysian art therefore is wont to exercise two kinds of influences on the Apollonian art-faculty: music incites to the *symbolic-intuition* of Dionysian universality, and music allows the symbolic image to emerge *in its highest significance.* From these facts, intelligible in themselves and not inaccessible to a more penetrating examination, I infer the capacity of music to give birth to *myth* (the most significant exemplar), and particularly the *tragic* myth: the myth which expresses Dionysian knowledge in symbols. In the phenomenon of the lyrist, I have shown how music strives to express its nature in Apollonian images. If now we reflect that music at its greatest intensity must seek to attain also to its highest symbolization, we must deem it possible that it also knows how to find the symbolic expression for its unique Dionysian wisdom; and where shall we seek for this expression if not in tragedy and, in general, in the conception of the tragic?

From the nature of art as it is usually conceived according to the single category of appearance and beauty, the tragic cannot honestly be deduced at all; it is only through the spirit of music that we can understand the joy involved in the annihilation of the individual. For only by the particular examples of such annihilation are we made clear as to the eternal phenomenon of Dionysian art, which gives expression to the will in its omnipotence, as it were, behind the *principium individuationis,* the eternal life beyond all phenomena, and despite all annihilation. The metaphysical joy in the tragic is a translation of the instinctive unconscious Dionysian wisdom into the language of the scene: the hero, the highest manifestation of the will, is disavowed for our pleasure, because he is only phenomenon, and because the eternal life of the will is not affected by his annihilation. "We believe in eternal life," exclaims tragedy; while music is the immediate idea of this life Plastic art has an altogether different aim: here Apollo dispels the suffering of the individual by the radiant glorification of the *eternity of the phenomenon:* here beauty triumphs over the suffering inherent in life; pain is in a sense obliterated from the features of nature. In Dionysian art and its tragic symbolism the same nature cries to us with its true, undissembled voice: "Be as I am! Amidst the ceaseless flux of phenomena I am the eternally creative primordial mother, eternally impelling to existence, eternally self-sufficient amid this flux of phenomena!"

17

Dionysian art, too, wishes to convince us of the eternal joy of existence: only we are to seek this joy not in phenomena, but behind them. We are to recognize that all that comes into being must be ready for a sorrowful end; we are forced to look into the terrors of the individual existence—yet we are not to become rigid with fear: a metaphysical comfort tears us momentarily from the bustle of the transforming figures. We are really for a brief moment Primordial Being itself, feeling its raging desire for existence and joy in existence; the struggle, the pain, the destruction of phenomena, now appear to us as a necessary thing, in view of the surplus of countless forms of existence which force and push one another into life, in view of the exuberant fertility of the universal will. We are pierced by the maddening sting of these pains just when we have become, as it were, one with the infinite primordial joy in existence, and when we anticipate, in Dionysian ecstasy, the indestructibility and eternity of this joy. In spite of fear and pity, we are the happy living beings, not as individuals, but as the *one* living being, with whose creative joy we are united.

The history of the rise of Greek tragedy now tells us with luminous precision that the tragic art of the Greeks was really born of the spirit of music, with which conception we believe we have done justice for the first time to the primitive and astonishing significance of the chorus. At the same time, however, we must admit that the meaning of tragic myth set forth above never became clearly apparent to the Greek poets, not to speak of the Greek philosophers; their heroes speak, as it were, more superficially than they act; the myth does not at all obtain adequate objectification in the spoken word. The structure of the scenes and the intuitively created images reveal a deeper wisdom than the poet himself can put into words and concepts: the same is also observable in Shakespeare, whose Hamlet, for instance, similarly, talks more superficially than he acts, so that the previously mentioned lesson of Hamlet is to be deduced, not from his words, but from a profound contemplation and survey of the whole. With respect to Greek tragedy, which of course presents itself to us only as worddrama, I have even intimated that the lack of congruity between myth and expression might easily lead us to regard it as shallower and less significant than it really is, and accordingly to predicate for it a more superficial effect than it must have had according to the testimony of the ancients: for how easily one forgets that what the word-poet did not succeed in doing, namely, to attain the highest spiritualization and ideality of the myth, he might very well succeed in doing every moment as creative musician! To be sure, we are forced to construct for ourselves by scholarly research the superior power of the musical effect in order to experience something of the incomparable comfort which must have been characteristic of

[*1040*]

true tragedy. Even this musical superiority, however, would only have been felt by us had we been Greeks; for in the entire development of Greek music—as compared with the infinitely richer music known and familiar to us—we imagine we hear only the youthful song of the musical genius modestly intoned. The Greeks, as the Egyptian priests say, are eternal children, and in tragic art too they are only children who do not know what a sublime plaything has originated in their hands and— is being demolished.

That striving of the spirit of music towards symbolic and mythical objectification, which increases from the beginnings of lyric poetry up to Attic tragedy, suddenly breaks off immediately after attaining a luxuriant development, and disappears, as it were, from the surface of Hellenic art: while the Dionysian world-view born of this striving lives on in the Mysteries and, in its strangest metamorphoses and debasements, does not cease to attract serious natures. Will it not some day rise once again out of its mystic depths as art?

Here we are detained by the question, whether the power, by virtue of whose opposing influence tragedy perished, has for all time sufficient strength to prevent the artistic reawakening of tragedy and the tragic world-view. If ancient tragedy was diverted from its course by the dialectical desire for knowledge and the optimism of science, this fact might lead us to believe that there is an eternal conflict between *the theoretic* and *the tragic world-view;* and only after the spirit of science has been pursued to its limits, and its claim to universal validity destroyed by the evidence of these limits may we hope for a rebirth of tragedy: for which form of culture we should have to use the symbol *of the music-practicing Socrates* in the sense spoken of above. In this contrast, I understand by the spirit of science the belief which first came to light in the person of

Socrates—the belief in the explicability of nature and in knowledge as a panacea.

He who recalls the immediate consequences of this restless urgent spirit of science will realize at once that *myth* was annihilated by it, and that, because of this annihilation, poetry was driven like a homeless being from her natural ideal soil. If we have been right in assigning to music the power of reproducing myth from itself, we may similarly expect to find the spirit of science on the path where it inimically opposes this mythopœic power of music. This takes place in the development of the *New Attic Dithyramb,* the music of which no longer expressed the inner essence, the will itself, but only rendered the phenomenon approximately, in an imitation by means of concepts; from which intrinsically degenerate music the genuinely musical natures turned away with the same repugnance that they felt for the art-destroying tendency of Socrates. The unerrring instinct of Aristophanes was surely right when it included Socrates himself, the tragedy of Euripides, and the music of the New Dithyrambic poets in the same feeling of hatred, recognizing in all three phenomena the signs of a degenerate culture. In this New Dithyramb, music is outrageously manipulated so as to be the imitative portrait of a phenomenon, for instance, of a battle or a storm at sea; and thus, of course, it has been utterly robbed of its mythopœic power. For it seeks to arouse pleasure only by impelling us to seek external analogies between a vital or natural process and certain rhythmical figures and characteristic sounds of music; if our understanding is to content itself with the perception of these analogies, we are reduced to a frame of mind which makes impossible any reception of the mythical; for the myth as a unique type of universality and truth towering into the infinite cries to be conspicuously recognized. The truly Dionysian music presents itself as such a general mirror of the universal will: the conspicuous event refracted in this mirror expands at once for our consciousness to the copy of an external truth. Conversely, such a conspicuous event is at once divested of every mythical character by the tone-painting of the New Dithyramb; music now becomes a wretched copy of the phenomenon, and therefore infinitely poorer than the phenomenon itself: through which poverty it still further reduces the phenomenon for our consciousness, so that now, for example, a musically imitated battle of this sort exhausts itself in marches, signal-sounds, etc., and our imagination is arrested precisely by these superficialities. Tone-painting is thus in every respect the antithesis of true music with its mythopœic power: through it the phenomenon, poor in itself, is made still poorer, while through Dionysian music the individual phenomenon is enriched and expanded into a picture of the world. It was a great triumph for the un-Dionysian spirit, when by the development of the New Dithyramb, it had estranged music from itself and reduced it to be the slave of phenomena. Euripides, who, though in a higher sense, must be considered a thoroughly unmusical nature, is for this very reason a passionate adherent of the New Dithyrambic Music, and with the liberality of a freebooter makes use of all its effective tricks and mannerisms.

In another direction also we see at work the power of this un-Dionysian myth-opposing spirit, when we turn our attention to the prevalence of *character representation* and psychological refinement in tragedy from Sophocles onwards. The character must no longer be expanded into an eternal type, but, on the contrary, must develop individually through artistic subordinate traits and shadings, through the nicest precision of all lines, in such a manner that the spectator is in general no longer conscious of the myth, but of the vigorous truth to nature and the artist's imitative power. Here also we observe the victory of the phenomenon over the Universal, and the delight in a unique, almost anatomical preparation; we are already in the atmosphere of a theoretical world, where scientific knowledge is valued more highly than the artistic reflection of a universal law. The movement in the direction of character delineation proceeds rapidly: while Sophocles still portrays complete characters and employs myth for their refined development, Euripides already draws only prominent individual traits of character, which can express themselves in violent bursts of passion; in the New Attic Comedy, however, there are only masks with *one* expression: frivolous old men, duped panders, and cunning slaves, recurring incessantly. Where now is the mythopœic spirit of music? What still remains of music is either excitatory music or associational music, that is, either a stimulant for dull and faded nerves, or tone-painting. As regards the former, it hardly matters about the text set to it: the heroes and choruses of Euripides are already dissolute enough when once they begin to sing; to what pass must things have come with his impertinent successors?

The new un-Dionysian spirit, however, reveals itself most plainly in the dénouements of the new dramas. In the Old Tragedy one could sense at the end that metaphysical comfort, without which the delight in tragedy cannot be explained at all; the reconciliating tones from another world sound purest, perhaps, in the *Œdipus at Colonus*. Now that the genius of music has fled from tragedy, tragedy, strictly speaking, is dead: for from what source shall we now draw this metaphysical comfort? The new spirit, therefore, sought for an earthly resolution of the tragic dissonance. The hero, after being sufficiently tortured by fate, earned a well-deserved reward through a splendid marriage or tokens of divine favor. The hero had turned gladiator. On him, after he had been nicely beaten and covered with wounds, freedom was occasionally bestowed. The *deus ex machina* took the place of metaphysical comfort. I will not say that the tragic world-view was everywhere completely destroyed by this intruding un-Dionysian spirit: we only know that it had to flee from art into the underworld as it were, in the degenerate form of a secret cult. Over the widest extent of the Hellenic character, however, there raged the consuming blast of this spirit, which manifests itself in the form of "Greek cheerfulness," which we have already spoken of as a senile, unproductive love of existence. This cheerfulness is the antithesis of the splendid "naïveté" of the earlier Greeks, which, according to the characteristic indicated above, must be conceived as the blossom of the Apollonian culture springing from a dark abyss, as the victory which the Hellenic will, through its mirroring of beauty, obtains over suffering and the wisdom of suffering. The noblest manifestation of that other form of "Greek cheerfulness," the Alexandrian, is the cheerfulness of the *theoretical man:* it exhibits the same characteristic symptoms that distinguished the spirit of the un-Dionysian: it combats Dionysian wisdom and art, it seeks to dissolve myth, it substitutes for a metaphysical comfort an earthly consonance, in fact, a *deus ex machina* of its own, the god of machines and crucibles, that is, the powers of the forces of nature recognized and employed in the service of the higher egoism; it believes that it can correct the world by knowledge, guide life by science, and actually confine the individual within a limited sphere of solvable problems, from which he can cheerfully say to life: "I desire thee: it is worth while to know thee."

[*1045*]

It is an eternal phenomenon: the insatiate will can always, by means of an illusion spread over things, detain its creatures in life and compel them to live on. One is chained by the Socratic love of knowledge and the delusion of being able thereby to heal the eternal wound of existence; another is ensnared by art's seductive veil of beauty fluttering before his eyes; still another by the metaphysical comfort that beneath the flux of phenomena eternal life flows on indestructibly: to say nothing of the more ordinary and almost more powerful illusions which the will has always at hand. These three planes of illusion are on the whole designed only for the more nobly formed natures, who in general feel profoundly the weight and burden of existence, and must be deluded by exquisite stimulants into forgetfulness of their sorrow. All that we call culture is made up of these stimulants; and, according to the proportion of the ingredients, we have either a dominantly *Socratic* or *artistic* or *tragic* culture: or, if historical exemplifications are wanted, there is either an Alexandrian or a Hellenic or a Buddhistic culture.

Our whole modern world is entangled in the net of Alexandrian culture. It proposes as its ideal the theoretical man equipped with the greatest forces of knowledge, and laboring in the service of science, whose archetype and progenitor is Socrates. All our educational methods have originally this ideal in view: every other form of existence must struggle on wearisomely beside it, as something tolerated, but not intended. In an almost alarming manner the cultured man was for a long time found only in the form of the scholar: even our poetical arts have been forced to evolve from learned imitations, and in the main effect, that of rhyme, we still recognize the origin of our poetic form from artistic experiments with a non-indigenous, thoroughly learned language. How unintelligible must *Faust,* the modern cultured man, who is in himself intelligible, have appeared to a true Greek—Faust, storming unsatisfied through all the faculties, devoted to magic and the devil from a desire for knowledge; Faust, whom we have but to place beside Socrates for the purpose of comparison, in order to see that modern man is beginning to divine the limits of this Socratic love of perception and yearns for a coast in the wide waste of the ocean of knowledge. When Goethe on one occasion said to Eckermann with reference to Napoleon: "Yes, my good friend, there is also a productiveness of deeds," he reminded us in a charmingly naïve manner that the non-theorist is something incredible and astounding to modern man; so that we again have need of the wisdom of Goethe to discover that such a surprising form of existence is not only comprehensible, but even pardonable.

Now, we must not hide from ourselves what is concealed at the heart of this Socratic culture: Optimism, with its delusion of limitless power! Well, we must not be alarmed if the fruits of this optimism ripen—if society, leavened to the very lowest strata by this kind of culture, gradually begins to tremble with wanton agitations and desires, if the belief in the earthly happiness of all, if the belief in the possibility of such a general intellectual culture is gradually transformed into the threatening demand for such an Alexandrian earthly happiness, into the conjuring up of a Euripidean *deus ex machina.* Let us mark this well: the Alexandrian culture, to be able to exist permanently, requires a slave class, but, with its optimistic view of life, it denies the necessity of such a class, and consequently, when the effect of its beautifully seductive and tranquillizing utterances about the "dignity of man" and the "dignity of labor" is over, it gradually drifts towards a dreadful destruction. There is nothing more terrible than a barbaric slave class, who have learned to regard their existence as an injustice, and now prepare to avenge, not only themselves, but all future generations. In the face of such threatening storms, who dares to appeal with any confidence to our pale and exhausted religions, whose very foundations have degenerated into "learned" religions?—so that myth, the necessary prerequisite of every religion, is already paralyzed everywhere, and even in this domain the optimistic spirit—which we have just designated as the destroying germ of society—has attained the mastery.

While the evil slumbering in the heart of theoretical culture gradually begins to disquiet modern man, while he anxiously ransacks the stores of his experience for means to avert the danger, though he has no great faith in these means; while he, therefore, begins to divine the consequences of his position: great, universally gifted natures have contrived, with an incredible amount of thought, to make use of the paraphernalia of science itself, in order to point out the limits and the relativity of knowledge generally, and thus definitely to deny the claim of science to universal validity and universal aims: with which demonstration the illusory notion was for the first time recognized as such, which pretends, with the aid of causality, to be able to fathom the innermost essence of things. The extraordinary courage and wisdom of *Kant* and *Schopenhauer* have succeeded in gaining the most difficult victory, the victory over the optimism hidden in the essence of logic, which optimism in turn is the basis of our culture. While this optimism, resting on apparently unobjectionable *æternæ veritates*, had believed in the intelligibility and solvability of all the riddles of the universe, and had treated space, time, and causality as totally unconditioned laws of the most universal validity, Kant, on the other hand, showed that in reality these served only to elevate the mere phenomenon, the work of Mâyâ, to the position of the sole and highest reality, putting it in place of the innermost and true essence of things, and thus making impossible any knowledge of this essence or, in Schopenhauer's words, lulling the dreamer still more soundly asleep. With this knowledge a culture is inaugurated which I venture to call a tragic culture; the most important characteristic of which is that wisdom takes the place of science as the highest end, wisdom, which, uninfluenced by the seductive distractions of the sciences, turns with unmoved eye to a comprehensive view of the world, and seeks to conceive therein, with sympathetic feelings of love, the eternal suffering as its own. Let us imagine a rising generation with this bold vision, this heroic desire for the magnificent, let us imagine the valiant step of these dragon-slayers, the proud daring with which they turn their backs on all the effeminate doctrines of optimism that they may "live resolutely," wholly, and fully: would it not be necessary for the tragic man of this culture, with his self-discipline of seriousness and terror, to desire a new art, the art of metaphysical comfort—namely, tragedy—to claim it as Helen, and exclaim with Faust:

"Und sollt' ich nicht, sehnsüchtigster Gewalt,
  Ins Leben ziehn die einzigste Gestalt?" [21]

---

[21] And shall not I, by mightiest desire,
  In living shape that sole fair form acquire?
  Faust, Swanwick's Trans.

But now that the Socratic culture can only hold the scepter of its infallibility with trembling hands; now that it has been shaken from two directions—once by the fear of its own conclusions which it at length begins to surmise, and again, because it no longer has its former naïve confidence in the eternal validity of its foundation—it is a sad spectacle to see how the dance of its thought rushes longingly on ever-new forms, to embrace them, and then, shuddering, lets them go suddenly as Mephistopheles does the seductive Lamiæ. It is certainly the sign of the "breach" which all are wont to speak of as the fundamental tragedy of modern culture that the theoretical man, alarmed and dissatisfied at his own conclusions, no longer dares entrust himself to the terrible icestream of existence: he runs timidly up and down the bank. So thoroughly has he been spoiled by his optimistic views that he no longer wants to have anything whole, with all of nature's cruelty attaching to it. Besides, he feels that a culture based on the principles of science must be destroyed when it begins to grow *illogical,* that is, to retreat before its own conclusions. Our art reveals this universal trouble: in vain does one depend imitatively on all the great productive periods and natures; in vain does one accumulate the entire "World-literature" around modern man for his comfort; in vain does one place one's self in the midst of the art-styles and artists of all ages, so that one may give names to them as Adam did to the beasts: one still continues eternally hungry, the "critic" without joy and energy, the Alexandrian man, who is at bottom a librarian and corrector of proofs, and who, pitiable wretch, goes blind from the dusty books and printers' errors.

19

We cannot indicate the essential modern content of this Socratic culture more distinctly than by calling it *the culture of the opera:* for it is in this department that this culture has expressed its aims and perceptions, with special naïveté, which is surprising when we compare the genesis of the opera and the facts of operatic development with the eternal truths of the Apollonian and Dionysian. I call to mind first of all the origin of the *stilo rappresentativo* and the recitative. Is it credible that this thoroughly externalized undevotional operatic music, could be received and cherished with enthusiastic favor, as a rebirth, as it were, of all true music, by the very age in which had appeared the ineffably sublime and sacred music of Palestrina? And who, on the other hand, would think of making only the diversion-craving luxuriousness of those Florentine circles and the vanity of their dramatic singers responsible for the love of the opera which spread with such rapidity? That in the same age, even among the same people, this passion for a half-musical mode of speech should awaken alongside of the vaulted structure of Palestrina harmonies which all medieval Christendom had been building up, I can explain to myself only by a co-operating, *extra-artistic tendency* in the essence of the recitative.

The listener, who insists on distinctly hearing the words under the music, has his desire fulfilled by the singer in that the latter speaks rather than sings, and by this half-song intensifies the pathetic expression of the words. By this intensification of the pathos he facilitates the understanding of the words and surmounts the remaining half of the music. The specific danger now threatening him is that in some unguarded moment he may stress the music unduly, which would immediately entail the destruction of the pathos of the speech and the distinctness of the words: while, on the other hand, he feels himself continually impelled to musical delivery and to a virtuose exhibition of vocal talent. Here the "poet" comes to his aid, who knows how to provide him with abundant opportunities for lyrical interjections, repetitions of words and sentences, etc.—at which places the singer, now in the purely musical element, can rest himself without paying any attention to the words. This alternation of emotionally impressive speech which, however, is only half sung, with interjections which are wholly sung, an alternation characteristic of the *stilo rappresentativo,* this rapidly changing endeavor to affect now the conceptional and representative faculty of the hearer, now his musical sense, is something so utterly unnatural and likewise so intrinsically contradictory both to the Apollonian and Dionysian artistic impulses, that one has to infer an origin of the recitative lying outside all artistic instincts. According to this description, the recitative must be defined as a mixture of epic and lyric delivery, not indeed as an intrinsically stable mixture, a state not to be attained in the case of such totally disparate elements, but as an entirely superficial mosaic conglutination, such as is totally unprecedented in the domain of nature and experience. *But this was not the opinion of the inventors of the recitative:* they themselves, together with their age, believed rather that the mystery of antique music has been solved by this *stilo rappresentativo,* in which, so they thought, was to be found the only explanation of the enormous influence of an Orpheus, an Amphion, and even of Greek tragedy. The new style was looked upon as the reawakening of the most effective music, the Old Greek music: indeed, in accordance with the universal and popular conception of the Homeric *as the primitive world,* they could abandon themselves to the dream of having descended once more into the paradisiacal beginnings of mankind, where music also must have had that unsurpassed purity, power, and innocence of which the poets, in their pastoral plays, could give such touching accounts. Here we can see into the internal development of this thoroughly modern variety of art, the opera: art here responds to a powerful need, but it is a need of the belief in the prehistoric existence of the artistic, of an unesthetic kind: the longing for the idyllic, good man. The recitative was regarded as the rediscovered language of this primitive man; the opera as the found country of this idyllically or heroically good creature, who simultaneously with every action follows a natural artistic impulse, who accomplishes his speech with a little singing, in order that he may immediately break forth into full song at the slightest emotional excitement. It is now a matter of indifference to us that the humanists of the time combated the old ecclesiastical conception of man as inherently corrupt and lost, with this newly created picture of the paradisiacal artist: so that opera is to be understood as the opposition dogma of the good man, but may also, at the same time, provide a consolation for that pessimism which, owing to the frightful uncertainty of all conditions of life, attracted precisely the serious-minded men of the time. For us, it is enough to have perceived that the essential charm, and therefore the genesis, of this new art-life lies in the gratification of an altogether unesthetic need, in the optimistic glorification of man as such, in the conception of the primitive man as the man naturally good and artistic: a principle of the opera that has gradually changed into a threatening and terrible *demand,* which, in face of contemporary socialistic movements, we can no longer ignore. The "good primitive man" wants his rights: what

[*1053*]

paradisiacal prospects! Beside this I place another equally obvious confirmation of my view that opera is based on the same principles as our Alexandrian culture. Opera is the birth of the theoretical man, the critical layman, not of the artist: one of the most surprising facts in the whole history of art. It was the demand of thoroughly unmusical hearers that before everything else the words must be understood, so that according to them a rebirth of music is to be expected only when some mode of singing has been discovered in which text-word lords over counterpoint like master over servant. For the words, it is argued, are as much nobler than the accompanying harmonic system as the soul is nobler than the body. It was in accordance with the laically unmusical crudeness of these views that the combination of music, picture and words was effected in the beginnings of the opera: and in the spirit of this esthetic the first experiments were made in the leading amateur circles of Florence by the poets and singers patronized there. The man incapable of art creates for himself a kind of art precisely because he is the inartistic man as such. Because he cannot divine the Dionysian depth of music, he changes his musical taste into an appreciation of the understandable word-and-tone-rhetoric of the passions in the *stilo rappresentativo,* and into the voluptuousness of the lyric arts; because he is unable to behold a vision, he forces the machinist and the decorative artist into his service; because he cannot comprehend the true nature of the artist, he conjures up the "artistic primitive man" to suit his taste, that is, the man who sings and recites verses under the influence of passion. He dreams himself back into a time when passion sufficed to generate songs and poems: as if emotion had ever been able to create anything artistic. The premise of the opera is a false belief concerning the artistic process, in fact, the idyllic belief that every sentient man is an artist. This belief would make opera the expression of the taste of the laity in art, dictating their laws with the cheerful optimism of the theoretical man.

Should we desire to combine the two conceptions just set forth as influential in the origin of opera, it would merely remain for us to speak of an *idyllic tendency of the opera:* in which connection we may avail ourselves exclusively of the phraseology and illustration of Schiller. "Nature and the ideal," he says, "are either objects of grief, when the former is represented as lost, the latter unattained; or both are objects of joy, in that they are represented as real. The first case furnishes the elegy in its narrower signification, the second the idyll in its widest sense." Here we must at once call attention to the common characteristic of these two conceptions in the genesis of opera, namely, that in them the ideal is not felt as unattained or nature as lost. In consonance with this sentiment, there was a primitive age of man when he lay close to the heart of nature, and, owing to this naturalness, had at once attained the ideal of mankind in a paradisiacal goodness and artistry. From this perfect primitive man all of us were supposed to be descended. We were, in fact, faithful copies of him; only we had to cast off some few things in order to recognize ourselves once more as this primitive man, on the strength of a voluntary renunciation of superfluous learnedness, of superabundant culture. It was to such a concord of nature and the ideal, to an idyllic reality, that the cultured Renaissance man let himself be led back by his operatic imitation of Greek tragedy. He made use of this tragedy as Dante made use of Vergil, in order to be conducted to the gates of paradise: while from this point he continued unassisted and passed over from an imitation of the highest Greek art-form to a "restoration of all things," to an imitation of man's original art-world. What a cheerful confidence there is about these daring endeavors, in the very heart of theoretical culture!—solely to be explained by the comforting belief, that "man-in-himself" is the eternally virtuous hero of the opera, the eternally fluting or singing shepherd, who must always in the end rediscover himself as such should he ever at any time have really lost himself; to be considered solely as the fruit of that optimism, which here rises like a sweetishly seductive column of vapor out of the death of the Socratic world-view.

Therefore, the features of the opera do not in any sense exhibit the elegiac sorrow of an eternal loss, but rather the cheerfulness of eternal rediscovery, the indolent delight in an idyllic reality which one can at least momentarily imagine as real. But in this process one may some day grasp the fact that this supposed reality is nothing but a fantastically silly dawdling, at which every one who could judge it by the terrible seriousness of true nature, and compare it with actual primitive scenes of the beginnings of mankind, would be impelled to call out with loathing: Away with the phantom! Nevertheless, it would be a mistake to imagine that it is possible merely by a vigorous shout to frighten away such a dawdling thing as the opera, as if it were a specter. He who would destroy the opera must take up the struggle against Alexandrian cheerfulness, which expresses itself so naïvely therein concerning its favorite conceptions; of which in fact it is the specific form of art. But what may art itself expect from the operation of an art-form whose beginnings lie entirely outside of the esthetic province? Which has rather stolen over from a half-moral sphere into the artistic domain, and has been able only occasionally to deceive us as to its hybrid origin? By what sap is this parasitic operatic-form nourished, if not by that of true art? Must we not suppose that the highest and, indeed, the truly serious task of art,—to release the eye from its gaze into the horrors of night and to deliver the "patient" by the healing balm of appearance from the spasms of the agitations of the will,—must we not suppose that this task will degenerate under the influence of its idyllic seductions and Alexandrian adulation to an empty and dissipating dilettanteism? What will become of the eternal truths of the Dionysian and Apollonian in such a *mélange de genres,* as I have shown to be the essence of the *stilo rappresentativo?* A style in which music is regarded as the servant, the text as the master, where music is compared with the body, the text with the soul? where at best the highest aim will be directed toward a paraphrastic tone-painting, just as formerly in the New Attic Dithyramb? where music is completely alienated from its true dignity of being the Dionysian mirror of the world, so that the only thing left to it, as the slave of phenomena, is to imitate the formal character of phenomena, and to arouse a superficial pleasure in the play of lines and proportions. Closely observed, this fatal influence of the opera on music is seen to coincide exactly with the universal development of modern music; the optimism lurking in the genesis of the opera and in the character of the culture thereby represented, has, with alarming rapidity, succeeded in divesting music of its Dionyso-cosmic mission and impressing on it a playfully formal and pleasurable character: a change to which the only analogy perhaps is the metamorphosis of the Æschylean man into the cheerful Alexandrian.

If, however, in the exemplification here indicated, we have rightly associated the disappearance of the Dionysian spirit with a most striking, but hitherto unexplained, transformation and degeneration of the Hellenic man—what hopes must revive in us when the most certain auspices guarantee *the reverse process, the gradual awakening of the Dionysian spirit* in our modern world! It is impossible that the divine strength of Heracles should languish for ever in voluptuous bondage to Omphale. Out of the Dionysian root of the German spirit a power has arisen which, having nothing in common with the primitive conditions of Socratic culture, can neither be explained nor excused by it, but which is rather felt by this culture as something terribly inexplicable and overwhelmingly hostile. I refer, of course, to *German music* as we must understand it, particularly in its vast solar orbit from Bach to Beethoven, from Beethoven to Wagner. Even under the most favorable circumstances what can the knowledge-craving Socratism of our days do with this demon rising from unfathomable depths? Neither by means of the zigzag and arabesque work of operatic melody, nor with the aid of the arithmetical counting-board of fugue and contrapuntal dialectic is the formula to be found, by whose thrice-powerful light one might subdue this demon and compel it to speak. What a spectacle, when our latter-day estheticians, with a net of "beauty" peculiar to themselves, pursue and clutch at the genius of music whirling before display activities which are not to be judged by the standard of eternal beauty any more than by the standard of the sublime. Let us but observe these patrons of music at close range, as they really are, indefatigably crying: "Beauty! beauty!" We may discover whether they really bear the stamp of nature's darling children who are fostered and nourished at the breast of the beautiful, or whether they are not rather seeking a deceptive cloak for their own rudeness, an esthetical pretext for their own impassive insipidity: I am thinking here, for instance, of Otto Jahn. But let the liar and the hypocrite beware of our German music: for amid all our culture it is really the only genuine, pure and purifying fire-spirit from which and towards which, as in the teaching of the great Heraclitus of Ephesus, all things move in a double orbit: all that we now call culture, education, civilization, must some day appear before the unerring judge, Dionysus.

Let us recollect further that Kant and Schopenhauer made it possible for the spirit of *German philosophy*, streaming from similar sources, to destroy scientific Socratism's complacent delight in existence by establishing its boundaries; how through this delimitation was introduced an infinitely profounder and more serious view of ethical problems and of art, which we may unhesitatingly designate as Dionysian wisdom comprised in concepts. To what then does the mystery of this oneness of German music and philosophy point if not to a new form of existence, concerning whose character we can only inform ourselves by surmise from Hellenic analogies? For to us who stand on the boundary line between two different forms of existence, the Hellenic prototype retains this immeasurable value, that therein all these transitions and struggles are imprinted in a classically instructive form: except that we, as it were, pass through the chief epochs of the Hellenic genius, analogically in *reverse* order, and seem now, for instance, to be passing backwards from the Alexandrian age to the period of tragedy. At the same time we have the feeling that the birth of a tragic age simply means a return to itself of the German spirit, a blessed self-rediscovery after powerful intrusive influences had for a long time compelled it, living as it did in a helpless and unchaste barbarism, to servitude under their form. Now at last, upon returning to the primitive source of its being, it may venture to stride along boldly and freely before the eyes of all nations without being attached to the leading-strings of a Romanic civilization: if only it can learn implicitly from one people—the Greeks, from whom to learn at all is itself a high honor and a rare distinction. And when were we in greater need of these highest of all teachers more than at present, when we are experiencing a *rebirth of tragedy* and are in danger alike of not knowing whence it comes and of being unable to make clear to ourselves whither it tends?

20

Some day before an impartial judge, it may be decided in what time and in what men the German spirit has thus far striven most resolutely to learn from the Greeks: and if we confidently assume that this unique praise must be accorded to the noblest intellectual efforts of Goethe, Schiller, and Winkelmann, we will certainly be compelled to add that since their time and subsequent to the more immediate consequences of their efforts, the endeavor to attain to culture and to the Greeks by a similar path has grown incomprehensibly feebler and feebler. That we may not despair utterly of the German spirit, must we not conclude that possibly, in some essential matter, even these champions could not penetrate into the core of the Hellenic nature, and were unable to establish a permanent alliance between German and Greek culture? So that perhaps an unconscious perception of this shortcoming might arouse also in more serious minds the disheartening doubt as to whether after such predecessors they could advance still farther on this path of culture, or could reach the goal at all. Accordingly, since that time, we see that opinions concerning the value of Greek contributions to culture have been degenerating in the most alarming manner; the expression of compassionate superiority may be heard in the most varied intellectual and non-intellectual camps: or elsewhere a totally impotent rhetoric plays with the phrases "Greek harmony," "Greek beauty," "Greek cheerfulness." And in those very circles whose dignified task it might be to draw indefatigably from the Greek reservoir for the good of German culture, in the teaching circles of the higher educational institutions, they have learned best to compromise with the Greeks easily and in good time, often to the extent of a skeptical abandonment of the Hellenic ideal and a total perversion of the true purpose of antiquarian studies. If there is any one at all in these circles who has not completely exhausted himself in his endeavor to be a dependable corrector of old texts or a natural-history microscopist of language, he perhaps is also seeking to take over Grecian antiquity "historically" along with other antiquities, and in any case according to the method and with the supercilious air of our present cultured historiography. Therefore, when the intrinsic efficiency of our higher educational institutions has perhaps never been lower or feebler than at present; when the "journalist," the paper slave of the day, triumphs over the professor in all matters pertaining to culture; and when there remains to the latter only the often previously experienced metamorphosis of now fluttering also like a cheerful cultured butterfly (to use the idiom of the journalist), with the "light elegance" peculiar to this sphere;—under these conditions, with what a painful confusion must the cultured persons of a period like the present gaze at the phenomenon which perhaps is to be comprehended analogically only by means of the profoundest principle of the hitherto unintelligible Hellenic genius, the phenomenon of the reawakening of the Dionysian spirit and the rebirth of tragedy. There has never been another art-period in which so-called culture and true art have been so estranged and opposed, as we may observe them to be at present. We can understand why so feeble a culture hates true art; it fears destruction from its hands. But must not an entire cultural-form, namely, the Socratic-Alexandrian, have exhausted itself after culminating in such a daintily tapering point as our present culture? If heroes like Goethe and Schiller could not succeed in breaking open the enchanted gate which leads into the Hellenic magic mountain; if with their most dauntless striving they could not go beyond the longing gaze which Goethe's Iphigenia casts from barbaric Tauris to her home across the ocean, what could the epigones of such heroes hope for?—unless the gate—amidst the mystic tones of reawakened tragic music—should open for them suddenly of its own accord, from an entirely different side, quite overlooked in all previous cultural endeavors.

Let no one attempt to trouble our faith in an impending rebirth of Hellenic antiquity; for in it alone we find our hope of a renovation and purification of the German spirit through the fire-magic of music. What else shall we name, that amid the present desolation and fatigue of culture might awaken any comforting expectation for the future? We look in vain for one single vigorous root, for one spot of fruitful healthy soil: Everywhere dust, sand, torpidity, languor! Under such circumstances a cheerless solitary wanderer could choose for himself no better symbol than the Knight with Death and the Devil, as Dürer has sketched him to us—the mail-clad knight, grim and stern of visage, who undisturbed by his gruesome companions, yet without hope, pursues his terrible path with horse and hound, alone. Our Schopenhauer was such a Dürerian knight: he was destitute of all hope, but he sought the truth. We have not his equal today.

But how suddenly this gloomily depicted wilderness of our exhausted culture changes when it is touched by the Dionysian magic! A hurricane seizes everything decrepit, decaying, broken, and stunted; enwraps it whirlingly in a red cloud of dust; and like a vulture carries it off into the air. Confused, we look for what has vanished: for what we see is something risen to the golden light as from a depression, so full and green, so luxuriantly vital, so ardent, so immeasurable. In the midst of this exuberance of life, sorrow and joy, Tragedy sits, in sublime ecstasy; she listens to a sad song, far away—it tells of the Mothers of Being, whose names are: *Wahn, Wille, Wehe*.[22]—Yes, my friends, have faith with me in Dionysian life and in the rebirth of tragedy. The time of the Socratic man is past: crown yourselves with ivy, take the thyrsus in your hand, and marvel not if tigers and panthers lie down fawning at your feet. Dare now to be tragic men, for ye shall be redeemed! Ye shall accompany the Dionysian festive procession from India to Greece! Arm yourselves for hard strife, but have faith in the wonders of your god!

21

Passing back from the hortatory tones to the mood befitting the contemplative man, I repeat that only from the Greeks can we learn what such a sudden and miraculous awakening of tragedy must signify for the inner fabric of a people's life. It is the people of the tragic mysteries who fight the battles with the Persians: and, conversely, the people who waged such wars required tragedy as a necessary healing potion. Who would have imagined that there was still such a uniformly powerful effusion of the simplest political sentiments, the most natural domestic instincts and the primitive manly de-

---

[22] Whim, will, woe.

light in battle in this very people after it had been agitated so profoundly for several generations by the most violent convulsions of the Dionysian demon? If with every noteworthy extension of the Dionysian life one always perceives that the Dionysian release from the shackles of the individual makes itself felt first of all in an increased encroachment on the political instincts, to the extent of causing indifference, yea, even hostility, it is certain, on the other hand, that the state-forming Apollo is also the genius of the *principium individuationis,* and that the state and the domestic sentiment cannot survive without an assertion of the individual personality. For any people there is but one road leading from orgasm—the way to Indian Buddhism, which, that its longing for nothingness may be at all endured, requires those rare ecstatic states raised high above space, time, and the individual; just as these in turn demand a philosophy which teaches one how to overcome the indescribable depression of the intermediate states by means of the imagination. With the same necessity, owing to the unconditional domination of political impulses, a people drifts into a path of extremest secularization, whose most magnificent but also most terrible expression is the Roman *imperium.*

Placed between India and Rome, and constrained to a choice, misleading in either case, the Greeks succeeded in devising in classical purity still a third form, not indeed for long private use, but just on that account destined for immortality.—For it holds true in all things that those whom the gods love die young, but, on the other hand, it is equally certain that they can live eternally with the gods. One should not require the noblest things to possess the durable toughness of leather; the staunch durability, for instance, which was inherent in the Roman national character, probably does not belong to the indispensable predicates of perfection. But if we ask what medicinal means enabled the Greeks, in their best period, despite the fury of their Dionysian and political impulses, neither to exhaust themselves in ecstatic brooding, nor in a consuming scramble for empire and worldly honor, but on the contrary to achieve the splendid mixture which we find in a noble, inflaming, and contemplatively disposing wine, we must remember the enormous power of *tragedy*, exciting, purifying, and releasing the entire life of a people; the highest value of which we shall divine only when, as with the Greeks, it presents itself as the essence of all the prophylactic healing forces, as the mediator arbitrating-between the strongest and most inherently fateful characteristics of a people.

Tragedy absorbs into itself the highest musical ecstasy so that it absolutely brings music to perfection among the Greeks, as among ourselves; but it then places beside it tragic myth and the tragic hero. The latter, like a mighty Titan, takes the entire Dionysian world on his shoulders and relieves us of the burden; while, on the other hand, by means of this same tragic myth, tragedy is able through the tragic hero, to deliver us from the intense longing for this existence, and to remind us with warning hand of another existence and a higher joy, for which the struggling hero prepares himself presentiently by his destruction, not by his victories. Tragedy sets a sublime symbol, the myth, between the universal authority of its music and the receptive Dionysian hearer, and produces in him the illusion that music is only the most effective means for the animating, the plastic world of myth. Relying upon this noble illusion, she may now move her limbs for the dithyrambic dance, and abandon herself unhesitatingly to an orgiastic feeling of freedom, in which, as music itself, without this illusion, she could not venture to indulge. The myth, while protecting us from the music, on the other hand, affords it the highest freedom. By way of return, music imparts to tragic myth an impressive and convincing metaphysical significance such as could never be attained by word and image, without this unique aid; and the tragic spectator in particular experiences thereby the sure presentment of supreme joy to which the path through destruction and negation leads; so that he imagines he hears the innermost abyss of things speaking audibly to him.

If with these last propositions I have succeeded in giving perhaps only a preliminary expression, intelligible to few at first, to this difficult idea, I must not here desist from stimulating my friends to a further attempt, or cease from beseeching them to prepare themselves, by a detached example of our common experience, for the recognition of the more generous proposition. In this example I must not appeal to those who make use of the pictures of the scenic processes, the words and the emotions of the performers, to approximate musical perception; for none of these speak music as their mother-tongue, and despite these aids get no farther than the outer precincts of musical perception, without ever being allowed to touch its innermost shrines; some of them, like Gervinus, do not even reach the precincts by this path. But I must address myself only to those who, being immediately allied to music, have it as it were for their mother's breast and are connected with things almost exclusively by unconscious musical relations. I ask the question of these genuine musicians: can they imagine a man capable of hearing the third act of *Tristan und Isolde* without any aid of word or scenery, purely as a vast symphonic period, without expiring by a spasmodic distention of all the wings of the soul? A man who has thus, so to speak, put his ear to the heart-chamber of the world-will, who feels the furious desire for existence issuing from it as thundering stream or gently dispersed brook, into all the veins of the world, would he not collapse all at once? Could he endure, in the wretched fragile tenement of the human individual, to hear the re-echo of countless cries of joy and sorrow from the "vast void of cosmic night," without flying irresistibly towards his primitive home at the sound of this pastoral dance-song of metaphysics? But if, nevertheless, such a work can be heard as a whole, without a renunciation of individual existence, and if such a creation could be created without demolishing its creator, where are we to find the solution of this contradiction?

Here between our highest musical excitement and the music in question are interposed the tragic myth and the tragic hero —in reality only as symbols of the most universal facts, of which only music can speak directly. If, however, we felt as purely Dionysian beings, myth as a symbol would stand by us absolutely ineffective and unnoticed, and would never for a moment prevent us from giving ear to the re-echo of the *universalia ante rem*. Here, however, the *Apollonian* power, with a view to the restoration of the almost shattered individuals, bursts forth with the healing balm of the blissful illusion: all of a sudden we imagine we see only Tristan, motionless, asking himself dully: "The old tune, why does it wake me?" And what once moved us like a hollow sigh from the heart of being now seems to tell us only how "waste and empty is the sea." And whereas, breathless, we once thought to expire by a convulsive distention of all our feelings, and only a slender tie bound us to our present existence, we now hear and see only the hero wounded to death, yet not dying, with his despairing cry: "Longing! Longing! In death still longing! for very longing not dying!" And whereas, formerly after such an excess and superabundance of consuming agonies, the jubilation of the horn rent our hearts almost like the very extreme of agony, the rejoicing Kurwenal now stands between us and this "jubilation as such," his face turned toward the ship which carries Isolde. However powerfully we are touched by fellow-suffering, it nevertheless delivers us in a manner from the primordial suffering of the world, just as the symbol-image of the myth delivers us from the immediate perception of the highest world-idea, just as the thought and the word deliver us from the unchecked effusion of the unconscious will. The glorious Apollonian illusion makes it appear as if the very tone-world presented itself to us as a plastic cosmos, as if even the fate of Tristan and Isolde had been merely formed and molded therein as out of some most soft and yielding material.

Thus does the Apollonian tear us away from Dionysian universality and make us delight in individuals; to these it attaches our sympathetic emotion; through these it satisfies our sense of beauty which longs for great and sublime forms; it presents us with biographical portraits, and incites us to a thoughtful comprehension of the essence of life dwelling within them. With the immense combined power of the image, the concept, the ethical teaching and the sympathetic emotion —the Apollonian influence uplifts man from his orgiastic self-annihilation and deceives him concerning the universality of the Dionysian process into the belief that he is seeing a detached picture of the world (Tristan and Isolde for instance), and that, *through music,* he will be enabled to *see* it with still more essential clearness. What can the healing magic of Apollo not accomplish when it can even excite in us the illusion that the Dionysian is actually in the service of the Apollonian and is capable of enhancing its effects, in fact, that music is essentially the representative art for an Apollonian content?

[*1068*]

By means of the pre-established harmony obtaining between perfected drama and its music, the drama attains the highest degree of conspicuousness, such as is usually unattainable in mere spoken drama. As all the animated figures of the scene in the independently evolved lines of melody simplify them-selves before us to the distinctness of a single curved line, the co-existence of these lines is also audible in the harmonic change which sympathizes in a most delicate manner as the process evolves: through which change the relations of things become immediately perceptible to us in a sensible and not at all abstract manner, as we likewise perceive that it is only in these relations that the essence of a character and of a melodic line manifests itself clearly. And while music thus compels us to a broader and more intensive vision than usual, and makes us spread out the curtain of the scene before our eyes like a delicate texture, the world of the stage is as infinitely expanded for our spiritualized, introspective eye as it is illumined out-wardly from within. How can the word-poet furnish anything analogous, who strives to attain this internal expansion and illumination of the visible stage-world by a much more imper-fect mechanism and by an indirect method, proceeding as he does from word and concept? Although musical tragedy also avails itself of the word, it can at the same time place beside it its basis and origin, and can make clear to us the development of the word, from within outwards.

Concerning the process just described, however, we may still make the definite statement that it is only a glorious ap-pearance, namely, the aforementioned Apollonian *illusion*, through whose influence we are to be delivered from the Dio-nysian obtrusion and excess. For, at bottom, the relation of music to drama is precisely the reverse; music is the essential idea of the world, drama is but the reflection of this idea, a

[*1069*]

detached adumbration of it. The identity between the melody and the living form, between the harmony and the character-relations of that form, is true in a sense opposite to what one would suppose on the contemplation of musical tragedy. We may agitate and enliven the form in the most conspicuous manner, and illuminate it from within, but it still remains merely a phenomenon, from which there is no bridge to lead us to the true reality, to the heart of the world. But out of this heart speaks music; and though countless phenomena of the kind might be passing manifestations of this music, they could never exhaust its essence, but would always be merely its externalized copies. Of course, as regards the intricate relation of music and drama, nothing can be explained, while everything may be confused by the popular and thoroughly false antithesis of soul and body; but the unphilosophical crudeness of this antithesis seems to have become—who knows for what reasons—a readily accepted Article of Faith with our estheticians, while they have learned nothing concerning an antithesis of the phenomenon and the thing-in-itself—or perhaps for equally unknown reasons they have not cared to learn anything about it.

Should our analysis have established the point that the Apollonian element in tragedy has by means of its illusion gained a complete victory over the Dionysian primordial element of music, and has made music itself subservient to its end, namely, the clearest possible elucidation of the drama, it would certainly be necessary to add a very important restriction: that at the most essential point this Apollonian illusion is dissolved and annihilated. The drama, which, aided by music, unfolds itself before us with such inwardly illumined distinctness in all its movements and figures, that we imagine we see the texture unfolding on the loom as the shuttle flies to and fro,—this drama attains as a whole an effect which *transcends all Apollonian artistic effects.* In the collective effect of tragedy, the Dionysian once again dominates. Tragedy closes with a sound which could never emanate from the realm of Apollonian art. And the Apollonian illusion thereby reveals itself as what it really is—the assiduous veiling during the performance of the tragedy of the intrinsically Dionysian effect: which, however, is so powerful, that it ends by forcing the Apollonian drama itself into a sphere where it begins to talk with Dionysian wisdom, and even denies itself and its Apollonian conspicuousness. So that the intricate relation of the Apollonian and the Dionysian in tragedy may really be symbolized by a fraternal union of the two deities: Dionysus speaks the language of Apollo; Apollo, however, finally speaks the language of Dionysus; and so the highest goal of tragedy and of art in general is attained.

22

Let the attentive friend picture to himself purely and simply, according to his experience, the effect of a true musical tragedy. I think I have so portrayed the phenomenon of this effect in both its phases that he will now know how to interpret his own experiences. For he will recollect that with regard to the myth which passed before him he felt himself exalted to a kind of omniscience, as if his visual faculty were no longer merely a surface faculty, but capable of penetrating into the interior, and as if he now saw before him, with the aid of music, the ebullitions of the will, the conflict of motives, and the swelling stream of the passions, almost sensibly visible, like a multitude of actively moving lines and figures; and he would feel as if he could thereby dip into the most delicate secrets of unconscious emotions. While he thus becomes conscious of the highest exaltation of his instincts for clarity and transfiguration, he nevertheless feels with equal definiteness that this long series of Apollonian artistic effects still does *not* generate that blessed continuance in will-less contemplation which the plastic artist and the epic poet, that is to say, the strictly Apollonian artists, evoke in him by their artistic productions: to wit, the justification of the world of the *individuatio* attained by this contemplation,—which is the climax and essence of Apollonian art. He beholds the transfigured world of the stage and nevertheless denies it. He sees the tragic hero before him in epic clearness and beauty, and nevertheless rejoices in his annihilation. He comprehends the action in the minutest detail, and yet loves to flee into the incomprehensible. He feels the actions of the hero to be justified, and is nevertheless still more elated when these actions annihilate their originator. He shudders at the sufferings which will befall the hero, and yet in them he anticipates a higher and much more overpowering joy. He sees more extensively and profoundly than ever, and yet wishes to be blind. Whence must we derive this curious internal dissension, this collapse of the Apollonian apex, if not from the *Dionysian* spell, which, though apparently exciting the Apollonian emotions to their highest pitch, can nevertheless force into its service this excess of Apollonian power? The *tragic myth* is to be understood only as a symbolizing of Dionysian wisdom through Apollonian art-media. The mythus conducts the world of phenomena to its boundaries, where it denies itself, and seeks to flee back again into the bosom of the true and only reality; where it then, like Isolde, seems to strike up its metaphysical swansong:

> "In des Wonnemeeres
> wogendem Schwall,
> in der Duft-Wellen
> tonendem Schaal,
> in des Weltathems
> wehendem All——
> entrinken—versinken—
> unbewusst—höchste Lust!" [23]

We may thus make real to ourselves through the experiences of the truly esthetic hearer the tragic artist himself as he creates his figures like a fecund divinity of individuation (in which sense his work can hardly be understood as an "imitation of nature") and when, on the other hand, his vast Dionysian impulse then absorbs this entire world of phenomena, in order to anticipate beyond it, and through its destruction, the highest artistic primal joy, in the bosom of the Primal Unity. Of course, our estheticians have nothing to say about this return in fraternal union of the two art-deities to the original home, nor of either the Apollonian or Dionysian excitement of the hearer, while they never tire of characterizing the struggle of the hero with fate, the triumph of the moral order of the world, or the purgation of the emotions through tragedy,

---

23 "In the sea of pleasure's
Billowing roll,
In the ether-wave's
Ringing sound,
In the world-breath's
Drifting whole—
To drown in, to sink—
Unconscious—extremest joy!"

as the properly Tragic: an indefatigability which makes me think that perhaps they are not esthetically sensitive men at all, but are to be regarded merely as moral beings when hearing tragedy. Never since Aristotle has an explanation of the tragic effect been offered, by which an esthetic activity of the hearer could be inferred from artistic circumstances. At one time pity and terror are supposed to be forced to an alleviating release through the serious action, at another time we are supposed to feel elevated and inspired at the victory of good and noble principles, at the sacrifice of the hero in the interest of a moral conception of the universe; and however sure I am that for countless men precisely this, and only this, is the effect of tragedy, it just as plainly follows that all these men, together with their interpreting estheticians, have had no experience of tragedy as the highest *art*. The pathological discharge, the catharsis of Aristotle, which philologists are at a loss whether to include under medicinal or moral phenomena, recalls a remarkable anticipation of Goethe. "Without a lively pathological interest," he says, "I too have never yet succeeded in elaborating a tragic situation of any kind, and hence I have rather avoided than sought it. Can it perhaps have been still another of the merits of the ancients that the deepest pathos was with them merely esthetic play, whereas with us the truth of nature must co-operate in order to produce such a work?" we can now answer this latter profound question in the affirmative after our glorious experiences, in which we have found to our astonishment in the case of musical tragedy itself, that the deepest pathos can in reality be merely esthetic play; and therefore we are justified in believing that now for the first time the proto-phenomenon of the tragic can be described with some degree of success. He who now still persists in talking only of those vicarious effects proceeding from extra-esthetic spheres, and does not feel himself raised above the patho-logical-moral process may despair of his esthetic nature: for which we recommend to him, by way of innocent equivalent, the interpretation of Shakespeare after the fashion of Gervinus, and the diligent search for poetic justice.

Thus with the rebirth of tragedy the *esthetic hearer* is also reborn, in whose place in the theater a curious *quid pro quo* was wont to sit with half-moral and half-learned pretensions —the "critic." Everything in his sphere hitherto has been artificial and merely glossed over with a semblance of life. The performing artist in fact was at a loss as to how to deal with a hearer who comported himself so critically; hence he, as well as the dramatist or operatic composer who inspired him, searched anxiously for the last remains of life in a being so pretentiously barren and incapable of enjoyment. Such "critics," however, have hitherto constituted the public; the student, the schoolboy, even the most harmless female, were already unwittingly prepared by education and by magazines for a similar perception of works of art. The nobler natures among the artists when dealing with such a public counted upon exciting their moral-religious emotions, and the appeal to the moral world-order operated vicariously, when actually some powerful artistic spell should have enraptured the true hearer. Or again, some imposing or at all events exciting trend of the contemporary political and social world was so vividly presented by the dramatist that the hearer could forget his critical exhaustion and abandon himself to similar emotions, as, in patriotic or war-like moments, or before the tribune of parliament, or at the condemnation of crime and vice—an estrangement of the true aims of art which could not but lead

directly now and then to a cult of such tendencies. But here
there took place what has always taken place with factitious
arts, an extraordinarily rapid degeneration of these tendencies,
so that, for instance, the tendency to use the theater as a means
for the moral education of the people, which in Schiller's time
was taken seriously, is already reckoned among the incredible
antiquities of an abandoned culture. While the critic got the
upper hand in the theater and concert-hall, the journalist in
the school, and the press in society, art degenerated into a
trivial topic of conversation, and esthetic criticism was used as
a means of uniting a vain, distracted, selfish and moreover
piteously unoriginal society, whose character is suggested by
Schopenhauer's parable of the porcupines: with the result that
art has never been so much talked about and so little esteemed.
But is it still possible to have intercourse with a man capable
of conversing on Beethoven or Shakespeare? Let each answer
this question according to his own feelings: he will at any
rate show by his answer his conception of "culture," provided
he at least tries to answer the question, and has not already
grown mute with astonishment.

On the other hand, many a being more nobly and delicately
endowed by nature, though he may have gradually become a
critical barbarian in the manner described, might have something to say of the unexpected as well as totally unintelligible
effect which a successful performance of *Lohengrin,* for
example, had on him: except that perhaps every warning and
interpreting hand was lacking to guide him; so that the incomprehensibly diffused and quite incomparable sensation
which then thrilled him remained isolated and became extinct,
like a mysterious star after a short period of brilliance. But it
was then that he had an inkling of what the esthetic hearer is.

23

He who wishes to test himself rigorously as to whether he is related to the true esthetic hearer, or whether he belongs rather to the community of the Socratic-critical men, need only examine sincerely the feeling with which he accepts the *wonder* represented on the stage: whether he feels his historical sense, which insists on strict psychological causality, insulted by it, whether with benevolent concession he admits the wonder as a phenomenon intelligible to childhood, but alien to him, or whether he experiences anything else from it. For in this way he will be able to determine on the whole how capable he is of understanding *myth,* the concentrated picture of the world, which, as abbreviature of phenomena, cannot dispense with wonder. It is probable, however, that almost every one, upon close examination, feels so broken up by the critico-historical spirit of our culture, that he can only make the former existence of myth credible to himself by learned means through intermediary abstractions. Without myth, however, every culture loses its healthy creative natural power: it is only a horizon encompassed with myths that rounds off to unity a social movement. It is only myth that frees all the powers of the imagination and of the Apollonian dream from their aimless wanderings. The mythical figures have to be the unnoticed omnipresent genii, under whose care the young soul grows to maturity, by the signs of which the man gives meaning to his life and struggles: and the state itself knows no more powerful unwritten law than the mythical foundation which vouches for its connection with religion and its growth from mythical ideas.

On the other hand, let us now think of the abstract man unguided by myth, the abstract education, the abstract morality, the abstract justice, the abstract state: let us picture to ourselves the lawless roving of the artistic imagination, unchecked by native myth: let us imagine a culture which has no fixed and sacred primitive seat, but is doomed to exhaust all its possibilities, and to nourish itself wretchedly on all other cultures— there we have the Present, the result of Socratism, which is bent on the destruction of myth. And now the mythless man remains eternally hungering amid the past, and digs and grubs for roots, though he have to dig for them even among the remotest antiquities. The terrible historical need of our unsatisfied modern culture, the assembling around one of countless other cultures, the consuming desire for knowledge— what does all this point to, if not to the loss of myth, the loss of the mythical home, the mythical maternal bosom? Let us ask ourselves whether the feverish and uncanny excitement of this culture is anything but the eager seizing and snatching at food of hungry man—and who would care to contribute anything more to a culture which cannot be satisfied no matter how much it devours, and at whose contact the most vigorous and wholesome nourishment habitually changes into "history and criticism"?

We should also have to regard our German character with sorrowful despair, if it had already become inextricably entangled in, or even identical with this culture, as we may observe to our horror is the case in civilized France; and that which for a long time was the great advantage of France and the cause of her vast superiority, to wit, this very identity of people and culture, might compel us at the sight thereof to congratulate ourselves that this so questionable culture of ours has hitherto had nothing in common with the noble heart of our people's character. On the contrary, all our hopes stretch out longingly towards the perception that beneath this rest-lessly palpitating civilized life and educational convulsion there is concealed a glorious, intrinsically healthy, primitive power, which, to be sure, stirs vigorously only at intervals in stupendous moments, and then continues to dream of future awakening. It is from this abyss that the German Reformation came forth: in the choral-hymn of which the future melody of German music first resounded. So deep, courageous, and spiritual, so exuberantly good and tender did this chorale of Luther sound—as the first Dionysian luring call breaking forth from dense thickets at the approach of spring. To it responded with emulative echo the solemnly wanton procession of Dionysian revelers, to whom we are indebted for German music—and to whom we shall be indebted for *the rebirth of German myth*.

I know that I must now lead the sympathizing and attentive friend to an elevated position of lonesome contemplation, where he will have but few companions, and I call out en-couragingly to him that we must hold fast to our shining guides, the Greeks. That we might clarify our esthetic knowl-edge, we previously borrowed from them the two divine forms, each of whom rules over a separate realm of art, and concerning whose mutual contact and exaltation we acquired a notion through Greek tragedy. Through a remarkable disrup-tion of both these primitive artistic impulses, the ruin of Greek tragedy seemed to be necessarily brought about: with which process a degeneration and a transformation of the Greek national character was quite in keeping, summoning us to earnest reflection as to how closely and necessarily art and the people, myth and custom, tragedy and the state, are rooted to-gether. The ruin of tragedy was at the same time the ruin of myth. Until then the Greeks had been involuntarily compelled to connect all experiences at once with their myths: indeed it was only through this association that they could understand them, so that even the most immediate present necessarily appeared to them *sub specie æterni* and in a certain sense as timeless. Into this current of the timeless, however, the state as well as art plunged in order to find repose from the burden and eagerness of the moment. A people—and, for that matter, also a man—is to be valued only according to its ability to impress on its experiences the stamp of eternity: for it is thus, as it were, desecularized; thus it reveals its unconscious inner conviction of the relativity of time and of the true, that is, the metaphysical significance of life. The contrary happens when a people begins to comprehend itself historically and to demolish the mythical bulwarks surrounding it: with which there is usually connected a marked secularization, a break with the unconscious metaphysics of its earlier existence, with all its ethical consequences. Greek art and especially Greek tragedy delayed above all the annihilation of myth: it was necessary to annihilate these also to be able to live detached from the native soil, unbridled in the wilderness of thought, custom, and deed. Even then this metaphysical impulse still endeavors to create for itself a form of apotheosis (weakened, no doubt) in the Socratism of science that urges to life: but in its lower stage the same impulse led only to a feverish search, which gradually lost itself in a pandemonium of myths and superstitions accumulated from all quarters: in the midst of which, nevertheless, the Hellene sat with a yearning heart till he contrived, as Græculus, to mask his fever with Greek cheerfulness and Greek levity, or to narcotize himself completely with some gloomy Oriental superstition.

We have been approaching this state in the most striking manner since the reawakening of Alexandrian-Roman antiquity in the fifteenth century, after a long, most easily describable, interlude. On the heights there is the same exuberant love of knowledge, the same insatiate happiness of the discoverer, the same tremendous secularization, and, with these, a homeless wandering, an eager intrusion at strange tables, a frivolous deification of the present or a dull senseless estrangement, all *sub specie sæculi,* of the present time: which same symptoms lead one to infer the same defect at the heart of this culture, the destruction of myth. It seems hardly possible to transplant a foreign myth with permanent success, without fatally injuring the tree which may occasionally be sufficiently strong and healthy to eliminate the foreign element after a terrible struggle; but which must ordinarily consume itself in a languishing and stunted condition or in a sickly luxuriance. So highly do we rate the pure and vigorous kernel of the German character that from it alone may we venture to expect this elimination of forcibly ingrafted foreign elements, and we deem it possible that the German spirit will reflect anew on itself. Perhaps many will be of opinion that this spirit must begin its struggle with the elimination of the Romanic element. Such people may recognize an external preparation for, and encouragement of, this struggle in the victorious bravery and bloody glory of the late war; but must seek the inner constraint in the emulative zeal to be eternally worthy of our sublime protagonists on this path, of Luther as well as of our great artists and poets. But let him never think he can fight such battles without the household gods, without his mythical home, without a "restoration" of all things German! And if the German should be looking around timidly for a guide to lead him back to his long-lost home, whose ways and paths he hardly knows any longer—let him but listen to the ecstatic luring call of the Dionysian bird, which hovers above him, and would fain point the way for him.

24

Among the peculiar artistic effects of musical tragedy we had to emphasize an Apollonian *illusion,* through which we are to be saved from an immediate oneness with the Dionysian music, while our musical excitement is able to discharge itself on an Apollonian domain and in an interposed visible middle world. It therefore seemed to us that precisely through this discharge this middle world of theatrical procedure, the drama generally, became visible and intelligible from within in a degree unattainable in all other forms of Apollonian art: so that here, where this art was as if winged and borne aloft by the spirit of music, we had to recognise the highest exaltation of its powers, and consequently, in the fraternal union of Apollo and Dionysus, the climax of the Apollonian as well as of the Dionysian artistic aims.

Of course, the Apollonian light-picture did not, precisely with this inner illumination through music, attain the peculiar effect of the weaker forms of Apollonian art. What the epos and the animated stone can do—constrain the contemplative eye to calm delight in the world of the *individuatio*—could not be realized here, notwithstanding a greater animation and distinctness. We contemplated the drama and penetrated with piercing glance into its inner agitated world of motives—and yet it seemed as if only a symbolic picture passed before us whose deepest meaning we almost believed we had divined, and which we desired to draw aside like a curtain in order to behold the original behind it. The greatest distinctness of the picture did not suffice us: for it seemed to reveal as well as veil something; and while with its symbolic revelation it seemed to invite the rending of the veil for the disclosure of the mysterious background, this illuminated all-consciousness itself enthralled the eye and prevented it from penetrating more deeply.

He who has not experienced this—to be constrained to view, and at the same time to long for something beyond the viewing—will hardly be able to conceive how clearly and definitely these two processes co-exist and are felt to co-exist in the contemplation of tragic myth; while the truly esthetic spectators will confirm my assertion that among the peculiar effects of tragedy this conjecture is the most noteworthy. Now let this phenomenon of the esthetic spectator be transferred to an analogous process in the tragic artist, and the genesis of *tragic myth* will have been understood. It shares with the Apollonian sphere of art the full delight in appearance and contemplation, and at the same time it denies this delight and finds a still higher satisfaction in the annihilation of the visible world of appearance. The substance of the tragic myth is first of all an epic event involving the glorification of the fighting hero: but how does it come about that the essentially puzzling trait, the suffering of the hero, the most painful victories, the most agonizing contrasts of motives, in short, the exemplification of the wisdom of Silenus, or, in esthetic terms, the ugly and unharmonious, are always represented anew in such countless and popular forms, and precisely at the most youthful and exuberant age of a people, unless there is really a higher delight experienced in all this?

For the fact that in life things actually take such a tragic course would hardly explain the original of a form of art; provided that art is not merely an imitation of the reality of nature, but in fact a metaphysical supplement to the reality of nature, placed beside it for purpose of conquest. Tragic myth, in so far as it really belongs to art, also fully participates in this transfiguring metaphysical purpose of art in general. What does it transfigure, however, when it presents the phenomenal world under the form of the suffering hero? Least of all the "reality" of this phenomenal world, for it says to us: "Look at this! Look carefully! It is your life! It is the hour-hand of the clock of your existence!"

And myth has displayed this life, in order thereby to transfigure it for us? If not, how shall we account for the esthetic pleasure with which even these representations are accompanied? I am inquiring concerning the esthetic pleasure, and am well aware that besides this pleasure many of these representations may occasionally create even a moral delectation, perhaps in the form of pity or of a moral triumph. But he who would derive the effect of the tragic exclusively from these moral sources, as indeed was usually the case far too long in esthetics, let him not think that he has done anything for Art thereby; for above all Art must insist on purity in her domain. The very first requirement for the explanation of tragic myth is that its characteristic pleasure must be sought in the purely esthetic sphere, without encroaching on the domain of pity, fear, or the morally sublime. How can the ugly and the unharmonious, the substance of tragic myth, excite esthetic pleasure?

Here it becomes necessary to raise ourselves with one daring bound into a metaphysics of Art. Therefore I repeat my former proposition that only as an esthetic phenomenon may existence and the world appear justified: and in this sense it is precisely the function of tragic myth to convince us that even the ugly and unharmonious is an artistic game which the will plays with itself in the eternal fullness of its joy. But this not easily comprehensible proto-phenomenon of Dionysian art becomes, in a direct way, singularly intelligible, and is immediately apprehended in the wonderful significance of *musical dissonance:* just as in general it is music alone, placed in contrast to the world, which can give us an idea as to what is meant by the justification of the world as an esthetic phenomenon. The joy aroused by the tragic myth has the same origin as the joyful sensation of dissonance in music. The Dionysian, with its primordial joy experienced in pain itself, is the common source of music and tragic myth.

Is it not possible that by calling to our aid the musical relation of dissonance, we may meanwhile have essentially facilitated the difficult problem of the tragic effect? For we now understand what it means to wish to view tragedy and at the same time to have a longing beyond that viewing: a frame of mind, which, referring to the artistically employed dissonance, we should have to characterize simply by saying that we desire to hear and at the same time have a longing beyond the hearing. That striving for the infinite, the beating wings of longing accompanying the highest delight in the clearly perceived reality, remind us that in both states we must recognize a Dionysian phenomenon, which reveals to us again and again the playful construction and demolishing of the world of individuals as the overflow of a primitive delight, just as Heraclitus the Obscure compares the world-building power to a playing child which places stones here and there and builds sandhills only to overthrow them again.

Hence, in order to form a true estimate of the Dionysian capacity of a people, we must think not only of their music, but equally of their tragic myth, the second witness of this capacity. Considering this close relationship between music and myth, we may now in like manner infer that a degeneration and depravation of the one involves a deterioration of the other: if it is at all true that the weakening of the myth is generally indicative of a debilitation of the Dionysian capacity. Concerning both, however, a glance at the development of the German genius should not leave us in any doubt; in the opera just as in the abstract character of our mythless existence, in an art degenerated to pastime as well as in a life guided by concepts, the inartistic as well as life-consuming nature of Socratic optimism had revealed itself to us. For our consolation, however, there have been some indications that nevertheless in some inaccessible abyss the German spirit still rests and dreams, undestroyed, in glorious health, profundity, and Dionysian strength, like a knight sunk in slumber: from which abyss the Dionysian song rises to our ears to let us know that this German knight even now is dreaming his primitive Dionysian myth in blissfully earnest visions. Let no one believe that the German spirit has forever lost its mythical home when it can still understand so plainly the voices of the birds which tell of that home. Some day it will find itself awake in all the morning freshness following a deep sleep: then it will slay the dragons, destroy the malignant dwarfs, waken Brunnhilde —and Wotan's spear itself will be unable to obstruct its course!

My friends, ye who believe in Dionysian music, ye also know what tragedy means to us. There we have tragic myth reborn from music—and in this birth we can hope for everything and forget what is most afflicting. What is most afflicting to all of us, however, is—the prolonged degradation in which the German genius has lived estranged from house and home in the service of malignant dwarfs. Ye understand my words— as ye will also, in conclusion, understand my hopes.

[*1086*]

25

Music and tragic myth are equally the expression of the Dionysian capacity of a people, and are inseparable from each other. Both originate in a sphere of art lying beneath and beyond the Apollonian; both transfigure a region in whose joyous harmony all dissonance, like the terrible picture of the world, dies charmingly away; both play with the sting of displeasure, relying on their most potent magic; both thereby justify the existence even of the "worst world." Here the Dionysian, as compared with the Apollonian, exhibits itself as the eternal and original artistic force, which in general calls into existence the entire world of phenomena; in the midst of which a new transfiguring appearance becomes necessary, in order to keep alive the animated world of individuation. If we could conceive of an incarnation of dissonance—and what else is man?—then, that it might live, this dissonance would need a glorious illusion to cover its features with a veil of beauty. This is the true artistic function of Apollo: in whose name we include all the countless manifestations of the fair realm of illusion, which at each moment render life in general worth living and impel one to the experience of the next moment.

At the same time, just as much of this basis of all existence —the Dionysian substratum of the world—is allowed to enter into the consciousness of human beings, as can be surmounted again by the Apollonian transfiguring power, so that these two art-impulses are compelled to develop their powers in strictly mutual proportion, according to the law of eternal justice. When the Dionysian powers rise with such strength as we are experiencing at present, there can be no doubt that, wrapped in a cloud, Apollo has already descended to us; whose fullest and most beautiful effects a coming generation may perhaps behold.

That this effect is necessary, however, each one would most surely perceive intuitively, if once he found himself carried back—even in a dream—into an Old-Hellenic existence. Walking under high Ionic colonnades, looking up towards a horizon defined by clear and noble lines, with reflections of his transfigured form by his side in shining marble, and around him solemnly marching or quietly moving men, with harmonious voices and rhythmical pantomime—in the presence of this perpetual influx of beauty would he not have to raise his hand to Apollo and exclaim: "Blessed race of Hellenes! How great Dionysus must be among you, when the Delian god deems such charms necessary to cure you of your dithyrambic madness!" To such a one, however, an aged Athenian, looking up to him with the sublime eyes of Æschylus, might answer: "Say also this, thou curious stranger: what must this people have suffered, that they might become thus beautiful! But now follow me to a tragic play, and sacrifice with me in the temple of both the deities!"